D1259351

THIS DAY IN
NORTH AMERICAN
INDIAN HISTORY

Important Dates in the History of North America's Native Peoples for Every Calendar Day

Phil Konstantin

DA CAPO PRESS
A Member of the Perseus Books Group

Copyright © 2002 by Phil Konstantin

Designed by Janice Tapia
Set in 10.5 point Goudy by The Perseus Books Group

Photo credits abbreviations: IMH—Institute of Military History, LOC—Library of Congress, NA—National Archives.

Cataloging-in-Publication data for this book is available from the Library of Congress.

First Da Capo Press edition 2002
ISBN 0-306-81170-7

Published by Da Capo Press
A Member of the Perseus Books Group
http://www.dacapopress.com

Da Capo Press books are available at special discounts for bulk purchases in the U.S. by corporations, institutions, and other organizations. For more information, please contact the Special Markets Department at the Perseus Books Group, 11 Cambridge Center, Cambridge, MA 02142, or call (800) 255-1514 or (617) 252-5298, or e-mail j.mccrary@perseusbooks.com.

1 2 3 4 5 6 7 8 9—06 05 04 03 02

For my teachers, who fostered my interest in history;

For my Cherokee ancestors stretching back into the mists of time;

For my father, Morris Benjamin Konstantin Jr., a true role model;

For my mother, Lila Beatrice Adair Konstantin,
a constant source of encouragement and the source
of my interest and pride in my Cherokee heritage;

For my brothers, Michael Edward Konstantin Sr.
and Milton Duncan Konstantin;

For my children, Ron, Heidi, and Sarah;

For Jo, for her encouragement, and the photo;

and

For Robyn . . .

Contents

Preface

This work is the result of thousands of hours of research over ten years. I have exchanged countless e-mails and had many discussions with members of different tribal groups. I have gone through hundreds of old books, journals, and reports. The geographic scope of the material in this book is limited to the North American continent. The subject matter includes events in the history of the native people of North America or events that affected them.

Throughout the book, I have listed events that could be traced to an exact date. Different authors may have recorded an event on different dates. This may have been due to poor record keeping, delays in reporting events, simple errors, or changes in the Gregorian calendar in the 1700s. When possible, I have tried to show which date is the most acceptable to the widest number of sources. In some cases, I have listed more than one date for the same event.

Even though some of my ancestors are American Indians, I have made an effort not to have too much of a bias when reporting the happenings in this book. Both the indigenous inhabitants and the nonnative colonizers have engaged in atrocities. At other times, and at different places, they both have meant well by their actions. Lies and schemes were perpetrated by both groups. Kind acts have been performed on both sides. It is not my goal to justify activities by any group. My personal sympathies are with the innocent of both groups. My effort is merely to report the happenings that involved the native peoples of the North American continent.

There are two intended exceptions to this. I have included the names of every member of the military who was given the Medal of Honor by the U.S. government while fighting American Indians. This is not intended as an indictment of the named military personnel. In many cases, they were fighting for their lives, and I felt that it was important to show how many of the country's highest military citations were issued for fighting Indians, regardless of the soldiers' intentions. The other intended bias on my part concerns the phrase "Native American." Unless it is part of a quote from an original source, I have avoided this title. My ancestry is mixed. I have both European and Cherokee forebears. I grew up considering myself part American Indian, not Native American. I have never liked, nor do I use, the contrivance.

THIS DAY IN
NORTH AMERICAN
INDIAN HISTORY

Soldiers march through the snow on the return from Wounded Knee. (NA)

JANUARY 1

1756: After the attack of the Christianized Indian village of Gnadenhutten (near modern Leighton, Pennsylvania) on November 24, 1755, by other Indians, British troops were sent in to patrol the area. Two groups of Delaware, one led by Chief Tedyuscung, attacked the troops and farms in the area. Twenty soldiers and several settlers were killed, and the village was burned. The Moravian missionaries abandoned the area. They and many of their Indian converts moved to Ohio and established another village named Gnadenhutten.

1838: Seminole Chief Osceola was transferred from St. Augustine to the prison at Fort Moultrie, South Carolina. Osceola eventually died there.

1839: At a site near what is modern Marlin, Texas, Europeans established several farms. A war party attacked the settlements, killing five people. Several children managed to hide and escape after the war party moved on.

1852: One in a series of treaties with California Indians was signed in Santa Isabel. The treaty was meant to reserve lands for the Indians and to protect them from Europeans.

1867: According to army records, members of the Third Cavalry fought with a band of Indians near Fort Stanton, New Mexico. One soldier was reported wounded, and five Indians were killed.

1868: Buffalo soldiers (black troops) of Troop E, Ninth Cavalry, skirmished with Indians near Fort Quitman, Texas.

1877: Colonel Nelson "Bear Coat" Miles and his forces from Fort Keogh (near modern Miles City in eastern Montana) were moving up the Tongue River in search of Crazy Horse and his followers. They had their first skirmish with Indians. According to army reports, there were 600 lodges on the Tongue River, which were abandoned as Miles moved through the area.

1889: Wovoka had a ghost dance vision.

1891: While pursuing Indians after the massacre at Wounded Knee, members of the Sixth Cavalry were encountering Indians and extremely cold weather. For their actions in "heading the advance across White River partly frozen, in a spirited movement to the effective assistance of Troop K," First Lieutenant Benjamin H. Cheever Jr. and Sergeant Joseph F. Knight, Troop F, would be awarded the Medal of Honor. Second Lieutenant Robert L. Howze, Company K, would also receive the award for "bravery in action." Captain John B. Kerr would also get the Medal of Honor "for distinguished bravery while in command of his troops in action against hostile Sioux Indians on the north bank of the White River, near the mouth of Little Grass Creek, South Dakota, where he defeated a force of 300 Brule Sioux warriors, and turned the Sioux tribe, which was endeavoring to enter the Badlands, back into the Pine Ridge Agency." With five men, Sergeant Fred Myers, Company K, held his position "against superior forces." He was also awarded the highest medal in the land. Corporal Cornelius Smith, Company K, was also awarded the Medal of Honor for his actions during the fighting.

1898: According to a new law, U.S. presidents must now approve Indian Council Acts.

1965: The Nisqually Nation in Washington State issued a proclamation denouncing their treatment by the United States. The document stated the United States had not lived up to its treaty agreements. The Nisqually Nation therefore declared that non-Nisqually people "no longer have the right to reside, tax or hunt or fish upon said lands or waters, within the ceded areas of the treaties made with the Indian peoples." They also compared the treatment of the Indian peoples by the U.S. government to Jews under Hitler.

1970: Indian tribes in San Diego County met at Grossmont College. They requested federal funds to find solutions to problems of low-income and minority people in the area. This was one of the first meetings of its kind in the area.

1975: Menominee Warrior Society members seized the Alexian Brothers Novitiate in Grisham, Wisconsin. They ended their occupation on February 2, 1975. The brotherhood agreed to give title to the grounds to the Menominee, but they changed their minds in July.

Every: Pueblo turtle dance.

JANUARY 2

1761: A small force of British soldiers moved into a blockhouse that would eventually be called Fort Sandusky, Ohio. This move unsettled the local Indians.

1791: Delaware and Wyandot Indians attacked Big Bottom Settlement on the Muskingum River in Morgan County, southeastern Ohio.

1823: Thirty-one Seminole signed a treaty with the United States (7 Stat. 224) on Moultrie Creek in Florida. Six chiefs were given large estates to get them to agree to the treaty. Those chiefs were: John Blunt, Eneah Emathla, Emathlochee, Tuski Hadjo, Econchattemicco, and Mulatto King. The Seminole gave up lands north of Tampa Bay and returned runaway black slaves. They received an annuity of $5,000. The lands set aside for the Seminole were poor at best. The Americans were represented by James Gadsden. The Treaty of Fort Moultrie would be ratified by the U.S. Senate in 1824.

Indians from the Makah Tribe near Port Townsend, Washington (NA)

1838: By this date, 3,538 Chickasaws arrived in eastern Indian Territory (present-day Oklahoma) at Fort Coffee.

1848: Peter Skene Ogden arranged for the release of captives during the Cayuse attack on the Whitman Mission.

1873: The Makah Reservation in Washington was enlarged by executive order.

1873: Elements of the Fifth Cavalry and the Twenty-Third Infantry were on Clear Creek, Arizona Territory. For "gallantry in action while engaging hostile Indians," Private James Lenihan, Company K, would be awarded the Medal of Honor.

1875: Indians fought with soldiers from the Fifth Cavalry and some Indian scouts near Camp Apache, Arizona. According to army documents, fifteen Indians were killed, and 122 were captured. This engagement lasted until February 23.

1881: According to army reports, Major George Ilges, a force of 300 men from the Seventh Cavalry, the Fifth, Seventh, and Eleventh Infantries, and two pieces of artillery encountered a group of approximately 400 Poplar Camp Sioux from Montana on the Missouri River. The Sioux fled into the woods, but a few cannon rounds induced them to surrender. Ilges captured 324 Sioux, 200 horses, sixty-nine guns of various types, and a sizable quantity of supplies. Eight Sioux were killed in the fighting, and sixty escaped.

1980: The acting deputy commissioner of Indian affairs, Theodore Krenzke, authorized an election to adopt a new constitution and bylaws for the residents of the Cold Springs Rancheria in Fresno County, California. It was approved by a vote of 12–3.

1985: The extreme eastern portion of the Havasupai Reservation formed a portion of the Rain Tank Allotment that was under grazing permit to a private rancher until January 2, 1985.

Every: The terms of members of the Air Pollution Control Commission (which oversees tribal environmental programs) start according to the Model Tribal Environmental Code from the Native American Rights Fund.

JANUARY 3

1541: Hernando de Soto visited the main Chickasaw town. He wanted to visit Caluca, and he got guides and interpreters from the Chickasaw.

1786: A treaty (7 Stat. 21) with the Choctaw was signed by Benjamin Hawkins for the United States. The Choctaw agreed to release all prisoners. They acknowledged the sovereignty of the United States and no other country. New boundaries for their lands were delineated. No U.S. citizens were allowed to settle on Choctaw lands without Choctaw permission. Only the United States was allowed to regulate trade with the Choctaw. Signatories: five Great Medal Chiefs, thirteen small Medal Chiefs, twelve Medal and Gorget Captains. It was signed at Hopewell River.

1818: An agreement with the Piankashaw was made.

1870: According to official army records, Indians skirmished with a group of soldiers from the Ninth Cavalry and Twenty-Fourth Infantry between the Pecos and Rio Grande Rivers in Texas.

No casualties were reported. The fighting lasted until February 6.

1875: Indians fought with soldiers from the Fifth and Nineteenth Infantries near Hackberry Creek, Kansas. According to army documents, four Indians were captured. The fighting lasted until January 6.

1877: Colonel Nelson Miles and his troops had a second skirmish with what were believed to be followers of Crazy Horse as the army moved up the Tongue River.

1879: U.S. Army Captain Henry Wessells at Fort Robinson in northwestern Nebraska received orders from General Sheridan and Secretary of the Interior Carl Schurz that stated that Dull Knife and his Cheyenne must return to their reservation.

1891: The frozen bodies of the Indians killed at Wounded Knee on December 29, 1890, were picked up.

1895: On November 25, 1894, a group of nineteen Hopi hostiles were placed under arrest by the

Some Sioux killed at the Battle of Wounded Knee were placed on burial platforms by their surviving relatives.

army for interfering with friendly Hopi Indian activities on their Arizona reservation. The nineteen prisoners were held in Alcatraz prison in California from January 3, 1895, to August 7, 1895.

1975: President Ford signed into law Senate Bill 1296, as Public Law 93–620. This act enlarged the Havasupai Indian Reservation by 185,000 acres and designated a contiguous 95,300 acres of the Grand Canyon National Park as a permanent traditional use area of the Havasupai people.

1990: The Coast Indian Community of the Resighini Rancheria adopted a constitution by a vote of 18–4.

JANUARY 4

1752: Spanish forces defeated a group of 2,000 Pima near Aribaca.

1818: After the fighting in Fowltown, on the Flint River in Georgia opposite Fort Scott, on November 21, 1817, most of the Creek abandoned the village. Forces under Andrew Jackson moved in and occupied the village. The soldiers methodically destroyed it to keep the Red Stick Creek from returning.

1837: Fourteen Texans, led by George B. Erath, were following the trail of a Caddo war party on the Little River, near the Three Forks. At sunset they found the camp of 100 Caddo warriors. They attacked the next day.

1839: Elijah Hicks's group of Cherokees arrived in the Indian Territory (present-day Oklahoma). Hicks's group was one of several that made their own arrangements to move to their new lands west of the Mississippi River. Hicks started with 748 Cherokees but picked up 110 other emigrants en route. A smaller than normal percentage of this group died on the trip, approximately thirty-four. The deaths included the elderly Chief White Path.

1845: A Creek and Seminole treaty (9 Stat. 821) was signed at the Creek Agency by many Indians. It called for the Seminole to live with the Creek.

1868: According to army records, members of the First Cavalry and some Indian scouts fought with a band of Indians near Owyhee River, Idaho. One Indian was killed, and fifteen were captured.

1874: Eskiminzin of the Aravaipa Apache, survivor of the Camp Grant massacre and arrested as a "military precaution," escaped from San Carlos with many of his band. He returned in four months because most of his people were sick and hungry.

1874: Indians fought with soldiers from the Fifth Cavalry and some Indian scouts near Wild Rye Creek in Arizona. According to army documents, four Indians were killed.

1883: President Chester Arthur, by executive order, established the Hualpai Reservation in Walapai Agency. Size: 1,142 square miles in Arizona Territory. Bounded by: Colorado River, five miles east of Tinnakah Spring, south twenty miles to the summit of the high mesa, forty degrees east for twenty-five miles to Music Mountains, east fifteen miles, north fifty degrees, east for thirty-five miles, north thirty miles to Colorado River.

1937: The constitution of the Yerington Paiute Tribe of Nevada was approved by Secretary of the Interior Harold Ickes.

1975: The Indian Self-Determination and Education Assistance Act became law.

1979: The Cheyenne River Sioux Tribe established a sanitary landfill for garbage and waste materials for the community of Eagle Butte.

JANUARY 5

1802: According to some sources, William Augustus Bowles, self-appointed director-general and commander in chief of the Muskogee nation, led a force of Seminole (Miccosukee) warriors against the Spanish in St. Marks in northern Florida. They gave up their attack and siege in a little over a week.

1820: A proposal for the United States to buy Choctaw lands was made in the Mississippi legislature.

1837: After tracking a war party the day before, fourteen Texans, with their leader George Erath, found a Caddo war party of 100 braves. This morning, despite the odds, the Texans attacked the camp just after sunrise. Each side lost a few men before the Texans fled the area.

1852: One in a series of treaties with California Indians was signed in Temecula. The treaty was to set aside land and to protect the San Luis Rey Indians from Europeans.

1878: According to army records, six men were killed sixty miles northwest of Presidio del Norte, Texas, near the Rio Grande, by Mescalero Apache from the Fort Stanton Reservation in central New Mexico.

1882: The Uncompahgre Reserve was modified by executive order.

1891: According to *Frank Leslie's Illustrated Weekly*, as an aftermath of Wounded Knee, 100 Indians attacked a wagon train between Wounded Knee and Rapid City, Dakota. The fighting lasted until the cavalry arrived approximately six hours later.

1910: Guion Miller submitted a "Supplemental Report and Roll" for the Eastern Cherokees.

1952: A new adoption ordinance for the Coeur d'Alene Tribe was passed by the Tribal Council. It was approved by the acting commissioner of Indian affairs.

1968: An amendment to the Havasupai constitution was approved by the secretary of the interior.

1973: The Confederated Salish and Kootenai Tribes of the Flathead Reservation amended several land ordinances.

1976: Amendments to the constitution of the Yerington Paiute Tribe of Nevada were approved by the area director of the Phoenix area office of the Bureau of Indian Affairs. The voting members of the tribe voted for the amendments on November 7, 1975.

1987: National Native News first aired.

Every: The Mason School powwow.

JANUARY 6

1542: On the site of what was once the village of T'ho, Spaniard Francisco de Montejo established the town of Mérida in the Yucatan of Mexico.

1706: The Spanish were trying to improve relations with the Pueblos of New Mexico. Governor Francisco Cuervo y Valdez and "Protector General for the Indians" Captain Alfonso Rael de Aguilar met with leaders of all the nearby tribes. Among the Indians was Don Domingo Romero Yuguaque. Yuguaque was Governor of the Tesuque Pueblo.

1864: To force the Navajos to move to the Bosque Redondo Encampment, the army got Kit Carson to mount an expedition against the Navajos in the Canyon de Chelly. Captain Albert Pfeiffer and a small force left Fort Canby to met Carson at the canyon. Carson was called Rope Thrower by the Indians.

1867: According to army records, members of the army's Indian scouts fought with a band of Indians near Crooked River, Oregon. One scout was reported wounded; twenty Indians were killed, and eight captured.

1870: According to official army records, Indians skirmished with a group of soldiers from the Ninth Cavalry in the Guadalupe Mountains in Texas. No casualties were reported.

1875: Indians fought with soldiers from the Fifth and Nineteenth Infantries near Hackberry Creek, Kansas. According to army documents, four Indians were captured. The fighting started on January 3.

1880: President R.B. Hayes expanded the lands set aside for the Navajo reservation.

1881: Lakota (or the incorrect but commonly used Sioux) were trying to avoid going to a reservation. A large group was captured and forced to march from Poplar to Fort Buford.

1891: Of all of the recorded attacks by Indians on wagon trains crossing the western half of the United States, the very last one happened on this day.

1895: Hawaiians trying to restore the native royalty staged a small revolt. The plan was passed along to the Republic of Hawaii. The revolt was quickly put down. (Also recorded as happening on January 7, 1895.)

1937: The secretary of the interior approved the constitution of the Tohono O'odham (Papago) Nation; it was adopted on December 12, 1936.

1959: According to Federal Register No. 24FR00282, Public Land Order No. 1773 was issued. This order revoked the executive order of December 16, 1882, which established the Hopi Reservation.

1975: The last full-blooded Mandan died in Twin Buttes, North Dakota. She was Mattie Grinnell, and she lived to be 108 years old.

Every: King's day for most Pueblos.

JANUARY 7

1781: The Mission San Pedro y San Pablo de Bicuner was established in modern Imperial County, California, where the Anza Trail crosses the Colorado River. This was on land claimed by the Quechan (Yuma) Indians.

1795: As a part of what would be called the Yazoo Fraud, where state legislators were bribed by land developers, the state of Georgia sold large sections of Indian land to settlers and speculators.

1802: President Thomas Jefferson believed Indians had more land than they needed. He felt that if they became indebted at the government trade houses, they would sell their lands to pay the debts. He also voiced the opinion that if they became farmers they would need less land. On this day, he addressed the Wea, Potawatomi, and Miami Indians on the latter issues. He extolled the virtues of renewable food and clothing supplies. "We will with pleasure furnish you with implements for the most necessary arts, and with persons who may instruct you how to make and use them."

1806: The first island in the Tennessee River, which was ceded by the Cherokees on October 27, 1805, was officially ceded to the United States.

1806: Black Fox (Inali) was the principal chief of the Cherokees and a signatory to the Treaty with the Cherokees (7 Stat. 1010). He received $100 a year as a part of the treaty. The Cherokees ceded almost 7,000 square miles in Tennessee and Alabama under this agreement. The treaty was repudiated by most Cherokees. Lands given away included the Great Island of the Holston River, which was originally ceded by the Cherokees on October 27, 1805. It was signed in Washington, D.C.

1814: Under orders from Andrew Jackson, a force of 600 Indians, primarily Chickasaws and Choctaws, led by Colonel John McKee, set out to attack a Red Stick Creek village near the falls of the Black Warrior River in Alabama. When they arrived at the village, they discovered that it had been abandoned. The village was burned to the ground.

1831: Eneah Micco (Fat King), principal Creek chiefs of the lower towns, and others decide on this day to send representatives to Washington, D.C. They wanted to talk to Secretary of War Lewis Cass about Alabama laws and about whites settling on their lands. The government's response was, as always in Indian removal questions of this time, "We cannot help you, go west."

1833: According to a government report, by this date 3,333 Choctaws reached the Red River settlements west of the Mississippi River.

1839: Almost 700 Cherokees who left the Tennessee Agency on October 11, 1838, reached their new lands in the Indian Territory (present-day Oklahoma). This group of Cherokees were supporters of the New Echota Treaty. Since they were not removed from their lands by force, they were well provisioned and would not be destitute upon their arrival. They picked up almost 150 stragglers en route. However, only 654 made it to their destination.

1865: Approximately 1,000 Indians, led by the Sioux, attacked Julesburg, Colorado, in the morning. The Indians soundly defeated the local garrison. They took some loot and left.

1877: Colonel Miles and his troops were still moving up the Tongue River in force. They were looking for Crazy Horse and his followers. They captured a warrior, and seven women and children, who were relatives of a Cheyenne head man. Several attempts were made by the Indians to rescue the captives. The army prepared for a large attack expected to come the next morning.

1878: Soldiers from the Sixth Cavalry, Eighth Infantry, and some Indian scouts fought a group of Indians near Tonto Creek in Arizona. According to army documents, three Indians were killed.

1895: Hawaiians trying to restore the native royalty staged a small revolt. The plan was passed along to the Republic of Hawaii. The revolt was quickly put down. (Also recorded as happening on January 6, 1895.)

1977: Ben Reifel, commissioner of Indian affairs, approved a constitution and bylaws for the Fort Mohave Tribe.

JANUARY 8

1700: Pierre le Moyne, Sieur d'Iberville, established a fort and trading post on the Mississippi River a few dozen miles south of present-day New Orleans. It was his hope to establish friendly relations with the lower Mississippi Valley Indians to keep them from allying with the English or the Spanish.

1756: According to some reports, a meeting over trade restrictions was held on this day and the next by representatives of the British in New Jersey and various Delaware bands.

1779: Virginia Governor Patrick Henry ordered the Virginia militia to mount a campaign against the Chickamauga, an offshoot of the Cherokee Nation. Former Cherokee Chief Dragging Canoe and his followers had joined the Chickamauga. They continued to attack American settlements despite peace treaties signed by conservative Cherokee chiefs.

1815: General Andrew Jackson fought the British in the Battle of New Orleans. Among Jackson's army were many Choctaw warriors.

1821: A treaty (7 Stat. 215 and 217) was signed in Indian Springs, Georgia. The Creek gave up 5 million acres of land between the Flint and Ocmulgee Rivers for payments totaling $200,000. The government paid claims against the Creek up to a maximum of $250,000.

1836: The treaties calling for the removal of the Seminole from Florida to Indian Territory (present-day Oklahoma) called for a date to be chosen when they should meet in Tampa Bay for transport. The government picked this day as that date.

1838: The Republic of Texas signed a treaty with the Lipan Apache at Live Oak Point.

1844: In northwestern Florida, a ship landed on an island in Phillips Inlet for repairs. Some Indians, led by Chief Old Joe, killed a few of the crew.

1863: Groundbreaking for the Central Pacific Railroad took place. The train's route went through Indian lands.

1865: In Tom Green County, Texas, Captain Cunningham and members of the Comanche County Company skirmished with the Kickapoo Indians at the Battle of Dove Creek.

1867: According to army records, members of the First Cavalry and Indian scouts fought with a band of Indians near Owyhee River, Idaho. No injuries were reported on either side.

1869: Major General Philip H. Sheridan marked out the boundaries for Fort Sill, Oklahoma. Fort Sill is one of the few forts built during the Plains Indian Wars to remain in service.

1869: According to army records, settlers fought with a band of Indians near Lake Station, Colorado. Two civilians were killed.

1869: According to army records, members of the Eighth Cavalry fought with a band of Indians in the Bill Williams Mountains of Arizona. One Indian was killed during the fighting, which lasted until January 15.

1874: Indians fought with soldiers from the Fifth Cavalry and some Indian scouts in Pleasant Valley near the headwaters of Cherry Creek in Arizona.

According to army documents, two Indians were killed.

1877: Colonel Nelson "Bear Coat" Miles caught up to Crazy Horse, Little Big Man, Hump, Two Moons, and their followers at Battle Butte in southeastern Montana. Miles's soldiers attacked through the three-foot-deep snow. The war chiefs occupied the soldiers while the women and children escaped during a blizzard. The weather caused Miles to disengage. According to army records, approximately 600 warriors approached the soldiers, and a five-hour battle started. The second half of the battle was fought in a "blinding" snowstorm. The army drove the Indians through the Wolf Mountains, toward the Bighorn Mountains. The army reported three soldiers killed, eight wounded. They estimated the Indians' losses to be high. Captains Edmond Butler and James S. Casey and First Lieutenant Robert McDonald, Fifth Infantry, would be awarded the Medal of Honor for their actions in the fighting. The troops then returned to Fort Keogh at the mouth of the Tongue River in east-central Montana.

1877: Fifth and Twenty-Second Infantry soldiers fought a group of Indians in the Wolf Mountains of Arizona. According to army documents, three soldiers were killed and eight were wounded.

1976: The Land Development Plan prepared by the Tribal Planning Board of the Eastern Band of Cherokee Indians would become the official development plan for future development of the Cherokee Reservation.

1996: The last native speaker of the Catawba language, Red Thunder Cloud, died in Worcester, Massachusetts. He was seventy-six years old.

JANUARY 9

1756: The British Indian Land Commission adopted a law saying it must approve all sales of Indian lands.

1789: The treaty (7 Stat. 33) with the Mohawk, Oneida, Onondaga, Tuscarora, Cayuga, and Seneca Nations, signed on this day, referred back to the treaty signed on October 22, 1784, and January 21, 1785. Two Indians were held as hostages until prisoners held by the Indians were returned. New tribal boundary lines were established. The Indians were able to hunt in the lands that were ceded in this treaty, if they did so peacefully. The governor of the Northwest Territory issued all trade licenses for trade with the Indians. No U.S. citizens were allowed to live on Indian lands without the Indians' approval. Lands set aside for trading posts in the earlier treaty were confirmed. It was signed by twenty-eight Indians and General Arthur St. Claire at Fort Harmar (near modern Marietta, Ohio). The Mohawks did not attend the meeting or sign the treaty.

1790: Spanish and Indian forces under Commanding General Juan de Ugalde attacked a group of 300 Lipan, Lipiyan, and Mescalero Apache at Arroyo de la Soledad. The Spanish soundly defeated the Apache. The Spaniards named the battlegrounds the Cañón de Ugalde in honor of their commander. Modern Uvalde, Texas, got its name from this spot.

1809: President Jefferson allowed Cherokee to go west of the Mississippi River to look at new lands.

1843: All of Pascofa's Apalachicola "Seminole" (actually Creek who had fled the Creek Wars and joined the Seminole) surrendered to Colonel Ethan Hitchcock in St. Marks, Florida. This brought an end to this Seminole war. The group included a total of fifty people.

1867: According to army records, members of the First Cavalry fought with a band of Indians near Malheur River, Oregon. Thirty Indians were reported captured.

1873: President Grant, by executive order, established the Tule River Preserve. At its height, it housed Kawia, Kings River, Monache, Tehon, Tule, and Wichumni Tribes from the Mission Tule Agency. It was seventy-six square miles. This order, and the preserve, were modified by further orders on October 3, 1873, and August 3, 1878.

1875: Indians fought with soldiers from the Eighth Infantry near Camp Apache, Arizona. According to army documents, no casualties were reported.

1876: Sixth Cavalry and Eighth Infantry soldiers and some Indian scouts fought some Indians near Camp Apache, Arizona. According to army documents, one Indian was killed and five were captured.

1877: Lieutenant J.A. Rucker, Troops H and L, Sixth Cavalry, and Company C, Indian scouts, battled with Indians in the Leidendorf Mountains of western New Mexico Territory. Ten Indians were killed, one captured. The army reported one soldier wounded.

1877: Sixth Cavalry soldiers and some Indian scouts fought a group of Indians in the Tonto Basin of Arizona. According to army documents, eighteen Indians were killed and twenty were captured. The fighting lasted through February 5.

1879: At Fort Robinson in northwestern Nebraska, the Cheyenne were being held in the barracks without food or wood because they would not return to their reservation. After five days, Captain Henry Wessells ordered Cheyenne chiefs to his quarters for a conference. Dull Knife did not go, but Left Hand, Crow, and Wild Hog attended. Wild Hog told the captain that the Cheyenne would never go to Indian Territory (present-day Oklahoma); they would rather die here. Captain Wessells ordered him put in irons and a fight ensued, with a soldier being stabbed. Left Hand, in manacles, made it outside and yelled aloud what was happening. Captain Wessells offered to let the women and children out of the barracks, but they said they would rather die at the fort than to be forced to go south. That evening, Cheyenne warriors recovered some hidden rifles, and just before 10 P.M. they opened fire on the soldier guards from their prison barracks. An army report called the barracks "like a den of rattlesnakes, into which it is certain death for any white man to go." While the shooting continued, the Cheyenne escaped from the fort. The soldiers pursued them, and a gunfight developed nearby. Only thirty-eight Cheyenne were not killed, wounded, or captured during this fight (Dull Knife's daughter was one of the killed). Most of these thirty-eight were killed or captured in the next few days. During the initial day of fighting, five soldiers were reported killed, and seven were wounded.

1881: Twenty Sioux were captured by Major Ilges's forces along the Missouri River.

1884: President Arthur, by executive order, canceled the initial order establishing the Yuma Reserve in California. This order reestablished the reserve in other areas. This order also removed Fort Yuma from the jurisdiction of the military and placed it under the authority of the Department of the Interior.

1949: Tom Longboat, a Canadian Iroquois, died. He was a world-class long-distance runner. In 1907, he won the Boston Marathon.

1967: Robert Bennett, commissioner of Indian affairs, approved an amendment to the constitution of the Comanche Indian Tribe.

1976: The commissioner of Indian affairs, Morris Thompson, ratified an election for a constitution and bylaws for the Manzanita Band of Mission Indians.

JANUARY 10

1591: Gaspar Castaño de Sosa was traveling through the Tewa Pueblo villages. In his journal he noted that he was received well in Jacona. He mentioned that Tewa villages were small but heavily populated. Jacona was eventually abandoned a little over 100 years later.

1786: A treaty (7 Stat. 24) with the Chickasaw was signed. The Chickasaw agreed to return all prisoners they held. The tribe recognized the sovereignty of the United States and no other. New tribal land boundary lines were established. No U.S. citizens were allowed to live on Chickasaw lands without Chickasaw approval. Only the

United States was allowed to regulate trade with the tribe. It was signed at Hopewell River by three Indians: Piomingo, Mingatushka, and Latopoia.

1806: President Thomas Jefferson addressed Cherokee chiefs. He applauded their efforts at becoming productive in their farming efforts. "Go on, my children, in the same way and be assured the further you advance in it the happier and more respectable you will be."

1839: John Benge and 1,103 other Cherokees arrived in the Indian Territory (present-day Oklahoma). They had started their trek with 1,200.

1852: According to the Oklahoma Law Enforcement Memorial, Chin-Chi-Kee, Captain, Chickasaw Lighthorse, attempted to arrest four whiskey smugglers south of Tishomingo, the capital of the Chickasaw Nation. A fought broke out, and Chin-Chi-Kee, armed only with a knife, killed three of the men before the fourth, a Seminole Indian named Bill Nannubbee, shot him in the head and killed him.

1874: Indians fought with soldiers from the Fifth Cavalry and some Indian scouts in Pleasant Valley near the headwaters of Cherry Creek in Arizona. According to army documents, two Indians were killed.

1879: President Rutherford Hayes, by executive order, added to the Gila River Reserve in Pima Agency. This reserve was established February 28, 1859. The order also added to the Pima and Maricopa Indian Reservation. This second part of this order was canceled on June 14, 1879.

1881: Gall and Crow were led into Fort Buford.

1886: Army Indian scouts under Captain Emmet Crawford fought a group of Indians near the Aros River in Sonora, Mexico. According to army documents, Captain Crawford was wounded. The fighting continued until the next day.

1929: By Executive Order No. 5023, the trust period on allotments to the "Iowa Indians in Kansas and Nebraska" was extended for ten years. A few plots of land were excepted because the person assigned to that land had died.

1949: According to Federal Register No. 14FR00471, an order was issued modifying the restoration of certain undisposed-of surplus lands on the Cheyenne River Reservation.

1961: The federal government restored certain nonmineral, unallotted, unreserved, and undisposed-of lands on the Fort Berthold Indian Reservation in North Dakota to tribal ownership of the three affiliated tribes.

1985: The Cherokee asked Arkansas and Missouri not to sell alcohol to Indians.

1992: The Rosebud Sioux Tribal Council approved the memorandum of understanding with the state of South Dakota and U.S. Environmental Protection Agency on implementation of Title III (Emergency Planning and Providing for Emergency Response) for release of hazardous substances and petroleum on the Rosebud Reservation.

JANUARY 11

1698: Four French missionaries had been staying with the Quapaw Indians, on the Mississippi River. They traveled downstream and reached a Tunica Indian village. Missionary Antoine Davion decided to stay with the Tunica to preach to them.

1790: George Washington wrote a letter to the Senate regarding a treaty with the Creek.

1803: The Creek Treaty (7 Stat. 68) of June 16, 1802, was publicly proclaimed.

1839: On January 1, 1839, an Indian war party attacked several settlements (near modern Marlin, Texas), killing five people. The war party returned. This time the Texans were ready. They killed seven of the Indians before the war party decided to give up the attack.

1851: As a part of the Mariposa Indian Wars in California, Sheriff James Burney led a force of settlers against the local Indians. The battle was a draw.

1870: According to official army records, Indians skirmished with a group of soldiers from the

Ninth Cavalry along the lower Pecos River in Texas. One Indian was killed.

1881: Crow King confronted Sitting Bull. After the confrontation, Crow King left.

1886: The First Infantry engaged Apache in the Sierra Madre Mountains near the Aros River in Sonora, Mexico. For his actions against hostile Indians under Geronimo and Natchez, First Lieutenant Marion Maus would be awarded the Medal of Honor. According to army documents, Captain Crawford was wounded. The fighting started one day earlier.

1962: John A. Carvey Jr., assistant secretary of the interior, ratified an amendment to the constitution and bylaws of the Miccosukee Tribe of Indians of Florida.

1972: Reverend Harold S. Jones, a Sioux from South Dakota, was the first American Indian to be made a bishop in the Episcopal Church.

1978: The Swinomish adopted amendments to their zoning ordinances.

1985: The National Tribal Chairmen Association rejected several federal proposals.

JANUARY 12

1825: James Hudson had been found guilty of murdering Seneca subchief Logan in Madison County, Indiana. Hudson was part of a group of settlers who killed eight other Seneca and Miami Indians in the Fall Creek Massacre on March 22, 1824. Two of the other attackers would also be hanged at a later date.

1864: The Navajos had been ordered to move to the Bosque Redondo Reservation in New Mexico. Many who decided not to go moved to the Canyon de Chelly. Kit "Rope Thrower" Carson had been directed to force the Navajos to move or to be killed as hostiles. Carson and Captain Pfeiffer advanced to the canyon. On this day, Carson entered the west end of the canyon. They encountered a band of Navajos and killed eleven of them. While in the canyon, Carson or-

dered the burning of the Navajos' food and cherished peach trees.

1866: Elements of the Second Cavalry from Fort McDermitt fought with Indians near Fish Creek, Nevada. Five soldiers were wounded. Thirty-four Indians were killed, according to army records.

1873: Indians fought with soldiers from the First Cavalry near Tule Lake, California, according to army documents. One soldier was wounded.

1877: Five soldiers from Troop A, Third Cavalry, fought a group of fourteen Indians on Elkhorn Creek, Wyoming. Three soldiers were wounded in the encounter. One of the wounded soldiers, Corporal Charles A. Bessey, would be awarded the Medal of Honor for his actions. Some government records show this happening on January 13.

1880: Major Albert Morrow and elements of the Ninth Cavalry buffalo soldiers (black troops) found and attacked Victorio and his Warm Springs Apache near the source of the Puerco River in southern New Mexico. The fighting lasted for about four hours, until sunset, when the Indians escaped. One soldier was killed, and one scout was wounded.

1938: Land disposal regulations were modified on the Rosebud Reservation in South Dakota.

1963: A land assignment ordinance was established by the Susanville Indian Rancheria in Lassen County, California. It was eventually replaced by a constitution.

1966: An amendment to the constitution of the Skokomish Indian Tribe was approved.

1971: The NAACP Legal Defense Fund alleged federal funds for Indian education were going to "every conceivable school need except aiding the 177,000 Indian children in public schools." Their study indicated that federal money was going to white schools or to lower whites' taxes.

1980: An election for amendments to the constitution and bylaws of the Fallon Paiute-Shoshone Tribe was held. They were approved by votes of 69–21, 57–36, and 62–32.

1990: The Colorado River Indian Tribal Council enacted Ordinance No. 90–1, which added article 2, covering the treatment and control of the Pink Bollworm to the agricultural code.

JANUARY 13

1729: Measles spread through New Spain. It struck the Pima workers at the mission San Ignacio de Caburica. The priest, Father Campos, baptized twenty-two Pima *in periculo mortis* because they were so close to death. This epidemic killed many Indians.

1756: For the next five days, Pennsylvania authorities and local Indians held a council in Carlisle, Pennsylvania. Governor Morris and several other prominent people represented the British. The Indians were represented by Aroas (Silver Heels), Belt of Wampum, Canachquasy, Isaac, Jagrea, Seneca George, and several others. These discussions led to the eventual declaration of war against the Delaware and the Shawnee by the British later in the year.

1832: Approximately 2,500 Choctaw bound for Indian Territory (present-day Oklahoma) were at Arkansas Post. They set out on foot and in wagons to Little Rock.

1834: Joseph Rutherford Walker left Monterey, California, en route to the east. He "discovered" Walker Pass through the southern Sierra Madre Mountains. This pass became part of a major pioneer trail to California.

1869: According to army records, members of the First Cavalry and the Thirty-Second Infantry fought with a band of Indians near Mount Turnbull, Arizona. One Indian was killed, and one was wounded.

1873: Captain Jack (Kintpuash, or Keintpoos) and his Modoc were hiding in the northeastern California lava beds. This day, his sentries spotted an army scouting party approaching their stronghold. The sentries sent a few shots in the army's direction. The scouting party withdrew.

1879: After Dull Knife's Cheyenne escaped from Fort Robinson in northwestern Nebraska, they were pursued by the army. They skirmished twice with Lieutenant James Simpson and elements of the Third Cavalry near Hat Creek Road. One soldier was killed and another wounded during the fighting.

1902: Commissioner W.S. Jones of the Department of the Interior, Office of Indian Affairs, sent out notification to federal agencies that Indian males should no longer be allowed to have long hair. He stated that it would be a great step in advance and certainly hasten their progress toward civilization.

1939: The Havasupai Nations approved a constitution. The assistant secretary of the interior approved the election on March 27, 1939.

1939: The assistant secretary of the interior authorized an election to amend the constitution and bylaws of the Oneida Tribe of Wisconsin. The election would be held on June 3, 1939.

1964: The assistant secretary of the interior authorized an election to amend the constitution of the Yerington Paiute Tribe of Nevada.

JANUARY 14

1784: The Treaty of Paris, ending the Revolutionary War, was ratified.

1830: The U.S. Senate passed a resolution that called for the government to survey lands west of the Mississippi and then parcel them out among the Creek, Cherokee, Choctaw, and Chickasaw Indians. Its intent was for the Indians to move there en masse.

1833: Reverend Samuel Worcester was a missionary to the Cherokee Nation in Georgia. The state of Georgia had ordered all whites living with Indians to swear allegiance to the state of Georgia. Reverend Worcester refused to do so. On September 16, 1831, Reverend Worcester was sentenced to four years at hard labor in a Georgia prison. Even though the Supreme Court ruled that it was unconstitutional for Georgia to jail Reverend Worcester, he was not released until this day.

1840: The Republic of Texas set aside two plots of land for the Alabama and Coushatta Indians in eastern Texas.

1846: A treaty was made and concluded at the Methodist mission in the Kansas country. Representing the United States were Commissioners Richard Cummins and Thomas Harvey. It was signed by the Woods and Mission Band of the Potawatomi.

1864: Kit Carson and Captain Pfeiffer joined forces in the Canyon de Chelly. Late in the evening, a small group of Navajo approached the army and told them the Navajo were freezing and hungry. They were willing to surrender. Carson gave them until the next day to surrender or be hunted down.

1868: According to army records, members of the Eighth Cavalry fought with a band of Indians near Difficult Canyon, Arizona. Two soldiers were wounded. Sixteen Indians were reported killed, and six were wounded.

1868: According to army records, members of the Eighth Cavalry fought with a band of Indians near Beale Springs, Arizona. Lieutenant J.D. Stevenson was wounded. Five Indians were reported killed.

1879: Dull Knife's Cheyenne escapees from Fort Robinson fortified a position twenty miles from the fort in northwestern Nebraska. They again fought with troops, who used artillery. The artillery was ineffectual, and the Indians escaped in the night. The army estimated their numbers at forty-five, including nineteen warriors. Cheyenne captured on January 22, 1879, said Dull Knife was probably killed during this fight.

1891: Many of the Plains Indians had left their reservations. The move was fostered by the Ghost Dance religion. On this day the army issued orders for all Indians to return to their reservations.

1893: Through January 17, the Hawaiian royalty had significant conflicts with non-Hawaiian settlers.

1913: Forty acres of land were "withdrawn from entry and set aside for administrative purposes" on the Flathead Reservation in Montana by executive order of President William Howard Taft.

1913: President Taft, by Executive Order No. 1682, set aside forty acres of the Fort Shaw School Reservation in Montana for administrative purposes.

1971: The U.S. government gave an old army base in Davis, California, to a group of Indians who had occupied the one-square-mile site in 1970.

1971: An election that adopted a constitution and bylaws for the Chitimacha Tribe of Louisiana was ratified by Assistant Secretary of the Interior Harrison Loesch. The election was held on November 7, 1970.

1971: An election that approved a constitution and bylaws for the San Pasqual Band of Mission (Diegueno) Indians in the San Pasqual Reservation was ratified by Assistant Secretary of the Interior Harrison Loesch. The election was held on November 29, 1970.

JANUARY 15

1704: On December 14, 1703, fifty South Carolina militia under Governor James Moore, allied with 1,000 Creek warriors, captured the Spanish Mission of Ayubale in northern Florida. The Spanish governor of Florida, Juan Ruiz Mexia, launched an expedition of Spanish soldiers and Apalachee Indians to recapture the mission. In the subsequent battle, the Carolina-Creek forces were victorious.

1756: After the Delaware uprising, many settlers moved to Bethlehem, Pennsylvania. A group of settlers and some friendly Indians left the village in hopes of returning to their farms. A group of Delaware attacked the party and killed all but one of the settlers and many of the Indians.

1808: The Treaty of Mount Dexter (7 Stat. 98; the Dinsmoor-Robertson treaty) with the

Choctaws, which ceded almost 5 million acres of land along the Florida border, was finally brought to the Senate by President Jefferson for ratification. The treaty had originally been negotiated on November 16, 1805.

1832: The Chickasaw met at their council house to discuss the removal proposal of President Jackson. They decided to approve the removal, but they would not cooperate with any efforts to have them share lands with the Choctaw.

1838: Ransom Gillet and Iroquois Indians signed a treaty (7 Stat. 550). The Iroquois gave up their lands in New York and Wisconsin. They were given five years to move to lands in Kansas. The Oneida did not move to the new lands.

1838: U.S. forces under Navy Lieutenant Levi Powell captured a Seminole woman. They forced her to lead them to a village in the Everglades. On this day the Americans attacked the village. By the time they retreated, four Americans had died, and fifteen others were wounded in the fighting. Seminole losses, if any, were not recorded in government records.

1864: Sixty starving Navajos surrendered to Kit Carson after the Canyon de Chelly fight.

1869: According to army records, members of the Eighth Cavalry fought with a band of Indians in the Bill Williams Mountains of Arizona. One Indian was killed during the fighting, which started on January 8.

1878: The forces of Major V.K. Hart and General John E. Smith, Fourteenth Infantry from Fort Hall (north of Pocatello, Idaho), surrounded two villages of hostile Bannock with thirty-two lodges at the Ross Fork Agency. Fifty-three warriors were captured and taken to the Bannock Indian Agency. Some 250 horses were also captured.

1877: Crazy Horse and his band of followers were camped on Prairie Dog Creek in Montana. They were hoping to avoid the army troops under Colonel Miles. On this day Sitting Bull arrived at the camp. According to some sources, he suggested a peaceful solution to the conflict.

1891: Kicking Bear surrendered, ending the Ghost Dance War. He eventually joined Buffalo Bill's Wild West Show.

1936: A constitution for the Tuolumne Band of Me-Wok Indians of the Tuolumne Rancheria was approved by Secretary of the Interior Harold Ickes. He also approved amendments to the constitution of the Oglala Sioux of the Pine Ridge Indian Reservation, the Manchester Band of Pomo Indians of the Manchester Rancheria, the Reno-Sparks Indian Community of Nevada, the Tule River Indian Tribe, and the Pyramid Lake Paiute Tribe of Nevada.

1936: The secretary of the interior authorized an election to approve a constitution and bylaws for the Santee Sioux Tribe of the Sioux Nation of the state of Nebraska. The election would be held on February 29, 1936.

1945: Jack C. Montgomery was a Cherokee and a first lieutenant with the 45th Infantry Division Thunderbirds. On February 22, 1944, near Padiglione, Italy, Montgomery's rifle platoon was under fire by three echelons of enemy forces when he single-handedly attacked all three positions, taking prisoners in the process. As a result of his courage, Montgomery's actions demoralized the enemy and inspired his men to defeat the Axis troops. He was awarded the Medal of Honor on this day.

1980: An election was held on a new constitution by the Skokomish Indian Tribe. The new constitution was approved by a vote of 41–21.

1981: An amendment to the constitution and bylaws of the Suquamish Indian Tribe of the Port Madison Reservation in the state of Washington was ratified by the area director, Bureau of Indian Affairs.

JANUARY 16

1714: According to some sources, a peace agreement was reached between representatives of the Abenaki Indians and the British in Massachusetts.

1792: Leading a force of 300 Creek and Seminole warriors, William Augustus Bowles had surrounded St. Marks, Florida. After holding out for several weeks, the Spanish surrendered to Bowles on this day. The Indians seized the supplies but were forced out by a Spanish force in a few months. Bowles conquered the fort again on May 19, 1800.

1831: Mushulatubbe (Determined to Kill) said he would step down as chief of the Northeastern District when the removal of the Choctaws to Indian Territory (present-day Oklahoma) began. He recommended that Peter Pitchlynn replace him as chief.

1832: Nitakeechi and 1,000 Choctaws, as part of their removal to Indian Territory (present-day Oklahoma), arrived in Little Rock, Arkansas, aboard the steamboat *Reindeer*. They camped outside of Little Rock at Camp Pope.

1839: Daniel Colon and 651 Cherokees arrived in the Indian Territory (present-day Oklahoma) as a part of their forced emigration from the east.

1847: The Treaty of Cahuenga was signed, ceding California to the United States.

1854: Citizens from Yreka, California, confronted Shasta Indians over stolen cattle. Four whites were killed. This helped to rekindle the Rogue River War.

1868: According to army records, members of the Eighth Cavalry fought with a band of Indians near Malheur River, Oregon. No injuries were reported on either side.

1873: More than 200 regular army soldiers and 100 California and Oregon militia approached the Modoc stronghold in the northeastern California lava beds. They visibly set up around Captain Jack's position in hopes that the Modoc would not fight in the face of obviously superior forces. The Modoc considered surrender, but only a few wished to do so, so all stayed.

1873: Indians fought with soldiers from the Fifth Cavalry in the Superstition Mountains of Arizona, according to army documents. Four Indians were killed, and twelve were captured.

1875: Lieutenant Hinkle and soldiers from the Fifth Infantry engaged in a short chase and captured four Cheyenne near the Smoky Hill River, southeast of Fort Wallace in western Kansas.

1878: Settlers fought a group of Indians in Mason County, Texas. According to army documents, two settlers were killed. In Brady City, Texas, another settler was killed by Indians.

1879: Regulations regarding the Shoshone Carlin Farms Reserve in Elko, Nevada, were modified.

1896: The state of Iowa passed a Sac and Fox tax law.

1911: An executive order restored certain Indian lands in New Mexico to the public domain.

1929: The trust period on allotments of the Rosebud Sioux Indians in South Dakota was extended by Executive Order No. 5028.

1936: Secretary of the Interior Harold Ickes authorized an election for a constitution for the Omaha Tribe of Nebraska. He also authorized a similar election for the Kashia Band of Pomo Indians of the Stewarts Point Rancheria.

1964: The assistant secretary of the interior authorized an election to approve an amendment to the constitution and bylaws of the Miccosukee Tribe of Indians of Florida. The election was held on April 12, 1964.

1967: The National Indian Education Advisory Commission was modified by the Bureau of Indian Affairs.

1979: An amendment to the constitution and bylaws for the Eskimos of the Native Village of Kwinhagak was approved in an election.

JANUARY 17

1524: Verrazano set sail from Europe; he eventually landed in North Carolina.

1800: Congress passed the Act for the Preservation of Peace with the Indian Tribes. One of its provisions was: "That if any citizen or other person residing within the United States, or the territory thereof, shall send any talk, speech, message or letter to any Indian nation, tribe, or chief, with an intent to produce a contravention or infraction of any treaty or other law of the United States, or to disturb the peace and tranquillity of the United States, he shall forfeit a sum not exceeding two thousand dollars, and be imprisoned not exceeding two years."

1813: As a part of the Detroit campaign, General James Winchester's force of 700 Kentucky soldiers attacked British and Indian forces at Monroe, Michigan, then called Frenchtown, on the Raisin River. They liberated the village. A counterattack was waged on January 22, 1813.

1836: On the Halifax River in Dunlawton, Florida, ten dozen Seminole battled forces from St. Augustine under Major Benjamin Putnam. The Seminole killed four of the militia and wounded thirteen others, and the soldiers retreated. After this battle, many settlers fled parts of Florida south of St. Augustine.

1837: John Caesar, a black Seminole, and fourteen others attacked a plantation not far from St. Augustine, Florida. They were run off by militia from the nearby town. Later that night, the militia found Caesar's camp and attacked. Caesar and two other Seminole were killed. The others escaped. As a longtime aide to Seminole Chief Philip, Caesar's skills in warfare were missed by the Seminole.

1837: The Chickasaws agreed to buy a large section of the western lands of the Choctaws in eastern Indian Territory (present-day Oklahoma) for $530,000. This was where the Chickasaws moved when they left Alabama. This was called the Treaty of Doaksville (11 Stat. 573).

1850: Cupeno Chief Antonio Garra had attacked the settlements at Warner Hot Springs in modern San Diego County, California. This and other similar attacks were in retaliation for the forced indentured servitude of many Indians. Garra was captured by a citizens' militia. They executed him.

1863: Mangas Colorado (Red Sleeves) was camped near the Mimbres River when he was sent a message from California volunteers Captain Edmond Shirland requesting a truce and a parley. Against the advice of his Apache followers, Mangas agreed to a meeting. Mangas entered the soldiers' camp (near modern Silver City in southwestern New Mexico) under a white flag, but he was seized immediately. He was transferred to old Fort McLane in southwest New Mexico.

1873: After a fight, during efforts to get the Modoc to return to their reservation, the Modoc moved into the northeastern California lava beds. Captain Jack, Hooker Jim, Curly Headed Doctor, Boston Charley, and Scarface were some of the Modoc who fought the soldiers from the First Cavalry, Twenty-First Infantry, California and Oregon volunteers, according to army documents. One the first day, nine soldiers were killed. Lieutenants David Perry, J.M. Kyle, and G.W. Roberts and twenty-seven soldiers were wounded. The Modoc suffered no fatalities. By placing himself in a position that was exposed to the Indians and surviving, Major John Green was able to motivate his troops. For his actions, Major Green was given the Medal of Honor. Contract Surgeon John O. Skinner was also awarded the Medal of Honor for rescuing a wounded soldier while under heavy fire.

1880: After escaping from the troops near the Puerco River, Victorio again fought with Major Albert Morrow's Ninth Cavalry troops in the San Mateo Mountains of New Mexico. Indian losses were unknown. Two scouts were wounded, and Lieutenant J. Hansell French was killed in the fighting, according to army files.

1881: Peter Pitchlynn, Choctaw chief during the Civil War, died in Washington, D.C. Pitchlynn served as Northeastern District chief for a short time during the removal process. He was buried in Congressional Cemetery.

1888: Big Bear, a Canadian Plains Cree, died. He was one of the last Cree to sign Treaty No. 6. Three years prior to his death, he was convicted of treason for his part in Riel's Rebellion. He was released from prison due to ill health. He died soon after his release.

1893: American settlers overthrew the royal government of Queen Lydia Paki Kamekeha Lili-uokalani in Hawaii. They established a provisional government under the leadership of Judge Sanford Dole.

1936: The territory of the Fort McDermitt Paiute and Shoshone Indian Reservation was established (Public Law No. 419, 74th Congress) near McDermitt in northwestern Nevada and southeastern Oregon.

1969: Boundary lines on the Colorado River Reservation were modified.

1975: A modification to the constitution of the Indians of the Tulalip Tribes in Washington was approved by the U.S. government.

JANUARY 18

1867: According to army records, members of the Eighth Cavalry fought with a band of Indians near Eden Valley, Nevada. One soldier was wounded, and two Indians were killed.

1870: From a marker in the Fort Buford (North Dakota) cemetery: "He That Kills His Enemies—Indian Scout—January 18, 1870—Died of Wounds . . . in a quarrel with a fellow scout on the 5th inst. received a penetrating [arrow] wound of the pelvis and abdomen. . . . Death occured January 18, 1870. An autopsy could not be obtained owing to the feelings of the relatives."

1873: Under a white flag, the army claimed its dead and wounded from the previous day's fight against the Modoc in California. The army then retreated.

1881: An act (21 Stat. 315) called for an official census of the Wisconsin Winnebago.

1938: Executive Order No. 7792 was issued regarding Indian lands in New Mexico. It modified Executive Order No. 4929, issued on July 7, 1928.

1956: Assistant Secretary of the Interior Wesley D'Ewart authorized an election to approve an

Jim Thorpe, Olympic medal winner, in football uniform, Carlisle Indian School (NA)

amendment to the constitution and bylaws of the Tule River Indian Tribe. The election would be held on February 25, 1956.

1958: The Lumbee broke up a Ku Klux Klan meeting in North Carolina and made national headlines.

1974: An election for amendments to the constitution for the Gila River Pima-Maricopa Indian Community was held. They were approved by a vote of 140–29, with 532 voters eligible.

1983: Jim Thorpe's Olympic medals were given to his heirs.

1986: The Tohono O'odham approved a new constitution by a vote of 1,236–944.

JANUARY 19

1777: A group of Oneida chiefs met with Colonel Elmore at Fort Schuyler. The wanted the army to tell the Mohawks that the great council fire of the Onondaga had been extinguished.

1821: The Senate ratified the Treaty of Doak's Stand made with the Choctaws on October 18, 1820.

1830: The Senate and House of Representatives of Mississippi passed a law making all state laws apply to all Indians and their lands within the state. The law effectively removed all federal privileges the Indians enjoyed.

1838: Seminole Chief Jumper and sixty-four of his followers left Tampa Bay en route to the Indian Territory (present-day Oklahoma). Jumper had surrendered to Colonel Zachary Taylor a month earlier.

1847: In Don Fernandez de Taos (present-day Taos, New Mexico), recently installed Governor George Bent was trying to keep Mexican and Pueblo Indians from revolting (an earlier revolt was prevented). A number of Pueblo Indians demanded the release of some Indians being held in jail. Words were exchanged, and a fight started. People were killed on both sides. Governor Bent was attacked, killed, and scalped. The Indians' plan was to kill all of the Americans they could find. Near Mora, eight Americans were captured, robbed, and shot. Many Mexicans joined the revolt against the Americans who had captured Santa Fe de San Francisco (present-day Santa Fe, New Mexico) on August 18, 1846.

1867: According to army records, members of the Fourth Cavalry fought with a band of Indians near Nueces River, Texas. Two Indians were reported killed.

1870: Brevet Colonel E.M. Baker and Troops F, G, H, and I, Second Cavalry, and fifty-five mounted infantry left Fort Shaw, near Great Falls, Montana. Their goal was to find, and punish, Mountain Chief and his band of Piegan, believed to be on the Marias River.

1891: The Sioux survivors of Wounded Knee arrived back at their reservation.

1937: Secretary of the Interior Harold Ickes ratified an election for a constitution and bylaws by the members of the Ute Indians of the Uintah, Uncompahgre, and White River Bands of the Uintah and Ouray Reservation.

1959: An amendment to the constitution and bylaws of the Fort Belknap Indian Community of the Fort Belknap Indian Reservation in Montana were adopted.

1963: An election on amendments to the constitution for the Wisconsin Winnebago was held. They were approved by a margin of 514–5.

1974: According to a report from Bureau of Indian Affairs Commissioner Morris Thompson, the Menominee tribe officially resumed receiving federal services. The tribe had previously been terminated as a federally recognized entity in 1961.

JANUARY 20

1814: Seven dozen men left Fort George (modern Astoria, Oregon) in canoes to retaliate for an attack on David Stuart's party at the Cascades portage last year.

1825: The Choctaw signed a treaty (7 Stat. 234) in Washington, D.C. One of the major provisions ceded most of the Choctaws' land in Arkansas. This was often called the Treaty of 1825.

1830: Red Jacket (Sagoyewatha) was a Seneca chief born around 1779. Although he was often called a coward in war, he was respected as a great speaker and for his refusal to adopt white ways. Following the way of many before him, he eventually became an alcoholic. He died on this day.

1856: Governor Stevens's Nez Perce honor guard was disbanded.

1857: An executive order from President Franklin Pierce modified the Nisqually Reserve. It allowed the Oregon territorial governor to move the Indian tribes to more suitable lands. This change was allowed under the treaty signed on December 26, 1854.

1870: According to some sources, buffalo soldier Troops C, D, I, and K, Ninth Cavalry, battled with Indians on Delaware Creek in the Guadalupe Mountains in Texas. Two soldiers were killed.

1872: Indians attacked a stage between Tucson and Camp Bowie in Arizona, according to official army records. Three people on the stage were killed, and one was wounded.

1873: Indians fought with soldiers from the Eighth Cavalry near the Lower Miembres in New Mexico, according to army documents. One Indian was killed.

1874: Indians fought with soldiers from the Fifth Cavalry and some Indian scouts near San Carlos, Arizona, according to army documents. A total of twenty-five Indians were killed, and seventeen were captured, in the fighting, which started on December 8, 1873.

1877: Elements of the Third Cavalry skirmished with hostile Indians at Bluff Station, Wyoming. For his actions over the next two days, Sergeant William Lewis, Company B, would be awarded the Medal of Honor.

1879: Major Andrew Evans and Troops B and D, Third Cavalry, fought with remnants of Dull Knife's Fort Robinson, Nebraska, escapees. The Indians were on some cliffs and managed to elude the army after a skirmish.

1891: Hawaiian King Kalakaua died. He would be one of the last native Hawaiian rulers.

1976: Commissioner of Indian Affairs Morris Thompson approved the election of a constitution for the Utu Utu Gwaitu Paiute Tribe of the Benton Paiute Reservation in California. The election was held on November 22, 1975.

1980: Commissioner of Indian Affairs William Hallett ratified the constitution of the Tonto Apache Tribe.

1984: The Jicarilla Apache tribal council enacted Ordinance No. 84–0–235, the Jicarilla Apache Environmental Protection Ordinance.

Seneca Chief Red Jacket

The purpose of this ordinance was to ensure "that proper and meaningful consideration of environmental, cultural, historical, and ecological factors is made by any person, the Bureau of Indian Affairs, or the Tribal Council prior to its approval of activities on the Jicarilla Apache Reservation that may significantly affect that environment." It became effective on April 13, 1984.

JANUARY 21

1634: Trader Captain John Stone was killed by Pequot. Stone was often considered a less than reputable character by both the settlers and the Indians.

1674: Father Pierre Millet "foretold" the coming of this day's lunar eclipse, using an almanac. He challenged Iroquois shamans to predict the time or date of the eclipse, which they did not. Millet made religious inroads among the Iroquois by his successful prediction.

1698: French missionary Father de Montigny reached the Taensa Indian village on the Mississippi River. He stayed with them to instruct them in his religion.

1731: Natchez Indians, led by Chief Farine, had built a fort in Louisiana near the Red River. French and Tunica forces, led by Louisiana Governor Etienne de Perier, attacked the fort. The fighting lasted for three days. Although the Natchez killed many of the allied forces, they were at a disadvantage because the French had a cannon. After three days of fighting, the Natchez promised to surrender the next morning. Many of the Natchez escaped during the night, including Chief Farine.

1785: A treaty (7 Stat. 16) signed by the Chippewa, Delaware, Ottawa, and Wyandot called for Indian hostages to be taken until all prisoners held by the Indians (white and black) were returned. The four tribes acknowledged the sole sovereignty of the United States. New tribal land boundaries were established. No U.S. citizens could live on Indian lands without Indian approval. Land for a military post was set aside at Detroit and Michilimackinac. It was signed by thirteen chiefs at Fort Macintosh in western Pennsylvania.

1866: According to army records, soldiers from the Second Cavalry fought with Indians near Cottonwood Springs, Arizona. Thirteen Indians were killed, and six were captured.

1953: Amendment 4 to the constitution and by-laws of the Lac du Flambeau Band of Lake Superior Chippewa Indians of Wisconsin was approved and became effective.

JANUARY 22

1599: On December 4, 1598, a fight broke out between Acoma Pueblo and Spaniards under Juan de Zaldivar when a soldier stole some turkeys. In retaliation, de Zaldivar's brother Vicente returned with seventy soldiers. After two days of fighting, the Acoma surrendered, and 500 were taken prisoner. Seventy Acoma were tried by Juan de Oñata,

Zaldivar's uncle. All seventy were found guilty on February 12, 1599.

1793: In Drippings Springs, Kentucky, Chickamauga Chief Captain Bench, Doublehead, and Pumpkin Boy attacked two men leading pack animals. After killing the two men, the Indians ate them.

1813: British Colonel Henry Proctor, with 600 soldiers and 600 Indian warriors, attacked General James Winchester and his 850 soldiers in Monroe (called Frenchtown at the time), Michigan. Winchester's forces were split up on both sides of the Raisin River. When the British and Indians attacked the forces on the south bank during a snowstorm, they killed almost 100 Americans. Winchester was taken prisoner. He surrendered his entire force of almost 500 men on this day, even though his troops on the north side of the river were virtually untouched by the fighting. Proctor marched his able-bodied captives to Fort Malden, Ontario, Canada, leaving sixty-four wounded Americans in Frenchtown under a limited guard. Angry Indians later attacked and killed most of the wounded. This attack was called the Raisin River Massacre, and it became a battle cry during the War of 1812.

1814: Andrew Jackson's forces of 900 soldiers and 200 Creek and Cherokee allies fought a major battle with 500 Red Stick Creek under William Weatherford (Lume Chathi—Red Eagle), along Emuckfau Creek in Alabama. The Creek sustained significant losses, but Jackson had to retreat as well.

1814: As a part of the Red Stick Creek War, Georgia General John Floyd was leading 1,700 soldiers and almost 400 Indian allies up the Calabee Valley near the Georgia-Alabama border. His army was attacked by Red Stick Creek. The Creek drove the army into the swamps. Lacking adequate defenses and knowledge of the area, Floyd eventually returned to Georgia.

1832: Major F.W. Armstrong, the new Choctaw Indian agent, arrived in Little Rock. He distributed arms and supplies to the Choctaws.

Indians stand in line for rations near Camp Supply. (NA)

1855: The Treaty of Point Elliot (12 Stat. 927) was signed. The Tulalip, Kalapuya, Swinomish, and Snoqualnoo Tribes of Whidbey Island, Washington, were among the signers.

1873: Elements of the Fifth Cavalry engaged with hostile Indians at Tonto Creek in Arizona. Private George Hooker, Company K, would be awarded the Medal of Honor for "gallantry in action in which he is killed." Seventeen Indians were killed, and one soldier was wounded.

1876: Seventeen men from Troop G, Fifth Cavalry, under Lieutenant H.S. Bishop had been tracking a group of Indians who had been stealing livestock near Camp Supply in the panhandle of Indian Territory (present-day Oklahoma). The troopers found, and attacked, the Indians on the Cimarron River, 125 miles east of Camp Supply. Three Indians were killed, and four were captured. Thirty-five horses and two mules were recovered.

1879: Captain Henry Wessells and troops A, E, F, and H, Third Cavalry, found Dull Knife's Fort Robinson escapees near the telegraph line from Fort Robinson to Hat Creek. The Indians did not surrender, so Wessells attacked. According to army reports, all of the remaining escapees were killed or wounded. Three soldiers were killed, and Captain Wessells and two other soldiers were wounded. Twenty-three Cheyenne were listed as killed, and nine were captured. The captured Cheyenne said Dull Knife was killed by artillery during a battle a few days before (probably on January 14).

1941: Wupatki National Monument was modified by Presidential Proclamation No. 2454.

1960: An election for amendments to the constitution for the Gila River Pima-Maricopa Indian Community was held. The amendments were approved by a vote of 761–476.

1976: Executive Order No. 11899 was issued. It was titled: "Providing for the protection of certain civil service employment rights of Federal personnel who leave Federal employment to be employed by tribal organizations pursuant to the Indian Self-Determination and Education Assistance Act."

JANUARY 23

1689: Saco, in southwestern Maine, was attacked by Abenaki Indians, one in a series of attacks on the settlement. Nine settlers were killed in the fighting.

1812: When Tecumseh visited the Creek, he told them to wait for a sign that would tell them it was time to begin their uprising against the Europeans. Tecumseh said he would stamp the ground and make every house in Tuckabatchee fall down. The Creek Nation was shaken by an earthquake. Many of the younger braves felt this was the awaited sign. They were cautioned by calmer heads to wait for a less ambiguous event.

1814: After a fight at Emuckfau Creek, Alabama, the day before, Andrew Jackson's army of Americans and Indian allies was forced to retreat. They reached the Creek village of Enitachopco, where they bivouacked for the night.

1837: U.S. forces under Colonel Cawfield surprised a group of Seminole under Chief Osuchee (Cooper) at Ahapopka Lake in Florida. The chief and several warriors were killed in the fighting.

1838: In Saginaw, Michigan, Henry Schoolcraft negotiated a treaty (7 Stat. 565) with the Chippewa. The treaty worked out the misunderstandings from previous treaties regarding the sales of Indian lands. Six Indians signed the document.

1847: General Sterling Price and his troops left Santa Fe for Taos to put down the revolt that started on January 19, 1847.

1870: Brevet Colonel E.M. Baker's Second Cavalry and Thirteenth Infantry troops discovered Bear Chief and Big Horn's camp ("action with Blackfeet Indians, Piegan Camp, Bear Chief, and Big Horn") after a night march. The surprise was complete when they attacked. A total of 173 Indians were killed, and twenty were wounded. The soldiers captured 140 women and children and more than 300 horses. While one group of soldiers destroyed the camp, the rest moved down the Marias River in Montana to Mountain Chief's camp. The soldiers found it abandoned. After burning the camp, the soldiers embarked for the Northwest Fur Company's fort. Only one soldier was killed in the engagement.

1877: Buffalo soldiers (black troops) Troop C, Ninth Cavalry, skirmished with Indians in the Florida Mountains, New Mexico. According to army documents, no casualties were reported.

1937: The original constitution of the Kickapoo Tribe was approved in a tribal election.

1975: Morris Thompson, Commissioner of Indian Affairs, ratified an election for amendments to the constitution and bylaws of the Reno-Sparks Indian Community.

Every: San Ildefonso Pueblo festival.

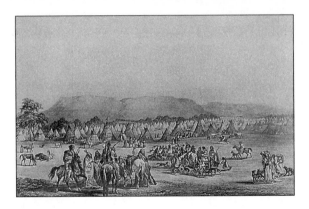

Sioux camp at Pine Ridge, South Dakota (NA)

JANUARY 24

1806: Cherokee Chief Doublehead and sixteen others signed a land-cession treaty in Washington. They gave up lands on the north side of the Tennessee River and near Chickasaw lands for a little more than $10,000, a cotton gin, and a gristmill. The chiefs did not represent the Cherokees. When the rest of the tribe heard of the treaty, it was repudiated at once. Doublehead was killed for making the agreement.

1814: Andrew Jackson's force of American soldiers and Indian allies hoped to spring a trap on the Red Stick Creek, led by William Weatherford. As Jackson's forces started to cross Enitachopco Creek in Alabama, they encountered the Red Stick Creek. Jackson's initial feint was unsuccessful because his troops did not hold their ground. After assuming personal command of the battle, Jackson rallied his troops and inflicted considerable losses on the Red Stick Creek. The Creek lost 189 warriors during this battle and the Battle of Emuckfau two days earlier. Jackson's force sustained twenty fatalities.

1826: Chief Opothleyoholo was one of the signers of the treaty that replaced the repudiated treaty signed by a few proremoval chiefs at Indian Springs on February 12, 1825. This treaty (7 Stat. 286) ceded most Creek lands in Georgia for $217,000 up front and $20,000 per year thereafter. Congress ratified the treaty only after the Creek agreed to gave up all lands in Georgia. This was called the first Treaty of Washington.

1835: Mexican Governor Figueroa in Monterey, California, wrote a letter to the *alcalde* of San José. He warned the local ranchers not to mount punitive expeditions against the local Indians. Some Indians had been raiding ranches to steal the horses. On more than one occasion, the Mexicans had killed innocent Tulare Indians in their efforts to punish the thieves.

1838: Forces under U.S. General Thomas Jesup fought as many as 300 Seminole in Lockahatchee, west of Jupiter Inlet, Florida. Seven soldiers were killed and thirty-one wounded in the fighting. The Seminole escaped into the swamps.

1845: The Texas senate ratified a trade and peace treaty signed on October 9, 1844, by Sam Houston and the Anadarko, Lipan Apache, Caddo, Cherokee, Comanche, Delaware, Hainai, Kichai, Shawnee, Tawakoni, and Waco.

1847: General Sterling Price, with just over 400 soldiers and volunteers, met a force of Mexicans and Pueblo Indians near La Canada. Cannon fire and a cavalry charge caused the rebels to flee. The Americans lost two men. Thirty-six rebels were killed, according to Sterling's report.

1848: Gold was found in a Maidu village on the American River.

1864: Colonel King Woolsey, with thirty soldiers and fourteen friendly Indians, arranged for a parley with the Gila Apache. During the talks, shots rang out, and Gila Chief Paramucka and eighteen other Gila Indians were killed. Only one white was killed in what was called the Pinal Treaty at Bloody Tanks.

1871: About four miles east of Salt Creek in Young County, Texas, two dozen Kiowa warriors attacked a wagon train led by Britton (Britt) Johnson. Johnson was killed in the fighting.

1877: A small detachment of soldiers from the Ninth Cavalry contacted a large group of "renegade" Apache in the Florida Mountains of New Mexico. Their mission was to get the Apache to surrender. The soldiers were surrounded, and fighting broke out. Corporal Clinton Greaves, Company C, "in the center of the savage hand-to-hand fighting, manages to shoot and bash a gap through the swarming Apache, permitting his companions to break free." For his actions, Greaves would be awarded the Medal of Honor.

1881: Sitting Bull decided to leave Crazy Horse's camp in Montana. He would return to Canada in hopes of finding a home there.

1881: Ninth Cavalry soldiers fought a group of Indians near Cañada Alamosa, New Mexico. According to army documents, one soldier was wounded.

1882: Boundary lines were modified on the Pine Ridge Sioux Reserve, Dakota Territory.

1894: The first Medal of Honor for actions against Cochise's Chiricahua was issued. It was given to assistant surgeon Bernard Irwin.

1895: Queen Liliuokalani was forced by representatives of the Republic of Hawaii to officially abdicate her throne.

1927: With the exception of a few people who had died, the trust period for land allotments for members of the Sac and Fox Tribes of Kansas and Nebraska was extended for an additional ten years by Executive Order No. 4571 from President Calvin Coolidge.

1935: The Santa Clara Pueblo, New Mexico, adopted a new constitution.

1936: Acting Secretary of the Interior Charles West ratified the results of an election for a constitution for the Indians of the Tulalip Tribes in Washington.

1955: Ira Hayes, the Pima who participated in the famous raising of the flag on Iwo Jima during World War II, died.

1974: An election for amendments to the constitution and bylaws of the White Mountain Apache Tribe was held. Of the 792 eligible voters, 399 voted for the changes, 104 against.

JANUARY 25

1692: Just before dawn, the village of York, Maine, was attacked by 150 Abenaki warriors led by Chief Madockawando. The Abenaki killed more than four dozen settlers, and up to eight were taken as prisoners, then sold or used as slaves. The village and surrounding farms were burned for miles. (This battle also recorded as happening on February 5.)

1832: Some 1,300 of Nitakechi's Choctaws started their march from Little Rock to the Red River. Nitakechi was ill and left later.

1851: Texas Ranger Andrew Jackson Walker attacked a small band of Comanche near Fort Merrill, Texas, west of Corpus Christi. He killed four of the Indians.

1856: The second half of the Quinault and Quileute treaty (12 Stat. 971) was signed in Olympia, Washington. The first half was signed on July 1, 1855.

1904: By executive order, a tract of land in Nebraska that had been set aside for the Pine Ridge School Reservation was placed back into the public domain. This order was modified on February 20, 1904.

1968: The United States Indian Claims Commission decreed that the Mescalero Apache of New Mexico should receive $8.5 million for lands taken from them in the 1800s. The Mescalero refused the largesse because, by law, they could not share the money with the Lipan and Chiricahua Apache. A future ruling would allow this.

1969: The assistant commissioner of Indian affairs had authorized an election for amendments to the constitution and bylaws of the Lac Courte Oreilles Band of Lake Superior Chippewa Indians of Wisconsin. The election results were 73–3 in favor.

Every: Picuris dances.

JANUARY 26

1598: An expedition to explore modern New Mexico led by Don Juan de Oñate left San Gerómino, New Spain (Mexico). The expedition members included 170 families and 230 single men.

1716: Cherokee Chief Caesar had told the English in South Carolina that he would never fight them. He also told the Europeans they had nothing to fear from the Creek, because they wanted peace, too. He offered to arrange for leading Creek to go to Charles Town to arrange a peace. On this day, sixteen Creek and Yamassee representatives arrived at the Cherokee village of Tugaloo in northeastern Georgia. The Creek and the Yamassee knew of the Cherokees' desire to remain neutral or at peace. Rather than talking about peace, the representatives urged the Cherokees to join them in their plan to attack the South Carolina settlements. This so angered the Cherokees that the representatives were killed.

1836: The Battle of Hitchity took place in Stewart County, Georgia. Creek warriors on the Chattahoochee River were attacked by the local militia.

1875: As many as forty "Mexican Indians–cattle thieves" allegedly attacked a corporal and four soldiers from Troop G, Ninth Cavalry, eighteen miles from Ringgold Barracks, Texas. Two of the troopers were killed in the attack. Colonel Edward Hatch and Troops B and G, Ninth Cavalry, captured several of the suspects. A coroner's jury found nine Mexicans guilty of murdering the troopers.

1877: Regulations for the White Mountain–San Carlos Reservation in Arizona were modified.

1973: An election to approve a constitution for the La Posta Band of Mission Indians of the La Posta Indian Reservation, California, was held. It was endorsed by a vote of 2–0.

1973: An election was authorized to approve an amendment to the constitution and bylaws for the Sokaogon Chippewa Community of Wisconsin by the secretary of the interior. The election would be held on July 19, 1973.

1974: An election to approve amendments to the constitution and bylaws of the Tule River Indian Tribe was held. Of the 74 people entitled to vote, the results were 22–10 in favor of Amendment 4 and 23–9 on Amendment 5.

1977: Vincent Little, the acting area director, Portland area office, Bureau of Indian Affairs, authorized an election to approve amendments to the constitution and bylaws for the Upper Skagit

Indian Tribe. The election would be held on March 26, 1977.

1978: The area director, Bureau of Indian Affairs, Charles Delaney, authorized an election to approve an amendment to the constitution and bylaws for the Fort Sill Apache Tribe of Oklahoma. The election would be held on March 11, 1978.

1982: The Sioux sued the Black Hills Mining Company.

JANUARY 27

1730: After the Battle of Fort Rosalie (modern Natchez, Mississippi), the French were determined to defeat the Natchez Indians. A French-Canadian named Jean Paul Le Sueur, who had lived with the local Indians for years, volunteered to recruit Indians from other tribes to fight the Natchez. With a force of approximately 700 Choctaws, Le Sueur arrived at the main Natchez village. Le Sueur's fighters forced the Natchez to take refuge in two forts they had constructed. They remained bottled up here until the main French force of 200 soldiers arrived in February. During the fighting, eighty Natchez warriors were killed. Le Sueur's forces rescued 166 prisoners held by the Natchez.

1756: As a part of the Pennsylvania Delaware uprising, a war party from Susquehanna attacked several settlements in Juanita and Perry Counties. During the series of attacks, the Delaware killed almost two dozen settlers.

1814: In modern Macon County, Alabama, U.S. forces of almost 1,000 militia and Indians were camped on Callabee Creek near the scene of the Battle of Autossee (November 1813). Red Stick Creek attacked their encampment. The Georgia militia and the friendly Indians sustained twenty-two deaths and almost 150 wounded. The Red Stick Creek suffered as well, but they forced the American expedition to leave the area.

1825: An Indian frontier line was established by the government.

1838: In Florida, a small group of Creek warriors attacked a barge on the Choctawhatchee River.

1863: General Patrick Connor and almost 300 California volunteers fought Bear Hunter's Northern Shoshone on Bear River, north of the Idaho-Utah border. The soldiers reported 224 of the warriors were killed in the fighting, including Bear Hunter. Other sources put the number nearer to 400, including many women and children. Connor was called "Star Chief" by the Indians. This was called the Battle of Bear River by the army. Others called it the Bear River Massacre. Most sources said this happens on January 29, 1863.

1936: The U.S. government ratified the constitution and bylaws of the Swinomish Indians of the Swinomish Reservation, Washington.

1940: An election to adopt a constitution for the Ketchikan Indian Corporation was held. They adopted it.

1943: Regulations regarding rights-of-way on the Flathead Reservation in Wyoming were modified.

1948: The assistant secretary of the interior had authorized an election to approve a constitution and bylaws for the Organized Village of Kake, Alaska. It was passed by a vote of 117–1.

1958: The U.S. government officially recognized the Everglades Miccosukee Tribe of Seminole Indians as an independent tribal group.

1959: The first variety of American corn was found (5600 B.C.).

1967: The associate commissioner of tribal affairs approved a plan that would distribute assets to individual members of the Rumsey Indian Rancheria. This list of individuals would also be used as an official roll of the tribal members.

1975: The acting deputy commissioner of Indian affairs authorized an election for amendments to the constitution and bylaws for the Covelo Indian Community of the Round Valley Reservation in California. The election would be held on May 3, 1975.

Every: San Juan Pueblo basket dance.

JANUARY 28

1833: A Cherokee commission of John Ross, John Baldridge, Richard Taylor, and Joseph Vann addressed the secretary of war in Washington, D.C. They again stated their unwillingness to negotiate with the federal government about removal while the federal government was not living up to its previous agreements to protect them from the illegal actions of the state of Georgia. The Cherokees were told their only hope was for removal. During subsequent discussions, President Jackson offered the Eastern Cherokees $3 million for all lands east of the Mississippi River, excluding North Carolina. John Ross asked the president how he would be able to protect the Cherokees in Indian Territory (present-day Oklahoma) if he could not protect them from Georgia. The commission felt the gold mines on Cherokee lands were worth more than the president's offer.

1854: In Oregon, thirty miners attacked a peaceful Indian village on the Coquille River. Sixteen Indians were killed.

1869: The Seventh Cavalry was scouting in the Solomon River settlements when they encountered a small band of hostile Indians. Two soldiers were wounded. The soldiers claimed six kills and ten Indians wounded.

1870: According to official army records, Indians skirmished with a group of soldiers from the First and Eighth Cavalry in the Dragoon Mountains of Arizona. Thirteen Indians were killed, and two were captured.

1877: According to some sources, buffalo soldier Troop C, Ninth Cavalry, fought with Indians in Sierra Boca Grande, Mexico.

1891: Illegal settlers were found in the Cherokee Strip of Indian Territory (present-day Oklahoma).

1908: As listed in Executive Order No. 744, the lands set aside for the Navajo Indians in New Mexico conflicted with the lands set aside for the Jicarilla Apache by executive order on November 11, 1907. This would be corrected.

1973: An election to approve an amendment to the constitution and bylaws for the Seneca-Cayuga Tribe of Oklahoma had been authorized by the acting commissioner of Indian affairs. It would be approved by a vote of 22–9.

1974: The acting deputy commissioner of Indian affairs authorized an election for an amendment to the constitution and bylaws of the Reno-Sparks Indian Community.

1974: John Artichoker Jr., area director for the Phoenix area office, Bureau of Indian Affairs, ratified an election for amendments to the constitution for the Gila River Pima-Maricopa Indian Community.

1978: An election for Amendment 3 to the constitution for the Papago (Tohono O'odham) was held. Of the 5,087 people who could vote, 1,622 pulled the lever for it, 408 against it.

JANUARY 29

1675: John Sassamon was found under the ice of Assawompsett Pond, fifteen miles from Plymouth. A Christian Indian educated at Harvard, Sassamon had recently left living with the whites to become King Philip's aide. He then left Philip and returned to the colony as a preacher for the local Indians. He told the colony of Philip's plans to attack, but he was not believed. After his body was found, witnesses testified in court that three Wampanoag murdered Sassamon. Some time later, one of the three confessed on the gallows, after his rope broke while being hanged. He was hanged anyway. This episode was the spark Philip needed for his war.

1832: David Folsom's Choctaw finally reached the Kiamichi River area, their new home. Several people, and lots of animals, died en route. Cholera struck all of the groups.

1847: Captain Burgwin, of General Sterling Price's command in New Mexico, attacked Pueblo and Mexican rebels in Embudo. They took the town from the rebels that night. One U.S. soldier and twenty rebels, including rebel leader Pablo Chaves, were killed, according to the official report.

1863: General Patrick Connor and almost 300 California volunteers fought Bear Hunter's Northern Shoshone on Bear River, north of the Idaho-Utah border. The soldiers reported 224 of the warriors were killed in the fighting, including Bear Hunter. Other sources put the number nearer to 400, including many women and children. Connor was called "Star Chief" by the Indians. This was called the Battle of Bear River by the army. Others called it the Bear River Massacre. (Also recorded as happening on January 27, 1863.)

1867: According to army records, members of the First Cavalry fought with a band of Indians near Camp McDowell, Arizona. One Indian was reported captured.

1869: According to army reports, Captain Edward Byrne and Tenth Cavalry troops were patrolling along Mulberry Creek in Kansas. They fought with some hostile Indians; two soldiers were wounded, and six Indians were killed. Buffalo soldiers (black troops) Troops C, G, H, and K, Ninth Cavalry, were also reported to have participated.

1881: The eight lodges of Iron Dog and sixty-three of his followers surrendered to Major George Ilges's forces near the Poplar River in Montana. Thirteen horses and five guns were seized by the troops. The weather remained bitterly cold.

1942: According to Federal Register No. 7FR00768, certain lands in Apache County, Arizona, were temporarily withdrawn from disposition of any kind by department orders.

1963: Executive Order No. 2508 was issued regarding the Big Bend Dam on the Crow Creek Sioux Reservation in South Dakota.

1974: John Artichoker Jr., the Phoenix area director, Bureau of Indian Affairs, ratified the results of an election for amendments to the constitution and bylaws of the White Mountain Apache Tribe held on January 24, 1974.

1991: Starting on this day and through the next, a revision of the Menominee constitution and by-

Seminole Chief Osceola

laws was introduced and approved by a vote of the Menominee people.

JANUARY 30

1712: Near New Bern, North Carolina, Tuscarora and Coree Indians had built a fort they called Narhantes. As a part of the Tuscarora War, several hundred Indians and a few dozen South Carolina settlers, led by Colonel John Barnwell, attacked the fort. The defenders suffered sixty-two fatalities, including ten women. The attackers lost six Indians and seven Europeans. Sixty of the attackers were wounded in the fighting, which lasted a little less than an hour.

1806: Future principal chief of the Choctaws, Peter Perkins Pitchlynn, was born in Mississippi.

1838: Seminole Chief Osceola died at Fort Moultrie in Charleston, South Carolina. It was believed he had some sort of throat disease; others said malaria, and some said he died of a broken heart.

1885: Demand for lands in Indian Territory (Oklahoma) kept increasing. In response to this, the secretary of the interior officially recommended that what he called "surplus" Indian lands be opened up to settlers.

1980: An election for a proposed Amendment 3 to the constitution and bylaws of the Hopi Tribe was held. Of the 977 people eligible to vote, 607 voted for the amendment, and 64 voted against.

JANUARY 31

1646: Jesuits "predicted" a lunar eclipse for the Huron of Ossossane. This accurate prediction, made with the use of an almanac, led to many religious conversions.

1699: The French expedition under Pierre le Moyne, Sieur d'Iberville, landed on Dauphin Island, Alabama. The expedition eventually moved inland. Dauphin Island temporarily served as the French capital on the Gulf Coast.

1786: The Shawnee Treaty (7 Stat. 26) was signed at Fort Finley, in modern Findley, northwestern Ohio, by eight Shawnees. Three Indians were held hostage until all U.S. citizens held as prisoners were returned. The Shawnee acknowledged the sovereignty of only the United States over the lands ceded by the British under the 1784 Treaty of Paris. New boundary lines were established for Shawnee lands. No U.S. citizens could stay on Indian lands without Indian approval.

1833: The Mi'kmaq Waycobah First Nation Reserve of Whycocomagh No. 2 was established in Nova Scotia, according to the Nova Scotia Councils.

1844: A treaty was signed between the Republic of Texas and the Anadarko, Biloxi, Cherokee, Chickasaw, Delaware, Hainai, Kichai, Tawakoni, and Waco on September 29, 1843. It was ratified by the Texas senate.

1862: A peace conference was held at the San Francis Ranch between the American settlers and local Paiute. Although agreements would be reached, the peace would last only a few months. This series of fights was often called the Owens Valley (California) Indian War.

1870: The first acts were taken to establish the White Mountain–San Carlos–Camp Apache Reserve in western Arizona Territory by the Military Division of the Pacific. Major Engineer H.M. Robert forwarded a map of the proposed reserve to military headquarters in San Francisco for consideration.

1870: Mission Indian reservations were established by executive order of President Grant in southern California in the Mission Tule Agency. Eventually, twenty-two reserves, totaling 282 square miles, housed the Diegen, Kawi, San Luis Rey, Serrano, and Temecula Tribes in the San Pasqual and Pala Valleys. The initial boundaries were rescinded by President Grant on February 17, 1871, based on public outcries from citizens of San Diego County, California.

1864: Delgadito persuaded 680 Navajos to go to Fort Wingate.

1869: According to army records, settlers fought with a band of Indians near the Saline River in Kansas. Two settlers were killed.

1874: An order establishing the Judith Basin Crow Reservation, made on August 16, 1873, was modified.

1876: United States Indian Inspector E.C. Watkins issued a report stating Indians should report to their reservations or be considered as hostiles.

1881: Sitting Bull returned to Wood Mountain in Canada.

1931: The trust period on allotments made to Indians of the Cheyenne River Reservation in South Dakota was extended by Executive Order No. 5546.

1940: Oscar Chapman, assistant secretary of the interior, authorized an election for amendments to the constitution and bylaws of the Confederated Tribes of the Warm Springs Reservation of Oregon. The election would be held on February 21, 1940.

FEBRUARY 1

1834: The state of Georgia had begun the process of seizing Cherokee property. Much of the land was given to white settlers under a lottery. The Cherokees were forced out at gunpoint, in many cases. Cherokees begin arriving at the Cherokee Agency in eastern Tennessee to be moved to Indian Territory (present-day Oklahoma). The first boats left the agency on March 14, 1834.

1839: Cherokee Chief John Ross and 228 other Cherokees arrived in Little Rock, en route to the Indian Territory (present-day Oklahoma), as part of their forced emigration. Quatie Martin Ross, Chief Ross's wife, died. She was buried in Little Rock.

1876: The secretary of the interior advised the secretary of war that any Indians who had not returned to their reservations were under his jurisdiction. The army could use any means to deal with the hostiles. This primarily involved the Plains Indians.

1876: Army Indian scouts fought with a group of hostile Indians near Chevelons Fork, Arizona. According to army documents, four Indians were killed, and six were captured.

1877: By executive order, 7,579.75 acres of land in Arizona were set aside for the use of the military. It was called Fort Apache.

1877: Colonel Nelson Miles sent a scout, and two of the Cheyenne he captured on January 7, 1877, out to tell the hostiles his terms for surrender. The Indians were informed they would be attacked if they did not comply.

1917: By executive order, the Papago Indian Reservation was established in Sells, Arizona. The act was amended on February 21, 1931, and on October 28, 1932.

1977: The Swinomish permanent zoning legislation was enacted.

FEBRUARY 2

1836: Benjamin Marshall and his fellow Creek reached Fort Gibson in eastern Indian Territory (present-day Oklahoma).

1839: Reverend Evan Jones and 1,033 Cherokees arrived in the Indian Territory (present-day Oklahoma). Seventy-one of their original parties died on the trail.

1848: The Guadalupe Hidalgo Treaty was signed. It was the policy of the United States, in keeping with the treaty's (9 Stat. 929) understanding and long-established custom, to provide certain necessary services and facilities to Native American Indians.

1874: An order was issued that canceled the executive order of May 29, 1873, regarding the Fort Stanton Indian Reserve set aside for the Mescalero Apache in New Mexico.

1874: Indians fought with soldiers from the Tenth Cavalry near Home Creek, Texas. According to army documents, no casualties were reported.

1887: A law was passed that prohibits the use of Indian languages in schools.

1911: By Executive Order No. 1296, the Camp McDowell Reservation was modified.

1911: An executive order set aside 17,315 acres of land, which eventually became part of the Fort Mojave tribal lands.

1945: In 1905, the Shoshone and Arapaho Tribes of the Wind River Reservation ceded a large part of their reservation to the United States. According to Federal Register No. 10FR02254, they got a small part of that land back.

Every: San Felipe Candelaria Day for many Pueblos.

FEBRUARY 3

1837: In southeastern Alabama, near Cowikee Creek, Creek warriors and Alabama militia exchanged a few shots.

1838: The Oneida signed a treaty (7 Stat. 566) in Washington, D.C. It ceded some of their land.

1847: General Sterling Price reached the fortified Taos Pueblo. A cannonade proved unfruitful in dislodging the rebels, so Price retreated to the city of Taos.

1876: The War Department acknowledged Sitting Bull's notice about having to report to a reservation.

1880: A band of Hunkpapa Sioux had attacked some civilians on the Powder River in Montana. Sergeant Thomas Glover, eight men from Troop B, Second Cavalry, and eleven Indian scouts pursued the Sioux for almost seventy miles and circled them on Pumpkin Creek. A fight ensued, and each side lost one man. Two Indians and one soldier were wounded. After reinforcements arrived, three of the Hunkpapa were captured.

1956: Assistant Secretary of the Interior Wesley D'Ewart ratified an election that approved an amendment to the constitution and bylaws for the Pyramid Lake Paiute Tribe of Nevada. The election was held on December 26, 1955.

1961: An amendment to the constitution and bylaws of the Coeur d'Alene Tribe of Idaho was approved by H. Rex Lee, deputy commissioner of Indian Affairs.

1975: The Department of the Interior determined that the Pit River Indian Tribe was to be designated as the "beneficial owner" of the XL Ranch.

FEBRUARY 4

1509: Cakchiquel (Kaqchikel) Maya King Lahuh-Noh took the throne.

1829: The Mississippi house of representatives passed a law to extend legal process into that part of the state now occupied by the Chickasaw and Choctaw Tribes of Indians.

1847: General Sterling Price returned to the fortified Taos Pueblo, and two hours of cannonade were again unsuccessful. Price's troops attacked and make some headway. The cannon was moved closer and breached a wall. The troops swarmed through a hole in the church and other buildings. Many of the Pueblo Indians tried to escape but were cut down by volunteers stationed to the east of the pueblo. One of the leaders of the revolt, Jesus de Tafoya, was killed in the fighting.

1861: John Ward's stepson, Feliz Tellez, was kidnapped by Indians from his ranch on Sonoita Creek in Arizona. Ward complained to the army, and it sent Second Lieutenant George Bascom and fifty-four soldiers to find him. On this day, Chiricahua Apache Chief Cochise was invited to talk with Bascom in Apache Pass in southwestern Arizona. Cochise brought some family with him to the parley in Bascom's tent. Cochise was shocked when Bascom accused him of kidnapping the boy. Cochise denied his involvement, but Bascom did not believe him. Bascom then told Cochise he was under arrest. Cochise cut a hole in the tent and escaped. Bascom kept Cochise's relatives as hostages. Cochise quickly seized several whites as hostages as well.

1869: According to army records, members of the First Cavalry and Indian scouts fought with a band of Indians in the Arivaypa Mountains in Arizona. Eight Indians were killed, and eight more were captured.

1960: Secretary of the Interior Roger Ernst approved the constitution of the Mission Creek Band of Indians of Mission Creek, California.

1994: The Osage Nation's constitution was ratified by a vote of 1,931–1,013.

FEBRUARY 5

1692: Canadians and Indians attacked the southern Maine town of York. Almost fifty settlers were killed, and at least another seventy become captives. (Also recorded as happening on January 25.)

1802: Orono was a Penobscot chief. During his life, he was converted to Catholicism. He fought in the French and Indian War against the British settlements in New England. He fought on the American side during the Revolutionary War, and he was believed to have been 108 years old when he died.

1832: Nitakechi and 200 Choctaws began the wagon-train march from Little Rock to the Red River area.

1847: The rebel Pueblo Indians and Mexicans of Taos surrendered to General Sterling Price. They handed over rebel leader Pablo Montoya. He was tried and shot on February 7, 1847.

1856: The Stockbridge and Munsee signed a treaty (11 Stat. 663). It involved the cession of lands in Wisconsin and Minnesota.

1869: According to army records, members of the Eighth Cavalry fought with a band of Indians on Black Mesa in Arizona. One Indian was killed.

1874: Lieutenant Colonel George Buell and Troops D and G, Tenth Cavalry, and men from Companies A, F, and G, Eleventh Infantry, found an encampment of Comanche on the Double Mountain Fork of the Brazos River in Texas. The army attacked, and eleven Indians were killed. The soldiers sustained only one wounded man. Sixty-five horses were seized.

1877: Sixth Cavalry soldiers and some Indian scouts fought a group of Indians in the Tonto Basin of Arizona. According to army documents, eighteen Indians were killed, and twenty were captured. The fighting started on January 9.

1881: Crow King surrendered at Fort Buford.

1881: Ninth Cavalry soldiers and Indian scouts fought a group of Indians in the Candelaria Mountains of Mexico. According to army documents, no casualties were reported.

1934: More than 400 Zuni held a mass meeting to discuss the selection of Pueblo officials.

1937: Based upon authority granted by an act of Congress (47 Stat.777) passed on January 27, 1933, a trust agreement was established with the Five Civilized Tribes.

1948: An act (62 Stat. 17) was passed by Congress to "empower the Secretary to grant rights-of-way for various purposes across lands of individual Indians or Indian tribes, communities, bands, or nations."

1973: The assistant secretary of the interior authorized an election for amendments to the constitution and bylaws for the Covelo Indian Community of the Round Valley Reservation in California. The election would be held on April 14, 1973.

1990: Deputy to the Assistant Secretary of Indian Affairs Hazel Elbert approved the results of an election by the Coast Indian Community of the Resighini Rancheria on a constitutional amendment.

Crow King, a Sioux Indian, wearing a U.S. Army jacket (NA)

FEBRUARY 6

1682: René Robert Cavelier, Sieur de La Salle, and a force of twenty-two French and thirty-one Indians reached the confluence of the Illinois and Mississippi Rivers. La Salle then sailed down the Mississippi to see if it emptied into the Gulf of Mexico. The expedition contacted many Indian tribes along the way. Based on this expedition, La Salle claimed the Mississippi Valley and Louisiana for the French. La Salle reached the Gulf of Mexico on April 9, 1682.

1740: A force of 180 French troops and 400 Choctaw and Iroquois, led by Captain Pierre Celeron, left Fort Assumption (modern Memphis) to arrange for a peace with Chickasaw Indians in the region. They arrived in the Chickasaw village on February 22.

1793: After William Blount gained the promise of Chickamauga chiefs to stop their raids and murdering of European settlers on May 29, 1792, the rampages continued. Blount returned to the Chickamauga at Coyatee with the same request and an offer for the principal chiefs to visit the "great white father" at Philadelphia. The chiefs considered the offer, but within the next few months the village was attacked by Europeans. This hardened the hearts of the Chickamauga and some of their Cherokee neighbors. The attack continued.

1854: The state of Texas passed a law that allowed the United States to pick sites for two Indian reservations in Texas. One was on the Main Fork of the Brazos River. The other was on the Clear Fork of the Brazos River.

1861: Cochise left Lieutenant George Bascom a note offering to exchange hostages. Bascom agreed to the exchange if Cochise included the kidnapped boy Feliz Tellez. Cochise said he never had the boy, and the exchange did not take place. Cochise's hostages were found dead in a few days.

1870: According to official army records, Indians skirmished with a group of soldiers from the Ninth Cavalry and Twenty-Fourth Infantry between the Pecos and Rio Grande Rivers in Texas. No casualties were reported. The fighting started on January 3.

1873: Indians fought with soldiers from the First Cavalry in Hell Canyon in Arizona, according to army documents. Two Indians were killed, and one was captured.

1880: On the Yellowstone River, Sioux Indians stole more than a dozen horses from the settlement at Pease's Bottom. They also stole horses from Terry's Landing. Crow Indian scouts tracked the Sioux and managed to retrieve or kill all of the horses near Porcupine Creek.

1945: According to Federal Register No. 10FR02812, the Wind River Reservation tribes returned some of the "undisposed of, ceded lands" that were given to the United States in the past.

1973: Local authorities had failed to charge the white killer of a local Oglala Indian named Wesley Bad Heart Bull with murder. Angered by this lack of action, several militant Indians set fire to the Chamber of Commerce building and the courthouse in Custer, South Dakota.

1979: Acoma Pueblo were listed among Indian tribal entities "that have a government-to-government relationship with the United States" in the Federal Register.

1998: Activist groups worldwide declared this day as "Free Leonard Peltier Day."

FEBRUARY 7

1778: According to some sources, Daniel Boone was captured by Shawnee warriors under Chief Blackfish near the Blue Licks in Kentucky while making salt.

1813: Instigated by the Spanish governor of Florida, Florida Indians had attacked settlements in Georgia. Seeking revenge, a force of 250 militia and volunteers from Tennessee, led by Colonel John Williams, began a series of attacks on Indian villages in Florida. They destroyed many villages and looted supplies.

1861: Convinced that they would get better treatment from a southern government than from the one in Washington, D.C., the Choctaw announced their support of the Confederacy.

1867: According to army records, members of the First Cavalry fought with a band of Indians near Camp McDowell, Arizona. One Indian was reported as captured.

1869: A group of Indians stole some livestock about three miles from Fort Selden, near Las Cruces, New Mexico. Troops from the fort attempt to catch up to the Indians, but the Indians disappeared into the local mountains.

1876: The War Department authorized General Sheridan to start operations against the Indians.

1979: Bernard Granum, area director of the Minneapolis Office of the Bureau of Indian Affairs, authorized an election for an amendment to the constitution of the Red Lake Band of Chippewa Indians of Minnesota.

1983: The Inuit Circumpolar Conference was held at the United Nations.

FEBRUARY 8

1837: During the Second Seminole War, a battle took place between Seminole and U.S. forces on the bank of Lake Monroe (near modern Sanford, Florida). The Americans were led by Colonel Alexander Fanning. More than 600 Seminole, led by Chiefs Philip and Wildcat (Coacoochee), participated in the fighting, which began with a Seminole attack before dawn. Both sides lost a considerable number of men. The deciding factor in the battle was the arrival of a steamship with a cannon. Fort Monroe was built on the site of the battle.

1876: General Sheridan ordered Generals George Crook and Alfred Terry to make ready for a campaign in the Powder River area against the Sioux and other tribes who had not reported to the reservation. General Crook was called "Three Stars" by the Indians. He was also called "Gray Wolf" by the Apache.

1887: The Dawes Severalty Act (24 Stat. 388–389) regarding land allotments took effect. Its official title was "An Act to Provide for the Allotment of Lands in Severalty to Indians on the Various Reservations, and to Extend the Protection of the Laws of the United States and the Territories over the Indians, and for Other Purposes."

1918: An executive order was issued to remove 160 acres from the Winnemucca Shoshone Indian Colony in Nevada.

1936: An election was held to approve a constitution and bylaws for the Manchester Band of Pomo Indians of the Manchester Rancheria. It passed by a vote of 33–4.

1936: An election was held to approve a constitution and bylaws for the Kashia Band of Pomo Indians of the Stewarts Point Rancheria. It was approved by a vote of 47–2.

1971: The commissioner of Indian affairs ratified the new constitution for the Reno-Sparks Indian Community.

1975: An election for amendments to the constitution of the Papago (Tohono O'odham) was held. Of the 3,251 eligible voters, 1,521 voted for the amendments, 690 against.

1978: John Artichoker Jr., Phoenix area director of the Bureau of Indian Affairs, ratified an election for Amendment 3 to the constitution for the Papago (Tohono O'odham). The election was held on January 21, 1978.

FEBRUARY 9

1526: Spaniards were living in the Cakchiquel (Kaqchikel) Maya town of Iximche' in modern Guatemala. A few decided to desert. They set a large fire as a diversion.

1607: There had been a long period of fighting between the Indian tribes of the Powhatan Confederacy and the English colonists in Virginia. While leading a Paspahegh war party near Jamestown, Chief Wochinchopunck was seen by the colonists. A fought ensued, and the chief was killed.

1690: Some 300 Indians and French sneaked into the stockade at Schenectady, New York, during a snowstorm. After posting warriors at each building, a signal was given, and the primarily Dutch occupants were attacked. Sixty settlers were killed, and twenty-seven were captured. Mohawk Indians attempted to rescue some of the captives as they were marched off to Canada, with little success.

1730: A large Choctaw force under French-Canadian Jean Paul Le Sueur had forced the Natchez to remain in two forts (called Fort de la Valeur and Fort de la Farine by the French) they had built in their main village (see January 27, 1730). Starting on this day French forces arrived and joined in the battle. The fighting continued until February 24.

1813: Members of the Red Stick Creek faction of the Creek Indians, who resisted adopting European customs, were attacked by a Mississippi militia group at Burnt Cork Creek, Mississippi Territory. The Red Stick Creek were transporting a wagon train loaded with ammunition they obtained from Spain.

1836: General Edmund Gaines and 1,100 troops landed in Tampa Bay. They were sent to quell the Seminole uprising, known as the Second Seminole War. They planned to march to Fort King.

1869: According to General Philip Sheridan's official report, from March 2, 1868, to February 9, 1869, in the Department of the Missouri (from Texas and New Mexico to Dakota and Minnesota), 353 officers, soldiers, and citizens were killed, wounded, or captured by Indians. Of the Indians, 319 were killed, 289 wounded, and fifty-three captured. Approximately 1,200 surrendered.

1870: Louis Riel was elected president of the Metis.

1872: Three soldiers from Troop B, Fourth Cavalry, were attacked by Indians on the North Concho River in Texas. No casualties were suffered on either side.

1874: Lieutenant L.H. Robinson, Fourteenth Infantry, and Corporal James Coleman were among several people "wantonly murdered" by Indians on Cottonwood Creek, near Laramie Peak, Wyoming. Robinson and Coleman were leading a wagon train of lumber returning from a sawmill when they were attacked. Army reports cited this attack as a signal for the start of numerous battles in the area.

1935: By Executive Order No. 6968, the federal government extended the trust period on allotments made to Indians of the Crow Creek Band of Sioux Indians in Dakota.

1987: The Lac du Flambeau Band of Lake Superior Chippewa Indians modified local codes regarding timber trespassing.

Indians of Santa Clara Pueblo, New Mexico, making pottery (NA)

FEBRUARY 10

1676: The Narragansett attacked Lancaster, Massachusetts. This battle in King Philip's War killed fifty settlers. Twenty-four whites were taken prisoner. One of the prisoners, Mary Rowlandson, escaped. She wrote a best-seller about her ordeal. Mary Rowlandson's narrative was the first in a series of true-life stories published by Indian captives. Participating in the raid was Chief Quinnapin.

1763: "The definitive Treaty of Peace and Friendship between his Britannick Majesty, the Most Christian King, and the King of Spain is concluded at Paris the 10th day of February, 1763." England claimed sovereignty over all Indians east of the Mississippi River as a part of the Treaty of Paris.

1824: The president was authorized to order surveys of what were now Indian lands.

1834: The Western Cherokees did not wish to share their current holdings in the Indian Territory (present-day Oklahoma) with the Cherokees remaining in the east if they decided to emigrate. Western Chiefs Black Coat, John Jolly, and Walter Webber signed a treaty with Indian Agent George Vashon that gave them more land, and larger annual payments, if the Eastern Cherokees did move to the Indian Territory. Federal authorities in the Indian Territory did not pass the treaty along to Washington, D.C.

1876: General Terry got his "anti-Sioux" orders.

1890: The South Dakota land grab took place. Parts of the Great Sioux Reservation were opened to settlers.

1890: President Benjamin Harrison announced that Indians had agreed to open their lands.

1913: By Executive Order No. 1700, lands in New Mexico were set aside as a reservation for the Santa Clara Pueblo Indians.

1972: The constitution of the Indians of the Tulalip Tribes in Washington was modified.

1982: The first Indian was appointed director of the Indian Health Service.

1991: The Campo Band of Kumeyaay (Mission) drafted a solid-waste management plan by the establishment of the solid waste code and solid waste regulations.

1994: The Osage Nation constitution was approved according to the constitution's first page.

February 11

1715: The Tuscarora (Coree) Indians led by Tom Blount signed a peace treaty with the English settlers in North Carolina. This ended much of the fighting in the area. Some sources report that it was signed at a fort known as Nooherooka to the Indians.

1805: Sacajawea gave birth to a baby boy.

1828: John Tipton, representing the United States, and members of the Eel River Band of the Miami Indians signed a treaty (7 Stat. 309). Under the Treaty of Wyandot Village, the Indians moved to a reservation and gave up lands along Sugartree Creek. They received $10,000 in supplies.

1837: The Potawatomi signed a treaty (7 Stat. 532) in Washington, D.C. The treaty agreed to give to the Potawatomi of Indiana a tract of country on the Osage River, southwest of the Missouri River, sufficient in extent and adapted to their habits and wants.

1856: The Menominee signed a treaty (11 Stat. 679) at Keshena. The treaty ceded some land.

1861: In Arizona, Lieutenant George Bascom had discovered the bodies of the six hostages that had been held by Cochise. The bodies were buried. On this day, three of Cochise's relatives whom Bascom held hostage, and three Coyotero Apache prisoners, were hanged over the graves of the white hostages.

1880: The president warned Indian-land usurpers to stop their illegal acts.

1887: The boundary lines of the Jicarilla Apache Reservation were established by executive order.

1890: Half of the Sioux Reservation was opened to the public.

1918: The federal government extended the trust period on allotments on Devils Lake Reservation, North Dakota.

1931: By Executive Order No. 5556, the trust period on allotments made to members of the Prairie Band of Potawatomi Indians of Kansas was extended.

1957: North Dakota state fish and game laws were imposed on Indians claiming treaty and other rights to hunt and fish.

1959: An election for a constitution for the Standing Rock Sioux Tribe was held. They voted in favor by a 409–182 margin.

1975: The commissioner of Indian affairs authorized an election for amendments to the constitution of the Shoalwater Bay Indian Organization in Washington State. The election would be held on April 19.

1978: Tribal members from across the United States joined other activists in a march across the country to Washington, D.C. This demonstration to protest the treatment of American Indians is known as the Longest Walk.

FEBRUARY 12

1599: Of the seventy Acoma tried for battling with Spaniards on December 4, 1598, all were found guilty. On this day, Juan de Oñate ordered their punishment. All men over twenty-five years old had one foot cut off and served as slaves for twenty years. Everyone from twelve to twenty-five only had a foot cut off.

1733: Oglethorpe founded Savannah.

1825: Upper Creek Chief Jim Fife signed the Treaty of Indian Springs, Georgia. This treaty (7 Stat. 237), signed by Creek who were in favor of moving west, exchanged the remaining Creek lands in Georgia and Alabama for land west of the Mississippi River. The treaty was repudiated by most Creek. Many of the Creek signers of this treaty eventually were killed by the Creek opposed to moving west.

1848: As a part of the efforts to fight the Cayuse who attacked the Whitman Mission in Oregon Country, soldiers and militia had been reporting to The Dalles. By this date, 537 men had arrived.

1854: Colonel Jesse Stem was a special Indian agent in Texas until he retired to become a rancher. While transporting some goods near Fort Belknap in north-central Texas, he was killed by Kickapoo Indians.

1874: An executive order established the boundaries of the reservation for the Moapa Band of the Paiute.

1875: President Grant established the Lemhi Valley Indian Reservation in central Idaho. This act was instigated by the effort of Chief Tendoy and his Lemhi followers.

1881: Major George Ilges and soldiers of the Fifth Infantry arrested 185 Yanktonai Sioux, including forty-three warriors in their camp at Redwater, Montana. Seven guns and fifteen horses were seized.

1937: A constitution and bylaws for the Yavapai Apache of the Camp Verde Reservation were approved by Secretary of the Interior Harold Ickes.

1974: Native fishing rights were upheld in court.

1980: The governing body of the Paiute-Shoshone Tribe of the Fallon Reservation and Colony adopted a resolution that added amendments to their constitution and bylaws.

1987: The area director of the Bureau of Indian Affairs ratified the Nez Perce election to amend their constitution and bylaws.

1992: The Pequot started a bingo hall.

FEBRUARY 13

1684: According to some sources, an agreement was reached by representatives of the Cusabu Indians for the South Carolina colonies to acquire some land.

1743: Schaghticook Sachem Mahwee was baptized in New York. He was the first of his tribe to do so.

1811: A very large earthquake was felt along the Mississippi River. Many tribes passed along stories of the quake for many years.

1861: In fighting that took place through January 14 in Arizona, assistant surgeon Bernard J.D. Irwin took command of a group of soldiers who went to the rescue of Lieutenant Bascom's troops, who were engaging Cochise. For his actions, Irwin would be awarded the Medal of Honor.

1864: A Civil War battle took place at Middle Boggy Depot in Indian Territory (modern Atoka County, Oklahoma). Union forces under Major Charles Willette surprised Confederate forces under Lieutenant Colonel John Jumper. Jumper commanded members of the Seminole Battalion, Company A, First Choctaw and Chickasaw Cavalry Regiment, and a detachment of the Twentieth Texas Regiment. The bluecoats won the fight.

1879: According to U.S. Army reports, Victorio and twenty-two Warm Springs Apache Indians surrendered to Lieutenant Charles Merritt of the

Ninth Cavalry at Ojo Caliente, New Mexico. The Apache lived in Mexico for years, eluding the army's attempts to move them to the San Carlos Reservation on September 2, 1877.

1907: Lands were set aside for the Robinson Rancheria in California by secretarial order.

1931: The trust period on allotments made to Indians on the Pine Ridge Reservation, South Dakota, was extended by Executive Order No. 5557.

1942: Fishing rights of Alaska Indians were addressed in court.

1942: An election for a constitution and bylaws for the Moapa Band of Paiute Indians was authorized by Assistant Secretary of the Interior Oscar Chapman.

1969: The undersecretary of the interior ratified an election that approved amendments to the constitution and bylaws of the Jicarilla Apache. The election was held on December 23, 1968.

FEBRUARY 14

1756: Several Delaware attacked settlers in Berks County, Pennsylvania. A dozen settlers, including six children, were killed. Two of the settlers killed were young women, sisters who had a premonition of evil tidings the previous day. One of the sisters died in her father's arms when he found her in his burned farm.

1776: The first Spanish arrived at what eventually became Needles, California.

1873: Congress created the office of Indian Inspector. The initial three inspectors were appointed by the president for four-year terms. They inspected the operations of Indian officers in the field.

1913: By an act of Congress (37 Stat. 675) "all non-mineral, unallotted, unreserved lands within the Standing Rock Indian Reservation are opened to settlement and entry, to be disposed of under the general provisions of the Homestead laws."

1931: Congress passed an act (Public Law No. 667, 71st Congress) that authorized the president to establish the Canyon de Chelly National Monument in the Navajo Indian Reservation in northeastern Arizona. Another act (46 Stat. 1106) was also passed. Its purpose was to "enable the Secretary to accept donations of funds or other property for the advancement of the Indian race. An annual report will be made to Congress on donations received and allocations made from such donations."

1938: Assistant Secretary of the Interior Oscar Chapman ratified a constitution and bylaws approved by the Confederated Tribes of the Warm Springs Reservation of Oregon in an election held on December 18, 1937.

1969: The Confederated Salish and Kootenai Tribe of the Flathead Reservation enacted a resolution prohibiting the hunting or killing of mountain sheep.

1973: Deputy Assistant Secretary of the Interior W.L. Rogers authorized the Nooksack Indian Tribe of Washington an election for a constitution and bylaws.

1989: As of this date, the residential population of Acoma Pueblo communities was as follows: Acomita, 2,342; Anzac, 200 (est.); McCarty's, 1,646; Old Acoma (Sky City), 150 (est.); total 4,338.

FEBRUARY 15

1831: The U.S. Senate passed a resolution asking President Jackson if he was going to live up to the Indian Trade and Intercourse Act passed on March 30, 1802. If he was not going to live up to this law, they wanted to know why. He responded a week later.

1866: Elements of the Second Cavalry engaged Indians near Guano Valley, Nevada. One soldier was killed, and seven were wounded. Ninety-six Indians were killed, fifteen were wounded, and nineteen were captured, according to army records.

1867: According to army records, members of the Eighth Cavalry fought with a band of Indians near Black Slate Mountains, Nevada. Five Indians were reported killed.

1870: The second intercontinental railroad started. It also went through Indian lands.

1901: The Reservation Land Definition Act was passed.

1907: The confines of the Robinson Rancheria in California were established.

1936: The Omaha Tribe of Nebraska voted on a constitution. By a vote of 311–27, they approved it.

FEBRUARY 16

1863: An act (12 Stat. 1652) stated that all treaties between the United States and the Sisseton, Wahpeton, Medawakanton, and Wahpakoota Bands of Sioux of Dakota were abrogated and annulled as far as occupancy or obligations in Minnesota were concerned. This act took away their lands in Minnesota because of the Santee Sioux Uprising.

1866: Elements of the Fourteenth Infantry fought some Indians near Jordan Creek, Oregon. One soldier was wounded; one Indian was killed according to army records.

1867: According to army records, members of the First Cavalry and Ninth Infantry fought with a band of Indians near Surprise Valley, California. Five Indians were reported killed, and two were captured.

1867: According to army records, members of the First Cavalry fought with a band of Indians near Warm Springs, Idaho. Two Indians were reported killed, and five were captured.

1878: According to Army files, Victorio Rios and Sevoriano Elivano were killed by Indians near Point of Rocks, Limpia Canyon, Texas.

1911: President Taft issued several executive orders that allowed the sale, use, or manufacture of alcoholic beverages in former Indian reservations that had been ceded to the United States. The tribes that had ceded the land were the Chippewa of Lake Superior, Pillager, Red Lake, Pembina; and the Lake Traverse Sioux. President Taft also issued

Executive Order No. 1299, which stated that Pillager Chippewa lands in Minnesota ceded to the United States by the Treaty of August 21, 1847, would no longer be held in trust as Indian lands.

1922: President Warren Harding issued an executive order that would "withdraw from settlement, entry, sale or other disposition" approximately 386.85 acres of Zia Pueblo Indian lands in New Mexico until March 5, 1924. This order replaced Executive Order No. 3351, issued on November 6, 1920.

FEBRUARY 17

1690: While traveling through the area, French explorer Henri de Tonti visited the Natchitoches Confederation (near modern Natchitoches, Louisiana).

1792: An addendum was made to the Holston River Treaty. Payment for ceded land went from $1,000 to $1,500 annually. The new treaty was signed in Philadelphia by six Cherokees, including Bloody Fellow. As a part of the ceremony. President Washington gave Bloody Fellow the new name of Iskagua (Clear Sky).

1792: Chickamauga Chief Glass attacked settler John Collingsworth and his family near Nashville, Tennessee. He killed them all except for an eight-year-old girl. When he returned to Lookout Town, Glass performed a scalp dance as a part of his celebration. Dragging Canoe's enthusiastic participation in this dance led to his death on March 1, 1792.

1793: In Pensacola, Florida, Creek Chief Alexander McGillivray died.

1829: Thomas McKenney, head of the Bureau of Indian Affairs, sent orders to Little Rock, Arkansas, Indian agent Major Edward DuVal. DuVal was instructed to prohibit white people from entering or settling on Indian lands without the Indians' approval.

1861: The Choctaw Council authorized their principal chief to appoint delegates to any future intertribal meeting to decide relations with the United States. If the United States ever split into two countries, the Choctaw delegates were authorized to open relations with the Confederacy. The chief was also instructed to let the southern governors know the Choctaw were inclined to support their cause.

1871: President Grant, by executive order, rescinded the initial boundaries of the Mission Indian Reservations, primarily in San Diego County, California. They were reestablished by other acts on December 27, 1875, and May 15, 1876.

1871: Indians attacked settlements near Fort Bayard in southwestern New Mexico, killing settlers, burning ranches, and seizing livestock. Cavalry troops pursued the Indians into the mountains. The soldiers burned villages and property. One soldier and fourteen Indians were reported killed. Two soldiers and twenty Indians were wounded, according to army reports.

1909: Geronimo (Goyathlay) died at Fort Sill, Oklahoma.

1912: Executive Order Nos. 1482 and 1483 modified the status of certain Indian lands in New Mexico.

1969: The acting assistant commissioner of Indian affairs authorized an election to amend the constitution and bylaws of the Kalispel Indian Community of the Kalispel Reservation. The election would be held on June 18, 1969.

FEBRUARY 18

1837: General Ellis Wool had been assigned the task of preventing the Cherokees from revolting after the passage of the New Echota Treaty on December 29, 1835. General Wool tried to get the Cherokees to acquiesce to the treaty, but to no avail. He reported opposition to the treaty was so prevalent that starving Cherokees would not take help from the government for fear that it might imply their consent to the treaty.

Geronimo, a Chiricahua Apache, with rifle (LOC)

1861: The Arapaho and Cheyenne signed a treaty (12 Stat. 1163) at Fort Wise in southeastern Colorado. The United States was represented by Albert Boone and F.B. Culver. It established a reservation bounded by Sand Creek and the Arkansas River. The Indians thought it allowed them the right to hunt freely outside of the reservation, but the treaty contained no such clause. Only six of the forty-four Cheyenne chiefs were present to sign, Black Kettle being one. Other than the Indians who signed on this day, no others ever signed it. The validity of the treaty was contested for a long time. The fort was renamed Fort Lyon.

1865: The second Julesburg, Colorado, skirmish takes place.

1867: The Sac and Fox signed a treaty (15 Stat. 495). They sold much of what remained of their reservation.

1876: Twenty-Fifth Infantry soldiers fought some Indians in the Carrizo Mountains in Texas. According to army documents, no casualties were recorded.

FEBRUARY 19

1725: Documents regarding the Delaware Walking Purchase Treaty were discovered.

1778: Virginia Governor Patrick Henry was upset by the actions of several white "frontiersmen" against the Indians. They had killed Shawnee Chief Cornstalk and four other Shawnees who had lived in peace with their neighbors. On this day Governor Henry wrote a letter to Colonel William Fleming suggesting that perhaps the murderers were British agents trying to instigate a fight with the Indians to divert troops away from the Revolutionary War.

1799: Congress passed "An Act Appropriating a Certain Sum of Money to Defray the Expense of Holding a Treaty or Treaties with the Indians."

1808: Congress passed "An Act Making Appropriations for Carrying into Effect Certain Indian Treaties."

1819: Congress passed an appropriation of $10,000 a year to be used for the education of some Indian tribes.

1867: The negotiations on a treaty (15 Stat. 505) were concluded. Article 3 set aside land in the North and South Dakota Lake Traverse Reservation. Eventually, the Sisseton Wahpeton Sioux Tribe occupied the land.

1877: Scout Colonel Nelson Miles, sent out on February 1, 1877, returned with nineteen chiefs and leading warriors. They wished to discuss specifics of Miles's terms of surrender. The terms were the same—unconditional surrender and return to designated agencies. The Indians left to council with their people.

1889: The Quileute Reserve was established by executive order.

1889: Gabriel Dumont was a Metis chief and actively participated in Riel's Rebellion. He received a government pardon for those actions.

1915: Lands that were set aside for the Arizona militia by executive order on July 23, 1914, were returned to Navajo tribal ownership.

1937: The Pawnee Indian Tribe of Oklahoma compiled an official census.

1968: Robert Kennedy was serving as chairman of the Senate subcommittee on Indian education. At a hearing in Twin Oaks, Oklahoma, Kennedy stated the opinion that cultural differences were a national resource, not a burden.

1976: An amendment to the constitution of the Tuolumne Band of Me-Wok Indians of the Tuolumne Rancheria was approved by a vote of 25 to 1.

1991: The Salamanca, New York, lease expired.

FEBRUARY 20

1755: General Edward Braddock reached Virginia (French and Indian War).

1832: Northeastern District Choctaw Chief Peter Pitchlynn and his followers arrived in Fort Smith in western Arkansas. Floods, cold weather, low rivers, and mud had delayed their trip considerably.

1863: Cherokee Chief John Ross had been arrested by Union forces and taken to Washington, D.C. In the interim, Stand Watie had been elected tribal chief at the First Confederate Cherokee Conference. At Cow Skin Prairie, Cherokees loyal to John Ross revoked the treaty with the South and pledged loyalty to the Union. They removed Confederates from office, emancipated slaves, and confirmed John Ross as principal chief.

1873: Indians fought with soldiers from the First Cavalry near Fossil Creek, Arizona, according to army documents. Five Indians were killed, and four were captured.

1874: Indians fought with soldiers from the Fifth Cavalry around the Bill Williams Mountains in Arizona. According to army documents, three Indians were killed during this engagement, which lasted until April 21.

1893: A congressional act modified the White Mountain–San Carlos–Camp Apache Reserve in western Arizona Territory. It was amended further on June 10, 1896. At its largest, it comprised 2,866 square miles and was occupied by Aravaipa, Chillion, Chiricahua, Coyotero, Membreno, Mogollon, Mohave, Pinal, San Carlos, Tonto, and Yuma Apache Tribes.

1904: The executive order issued on January 25, 1904, returning a tract of land set aside for the Pine Ridge School Reservation to the public domain was modified.

1949: The Oneida Tribe of Indians of Wisconsin's Tribal Council delegated to an executive committee the powers exercised by the general council in article 4 of their constitution.

1973: The deputy assistant secretary of the interior authorized an election to amend the revised constitution and bylaws for the Sisseton Wahpeton Sioux Tribe of South Dakota. The election would take place on March 16 and 17, 1973.

FEBRUARY 21

1756: According to some reports, an agreement covering alliances and fort construction was reached by representatives of the British in Virginia and the Catawba.

1803: President Thomas Jefferson submitted a treaty between the United States and the Tuscarora of North Carolina to the U.S. Senate. The treaty was signed in Raleigh, North Carolina, on December 4, 1802.

1828: Elias Boudinot (Buck Watie), as editor, established the *Cherokee Phoenix* newspaper in New Echota.

1861: The rich members of the Navajo tribe (the so-called Rico leaders) met with Colonel Edward Canby at the new Fort Fauntleroy in western New Mexico. The meeting included such leaders as Manuelito, Delgadito, Armijo, Barboncito, and Herrero Grande. During the meeting, the Navajos choose Herrero Grande as the head chief of the Navajo. The parley led to a "treaty" whereby the

Fort Griffin, Texas, located near Camp Cooper close to the Brazos River (author photo)

Navajos promised to live in peace with their non-Indian neighbors. The fort later was renamed Fort Lyon, then Fort Wingate.

1861: Camp Cooper was officially decommissioned and abandoned. It was located on the Clear Fork of the Brazos River, not far from Fort Griffin in modern Throckmorton County, Texas. The camp was established to keep watch over a nearby Comanche Reservation.

1864: After the battles in the Canyon de Chelly, Herrero Grande and 300 of his followers turned themselves in to army authorities. They eventually participated in the Long Walk to the Bosque Redondo Reservation in New Mexico.

1876: Forty-six people were trapped in the trading post at Fort Pease in central Montana by hostile Indians. On this day, Major James Brisbin and 221 officers, soldiers, and volunteers left Fort Ellis, Montana, to rescue the party (see March 4, 1876).

1911: Comanche Chief Quanah Parker died. He was eventually buried at Fort Sill in south-central Oklahoma. His headstone reads, "resting here until day breaks and darkness disappears is Quanah Parker, the last Chief of the Comanche. Died

Eskimo spear and lance maker, Point Barrow, Alaska (NA)

Feb. 21,1911, age sixty-four years." (Also recorded as February 23.)

1931: The Papago Reservation in Sells, Arizona, was modified.

1935: The Inuit of the Mackenzie Delta had decided to raise reindeer as an economic enterprise. A herd of 2,300 reindeer, herded by Lapps and Eskimos, arrived at the Mackenzie Delta. The effort proved to be very successful.

1940: An election was held on two proposed amendments to the constitution and bylaws of the Confederated Tribes of the Warm Springs Reservation of Oregon. The constitution was approved in an election held on December 18, 1937. Amendment 1 was passed 93–68. Amendment 2 was passed 149–15.

1956: Land ownership on Tulalip Reservation in Washington was questioned.

1978: The area director of the Sacramento office of the Bureau of Indian Affairs authorized an election for an amendment to the constitution of the Utu Utu Gwaitu Paiute Tribe of the Benton Paiute Reservation in California. The election would be held on May 27, 1978, according to a government document.

FEBRUARY 22

1637: Lieutenant Lion Gardiner was commander of some of the forces at Fort Saybrook, Connecticut. He led some men out to get rid of the undergrowth that might hide approaching Indians. They were attacked by Pequot. Two of the settlers were killed in the fighting.

1676: According to some sources, 300 Indians attacked Medfield, Massachusetts, near Boston. They killed twenty settlers and took many more captive. Some settlers said King Philip was involved.

1740: After leaving Fort Assumption (modern Memphis) with a force of 180 French troops and 400 Choctaws and Iroquois, French Captain Pierre Celeron finally arrived at one of the main fortified Chickasaw villages in the region. After a brief exchange of gunfire by Celeron's allies and the Chickasaw, a conference was arranged. Believing Celeron's expedition was only the precursor of a major French expedition, the Chickasaw agreed to return captives, destroy the bulwarks of their forts, and come to Fort Assumption for formal peace talks. Celeron's forces remained in the Chickasaw villages until March 15.

1819: The "Treaty of Amity, Settlement, and Limits Between the United States of America and His Catholic Majesty" of Spain was signed. It was regarding Florida.

1831: The state of Georgia had seized Cherokee lands. Cherokee leaders had complained to many federal government officials. On February 15, the U.S. Senate officially asked President Andrew Jackson if he was going to live up to the Indian Trade and Intercourse Act passed in March 1802. On this day, President Jackson responded to the Senate's inquiry. Unequivocally, Jackson stated he sided with the state of Georgia and he would not enforce any law giving precedence to the Cherokees over Georgia.

1838: Mikanopy, King Philip, Coahadjo, Little Cloud, and almost 220 other Seminole boarded a ship in Charleston, South Carolina, bound for New Orleans and the Indian Territory (present-day Oklahoma).

1838: Cherokee Chief John Ross presented to Congress a petition signed by 15,665 Cherokee (there were approximately 18,000 Cherokees in all) repudiating the New Echota treaty. They reminded Congress that when a similar rigged treaty was ratified in 1825 then–President Adams had it nullified. The Senate did not act on the petition.

1855: The Sandy Lake Indian Reservation was created in Minnesota as a part of a treaty (10 Stat. 1165). This treaty was signed in Washington, D.C., by the "Mississippi, Pillager and Lake Winnebigoshish Bands of Chippewa Indians."

1856: Many Rogue River War volunteers were at a party away from camp when Indians attacked the camp. Twenty-four whites were killed, including a captain and an Indian agent. This was the beginning of a series of raids along the river.

1866: Elements of the Fourteenth Infantry fought some Indians near Jordan Creek, Oregon. One soldier was killed, another wounded. Eighteen Indians were killed, and two were wounded, according to Fourteenth Infantry records.

1872: Indians skirmished with a group of settlers near Cullumber's Station, Arizona, according to official army records. Two settlers were killed.

1876: Second Cavalry and Seventh Infantry soldiers fought some Indians near Fort Pease, Montana. According to army documents, six civilians were killed and eight were wounded. The fighting lasted through March 17.

1877: Settlers fought a group of Indians in the Staked Plain (Llano Estacado) of northern Texas. According to army documents, one settler was killed.

1944: Jack C. Montgomery, a Cherokee, was a first lieutenant with the Forty-fifth Infantry in Italy. For his solo actions against three different enemy positions, he would be awarded the Medal of Honor.

1981: The Vietnam-era Veterans Intertribal Association held formal meetings.

FEBRUARY 23

1540: According to some sources, the Coronado expedition began preparations to get under way.

1832: Chickasaw Chief Levi Colbert told President Jackson the Chickasaw agreed to the removal to Indian Territory (present-day Oklahoma). He informed the president they could not reach an agreement with the Choctaws on sharing lands, so the provisional treaty of September 1, 1830, was void.

1833: According to a government report, by this date it was estimated approximately 6,000 Choctaws had been removed to the west. Some 1,000 Choctaws had gone on their own, without having to be removed by the government.

1836: Cherokees in Texas signed a treaty with the local settlers. It was eventually repudiated by then–Texas President Mirabeau B. Lamar.

1839: Almost 900 Cherokees under the leadership of fellow Cherokee Reverend Jesse Bushyhead arrived in Indian Territory (present-day Oklahoma). They sustained thirty-eight deaths while on their forced emigration.

1865: Major General G.M. Dodge, in St. Louis, sent the following message by telegram to Colonel Ford at Fort Riley: "The military have no authority to treat with Indians. Our duty is to make them keep the peace by punishing them for their hostility. Keep posted as to their location, so that as soon as ready we can strike them. 400 horses arrived here for you."

1867: The Quapaw gave up their lands in Kansas and a large part of their lands in northern Indian Territory (present-day Oklahoma).

Ira H. Hayes, shown here at age nineteen, helped raise the flag on Iwo Jima. (NA)

1867: According to army records, members of the First Cavalry fought with a band of Indians near Meadow Valley, Arizona. One soldier was reported wounded.

1867: According to a treaty (15 Stat. 513), all members of the Miami tribe could become citizens of Kansas if they wished to do so. Those who did not wish to do this had to move to Indian Territory (present-day Oklahoma).

1875: Indians fought with soldiers from the Fifth Cavalry and some Indian scouts near Camp Apache, Arizona. According to army documents, fifteen Indians were killed, and 122 were captured. This engagement started on January 2.

1875: Lieutenant Colonel J.W. Davidson's troops of the Tenth Cavalry captured sixty-five Kiowa men, and 175 women and children, on the Salt Fork of the Red River in Texas. Also taken

were 300 horses and mules. Among the captured were Lone Wolf, Red Otter, and Lean Bull, according to army reports.

1877: Lieutenant J.F. Cummings and Troop C, Third Cavalry, attacked a group of hostile Indians near Deadwood, Dakota Territory. One Indian was killed; 624 head of livestock were recovered.

1878: Army reports say R.W. Barry and Juan Dial were killed by Indians twenty-three miles from Fort Duncan, near Eagle Pass, Texas, on the Laredo Road.

1889: Congress approved an agreement signed by Lemhi Chief Tendoy and several others to move from the Lemhi Reservation in Idaho to Fort Hall. The agreement was signed on May 14, 1880. The Lemhi would not actually move until 1909.

1939: Land acquired on June 16, 1933, under the National Industrial Recovery Act was transferred from the jurisdiction of the secretary of agriculture to the secretary of the interior, by executive order, as a part of the Milk River Land Utilization Project on the Fort Peck Indian Reservation in Montana.

1945: Ira Hayes participated in the flag-raising on Iwo Jima.

1962: Assistant Secretary of the Interior John A. Carver Jr. ratified an election that approved an amendment to the constitution and bylaws for the Pyramid Lake Paiute Tribe of Nevada. The election was held on December 26, 1961.

1970: The Pueblo of Isleta approved a new constitution by a vote of 347–29. It would go into affect on April 10, 1970.

FEBRUARY 24

1730: With both sides running out of ammunition, the French and the Natchez Indians agreed on a peace settlement. The Natchez released all of their prisoners, and the French withdrew to the Mississippi River. The French were anxious to make the agreement because their Choctaw allies expressed a desire to quit the fight. The prisoners were released to the Choctaw, who demanded a ransom for their services. The Natchez eventually escaped into the woodlands.

1831: The Choctaw Dancing Rabbit Creek Treaty (11 Stat. 537) was ratified by the U.S. Senate. The Choctaw left Mississippi for Indian Territory (present-day Oklahoma). While many Choctaw were opposed to the treaty, they lacked organization. It was publicly proclaimed on May 26, 1831.

1848: As a part of the war against the Cayuse who attacked the Whitman Mission in Oregon Country, a fight took place. The Cayuse lost eight men, including Chief Gray Eagle, and had five warriors wounded. Lieutenant Colonel Waters and four other soldiers were wounded.

1897: Api-kai-ees (Deerfoot) was a Siksika (Blackfoot) man known for his ability as a long-distance runner. He was well known in the Calgary area, where a modern local freeway bears his name. He died on this day.

1954: Starting the day before, and continuing on this day, an election was held to approve an amended constitution and bylaws for the San Carlos Apache Tribe. It would be approved by a vote of 405–402.

1976: William Finale, area director of the Sacramento area office of the Bureau of Indian Affairs, approved an election for amendments to the constitution of the Tuolumne Band of Me-Wok Indians of the Tuolumne Rancheria. They were enacted.

FEBRUARY 25

1643: For the last two years there had been several incidents sparked by both Indians and settlers that had led to bloodshed in the area around modern New York City. The only Indians in the area were some peaceful Indians seeking refuge from the Mohawks. Through the next day, New

Amsterdam citizens, with the approval of Dutch Director Kieft and led by Maryn Adriaensen, attacked a peaceful Wecquaesgeek village at Corlaer's Hook near the Pavonia settlements (near modern Jersey City). The Dutch soldiers killed not only the warriors but all of the eighty Indians in the camp, including women and children. This fight became known as the Pavonia Massacre, and it incited numerous reprisals. Adriaensen was exiled to Holland for three years as punishment for leading the attack once the population learned of the fight. He would return, and receive a land grant from Director Kieft, three years later. Some accounts say only thirty Indians were killed.

1689: According to some sources, an agreement of alliance and allegiance was reached between representatives of the Five Nations and the British in New York.

1779: Indians left Vincennes.

1799: Congress passed "An Act Making Appropriations for Defraying the Expenses Which May Arise in Carrying into Effect Certain Treaties Between the United States and Several Tribes or Nations of Indians."

1825: Under a treaty signed on this day, the United States had specific trust responsibilities to protect the property, persons, and lives of the Oglala Sioux people. The United States agreed to receive the Oglala Band into friendship and under its protection.

1839: Captain Jacob Burleson and fifty-three other Texas Rangers fought a group of Comanche near Brushy Creek (near modern Taylor, Texas). The Indians gained the upper hand. Later the next day, other Rangers arrived and pursued the fleeing Indians. Burleson was killed in the fighting.

1858: A group of Bannock and a few Shoshone stole some cattle from the local Mormon settlers near Fort Limhi, Idaho. This led to a brief battle with a couple of settlers being killed. The fort would be abandoned on March 27, 1858.

Lone Wolf, chief of the Kiowa (NA)

1871: Colonel Ranald S. Mackenzie took over command of the Fourth Cavalry at Fort Concho (modern San Angelo, Texas).

1874: Regulations regarding the Skokomish Reserve were written.

1875: After the battle of Palo Duro Canyon, Lone Wolf and his followers headed across the plains. But after a relentless search by the army, on this day Lone Wolf and 252 Kiowa finally surrendered at Fort Sill in south-central Oklahoma. Lone Wolf eventually was sent as a prisoner of war to Fort Marion in St. Augustine, Florida.

1956: An election to approve an amendment to the constitution and bylaws of the Tule River Indian Tribe was held. The vote was 36–11 in favor of Amendment 3.

1983: The state of Virginia officially recognized the Chickahominy, Eastern Chickahominy, Mattaponi and Upper Mattaponi, Monacan, Nansemond, Pamunkey, and United Rappahanock Tribes.

1987: The legality of Indian bingo was upheld by courts in California.

1998: The Oglala Sioux Tribal Council declared the twenty-fifth anniversary of the Wounded Knee occupation a tribal holiday. It designated the occupation a historic and cultural event that brought attention to Indian issues.

1998: The U.S. Supreme Court ruled against the Native Village of Venetie tribal governments, stating there was no Indian country in Alaska, save one reservation. This ruling was part of an effort of this tribe to tax a company in their "territory."

FEBRUARY 26

1757: Built by Pennsylvania troops at Shamokin on the Susquehanna River at the juncture of several Indian trails, Fort Augusta was surrounded and briefly held under siege by Indians. The Indians left after a few days but would return in a few months.

1860: The Wiyot lived on the upper California coast between the Little River and the Bear River. An annual ceremony lasting over a week was held in the village of Tutulwat on an island in the river in what is now Eureka, California. By Wiyot tradition, everyone was welcome at the ceremony, including whites. Tonight, after the ceremonies were finished, a group of men from Eureka sneaked into the village and attacked the participants. Several other nearby villages were also attacked. An estimated eighty to 100 Indians were killed in the sneak attack. An annual vigil is now held on a nearby island to commemorate the event.

1871: Indians attacked a hunter's camp, stole the stock, and burned the camp near Grinnell, Kansas.

1872: Indians skirmished with a group of settlers near Camp Bowie, Arizona, according to official army records. One settler was killed, and one was wounded.

1873: Indians fought with soldiers from the Eighth Cavalry near Angostura, New Mexico, according to army documents. Five Indians were killed, and seven were wounded.

1881: According to army records, 325 Sioux, believed to be primarily from Sitting Bull's camp, surrendered to Major David Brotherton, Seventh Infantry, at Fort Buford, near the North Dakota–Montana line. Some 150 horses and forty guns were turned in by the Indians.

1937: The secretary of the interior approved a constitution for the Kickapoo Tribe.

1937: The constitution of the Iowa Tribe of Kansas and Nebraska was approved.

FEBRUARY 27

1699: Fearing an English takeover of the Mississippi Valley, Frenchman Pierre le Moyne, Sieur d'Iberville, was granted permission to establish a series of forts along the lower Mississippi River. He began his voyage up the Mississippi. (Also recorded as happening on March 3.)

1754: In a letter to Pennsylvania Governor James Hamilton, the Pennsylvania assembly assailed the European traders cheating the local Indians. The traders were equated with the worst of European criminals.

1760: Tonight there was a skirmish at Fort Dobbs (modern Salisbury, North Carolina). A war party of Cherokees attacked the fort. Troops led by Captain Hugh Waddell beat back the attack, killing almost a dozen warriors. Waddell posted no losses to his force.

1798: Congress passed "An Act Appropriating a Certain Sum of Money to Defray the Expense of Holding a Treaty or Treaties with the Indians."

1803: President Thomas Jefferson wrote a letter to William Henry Harrison. He expressed his belief that promoting trading houses among the Indians led to the Indians incurring greater debts. He felt these debts could lead to the United States acquiring more lands to pay off the debts.

1819: The Cherokee signed a treaty (7 Stat.195). The United States was represented by Secretary of War John C. Calhoun.

1836: General Edmund Gaines had marched from Tampa Bay to Fort King in central Florida to put down the Seminole Uprising. When he arrived in Fort King, he did not find enough supplies to feed his troops or mounts. Gaines ordered his 1,100 troops to return to Tampa Bay. While attempting to cross the Withlacoochee River, Gaines was attacked by a Seminole force of 1,500 warriors. Gaines built a stockade and sent for reinforcements during the battle. After ten days of fighting, both sides agreed to a truce, with formal peace talks to come later.

1839: Reverend Stephen Foreman and 911 fellow Cherokees arrived in the Indian Territory (present-day Oklahoma). They had lost fifty-seven of their group to deaths along the trail. There were nineteen births during the trip.

1866: President Andrew Johnson issued an executive order that set aside additional lands for the Santee Sioux in Nebraska.

1867: An act (15 Stat. 531) was passed regarding the reservation occupied by the Prairie Band of Potawatomi Indians. It covered 29.75 square miles of territory in Kansas.

1867: According to army records, members of a hunting party from near Fort Reno, Dakota Territory, fought with some Indians. Three soldiers were reported as wounded.

1869: According to army records, members of the Fourteenth Infantry fought with a band of Indians near Camp Grant. Two civilians were killed, and one soldier was wounded.

1885: "That tract of country in the Territory of Dakota, known as the Old Winnebago Reservation and the Sioux on Crow Creek Reservation, and lying on the east bank of the Missouri River" was modified by law.

1925: Laws were enacted affecting Phoenix Indian School land in Arizona.

1958: Randall Dam and Reservoir Project required condemnation actions in South Dakota.

1973: The siege of Wounded Knee began. It lasted until May 8, 1973.

1973: An election to approve a constitution and bylaws for the Cortina Band of Indians on the Cortina Indian Rancheria in Colusa County, California, was authorized by the deputy assistant secretary of the interior. The election occurred on July 18, 1973.

1979: The area director of the Sacramento office of the Bureau of Indian Affairs, William Finale, approved an amendment for the constitution for the Utu Utu Gwaitu Paiute Tribe of the Benton Paiute Reservation in California.

FEBRUARY 28

1675: The Mission Santa Cruz de Sabacola El Menor was dedicated. The mission was for the Sawoklis Indians on the Apalachicola River.

1681: The charter for the province of Pennsylvania was issued by King Charles II. It included mostly lands claimed by Indian tribes.

1683: According to some sources, a land cession agreement was reached between representatives of the Wimbee Indians and South Carolina colonies.

1704: On this day and through the next day, in what was the first American battle in Queen Anne's War, Deerfield in central Massachusetts was attacked by Indians and French under Major Hertel de Rouville. Of the almost 300 inhabitants, about fifty were killed, and as many as 180 were taken prisoner.

1780: The village of Nashborough (Nashville) was started.

1809: Congress passed "An Act for the Relief of Certain Alibama and Wyandot Indians."

1837: A few Creek Indians attacked the Alberson homestead on the Alabama-Florida border. The Creek were reported to have killed the entire family.

1859: By government act, 558 square miles were set aside for the establishment of the Gila River Reserve in the Pima Agency south of Phoenix, Arizona. It was occupied by the Maricopa and Pima Tribes.

1873: After the first battle in the northern California lava beds, Captain Jack's cousin, Winema, and some friendly local whites came to visit him. Winema had married a white settler. In a council on this night, the white men told Captain Jack that peace commissioners wanted to meet with them. When asked, they also said that Hooker Jim would not be tried for his killing raid in Oregon but was to be sent to a reservation in Oklahoma instead. Captain Jack agreed to meet with the commissioners and to hear what they had to say.

1877: The Standing Rock Sioux Reservation had been created by the Treaty of April 29, 1868, and an act of Congress (19 Stat. 254) in Dakota Territory. It covered 4,176 square miles and was occupied by "Blackfeet, Hunkpapa, Lower and Upper Tanktonai Sioux." Article 8 of the act provided that each individual Oglala Sioux person "shall be protected in his rights of property, person and life."

1929: The Northwestern Shoshone Jurisdictional Act was modified.

1941: According to Federal Register Nos. 6FR01229 and 6FR01230, Executive Order Nos. 8696 and 8670 were issued. They transferred the jurisdiction of certain Pueblo Indian lands in New Mexico from the secretary of agriculture to the secretary of the interior.

FEBRUARY 29

1704: The battle started the day before at Deerfield, Massachusetts, continued.

1836: General Edmund Gaines and 1,100 soldiers had been engaged in a battle with a force of 1,500 Seminole under Chief Osceola since February 27. The Americans built a stockade on February 27. The Seminole mounted a major attack on the stockade. Many men were wounded on both sides during the attack. The fighting continued until March 6, 1836.

1936: An election was held to approve a constitution and bylaws for the Santee Sioux Tribe of the Sioux Nation of the state of Nebraska. The vote was 284–60 in favor.

MARCH 1

1524: Giovanni da Verrazano, sailing for France, anchored near Wilmington, North Carolina, in the *Dauphine*. He kidnapped an Indian child they encountered to bring back to Europe. (Also recorded as happening on March 7.)

1781: The U.S. Articles of Confederation went into effect.

1792: In the past few days, the Chickamauga had staged several successful raids on European settlements. Last night they started a victory dance. Chief Dragging Canoe danced the night through. This morning, Dragging Canoe died at the approximate age of sixty-two. He was replaced as war chief by John Watts (Young Tassel).

1793: Congress passed "An Act to Regulate Trade and Intercourse with the Indian Tribes." It also passed "An Act Making an Appropriation to Defray the Expense of a Treaty with the Indians Northwest of the Ohio."

1831: According to a Georgia law, this date was the deadline for all whites to be out of Cherokee lands.

1832: A large group of Creek Indian leaders left Alabama to go to Washington, D.C., to again protest Alabama laws. Secretary of War Lewis Cass again told them their only hope was to go west. The federal government could not help them.

1833: One of the first books for Indians about Christianity was published.

1851: California Governor McDougal wrote to the president stating there were more than 100,000 hostile Indians in California. He informed the president an uprising was going on. This information was false, and the governor never specified who was revolting or where the uprisings were located. He requested permission to call out the militia as U.S. troops.

1856: A big peace conference with the Sioux was begun by General William S. "White Whiskers" Harney.

1873: Not waiting for Captain Jack to meet with the commissioners, Hooker Jim and his followers

Secretary of War Lewis Cass (IMH)

went to the Fairchild Ranch to talk directly to them. Hooker Jim told them he wished to surrender as a prisoner of war. While in the camp, Hooker Jim met an Oregon settler who said he would take them to Oregon to be tried for murder. Jim and his followers fled the camp and returned to the lava beds. They warned Captain Jack not to meet with the commissioners because it was a trap.

1873: The Lac Courte Oreilles Reservation was established by an act in Wisconsin.

1876: General George Crook's forces of ten troops of the Second and Third Cavalry, and two companies of infantry, left Fort Fetterman in east-central Wyoming to look for hostile Indians near the sources of the Powder, Tongue, and Rosebud Rivers.

1883: An act was passed that enabled the president to consolidate tribes, or agencies, without the Indians' consent. The government used this law to take more lands when they wanted to intimidate the Indians during negotiations.

1907: A congressional act set aside lands in the Blackfeet Indian Reservation, Montana, for the purposes of establishing townsites.

Pine Ridge Indian Agency buildings (NA)

1907: An act of Congress (34 Stat. 1016) authorized the president to divert appropriations made for certain purposes to other uses for the benefit of the several Indian tribes, "Provided, that the Secretary of the Interior shall make to the Congress reports required in connection with action taken by him under this provision."

1910: Executive Order No. 1172 was issued. It modified some of the landholdings within the Mescalero Apache Indian Reservation.

1954: The "Buckskin Declaration of Independence" was presented in Washington, D.C. It was a document from the Miccosukee Seminole Nation requesting President Eisenhower to "to dispense the justice which will preserve our freedom, property rights and independence."

1972: The Articles of Association were adopted by the Twenty-Nine Palms Band of Mission Indians.

MARCH 2

1793: Sam Houston was born. He lived with the Cherokees for many years, where he was known as Raven.

1805: The United States acknowledged some old land grants.

1811: Congress passed "An Act for Establishing Trading Houses with the Indian Tribes."

1839: Mose Daniels and 924 fellow Cherokees arrived in the Indian Territory (present-day Oklahoma) after their forced emigration. Forty-eight members of this group died on the march.

1847: The Meusebach-Comanche Treaty was signed by Buffalo Hump, Santana, and other Comanche leaders in Texas.

1867: An act was passed that purchased a reserve for Sac and Fox of 4.5 square miles.

1867: An agreement had been reached between the United States and the Shawnee Tribe of Indians.

1876: William W. Belknap, the secretary of war, was impeached for taking bribes to make political appointments.

1889: Indian lands went public.

1889: The original confines of the Pine Ridge Indian Reservation were defined by an act (25 Stat. L. 888) according to the constitution of the Oglala Sioux Tribe of the Pine Ridge Indian Reservation. Section 11 of the act allocated lands to individual tribal members and provided that "the United States does and will hold the land thus located for a period of twenty-five years, in trust for the sole use and benefit of the Indian to whom such allotment shall have been made."

1889: The boundaries of the Lower Brule Reservation and the Rosebud Sioux Reservation were established.

1895: The Miami Tribe Annuity Pay-Roll was authorized by an act of Congress (28 Stat. 903). It also served as a tribal roll.

1929: An act (45 Stat. 1481) was passed that modified the election and terms of the Osage Tribal Council.

1974: The Shoalwater Bay Indian Organization in Washington State established a 3 percent privilege fee based on earnings on their reservation.

1989: The Navajo Code Talker Monument was erected.

1992: Executive Order No. 6407 was issued by President George Bush. It declared 1992 as "The Year of the American Indian."

MARCH 3

1513: Ponce de Leon left Puerto Rico. His destination was Florida and the Fountain of Youth. De Leon claimed Florida for Spain.

1540: Hernando de Soto had found some gold in one of the southern Florida Indian villages he had "discovered." He broke his winter camp at Iniahica (near modern Tallahassee) and began the second season of his expedition, searching for gold in the north.

1699: Fearing an English takeover of the Mississippi Valley, Frenchman Pierre le Moyne, Sieur d'Iberville, was granted permission to establish a series of forts along the lower Mississippi River. He began his voyage up the Mississippi. (Also recorded as happening on February 27.)

1791: An act of Congress gave the Kaskaskia Indians a 320-acre tract of land near Kaskaskia Township.

1795: Congress passed "An Act Making Provision for the Purposes of Trade with the Indians."

1799: Congress enacted "An Act [1799] to Regulate Trade and Intercourse with the Indian Tribes, and to Preserve Peace on the Frontiers."

1805: Congress passed "An Act Making Appropriations for Carrying into Effect Certain Indian Treaties, and for Other Purposes of Indian Trade and Intercourse."

1807: Congress passed "An Act Making Appropriations for Carrying into Effect a Treaty Between the United States and the Chickasaw Tribe of Indians and to Establish a Land Office in the Mississippi Territory." It also passed "An Act Making Appropriations for Carrying into Effect Certain Treaties with the Cherokee and Piankeshaw Tribes of Indians."

1809: Congress enacted a supplemental act to "An Act for Establishing Trading Houses with the Indian Tribes."

1811: Congress passed "An Act Making Appropriations for Carrying into Effect a Treaty Between the United States and the Great and Little Osage Nation of Indians, Concluded at Fort Clarke, on the Tenth day of November, One Thousand Eight Hundred and Eight, and for Other Purposes."

1819: The United States started its Indian "civilization" program.

1820: The Mi'kmaq Afton First Nation Reserve of Pomquet-Afton was established in Nova Scotia. The Bear River First Nation Reserve of Bear River was also established.

1837: Dr. John Young loaded 466 Cherokees and five Creek onto eleven boats at the site of Chattanooga, Tennessee. They were the first Cherokees to emigrate to the Indian Territory (present-day Oklahoma) by the government under the New Echota Treaty. Included in the group was Chief Major Ridge (Kahnungdaclageh). Half of the Cherokees were children. They reached Fort Coffee in eastern Indian Territory on March 29.

1847: An act was passed by Congress that gave the president, or the secretary of war, discretionary power to pay annuities to people other than tribal chiefs. With Indian consent, the president could also spend the annuities to promote the prosperity and happiness of the tribe. No moneys would be given to intoxicated persons. It also authorized funds to pay for the Texas Treaty signed at Council Springs.

1849: The Bureau of Indian Affairs was transferred to the Home Department from the War Department.

1851: The Mi'kmaq Anapolis Valley First Nation Reserve of St. Croix was established in Nova Scotia.

1863: The Idaho Territory bill passed, and funding was okayed to finance new treaty meetings.

1865: A governmental act (13 Stat. 559) established the Colorado River Agency. It was 376 square miles in size and became home to the Chemehuevi, Walapai, Kowia, Cocopah, Mohave, and Yuma Tribes.

1865: The Mi'kmaq Afton First Nation Reserve of Franklin Manor was established in Nova Scotia.

1867: The Mi'kmaq Millbrook First Nation Reserve of Beaver Lake No. 17 was established in Nova Scotia.

1869: According to army records, members of the Thirty-Second Infantry fought with a band of Indians near Oak Grove, Arizona. One Indian was killed.

1871: The U.S. House of Representatives was unhappy because it was not involved in the treaty-making process (only the Senate votes on treaties). It passed an act whereby Indian nations were not considered sovereign nations. The act read that the Indians would not be "acknowledged or recognized as an independent nation, tribe or power with whom the United States may contract by treaty." This terminated the president's authority to make treaties with Indian nations.

1873: Congress passed an act to remove certain lands from the Round Valley Reservation in Mendocino County, California. President Grant issued an executive order, based on this act, on April 8, 1873.

1875: The federal government passed an act that extended the Homestead Act to Indians who gave up their tribal affiliations. The head of the household was entitled to 160 acres.

1875: An act of Congress (18 Stat. 420) modified the boundaries of the Paiute Indians' Moapa Band Reservation.

1885: An order was issued modifying the boundaries of the Zuni Pueblo Reservation in New Mexico Territory.

1886: The Mi'kmaq Millbrook First Nation Reserve of Millbrook No. 27 was established in Nova Scotia.

1891: The boundaries of the Fort Berthold Reservation were defined by act of Congress (26 Stat. 1032).

1893: Congress passed a law that purchased the Cherokee Strip (6,574,487 acres) for $8,595,736.12, or approximately $1.31 an acre. The government

basically forced the Cherokee Nation to sell the land. The "run" for the Cherokee Strip was held on September 16, 1893.

1893: An act of Congress (27 Stat. 656) was approved. It established a commission to "negotiate agreements with the Cherokee, Choctaw, Chickasaw, Creek, and Seminole Tribes providing for the dissolution of the tribal governments and the allotment of land to each tribal member." Senator Henry L. Dawes of Massachusetts was appointed as chairman. It became known as the Dawes Commission.

1901: An act (31 Stat. 1066) was passed by Congress. Its purpose was to "require that any person seeking to trade with the Indians on any Indian reservation must satisfy the Commissioner of Indian Affairs that he is a proper person to engage in such trade and must do so under such rules and regulations prescribed for the protection of the Indians."

1904: The Mi'kmaq Millbrook First Nation Reserve of Truro No. 27A was established in Nova Scotia.

1906: The federal government dissolved the Cherokee tribal government.

1907: The Mi'kmaq Horton First Nation Reserve of Horton was established in Nova Scotia. The Millbrook First Nation Reserve of Truro No. 27B was also set up.

1909: In Nova Scotia, Truro No. 27C Reserve was established for the Mi'kmaq Millbrook First Nation.

1921: An act of Congress (41 Stat. 1355) set aside land on the Fort Belknap Indian Reservation in Montana to establish the townsite of Lodge Pole. It also established a census of the tribes there.

1927: A congressional act (44 Stat. 1347) was passed. It gave the commissioner of Indian affairs the authority to set aside lands to be used as reservations. It also authorized "oil and gas mining leases upon unallotted lands within Executive Order Indian reservations; and to prevent changes in boundaries of E.O. reservations except by the Congress."

1933: By Proclamation No. 2036, the president announced the establishment of the Canyon de Chelly National Monument in the Navajo Indian Reservation in northeastern Arizona.

1936: The secretary of the interior authorized an election for a constitution and bylaws for the Shoshone-Paiute Tribes of the Duck Valley Reservation in Nevada. The election would be held on March 21, 1936.

1938: The Mi'kmaq Bear River First Nation Reserve of Bear River No. 6A was established in Nova Scotia.

1988: The Alaska Native Claims Act was amended.

MARCH 4

1541: Chickasaw Indians attacked de Soto's forces. They set fire to the huts de Soto's men were using. Approximately twelve Spaniards were killed. They lost a considerable number of their horses and livestock. The Chickasaw suffered only minimal losses.

1629: The Charter of Massachusetts Bay was issued.

1643: The Canarsee Indians negotiated a peace with the Dutch in Fort Amsterdam. The Canarsee were the Indians who sold Manhattan to Peter Minuit for $24 in trinkets, even though they did not own it.

1805: Some Assinibois tried to steal Minnetaree horses.

1829: President Jackson gave his "just policy for Indians" speech.

1844: In Oregon City, Oregon, a large fight broke out along the Willamette River. One Molalla Indian and two settlers were killed in the fighting. The fight became known as the Cockstock Affair.

1847: In Oregon Country, the *Spectator* newspaper had mentioned several reports of Indians stealing horses. It told of a man named Newton who was killed by Indians in the Umpqua area.

1855: The Second Cavalry was established. Its primary function was to protect Texas settlers from hostile Indians.

1870: Louis Riel's Metis had taken over the government in the Red River Colony. They executed Thomas Scott for "taking up arms" against Riel's government. This execution helped to speed up an expedition against Riel's Metis.

1876: Major James Brisbin and his troops from Fort Ellis, Montana, arrived at Fort Pease, just north of present-day Custer in central Montana, where forty-six people had been besieged by Indians. After Brisbin's Rescue had been completed, six whites had been killed, with eight wounded; thirteen had escaped. Brisbin escorted the remaining nineteen to safety.

1917: The McLaughlin Roll of the Santee Sioux Tribe of the Sioux Nation of the state of Nebraska was made under the auspices of an act of Congress (39 Stat. 1195).

1930: The Coolidge Dam was dedicated. It swamped Indian lands.

1963: Several amendments were made to the constitution of the Pawnee Indian Tribe of Oklahoma.

1974: Secretary of the Interior Rogers Morton ratified the results of an election that approved two amendments to the constitution and bylaws of the Tule River Indian Tribe. The election was held on January 26, 1974.

MARCH 5

1712: As a part of the Tuscarora War, a force of 600 militia entered the Tuscarora village of Catechna (near Grifton). They discovered it had been abandoned.

1766: The Spanish governor had arrived in Louisiana.

1781: What was believed to be a Shawnee war party was roaming the woods in northwestern Virginia. They came across the Thomas family farm on Booth's Creek. The war party killed eight members of the family and took one small boy prisoner.

1792: A new general was appointed in the Northwest Territory.

1831: The Supreme Court decided the case of *Cherokee Nation v. Georgia.* The court decided that the Cherokees were not a "foreign state," and therefore the court had no jurisdiction in the dispute. However, the court did decide that the Cherokees were a distinct political society capable of governing itself and managing its own affairs. See March 3, 1832.

1839: James Brown and 717 fellow Cherokees arrived in their new lands in the Indian Territory (present-day Oklahoma). Thirty-four deaths occurred on the trip.

1856: This day marked the end of the peace conference with the Sioux headed by General William Harney.

1861: The Confederacy appointed Albert Pike of Arkansas to negotiate treaties with the Indians in the region. He established the "United Nations of the Indian Territory" as an Indian confederacy to oppose the federal government under President Abraham Lincoln.

1866: The U.S. Senate ratified the treaty signed by the United States and the Oglala Band, Upper Yanktonai Band, of the Sioux Indians on October 28, 1865 (14 Stat. 747).

1876: Fourth Infantry soldiers, as a part of General George Crook's Bighorn expedition, fought some Indians near the Dry Fork of the Powder River in Wyoming. According to army documents, one soldier was wounded.

1880: Lieutenant Samuel Miller, nine soldiers of the Ninth Mounted Infantry, and eight Indian scouts discovered a party of hostiles thirty miles west of the Rosebud River in Montana. During the subsequent fighting, two scouts and three Indians were killed. The Indians' camp was destroyed, and significant stores of supplies and ammunition were seized. The hostiles escaped across the Yellowstone River.

1891: The city of Phoenix, Arizona, offered a $200 bounty for dead Indians.

1907: This day was the final day to be listed in the tribal membership rolls for the Cherokee, Choctaw, Chickasaw, Creek, and Seminole Tribes that were being compiled by the Dawes Commission.

1971: The Winnemucca Shoshone of Nevada adopted a constitution and bylaws on December 12, 1970. Harrison Loesch, assistant secretary of the interior, approved the election.

1976: The area director, Portland area office, Bureau of Indian Affairs, authorized an election to amend the constitution and bylaws of the Kalispel Indian Community of the Kalispel Reservation. The election would be held on May 22, 1976.

MARCH 6

1760: The British had established a fort and settlement ninety-six miles along the trail from Keowee (Fort Prince George), South Carolina, to the Cherokee villages. The settlement was called Ninety-Six, South Carolina. The month before, British forces had killed Cherokee hostages at Fort Prince George. Seeking revenge, a force of 200 Cherokee warriors, led by Chief Oconostota, attacked the fort, which was defended by a few dozen soldiers. A few people were killed on both sides. The Cherokees eventually gave up the assault.

1777: Seventy Shawnee warriors, led by Chief Blackfish, attacked some settlers near Harrodsburg, Kentucky. One of the men, James Ray, managed to escape and warn the settlement of the war party. The Shawnee attacked Harrodsburg the next day.

1813: Heads of the Cherokee Nation—Tocha Lee and Chu Lioa—wrote a letter for publication. It was addressed to the citizens of the United States. The letter expressed the Cherokees' concern for the actions of whites against them. "Backwoodsmen" continued to attack the Cherokees, with little fear of reprisal. The Cherokees wished the United States well in its ongoing battle with

Britain. They also asked for the assistance of the United States to stop the crimes against them.

1836: On February 27, General Edmund Gaines's troops were forced into a battle on the Withlacoochee River, in central Florida, with the Seminole. They had continued fighting until this date, when the Seminole requested a conference. While the talks were being held, General Duncan Clinch and his troops arrived. These troops were a decisive force, the battle was broken off, and the Seminole retreated.

1837: General Thomas Jesup and Seminole Chiefs Jumper and Holahtochee signed a treaty to end the fighting and agreed to removal to Indian Territory (present-day Oklahoma). Jesup agreed to allow the free blacks living with the Seminole to go with them to their new lands. The Seminole agreed to come to Tampa Bay by April 10, 1836, for transport. The Seminole agreed to having Chief Mikanopy, who was not at the conference, held as a hostage until the transport was arranged. Mikanopy turned himself in several days later.

1848: Beginning on this day, the Nez Perce arrived for a conference at Waiilatpu.

1861: According to the constitution of the Iowa Tribe of Kansas and Nebraska, "The jurisdiction of the Iowa Tribe shall extend to the territory within the confines of the Iowa Reservation as defined in the Treaty of March 6, 1861."

1864: After surrendering to the army at Forts Canby and Wingate, on the New Mexico–Arizona border, the first group of Navajos set out to the Bosque Redondo Reservation. More than 1,400 made this first trip, with several dying along the trail.

1865: The Winnebago signed a treaty (14 Stat. 671) in Washington, D.C., that ceded some of their land.

1866: According to army records, soldiers from the First Arizona Infantry fought with some Indians through March 9. The fighting took place near Fort McDowell, Arizona. The soldiers reported killing twenty Indians and wounding seven.

1868: According to army records, members of the Sixth Cavalry fought with a band of Indians near Paint Creek, Texas. Two soldiers were wounded and seven Indians were killed.

1873: After hearing from Hooker Jim of the "trap" at the Fairchild Ranch, Modoc Captain Jack had his sister Mary write a letter to the commissioners. The letter stated Captain Jack's wish for both sides to forget the killings on both sides and for the slate to be wiped clean. Captain Jack wanted no more killing, but he would not give up his people to be hanged. He stated he had not asked for the whites who had killed his people.

1961: Lands had been set aside for townsites in the Blackfeet Indian Reservation in Montana. By Public Land Order No. 2290, certain undisposed of lands within the townsite of "Blackfoot" were returned to tribal ownership.

1968: President Lyndon Johnson started a new Indian program.

1986: Deputy Assistant Secretary of Indian Affairs Ronald Esquerra approved a new constitution for the Tohono O'odham Nation.

March 7

1524: Giovanni da Verrazano, sailing for France, anchored near Wilmington, North Carolina, in the *Dauphine*. He kidnapped a child they encountered to bring back to Europe. (Also recorded as happening on March 1.)

1539: Mexican Viceroy Don Antonio de Mendoza had decided to send an expedition to search for wealthy cities north of Mexico. Friar Marcos de Niza left from Culiacan on this day. He would "discover" Cibola, although he never set foot in the pueblo. His report would lead to future expeditions looking for the Seven Cities of Gold.

1712: A force led by John Barnwell signed a treaty with the Tuscarora at their fort in Catechna villages (near Grifton). He later broke the treaty by attacking the fort on April 7.

1776: Congress authorized Colonel Nathaniel Gist to organize and equip 200 Indians in Virginia and the Carolinas to fight in the Revolutionary War.

1777: One day earlier, a Shawnee war party of seventy men, led by Chief Blackfish, attacked a few men en route to Harrodsburg, Kentucky. One of the men, James Ray, escaped and ran to warn the settlement. The Shawnees reached Harrodsburg and attacked. Given the forewarning, the settlers held off the Shawnees, who prepared for a siege. The Shawnee eventually gave up the siege.

1782: Moravian missionaries had converted many Delaware, Mahican, and Munsee Indians to Christianity. They had established villages in Pennsylvania in 1746 but moved them to the Muskingum River in Ohio in 1773 after their old villages were attacked by other Indian tribes. Unfortunately, at the outbreak of the Revolutionary War, the "Moravian" Indians found themselves directly between American and British forces and their allies. Both sides believed the Moravians were helping the other. On this day, American Colonel David Williamson and soldiers from Pennsylvania surrounded the peaceful village of Gnadenhutten (the second village of the same name; the first had been in Pennsylvania) and herded the occupants into two houses. While some of the militia refused to participate, the majority of the soldiers decided to kill all of the Moravians. After allowing the victims a final prayer, the soldiers killed ninety-six Indian men, women, and children in cold blood. (Also recorded as happening on March 8.)

1834: The Chickasaw Council appointed a commission to go to Washington, D.C., to discuss a removal treaty. They eventually signed a treaty (7 Stat. 450) on May 24, 1834.

1862: The Civil War's Battle of Pea Ridge, Arkansas, started on this day and continued through the next. Many Indians were fighting on both sides. The Cherokees had a large contingent (including the author's great-great-grandfather).

1865: During an investigation into the Sand Creek Massacre (November 29, 1864), Indian Agent Samuel G. Colley was questioned. He estimated there were 200–300 Cheyenne and 200 Arapaho lodges in the reservation area near Fort Lyon. A lodge averaged five people, according to Colley.

1877: Settlers fought a group of Indians near Fort Davis in western Texas. According to army documents, two settlers were killed.

1890: During a skirmish with Apache in Arizona, Sergeant James T. Daniels, Company L, Fourth Cavalry, would earn the Medal of Honor for "untiring energy and gallantry under fire." Sergeant William McBryar, Company K, Tenth Cavalry, would also win the medal for "coolness, bravery, and marksmanship." Indian scout Rowdy would earn the nation's highest award for bravery.

1960: New York State wished to build a dam that would flood lands belonging to the Tuscarora (one of the six Iroquois Nations). The Indians took the issue to court as a violation of the Treaty of 1794. After the Tuscarora won several lower-court decisions, the Supreme Court issued a 6–3 decision against them. In the dissenting opinion, Justice Hugo Black says, "I regret that this court is the agency that breaks faith with this dependent people. Great nations, like great men, should keep their word."

1960: The commissioner of Indian affairs approved the Articles of Association of the Pala Band of Mission Indians of California.

1972: Raymond Little Thunder had been murdered. Local Indians felt local authorities were not doing enough to bring the murderer to justice. Some 1,000 Indians staged a march on Gordon, Nebraska, to demonstrate their dissatisfaction.

1975: The acting deputy commissioner of Indian affairs authorized an election for amendments to the constitution and bylaws for the Covelo Indian Community of the Round Valley Reservation in California. The election would be held on May 3, 1975.

1988: The Lac du Flambeau Band of Lake Superior Chippewa Indians modified their local codes regarding timber trespassing.

MARCH 8

1712: According to some sources, forces under John Barnwell established Fort Barnwell on the Neuse River between New Berne and Kinston as a part of the Tuscarora War in North Carolina.

1782: Moravian missionaries had converted many Delaware, Mahican, and Munsee Indians to Christianity. They had established villages in Pennsylvania in 1746 but moved them to the Muskingum River in Ohio in 1773 after their old villages were attacked by other Indian tribes. Unfortunately, at the outbreak of the Revolutionary War, the "Moravian" Indians found themselves directly between American and British forces and their allies. Both sides believed the Moravians were helping the other. On this day, American Colonel David Williamson and soldiers from Pennsylvania, surround the peaceful village of Gnadenhutten (the second village of the same name; the first had been in Pennsylvania) and herded the occupants into two houses. While some of the militia refused to participate, the majority of the soldiers decided to kill all of the Moravians. After allowing the victims a final prayer, the soldiers killed ninety-six Indian men, women, and children in cold blood. (Also recorded as happening on March 7.)

1813: At the Cherokee Agency, Highwassee Garrison, an agreement was signed. In part, it said, "We, the undersigned Chiefs and Councillors of the Cherokees in full council assembled, do hereby give, grant, and make over unto Nicholas Byer's and David Russell, who are agents in behalf of the states of Tennessee and Georgia, full power and authority to establish a Turnpike Company are hereby fully authorized by us, to lay out and open a road from the most suitable point on the Tennessee River, to be directed the nearest and best way to the highest point of navigation on the Tugelo River."

1837: By this day, almost 4,000 Creek were assembled near Montgomery, Alabama, preparing to be removed to Indian Territory (present-day Oklahoma). Most were family members of the Creek fighting for the government against the Seminole in Florida. The government promised to protect them in Alabama until the Creek soldiers returned. The government did not live up to this promise.

1857: Inkpaduta and about a dozen Wahpakoota Sioux warriors attacked a series of settlements in northwestern Iowa along Spirit Lake. As many as forty settlers were killed.

1859: The Quinault and Quileute Treaties, signed on July 1, 1855, and January 25, 1856, were ratified by the U.S. Senate.

1865: The Winnebago signed a treaty (14 Stat. 671) regarding the Omaha Reservation.

1874: Indians fought with soldiers from the Fifth Cavalry and some Indian scouts in the Pinal Mountains of Arizona. According to army documents, twelve Indians were killed and twenty-five were captured.

1880: Company K, Fifth Mounted Infantry, from Fort Keogh in east-central Montana, had been pursuing a band of Indians with stolen horses for sixty miles near Porcupine Creek, Montana. They managed to cut off the Indians and captured thirteen horses and sixteen mules north of the Yellowstone River. On Rosebud Creek, the Fifth and some Indian scouts also encountered some hostile Indians. Two soldiers and three Indians were killed. One soldier was wounded.

1941: The constitution of the Indians of the Tulalip Tribes in Washington was modified.

1965: The acting secretary of the interior authorized an election for an amendment to the constitution and bylaws of the Kaibab Band of Paiute Indians of Arizona. The election would be held on May 1, 1965.

MARCH 9

1728: The Yamassee had left their old lands in South Carolina and moved to Florida. Many were living near the Spanish Mission of Nombre de Dios near St. Augustine. Their anger at the Carolinians had not abated, and they continued raiding British settlements. A force of 250 volunteers from Carolina under Colonel John Parker attacked the mission. Thirty warriors were killed, and many Yamassee were taken as slaves.

1768: According to some sources, Shawnee Pucksinwah's third child, Tecumseh (Panther Passing Across), was born. His mother was Methotasa (Turtle Laying Her Eggs in the Sand).

1804: Northern Louisiana became part of the United States. This included many Indian lands.

1824: In Monroe County, Alabama, Red Stick Creek Chief William Weatherford (Lume Chatki) died. Having just returned from a bear hunt, he collapsed.

1837: The president named A.M.M. Upshaw as the superintendent of the Chickasaw removal from Alabama to Indian Territory (present-day Oklahoma).

1869: Near Fort Harker in central Kansas, U.S. Army troops overtook a band of Indians with stolen livestock. The soldiers recovered all of the livestock and captured five Indians.

1870: According to official army records, Indians skirmished with a group of soldiers from the Eighth Cavalry on the Reno Road near Camp McDowell, Arizona. One soldier and one civilian were wounded. Four Indians were killed.

1880: Captain Frank Baldwin, with elements of the Fifth Infantry, and the Second Cavalry had been pursuing Indians who escaped from the fight near the Rosebud River on March 5, 1880. He found them on Little Porcupine Creek. After a thirty-mile chase, the army captured all of the Indians' loose horses.

1935: Officers of tribes were now considered U.S. officers.

1951: Raymond Harvey, a Chickasaw, earned the Medal of Honor for his actions during the Korean War.

1974: Tribal members of the Sherwood Valley Rancheria approved a constitution and bylaws by a vote of 14–0.

MARCH 10

1675: According to some sources, a land-cession agreement was reached between representatives of the Kiawah Indians and the South Carolina colonies.

1760: The Mi'kmaq of Richibuto and Mouscadaboet signed a treaty with the British of Nova Scotia.

1808: President Jefferson wrote to the U.S. Senate, recommending that it ratify a treaty for land with the Cherokees. The 4,000 acres of land was on the Tennessee River and had iron-ore deposits. The Cherokees received $1.30 an acre for the land.

1848: The Guadalupe-Hidalgo Treaty was ratified. Many Indians lived in the covered area.

1865: The Ponca signed a treaty regarding 30,000 acres of land (14 Stat. 675).

1868: According to army records, members of the Fourth Cavalry fought with a band of Indians near the Colorado River in Texas. One Indian was reported to have died in the fighting.

1930: Under authority of an act passed by Congress (24 Stat. 388–389) on February 8, 1887, an executive order was issued that extended the trust period on land allotments made to members of the Prairie Band of Potawatomi Indians in Kansas.

1957: The Dalles Dam flooded sacred fishing areas on the Columbia River.

1960: An amendment to the Indian Act and the Canadian Elections Act was introduced. It allows Canadian "First People" who live on reserves to vote in national elections without losing their income-tax exemption.

1971: The commissioner of Indian affairs authorized an election for a constitution and bylaws for the

Shoalwater Bay Indian Organization in Washington State. The election would be held on May 22.

1992: The Aitkin County, Minnesota, board of commissioners voted to support the separation of the Sandy Lake Band of Ojibwe from the Mille Lacs Band of Chippewa. The federal government believed the Mille Lacs Band had authority over tribal lands that the Sandy Lake Band claimed.

MARCH 11

1583: A Spanish expedition traveling through modern New Mexico camped at the base of what would eventually be known as Inscription Rock.

1793: Thirty Creek warriors from Coweta, led by adopted Creek John Galphin, attacked a trading post in Georgia on Saint Mary's River. They killed a half-dozen settlers and stole a large amount of goods and slaves. This was called the Trader's Hill Massacre by some.

1824: Secretary of War John C. Calhoun created the Bureau of Indian Affairs within the War Department. Thomas McKenney was appointed its first head.

1836: Secretary of War Lewis Clark ordered J.B. Hogan to "vigorously" investigate the frauds being perpetrated against the Creek. The investigation was under way when Creek retaliated for the attack on them by Georgia militia in January.

1848: As a part of the Cayuse War, a fight took place. Captain McKay and a force of 268 were ambushed by approximately 400 Palouse. The Palouse were allied with the Cayuse.

1856: The Nez Perce joined Colonel Cornelius for a fight against the Yakima.

1859: According to his journals, Reverend Pierre De Smet arrived at the Mission St. Ignatius. He was there to minister to the Pend d'Oreille.

1863: The United States signed a treaty (12 Stat. 1249) with three different bands of the Chippewa Nation in Washington, D.C.

1863: As a part of the Owens Valley War in California, the small cavalry detachment fought more than 100 Paiute near the area known as Black Rocks. The army reported one soldier killed and four wounded.

1867: According to army records, members of the First Cavalry fought with a band of Indians near Arab Canyon in the Coso Mountains of California. Twelve Indians were reported killed.

1868: In New Mexico, near Tularosa, Apache raided several local settlements, killing eleven men and two women. Two children were kidnapped, and 2,200 sheep and other livestock were stolen. Lieutenant P.D. Vroom, Troop H, Third Cavalry, pursued the Apache, but they escaped into the Guadalupe Mountains.

1890: Fourth and Tenth Cavalry soldiers and Indian scouts fought a group of Indians near the mouth of Cherry Creek on the Salt River in Arizona. According to army documents, two Indians were killed and three were captured.

1891: The army tried to recruit Indians as troops.

1907: According to the Indians' constitution, the land known as the Kelsey Tract was added by a grant deed containing 235 acres for the Pechanga Indian Reservation–Temecula Band of Luiseno Mission Indians.

1907: Chaco Canyon (New Mexico) was officially designated as the Chaco Canyon National Monument. It was the home of many Anasazi ruins.

1920: Land for the Shingle Springs Rancheria in El Dorado County, California, was purchased by the U.S. government.

1936: The secretary of the interior approved the constitutions and bylaws of the Manchester Band of Pomo Indians of the Manchester Rancheria and the Kashia Band of Pomo Indians of the Stewarts Point Rancheria. They both took effect.

1936: The secretary of the interior authorized an election for the approval of a constitution and bylaws for the Muckleshoot Indian Tribe of the Muckleshoot Reservation to be held on April 4, 1936.

1949: The assistant secretary of the interior ratified an election that approved an amendment to the constitution and bylaws for the Quileute Tribe of Washington.

1978: Charles Delaney, the acting area director, Bureau of Indian Affairs, had authorized an election to approve an amendment to the constitution and bylaws for the Fort Sill Apache Tribe of Oklahoma. It was approved by a vote of 31–6.

MARCH 12

1676: Wampanoag Sachem Totoson led an attack on Clark's Garrison on the Eel River near Plymouth.

1771: Spaniards under Father Junipero Serra began construction of the Presidio (fort) in what became San Diego, California. It was built on the bluffs above the Kumeyaay village of Cosoy.

1798: According to Hudson's Bay Company records, two Kootenai Indians arrived at Edmonton House in Canada. The Indians made their way through the Rockies during winter to seek trade.

1803: An American fur-trading ship, the *Boston*, anchored in Nootka Sound on Vancouver Island. The crew traded with the Nootka Indians. They got along peacefully during the ten-day visit.

1816: In a meeting with Secretary of War William Crawford, Cherokee chiefs expressed their extreme frustrations. They had suffered under land grabs, trespassers, and many other grievances and yet they still aided the United States in the Creek War. Now the United States wished to impose a new treaty line through Cherokee lands without their approval.

1831: Claiming that some interlopers had not sworn an allegiance to Georgia, and did not have the mandated state permit to be allowed to be in Cherokee areas, Georgia militia arrested several

missionaries and teachers in the cities of New Echota, Hightower, and Carmel. The missionaries had been supporting the Cherokees in their legal fights with Georgia. One of the ministers, Samuel A. Worcester, appealed his conviction to the Supreme Court. The court ruled that all of the actions of Georgia against the Cherokees were illegal. (See June 24, 1832.)

1848: Throughout his life, Cherokee Chief Tahchee, or Captain William Dutch, was known as a fearless warrior. Tahchee was one of the original groups of Cherokees to move west of the Mississippi River. He became a major political force in the "old settler party." He fought many fights with the Osage Indians who lived near the Cherokees. Eventually, he became a scout for the U.S. Army, where he reached the rank of captain. Tahchee died in Indian Territory (present-day Oklahoma).

1858: The Ponca signed a treaty (12 Stat. 997) that granted them a permanent home on the Niobrara River and protection from their enemies, both whites and Indians. For these privileges, the Ponca gave up a part of their ancestral lands. Unfortunately, several years later, a mistake by a government bureaucrat forced them to share land with the Sioux. Repeated protestations over this error went unheard. The Ponca lived in constant fear of attacks from the Sioux.

1867: According to army records, members of the Fourth Cavalry fought with a band of Indians on the Pecos River in Texas. One soldier and one civilian were reported killed. Two soldiers were wounded, and twenty-five Indians were killed.

1930: In Montana, as a part of the Dawes Severalty Act of February 8, 1887, a trust period on allotments made to Crow Indians on their reservation in Montana was established and scheduled to expire in 1930. Executive Order No. 5301 extended that trust period. Executive Order No. 5302 extended the trust period on allotments on the Rosebud Indian Reservation in South Dakota. Executive Order No. 5303 extended the trust period for allotments on the Devil's Lake Reservation in North Dakota as well.

1969: Regulations regarding Indians undertaking law-and-order functions in New Mexico were changed.

1970: The secretary of the interior authorized an election on amendments to the constitution of the Zuni Tribe.

1975: The acting deputy commissioner of Indian affairs authorized an election for amendments to the constitution and bylaws for the Covelo Indian Community of the Round Valley Reservation in California. The election would be held on May 3, 1975.

MARCH 13

1857: The U.S. Senate rejected six different treaties made with Indians of the American Southwest.

1862: A treaty (12 Stat. 1221) was concluded between the United States and the Kansa Indians at the Kansa Agency.

1864: The first group of Navajos finished the Long Walk to Fort Sumner on the Bosque Redondo Reservation in east-central New Mexico. During their march, thirteen of the 1,430 who started the trip were kidnapped by Mexicans or died.

1869: According to army records, members of the Thirteenth Infantry fought with a band of Indians near the Shields River in Montana. Two civilians and four Indians were killed.

1880: Settlers fought a group of Indians near Russell's Ranch in Texas. According to army documents, one citizen was killed.

1936: The secretary of the interior authorized an election to approve a constitution and bylaws for the Shoshone-Bannock Tribes of the Fort Hall Reservation. The election would be on March 31, 1936.

1970: A legal inquiry into the boundaries of the Fort Berthold Indian Reservation in North Dakota was made.

1975: Commissioner of Indian Affairs Morris Thompson authorized an election for a constitution and bylaws for the Manzanita Band of Mission Indians. The election would be held on July 12, 1975.

MARCH 14

1493: Columbus wrote a letter describing the generous nature of the Indians he had encountered. He described them as "men of great deference and kindness."

1629: The Massachusetts Bay Company was chartered.

1697: The last of the independent Maya tribes, called the Itza, were finally conquered by the Spanish. The Spanish attacked and defeated the Itza at their capital city of Tayasal (Guatemala).

1699: French explorer Pierre le Moyne, Sieur d'Iberville, was exploring Louisiana, hoping to establish a series of French forts to keep the British out of the area. He reached, by boat, a village of Bayogoula and Mugulasha Indians on the Mississippi River.

1775: The Transylvania Company bought Cherokee land. (See March 17.)

1833: The secretary of war had the Indian Department issue orders, again, to U.S. Marshals to remove whites from Creek lands in the Southeast.

1834: The first boats left the Cherokee Agency in eastern Tennessee, on the Hiwassee River (present-day Calhoun), to take the Eastern Cherokees to the Indian Territory (present-day Oklahoma). Measles and cholera break out among the emigrants almost immediately. Many Cherokees died during the trek westward.

1835: The Reverend John Schermerhorn negotiated and signed an agreement with some Cherokees led by Major John Ridge. The treaty paid the Cherokees $4.5 million for all of their land east of the Mississippi River. However, the treaty contained a provision that it must be ratified by the Cherokees in a full tribal council (there were divi-

Fort McKavett, Texas (author photo)

sions among the Cherokees, from those willing to leave to those who would rather die than move west). Although Schermerhorn made considerable efforts, the treaty was not approved by the Cherokee Council, with a majority voting against it, including John Ridge. John Ross felt their land was worth at least $20 million.

1839: George Hicks and 1,039 of his fellow Cherokees arrived in the Indian Territory (present-day Oklahoma). This group was originally 1,118 in number.

1852: Fort McKavett was established in Texas to protect the local settlers from local Indians, mostly Comanche.

1868: According to army records, members of the First and Eighth Cavalries and the Twenty-Third Infantry fought with a band of Indians near Dunder and Blitzen Creek in Oregon. One soldier and two civilians were wounded. Twelve Indians were killed, and two were captured. Lieutenant Colonel George Crook was commanding the expedition.

1884: Sitting Bull visited St. Paul.

1959: The constitution of the Indians of the Tulalip Tribes in Washington was modified.

1985: The Lac du Flambeau Band of Lake Superior Chippewa Indians modified their local codes regarding timber trespassing.

MARCH 15

1697: The northwestern Massachusetts town of Haverhill was attacked by Abenaki Indians. Hannah Dustin, her newborn child, and their nurse were among the captives. While leaving the area, an Indian killed the child for fear its crying would give them away. In one of the most famous escapes of the era, Dustin bided her time for a month and a half. Finally seeing an opportunity, Dustin and the nurse killed all of their sleeping captors, except an old woman and a child, with an ax. Dustin brought back her captors' scalps; for that she was paid twenty-five pounds by the Massachusetts government.

1740: After getting the Chickasaw to agree to tear down their stockades, to release prisoners, and to come to Fort Assumption (modern Memphis), Captain Pierre Celeron and his force of 180 French soldiers and 400 Choctaw and Iroquois left the villages to return to Fort Assumption.

1749: England gave land grants in the Ohio Valley.

1767: Andrew Jackson was born.

1858: After fighting the Americans for almost twenty-five years, one of the last of the Seminole leaders, Billy Bowlegs, surrendered with 163 of his followers. They were shipped west.

1869: Colonel George Custer and his troops discovered two Cheyenne villages, including more than 250 lodges, on Sweetwater Creek near the Texas-Oklahoma border. The Cheyenne had been ordered to report to their reservation. Custer captured four chiefs. He threatened to hang the chiefs unless the Cheyenne surrendered. Both of the villages decided to give up.

1870: According to official army records, Indians skirmished with a group of soldiers from the Twenty-First Infantry near Sol's Wash, Arizona. Two Indians were killed. The fighting lasted until the next day.

1874: Indians fought with soldiers from the Fifth Cavalry in the Pinal Mountains in Arizona. According to army documents, two soldiers were wounded.

1880: Settlers fought a group of Indians near Blazer's Mill, New Mexico. According to army documents, one citizen was killed.

1910: The U.S. Supreme Court issued a final decree regarding the official tribal rolls and a distribution of a $1 million fund for the Eastern Cherokees.

1942: An election for a constitution and bylaws for the Moapa Band of Paiute Indians was held. It was approved by a vote of 55–2.

1966: In an election, there was an amendment to the constitution and bylaws of the Confederated Tribes of the Warm Springs Reservation of Oregon.

1978: Congress passed an act that allowed the Zuni Nation to seek redress for lands taken from them without compensation, through the U.S. Court of Claims. This act also added the Zuni Salt Lake to the lands held in trust for the tribe.

MARCH 16

1621: Samoset met the Pilgrims.

1649: Jesuit Father Jean de Brebeuf was killed by Iroquois Indians at the Saint Ignace Mission in Canada.

1700: According to records kept by French missionaries, lightning struck the temple in the Taensa village on Lake Saint Joseph (near modern Newellton, Louisiana). The temple caught fire. The tribal shaman told the women of the tribe to throw their small children into the fire to appease the angry god who started the fire. French priest Francois Joliet de Montigny attempted to stop the women.

1758: More than 2,000 Comanche and other Indians attacked the Santa Cruz de San Sabá Mission (near modern Menard, Texas). They killed eight of the inhabitants and destroyed most of the buildings. Father Miguel Molina was the sole survivor.

1779: General Washington ordered General Edward Hand to lead an expedition into Indian country in Pennsylvania. They were to subdue the Iroquois who were attacking the settlers.

1830: After some "politicking," Greenwood le Flore was elected as chief of the Choctaw Nation during a "rump" council. Previously, there were three regional chiefs. Le Flore was in favor of selling the Choctaw lands and moving to Indian Territory (present-day Oklahoma). (Also recorded as happening on April 9.)

1855: David Meriwether was informed by the president that he was authorized to establish conventions that granted land rights to the Apache, Navajo, and Ute.

1869: According to army records, members of the Twenty-Second Infantry fought with a band of Indians near Fort Randall, Dakota Territory. One soldier was killed.

1869: Ranald Mackenzie arrived at Fort McKavett (near modern Menard, Texas) to assume command of the unit there.

1870: According to official army records, Indians skirmished with a group of soldiers from the Twenty-First Infantry near Sol's Wash, Arizona. Two Indians were killed. The fighting started the day before.

1875: The Standing Rock Sioux Reservation in Dakota Territory was modified.

1877: Regulations regarding the Zuni Pueblo Reserve in New Mexico were changed.

1938: Assistant Secretary of the Interior Oscar Chapman authorized an election for a constitution

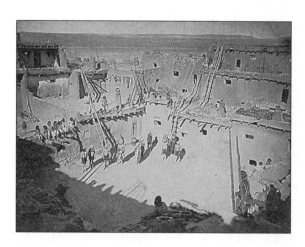

Zuni Pueblo, New Mexico (NA)

and bylaws of the Tonkawa Tribe of Indians of Oklahoma. The election would be on April 21, 1938.

1962: An act of Congress increased the size of the Zuni Reservation in Arizona and New Mexico.

1973: An election to amend the revised constitution and bylaws for the Sisseton Wahpeton Sioux Tribe of South Dakota was held. The results were 151–18 in favor.

MARCH 17

1649: Jesuit Father Gabriel Lalemant was killed by Iroquois Indians at the Mission Saint Louis in Canada.

1756: According to some reports, an agreement covering alliances and education of Indians was reached by representatives of the British in Virginia and the Cherokees.

1775: The Sycamore Shoals Treaty was signed (near modern Elizabethton, Tennessee). The Transylvania Company, headed by North Carolina Judge Richard Henderson, purchased most of western and central Kentucky and north-central Tennessee from the Cherokees. They traded $10,000 in goods and $2,000 cash for this very large parcel. The Cherokees were represented by Chiefs Attakullaculla and Oconostota. The treaty was revoked by the governments of Virginia and North Carolina as far as a private company owning the land. However, the treaty was used by the governments as a claim on Cherokee lands.

1830: Members of the Choctaw "rump" council signed a treaty selling Choctaw lands and agreeing to the move west. The paper eventually went to Washington, along with protests from the "non-rump" Indians. The treaty did not receive Senate approval.

1830: A large meeting was held in Natchez, Mississippi. Attendees protested the efforts of the Mississippi government to force the Choctaws to give up their lands within the state.

1842: The Wyandot signed a treaty (11 Stat. 581) in Kansas City. They gave up their lands in Ohio for lands west of the Mississippi River and $17,500 per year.

1853: Joel Palmer became superintendent of Indian affairs in Oregon. He guided the creation of the Oregon Indian reservations.

1854: Kickapoo Indians had determined that two men of their tribe, Thunder (Piawataka) and Polecat (Chekaquah), killed Colonel Jesse Stem on February 12, 1854. Thunder was captured by the Kickapoo. While they were taking him to a nearby fort, a fight broke out, and Thunder was killed (see March 29).

1862: Camp Cureton was built by the Confederate Army to defend the area from Indian attacks. It was located where the Gainesville–Fort Belknap Road crossed the West Fork of the Trinity River southeast of Archer City, Texas.

1869: Apache had killed some whites near Fort Bayard in southwestern New Mexico. Troops from the fort pursued the Apache to their village. The soldiers burned the village and its contents. No one was killed, but five Indians were wounded.

1869: According to army records, members of the Thirty-Second Infantry fought with a band of Indians near Camp Goodwin, Arizona. Two Indians were killed. Occasional skirmishes would last until March 30.

1872: Indians skirmished with a group of settlers near Camp Verde, Arizona, according to official army records. One settler was killed.

1876: General George Crook's advance forces, led by Colonel Joseph Reynolds, encountered a hunting-party camp of Cheyenne and Sioux near the confluence of the Powder River and the Little Powder River. Three troops of cavalry swooped down on the sleeping camp of 105 lodges. Among the Indians were White Bull, Old Bear, Two Moons, Maple Tree, Little Wolf, Wooden Leg, and Low Dog. The warriors tried to hold off the troops while the women, children, and old men made it to safety across the Powder River. The soldiers rounded up almost 1,500 of the Indians' horses, but later that night the Indians sneaked up on the army's camp and stole them back. Crook reported the attack as being against Crazy Horse. However, Crazy Horse's camp was several miles away. Four soldiers and six Indians were killed during the fighting. Hospital steward William C. Bryan participated in the charge on the village, and he brought back two of the wounded soldiers. Blacksmith Albert Glavinski, Company M, Third Cavalry, was cited for his bravery as a part of the rear guard. Private Jeremiah Murphy, Company M, was cited for trying to save a wounded comrade. For their actions, all would be awarded the Medal of Honor. According to army records, it was so cold that thermometers did not register. The troops returned to Fort Fetterman in east-central Wyoming and other stations to wait out the winter.

1877: A flood destroyed much of Sitting Bull's camp on the Missouri River.

1960: Assistant Secretary of the Interior Roger Ernst ratified an election for amendments to the constitution for the Gila River Pima–Maricopa Indian Community.

1967: The acting deputy commissioner of Indian affairs authorized an election to approve amendments to the constitution and bylaws for the Kashia Band of Pomo Indians of the Stewarts Point Rancheria.

1980: Commissioner of Indian Affairs William Hallett ratified an election on a new constitution for the Skokomish Indian Tribe.

MARCH 18

1819: Choctaw James Pitchlynn wrote a letter to Andrew Jackson. He stated that many Choctaw families were willing to move west of the Mississippi River if a treaty could be written.

1837: As a part of the treaty signed on March 6, Seminole Chief Mikanopy surrendered to General Jesup. He was prepared to move to the Indian Territory (present-day Oklahoma).

1839: John Drew and 219 of his original 231 fellow Cherokees arrived in the Indian Territory (present-day Oklahoma) as part of their forced emigration.

1868: According to army records, members of the Eighteenth Infantry fought with a band of Indians near Fort Fetterman, Dakota Territory. One soldier was killed.

1871: Indians made several sorties on a government wagon trail near Fort Dodge in southwestern Kansas. Three citizens were killed; five Indians were wounded.

1877: More Indians visited Colonel Nelson Miles to see if he would negotiate surrender terms. Miles informed the large group of chiefs that his terms had not changed, with the exception that they could surrender at an alternative agency than originally stated. Miles also informed them that he would wait no longer for a reply. If the Indians did not surrender soon, his troops would be deployed against them. Little Hawk, Crazy Horse's uncle, agreed to bring the Indians into Miles's camp or one of the agencies. Nine important Indians remained with Miles as hostages as a sign of good faith.

1877: The Battle of Yellow House Canyon took place near modern Lubbock, Texas. It involved over 150 Quahadi Comanche, led by Black Horse, and about fifty local hunters. Black Horse had killed a buffalo hunter who had shot and killed a large number of buffalo in the area. Black Horse was infuriated by the slaughter of his tribe's economic mainstay. The buffalo hunters sneaked up on Black Horse's camp and attacked it in retaliation for the killing of the hunter. Some sources cited this as the last significant Indian fight in the Texas Panhandle.

1879: Boundary lines for the White Earth Reserve were modified.

1903: A school reserve was established by executive order for the Fort Mohave Tribe. It contained approximately 7,000 acres of land.

1915: Certain lands were removed from "settlement, entry, sale, or other disposition" to be used in connection with the San Carlos Apache Indian dam and irrigation project.

1930: Executive Order No. 5306 extended the trust period on certain allotments made to members of the Seneca Nation.

1948: William Warne, assistant secretary of the interior, authorized an election for amendments to the constitution and bylaws of the Confederated Tribes of the Warm Springs Reservation of Oregon. The election would be held on April 24, 1948.

1954: Charles George, a Cherokee, was posthumously awarded the Medal of Honor. On November 30, 1952, he jumped on a grenade during the Korean War. He was killed, but he saved the lives of his fellow soldiers.

1976: Commissioner of Indian Affairs Morris Thompson ratified an election that approved a constitution and bylaws for the Rumsey Indian Rancheria (Yocha Dehe), Yolo County, Brooks, California. The election resulted in a vote of 15–0 in favor.

1987: The Lac du Flambeau Band of Lake Superior Chippewa Indians modified their local codes regarding timber trespassing.

MARCH 19

1784: Congress decided it did not want one big meeting with Indian representatives.

1840: The Southern Cheyenne and Comanche held several white prisoners. They requested a meeting to discuss peace and to trade prisoners. Sixty-five Comanche, including Muguara and eleven other chiefs, brought one prisoner, Matilda Lockhart, to the San Antonio council house. They told the white representatives, Hugh McCloud (adjutant general of the Texas Army), William Cooke, and William Fisher, that each prisoner must be released through an additional meeting. Lockhart was mutilated while in Comanche hands, and this incensed the whites. Armed men surrounded the Indians and told them they were hostages until all white prisoners were released. A fight erupted, and seven whites and

thirty-three Comanche, including all of the chiefs, were killed. The other Comanche were captured, but the story got back to their tribe. This became known as the Council House Fight.

1851: According to sources, one in a series of treaties with California Indians was signed at Camp Fremont. These treaties purported to set aside lands for the Indians and to protect them from angry whites. The Americans were represented by George W. Barbour, Redick McKee, and Oliver M. Wozencraft.

1867: Santee Sioux agreed to go to a reservation in Dakota Territory.

1873: Indians fought with soldiers from the Fifth Cavalry Infantry in the Mazatzal Mountains in Arizona, according to army documents. Eight Indians were killed, and five were captured.

1885: Louis Riel's Metis established a government at Batoche. They also declared themselves independent from Canada. This was a significant event in Riel's Rebellion.

1900: The size of the Northern Cheyenne Reservation was changed by executive order.

1963: Assistant Secretary of the Interior John A. Carver Jr. ratified an election for amendments to the constitution for the Wisconsin Winnebago.

1988: The Hayfork Norelmuk Band of Wintu Indians' constitution was approved by a tribal vote.

Every: St. Joseph's Feast celebrated in Old Lahuna Village.

MARCH 20

1699: Continuing his exploration up the Mississippi River, French explorer Pierre le Moyne d'Iberville visited the village of the Houma Indians.

1760: Tensions had been rising between the Cherokees and the British in southeastern Tennessee. The Cherokees opened fire and staged a four-day attack on Fort Loudoun (near modern Vonore, Tennessee). This also marked the beginning of a siege of the fort.

1837: According to government reports, between this date and July 31, 177 of the 4,000 Creek held at Mobile Point died at the camp or in transit. The conditions at Mobile camp led to the rapid spread of disease.

1837: About 1,600 Creek boarded two steamers to start their journeys to Indian Territory (present-day Oklahoma). They were first taken to a camp at Mobile Point.

1847: Robert S. Neighbors was appointed as a special federal Indian agent for Texas.

1862: As a part of the Owens Valley Indian War in California, a group of settlers attacked a Paiute Indian village north of Owens Lake. Almost a dozen Indians were killed; white settlers suffered only a few injuries.

1864: About 800 Navajos, mostly women, children, and old men, began the 300-mile march to Fort Sumner and the Bosque Redondo Reservation in east-central New Mexico. The group picked up 146 additional Navajos during the march. A powerful snowstorm struck the ill-equipped marchers during the trip. By the time they reached the new reservation, 110 Navajos had perished.

1866: Soldiers from the First Arizona Infantry fought with a band of Indians until March 25. The fighting took place near the headwaters of the Salt River in Arizona. The soldiers reported killing twenty two Indians, wounding seven, and capturing two.

1868: According to army records, settlers fought with a band of Indians near the Horseshoe and Twin Springs Ranch in Dakota Territory. Three settlers were killed.

1884: The Standing Rock Sioux Reservation had additions made to its boundaries.

1973: An ordinance passed by the Quechan Indian Tribe of Fort Yuma, California, created a zoning and planning commission.

1974: The area director of the Bureau of Indian Affairs authorized an election for an amendment to the constitution and bylaws of the Lower Brule Sioux Tribe of the Lower Brule Reservation. The election would be held on May 28, 1974.

1975: An election was held for proposed amendments to the Yankton Sioux constitution. The results were (with all four amendments passing): Amendment 1: 147–5 ; Amendment 2; 175–25; Amendment 3: 164–41; and Amendment 4: 180–19.

MARCH 21

1841: According to government documents, 220 Tallahassee Seminole prisoners boarded a boat in Tampa Bay. They were being sent to the Indian Territory (present-day Oklahoma). Fifteen of the Indians died in transit.

1842: General Zachary Taylor estimated that by this date 2,833 Seminole had relocated to the Indian Territory (present-day Oklahoma).

1866: The Seminole signed a treaty (14 Stat. 755) in Washington, D.C. This treaty was necessary because of the Seminole treaty with the Confederacy during the Civil War.

1868: According to army records, members of the Fourteenth Infantry escort fought with a band of Indians near Camp Willow Grove, Arizona. Two soldiers were reported killed.

1870: Indians attacked a railroad work gang at Eagle Tail station, Kansas. Before anyone was injured, the station's military guard ran off the Indians.

1873: General Canby decided not to wait for the Modoc to meet with him and the peace commissioners at Fairchild Ranch. Instead, he led a small detachment to Captain Jack's lava-bed stronghold. Jack agreed to meet Canby, and they discussed several matters. Canby promised to treat the Modoc well if they came out of the lava beds. Captain Jack asked the soldiers to leave, because all they wanted was to continue their normal lives. With no headway being made on either side, the meeting ended.

1883: Chiricahua Apache were raiding American locations then returning to Mexico. Chato,

Man and woman of Laguna Pueblo, New Mexico (NA)

Bonito, and Chihuahua raided a mining town near Tombstone, twelve miles south of Fort Huachuca, Arizona. According to army documents, four settlers were killed. This was the pretext General George Crook needed to mount a raid into Mexico to find the Apache.

1917: Federal regulations regarding the Laguna Pueblo in New Mexico were changed.

1936: Secretary of the Interior Harold Ickes authorized an election to adopt a constitution and bylaws for the Makah Indian Tribe of the Makah Indian Reservation Washington. The election would be held on April 18, 1936.

1936: The secretary of the interior had authorized an election for a constitution and bylaws for the Shoshone-Paiute Tribes of the Duck Valley Reservation in Nevada. It was approved by a vote of 183–57.

1940: The constitution and bylaws of the Shivwits Band of Paiute Indians was approved by the secretary of the interior.

1956: Assistant Secretary of the Interior Wesley D'Ewart ratified an election that approved Amendment 3 to the constitution and bylaws of the Tule River Indian Tribe. The election was held on February 25, 1956.

1978: An amendment to the constitution and bylaws of the Suquamish Indian Tribe of the Port Madison Reservation in the state of Washington was passed in an election.

1979: An election to approve a constitution and bylaws for the Choctaw Nation of Oklahoma was authorized by the acting deputy commissioner of Indian affairs. The election would be held on May 17, 1979.

MARCH 22

1621: Massasoit, Quadequina, Samoset (a Pemaquid), Squanto, and sixty warriors visited the Plymouth colony with great ceremony. They freely gave lands to the Pilgrims. According to some calendars, this happened on April 1 or 2.

1622: Opechancanough was Chief of the Pamunkey Indians, part of the Powhatan Confederacy. They attacked the English on this day, Good Friday, at Jamestown. An Indian named Chanco warned his stepfather, Richard Pace, of the impending attack. The town was warned, and the outer settlements suffered the brunt of the attack. Of the 1,240 English, 347 were killed in the fighting, the first large massacre by Indians in North America.

1682: The Taensa were first visited by an organized European force—La Salle of France—along the Mississippi River. Explorer Henri de Tonti was impressed by their use of cabins with mud walls two feet thick and twelve feet high. La Salle returned to the village on Lake Saint Joseph (near modern Newellton, Louisiana) on April 30, 1682, for a four-day stay.

1752: In an effort to end the fighting between the Spanish and the Pima, Pima chief Luis Oacpicagigua surrendered to Captain Díaz del Carpio.

1764: A slave held by the English fled and took refuge with the Tunica Indians. The English set up

Squanto with Plymouth colonist

a small expedition to retrieve the slave. On this day, Tunica, Ofo, Avoyel, and some Choctaw Indians attacked a group of small boats carrying the English. Six of the English were killed, and they abandoned their attempt.

1803: On March 12, the American fur-trading ship *Boston* anchored in Nootka Sound, Vancouver Island. The crew began trading with the Nootka Indians. On this day, the ship's captain insulted a Nootka chief. The Nootka attacked the ship's crew. Only two crew members survived.

1811: Tonquin landed in the Columbia estuary.

1816: The Cherokees ceded the last of their lands in South Carolina. The treaty (7 Stat. 139) was signed by Chief John Ross.

1824: A group of six settlers attacked and killed nine Seneca and Miami Indians in Madison County, Indiana. The attack took place near Fall Creek. The unprovoked attack was often called the Fall Creek Massacre. One of those killed was a Seneca subchief named Logan. Several of the at-

tackers were tried and sentenced to die for the murders.

1875: General George Crook was relieved as commander of Arizona. He was replaced by Colonel Kautz. Crook was sent farther north to engage the Sioux.

1866: Soldiers from the Fourteenth Infantry fought with a band of Indians near Cottonwood Springs in Arizona. According to army records, Captain J.F. Miller and surgeon Benjamin Tappan were killed in the fighting.

1869: According to army records, members of the Thirtieth Infantry fought with a band of Indians near Fort Fred Steele in Wyoming. Five Indians were killed.

1883: Miners fought a group of Indians at the Total Wreak Mine on the west side of Whetstone Mountain in Arizona.

1896: The Bureau of Indian Affairs was authorized to appoint Indians to reservation posts.

1956: The departmental order of September 1, 1939, which placed lands under the jurisdiction of the commissioner of Indian affairs for use by Navajo Indians, was partially revoked.

1967: Executive Order No. 11336 authorized the secretary of agriculture, under circumstances of chronic economic hardship, to offer economic relief to Indian tribes in the form of emergency livestock feed.

MARCH 23

603: The Maya king of Palenque, Hanab Pakal (Pacal) II was born. According to other inscriptions, he died on August 18, 683.

1730: In Keowee, in western North Carolina, Sir Alexander Cuming held a conference with 300 Cherokee chiefs. Using threats and gifts, Cuming got the Cherokees to agree to acknowledge King George II of England as their sovereign.

1838: S.T. Cross started an additional emigrant removal from Mississippi. They arrived at Choctaw Landing in May. A special act of Congress allowed for this trip, in hopes the Choctaws in Mississippi would not get involved in the Creek agitation.

1859: Fort Stockton, in western Texas, was established on the San Antonio–El Paso Road where it crosses the Comanche war trail. The fort was named in honor of Commodore Robert Stockton, "who captured California for the United States." The fort was abandoned by U.S. Army troops during the Civil War and reoccupied in 1867. It was permanently abandoned on June 30, 1886.

1869: According to army records, members of the Thirty-Second Infantry fought with a band of Indians near Camp Grant, Arizona. One civilian was killed and two soldiers were wounded.

1879: The second council on the Sioux-versus-Crow problem was held.

1883: Settlers fought a group of Indians near Point of Mountain, the south end of the Galiuro Range in Arizona. According to army documents, two settlers were killed.

1889: President Benjamin Harrison said part of Oklahoma would be opened to the public.

1914: An executive order established the boundaries of the Kalispel Indian Reservation.

MARCH 24

1617: King James I of England decided the Indians of Virginia must be educated. He directed the Anglican Church to collect funds to build churches and schools.

1663: The Charter of Carolina was issued.

1756: As a part of the Pennsylvania Delaware Uprising, several farms were attacked near Reading. Approximately ten settlers were killed in the fighting.

1832: The Creek signed a treaty (7 Stat. 366) with the United States and ceded more than half of their lands east of the Mississippi River. They were allowed sections of land to live on for a maximum of five years unless they sold it first. All white interlopers were to be removed during this five-year period. The Creek who decided to stay permanently

in Alabama were subject to Alabama laws. The temporary land areas granted to the Creek amounted to 2,187,200 acres of their original 5.2 million acres. The rest were ceded immediately. This was called the Second Treaty of Washington.

1837: There were a few hundred Creek Indians hiding in the swamps near the Alabama-Georgia line. General Carlton Welborne and several hundred state militia found some of these Creek and attacked. The Creek were half-starved and poorly armed, if at all. The Indians sustained as many as eighty fatalities; the militia lost two.

1839: Richard Taylor and 944 of his original group of 1,029 Cherokee forced emigrants arrived in Indian Territory (present-day Oklahoma). Taylor's group suffered fifty-five deaths and saw fifteen births during the trek.

1880: Three dozen Sioux made off with thirty horses belonging to Crow Indian scouts at Fort Custer in south-central Montana. Captain John Mix and forty-four soldiers from Troop C, Second Cavalry, covered sixty-five miles in eleven hours to catch the Sioux. During a skirmish, sixteen of the stolen horses were recovered.

1883: The Fort Stanton Reserve (for the Mescalero Apache) in New Mexico was modified.

1978: The case of *Mashpee Tribe v. the City of Mashpee, Massachusetts*, was in court.

1989: The *Exxon Valdez* crashed in Prince William Sound, Alaska. Many Indian lands were affected by this disaster.

MARCH 25

1713: European and Indian forces under General James Moore, son of South Carolina Governor James Moore, had been attacking the Tuscarora fort of Nohoroco, North Carolina, for several days. They finally captured the fort. During the fighting, 192 Tuscarora were killed, and almost 400 were taken prisoner. After this defeat, the Tuscarora would not be a significant force in North Carolina.

1837: Creek warriors had a camp set up in the swamp near the Hobdy Bridge on the Pea River in Alabama. Alabama militiamen attacked the camp. As many as four dozen Creek were killed in the fighting.

1839: Peter Hilderbrand and 1,312 of his original group of 1,776 forced Cherokee emigrants arrived in Indian Territory (present-day Oklahoma). This was the last of the major groups of arriving Cherokees in the Indian Territory. The migration was called the Trail of Tears. Although figures vary according to the source, it is believed that almost 12,000 Cherokees survived the trek; almost 4,000 died en route.

1868: The military received reports of an Indian raid upon the settlers of Bluff Creek, Kansas. The settlers were reported to have been attacked and driven from their homes.

1868: According to army records, members of the Fourteenth Infantry fought with a band of Indians near Cottonwood Springs, Arizona. One soldier and two Indians were wounded. One Indian was also killed.

1873: At Turret Mountain, Arizona, members of the Fifth Cavalry engaged the local Indians in a fight. According to army records, "for gallantry in the engagement," Sergeant Daniel Bishop, First Sergeant James M. Hill, and Private Eben Stanley, Company A, would be awarded the Medal of Honor. Ten Indians were killed, and three were captured.

1874: An order was issued that modified the boundaries of the Jicarilla Apache Indian Reservation in New Mexico Territory. It covered 447.5 square miles.

1874: Indians fought with soldiers from the Fifth Cavalry in the Superstition Mountains of Arizona. According to army documents, twelve Indians were killed and two were captured. The fighting lasted through the next day.

1879: Little Wolf and a small band of Northern Cheyenne had managed to elude capture by army troops since they split off from Dull Knife's group when they were captured during a fight on October 23, 1878. Lieutenant William Clark (called "White Hat" by the Cheyenne), Troops E and I, Second Cavalry, as well as some infantry, Indian scouts, and artillery discovered Little Wolf's band near Box Elder Creek in Dakota. The group of thirty-three men, forty-three women, and thirty-eight children surrendered. The army seized thirty-five lodges, all the Cheyenne weapons, and 250 horses. This last significant group of "free" Northern Cheyenne was marched to Fort Keogh in east-central Montana.

1886: After escaping from the San Carlos Reservation, Geronimo and his followers went to Mexico. However, the Mexican army had orders to kill the Apache. U.S. General George Crook's orders were to kill them if they did not peacefully surrender. Geronimo decided to talk to Crook about returning to the reservation. On this day, they met in the Canyon de los Embudos, a few miles into Mexico. Geronimo asked Crook his terms for surrender. Crook explained that surrender had to be unconditional and probably included being shipped to Indian Territory (present-day Oklahoma) or Florida as prisoners. Geronimo asked if they could be returned to San Carlos after two years. Crook felt this was a good compromise and was sure he could convince his supervisors of its validity, so he agreed. However, Crook was unable to convince Washington to accept Geronimo's suggestion. Although many of his followers surrendered, Geronimo did not.

1899: Moses, chief of the Middle Oregon Tribes for the last forty years, died. He was buried in Coleville Agency near Nespelem, Washington.

1916: Yahi Indian Ishi (portrayed in the film *The Last of His Tribe*) died.

1971: William John Gobert, a Blackfoot, was named the "Outstanding Handicapped Worker of the Year" by the Department of Health, Education, and Welfare. He was presented his award by Pat Nixon, wife of the president. Gobert worked as an instructor for the Indian Health Service in Tucson, Arizona.

1976: An election for an amendment to the constitution and bylaws for the Lower Elwha Tribal Community of the Lower Elwha Reservation in Washington State was authorized by the commissioner of Indian affairs. The election would be held on May 22, 1976.

MARCH 26

1676: The English attacked Chief Canonchet and his Narragansett followers at Patuxet. Many of the English were killed in the fighting.

1682: On the Mississippi River, La Salle's expedition first met the Natchez Indians. This was the first recorded meeting of Europeans with the Natchez. Fellow explorer Henri de Tonti was the first member of the expedition to meet them.

1765: According to some reports, a meeting was held by people representing the British and the Chickasaw and the Choctaw regarding questions on boundary lines and land cessions.

1776: Juan de Ugalde was appointed governor of San Francisco de Coahuila, Mexico. He was renowned as an Indian fighter.

1777: Henry Hamilton was the British lieutenant governor of Detroit. He received orders to dispatch his Indian allies against American settlers in Ohio.

1793: James McFarland was leading a group of fifteen settlers along the Wilderness Road in Kentucky. Near an area called the Hazel Patch, a Chickamauga war party attacked. All but four people were killed in the fighting. One girl was eventually rescued by frontiersmen.

1804: Congress passed "An Act to Make Further Appropriations, for the Purpose of Extinguishing the Indian Claim."

1836: The Potawatomi signed a treaty (7 Stat. 490). It involved the ceding of land. Six Indians signed the document.

1839: In October 1838, a group of Cherokees started their forced emigration to Indian Territory (present-day Oklahoma). They arrived at their destination, according to the journal of John G. Burnett, one of the soldiers who accompanied them. Burnett was extremely saddened by the entire episode, especially by the death of Chief John Ross's wife.

1854: Command of Fort Phantom Hill, north of Abilene, Texas, changed hands from Major H.H. Sibley to First Lieutenant Newton C. Givens. The fort was often visited by the local Comanche, Lipan Apache, Kiowa, and Kickapoo.

1855: The First Cavalry Regiment was formed at Jefferson Barracks, Missouri. Its main function was to seek out hostile Plains Indians. In 1861, it was renamed the Fourth Cavalry.

1856: As a part of the Battle of the Cascades, local Indians under the instructions of Yakima Chief Kamiakin attacked Fort Cascade. The militia in the fort, near the modern Cascade Locks and the Bridge of the Gods, would hold out until March 28, when a boatload of soldiers from Fort Vancouver arrived. The soldiers, led by Lieutenant Phil Sheridan, defeated the Indians. This was one of the last fights in Kamiakin's War.

1868: According to army records, members of the Eighth Cavalry fought with a band of Indians near Owyhee River, Oregon. One Indian was reported killed.

1874: Indians fought with soldiers from the Fifth Cavalry in the Superstition Mountains of Arizona. According to army documents, twelve Indians were killed, and two were captured. The fighting started a day earlier.

1876: Colonel Reynolds returned to Fort Fetterman.

1885: The Duck Lake Fight took place in Canada. Louis Riel's Metis had taken over the village at Duck Lake, Saskatchewan. Metis representatives and Superintendent Lief Crozier of the Northwest Mounted Police met to discuss the situation. Somehow, a fight broke out and shots were fired. Five Metis and twelve Mounties or volunteers were killed. This was one of the first major fights in the North-West Rebellion.

1973: A Native American mass was held in New York City at Saint John the Divine Cathedral. Almost 4,000 people attended.

1977: Vincent Little, the acting area director, Portland area office, Bureau of Indian Affairs, had authorized an election to approve an amendment to the constitution and bylaws for the Upper Skagit Indian Tribe. It was approved by a vote of 50–3.

MARCH 27

1756: Lieutenant Gaspard-Joseph Chaussegros de Lééry was leading a force of 251 Canadians and 103 Iroquois, Abenaki, and Nepissing Indians. They attacked the British garrison of seventy soldiers at Fort Bull (also called Wood Creek Fort, near modern Rome, New York). All but twenty-eight of the soldiers were killed in the fighting. Knowing reinforcements would soon be arriving from nearby Fort William, Lééry left soon after destroying most of the fort's supplies. Due to the vicious nature of the fighting, the British called this the Massacre at Fort Bull.

1814: At a site east of what is modern Alexander City, Alabama, Andrew Jackson and 2,000 whites, Cherokees, Choctaws, and White Stick Creek discovered a fort built by Red Stick Creek at the village of Tohopeka on a horseshoe bend in the Tallapoosa River. The Red Stick Creek were antiwhite; the White Stick Creek were prowhite. Jackson attacked 800–1,000 Red Stick Creek, who were led by Chief Menewa. The Creek village and defenses covered approximately 100 acres on the peninsula made by the bend in the river. To cross the river, Jackson's Cherokee allies, led by Chief Junaluska, swam the river to steal Creek canoes. Jackson's forces eventually set fire to the Red Stick Creek's wooden barricade. In the end, only about fifty of the Red Stick Creek survived the battle. Jackson's forces lost forty-nine soldiers and twenty-three warriors killed; 157 soldiers and forty-seven warriors were wounded. Jackson's forces captured approximately 300 women and children. The Red Stick Creek leader William Weatherford was not at the battle. Weatherford would turn himself in later. This defeat led to the Treaty of Horseshoe Bend, signed on August 9, 1814, whereby the Creek gave up 23 million acres of land to the United States.

1851: As a part of the Mariposa Indian Wars in California, two companies of the Mariposa Battalion discovered a valley where Yosemite and Chowchilla (both Miwok) Indians lived.

1858: A group of Bannock and a few Shoshone stole some cattle from the local Mormon settlers near Fort Limhi, Idaho, on February 25. This led to a brief battle, with a couple of settlers being killed. Under orders from Brigham Young, the fort was abandoned and the settlers returned to safer territory. Eventually, the name "Limhi" would evolve into "Lemhi" and became a common place name in central Idaho.

1873: According to Kansas House Concurrent Resolution No. 5014, Creek leader Opothle Yahola died. He was buried near Fort Belmont, Kansas.

1872: Sergeant William Wilson and soldiers from Troop I, Fourth Cavalry, were near Fort Concho, modern San Angelo in west-central Texas, when they were attacked by Indians. The troopers were uninjured, but the Indians tallied two killed, three wounded, one captured, and nineteen horses lost. The fighting lasted through the next day.

1873: Captain George Randall led the Fifth Cavalry, the Twenty-Third Infantry Regiment, and some Indian scouts in a fight with Apache at Turret Peak, south of Camp Verde, in central Arizona. This was one of the last Apache battles. First Sergeant William Allen of Company I would win the Medal of Honor for his actions in this battle. Twenty-three Indians were killed, and ten were captured.

1876: Indian scouts fought with some hostile Indians in Tonto Basin, Arizona. According to army documents, sixteen Indians were killed. The fighting lasted through the next day.

1939: The assistant secretary of the interior approved the election of a new constitution for the Havasupai Nations that was held on January 13, 1939.

1947: The Pueblo of Isleta established a constitution.

1967: The Lac du Flambeau Tribal Council adopted numerous zoning ordinances.

1973: Sacheen Littlefeather refused Marlon Brando's Oscar as a protest against media and government mistreatment of American Indians.

1973: The U.S. Supreme Court ruled that states cannot charge income taxes to Indians who earn all of their income on reservations.

MARCH 28

1513: According to some sources, Ponce de Leon landed in Florida. It was also recorded as April 2 and May 2.

1634: According to some sources, the Yaocomico sold some of their land on the St. Marys River to Leonard Calvert. This helped to establish their colony in Maryland.

1676: After attacking a military group near the town two days before, King Philip's forces attacked the village of Rehoboth, Massachusetts. Most of the townspeople survived in barricaded homes, but much of the town was razed.

1833: Several Seminole had been sent to Indian Territory (present-day Oklahoma) to look over the areas proposed as their new lands. The Seminole in Indian Territory were sent to only look at the land, but the government had them sign an agreement that the land was adequate and committing the Seminole to removal. The agreement was signed at Fort Gibson in western Oklahoma and was called the Fort Gibson Treaty (7 Stat. 423). The Payne's Landing Treaty (7 Stat. 368) of May 9, 1832, stated that the Seminole had to be satisfied with the report of the delegation to Indian Territory before they agreed to move. The government worded the new agreement so that the Seminole in Florida did not get to discuss the matter. The Seminole delegation was satisfied with the lands; being with their former kin, the Creek, they were not satisfied with the proximity of the belligerent Plains Indians. Upon the return of the delegation to Florida, the Seminole Nation repudiated the agreement, with the exception of John Blunt and his Apalachicola followers. The enforcement of this illegal treaty by the U.S. government led to the start of the Second Seminole War.

1835: Captain John Page arrived at the Western Creek Agency near Fort Gibson in eastern Indian Territory (present-day Oklahoma). He was with 469 Creek survivors of the 630 Creek who started this removal trek in December 1834.

1836: The Ottawa and Chippewa signed a treaty (7 Stat. 491) in Washington, D.C. It involved the ceding of land and the sharing of a reservation.

1836: The Bay Mills Reservation territory (Michigan) was altered by an act of Congress (7 Stat. 491).

1840: After hearing of the fight in San Antonio on March 19, 1840, the remaining Comanche were outraged. Chief Isimanica and 300 Comanche rode up to San Antonio. Isimanica and one warrior rode into the central square and challenged anyone to a fight. The civilians declined but told him that the army was at the San Jose Mission.

1843: This day marked the first of what became known as the Tehuacana Creek councils. These were meetings between Texas officials and members of the Lipan Apache, Caddo, Delaware, Tawakoni, Tonkawa, and Waco Indians. Tehuacana Creek was south of what is modern Waco.

1856: As a part of the Battle of the Cascades, local Indians under the instructions of Yakima Chief Kamiakin attacked Fort Cascade on March 26. The militia in the fort, near the modern Cascade Locks and the Bridge of the Gods, would hold out until this date, when a boatload of soldiers from Fort Vancouver arrived. The soldiers, led by Lieutenant Phil Sheridan, defeated the Indians. This was one of the last fights in Kamiakin's War.

1866: Soldiers from the First New Mexico Cavalry fought with a band of Indians near Rita Mangas in southern New Mexico. The soldiers reported killing one Indian and wounding six.

1867: According to army records, members of the Eighth Cavalry fought with a band of Indians near Murderers' Creek, Oregon. No injuries were reported on either side.

1872: Indians skirmished with a group of soldiers from the Fourth Cavalry near Fort Concho, Texas, according to official army records. Two Indians were killed, three were wounded, and one was captured. The fighting lasted through the next day.

1872: A band of Indian and Mexican thieves was attacked by troopers from Fort Concho in west-central Texas. One hostile Indian was captured, three wounded, and two killed during the fight.

1876: Indian scouts fought with some hostile Indians in Tonto Basin, Arizona. According to army documents, sixteen Indians were killed. The fighting started one day earlier.

1879: Indians kill two white men in Montana, according to army records. One, H.D. Johnson, was killed near the mouth of the Bighorn River. The other, Dave Henderson, was killed near Buffalo Springs on the Yellowstone River.

1883: Settlers fought a group of Indians between Silver City and Lordsburg, New Mexico. According to army documents, two settlers were killed.

1885: Fighting in the Second Riel Rebellion took place as Poundmaker led the Cree against settlers in Battleford, Saskatchewan.

1929: The railroad ran through the San Carlos Reservation in Arizona.

1953: Jim Thorpe died.

1957: A court rules that Montana state courts "are without jurisdiction to try an Indian for the crime of larceny committed somewhere within the external boundaries of the Blackfeet Indian Reservation, although conceivably the offense could have been committed within the town of Browning, Montana located on the reservation."

1968: The acting assistant commissioner of Indian affairs authorized an election for a new constitution for the Havasupai Indian Tribe.

1975: Commissioner of Indian Affairs Morris Thompson ratified an election that approved the revised constitution and bylaws of the Mississippi Band of Choctaw Indians. The election was held on December 17, 1974.

1989: The St. Regis Mohawk reached an agreement with the U.S. Environmental Protection Agency to implement environmental standards and regulations on their reservation.

MARCH 29

1542: Hernando de Soto's expedition reached the territory of the Anilco Indians. As with many of his previous encounters, a battle was fought.

1676: As a part of King Philip's War, a band of Narragansett Indians attacked Providence, Rhode Island. All but one of the settlers retreated to the garrison. The remaining settlers were killed. Many of the other structures in the village were burned to the ground.

1778: Captain James Cook anchored his two ships, HMS *Discovery* and HMS *Resolution*, in Nootka Sound. He worked on the ships and traded with the Nootka for the next month.

1797: The Mohawk Treaty (7 Stat. 61) was signed in Albany by five Indians, including Joseph Brandt. All of their lands in New York were ceded for $1,000.

1835: Members of the treaty faction of the Cherokees signed a treaty, in secret, at the home of *Cherokee Phoenix* editor Elias Boudinot. When more conservative Cherokees heard of the event, they became furious. The tribal council did not ratify the treaty.

1837: The first group of Cherokees to emigrate from the east under the terms of the New Echota

Treaty, under Dr. John Young's supervision, arrived at Fort Coffee in eastern Indian Territory (present-day Oklahoma).

1854: The second Kickapoo implicated in the murder of former Texas Indian agent Colonel Jesse Stem, on February 12, 1854, was killed by his brother. A large group of Kickapoo brought Polecat's head to army officials at Fort Arbuckle in Indian Territory (present-day Oklahoma).

1858: According to some sources, Major Robert S. Neighbors, Texas Indian agent, recommended the abolishment of the Indian reservations on the Brazos River and the Comanche Reservation. This was because of the hostility of the nearby settlers and the reluctance of government forces to defend the Indians.

1866: The Potawatomi signed a treaty (14 Stat. 763). It extended the provisions of previous treaties to both genders.

1884: The executive order establishing the Turtle Mountain Reserve in Dakota Territory for the Turtle Mountain Band of Chippewa Indians was modified.

1885: According to the Oklahoma Law Enforcement Memorial, Captain Thomas Cloud and Officer Sam Cudgo were part of a Seminole Lighthorse posse. The posse attempted to arrest Rector Roberts when he barricaded himself in a hut and opened fire on the posse. The first shot hit Officer Cudgo in the stomach and the next bullet stuck Captain Cloud in the left leg. The rest of the posse returned fire and killed Roberts. Officer Cudgo died within the hour. Captain Cloud died two days later.

1965: New York State wanted to convert a two-lane road into a limited-access freeway. The freeway would divide the Seneca Reservation in two. The Seneca took the matter to court. The Supreme Court ruled that eminent domain laws applied to reservations, as well as all other lands. It was five years before Congress allocated the funds to pay for the lands that were lost. The Seneca called the freeway the Berlin Wall.

1976: An amendment to the constitution of the Comanche Indian Tribe was enacted.

1979: The rules for the election of delegates to the Official Central Council of the Tlingit and Haida Indian Tribes of Alaska were amended through March 31.

MARCH 30

1791: The Knoxville Road through Indian lands was started.

1802: Congress passed the Indian Trade and Intercourse Act. It was titled "An Act to Regulate Trade and Intercourse with the Indian Tribes, and to Preserve Peace on the Frontiers." One of its provisions was "to promote civilization among the aborigines."

1817: William Clark, Auguste Chouteau, Ninian Edwards, and representatives of the Menominee Indians signed a treaty (7 Stat. 153) in St. Louis. The treaty called for the return of prisoners and the affirmation of earlier land cessions.

1824: Southern officials felt that the U.S. government should remove the Indians from their states. Georgia asked President James Monroe to remove the Indians based on an agreement whereby Georgia released western lands it claimed to the United States. Monroe said the U.S. government was not required to do so: "Indian title was in no way affected by the compact with Georgia."

1854: Indians successfully attacked and defeated a company of dragoons (Lieutenant J.W. Davidson, with Company I, and sixteen men of Company F) at Cieneguilla, New Mexico.

1866: Soldiers from the First Arizona Infantry fought with a band of Indians until March 25. The fighting took place near Pimas Village in Arizona. The soldiers reported killing twenty-five Indians and capturing sixteen. One soldier was killed, and two were wounded.

1867: The United States obtained Alaska from Russia.

1869: According to army records, members of the Thirty-Second Infantry fought with a band of Indians near Camp Goodwin, Arizona. Two Indians were killed. Occasional skirmishes started on March 17.

1870: Based on the congressional act of April 8, 1864, and this date's executive order by President Grant, Round Valley Reservation was established in Mendocino County, California. In time it would house Clear Lake, Concow, Little Lake, Nomelaki, Pit River, Potter Valley, Redwood, Wailaki, and Yuki Tribes within approximately fifty square miles of land.

1893: The "agreement" forced on the two Kickapoo chiefs on September 9, 1891, was approved by Congress. An investigation held many years later showed the signatures of many dead Indians or fictitious names.

1936: Secretary of the Interior Harold Ickes ratified a constitution for the Omaha Tribe of Nebraska.

1972: The deputy commissioner of Indian affairs authorized an election to approve amendments to the constitution and bylaws of the Cree Tribe of the Rocky Boy's Reservation in Montana. The election would be held on April 22, 1972.

1976: The area director of the Phoenix office of the Bureau of Indian Affairs authorized an election that approved an amendment to the constitution and bylaws for the Pyramid Lake Paiute Tribe of Nevada. The election was held on July 1, 1976.

1986: The secretary of the interior ratified a new constitution for the Omaha Tribe of Nebraska. It went into effect.

MARCH 31

1793: Moses Cockrell and a few whites were leading pack animals across Powell's Mountain. They were attacked by Chickamauga Chief Captain Bench and his followers. All of the Europeans were killed except Cockrell, who escaped after outrunning Bench.

1826: A supplemental article (7 Stat. 289) was added to the treaty with the Creek signed on January 24.

1877: In Arizona, parts of the White Mountain–San Carlos Reservation were restored to the public domain.

1882: The Havasupai Reservation boundaries in Arizona were modified.

1885: According to the Oklahoma Law Enforcement Memorial, Captain Thomas Cloud and Officer Sam Cudgo were part of a Seminole Lighthorse posse. On March 29, the posse attempted to arrest Rector Roberts when he barricaded himself in a hut and opened fire on the posse. The first shot hit Officer Cudgo in the stomach and the next bullet struck Captain Cloud in the left leg. The rest of the posse returned fire and killed Roberts. Officer Cudgo died within the hour on March 29. Captain Cloud died on this day.

1936: The ownership of an island within the Fort Berthold Reservation in North Dakota was contested.

1936: The secretary of the Interior had authorized an election to approve a constitution and bylaws for the Shoshone-Bannock Tribes of the Fort Hall Reservation. It was approved by a vote of 358–86.

1977: The commissioner of Indian affairs ratified an election that approved Amendment 6 to the constitution and bylaws of the Miccosukee Tribe of Indians of Florida by a vote of 58–18.

1979: The constitution of the central council of the Tlingit and Haida Indian Tribes of Alaska was amended.

APRIL 1

1536: After being shipwrecked in Galveston, Texas, Cabeza de Vaca and a few men marched across the continent to California. They were the

Indians meet Plymouth colonists

first "white men" to visit many Indian tribes. On this day, Cabeza de Vaca reached "civilization" again at San Miguel in New Galicia.

1621: Massasoit, Quadequina, Samoset (a Pemaquid), Squanto, and sixty warriors visited the Plymouth colony with great ceremony. They freely gave lands to the Pilgrims. According to some calendars, this happened on March 22 or April 2.

1727: According to some sources, a land cession agreement was reached between representatives of the British in North Carolina and the Mattamuskeet Indians.

1756: A large band of Delaware, led by Chief Shingas, attacked Fort McCord near Loudon, Pennsylvania. Of the twenty-seven defenders, all were either killed or captured. After burning the fort, Shingas fled the area. Several groups of settlers and soldiers pursued Shingas. At Sideling Hill, the Europeans caught up with the Delaware, and a battle was fought. Twenty-one Europeans and seventeen Delaware were killed. Twenty-one Indians and seventeen settlers were wounded in the engagement.

1757: According to some reports, a conference regarding various alliances was held through May 22 by representatives of the British in Pennsylvania and the Delaware, Nanticoke, Six Nations, and Susquehannock Indians.

1775: Boonesborough was founded.

1850: The Wyandot signed a treaty (9 Stat. 987) in Washington, D.C. As a part of the agreement, they sold 148,000 acres of land for $185,000.

1866: Congress overrode President Andrew Johnson's veto of the Civil Rights Bill of 1866. The bill gave equal rights to all persons born in the United States. The one exception: Indians were excluded.

1868: According to army records, members of the Eighth Cavalry Infantry fought with a band of Indians in the Pinal Mountains of Arizona. One Indian was killed.

1877: Seminole Negro scouts under Lieutenant J.L. Bullis fought a group of Indians on the Rio Grande near Devil's River in Texas. According to army documents, no casualties were reported.

1880: Captain Eli Huggins and Troop E, Second Cavalry, from Fort Keogh in east-central Montana surprised a band of hostile Sioux. During a brief battle, the soldiers captured five Indians, forty-six horses, and some weapons. Lieutenant John Coale and Troop C, Second Cavalry, from Fort Custer in south-central Montana had a skirmish with Sioux on O'Fallon's Creek. One soldier was killed in the fighting. According to army reports, some of these Indians were believed to have been involved in the theft of Crow Indian scout horses from Fort Custer on March 24, 1880. For his part in cutting off the Indians' herd of ponies through the use of "fearless exposure and dashing bravery," Second Lieutenant Lloyd M. Brett was awarded the Medal of Honor. Captain Huggins would also be awarded the Medal of Honor for his actions in the fighting.

1899: Under the Curtis Act, passed in 1898, the allotment of Creek lands began.

1940: The Moapa Band of Paiute Indians conducted an official census.

1968: According to the constitution of the To-hono O'odham Nation, the Indian Civil Rights Act (82 Stat. 77) was enacted.

1969: The acting assistant commissioner of Indian affairs authorized an election to approve a constitution and bylaws for the Hoh Indian Tribe. It would be held on May 24, 1969.

1986: The constitution and bylaws of the Nanti-coke Indian Association were adopted by the tribe.

1991: The Campo Band of Kumeyaay (Mission) Indians drafted a solid waste management plan.

APRIL 2

1513: According to some sources, Ponce de Leon "discovered" Florida. He landed south of St. Johns River and claimed Florida for Spain. There was considerable debate as to the exact date of this event.

1621: Massasoit, Quadequina, Samoset (a Pe-maquid), Squanto, and sixty warriors visited the Plymouth colony with great ceremony. They freely gave lands to the Pilgrims. According to some calendars, this happened on March 22 or April 1.

1676: Canonchet, a Narragansett sachem, was sentenced to death for his part in King Philip's War.

1781: Established on the heights above the Cumberland River, Fort Nashborough served as a central point of defense for the settlers in the area that eventually became Nashville, Tennessee. The fort was the scene of almost continuous sniping by local Indians over a twenty-year period. A Cherokee war party attempted to capture the fort. Using a few exposed warriors as bait, they lured twenty woodsmen out of the fort. The main body attacked the Europeans, killing five. The fort let loose a pack of hunting dogs that attacked the Cherokees. The surviving woodsmen made their escape while the Cherokees fought off the dogs. This attack was the last serious attack on the fort by the Cherokees.

1786: In a council of the Creek chiefs, war was officially declared against the United States. Sub-sequent fighting along the Georgia borders killed eighty-two whites, wounded twenty-nine, and captured 140.

1870: According to official army records, Indians skirmished with a group of settlers near the headwaters of the Sweetwater River in Wyoming. Six settlers were killed.

1873: Captain Jack and several of his Modoc warriors and women met with several of the peace commissioners about halfway between the soldiers' and Jack's camps in northern California. After the meeting on March 21, instead of moving the soldiers away, Canby brought in reinforcements. Captain Jack questioned Canby on this action. Canby said the soldiers made him feel safer during councils with the Modoc. Captain Jack asked for them to go away. They discussed the matter of Hooker Jim's killing of white settlers. A sudden rainstorm interrupted the meeting, and the parties left without resolving any of the issues.

1874: During a skirmish with hostile Indians at Apache Creek, Arizona, Sergeant George Deary, Company L, Fifth Cavalry, would earn the Medal of Honor for "gallantry in action." According to army documents, thirty-one Indians were killed, and fifty were captured.

1880: Lieutenant Calvin Esterly, leading troopers from Troops F and L, Tenth Cavalry, had been tracking a band of Indians from near Pecos Falls, Texas. The Indians were accused of stealing stock from local settlers. The army found its quarry. One Indian was killed, and eight of the stolen livestock were seized.

1885: An incident in the Second Riel Rebellion took place. Several Cree and Assiniboin warriors attacked settlers in the village of Frog Lake. They killed nine men, including the local Indian agent. Cree Chief Big Bear was unsuccessful in preventing the attack.

1936: A constitution and bylaws were approved for the Santee Sioux Tribe of the Sioux Nation of the state of Nebraska.

1938: The secretary of the interior authorized an election for a constitution for the Skokomish Indian Tribe.

1948: The assistant commissioner of Indian affairs authorized the Nez Perce to vote on a constitution and bylaws.

1970: Four hundred acres of Indian land were withdrawn from a land reclamation project in New Mexico according to Federal Register No. 35FR05813.

1975: A three-day National Conference on Indian Water Rights was convened in Washington, D.C. Representatives from almost 200 tribes attended the meeting.

1977: The area director of the Bureau of Indian Affairs had authorized an election for an amendment to the constitution and bylaws of the Tonkawa Tribe of Indians of Oklahoma. It was approved by a vote of 17–1.

April 3

1730: In the Cherokee village of Nequassee (modern Franklin, North Carolina), Sir Alexander Cuming oversaw a ceremony making Chief Moytoy the "Emperor of the Cherokees." This was his final step in having the Cherokees acknowledge the sovereignty of King George II of England.

1792: The president ratified an article to pay the Iroquois Six Nations $1,500 annually for their land.

1861: Whites had started settling on Sioux lands near New Ulm, Minnesota. In an effort to improve their illegal standing, they petitioned President Lincoln for protection against the Indians.

1867: According to army records, soldiers under Captain Guido Ilges of the Fourteenth Infantry fought with a band of Indians in Tonto Valley, Arizona. Three Indians were reported killed, and one was captured.

1868: According to army records, a "wood chopping party" fought with a band of Indians near Rock Creek, Wyoming. One Indian was killed.

1870: According to official army records, Indians skirmished with a group of soldiers from the Ninth Cavalry near San Martine Springs, Texas. One Indian was killed. Fourth Cavalry troopers also fought with some Indians near North Hubbard Creek in Texas. Two Indians were killed and four were wounded in this fight.

1874: Indians fought with soldiers from the Fifth Cavalry and some Indian scouts in the Pinal Mountains of Arizona. According to army documents, fourteen Indians were killed, and twenty-eight were captured in the fighting, which lasted until April 14.

1880: Tenth Cavalry soldiers fought a group of Indians near Pecos Falls, Texas. According to army documents, one Indian was killed.

1936: Harold Ickes, the secretary of the interior, approved a constitution and bylaws for the Santee Sioux Tribe of the Sioux Nation of the state of Nebraska.

1959: Assistant Secretary of the Interior Fred Aandahl authorized an election for the proposed Amendment 7 to the constitution and bylaws of the Confederated Tribes of the Warm Springs Reservation of Oregon. The election would be held on April 25, 1959.

1969: The constitution and bylaws of the Lac Courte Oreilles Band of Lake Superior Chippewa Indians of Wisconsin was amended.

1975: An amendment to the constitution and bylaws of the Turtle Mountain Band of Chippewa Indians of North Dakota was approved by Harley Zephier, acting area director of the Aberdeen area office of the Bureau of Indian Affairs.

1975: Gerald Tailfeathers, a Blood from Alberta, Canada, was an accomplished artist. He died on the Blood Reserve.

1992: The Dickson Mounds Museum closed.

April 4

1840: Comanche Chief Piava arranged an exchange of two prisoners with the residents of San

Antonio, Texas. Two captives from each side were released.

1856: According to a report written by Lieutenant Philip Sheridan, six Vancouver Indians were murdered near his fort in the Lower Cascades, Washington Territory. The murders were reported to have been committed by six well-armed settlers seen following the Indians. The victims, including a three-year-old boy, were family members of Chief Spencer.

1862: As a part of the Owens Valley War in California, approximately three dozen Paiute were attacking the Putnam Trading Post. Colonel Evans arrived with the cavalry, and the Indians fled.

1874: Sioux warriors attacked the Yellowstone Wagon Road and a prospector's expedition.

1879: According to army files, a group of Indians stole almost thirty horses from Countryman's Ranch on the Yellowstone River. Local citizens and friendly Crow Indians pursued them. They were found on April 22, 1879.

1894: Cheyenne fought in Oklahoma.

1936: An election for the approval of a constitution and bylaws for the Muckleshoot Indian Tribe of the Muckleshoot Reservation was held. It passed by a vote of 46–2.

1966: An election for an amendment to the constitution and bylaws of the Moapa Band of Paiute Indians held on November 20, 1965, was ratified by Assistant Secretary of the Interior Harry Anderson.

April 5

1614: Representatives of the British Colony in Virginia and Chickahominy tribe signed a treaty of friendship and alliance.

1800: William Augustus Bowles, the self-proclaimed "Director General and Commander-In-Chief of the Muskogee Nation," declared war on Spain. (Also recorded as happening on May 5, 1800.)

1832: After being removed from Illinois in 1831, Black Hawk and his Sac followers lived in Iowa. Wanting to return to their old homeland, Black Hawk and almost 1,000 of his tribe crossed the Mississippi River back into Illinois. Not much later, they were attacked by the whites. (See April 6.)

1868: According to army records, members of the First and Eighth Cavalry and Twenty-Third Infantry fought with a band of Indians near Malheur River, Oregon. Thirty-two Indians were reported killed, and two were captured.

1879: Having been cast out of Little Wolf's Band of Cheyenne for killing two of their fellow Northern Cheyenne, a group of eight Indians were moving on their own. They attacked a sergeant and a private, of the Second Cavalry, on Mizpah Creek. The sergeant was seriously wounded, and the private was killed.

1880: Ninth Cavalry soldiers fought a group of Indians in Miembrillo Canyon in the San Andreas Mountains of New Mexico. According to army documents, one soldier and one civilian were wounded.

1935: An extension on the trust period on allotments made to Indians of the Crow Reservation made by the Dawes Severalty Act on February 8, 1887, was extended by Executive Order No. 7001.

1943: A "Tribal Land Enterprise" was established by the tribe pursuant to the bylaws of the Rosebud Indian Reservation. It was adopted by the Tribal Council on this day through April 7. It was approved by the secretary of the interior on July 8, 1955, as amended.

April 6

1728: For the past month representatives from Virginia and the Carolinas had been running a survey to separate the two colonies. They had decided to stop their efforts until after summer was over. Several members of the Virginia Boundary Commission visited the Indian village of Nottaway Town. They enjoyed a dance and the "favors" of several Indian women.

1792: Chickamauga Chief Captain Bench and followers attacked settlements near Holston. After killing four people, he left a declaration of war beside the bodies. He was a former friend to Europeans, but his heart turned to war following the death of his great-uncle, Old Tassel, at the hands of whites.

1794: Chickamauga Chief Captain Bench and his followers were continuing their attacks on European settlements. Near Mendota, Virginia, they attacked several farms in the area. After killing or capturing thirteen members of the Livingstone families, Captain Bench left the area. Remaining members of the Livingstone families and other local settlers followed Bench's trail. They eventually caught up to them. Vincent Hobbs shot and killed Captain Bench.

1830: U.S. Senator Hugh White proposed that the Senate begin discussions on an act to move Indians to lands west of the Mississippi River. The debate continued for almost three weeks.

1831: Secretary of War John C. Calhoun resigned. He would have overseen the implementation of many of the policies that forced the Indians of the Southeast to move west of the Mississippi River. He was eventually replaced by Lewis Cass.

1832: Black Hawk returned to Illinois, according to some sources.

1854: Fort Phantom Hill, north of Abilene, Texas, was abandoned. The fort was often visited by the local Comanche, Lipan Apache, Kiowa, and Kickapoo.

1863: Representatives of the Apache, Cheyenne, Comanche, and Kiowa signed a treaty in Washington.

1869: According to army records, members of the Fourth Infantry fought with a band of Indians near La Bonte Creek, Wyoming. Two soldiers were killed.

1870: According to official army records, Indians skirmished with a group of soldiers from the Tenth Cavalry near Clear Creek, Texas. One Indian was killed, and ten were captured.

1870: According to official army records, Indians skirmished with a group of soldiers escorting a train near Bluff Creek, Kansas. Three Indians were wounded.

1875: Black Horse was one of several Southern Cheyenne Indians being sent to prison from the Cheyenne and Arapaho Agency (later called Fort Reno) in west-central Indian Territory (present-day Oklahoma) to St. Augustine, Florida, for his part in the uprisings in Indian Territory and Texas. While handcuffed, he attempted to escape into the rest of his tribe. He was pursued and mortally wounded by the army guards under Captain Andrew Bennett, Fifth Infantry. Several of the shots at Black Horse missed him and hit other Indians in the crowd. The Indians retaliated with a hail of bullets and arrows. Almost half of the Cheyenne fled the agency to some hills south of the Canadian River. Lieutenant Colonel T.H. Neill, with one company of infantry, and cavalry troops pursued the Cheyenne. A fight began when the soldiers caught up to the Cheyenne. The fight continued until after sunset. The next day, eleven Indians were found dead. Nineteen Indians were wounded in the engagement. Most of the Cheyenne eventually returned to the agency. Another group of sixty to seventy Cheyenne, characterized as some of the worst criminal elements of the tribe by the army, fled north to the Platte River country.

1879: According to army records, Indians attacked the Sebezzo and Peterson Ranches near Powder River in Montana. One rancher was killed. The Indians were believed to be Gros Ventre from the Northwest Territory.

1880: Ninth Cavalry soldiers fought a group of Indians in Miembrillo Canyon in the San Andreas Mountains of New Mexico. According to army documents, Captain H. Carroll and seven soldiers were wounded. The fighting continued through April 9.

1974: The constitution of the Indians of the Tulalip Tribes in Washington was modified.

APRIL 7

1712: As a part of the Tuscarora War, on March 7 John Barnwell signed a treaty with the Tuscarora at their fort in the village of Catechna (near Grifton). He and a force of militia broke the treaty by attacking the fort.

1781: General Daniel Broadhead and 300 troops attacked a peaceful Delaware village at Coshocton, Ohio. The town was burned to the ground. After the fighting, the soldiers murdered fifteen prisoners, earning the Delaware Indians' wrath.

1788: Marietta, Ohio, was founded.

1830: President Jackson had submitted a bill that called for the removal of most of the Indians in the Southeast to lands west of the Mississippi. In a speech, U.S. Senator Theodore Frelinghuysen denounced the bill. He asked the Senate when was it ever proclaimed "that the right of discovery contained a superior efficacy to all prior titles?"

1864: Colonel John Chivington, commander of the District of Colorado, reported to his supervisor, Major General Samuel Curtis, that Cheyenne had stolen 175 cattle from a ranch on the Smokey Hill stage-coach route. An investigation conducted much later showed no proof that Indians were involved in any such activity.

1869: Captain E.W. Clift, commanding Thirteenth Infantry Companies D, F, and G, was on the Mussellshell River in Montana. They encountered some Indians, and a fight developed. One soldier and nine Indians were killed.

1873: In a Modoc council in the lava beds, Hooker Jim, Black Jim, Schonchin John, and others told Captain Jack that the peace commissioners were just buying time to bring in more soldiers. They said that the commissioners just wanted to trick the Modoc. They demanded that Captain Jack, as tribal chief, kill Commissioner General Canby during the peace conference. Captain Jack was against the idea, but he agreed to do so.

1876: According to a marker in the Fort Bowie cemetery in Arizona, O.O. Spence was killed by Indians.

Grave marker for O.O. Spence in Fort Bowie cemetery, Arizona (author photo)

1971: The commissioner of Indian affairs approved an election for an amendment to the constitution of the Pawnee Indians of Oklahoma.

1984: The first meeting between the Eastern and Western Cherokees since the 1800s was held.

APRIL 8

1665: According to some sources, a land-cession treaty was reached between representatives of the Narragansett Indians and the Massachusetts Colony.

1676: As a part of King Philip's War, 500 Indians attacked a force of fifty soldiers led by Captain Samuel Wadsworth near Sudbury, Massachusetts. Most sources said all of the English and more than 100 Indians were killed.

1756: Governor Robert Morris declared war on the Delaware and Shawnee Indians. As a part of his declaration, he offered the following cash bounties: prisoners: men over twelve = 150 Spanish pieces of eight, women or boys = 130; scalps:

Office and sutler store, Round Valley Agency, California (NA)

men = 130, women and boys = 50. The bounty on scalps led to the killing of many innocent Indians who were members of neither tribe. The legislation for this was called the Scalp Act. (Also recorded as happening on April 14.)

1864: Congress passed an act authorizing the establishment of four tracts of land in northern California for Indian reservations.

1873: Based on the congressional act of March 3, 1873, President Grant, by executive order, withdrew some of the land from the Round Valley Reserva-

Warm Springs Apache scouts (NA)

84

tion in Mendocino County, California. Established on March 30, 1870, the reservation was further modified on May 18, 1875, and July 26, 1876.

1880: Colonel Edward Hatch, with 400 troops of the Ninth Cavalry, sixty infantry troops, and seventy-five Indian scouts, attacked Victorio's fortified camp in Hembrillo Canyon in the San Andreas Mountains of New Mexico. According to the army report, Victorio's force included Warm Springs Apache, Mescalero, and Comanche. Three Indians were killed in the fighting. Captain Henry Carroll, Ninth Cavalry, and seven other soldiers were wounded. Twenty-five of the soldiers' horses and mules were killed.

Lt. Ernest Childers, a Creek Indian and Medal of Honor winner in World War II (US Army)

1944: Ernest Childers received the Medal of Honor.

1948: An order returning surplus or ceded lands on the Fort Berthold Reservation in North Dakota was modified, according to Federal Register No. 13FR02416.

1953: An official roll of the members of the Lac du Flambeau Band of Lake Superior Chippewa Indians of Wisconsin was taken.

1963: According to Federal Register No. 28FR03655, certain lands in the township of Parshall were returned to tribal ownership in the Fort Berthold Indian Reservation in South Dakota.

1977: Vincent Little, the acting area director of the Portland area office, Bureau of Indian Affairs, ratified an amendment to the constitution and bylaws for the Upper Skagit Indian Tribe.

APRIL 9

1682: The expedition of French and Indians under La Salle reached the mouth of the Mississippi River. Based on his expedition along the Mississippi from its confluence with the Illinois River, La Salle claimed the Mississippi Valley, and what became Louisiana, for the French.

1772: Whites could now buy Indian land in Oklahoma without government approval.

1830: After some "politicking," Greenwood le Flore was elected as chief of the Choctaw Nation during a "rump" council. Previously, there were three regional chiefs. Le Flore was in favor of selling the Choctaw lands and moving to Indian Territory (present-day Oklahoma). (Also recorded as happening on March 16.)

1862: As a part of the Owens Valley War in California, Colonel Evans led the cavalry up to the canyon where Bishop Creek flows from the Sierra Nevada. A large group of Paiute was suspected to be in the canyon. Fighting soon broke out. It appeared that only a small number of Paiute were there. They acted as a diversion while a larger group of Indians fled the area.

1865: According to some sources, the Black Hawk Indian War began in Manti, Sanpete County, Utah. It began as a dispute over cattle between some Ute and local Mormon settlers. Black Hawk, a young Ute warrior, eventually became the Indians' leader during the fighting.

1874: Lands in New Mexico Territory were withdrawn from public sale and set aside for whatever Indians the secretary of the interior felt

Black Hawk, Ute leader during the fighting in Utah (NA)

should be placed here. This area was called the Hot Springs Reserve.

1880: Captain Thomas Lebo and Troop K, Tenth Cavalry, attacked a band of Indians at Shakehand Spring, forty miles south of Penasco, Texas. During the fighting, the village chief was killed. Four women and one Indian child were captured. A Mexican boy named Coyetano Garcia, held prisoner by the Indians, was freed.

1880: Ninth Cavalry soldiers fought a group of Indians in Miembrillo Canyon in the San Andreas Mountains of New Mexico. According to army documents, Captain H. Carroll and seven soldiers were wounded. The fighting started on April 6. Also in the San Andreas Mountains, Sixth Cavalry soldiers and some Indian scouts fought a group of Indians near San Andreas Springs. According to army documents, no casualties were reported.

1884: A woman, identified by local missionaries as Sacajawea, died in Wyoming. If this was the

Sacajawea of the Lewis and Clark expedition, she would be almost 100 years old.

1954: The federal government set aside some lots of land on the Blackfeet Indian Reservation in Montana for administrative purposes.

1960: An election for amendments to the constitution of the Papago (Tohono O'odham) was held. The vote was 1,286–199 for approval.

1977: Stanley Speaks, area director of the Bureau of Indian Affairs, had authorized an election to approve an amendment to the constitution and bylaws for the Fort Sill Apache Tribe of Oklahoma. It was approved by a vote of 32–8.

Arapaho camp near Fort Dodge (NA)

APRIL 10

1671: According to some sources, a treaty of allegiance was reached between the Wampanoag Indians and the Plymouth Plantation. The Indians also agreed to surrender some arms.

1685: According to some sources, a treaty of friendship was reached between representatives of the Five Nations and the Maryland colonies.

1758: As of this date, British General John Forbes reported he had gathered 500 Indians at his fort in southwestern Pennsylvania (present-day Bedford). He hoped to make use of the Indians in his maneuvers against the French, but delays caused many of the Indians to leave.

1830: The first wagons appeared on the Oregon Trail.

1837: As part of the treaty signed on March 6, the Seminole were to report to Tampa Bay no later than this date for transport to the Indian Territory (present-day Oklahoma). Prior to this date, General Jesup reneged on one of the provisions of the treaty. He allowed whites to come among the Indians to seek out blacks who they claimed were runaway slaves. This made the Seminole doubt whether the United States would live up to the agreement. Many of the Seminole disappeared into the woods.

1838: The Republic of Texas signed a treaty with the Tonkawa (near modern Houston).

1861: The Nez Perce held a conference on gold-miner trading.

1865: Captain Henry Pierce, Eleventh Kansas Cavalry, established Fort Dodge (a few miles southeast of modern Dodge City, Kansas). The fort was designed to protect travelers on the Santa Fe Trail from hostile Indians. The fort was abandoned in 1882.

1867: According to army records, members of the Eighth Cavalry fought with a band of Indians in the Black Mountains of Arizona. Three Indians were reported killed.

1869: A congressional act of April 10, 1869, authorized the president to establish the Board of Indian Commissioners of up to ten people known for their intelligence and philanthropy. These positions were unpaid, and commissioners assisted in the control of Indian appropriations. The president formally established the board by executive order on June 3, 1869.

1871: Apache raided the San Xavier Mission south of Tucson and stole livestock.

1873: Hoping to avoid fulfilling his promise to kill General Canby, Captain Jack talked to his warriors in northern California. He told them that such an act would only kill them all. But when he asked his warriors to voice their opinion, only a few supported him. As a last resort, Captain Jack asked if they would let Canby live if he agreed to all of the Modoc's terms. To this, the warriors agreed.

1876: Sixth Cavalry soldiers fought some Indians in the San Jose Mountains near the Mexico border in Arizona. According to army documents, no casualties were reported.

1877: The Beaver Creek Council was held.

1879: The small group of eight Northern Cheyenne who were thrown out of Little Wolf's Band and attacked two soldiers on April 5, 1879, were captured by Sergeant Thomas Glover, ten men from the Troop B, Second Cavalry, and three Indian scouts from Fort Keogh. For his actions, Sergeant Glover would be awarded the Medal of Honor.

1883: Commissioner of Indian Affairs Hiram Price established the rules that established the Courts of Indian Offenses.

1947: The Kootenai Tribe of Idaho approved a constitution and bylaws by a vote of 24–2.

1969: According to Federal Register No. 34FR06583, Public Land Order No. 4593 was issued. It partially revoked Land Order No. 2198 issued on August 26, 1960.

1970: Assistant Secretary of the Interior Harrison Loesch approved a new constitution for the Pueblo of Isleta. It became effective.

1973: Chicago's Newberry Library dedicated a new center for the history of the American Indian.

APRIL 11

1713: This day marked the end of Queen Anne's War.

1832: Secretary of War Lewis Cass, after repeated inquiries and complaints, promised the Cherokees already in Indian Territory (present-day Oklahoma) to keep the government's promises made in the Treaty of May 6, 1828. The government had promised to provide funds or supplies for a printing press, a sawmill, a grist mill, and schools. None of these promises had been fulfilled yet.

1836: Lieutenant Joseph W. Harris and 407 friendly Seminole left Tampa Bay en route to the Indian Territory (present-day Oklahoma). They sustained considerable losses during their journey. They reached their new lands on June 5.

1859: The Quinault and Quileute Treaties signed on July 1, 1855, and January 25, 1856, were officially proclaimed by the president of the United States.

1862: Twenty members of the Alabama-Coushatta Tribe enlisted in the Confederate Army. One of them, John Scott, eventually became chief of the tribe.

1866: Soldiers from the First Arizona Infantry fought with a band of Indians between Forts Lincoln and Whipple in Arizona. The soldiers reported killing sixteen Indians.

1873: Captain Jack and several of his warriors arrived at the peace conference site between the lava beds and the soldiers' camp in northern California. The army was composed of soldiers from the First Cavalry, Twelfth and Twenty-First Infantry, Fourth Artillery, and some Indian scouts. A little before noon, General Canby, who convinced Manuelito and his Apache followers to sign a peace treaty, and his peace commissioners arrived at the meeting place. Canby said he wanted to help the Modoc find good land for a

Modoc chief Captain Jack shooting General Canby as they were negotiating peace during the Modoc War

reservation. Captain Jack told him he wanted land near the lava beds and Tule Lake. Captain Jack repeated his request for the soldiers to be removed before they continued talks. Angry words were then passed between Schonchin John, Hooker Jim, and commissioner Alfred Meacham. General Canby said that only the "Great Father in Washington" could order the soldiers to leave. Captain Jack, again, repeated his demands to be given lands nearby and to do it this date. Meacham told Canby to promise him the land. Captain Jack suddenly jumped up, pointed his pistol at Canby, and fired, mortally wounding Canby. Boston Charley shot and killed Commissioner Reverend Eleazar Thomas. The other commissioners escaped. Six soldiers were also killed. Two officers, thirteen soldiers, and two civilians were wounded during fighting that lasted until April 26.

1874: Indians fought with soldiers from the Sixth Cavalry near Bull Bear Creek in Indian Territory (present-day Oklahoma). According to army documents, no casualties were reported.

1881: Major David Brotherton reported the surrender of 135 hostile Sioux, including forty-five warriors and their weapons and horses, at Fort Buford in western North Dakota. Among the warriors was Lone Dog.

1892: By executive order, the Lake Traverse Reservation in Dakota was modified.

1968: The American Indian Civil Rights Act was passed.

1969: The acting assistant commissioner of Indian affairs authorized an election to amend the constitution and bylaws of the Oneida Tribe of Indians of Wisconsin. The election would be held on October 18, 1969.

1970: The residents of the Cold Spring Rancheria in Fresno County, California, adopted articles of association under the name of the Sycamore Valley Association.

1970: An act (84 Stat. 120) was passed by Congress to "provide [agricultural] loans to Indian tribes, and for other purposes."

1980: The commissioner of Indian affairs ratified a new constitution and bylaws for the Spokane Tribe of the Spokane Reservation in Wellpinit, Washington.

APRIL 12

1676: As a part of King Philip's War, 500 Indians attacked Sudbury, Massachusetts. Most of the settlers escaped into fortified structures. The Indians burned many of the outlying buildings. Hearing of the attack, three relief forces consisting of a total of approximately 100 men from Concord, Watertown, and Marlborough converged on the settlement. In one battle, the Indians started grass fires to strike at the Europeans. At least thirty whites were killed in the fighting, and much of the town was destroyed before the Indians withdrew.

1678: According to some sources, a peace treaty was signed in Casco (modern Portland), Maine. It required the Abenaki to release all of their prisoners and to pay an annual fine of corn to the local inhabitants.

1811: John Jacob Astor's people started building Astoria in what eventually became Oregon. Donald McDougal and David Stuart returned to the ship with Chief Comcomly of the Chinook and reported a better site for a post at a spot later named George Point.

1836: Since April 5, 1836, a blockhouse twelve miles from the mouth of the Withlacoochee had been staffed by Captain Holleman and fifty volunteers from the Florida militia. They were attacked by up to 1,000 Seminole warriors. The attack on the blockhouse continued for the next two months.

1844: Part of Texas was sold to the United States.

1870: By executive order, certain lands in Montana and Dakota Territory would be set aside for the Arickaree, Gros Ventre, and Mandan Tribes. Together the reservation would be known as the Fort Berthold Reservation.

1875: Sergeant Alchesay, Corporal Elsatsoosu, Kelsay, Kosoha, Machol, Nannasaddie, and Nantaje of the Indian scouts would be awarded the Medal of Honor for their service to the U.S. Army during "campaigns and engagements with Apache" during the winter of 1872–1873.

1881: One Bull arrived at Fort Buford as representative for Sitting Bull.

1886: Due to General George Crook making an agreement with Geronimo about his surrender terms that his supervisors would not honor, Geronimo did not surrender. This angered Washington, and Crook was replaced on this day by Nelson "Bear Coat" Miles. Miles eventually took a large force into the field to hunt down Geronimo and his twenty-four holdouts.

1893: The Ozette Reserve was established.

1944: In Wyoming, a small part of the Shoshone-Arapaho tribal lands on the Wind River Reservation that were ceded to the United States in 1905 was returned.

1960: According to the Arizona Law Enforcement Memorial, San Carlos Apache Tribal Chief of Police Dennis Titla was killed while on duty.

1964: The assistant secretary of the interior had authorized an election to approve an amendment to the constitution and bylaws of the Miccosukee Tribe of Indians of Florida. It passed 36–2.

1972: The deputy commissioner of Indian affairs authorized an election for an amendment to the constitution of the Minnesota Chippewa Tribe, consisting of the Chippewa Indians of the White Earth, Leech Lake, Fond du Lac, Bois Forte (Nett Lake), and Grand Portage Reservations.

1974: The Indian Financing Act (Public Law 93–262) was passed by Congress. It was intended to "provide capital on a reimbursable basis to help develop and utilize Indian resources, both physical and human, to a point where the Indians will fully exercise responsibility for the utilization and management of their own resources and where they will enjoy a standard of living from their own productive efforts comparable to that enjoyed by non-Indians

in neighboring communities." Another act (88 Stat. 78) was also passed to "provide for the taking into trust of certain lands within a reservation or approved tribal land consolidation area or where prior trust interests existed which is purchased by tribes or individuals with revolving loan funds. To permit the escheating of restricted estates or homestead on the public domain to the U.S. if an Indian dies intestate, with no heirs unless the Secretary determines that the land is within or adjacent to an Indian community and can be used for Indian purposes, then land will transfer to the U.S. in trust for the tribe. To require a mediator to be appointed to assist in negotiations for the settlement and partition of land of the Navajo and Hopi Tribes."

APRIL 13

1788: According to some sources, Tecumseh's older brother, Chiksika, was killed in a battle.

1846: The two Cherokee factions (old settlers and new emigrants) continued to feud over who had legal control of the Cherokee Nation. Based on appeals from the old settlers and the agreement of the Bureau of Indian Affairs, President James Polk asked Congress to approve the creation of separate reservations for the two sides. The new emigrants opposed the proposal. An agreement was reached by both sides on August 6, 1846.

1851: As a part of the Mariposa Indian Wars, California soldiers attacked a Chowchilla Indian village. Although much of the village was destroyed, most of the Indians escaped.

1871: Apache Indians made a raid near San Pedro, east of Tucson. Four whites were killed. Although most evidence indicated this was the work of Indians living in or near Mexico, some residents of Tucson blamed the raid on Eskiminzin's Aravaipa Apache near Camp Grant.

1875: In Montana, an additional tract of land was set aside by executive order for the existing reservation for the Gros Ventre, Piegan, Blood, and Blackfeet in Montana.

1876: Fourth Cavalry soldiers fought some Indians near Fort Sill, Indian Territory. According to army documents, six Indians were captured.

1878: Indian "hostages" were sent to school.

1940: The assistant secretary of the interior approved an election for amendments to the constitution of the Tuolumne Band of Me-Wok Indians of the Tuolumne Rancheria, the Kashia Band of Pomo Indians of the Stewarts Point Rancheria, and the Tule River Indian Tribe.

1946: Congress created the Indian Claims Commission, established to hear and decide claims made by Indians based on land losses from treaties.

1984: Jicarilla Apache Tribal Council Ordinance No. 84–0–235, titled the "Jicarilla Apache Environmental Protection Ordinance," went into effect.

1988: The constitution of the Indians of the Tulalip Tribes in Washington was modified.

APRIL 14

1524: Spaniards under Pedro de Alvarado were welcomed as they entered the Cakchiquel (Kaqchikel) Maya town of Iximche' (Guatemala).

1528: Panfilo de Narvaez, with four or five ships and 400–500 men, including Cabeza de Vaca, sighted land on the western coast of Florida. This was the first significant exploration of Florida.

1614: John Rolfe married Pocahontas.

1665: A deed for Indian land was registered in New England. It said, "articles of agreement, and a firme bargaine agreed and confirmed between the Sachem of Setaucet, Warawakmy by name."

1756: Governor Robert Morris declared war on the Delaware and Shawnee Indians. As a part of his declaration, he offered the following bounties: prisoners: men over 12 = 150 Spanish pieces of eight, women or boys = 130; scalps: men = 130, women and boys = 50. The bounty on scalps led to the killing of many innocent Indians who were members of neither tribe. The legislation for this was called the Scalp Act. (Also recorded as happening on April 8.)

1869: According to army records, members of the Thirty-Second Infantry fought with a band of Indians near Cienega, Arizona. Two soldiers were wounded.

1873: Three days after the murder of General Canby and Reverend Thomas, the army moved troops and artillery up to the Modoc's lava-bed fortress. When the soldiers rushed up on the stronghold, they discovered it to be abandoned. Using reservation Tenino Indians as scouts, the army began a search for Captain Jack and his people. The Modoc fought a brief battle with the Tenino, but they soon scattered to avoid the rapidly approaching army.

1874: Indians fought with soldiers from the Fifth Cavalry and some Indian scouts in the Pinal Mountains of Arizona. According to army documents, fourteen Indians were killed, and twenty-eight were captured in fighting that started on April 3.

1877: Expecting to be given a reservation in the Powder River area and to avoid General George "Three Stars" Crook, Touch the Clouds and many Minneconjou and Sans Arc surrendered at the Spotted Tail Agency in Nebraska. Although many of these people were from Crazy Horse's village, Crazy Horse would not surrender for a few weeks.

1883: Soldiers encountered a group of Indians near Beaver Creek, Montana. According to army documents, sixty-nine Indians were captured.

1945: An election approved Amendment 2 to the constitution and bylaws of the Lac du Flambeau Band of Lake Superior Chippewa Indians of Wisconsin.

1954: The assistant secretary of the interior had authorized an election for amendments to the constitution for the Omaha Tribe of Nebraska.

1973: The assistant secretary of the interior authorized an election for amendments to the constitution and bylaws for the Covelo Indian Community of the Round Valley Reservation in California. It took place on this day. The results were 37–11 in favor.

1976: The constitution of the Central Council of the Tlingit and Haida Indian Tribes of Alaska was amended.

1979: An amendment to the constitution of the Comanche Indian Tribe was enacted.

April 15

1614: Over the past six days, representatives of the British colony in Virginia and representatives of the Powhatan Confederacy had conferred. They agreed to a treaty of friendship and allegiance.

1715: Many European settlers had moved onto Yamassee lands without permission. The Yamassee had also been cheated by many traders. The British authorities had ignored almost all of the Yamassee complaints. Yamassee Indians attacked settlements near the southeastern Georgia–South Carolina border. Several hundred settlers were killed. Among the dead were Indian agent Thomas Naire and trader William Bray, who had been engaged in a conference at the Indian village of Pocotaligo. Bray had settled, without permission, on Yamassee lands and established a trading post. After amassing debts that the Indians could not pay, Bray suggested the Yamassee pay their debts by giving him slaves from other Indian tribes. This slave trade—and Bray's habit of capturing Indians and selling them as slaves—was a significant factor in the war.

1777: American settlers in Boonesborough survived an attack by the Shawnees. The fortifications of the town proved to be too much for the Indians to surmount. The Shawnees tried again on July 4, 1777.

1834: Lieutenant Joseph Harris was leading 500–600 Cherokees to Indian Territory (present-day Oklahoma). They had reached the confluence of the Arkansas and Cadron Rivers, about twenty-five miles northwest of Little Rock. The river was very low, so they were making no headway in their boats. The Cherokees got off the boats to wait for the river to rise or, for the impatient, to travel overland. Among those waiting for the river to rise, a virulent form of cholera struck. As many as a dozen Indians would die each day for several days. Eventually, they started moving overland toward Indian Territory. They reached their new lands on May 8.

1836: Captain Holleman and his four dozen Florida militia volunteers were still under siege in a small blockhouse twelve miles from the mouth of the Withlacoochee River. They saw the second major attack by almost 1,000 Seminole since they occupied the site on April 5, 1836. During the fighting, the militia killed a significant number of the Seminole warriors, including at least one chief. One story among the Seminole was that the defenders were using magic to defend themselves. Unfortunately for the soldiers, when the remainder of their volunteer militia unit was disbanded, this outpost was forgotten. It was June before a rescue was organized and reached the outpost. Five militiamen, including Captain Holleman, were killed before the relief column rescued them.

1846: The treaty of January 14, 1846, between the United States and the Kansa Indians of Kansas was ratified by the U.S. Senate.

1859: The Winnebago signed a treaty (12 Stat. 1101) regarding reservation lands.

1859: Traditional full-blood and mixed-blood Cherokees organized the Keetoowah Society.

1866: After serving as an outpost on the mountain branch of the Santa Fe Trail in Hamilton County, Kansas, for many months, Fort Aubrey was abandoned. With the cessation of the "Indian troubles" in the area, the army closed the fort located between modern Kendall and Syracuse, Kansas.

1867: According to army records, members of the Seventh Cavalry fought with a band of Indians near Fort Lyon, Colorado. One soldier was reported wounded in the encounter.

1873: The Indian peace policy was explained in an open letter from Secretary Delano to L.L. Crounse. It had five major provisions: (1) put the

Indians on reservations as soon as possible where they could be provided for; (2) punish Indians who were unwilling to go onto the reservations and who fought until they were willing to go and live peacefully; (3) furnish supplies at fair prices; (4) appoint "competent, upright, moral, and religious" agents; and (5) establish regular schools and Sunday schools so Indians could become citizens.

1879: On February 13, 1879, Victorio and twenty-two Warm Springs Apache Indians surrendered to Lieutenant Charles Merritt at Ojo Caliente, New Mexico. Eventually, thirty-nine Apache came into the camp in west-central New Mexico. With fears of being sent to a reservation, Victorio led all of the Indians on an escape from Ojo Caliente to return to Mexico.

1880: Settlers fought a group of Indians near Pato Springs, New Mexico. According to army documents, one citizen was killed.

1885: Under the Treaty of Fort Laramie, many of the lands allocated to the Santee Sioux were required to be divided into individual plots. By executive order, this date was the deadline for that requirement. All unclaimed plots became available for public sale on May 15, 1885. A total of 72,000 acres were eventually divided into 853 plots.

1892: A land rush took place on the Sisseton Reservation.

1940: The Miami of Oklahoma Corporation was chartered.

1964: An election to amend the constitution of the Yerington Paiute Tribe of Nevada was held. The voting members approved the amendment.

APRIL 16

1519: According to some sources, after landing on the Mexican mainland Hernán Cortés and his army started their travels toward Tenochtitlán (modern Mexico City).

1528: Panfilo de Narvaez sighted Indian houses near Tampa Bay, Florida. He anchored his boats in the area. Seeing Narvaez, the Indians aban-

Hernán Cortés, leader of the Spanish conquistadors

doned their village. Narvaez held Spanish royal title to the land between the Rio de Las Palmas and the Cape of Florida.

1550: King Charles V ordered a stop to Indian land conquests.

1605: Spanish explorer Don Juan de Oñate stopped at a popular Spanish camping area in western New Mexico. At the base of a cliff, he carved a message about his discovery of the "Southern Sea." Others would also carve messages on the rock over the years. It would eventually become called Inscription Rock.

1754: With a force of 1,000 French and Indians, Captain Contrecoeur demanded the surrender of Fort Trent on the Ohio River. The unfinished fort was defended by forty militia, and they promptly surrendered. This was one of the first actions of the French and Indian War. The French completed the fort and named it Fort Dusquesne. It was later called Fort Pitt. (Also recorded as happening on April 18.)

1806: William Clark spent the night at a Skiloot village.

1813: Creek leaders, including Tustunnuggee Thlucco, and local Europeans finish executing members of the Red Stick Creek faction believed to be involved in the unprovoked murders of European settlers. Between April 16 and this date they had executed eleven Creek. The Red Stick Creek had been motivated by the teachings of Tecumseh.

1856: The Mendocino Reserve, 25,000 acres of land northwest of Clear Lake in California, was established.

1867: According to army records, members of the Eighth Cavalry fought with a band of Indians in the Black Mountains of Arizona. Twenty Indians were reported killed.

1869: Outside Fort Wallace in west-central Kansas, an officer and his escort encountered some Indians. The Indians chased the soldiers until they reached safety at the fort. No one was injured on either side.

1874: Louis Riel was expelled from the Canadian House of Commons.

1877: Sitting Bull reached the Milk River big bend on his trip to Canada.

1880: Colonels Edward Hatch and Benjamin Grierson and their troops arrived at the Mescalero Agency on the Fort Stanton Reservation in eastern New Mexico. An effort to disarm the Indians, and to take their horses, led to bloodshed. Ten warriors were killed while trying to escape. Forty warriors successfully fled the agency. Some 250 Indian men, women, and children were held in the agency. Also, 200 horses and mules and two dozen guns were seized. Troops pursuing the escaping Indians engaged in fights at Dog Canyon other locations. Four Indians died in these engagements. Ninth Cavalry and Fifteenth Infantry soldiers under Captain Charles Steelhammer encountered a group of Indians near "South Fork, New Mexico." According to army documents, one Indian was killed and 300 were captured. Also in New Mexico, the Ninth and Tenth Cavalries and the Twenty-Fifth Infantry skirmished with some Indians. Ten Indians died in the fighting.

1914: The federal government extended the trust period on all allotments of the Sisseton and Wahpeton Bands of Sioux Indians in Dakota.

1928: Executive Order No. 4858 dealing with the trust period for the Prairie Band of Potawatomi Indians in Kansas was modified.

1934: The Johnson-O'Malley Act passed. It provided the secretary of the interior with the authority to arrange with the states or territories for the education, medical attention, agriculture assistance, relief of distress, and social welfare of the Indians and for other purposes.

1987: The constitution of the Central Council of the Tlingit and Haida Indian Tribes of Alaska was amended.

APRIL 17

1528: Panfilo de Narvaez began his exploration of Florida by coming ashore near Tampa Bay. He visited an Indian house that was big enough to hold 300 people, in his opinion. He also found a "rattle" made of gold in the abandoned house. This discovery of gold spurred Narvaez onward across Florida.

1680: Born at a site near what is modern Auriesville, New York, in 1656, Tekawitha was the niece of a Mohawk chief who raised her after her parents died. She eventually met a Jesuit missionary who baptized her as Kateri (Catherine). She was shunned by her Mohawk tribe, and she moved to a village of Iroquois Indians in 1677. It was at this time that she became a Catholic nun, the first of her tribe to did so. She died on this day. Many cures were attributed to prayers made in her name. She was recommended for canonization in 1844, and she was beatified in 1980.

1766: The Proclamation of 1763, which set aside lands west of the Appalachian Mountains for Indians, was overturned.

1818: Jackson set out for Florida to fight the Seminole.

1824: Russia agreed to the 54–40' boundary with the United States.

1868: According to army records, members of the Twenty-Third Infantry fought with a band of

Indians at Camp Three Forks near the Owyhee River in Oregon. Five Indians were reported killed, and three were captured.

1868: Army troops from H Troop, Third Cavalry, under command of Sergeant Glass skirmished with Indians near Tularosa, New Mexico. The troopers reported one soldier and five civilians wounded, ten Indians killed, and twenty-five Indians wounded.

1872: Indians skirmished with a group of soldiers from the Twenty-First Infantry near Camp Apache, Arizona, according to official army records. One soldier was killed.

1879: Lieutenant Samuel Loder, sixteen soldiers of the Third and Seventh Infantries, and six Indian scouts were following a band of renegade Sioux in Montana. Near Careless Creek, at Musselshell Canyon, the two groups met and fought. Eight Sioux were killed. Two scouts were killed, and one was wounded.

1880: Sixth and Ninth Cavalry soldiers and some Indian scouts fought a group of Indians near Dog Canyon, New Mexico. According to army documents, three Indians were killed.

1881: One Bull arrived back at Sitting Bull's camp with a report on fort conditions.

1937: As a part of the Indian Re-Organization Act, the Shoshone-Bannock Tribes became a federally chartered corporation.

1940: The Shoshone and Arapaho Tribes of the Wind River Reservation in Wyoming ceded a large part of their reservation to the United States in 1905. They received a small part of that land back, according to Federal Register No. 5FR01805.

1942: An election for a constitution and bylaws for the Moapa Band of Paiute Indians on March 15 was ratified by Assistant Secretary of the Interior Oscar Chapman.

1950: The U.S. government ratified the addition of Amendment 1 to the constitution and bylaws of the Swinomish Indians of the Swinomish Reservation in Washington.

1973: The constitution of the Central Council of the Tlingit and Haida Indian Tribes of Alaska was amended.

1990: The Supreme Court ruled on the use of peyote by the Native American Church.

1991: The Pueblo of Acoma adopted an Emergency Response Plan for hazardous materials releases.

April 18

1528: Panfilo de Narvaez claimed Florida for Spain. He had just landed on the western coast of Florida.

1637: The Massachusetts General Court authorized a tax to generate money to cover the costs of a war against the Pequot.

1644: Forces under ninety-nine-year-old Opechancanough, a leader of the Powhatan Confederacy, attacked the English along the Pamunkey and York Rivers, twenty-two years after his first attack at Jamestown. His followers killed almost 400 Virginia colonists.

1754: With a force of 1,000 French and Indians, Captain Contrecoeur demanded the surrender of Fort Trent on the Ohio River. The unfinished fort was defended by forty militia, and they promptly surrendered. This was one of the first actions of the French and Indian War. The French completed the fort and named it Fort Dusquesne. It was later called Fort Pitt. (Also recorded as happening on April 16.)

1838: Although being held captive in Fort Peck in New Orleans, former Red Stick Creek and now Seminole Chief Jumper (Ote Emathla) died of "consumption." Jumper was en route to the Seminole's territory in Oklahoma.

1855: The Nez Perce raise a U.S. flag at Lapwai.

1856: On April 4, according to a report written by Lieutenant Philip Sheridan, six Vancouver Indians were murdered near Sheridan's fort in the Lower Cascades, Washington Territory. The murders were reported to have been committed by six well-armed settlers seen following the Indians. The victims, including a three-year-old boy, were family members of Chief Spencer. Sheridan buried the six Indians.

1867: According to army records, members of the Eighth Cavalry fought with a band of Indians on the Rio Verde in Arizona. One soldier was reported killed, and one was wounded. Thirty Indians were killed.

1878: According to a report by the army commander at San Diego, Texas, Indians killed one man at Rancho Soledad, a man and a woman near Rancho Soledad, and a man at Charco Escondido, Duval County.

1879: After the Custer disaster at Little Bighorn, the U.S. government decided to punish the Plains Indians. Although the Ponca had no part in the Custer battle, they had erroneously been placed in a reservation with the Sioux. When it was decided to force the Sioux to go to Indian Territory (present-day Oklahoma), the Ponca were ordered to go as well. Many Ponca started to walk back to their old reservation from Indian Territory. Eventually, General George Crook sympathized with the Ponca and one of their chiefs, Standing Bear. Seeking public support to avoid being ordered to send Standing Bear back to Indian Territory, General Crook contacted the press about the Ponca plight. Many editorials were written in support of the Ponca, and several lawyers volunteered their services for free. Judge Elmer Dundy, with Crook's blessing, issued a writ of habeas corpus to the general to produce the Ponca and show why he was holding them. A U.S. district attorney argued that the Ponca could not be served a writ because they had no legal standing, or were not recognized as people, under the law. On this day the trial began to determine if Indians, and particularly Standing Bear, were people under U.S. laws and could enjoy constitutional rights and privileges. The judge eventually ruled that Standing Bear was indeed a person and could not be ordered to a reservation against his will. Although this decision seemed to

Arapaho ghost dance

prevent keeping any Indians on any particular reservation against their will, the eventual course of the U.S. government was to say that the ruling applied only to Standing Bear and to no one else.

1881: Sitting Bull confronted a group of Cree at the police compound.

1881: Lieutenant Colonel J.N.G. Whistler reported the surrender of forty-seven Sioux men, thirty-nine women, twenty-five boys, and forty-five girls at Fort Keogh in east-central Montana. They turned in thirty-two lodges, fifty-seven horses, and nineteen guns of various types.

1892: The last formal ghost dance was held in Oklahoma.

1936: An election to adopt a constitution and bylaws for the Makah Indian Tribe of the Makah Indian Reservation in Washington was held. It passed by a vote of 58–15.

1971: Acting Associate Commissioner of Indian Affairs Eugene Suarez Sr. had authorized an election for an amendment to the constitution and bylaws of the Paiute-Shoshone Tribe of the Fallon Reservation and Colony. It would be held on June 22, 1971.

1981: Navajo and Hopi lands were divided by the government.

1985: President Ronald Reagan signed House Bill 730, which increased the size of the Cocopah Indian Reservation. The reservation, south of Yuma, Arizona, increased from 1,772 to 6,009 acres.

1987: The rules for the election of delegates to the Official Central Council of the Tlingit and Haida Indian Tribes of Alaska were amended.

APRIL 19

511: Maya royalty "Lady of Tikal" was named a Queen in Tikal, Guatemala.

1519: Shortly after arriving in Mexico, Hernán Cortés met with a representative of Montezuma in the Yucatan. The representative, Teudile, delivered Montezuma's best wishes and some gifts. Cortés said he represented the ruler of most of the world (the king of Spain). He demonstrated the might of his soldiers. Teudile was impressed by the power of the conquistadors. (Also recorded as happening on April 20.)

1735: A force of eighty French and more than 200 Indian warriors started a four-day attack on a Sac and Fox village on the Mississippi River near the Des Moines River. The expedition, led by Captain Nicolas de Noyelles, was not prepared for siege warfare and abandoned the attack.

1746: French and Indian warriors attacked Fort Number 4 on the Connecticut River (near modern Charlestown, New Hampshire). This attack, and several others in the months to follow, proved unsuccessful.

1786: Near Louisville, Kentucky, the Chickamauga had been attacking local settlements. Militia Colonel William Christian, with twenty men, crossed the Ohio River to find the Indian warriors. They came across a war party led by Chief Black Wolf. During the fighting, both Black Wolf and Christian were killed.

1842: Miccosukee Seminole Hallack Tustenuggee was chief of one of the last groups of Seminole still fighting U.S. forces. His band engaged 400 soldiers under Colonel William Worth at Peliklakaha Hammock near Lake Ahapopka, Florida.

Leaving their provisions behind, many of the Seminole escaped. Many historians consider this to be the last major battle of the Second Seminole War.

1858: The Yankton Sioux signed a treaty (11 Stat. 743) in Washington, D.C. Article 8 provided for the Indians to retain access and use of the red pipestone quarry in southwestern Minnesota.

1859: Fort Mohave was established to "protect" the area from the Mohave and the Paiutes.

1867: According to army records, members of the Seventh Cavalry fought with a band of Indians near Cimarron Crossing, Kansas. One soldier was wounded and six Indians were reported killed.

1871: This day marked the start of a series of raids by the Kiowa near Fort Richardson in north-central Texas. The Kiowa ambushed numerous settlers and travelers in the Salt Creek prairie between Fort Richardson and Fort Belknap. The Kiowa were led by Mamanti, Satank, Satanta, Big Tree, Eagle Heart, and others.

1881: Sitting Bull broke camp at Wood Mountain.

1882: Another fight in the Apache resistance took place against Colonel Forsythe.

1883: Second Cavalry soldiers fought a group of Indians at Wild Horse Lake in Montana near the Canadian border. According to army documents, two Indians were killed.

1884: The Indian Act was amended to outlaw the Potlatch ceremony practiced by many Northwest Coast Indians. This prohibition remains in effect until 1951.

1949: A resolution was passed that established a roll of the members of the United Keetoowah Band of Cherokee Indians in Oklahoma.

1954: An election for an amended constitution and bylaws for the San Carlos Apache Tribe was ratified by Secretary of the Interior Douglas McKay. The election had been held on February 23–24, 1954.

1975: An election for amendments to the constitution for the Shoalwater Bay Indian Organization in Washington State was held. They were approved by votes of 14–5, 12–7, and 17–2.

1977: An election was authorized to approve an amendment to the constitution and bylaws for the Lower Sioux Indian Community of Minnesota by the area director of the Bureau of Indian Affairs. The election would be held on June 20, 1977.

1991: Mississippi Choctaw voted on a dump.

Every: Northern Pueblos' spring art show.

APRIL 20

1519: Shortly after arriving in Mexico, Hernán Cortés met with a representative of Montezuma in the Yucatan. The representative, Teudile, delivered Montezuma's best wishes and some gifts. Cortés said he represented the ruler of most of the world (the king of Spain). He demonstrated the might of his soldiers. Teudile was impressed by the power of the conquistadors. (Also recorded as happening on April 19.)

1537: Hernando de Soto received royal permission to "conquer, pacify, and people" the land from Rio de la Palmas to Cape Fear (Florida) on the Atlantic.

1598: The entire expedition lead by Juan de Oñate reached El Rio del Norte or the Rio Grande (south of modern El Paso, Texas).

1606: According to the first charter of Virginia, part of the colonists' goals were to civilize the natives "and may in time bring the infidels and savages, living in those parts, to human civility."

1769: According to some reports, Pontiac was killed by a Kaskaskia warrior in St. Louis. Pontiac, an Ottawa chief, was best known for the 1763 uprising that bears his name.

1865: As a part of the investigation into the Sand Creek Massacre (November 29, 1864), Lieutenant James Olney appeared before the commission at Fort Lyon, Colorado. He testified he witnessed a specific incident of brutality. "Three squaws and five children, prisoners in charge of some soldiers; that, while they were being conducted along, they were approached by Lieutenant Harry Richmond, of the third Colorado cavalry; that Lieutenant Richmond thereupon immediately killed and scalped the three women and the five children while they [prisoners] were screaming for mercy; while the soldiers in whose charge the prisoners were shrank back, apparently aghast."

1869: According to army records, members of the Thirty-Second Infantry fought with a band of Indians near Camp Crittenden, Arizona. One soldier was killed.

1872: Captain Michael Cooney and Troops A and H, Ninth Cavalry, attacked a group of hostile Indians near Howard's Well in Texas. Six Indians and Lieutenant F.R. Vincent were killed in the fighting.

1877: The Nez Perce attended a conference at Fort Walla Walla on this day and the next day.

1877: Settlers fought a group of Indians near Fort Clark, Texas. According to army documents, three settlers were killed. The fighting lasted until April 22.

1880: Tenth Cavalry soldiers fought a group of Indians in the Sacramento Mountains of New Mexico. According to army documents, one Indian was killed.

1882: Sixth Cavalry soldiers fought a group of Indians near Fort Thomas, Arizona. According to army documents, one Indian was wounded.

1936: A constitution and bylaws for the Shoshone-Paiute Tribes of the Duck Valley Reservation in Nevada was approved by Secretary of the Interior Harold Ickes.

1960: The assistant secretary of the interior authorized an election for an amendment to the constitution and bylaws of the Lower Brule Sioux Tribe of the Lower Brule Reservation. The election would be held on June 14, 1960.

1960: An amended constitution and bylaws were submitted for ratification by the members of the Northern Cheyenne Tribe of the Northern Cheyenne Indian Reservation in Montana. It would be approved by a vote of 273–67.

1966: Assistant Secretary of the Interior Harry Anderson authorized an election for amendments to the constitution and bylaws of the Lac Courte Oreilles Band of Lake Superior Chippewa Indians of Wisconsin. The election would be held on September 3, 1966.

1974: The acting deputy commissioner of Indian affairs had authorized an election to approve an amendment to the constitution of the Grindstone Indian Rancheria in Glenn County, California. The amendment was approved by a vote of 14–3.

1988: The Termination Resolution of 1953, whereby Congress ended the federal trust relationship with certain tribes, was repealed.

APRIL 21

1806: The Department of War established the office of superintendent of Indian trade, a position appointed by the president. The job entailed the purchase of goods for and from the Indians.

1806: Congress passed "An Act for Establishing Trading Houses with the Indian Tribes" and "An Act Making Appropriations for Carrying into Effect Certain Indian Treaties."

1864: Based on a congressional act of April 8, 1864, Austin Wiley, superintendent of Indian affairs for the state of California, proclaimed the proposed establishment of the Hoopa Valley Reserve on the Trinity River. It was located in Klamath County, California, and settlers were advised not to make further improvements to their properties or to move into the area. This proposal required presidential approval.

1865: After the killing of Mangas at Fort McLane in southwestern New Mexico in January 1863, Cochise vowed revenge. They began a series of raids throughout Arizona and New Mexico. On this day, Victorio and Nana met with a U.S. government agent. They told him that they wished for peace between the two peoples. The agent said the only way the Apache could have peace was to go to the Bosque Redondo Reservation and surrender. Victorio asked to meet the agent again in a few days, when he started his trek to the reservation.

1868: According to army records, members of the Eighth Cavalry fought with a band of Indians near Camp Grant, Arizona. Two Indians were reported killed.

1868: According to army records, a settler was killed in a fight with a band of Indians near the Upper Yellowstone River in Montana.

1869: Donehogawa (Ely Samuel Parker) was the first Indian appointed to be commissioner of Indian affairs. Donehogawa, a Seneca Iroquois, was trained as a lawyer and a civil engineer. Unable to find work in the white world, Donehogawa contacted his old friend, Ulysses Grant. Grant made him an aide, and they worked together through much of the Civil War. Because of his excellent penmanship, Donehogawa drew up the surrender papers that Confederate General Robert E. Lee signed at Appomattox to end the war. Promoted to brigadier general, Ely Parker worked to settle many conflicts between whites and Indians. After Grant became president, he was appointed as Indian Commissioner on this day.

1874: Indians fought with soldiers from the Fifth Cavalry around the Bill Williams Mountains in Arizona. According to army documents, three Indians were killed during this engagement, which started on February 20.

1904: "White lands" were bought for the Yavapai Reserve.

1936: Lands within the Flathead Indian Reservation in Montana had been set aside to establish the townsite of Blue Bay. As listed in Federal Register No. 1FR00666, "undisposed of" land within the townsite of Blue Bay was returned to tribal ownership.

1938: In an election a constitution and bylaws for the Tonkawa Tribe of Indians of Oklahoma was approved by a vote of 9–7.

APRIL 22

1758: According to some reports, a land-settlement agreement was reached by representatives of the British and the Creek.

1800: Congress passed "An Act Supplementary to the Act to Regulate Trade and Intercourse with the Indian Tribes, and to Preserve Peace on the Frontiers."

1836: Two treaties (7 Stat. 500) were concluded with the Potawatomi.

1839: General Alexander Macomb, the new military commander in Florida, met with several Seminole chiefs, including Chitto and Hallack Tustenuggee. The council agreed that the Seminole could remain in Florida if they stayed near Lake Okeechobee.

1847: Punnubbee and 342 Choctaws from six towns in Mississippi arrived at Fort Towson in southeastern Indian Territory (present-day Oklahoma).

1866: Soldiers from the First Cavalry, Fifth Infantry, and the First New Mexico Cavalry fought with a band of Indians in the Canyon de Chelly in Arizona. Captain Edmond Butler reported killing twenty six Indians, wounding thirty, and capturing nine.

1868: According to army records, ranchers fought with a band of Indians near Fort McPherson, Nebraska. Six civilians were killed.

1869: An army scouting party caught up to a band of hostile Indians in Sangre Canyon, New Mexico. When the shooting was over, five Indians were wounded; the army recovered nineteen stolen horses and a stolen check for $500.

1877: Settlers fought a group of Indians near Fort Clark, Texas. According to army documents, three settlers were killed. The fighting started on April 20.

1877: Two Moons, Hump, and 300 other Indians surrender to Colonel Nelson Miles. Most of the rest of Crazy Horse's followers surrender on May 6, 1877, at the Red Cloud and Spotted Tail Agencies.

1879: Crow Indian scouts caught, and attacked, Indians who stole a herd of horses from Countryman's Ranch on April 3, 1879. One of the hostiles was killed.

1889: The Oklahoma land rush began.

1953: An adoption ordinance for the Coeur d'Alene Tribe had been passed by the tribal council. It was approved by the assistant secretary of the interior.

1972: The deputy commissioner of Indian affairs had authorized an election to approve amendments to the constitution and bylaws of the Cree Tribe of the Rocky Boy's Reservation in Montana. The election was held, and three amendments were approved.

1978: Non-Indians were not allowed on the Fort Hall Reservation as of this date.

1999: The Mi'kmaq Education Act became law in Canada. It allowed local tribes to control certain aspects of their educational institutions.

APRIL 23

1520: An expedition under Panfilo de Narvaez landed at what would eventually become Vera Cruz, Mexico. Narvaez represented a Spanish faction that hoped to arrest Hernán Cortés and remove him from Mexico.

1637: Wongunk Chief Sequin gave settlers the land on which to establish the village of Wethersfield, north from Saybrook on the Connecticut River. After he was ordered out of the area—even though he was promised protection as a part of the agreement—he led an attack on the settlement. With the help of 200 Pequot warriors, Sequin's force killed nine settlers and took two more

William Penn, founder of Pennsylvania colony and the city of Philadelphia

hostage. Other sources said the fighting was because settlers took the land from Indian Sachem Sowheag even though they had promised him he could live there.

1662: The Charter of Connecticut was issued.

1701: William Penn signed the Articles of Agreement (a treaty of friendship) at Philadelphia with representatives of the Susquehanna, Shawnee, Ganawese, and Iroquois. All parties agreed to act peaceably with each other.

1786: Creek chiefs agreed to remove squatters.

1835: After the end of the First Seminole War, many Seminole had refused to leave Florida. A conference was held between almost two dozen Seminole chiefs and General Duncan Clinch. Clinch told the Indians they would be forced to leave Florida if they did not leave voluntarily as required by the Treaty of Payne's Landing.

1836: The Wyandot signed a treaty (7 Stat. 502) that reduced their total land holdings to 109,144 acres in Ohio.

1838: During the Second Seminole War, many Indians fought on the side of the U.S. forces. Service for members of Richard's Company of Friendly Indians ended.

1850: Thousands of prospectors were flooding into California. Quechan attacked a ferry that transported the goldseekers across the Colorado River. This attack would lead to the eventual construction of Fort Yuma.

1865: Victorio agreed to met with the agent on this day and to begin his trip to the Bosque Redondo Reservation. But Victorio did not attend the meeting or start out for the reservation.

1868: According to army records, Indian scouts fought with a band of Indians near Camp Hearny, Oregon. One Indian was reported killed.

1868: According to army records, a settler was killed in a fight with a band of Indians near Fort Ellis, Montana.

1874: Indians fought with soldiers from the Seventh Cavalry near Fort Abraham Lincoln, Dakota Territory. According to army documents, one Indian was wounded.

1875: President Grant issued an executive order revoking the Camp Verde Indian Reservation in Arizona Territory. The land returned to the public domain.

1875: The group of Southern Cheyenne who fled north toward the Platte River country after the fight at their agency in Indian Territory (present-day Oklahoma; see April 6, 1875) were discovered by Lieutenant Austin Henely and forty troopers from the Sixth Cavalry. The troopers flanked twenty-seven of the warriors on the north fork of Sappa Creek, southeast of Fort Wallace, in western Kansas. The Indians were ordered to surrender, but they refused. When the shooting was over, nineteen Indians and two troopers were killed. Two chiefs and a medicine man were among the dead. About 125 horses were seized, and the Indians' lodges were burned. The rest of the Cheyenne escaped. The army would issue Congressional Medals of Honor to the following soldiers: Private James F. Ayers, Company H, for "rapid pursuit, gallantry, energy and enterprise"; trumpeter Michael Dawson, Company H, for "gallantry in action"; Sergeants Frederick Platten and

Richard Tea and Privates Peter W. Gardiner, Simpson Hornaday, James Lowthers, and Marcus Robbins, Company H, for their efforts in breaking the Cheyenne resistance by wading in mud and water through a creek to come up behind an entrenched Cheyenne position.

1882: Lieutenant David McDonald, six Fourth Cavalry troopers, and six Indian scouts were attacked by a large group of Chiricahua Apache, led by Loco, twenty miles south of Stein's Pass, Arizona. Four of the scouts were killed, but one managed to escape in order to get help. Lieutenant Colonel George Forsyth and Troops C, F, G, H, and M, Fourth Cavalry, rode to Lieutenant Mc-Donald's rescue. The soldiers chased the Apache into Horseshoe Canyon, New Mexico. After a fight here, the Indians scattered. The army estimated thirteen Indians were killed in the fighting. For their actions in rescuing an injured soldier during the fighting at Horseshoe Canyon, First Lieutenant Wilber Wilder and wagoner John Schnitzer, Troop G, would be awarded the Medal of Honor. Lieutenant J.W. Martin and six soldiers were wounded.

1897: Congress had created the Dawes Commission in 1893. One of its primary duties was to bring about the breakup of the reservations in Indian Territory (present-day Oklahoma). The method was to allot individual tribal members a certain amount of land each. The remaining lands were opened up to white settlers. The commission reached an agreement with the Choctaws and the Chickasaws to these ends.

1936: The secretary of the interior authorized an election to approve a constitution and bylaws for the members of the Minnesota Mdewakanton Sioux of the Prairie Island Indian Community in Minnesota. It would be held on May 23, 1936.

1937: A federal corporation charter was issued for three affiliated tribes.

1966: A constitution and bylaws of the Shoshone-Paiute Tribes of the Duck Valley Reservation in Nevada were approved.

APRIL 24

1754: Delaware Chief Teedyuscung led a group of seventy Christian Indians out of the village of Gnadenhuetten. They left to live in the village of Wyoming, Pennsylvania.

1802: The state of Georgia ceded its western lands to the United States, with the proviso that the federal government obtain the title to Indian lands as soon as "can be peaceably obtained on reasonable terms."

1806: The Wyandot Treaty of July 4, 1805, and the Delaware Treaty of August 21, 1805, were publicly proclaimed.

1820: The price for government land went down.

1838: In the swamps of Florida, Colonel William Harney, leading a force of 100 soldiers, attacked the Mikasuki Seminole camp of seventy-year-old Chief Sam Jones. Although the plan was to kill or capture Jones, he managed to escape. Only one Seminole was killed in the fighting.

1867: According to army records, members of the Eighth Cavalry and Fourteenth Infantry fought with a band of Indians near Fort Mojave, Arizona. Five Indians were killed, and five were wounded.

1885: The Fish Creek Fight took place between Canadian forces under Major General Frederick Dobson Middleton and 150 Metis under Gabriel Dumont. This was one of the more significant fights of Riel's Rebellion.

1943: An election approved Amendment 3 to the constitution and bylaws of the Lac du Flambeau Band of Lake Superior Chippewa Indians of Wisconsin.

1948: An election on proposed Amendment 3 to the constitution and bylaws of the Confederated Tribes of the Warm Springs Reservation of Oregon was held. The amendment passed on a vote of 199–34.

1959: A modification to the constitution of the Indians of the Tulalip Tribes in Washington was approved by the U.S. government.

1959: A constitution and bylaws were approved for the Standing Rock Sioux Tribe.

1971: This day was the end of a three-day tribal chairmen's conference in Pierre, South Dakota. Eighteen leaders from the National Tribal Chairman's Association met to assure representation for all federally recognized tribes, with and without reservations.

1973: The area director, Bureau of Indian Affairs, ratified an election that approved an amendment to the constitution and bylaws of the Coeur d'Alene Tribe. The election was held on November 18, 1972.

April 25

1541: Coronado left Alcanfor en route to Quivira. While in Quivira, Coronado killed many of the inhabitants of Tiguex Pueblo.

1704: Indians attacked Wells, Maine. Most of the settlers escaped to fortified homes, but two were killed and one captured.

1774: Michael Cresap was one of many "frontiersmen" in Kentucky who wished to instigate a war with the local Indians. He hoped the Indians would lose the war and be forced off their highly coveted lands. Cresap and a few friends came across a Shawnee and a Delaware Indian traveling through the woods. Cresap's group killed them both.

1839: Abraham, a former slave to the Seminole and later freed and elevated to "Sense Bearer," or counselor, and his family were shipped to Oklahoma. During his lifetime, he was an interpreter and a warrior. He also influenced other blacks to flee from their owners and to join the growing band of black Seminole.

1870: According to official army records, Indians skirmished with a group of soldiers from the Ninth Cavalry near Crow Springs, Texas. No casualties were reported.

1873: Indians met with soldiers from the First Cavalry and the Twenty-Third Infantry near

Canyon Creek in Arizona, according to army documents. Del Chey and his band surrendered.

1875: Indians fought with "Seminole Negro Scouts" at the Eagle Nest crossing of the Pecos River in Texas. According to army documents, three Indians were killed, and one was wounded.

1878: Lieutenant Frank Baldwin and a small contingent from the Fifth Infantry accepted the surrender of a small group of Indians at Fort Peck in northeastern Montana. He believed they were followers of Sitting Bull.

1881: Sitting Bull had a feast and conference with Leaguer at Willow Bunch.

1890: Blackfeet Chief Isapo-Muxika (Crowfoot) died on a reserve near Gleichen, Alberta, Canada. He was one of the signers of Treaty Number 7.

1943: An election approved Amendment 1 to the constitution and bylaws of the Lac du Flambeau Band of Lake Superior Chippewa Indians of Wisconsin.

1951: Mitchell Red Cloud received the Medal of Honor.

1959: An election to approve Amendments 6 and 7 to the constitution and bylaws of the Confederated Tribes of the Warm Springs Reservation of Oregon was held. Amendment 6 was approved by a vote of 198–117. Amendment 7 won 186–137.

1981: An amendment to the constitution of the Comanche Indian Tribe was enacted.

April 26

1706: Indians attacked a small group of buildings outside the Oyster River settlement at the site of modern Durham, New Hampshire. Eight men were killed before female settlers drove the Indians off with gunfire.

1778: Last month, Captain James Cook anchored his two ships, the HMS *Discovery* and the HMS *Resolution*, in Nootka Sound. He had worked on the ships and traded with the Nootka since then. On this day, he left the area of British Columbia.

1867: According to army records, members of the Twenty-Seventh Infantry fought with a band of Indians near Fort Reno, Dakota Territory. One soldier was reported killed.

1872: Captain Charles Meinhold and Troop B, Third Cavalry, encountered an Indian war party on the South Fork of the "Loup" River, Nebraska. A fight ensued in which three Indians were killed. Scout William F. "Buffalo Bill" Cody, Sergeant John H. Foley, and Privates William Strayer and Leroy Vokes would be given the Medal of Honor for "gallantry in action" during this engagement.

1873: Another battle in the Modoc War took place. Captain Evan Thomas, Lieutenant Albion Howe, Lieutenant Arthur Cranston, Lieutenant T.F. Wright, and eighteen soldiers were killed. One officer, sixteen soldiers, and one civilian were wounded.

1875: Lieutenant John Bullies and three men from the Twenty-Fourth Infantry sneaked up on and attacked a group of twenty-five Comanche on the Pecos River. Three Indians were killed and one was wounded in the fight. Sergeant John Ward, Private Pompey Factor, and Trumpeter Isaac Payne of the Indian scouts would be awarded the Medal of Honor for their actions.

1906: A law was passed (34 Stat. 139) that authorized the president to remove from office the principal chief of the Choctaw, Cherokee, Creek, or Seminole Tribe or the governor of the Chickasaw Tribe to declare any such office vacant and to fill any vacancy in any such office arising from removal, disability, or death of the incumbent.

1906: An act of Congress (34 Stat. 370) established a deadline for enrolling in the Dawes Commission official tribal membership rolls for the Cherokee, Choctaw, Chickasaw, Creek, and Seminole Tribes.

1937: An election to approve a constitution and bylaws for the Seneca-Cayuga Tribe of Oklahoma was authorized by the secretary of the interior. The election would be held on May 15, 1937.

1943: In 1905, the Shoshone and Arapaho Indians of the Wind River Reservation in Wyoming ceded a large section of their reservation to the United States. According to Federal Register No. 8FR06857, they got a small part of that land back.

1962: An amendment to the constitution and bylaws of the Turtle Mountain Band of Chippewa Indians of North Dakota was approved.

1969: The constitution of the Central Council of the Tlingit and Haida Indian Tribes of Alaska was amended.

APRIL 27

1763: Pontiac held a council with a large group of Ottawa, Wyandot, and Potawatomi Indians. He told them of his plans to attack Fort Detroit. He extolled the virtues of returning to the old Indian ways before the coming of the Europeans.

1774: Still trying to instigate a war with local Indians in Kentucky, with hopes of seizing their lands as spoils of war, Michael Cresap and some followers attacked a party of peaceful Shawnees returning home from a conference at Fort Pitt. These "frontiersmen" killed several of the Indians. This was one of the fights that eventually led to what was commonly called Dunmore's War. This series of battles was occasionally called Cresap's War.

1813: Ending this date, Creek leaders, including Tustunnuggee Thlucco, and local Europeans finished executing members of the Red Stick Creek faction believed to be involved in the unprovoked murders of European settlers. Between April 16 and this date they had executed eleven Creek. The Red Stick Creek had been motivated by the teachings of Tecumseh.

1852: Command of Fort Phantom Hill north of Abilene, Texas, changed hands from Colonel J.J. Abercrombie to Lieutenant Colonel Carlos A. Waite. The fort was often visited by the local Comanche, Lipan Apache, Kiowa, and Kickapoo.

1867: According to army records, members of the Eighth Cavalry fought with a band of Indians near Lake Harney, Oregon. Six Indians were killed.

1868: The Cherokee signed a treaty (16 Stat. 727) covering 800,000 acres of land.

1873: Indians fought with soldiers from the Twenty-Fifth Infantry near Eagle Springs, Texas, according to army documents. No casualties were reported.

1877: General George Crook contacted Red Cloud with a message for Crazy Horse. Crook promised that if Crazy Horse surrendered he would get a reservation in the Powder River area. On this day, Red Cloud delivered the message to Crazy Horse. Crazy Horse agreed and headed to Fort Robinson in northwestern Nebraska, where he surrendered to the U.S. Army.

1880: Settlers fought a group of Indians near Ojo Caliente, New Mexico. According to army documents, three citizens were killed.

1966: The U.S. government ratified the addition of Amendments 2–8 to the constitution and bylaws of the Swinomish Indians of the Swinomish Reservation, Washington.

1972: An amendment to the constitution of the Skokomish Indian Tribe and a modification to the constitution of the Indians of the Tulalip Tribes in Washington were approved by the U.S. government.

1974: A modification to the constitution of the Indians of the Tulalip Tribes in Washington was approved by the U.S. government.

APRIL 28

1659: The Quinebaug Indians lived in Connecticut. Chiefs Allumps, Ma-Shan-Shawitt, and Aguntus sold their lands in the area around modern Plainfield and Canterbury. There was a provision in the deed to allow the tribe the privilege of "hunting, fishing and convenient planting" forever.

1835: The U.S. government issued orders to stop certifying Creek land sales. After a year of re-

ceiving complaints from Creek and honest whites, the government also agreed to investigate fraud in previous sales. Numerous scams had developed to get Creek land. Indians were paid to represent another Indian in a land sale, or they were made drunk and tricked into signing papers. These were just two of the many schemes going on.

1866: The Choctaws and the Chickasaws signed a treaty (14 Stat. 769).

1871: Either convinced that Eskiminzin's Apache were responsible for raids near Tucson, or just looking for an excuse to attack the Aravaipa, William Oury set out with 140 armed whites and Indians for the Apache camp near Camp Grant.

1874: Indians fought with soldiers from the Fifth Cavalry in the Arivaypa Mountains in Arizona. According to army documents, twenty-three Indians were killed, and twelve were captured.

1875: Kotsoteka Comanche Chief Mow-way and 200 followers surrendered to Ranald Mackenzie at Fort Sill, Indian Territory (present-day Oklahoma).

1876: Lieutenant Charles H. Heyl and nine men from Company A, Twenty-Third Infantry, encountered and fought a group of Indians near Fort Hartsuff and Grace Creek, Nebraska. One Indian was killed and several were wounded. One soldier, a sergeant, was killed while charging up a hill. Lieutenant Heyl would be awarded the Medal of Honor for leading this charge. Corporal Patrick Leonard would be awarded his second Medal of Honor for his actions in the fighting. Corporal Jeptha Lytton would also get the Medal of Honor.

1880: Settlers fought a group of Indians near the head of Rio Gilitfe, New Mexico. According to army documents, six citizens were killed.

1881: Sitting Bull left Willow Burch for Fort Qu'Appelle northeast of Regina, Saskatchewan, Canada.

1882: Remnants of Loco's Chiricahua Apache who fought in the battles south of Stein's Pass and in Horseshoe Canyon on April 23, 1882, were attacked by Captain Tullius Tupper, Troops G and

M, Sixth Cavalry, and a company of Indian scouts twenty-five miles south of Cloverdale, Arizona. Six Apache were killed, and seventy-two head of livestock were seized, according to army reports. The surviving Indians headed toward Mexico. Sixth Cavalry soldiers and Indian scouts fought a group of Indians near the Mexican border in the Hatchet Mountains of New Mexico. According to army documents, one soldier and six Indians were killed. Two soldiers were wounded.

1882: The Mi'kmaq Membertou First Nation Reserve of Caribou Marsh was established in Nova Scotia.

1897: The Dawes Commission divided Chickasaw and Choctaw lands.

1924: An act (43 Stat. 111) was passed by Congress to "authorize leasing for mining purposes cemetery lands not needed, school and agency land on the Kaw Reservation."

1980: The area director of the Phoenix area office of the Bureau of Indian Affairs, LaFollette Butler, ratified an election for an amendment to the constitution and bylaws of the Walker River Paiute Tribe of Nevada. The election was held on August 7, 1979. Also, the area director of the Phoenix area office of the Bureau of Indian Affairs, LaFollette Butler, ratified an election for amendments to the constitution and bylaws of the Fallon Paiute-Shoshone Tribe of Nevada. The election was held on January 12, 1980.

1988: The Indian Education Amendments (102 Stat. 130) of April 28, 1988, were passed by Congress. They were meant to improve elementary and secondary education programs, to make clarifying, corrective, and conforming amendments to laws relating to Indian education, and to establish programs of drug abuse education and prevention through provision of federal financial assistance.

APRIL 29

1700: Pierre le Moyne d'Iberville visited a Pascagoula Indian village, one day's walk from the French post at Biloxi. The Pascagoula had been hit hard by disease brought by the Europeans. D'Iberville was impressed by the beauty of the Pascagoula women.

1818: Although pursuing Seminole Creek, Andrew Jackson entered western Florida, which was Spanish territory. Jackson continued into the Spanish garrison of St. Mark and captured some Creek and British traders. He ordered the executions of two Creek chiefs and two British traders for helping the Creek.

1837: Near Battle Creek in Florida, Creek warriors and Florida militia fought. The militia killed or captured all of the warriors.

1842: After losing most of their provisions during a fight near Lake Ahapopka, Florida, ten days earlier, Mikasuki Seminole Chief Hallack Tustenuggee and his followers were starving. Hallack came to the camp of Colonel William Worth for talks. Worth offered food and alcohol to any Seminole who came into the camp. Many of the Seminole came into the camp. At a signal, soldiers captured forty-three warriors and seventy-one women and children. The Seminole were forced to leave Florida for Oklahoma.

1851: One in a series of treaties with California Indians was signed at Camp Barbour. These treaties promised to set aside lands for the Indians and to protect them from Americans.

1855: Colonel Fauntleroy and four companies from Fort Massachusetts in southern Colorado attacked the Ute on the Arkansas River near Chalk Creek. Forty Indians were killed, children were captured, and supplies were seized.

1868: Twenty-five Brule Sioux signed the treaty (15 Stat. 635) at Fort Laramie in eastern Wyoming. Many other Indians signed it later in the year. The Sioux Standing Rock Reservation was established by the treaty. It covered 4,176 square miles and was occupied by "Blackfeet, Hunkpapa, Lower and Upper Yanktonai Sioux" in Dakota Territory. Other tribes would sign the treaty over the next several months.

1868: According to army records, members of the Eighth Cavalry fought with a band of Indians near Camp Winfield Scott in Paradise Valley, Nevada. Lieutenant P. Hunter and one enlisted man were wounded.

1868: Four soldiers from Company A, Eighth Cavalry, were on patrol in Arizona Territory. They were attacked by seventeen hostile Indians. Private James C. Reed would be awarded the Medal of Honor for his actions during the fighting.

1868: According to army records, members of the Twenty-Third Infantry fought with a band of Indians south of the Warner Mountains in Oregon. Two soldiers were wounded.

1869: According to army records, members of the First Cavalry, Fourteenth and Thirty-Second Infantries, and Indian scouts fought with a band of Indians on Turnbull Mountain in Arizona. Twenty-eight Indians were killed, and eight were captured.

1874: An act of Congress was approved that guaranteed the Ute all of Uncompahgre Park in their reservation.

1880: Settlers fought a group of Indians in the Mogollon Mountains, New Mexico. According to army documents, three citizens were killed.

1881: Ninth Cavalry soldiers and some Indian scouts fought a group of Indians near the Mexican border. According to army documents, one soldier was killed.

1882: Lieutenant George Morgan and six men from Troop K, Third Cavalry, were ordered to arrest "Ute Jack," a chief of the White River Ute. Jack had a knife and resisted. He was shot in the arm by a soldier. Escaping to a nearby tepee, Jack found a rifle and shot the detachment sergeant. Major Julius Mason, Third Cavalry arrived, and according to army reports, "measures are taken resulting in the capture and death of the Indian." Third Cavalry soldiers and Indian scouts fought a group of Indians near Fort Washakie, Wyoming. According to army documents, one soldier and one Indian were killed.

1907: In a decree, the U.S. Supreme Court changed part of an earlier decision that appointed Guion Miller, then special agent of the Interior Department, as a special commissioner of the U.S. Court of Claims. He conducted an official tribal roll of the Eastern Cherokee, eventually called the Miller Rolls. The decision also set up a fund of $1 million for all Cherokee Indians who were still alive on May 28, 1906, and who could prove that at the time of the original treaties they were members of the Eastern Cherokee Tribe of Indians.

1968: The constitution and bylaws of the Lower Elwha Tribal Community of the Lower Elwha Reservation in Washington State were approved by Harry Anderson, assistant secretary of the interior.

1987: The Northwestern Band of Shoshoni Nation of Utah adopted a constitution.

1994: An executive memorandum was issued regarding "Government-to-Government Relations with Native American Tribal Governments."

April 30

1598: Don Juan de Oñate claimed all lands in modern New Mexico, including those of the resident Pueblos, for Spain. The event, known as "La Toma," took place near San Elizario.

1682: La Salle stayed with the Taensa Indians for four days, starting on this day, on Lake Saint Joseph in Louisiana. He signed a peace treaty with them.

1774: At the confluence of the Ohio River and Yellow Creek near Wheeling, Virginia, settlers had moved in near the Mingo. Among the settlers were many who hated the Indians. Daniel Greathouse and thirty-two confederates gathered at Baker's Tavern. They invited a dozen Indians in to drink with them. When the Mingo, including Mingo Chief Logan's sister, were intoxicated, the frontiersmen attacked. All of the Mingo were killed, except for a young girl. This massacre put Chief Logan on the warpath. His retaliatory attacks were an instigating factor in Lord Dunmore's War. (Also recorded as happening on May 3.)

1832: In a report written on this day, army supply agent Lieutenant J.R. Stephenson noted that 3,749 Choctaws had registered at four different posts in Indian Territory (present-day Oklahoma) after their trip from their old lands.

1860: Fort Defiance in northwestern Arizona was the first fort to be build in Navajo country. Built near land used by Manuelito's Navajos to graze their horses, an inevitable conflict began when the army claimed the grazing land for their own mounts. A series of raids on both sides led to a full-scale attack. Manuelito and nearly 1,000 warriors attacked Fort Defiance. The Navajos captured a few outbuildings, but the soldiers soon regrouped, and volleys were exchanged throughout the rest of the day. The Navajos left that night, considering the message delivered. The army eventually retaliated.

1861: Anticipating their need elsewhere in the Civil War, federal troops abandoned forts in Indian Territory (present-day Oklahoma).

1870: According to official army records, Indians skirmished with a group of soldiers from the First and Third Cavalry and the Twenty-First Infantry in the Pinal Mountains near San Carlos, Arizona. Eleven Indians were killed, and four were captured.

1871: William Oury, a veteran Indian fighter from Tucson, and 140 men, including ninety-two Papago Indians, found the unarmed camp of Eskiminzin's Aravaipa Apache living near Camp Grant. Believing them to be the raiders of San Xavier Mission (fifty miles away, near Tucson) on April 10, the group attacked the unsuspecting village. A total of 144 Indians were killed during the massacre. Twenty-seven children survived, all sold into slavery in Mexico by the Papago. Lieutenant Royal Whitman of Camp Grant heard of the expedition against the Indians, but his message of warning arrived a few hours after the fighting began. Lieutenant Whitman, believing the Aravaipa to be innocent, eventually got the Tucson men

brought to trial in Tucson. Many army members testified that the Aravaipa could not possibly have been involved in the raids, but after the five-day trial and a deliberation of less than half an hour, the Tucson men were acquitted.

1871: According to army records, Indians from Arizona staged raids in Colorado. They were reported to have killed twenty whites.

1875: Indians fought with soldiers from the Eighth Cavalry near La Luz Canyon, New Mexico. According to army documents, nine Indians were captured.

1882: While tracking Loco's Chiricahua Apache involved in the fights on April 23, 1882, and April 28, 1882, Lieutenant Colonel George Forsyth met Colonel Garcia of the Mexican army. Garcia did not let Forsyth follow the Apache into Mexico. However, Colonel Garcia led Forsyth to the scene of his own recent battle with the Apache. During the five-hour battle in Mexico, twenty-one Mexicans were killed and thirteen were wounded. Seventy-eight Indians were killed, and thirty-three women and children were captured. Compiling all of his sources of information, Lieutenant Colonel Forsyth estimated the fighting since April 23 had led to ninety-eight Indians dead and thirty wounded. A total of 205 Apache horses and mules were killed or captured.

1908: The 160-acre Shingle Springs Rancheria was located in El Dorado County, California. It was established by acts this date and on June 21, 1906. The land was purchased by the U.S. government on March 11, 1920.

1936: A constitution and bylaws for the Shoshone-Bannock Tribes of the Fort Hall Reservation were approved by Secretary of the Interior Harold Ickes.

1938: The Nez Perce approved a constitution and bylaws in a general assembly.

1974: Ralph Steinhauer was appointed lieutenant governor of Alberta. A Cree, he was the first "First Person" to become the lieutenant governor of a Canadian province.

MAY 1

1528: Panfilo de Narvaez and 300 men started marching inland from near Tampa Bay.

1540: Hernando de Soto's expedition reached the river across from the village of Cofitachequi. Among the high chiefs who were rowed across the river to meet de Soto was the "Lady of Cofitachequi. She was carried on a litter. The lady" spoke with de Soto and gave him a string of pearls. Eventually, de Soto's men "liberated" approximately 200 pounds of pearls from a temple in the town. It is believed this village was near present-day Silver Bluff, South Carolina.

1598: Oñate's expedition continued along the Rio Grande near El Paso. They met a group of people they called the Manso Indians.

1637: After numerous incidents and incursions on both sides, English settlers in Connecticut declared war on the Pequot Indians. Most of the fighting took place in Connecticut and Massachusetts.

1691: According to some sources, a peace agreement and the delivery of captives was agreed upon by representatives of the Five Nations and the British in New York.

1718: Martin de Alarcon founded the San Antonio de Valero Mission in what became modern San Antonio, Texas.

1740: Pierre and Paul Mallet, French traders and brothers, explored the Pecos Valley.

1758: According to some reports, a land-cession agreement was reached between representatives of Great Britain and the Creek.

1810: Congress passed "An Act Making Appropriations for Carrying into Effect Certain Indian Treaties."

1825: As a White Stick Creek, Chief William McIntosh fought with Andrew Jackson at Horseshoe Bend. He was eventually promoted to the rank of brigadier general. Although he once was a principal supporter of a law requiring death for any Creek who sold their lands, McIntosh helped prepare the documents that transferred the last of the Creek lands east of the Mississippi River. Before accepting payment for Creek lands, McIntosh was

warned the law would be carried out by antiremoval Creek. McIntosh ignored the warnings. On this day, Chief Menewa and over 100 Ockfuskee Creek warriors surrounded McIntosh's home. They set fire to the building. When McIntosh ran out of the house, he was shot to death.

1833: A census of the Creek upper towns showed 14,142 people, including 445 black slaves.

1833: According to a government memorandum, the Cherokees claimed to own 7.2 million acres of land east of the Mississippi River.

1863: Brigadier General James H. Carleton, in Santa Fe, New Mexico, wrote a letter to Major Joseph Smith, the commander of the Fifth Infantry California Volunteers at Fort Stanton. The letter said: "Major: No Mescaleros will have a right, even with a pass, to come back from Fort Sumner into their country to make mescal. I wish you would write this to Captain Updegraff. Nor will any woman or child return from Fort Sumner. One or two were to be permitted to come to tell the rest of the tribe to come in. . . . You will kill every Mescalero man that can be found without a passport."

1867: According to army records, members of the Second Cavalry fought with a band of Indians near La Prelle Creek, Dakota Territory. One soldier was killed.

1868: According to army records, members of the First Cavalry fought with a band of Indians near Camp Crittenden, Arizona. One soldier was wounded.

1868: According to army records, members of the First Cavalry fought with a band of Indians near the San Pedro River in Arizona. Three Indians were killed.

1868: According to army records, members of the Eighth Cavalry fought with a band of Indians on the Gila River near Camp Grant, Arizona. Six Indians were killed, and four were wounded.

1868: According to army records, members of the Eighth Cavalry and Ninth Infantry fought with a band of Indians near Hoag's Bluff in Warner Valley,

Oregon. One civilian was killed. Lieutenant Hayden De Lany and one soldier were wounded.

1877: Colonel Nelson Miles, Troops F, G, H, and L, Second Cavalry, Companies E and H, Fifth Infantry, and Companies E, F, G, and H, Twenty-Second Infantry, mounted a campaign to find Lame Deer and his primarily Minneconjou followers, who had changed their minds about surrendering. Miles started moving up the Tongue River to search for the escapees.

1879: Settlers fought a group of Indians between Fort Ewell and Corpus Christi, Texas. According to army documents, one citizen was killed. Near Fort McIntosh, a teamster was also killed by Indians.

1883: An order was issued to resolve some conflicts in the boundary lines established for the Zuni Pueblo Reservation in the executive order of March 16, 1877.

1888: Congress created the Fort Belknap Reservation.

1936: The Indian Reorganization Act was modified (49 Stat. 1250).

1965: An election for an amendment to the constitution and bylaws of the Kaibab Band of Paiute Indians of Arizona was held. It was approved by a vote of 36–1.

1971: The Pawnee of Oklahoma approved several amendments to their constitution with just under 200 members voting.

Every: The San Felipe Pueblo celebrates St. Philip Day and does the Green Corn dance.

Every: Some groups celebrate the birthday of Delaware chief Tamenend (Tammany).

May 2

1670: King Charles of England gave all trade rights to "all the Landes Countreyes and Territoryes upon the Coastes and Confynes of the Seas" lying within the Hudson Strait to the Hudson's Bay Company. This monopoly remained in effect until 1859.

1803: The Louisiana Purchase was signed.

1833: Secretary of War Lewis Cass assigned Colonel John Abert and General Enoch Parsons to approach the Creek about a new treaty to start the immediate removal to Indian Territory (present-day Oklahoma).

1841: A group of local Oregon Indians paddled up to the U.S. ship *Vincennes* anchored at Discovery Bay. One of the Indians spoke English. He asked if the sailors were "Boston" (American) or "King George" (British).

1867: The treaty of February 19, 1867, with the Sisseton and the Wahpeton Sioux was publicly proclaimed.

1869: Indians ambushed a wagon train guarded by soldiers near San Augustine, New Mexico. During fierce fighting, two soldiers and five Indians were killed. Four soldiers and ten Indians were wounded, according to the official army report on the incident. The Indians were unsuccessful in their attempt to seize the wagon train.

1869: According to army records, members of the Eighth Cavalry fought with a band of Indians in the Val de Chino Valley in Arizona. Two Indians were killed in fighting that lasted until May 9.

1871: Indians raided settlements near Fort Selden in southern New Mexico. According to army records, cavalry troops chased them for 280 miles, but they did not catch them.

1873: The treaty agreement of February 19, 1867, between the United States and the Sisseton and Wahpeton Bands of Dakota or Sioux Indians was amended. It covered the annual appropriations for the Sisseton and Devil's Lake Agencies.

1874: Lieutenant Quincy Gillmore and troopers from the Tenth Cavalry attacked a band of hostile Indians between the Red River and the Big Wichita River in Texas. No casualties were reported on either side.

1876: Sioux warriors stole horses near Fort Pease.

1880: Settlers fought a group of Indians near San Francisco River, New Mexico. According to army documents, seven citizens were killed.

1921: The trust period on allotments made to Kickapoo Indians on the Kickapoo Reservation in Kansas was extended.

MAY 3

679: Maya forces from Dos Pilas, Guatemala, attacked and defeated the forces at Tikal. Tikal King Nun Bak Chak was killed in the fighting.

1772: According to some sources, the Moravians established a mission for the Delaware at Schonbrunn, Ohio.

1774: At the confluence of the Ohio River and Yellow Creek, near Wheeling, Virginia, settlers had moved in near the Mingo. Among the settlers were many who hated the Indians. Daniel Greathouse and thirty-two confederates gathered at Baker's Tavern. They invited a dozen Indians in to drink with them. When the Mingo, including Mingo Chief Logan's sister, were intoxicated, the frontiersmen attacked. All of the Mingo were killed, except for a young girl. This massacre put Chief Logan on the warpath. His retaliatory attacks were an instigating factor in Lord Dunmore's War. (Also recorded as happening on April 30.)

1779: Starting on this day, Juan de Ugalde, governor of San Francisco de Coahuila, Mexico, launched the first of four expeditions against the Apache. Although the raids did not net many killed or captured, it forced many Apache to leave the area.

1871: Indians staged a raid on settlements near Cimarron, New Mexico. Three settlers were killed, and 950 head of livestock were seized. Cavalry troops pursued the Indians and captured twenty-two. The army also recovered 757 head of livestock.

1876: John Clum was the agent on the San Carlos Reservation. He was able to establish a livable system for the Apache there. He also established an Indian police force, which was an unheard-of plan for the era. When the Chiricahua Indians began to get beyond the control of their agent, the commissioner of Indian affairs decided to have Clum take over. Clum received a telegram with orders to go to the Chiricahua Reservation, relieve the local agent, and bring the Chiricahua to the San Carlos Reservation in the White Mountains of Arizona.

1877: General Oliver Howard held a conference at Lapwai. Some of the nontreaty Nez Perce agreed to move to a reservation.

1881: "Seminole Negro Scouts" fought a group of Indians in the Sierra Burras Mountains in Mexico. According to army documents, four Indians were killed and two were captured.

1886: U.S. troops had chased "renegade Apache" into Mexico. In a fight in the Pinito (Penito) Mountains of Sonora, Mexico, Second Lieutenant Powhatan H. Clarke earned the Medal of Honor for rescuing an injured soldier. According to army documents, one soldier and two Indians were killed. One soldier and one Indian were wounded.

1903: Armed federal troops forced the Cupeno group of Indians to relocate from Warners Hot Springs to the Pala Reservation in northern San Diego County, California. The Cupeno were allowed to take only what they could personally carry on the three-day trip through the mountains. Many lost most of their possessions. Several of the Cupeno were able to escape and joined Indians at other reservations in the area.

1922: According to the *Foss Enterprise* newspaper in Oklahoma, "Chief Little Wolf, the most noted Indian of the Cheyenne tribe," died one mile south of Clinton, Oklahoma.

1938: The constitution of the Skokomish Indian Tribe was approved by the secretary of the interior.

1973: Commissioner of Indian Affairs William Rogers ratified an election that approved a constitution for the La Posta Band of Mission Indians of the La Posta Indian Reservation, California. The election was held on January 26, 1973.

1975: The acting deputy commissioner of Indian affairs had authorized an election for amendments to the constitution and bylaws for the Covelo Indian Community of the Round Valley

Reservation in California. It took place on this day. The results were 47–9 in favor.

Every: Cochiti and Taos Pueblos celebrate Santa Cruz day.

MAY 4

1598: Oñate's expedition crossed the Rio Grande, with the help of the Manso Indians, north of El Paso.

1730: Sir Alexander Cuming and seven prominent Cherokees left Charlestown, South Carolina, en route to visit King George II of England. The two Cherokee chiefs in the group were Oukah-Ulah and Attakullaculla (Little Carpenter).

1781: A settlement had been established by the McAfee brothers near Harrodsburg, Kentucky, at the Boiling Springs of the Salt River. Indians attacked the station. One settler and one Indian were killed in the fighting. The Indians dispersed when reinforcements arrived from Harrodsburg.

1805: Pascagoula and Biloxi Indians sold their lands along the Gulf Coast to "Miller and Fulton," who were among the first settlers in the Rapides Parish area. The documents, signed by six Indians, were confirmed. The Pascagoula moved to the Red River area.

1847: Baptist and 123 other Choctaws from near Mobile, Alabama, arrived at Fort Towson in eastern Indian Territory (present-day Oklahoma).

1863: After the Minnesota Uprising of the Santee Sioux and their subsequent defeat, their lands were forfeited. The surviving Indians, including those who opposed the uprising and helped the whites, were ordered to be shipped to a reservation in Dakota Territory. A total of 770 Santee Sioux boarded a steamboat in St. Paul for the journey west. Eventually, 1,300 Santee Sioux were transported to an area that could hardly support life. During the first year, 300 Santee died.

1864: Henry Connelly, governor and commander in chief of the New Mexico militia, issued a proclamation. In part, it said hostilities between the citizens of New Mexico and the Navajo were to cease. It also prohibited "further traffic in captive Indians."

1870: Captain D.S. Gordon, commanding Troop D, Second Cavalry, engaged in a fierce battle with Indians near Miner's Delight, near Twin Creek, Wyoming. During the engagement, seven Indians were killed and one was wounded. Two soldiers, including Lieutenant Charles B. Stambaugh, were killed.

1877: Captain Philip L. Lee and Troop G, Tenth Cavalry, fought with Comanche Indians near Lake Quemado, Texas. Four Indians and one soldier were killed. Six Indians and sixty-nine head of livestock were captured. Twelve lodges and numerous articles of Indian property were destroyed. One of the killed was Ekawakane (Red Young Man). Many of these Comanche were believed to have been involved in the Battle of Yellow House Canyon on March 18, 1877.

1880: Settlers fought a group of Indians near Las Lentes, New Mexico. According to army documents, six citizens were killed.

1917: Under authority of an act of Congress (24 Stat. 388), an executive order was issued that extended the trust period on land allotments to the Sac and Fox Indians of Kansas and Nebraska.

1959: The assistant secretary of the interior authorized an election for amendments to the constitution of the Papago (Tohono O'odham). The election would be held on April 9, 1960.

1961: Lands on the Flathead Indian Reservation in Montana had been set aside to establish townsites. As reported in Federal Register No. 26FR04015, "a number of undisposed of lots within the townsites" were returned to tribal ownership by the Confederated Salish and Kootenai Tribes on the Flathead Reservation.

MAY 5

1541: Coronado left Cicuye (Cibola) to go to Texas.

1718: Martin de Alarcon established what eventually became the city of San Antonio, Texas. He brought with him seventy-two people to colonize the area.

1763: Near Fort Detroit, Ottawa Chief Pontiac addressed a group of Huron, Ottawa, and Potawatomi warriors. He asked them to join him in his fight against the British.

1785: The Cherokee Dumpling Creek Treaty was signed.

1875: Indians fought with soldiers from the Tenth Cavalry near Battle Point, Texas. According to army documents, one Indian was wounded.

1800: William Augusta Bowles was an adventurer in the southeastern part of the United States. With Creek and Cherokee supporters, he proclaimed a new nation, Muskogee, out of lands claimed by Spain along the Gulf Coast, with himself as "director-general." Bowles declared war on Spain and began a campaign against their outposts in his "nation." (Also recorded as happening on April 5, 1800.)

1864: Ute land was sold.

1867: According to army records, members of the First Cavalry fought with a band of Indians near Camp Watson, Oregon. One Indian was killed.

1871: The Third Cavalry engaged hostile Indians in the Whetstone Mountains of Arizona. For "gallantry in action" Sergeant John Mott and Privates Hermann Fichter, John Kilmartin, Daniel Miller, and John Yount, Company F, would be awarded the Medal of Honor. Lieutenant H.B. Cushing, one enlisted man, and thirteen Indians were killed. One soldier was wounded.

1875: Sergeant John Marshall and men from Troop A, Tenth Cavalry, attacked a group of Indians at Battle Point, Texas. One Indian was wounded, and his horse was seized.

1877: Sitting Bull and his followers escaped into Canada. (Also recorded as happening on May 6.)

1882: President Chester Arthur, by executive order, added additional land to the Gila River Reserve in the Pima Agency for the Pima and Maricopa Indian Reservation. This reservation was established on February 28, 1859. Lands already homesteaded in the new areas were exempted.

1916: The last fight by U.S. Army Indian scouts, who were part of the Eleventh Cavalry, took place. The scouts fought Pancho Villa's troops at Ojos Azules Ranch in Mexico. None of the scouts were killed, but Villa lost forty-four men.

1961: The Nez Perce voted 74–58 to approve amendments to their constitution and bylaws.

1969: N. Scott Momaday won the Pulitzer Prize for *House Made of Dawn*. He was the first American Indian to do so.

1971: The Kicking Horse Regional Manpower Center, in Ronab, Montana, was dedicated. It was the first all-Indian Job Corps Center.

MAY 6

1626: The purchase of Manhattan took place. Either the Shinnecock or the Canarsee Indians, according to sources, sold it to Peter Minuit.

1796: Congress passed "An Act Making Appropriations for Defraying the Expenses Which May Arise in Carrying into Effect a Treaty Made Between the United States and Certain Indian Tribes, Northwest of the River Ohio."

1822: As of this date, all nonprofit government trading houses were closed on or near Indian lands. All future trading posts were commercial enterprises.

1851: The Cherokee Nation opened its men's seminary (high school) near Park Hill in the eastern part of Indian Territory (present-day Oklahoma). The Cherokees provided all of the funding for the school. The female seminary opened the next day.

1859: Gold was discovered in Colorado.

1867: According to army records, members of the Fourteenth and Thirty-Second Infantry fought with a band of Indians near Mazatzal Mountains, Arizona. Two Indians were killed, and one soldier was wounded.

1869: According to army records, members of the Eighth Cavalry and Fourteenth Infantry fought with a band of Indians near Camp Verde on Grief Hill in Arizona. Five soldiers were wounded.

1872: Lieutenant J.D. Stevenson and Troops E and K, Eighth Cavalry, were at Tierra Amarilla, New Mexico Territory, when they were attacked by Ute Indians.

1873: Elements of the First Cavalry were engaging hostile Indians in the Santa Maria Mountains of Arizona. Bugler Samuel Hoover, Company A, would be awarded the Medal of Honor for "gallantry in action" during this date's activity. Four Indians were killed in the fighting.

1877: According to Canadian sources, Sitting Bull and his followers crossed into Canada from Montana. They were heading for Wood Mountain in Saskatchewan.

1877: Crazy Horse and Dull Knife, plus as many as 1,000 of their followers, surrendered at the Red Cloud Agency near Fort Robinson in northwestern Nebraska.

1877: Captain Philip L. Lee and Troop G, Tenth Cavalry, fought with more Indians in the Canyon Resecata.

1936: Secretary of the Interior Harold Ickes authorized an election to establish a constitution for the Fort McDermitt Paiute and Shoshone Tribes in Nevada.

1947: The acting commissioner of Indian affairs authorized an election to approve a constitution for the Coeur d'Alene Tribe of Idaho.

1991: David Sohappy, a fishing rights activist on the Columbia River, died.

MAY 7

755: According to a sculptured lintel in the ruins at Yaxchilan in Mexico, a battle took place. The lintel depicts Maya warriors Jeweled Skull and Bird Jaguar taking captives. The date is established by the Mayan glyphs also on the sculpture.

Dull Knife, chief of Northern Cheyenne at the Battle of Little Bighorn (NA)

1763: Pontiac attempted to enter Fort Detroit with a large group of armed Indians. However, his plans were leaked to the fort commanders, and they only met with Pontiac and a few chiefs. The next day, he attempted to distract the soldiers with a lacrosse game outside the fort, but the soldiers would not be distracted. Pontiac delayed his plans for a few days. Pontiac would later start the siege of Fort Detroit. The siege lasted until late October.

1851: The day before, the Cherokee Nation opened a seminary (high school) for men. On this day they opened a seminary for females north of Park Hill on the Cherokee Reservation in Indian Territory (present-day Oklahoma).

1864: A treaty (13 Stat. 693) with four different bands of the Chippewa Nation was signed in Washington, D.C.

1868: An act (15 Stat. 649) established the Crow Indian Reservation in Montana.

1869: According to army records, members of the Thirty-Fifth Infantry and some Indian scouts fought with a band of Indians on Paint Creek in Texas. Fourteen Indians were killed.

1869: According to army records, members of the Third Cavalry fought with a band of Indians near San Augustine Pass in New Mexico. One soldier was killed. One soldier and one civilian were wounded.

1873: Lieutenant Colonel William Carlin and Company B and C, Sixth Infantry, and Company H, Seventh Infantry, and Ree Indian scouts were stationed at Fort Abraham Lincoln (formerly Fort McKeen), near Bismarck, North Dakota. One hundred Sioux attacked the fort. The soldiers repelled the attack with one soldier killed and three wounded.

1877: Colonel Nelson Miles and his force of four cavalry troops and six infantry companies found Lame Deer and his followers on Muddy Creek, near the Rosebud River. Nelson surprised the village with a charge. Lame Deer and Iron Star parleyed with Miles about a peaceful settlement, but after they returned, the fight erupted again. The battle continued and proceeded toward the Rosebud. Lame Deer, Iron Star, and twelve other Indians were killed. Four soldiers were killed. Lieutenant Alfred M. Fuller and six soldiers were wounded. Almost 450 mounts were seized. The camp supplies and many lodges were also captured. Corporal Harry Garland and Private William Leonard, Company L, and Private Samuel Phillips, Company H, Second Cavalry, would win the Medal of Honor for "gallantry in action" as a part of the battle. Company L First Sergeant Henry Wilkens and farrier William H. Jones would also be awarded the Medal of Honor for their gallantry in this date's battle and for actions against the Nez Perce on August 20, 1877.

1880: Sixth Cavalry soldiers and some Indian scouts fought a group of Indians near Ash Creek Valley, Arizona. According to army documents, one soldier was killed and another was wounded.

1908: Congress passed an act removing tax exemption restrictions on lands owned by members of the "five civilized tribes" who were less than one-half blood. Other minor matters were also modified.

1964: An amendment to the constitution and bylaws of the Miccosukee Tribe of Indians of Florida was approved by Secretary of the Interior Stewart L. Udall.

1970: An act (84 Stat. 203) was passed by Congress to "provide that the estates of intestate members of the Cherokee, Chickasaw, Choctaw, and Seminole Nations of Oklahoma without heirs who own trust or restricted lands shall escheat to the tribes."

1973: According to the Federal Bureau of Investigation, at 10:19 A.M. this morning the occupation of Wounded Knee ended. The occupation started on February 27, 1973.

1983: The Nez Perce amended their constitution and bylaws.

MAY 8

1541: Hernando de Soto's expedition came upon the Mississippi River near the Indian village of Quizquiz in north-western Mississippi.

1716: The French had learned that the Natchez Indians had killed five Frenchmen. The French commander Bienville had established a makeshift fort on an island on the Mississippi River near a Tonica village. Bienville had the Tonica summon the Natchez for a conference. Believing that the Natchez were planning a surprise attack, Bienville planned his own surprise. Thirty-two Natchez rowed up to Bienville's camp. After a brief period of ceremonies, Bienville had the Natchez surrounded and manacled. Bienville informed the Natchez chiefs that they must bring him the heads of those who killed the five Frenchman and those chiefs who ordered it done. Bienville threatened the Natchez with destruction if they did not comply with his demands. The next morning, a group of Natchez and a dozen French soldiers set out for the Natchez village. (See May 14.)

1725: In one of the last battles of Lovewell's (or Father Rasle's) War, Pigwacket Indians defeated a British army under Captain John Lovewell at Fryeburg, Maine.

1765: According to some reports, a peace agreement was reached by representatives of the British and the Delaware.

1785: Congress passed the Land Ordinance of 1785.

1792: The Draft Act was issued against the Indians.

1820: The Mi'kmaq Acadia First Nation Reserve of Gold River was established in Nova Scotia. The Shubenacadie First Nation Reserve of Indian Brook No. 14 was also set up.

1827: Cherokee Chief Richard Fields and many of his Cherokee followers in Texas decided to join the Fredonian Revolution against Mexico. After a few efforts of rebellion were thwarted, Fields reconsidered his participation in the revolt. On this day, several antirevolution Cherokees killed Fields for his part in the revolt.

1827: Cantonment Leavenworth was established as a military base to protect travelers on the Santa Fe Trail from hostile Indians. Eventually renamed Fort Leavenworth, the base housed many army expeditions against the Indians of the Central Plains. The fort was the oldest permanent U.S. Army military base west of the Missouri River.

1834: Lieutenant Joseph Harris and his contingent of Cherokees who left the Tennessee Cherokee Agency on March 14 arrived in their new lands in Indian Territory (present-day Oklahoma). They moved on to the Dwight Mission.

1865: The Mi'kmaq Acadia First Nation Reserve of Medway was established in Nova Scotia.

1950: Assistant Secretary of the Interior William Warne authorized an election to approve a constitution and bylaws for the United Keetoowah Band of Cherokee Indians of Oklahoma. The election would be held on October 3, 1950.

1961: An election to approve a resolution to adopt a constitution and bylaws for the Wichita Indian Tribe of Oklahoma was held. It would be passed by a vote of 32–0.

1975: Amendments to the constitution and bylaws of the Covelo Indian Community were approved.

MAY 9

1735: The first debate on the Walking Purchase took place in Pennsbury. Thomas Penn and James Logan met with Delaware chiefs, including Nutimus and Tedyuscung.

1813: A battle took place at Fort Meigs (modern Perrysburg), Ohio.

1832: The Seminole were told that they must move to the Indian Territory (present-day Oklahoma). If they did not agree to a removal treaty, their annuities from their treaty of September 18, 1823, would be paid to the Creek. The U.S. government still considered the Seminole to be Creek. At Payne's Landing, Florida, they signed the Removal Treaty (7 Stat. 368). The treaty contained the provision that some Seminole would be sent to Indian Territory first and report back to tribal leaders. If the leaders decided the lands were adequate, they would agree to move to the Indian Territory. They were promised a shirt and a blanket when they arrived there. The Americans were represented by Colonel James Gadsden. In many minds, the Second Seminole War was fomented by disagreements over this treaty and its implementation.

1869: According to army records, members of the Eighth Cavalry fought with a band of Indians in the Val de Chino Valley in Arizona. Two Indians were killed in fighting that started on May 2.

1885: On this day through May 12, events in the Second Riel Rebellion took place in Canada. Major General Frederick Middleton and a force of 800 soldiers attacked the Metis and Cree Indians holding the village of Batoche. The fighting continued until the soldiers finally overran Batoche.

1907: Lemhi Chief Tendoy died when he fell off a horse while crossing a cold mountain stream in Idaho. He was believed to be seventy-three years old. (Also recorded as happening on May 10.)

1941: A modification to the constitution of the Indians of the Tulalip Tribes in Washington was approved by the U.S. government.

1960: The assistant secretary of the interior ratified an election for amendments to the constitution of the Papago (Tohono O'odham). The election was held on April 9, 1960.

1981: Commissioner of Indian Affairs William Hallett had authorized an election to approve a constitution and bylaws for the Jamul Indian Village in San Diego County, California. It was approved by a vote of 16–0.

1983: An amendment to the constitution and bylaws of the Suquamish Indian Tribe of the Port Madison Reservation in the state of Washington was passed.

MAY 10

1534: Jacques Cartier spotted Newfoundland.

1637: Approximately ninety Boston troops under John Mason and sixty Mohegan under Uncas marched toward the Pequot fort at Sassacus, on Pequot Harbor.

1676: Captain Turner and 100 men from Boston approached Deerfield in central Massachusetts. The Wampanoag had moved into the deserted city and planted crops in the fields. Turner's attack was a complete surprise, and he routed the Indians. One soldier was killed in the fighting; Turner reported he dispatched 300 Indians. Later, on May 18, Turner met another group of Indians. In the fighting, Turner and a third of his men were killed.

1765: Shawnees delivered white captives to Fort Pitt.

1816: Fort Howard was founded on Green Bay in Wisconsin.

1832: Settlers started construction of what was called Fort Blue Mounds (near modern Madison,

Wisconsin); the fort was built to protect settlers from attacks by the Winnebago.

1834: Lieutenant Joseph Harris left his first contingent of Eastern Cherokees, who left the Tennessee Cherokee Mission on March 14, at the Dwight Mission in the Cherokee lands of the Indian Territory (present-day Oklahoma). During this trip, eighty-one Cherokees died; almost half were children under ten. Fifty of the Cherokees died of cholera. Before the end of 1834, almost half of Harris's group of 500–600 Cherokees died of disease, illness, starvation, extreme weather conditions, or natural disasters.

1838: General Winfield Scott had been ordered to force any Cherokees remaining east of the Mississippi River to emigrate to the Indian Territory (present-day Oklahoma). He set up his headquarters at the Cherokee capital of New Echota in northwestern Georgia. On this day, he warned the Cherokees that if they had not started moving west by the deadline of May 28 he and his troops would use whatever means necessary to make them leave.

1839: Asa Smith was a missionary. He moved to an area in Idaho (near modern Kamiah) in order to learn the Nez Perce language. There he met Nez Perce leader Lawyer, who helped him.

1842: The U.S. government authorized Colonel William Worth to contact the remaining Seminole in Florida about establishing reservations. Worth offered the Seminole two choices: move to lands west of the Mississippi, or live on reservations in Florida. Most of the Seminole chose reservation life in Florida over moving.

1864: Cherokee Stand Watie was promoted to the rank of brigadier general in the Confederate Army. He was the first Indian to reach that rank. He would also be the last Confederate general to surrender at the end of the Civil War.

1869: One of the most devastating events in the lives of the Plains Indians was the crossing of their lands by the railroads. The railroads brought settlers and hunters and separated the buffalo herds.

The "iron horses" of the Central Pacific and the Union Pacific met at Promontory Point, Utah, completing the first crosscontinent railroad in the United States.

1869: Indian prisoners at Fort Hays in central Kansas attempted to escape. They attacked their guards with a knife. The sergeant of the guards was mortally wounded. The superior forces of the army overcame the Indians, and their escape attempt was foiled, according to army reports.

1873: Indians fought with soldiers from the First Cavalry, the Fourth Artillery, and some Indian scouts near Lake Soras, California, according to army documents. Two soldiers and one Indian were killed. Seven soldiers and two Indians were wounded.

1883: Sitting Bull arrived at Fort Yates.

1907: Lemhi Chief Tendoy died when he fell off a horse while crossing a cold mountain stream in Idaho. He was believed to be seventy-three years old. (Also recorded as happening on May 9.)

1926: The Kootenai Tribe of Idaho acquired additional trust lands (44 Stat. 202).

MAY 11

1704: As a part of Queen Anne's War, Indians attacked settlers near the New Hampshire border in Wells, Maine. Two settlers were killed, and one was captured, before the Indians withdrew.

1792: Robert Gray and the ship *Columbia* crossed the treacherous sandbar at the mouth of the Columbia River and explored the waterway. He "discovered" the Columbia River.

1832: Elisha W. Chester was appointed by President Jackson to go to the Eastern Cherokees. He was charged with determining whether the Cherokees would accept the government's plans for their removal.

1854: In an effort to end the fighting in the Walker War in southern Utah, Paiute Chief Walkara and Utah Governor Brigham Young met in Juab County, Utah. The meeting would end the

Navajo family in Canyon de Chelly (NA)

ongoing fighting; however, fighting would flare up again later.

1858: Colonel Albert Sidney, Second Cavalry, Colonel John S. "Rip" Ford with 100 Texas Rangers, Chief Placido, and 111 Tonkawa fought Buffalo Hump's Comanche in the Antelope Hills on the Canadian River in Indian Territory (present-day Oklahoma). The Rangers reported seventy-five Comanche warriors and two Rangers killed in the fighting. (Also reported on May 12.)

1864: The third group of Navajos to make the Long Walk from the Canyon de Chelly to the Bosque Redondo Reservation finally arrived at their destination. Of the 946 who started the trip, 110 died en route due to severe winter weather conditions and inadequate provisions.

1871: Major William Price and members of the Eighth Cavalry chased a band of raiding Navajos. According to official army records, they captured two "prominent" chiefs and lots of stolen livestock.

1889: Tenth Cavalry and Twenty-Fourth Infantry soldiers were escorting a payroll when they were attacked by a group of Indians near Cedar

Springs, Arizona. According to army documents, nine soldiers were wounded.

1968: The constitution of the Indians of the Tulalip Tribes in Washington was modified.

1974: The acting deputy commissioner of Indian affairs had authorized an election for amendments to the constitution and bylaws of the Lac Courte Oreilles Band of Lake Superior Chippewa Indians of Wisconsin. The amendments were voted in.

MAY 12

1676: Narragansett under Pumham attacked the New England village of Hatfield. They made off with six dozen head of cattle.

1838: S.T. Cross and 177 Choctaws arrived in eastern Indian Territory (present-day Oklahoma) at Choctaw Landing, near Fort Coffee. Many of the Choctaws were sick, lame, or old.

1854: The Menominee signed a treaty (10 Stat. 1064) at the Falls of the Wolf River. It involved the ceding of land.

1858: Comanche Chief Iron Jacket (Po-hebit-squash) was killed in a fight with Texas Rangers on the Canadian River.

1859: Captain Earl Van Dorn and members of the Second Cavalry attacked Comanche forces at Crooked Creek, Kansas Territory. Robert E. Lee was wounded during this fight.

1860: A battle in the Paiute War took place in Nevada at Big Bend in the valley of the Truckee River. Major William Ormsby's Nevada militia were attacked by Paiute under War Chief Numaga.

1865: Indians had attacked the stockade at Gilman's Ranch, Nebraska. For his actions in defending the government installation, Private Francis Lohnes, Company H, First Nebraska Veteran Cavalry, would be awarded the Medal of Honor.

1871: After a raid of livestock near Red River, Texas, troops from Fort Sill, Indian Territory (present-day Oklahoma), found the Indians and attacked. Three Indians were killed and four were wounded in the fighting.

1872: Captain J.A. Wilcox and troopers from the Fourth Cavalry attacked a group of Kiowa Indians between the Big and Little Wichita Rivers in Texas. Two Indians were killed and one soldier was wounded.

MAY 13

1540: Hernando de Soto left Cofitachequi. He took the "Lady of Cofitachequi" with him against her will.

1614: The Viceroy of Mexico found Spanish explorer Juan de Oñate guilty of atrocities against the Indians of New Mexico. As a part of his punishment, he was banned from entering New Mexico again.

1675: According to some sources, a peace agreement was reached between representatives of the Delaware Indians and the New Jersey Colony.

1704: Seventy-two Indian warriors and French soldiers attacked Pascommuck (modern Easthampton), Massachusetts. The village was taken by surprise, and twenty settlers died during the fighting. The remaining thirty settlers were captured. Nineteen of the captives were killed while the Indians were fleeing the area. Eight captives were rescued.

1800: Congress passed "An Act to appropriate a certain sum of money to defray the expense of holding a treaty or treaties with the Indians," and "An Act to Make Provision Relative to Rations for Indians, and to Their Visit to the Seat of Government."

1816: William Clark, Auguste Chouteau, and Ninian Edwards signed a treaty (7 Stat. 141) with the Rock River Sac and Fox Indians at St. Louis. This treaty ratified the Treaty of 1804 and dealt with property concerns of white settlers. Black Hawk signed the treaty, but later he said he was misled as to what he was signing.

1833: After moving to the Caddo lands along the Red River, the Quapaw were miserable and so returned to their former territory. After strong complaints from the settlers, they signed a treaty (7 Stat. 424) giving them lands in southern

Kansas and northern Indian Territory (present-day Oklahoma).

1833: A census of the Lower Creek towns showed 8,552 Creek, including 457 black slaves.

1851: Treaties were signed in California at Camp Belt and Camp Keyes regarding guaranteed reserved lands for Indians in California.

1859: Captain Earl Van Dorn's forces attacked a band of Comanche. Forty-nine Comanche warriors were killed and the remaining five were wounded in the fight at Crooked Creek in southwestern Kansas. The army had two soldiers killed in the fighting. Thirty-two Comanche women were taken prisoner.

1861: Union representatives signed a peace treaty with the Comanche at Alamogordo, New Mexico. Neither side kept the peace for long.

1868: According to army records, two settlers were killed in a fight with a band of Indians near Fort Buford, Dakota Territory.

1869: General Eugene Carr and seven troops of the Fifth Cavalry were scouting the area of Beaver Creek looking for hostile bands of Indians. Eight miles from Elephant Rock, a scouting party under the command of Lieutenant Edward Ward spotted the smoke of a large Indian village. A hunting party from the village saw Ward's troops. Ward charged through the hunting party and galloped back to the main army force. The main body of the army proceeded rapidly to the village and attacked. Although the women and children attempted to escape, the Indian warriors fought the soldiers. According to General Sheridan's official report, the army made a "brilliant charge" against the Indians. Three soldiers and twenty-five Indians were killed. Four soldiers and fifty Indians were reported to have been wounded.

1880: Settlers fight a group of Indians near Bass Canyon, Texas. According to army documents, two citizens were killed and two were wounded.

1904: The president of the United States issued a proclamation regarding Indian lands in South Dakota.

1916: The Society of American Indians established Indian Day to recognize, honor, and improve Indians' conditions.

1936: Secretary of the Interior Harold Ickes ratified an election for the approval of a constitution and bylaws for the Muckleshoot Indian Tribe of the Muckleshoot Reservation, which was held on April 4, 1936.

1974: An election for amendments to the constitution and bylaws of the Turtle Mountain Band of Chippewa Indians of North Dakota was held. They were approved by a vote of 752–640, 829–565, and 965–600.

Every: St. Anthony Feast Day for some Pueblos.

MAY 14

1716: The delegation under Bienville sent to the Natchez village on May 9, 1716, returned to the French camp. They were bearing the heads of three Natchez men. Bienville was upset because one of the heads did not belong to any of the murderers of five Frenchmen. The Natchez explained the third head was the brother of one of the murderers who escaped. Bienville demanded the head of the chief, Oyelape, who ordered the killings.

1741: According to some sources, a land-cession agreement was reached by representatives of the British in New York and the Seneca.

1833: After meeting with federal officials in Washington, D.C., in January about their removal to the Indian Territory (present-day Oklahoma), the Cherokee delegates met with the Cherokee council. Feelings were split on President Jackson's offer of $3 million for all of the Eastern Cherokee lands excepting North Carolina. A meeting of the Cherokee Nation in October would ask the delegates to return to Washington to continue talks with the federal government, including their friends in Congress.

1832: Near the Kyte River, Major Isaiah Stillman and 275 soldiers were patrolling the area on the lookout for Black Hawk. Weary of fighting, Black

Hawk sent a few representatives to Stillman's camp to negotiate the surrender of his four dozen warriors. When the soldiers fired on Black Hawk's representatives, a few managed to escape. With the soldiers in pursuit, Black Hawk set up an ambush. Becoming confused by the sudden attack, Stillman's troop panicked and fled the area. Eleven soldiers and three Indians were killed in the fighting. However, the soldiers report a massacre of troops. The "battle" was called Stillman's Run.

1841: Cherokee warrior James Foreman was believed to have been one of the men who killed Major Ridge on June 22, 1839, for signing the Treaty of New Echota that gave up the Cherokee lands east of the Mississippi River. Major Ridge's nephew, Chief Stand Watie, killed Foreman. Stand Watie was found not guilty based on self-defense.

1869: Most of the Indians who were left in the village on Beaver Creek escaped during the night. The village and all the property left behind by the Indians were destroyed by the troops. The troops then prepared to pursue the Indians who escaped.

1880: Sergeant George Jordan, Company K, Ninth Cavalry, was in charge of a detachment of twenty-five men at Old Fort Tularosa, New Mexico. The fort was attacked by over 100 hostile Indians. For his efforts in repulsing the Indians, Jordan would be awarded the Medal of Honor.

1880: Lemhi Chief Tendoy and several others signed an agreement to leave the Lemhi Reservation in Idaho. The agreed to go to Fort Hall. It would be nine years before Congress approved the agreement. The Lemhi would not actually move until 1909.

1900: Government regulations regarding the Hualpai (Walapai) Reserve in Arizona were modified.

1936: A constitution for the Gila River Pima–Maricopa Indian Community was approved by the U.S. government.

1971: San Carlos Reservation community radio station SCCR was dedicated. It was advertised as the first radio station on an American Indian reservation.

MAY 15

1637: Mason and Uncas's forces arrived at Saybrook. Almost immediately, Uncas led many of his Mohegan warriors against the Pequot and Niantic. Uncas claimed to have killed around a half-dozen men while having only one of his warriors wounded.

1649: Fleeing before advancing Iroquois, the Huron and then the Jesuits abandoned the mission at Sainte-Marie, Canada. The Jesuits burned the mission before leaving.

1658: According to some sources, a land-cession treaty was reached between representatives of the Plymouth Indians and the Plymouth Plantations.

1716: French commander Bienville sent three Natchez Indians to their village to bring back the head of a chief, Oyelape, who had ordered the killings of five Frenchmen. Bienville held several other Natchez as hostages. From friendly Tonica Indians, Bienville learned that the Natchez were planning an attack on his makeshift fort on an island in the Mississippi River.

1762: Cherokee Chiefs Ostenaco, Pouting Pigeon, and Stalking Turkey departed Hampton, Virginia, en route to England to visit King George III. They arrived on June 5.

1832: Secretary of War Lewis Cass issued orders reducing the amount of money the U.S. government spent in resettling Indians forcibly moved to lands west of the Mississippi River.

1836: Creek warrior Jim Henry and 200–300 followers attacked the Georgia town of Roanoke. A little over a dozen of the townspeople were killed in the fighting.

1846: A treaty was signed by Texas Governor Pierce Butler and Colonel M.G. Lewis (Meriwether Lewis's brother) and sixty-three Indians of the Aionai, Anadarko, Caddo, Comanche, Kichai (Keehy), Lipan (Apache), Longwha, Tahuacarro

(Tahwacarro), Tonkawa, Waco, and Wichita Tribes. It was ratified on February 15, 1847, and signed by President Polk on March 8, 1847.

1868: According to army records, two settlers were killed in a fight with a band of Indians between Fort Stevenson and Fort Totten, Dakota Territory.

1869: According to army records, members of the First Cavalry fought with a band of Indians near Fort Lowell, Arizona. One soldier was wounded.

1870: For their actions in this date's fight, Sergeant Patrick Leonard, Company C, and Privates Michael Himmelsback, Thomas Hubbard, and George Thompson would be awarded the Medal of Honor.

1876: The following reservations were established by President Grant, by executive order, in San Bernardino County, California, for the Mission Indians of Southern California: Portrero, Mission, Agua Caliente, Torros, Village, and Cabezon.

1880: Settlers fought a group of Indians near Kelly's Ranch, New Mexico. According to army documents, three citizens were killed.

1883: George Crook's forces attacked Chato. Indian scouts under Captain Emmet Crawford fought a group of Indians near the Bapispe River in the Sierra Madre Mountains of Mexico. According to army documents, nine Indians were killed and five were captured.

1884: An order restored to the public domain certain lands set aside for the Jicarilla Apache by the executive order of September 21, 1880.

1885: Louis Riel surrendered to Major General Frederick Middleton.

1885: Under the Treaty of Fort Laramie, much of the lands allocated to the Santee Sioux were required to be divided into individual plots. By executive order the deadline for that requirement was April 15, 1885. All unclaimed plots became available for public sale on this day.

1886: American troops had chased hostile Apache into Mexico. In a fight in the Pinto or Santa Cruz Mountains, Sergeant Samuel H. Craig, Company D, Fourth Cavalry, earned the Medal of Honor for "conspicuous gallantry during an attack on a hostile Apache Indian camp." According to army documents, two soldiers were killed and two were wounded.

1890: Rowdy received the Medal of Honor.

1937: An election to approve a constitution and bylaws for the Seneca-Cayuga Tribe of Oklahoma was held. It was approved by a vote of 186–0.

1940: Assistant Secretary of the Interior Oscar Chapman ratified amendments to the constitution and bylaws of the Confederated Tribes of the Warm Springs Reservation of Oregon approved in an election held on February 21, 1940.

1951: An election to approve a constitution and bylaws for the Kaibab Band of Paiute Indians of Arizona was held. It was approved by a vote of 26–5.

1965: The secretary of the interior had authorized an election to approve a constitution and bylaws for the Squaxin Island Tribe of the Squaxin Island Indian Reservation in Washington State. The election took place. It was approved by a vote of 29–8.

1979: The area director of the Phoenix area office of the Bureau of Indian Affairs authorized an election for an amendment to the constitution and bylaws of the Walker River Paiute Tribe of Nevada. The election was held on August 7, 1979.

1987: A criteria manual for the Seminole Water Rights Compact was published.

MAY 16

1661: A second treaty was signed between the Susquehannock and the British in Maryland.

1677: Mugg, an Arosaguntacook Indian chief, died in Black Point, Maine. At the outset of King Philip's War, Mugg attempted to arrange a peace treaty with the British. Instead, they jailed him for a short time and gained a bitter enemy. He destroyed much of Black Point, Maine, in a raid on

October 12, 1676. Later he captured a few ships and staged a brief naval war before his death.

1704: After the Pennsylvania assembly passed a law prohibiting the sale of rum to local Indians, the rum traders ignored the law. In Philadelphia, Susquehanna Chief Oretyagh addressed the Pennsylvanians about the depredations that alcohol had caused his people. His speech was moving, but the traders still sold their wares.

1760: Creek warrior Chief Hobbythacco (Handsome Fellow) had often supported the English, but at the outbreak of the Cherokee War he decided to support the Cherokees. He led an attack on a group of English traders in Georgia. Thirteen of the traders were killed during the fighting. Creek Chief The Mortar also participated in the fighting.

1763: A group of Ottawa and Wyandot Indians gained entry to Fort Sandusky on Lake Erie in Ohio. They killed the small garrison of sixteen men, with the exception of its commander, Ensign Christopher Pauli, whom they took captive. Pauli was taken to Detroit to Pontiac's camp.

1836: On the road to Tuskegee, a party of approximately fifty Creek Indians attacked a stagecoach carrying mail west of Columbus. Some of the passengers were killed.

1838: In a meeting held in Pennsylvania Hall, thousands of Philadelphians protested the forced removal of Cherokees from their lands east of the Mississippi River.

1858: Colonel Steptoe and his expedition met with the Spokane, Palouse, Coeur d'Alene, Yakama, and various other tribes at the place known as Te-hots-Ne-Mah.

1864: After the Treaty of Fort Wise (12 Stat. 1163), the Cheyenne thought they would be able to hunt in their old hunting grounds if they lived in an area bounded by the Arkansas River and Sand Creek. The actual terms were considerably different. Although on a routine hunting trip near Ask Creek, Black Kettle, Lean Bear, and others heard of a group of soldiers approaching their camp. Lean Bear and a small party rode out to see the soldiers. Lean Bear had visited Washington the year before, and he was presented medals and certificates stating he was a "good Indian." Carrying his credentials, Lean Bear rode his horse toward the army. When he was about 100 feet from the soldiers, they opened fire. Lean Bear was killed. The soldiers then directed their fire on Lean Bear's party. The Indians fought back. As more Indians rode in from the camp, the army opened fire with grapeshot from their cannons. Black Kettle responded to the scene and exhorted the Indians to stop fighting. Eventually the Indians stopped shooting, and the soldiers retreated. The army unit was headed by Lieutenant George Eayre, who was in Colonel Chivington's command (Sand Creek Massacre). The army was composed of Colorado volunteers. The battle was in Kansas, out of their jurisdiction.

1869: Lieutenant William Volkmar, Fifth Cavalry, was leading General E.A. Carr's advance troops, seeking the survivors of the fight at Beaver Creek on May 13, 1869. On Spring Creek in Nebraska, Volkmar finally caught up to the Indians. Volkmar's patrol was attacked by approximately 400 warriors, according to the army report. Fighting from behind the bodies of their dead horses, the troops were able to hold off the Indians until General Carr's main body arrived. The main body chased the Indians for almost fifteen miles to the Republic River, where the Indians split up into small groups. General Carr believed the warriors to be Cheyenne Dog Soldiers. The army would issue a Medal of Honor to First Lieutenant John B. Babcock.

1869: A dozen cowboys engaged in a day-long skirmish with Comanche (near modern Jean, Texas).

1870: Ten citizens were killed during a raid by Indians along a thirty-mile stretch of the Kansas Pacific railroad line. Cavalry chased the Indians to the Republican River, but they did not catch them. The Indians ran off 300 mounts.

1870: According to some sources, an army post was set up near the town of Whitewater in modern Arizona. It was eventually called Fort Apache.

1936: Secretary of the Interior Harold Ickes ratified a constitution and bylaws of the Makah Indian Tribe of the Makah Indian Reservation Washington that had been adopted by them in an election held on April 18, 1936.

1936: An election to approve a constitution and bylaws for the Lower Sioux Indian Community of Minnesota was held. It was passed by a vote of 54–6.

1947: According to Federal Register No. 12FR03239, Public Land Order No. 9854 transferred part of the Phoenix Indian School reserve to the control and jurisdiction of the Veterans Administration.

1955: Prior to this date, Indians could not sell their allotted lands if the sale would "destroy or jeopardize a timber unit or grazing area." If they sold the land along a river, the nearby, unirrigated grazing land and farmland would become useless after a few seasons. This protective restriction was canceled by an order of Commissioner of Indian Affairs Glenn L. Emmons.

MAY 17

1629: According to a deed, Sagamore Indians, including Passaconaway, sold a piece of land in what became Middlesex County, Massachusetts.

1673: Father Jacques Marquette and Louis Joliet begin their expedition from the Straits of Michilimackinac. Eventually, they explored much of the Mississippi River.

1790: Colonel Marinus Willett invited Alexander McGillivray and other Creek chiefs to come to New York City to conduct a council.

1836: The Senate ratified the illegal Cherokee Removal Treaty.

1838: Pending the forced removal of the Cherokees from their lands east of the Mississippi River, General Winfield Scott issued orders to his troops on how to handle the Cherokees. Scott ordered

Art class, Phoenix Indian School (NA)

the troops to show "every possible kindness . . . to by far the most interesting tribe of Indians in the territorial limits of the United States."

1842: The last soldier to die in the Seminole War was shot by a Seminole warrior. His name was Private Jesse Van Tassel. He died of his wounds on May 27.

1849: A Canadian court heard a charge against four Metis men who were accused of selling furs despite the Hudson Bay Company's monopoly. The Metis believed they had the right to sell furs as part of the rights as "First People." Only one of the men was found guilty, and he was not punished. From this day forward, the Hudson Bay Company no longer operated under the assumption they had a monopoly on fur trading.

1853: The army base that eventually became Fort Riley was established in Kansas. The fort was home to many different cavalry units during the Indian Wars.

1854: The Iowa signed a treaty (10 Stat.1069) in Washington, D.C., with George Manypenny.

1858: The battle against E.J. Steptoe and his troops began and ended disastrously for Steptoe. The battlefield became known afterward as Steptoe Butte. Brevet Lieutenant Colonel Steptoe had organized an expedition from Fort Walla Walla in southeastern Washington into the Coleville country to seek out hostiles. With 158 soldiers and thirty civilian volunteers, Steptoe encountered hundreds of Spokane and Coeur d'Alene Indians. Steptoe retreated and fought a running battle. Many lives were lost on both sides. The battle was fought about thirty miles south of present-day Spokane.

1870: Along Little Blue or Spring Creek in Nebraska, approximately fifty Indians attacked Sergeant Patrick Leonard and four men of Troop C, Second Cavalry. The soldiers escaped uninjured while inflicting one fatality and wounding seven of their attackers.

1871: The Kiowa and the Comanche were becoming very concerned about the number of settlers in their native Texas. Upon the urging of Mamanti (Sky Walker), a medicine man, they left their reservation in Indian Territory (present-day Oklahoma) and entered Texas. On this day they reached the Butterfield stagecoach road between Forts Richardson and Belknap in north-central Texas. They settled in to wait for something to pass by worth fighting. They hoped to find some weapons.

1871: Chief Satauk was killed in a fight with some soldiers from Fort Sill in Indian Territory. Chiefs Satanta and Big Tree were arrested, according to official army records. One soldier was wounded.

1873: Indians fought with soldiers from the First Cavalry, the Fourth Artillery, and some Indian scouts near Butte Creek, Oregon, according to army documents. Two Indians were killed.

1873: Colonel R.S. Mackenzie and Troops A, B, C, E, I, and M, Fourth Cavalry, and Lieutenant John Bullis, commanding Seminole Indian scouts, started a quick march at 1:00 P.M. to surprise a Kickapoo and Lipan Indian village seventy-five miles away near Remolina, Mexico. Mackenzie was called "Three Fingers" by the Indians. (Also recorded as happening on May 18.)

1876: General Alfred Terry and approximately 900 men, including Colonel Custer and Major Reno, left Fort Abraham Lincoln in central North Dakota for the mouth of the Powder River looking for hostile Indians.

1882: An act of Congress (22 Stat. 88, as amended; 25 U.S.C. 63), allowed the president to consolidate two or more Indian agencies into one, to consolidate one or more Indian tribes, and to abolish such agencies thereby rendered unnecessary.

1885: At the San Carlos Reservation, Geronimo was following the rules set up by General George Crook. However, angry citizens, and particularly local newspapers, vilified Crook for his "lenient" rule over the Apache. Geronimo was also accused of many atrocious and untruthful acts while on the reservation. One local paper suggested Geronimo be hanged by the citizens if the government did not do it. These threats, plus the routine nature of reservation life, agitated Geronimo. On this day, Geronimo, Nana, Mangas, and others were drinking bootleg *tiswin*, or Apache corn liquor. They decided to go to Mexico and try to convince others to go with them. Chato decided to stay, and he and Geronimo almost came to blows over the decision. Geronimo and his conspirators, about 130 in all, fled the reservation, cutting the telegraph wires as they did so. This "escape" sent a shock wave through the local settler communities.

1893: Pressured by the government to sell the Cherokee Strip section of Indian Territory (present-day Oklahoma), the Cherokee Nation ratified the sale of the land. They received approximately $1.31 an acre for over 6.5 million acres of land. The run for this land happened on September 16, 1893.

1948: The assistant secretary of the interior authorized an election to approve a constitution and bylaws for the Organized Village of Holikachuk, Alaska. The election was held on September 10, 1948.

1957: On May 29, 1908, lands on the Cheyenne River Indian Reservation in South Dakota were set aside to create the townsite of Timber Lake. According to Federal Register No. 22FR03693, several lots that were undisposed of were returned to tribal ownership of the Cheyenne River Sioux Tribe.

1974: An election for a proposed amendment to the constitution of the Standing Rock Sioux Tribe was held. The first proposal was approved by a vote of 164–89, the second by 151–102, the third by 170–84, the fourth by 168–85, the fifth by 182–69, and the sixth by 180–65.

1979: An election to approve a constitution and bylaws for the Choctaw Nation of Oklahoma as authorized by the acting deputy commissioner of Indian affairs was held. It was approved by a vote of 1,528–1,226.

MAY 18

1644: A battle in the Powhatan Wars took place.

1661: Captain John Odber was ordered by the Maryland general assembly to take fifty men and go to Susquesahannough Fort. According to a treaty signed on May 16, Maryland was required to help protect the Susquehannock from raids by the Seneca. Odber's force was to fulfill that part of the treaty.

1676: After the fight at Deerfield, Captain William Turner set out to attack a large gathering of Indians near the falls of the Connecticut River. Leading a force of 160 settlers, Turner attacked a sleeping camp. Many of the few Indians who escaped the fighting made their way to the river. Once on the river, many of the Indians died when they plunged over the falls. At least 100 Indians were killed or drowned. Later in the day, as survivors contacted other Indians along the river, a large band of warriors gathered and attacked Turner. During Turner's retreat to Deerfield, he and forty men were killed. (Also recorded as happening on May 19.)

1778: Settlers living in the Path Valley of Cumberland County asked the Supreme Executive Council of Pennsylvania for arms because the British had been trying to get the Indians around Kittanning to attack the American settlers.

1839: General Alexander Macomb announced peace terms with the Seminole. The Seminole were able to stay in Florida if they remained near Lake Okeechobee.

1854: Two treaties were signed regarding the Sac and Fox of Missouri Reserve (10 Stat. 1074). Most of their lands there were ceded back to the United States, except for fifty sections of 640 acres each.

1854: The Kickapoo signed a treaty (10 Stat. 1078) that ceded a large section of their reservation to the United States.

1859: According to his journals, Reverend Pierre De Smet would participate in a conference between the army (General William S. Harney) and local Indians at Fort Vancouver. Indian participants would include chiefs from the Pend d'Oreille, Kalispel, Flathead, Schuyelpi, Coeur d'Alene, Yacoman, and Spokane Tribes.

1868: According to army records, members of the Eighth Cavalry fought with a band of Indians near Rio Salinas, Arizona. Six Indians were reported killed.

1869: After Indians stole livestock from near Fort Bayard in southwestern New Mexico, troops pursued them. Upon arriving at the Indians' village, the troops destroyed it.

1869: From a marker in the Fort Buford (North Dakota) cemetery: "Blue Horn—Indian Scout—May 18, 1869—Killed by hostile Indians war party of Tetons, Santees, and Yanktonnais numbering from sixty to seventy-five attacked the guard over the cattle herd this AM about one mile east of the fort. The attacking party was discovered before they made their charge and were repulsed and driven back across the Missouri River with a loss of one killed and several wounded. We lost one scout killed, an Assiniboine named Blue Horn."

1869: According to army records, members of the Third Cavalry fought with a band of Indians in the Black Range of New Mexico. No casualties were reported. The fighting lasted until May 26.

1870: Lake Station, Colorado, was attacked by Indians. A cavalry unit ran off the Indians but could not capture them.

1871: After waiting overnight on a hill on the Salt Creek Prairie between Fort Richardson and Fort Belknap in north-central Texas, Mamanti and his Kiowa and Comanche followers sighted a small army patrol. Mamanti decided to wait for better pickings. Unknown to Mamanti, General William "Great Warrior" Sherman was one of the members of the patrol. Later in the day, Henry Warren and ten wagons loaded with corn came down the Butterfield Trail. Suspecting a great prize, Mamanti signaled the attack. The Indians killed most of the drivers and then ransacked the wagons. They were disappointed that the wagons contained no weapons. Mamanti and his followers, frustrated, rode back north of the Red River.

1873: This morning at 6:00 A.M. Colonel R.S. Mackenzie and his Fourth Cavalry and Indian scouts reached a Kickapoo and Lipan Indian village of approximately fifty-five lodges near Remolina, Mexico. During the fighting nineteen Indians were killed and forty were captured. A little over fifty horses were seized. The Lipan Principal Chief Costilietos was one of those captured in the fight.

1895: The "surplus lands" of the Kickapoo Indians in Indian Territory (present-day Oklahoma) were opened to the public in another land rush. These prime lands were secured from the Kickapoo by forgeries and deceit in an agreement forced on the Kickapoo on September 9, 1891.

1905: The Supreme Court decided in favor of the Eastern Cherokees and instructed the secretary of the interior to ascertain and identify the persons entitled to participate in the distribution of more than $1 million appropriated by Congress on June 30, 1906, for use in payment of the claims.

1931: The trust period on allotments made to Kickapoo Indians on the Kickapoo Reservation in Kansas was extended again.

1961: The Mi'kmaq Pictou Landing First Nation Reserve of Boat Harbour No. 37 was established in Nova Scotia.

1987: The Lac du Flambeau Band of Lake Superior Chippewa Indians modified their local codes regarding timber trespassing.

MAY 19

1700: Accompanied by missionaries de Montigny and Antoine Davion, a Natchez chief, with twelve followers and two Tunica chiefs and two other Tunica, visited the French outpost at Biloxi on the Mississippi River.

1712: According to some sources, a friendship agreement was reached between representatives of Pennsylvania and the Delaware Indians.

1749: The English gave land grants in the Ohio Valley.

1795: A treaty was signed between the Chippewa and the Canadian government. Second Lieutenant J. Givins represented the crown, and several Chippewa chiefs were present. It was signed at "York in the Province of Upper Canada" (Penetanguishene, Ontario).

1796: Congress passed "An Act Making Appropriations for Defraying the Expenses Which May Arise in Carrying into Effect a Treaty Made Between the United States and Certain Indian Tribes, Northwest of the River Ohio."

1800: As a part of his war with Spain, William Bowles, self-proclaimed "Director-General" of "Muscogee" along the Gulf Coast, attacked the fort at St. Marks, Florida, for a second time. He took over the fort after a siege on January 16, 1792. On this day, he and his Creek and Cherokee followers accepted the surrender of the fort. Spanish forces recaptured it a few months later. (Also recorded as happening on May 10.)

1830: Congressman Davy Crockett, frontiersman and later "hero" at the Battle of the Alamo, and Vermont Representative Horace Everett spoke out in Congress against President Jackson's bill to remove the Indians to west of the Mississippi River.

1835: White citizens in Macon County, Alabama, sent a resolution to President Jackson renouncing the persons who had defrauded the Creek out of most of their lands. They asked the president to withhold certification of all land sales until an investigation could be held.

1836: Several hundred Comanche warriors, under a flag of truce, approached the fort built by the Parker brothers on the Navasota River (near modern Navasota, Texas). They demanded a cow. The settlers refused, and the Comanche stormed the fort. Seven settlers were killed. Two children, Cynthia Ann and John Parker, were kidnapped. John would, one day, leave the tribe as an adult. Cynthia would marry a Comanche chief, Peta Nacona, and had two sons, Pecos and Quanah, and one daughter, Prairie Flower. Cynthia would eventually be rescued against her will on December 18, 1860. Quanah Parker would become a Comanche war chief.

1836: According to some sources, General Thomas Jesup took over command of western forces in the Creek War.

1837: In Florida, Creek warriors and Florida militia fought along Battle Bay on the Choctawhatchee River. The fighting lasted for several days. Most of the Creek were eventually killed or captured.

1838: Seminole Chiefs Mikanopy, King Philip, Coahadjo, and Little Cloud and 453 other Seminole left New Orleans on the steamboat *Renown*, bound for the Indian Territory (present-day Oklahoma).

1840: A group of Seminole warriors were waiting in ambush near Micanopy, Florida. Thirteen soldiers entered the trap. Ten of the soldiers were killed in the fighting.

1868: According to army records, members of the Thirteenth Infantry fought with a band of Indians near the mouth of the Musselshell River in Dakota Territory. Ten Indians were wounded.

1870: According to official army records, Indians skirmished with a group of soldiers from the Ninth Cavalry near Kickapoo Springs, Texas. Four Indians were wounded. The fighting lasted until the next day.

1872: A group of Kiowa Indians attacked a party of citizens, twenty-five miles from Fort Belknap in north-central Texas. One white and two Indians were killed. Two Indians were wounded.

1882: Fort Stanton Reserve (Mescalero Apache) boundary lines in New Mexico were modified.

1936: Jicarilla Apache Reservation lines in New Mexico were modified.

1939: Pope Pius XII approved the beatification of Kateritekawitha, a Mohawk from Ossernenon, New York.

1940: An election to approve amendments to the constitution and bylaws for the Kashia Band of Pomo Indians of the Stewarts Point Rancheria was held. Two were approved by a majority of the twenty-two people voting.

1971: The associate commissioner of Indian affairs authorized an election to approve an amendment to the constitution of the Grindstone Indian Rancheria in Glenn County, California. The election was held on June 27, 1971.

1974: Rod Curl (Wintu) won a golf tournament.

MAY 20

1493: A civil war battle among the Cakchiquel (Kaqchikel) Maya took place on this day in what is present-day Guatemala.

1636: British trader John Gallop spotted John Oldham's ship near Block Island. The decks were covered with Indians. Oldham was not in sight. Gallop attacked the ship and the Indians. Most got away. Gallop found Oldham's body on the boat. This was one of the first fights of the Pequot War.

1702: Franciscans had established the Santa Fe de Toluca Mission at one of the largest Timucua villages in northern Florida. Apalachicola Indians fought a battle with Spanish and Mission Indians.

Both sides lost a considerable number of fighters before the Apalachicola finally gained the upper hand.

1777: When Dragging Canoe and his followers left the area, older chiefs arranged a peace treaty that was signed by the Cherokees and representatives of the American colonies in the South. The Americans forced the Cherokees to cede all of their lands (more than 5 million acres) in South Carolina. This created a great rift in the tribe. Many Cherokees joined the offshoot Chickamauga tribe. General Andrew Williamson was one of the American representatives. This was called the Treaty of De Witt's Corner.

1777: In 1775, Benjamin Logan established an outpost at what became present-day Stanford, Kentucky. Logan's Station would eventually attract other settlers. Shawnees mounted an attack on the station. One settler, William Hudson, was killed; Logan rescued another. The Shawnees established a siege that lasted until a column of frontiersmen arrived in late June.

1832: Forces under Black Hawk were reported to have attacked a settlement on Indian Creek. Fifteen settlers were killed. This was also reported to have happened on May 20.

1858: Reverend Pierre De Smet left St. Louis to go west. He would visit many different tribes during this trip while serving as chaplain for an army expedition.

1862: Congress passed the Homestead Act. This act allowed settlers to buy 160 acres of western, formerly Indian, land for $1.25 an acre. This brought in a new wave of settlers to the west.

1863: A new Northwest Reservation Conference started. It lasted through June 9.

1870: Although scouting for Indians at Kickapoo Springs, Texas, Sergeant Emanuel Stance encountered a group of hostile Indians. For his actions during the ensuing fight, he would be awarded the Medal of Honor. Four Indians were wounded in the encounter. The fighting started the day before, according to army records.

1871: Indians skirmished with a group of soldiers from the Fourth Cavalry in the divide between the Brazos and Big Wishita Rivers in Texas, according to official army records. One Indian was killed and one soldier was wounded.

1872: Lieutenant Gustavus Valois, troops from the Ninth Cavalry, and eight Indian scouts attacked a small group of Kickapoo Indians at La Pendencia, Texas. Official army records did not report the outcome of the battle.

1878: Seventh Infantry soldiers fought a group of Indians near the head of White's Gulch, Montana. According to army documents, one Indian was killed and two were wounded.

1948: Assistant Secretary of the Interior William Warne ratified a constitution and bylaws approved by the Confederated Tribes of the Warm Springs Reservation of Oregon in an election held on April 24, 1948.

1966: The assistant secretary of the interior ratified an amendment to the constitution and bylaws for the Shoshone-Paiute Tribes of the Duck Valley Reservation in Nevada.

1968: An election by the Havasupai Nation for an amendment to their constitution was held. The result was approval for three new amendments by a majority of the twenty-five tribal members voting.

1972: Mt. Adams reverted back to the Yakima.

MAY 21

1542: Hernando de Soto died with a high fever in the village of Guachoyo, along the Mississippi River. Before his death, he appointed Luis de Moscoso to be his replacement. Fearing that the Indians might exhume his body, Moscoso had de Soto's body weighted down and deposited in the Mississippi River.

1733: According to some sources, an agreement covering amity, land cession, and trade was reached by representatives of the British in Georgia and the Lower Creek, Yamacraw, and Yuchi Indians.

1751: The French suggested that Indians should abandon the British.

1803: Chiefs of the four Southern Tribes met at Hickory Grounds (near modern Wetumpka, Alabama). They talked with American representatives Stephen Folch, John Forbes, and Benjamin Hawkins about land, money, and William Bowles's efforts to unite the Indians into a new country, with him as its leader and with British support.

1832: As a part of Black Hawk's War, a group of approximately fifty Potawatomi attacked a settlement on Indian Creek (near modern Ottawa, Illinois). Fifteen settlers were killed in the fighting. This was often called the Indian Creek Massacre. This was also reported to have happened on May 20.

1869: According to army records, members of the Fourth Infantry fought with a band of Indians near Fort Fred Steele, Wyoming. No casualties were reported.

1871: Indians skirmished with a group of soldiers from the Twenty-Fifth Infantry near Camp Melvin Station, Texas, according to official army records. Two soldiers were wounded.

1877: In retaliation for the Custer defeat, the Sioux and Ponca were ordered to go to a new reservation in Indian Territory (present-day Oklahoma). The Ponca had nothing to do with the war, and they continued their complaints about the bureaucratic error that placed them on a reservation with the Sioux in the first place. The government did not bend, and the Ponca began their march to Indian Territory.

1879: In the *Standing Bear* case, the courts decided that Indians were people in the eyes of the law and no Indian could be held on a particular reservation against his will. Big Snake, Standing Bear's brother, decided to test the law. He asked his agent for permission to visit Standing Bear. His request was denied. He decided to leave the Ponca Reservation in Indian Territory (present-day Oklahoma) to visit the Cheyenne Reservation, also

in Indian Territory. Big Snake asked for permission to leave from his agent, William Whiteman. Whiteman again refused the request. Big Snake and thirty other Ponca left anyway. On this day, Agent Whiteman telegraphed the commissioner of Indian affairs of Big Snake's exit, with the request that Big Snake be arrested at Fort Reno in central Indian Territory.

1928: An act of Congress (45 Stat. 618) acquired twenty acres for the Winnemucca Shoshone Indian Colony in Nevada.

1979: An election that approved a constitution and bylaws for the Choctaw Nation of Oklahoma was ratified by Acting Deputy Commissioner of Indian Affairs Martin E. Seneca Jr. The election was held on May 17, 1979.

1980: The secretary of the interior authorized an election for an amendment to the constitution and bylaws of the Lac Courte Oreilles Band of Lake Superior Chippewa Indians of Wisconsin. The election was held on August 16, 1980.

1983: The bylaws of Kootznoowoo Incorporated were amended.

1990: Amendments to the Menominee constitution and bylaws were introduced and approved by a vote of the Menominee people starting this date through May 24, 1990.

MAY 22

1836: The town of Irwinton (modern Eufaula), Alabama, was attacked by Creek warriors. They were beaten back by the settlers.

1838: A total of 674 Seminole boarded the steamer *South Alabama* in New Orleans. They were bound for the Indian Territory (present-day Oklahoma).

1851: As one of the last conflicts in the Mariposa Indian Wars in California, a large group of Yosemite Indians was captured at Lake Tenaija.

1854: The House of Representatives passed the Kansas-Nebraska Act.

Paiute Indian with bow and arrow (NA)

1863: As a part of the Owens Valley War in California, Paiute Chief Captain George arrived at Camp Independence. He told the soldiers the Paiute wanted peace. This effectively ended the war.

1869: According to army records, members of the First Cavalry, Thirty-Second Infantry, and Indian scouts fought with a band of Indians near Mineral Springs, Arizona. Four Indians were killed and four were captured. The fighting lasted until May 28.

1872: Members of Troop E, Sixth Cavalry, acting as couriers between Fort Dodge in southwestern Kansas and Fort Supply in northwestern Indian Territory (present-day Oklahoma), were attacked by Indians. One soldier was killed and one was wounded.

1872: Indians skirmished with a group of settlers near Sonoita Valley, Arizona, according to official army records. One settler was killed.

1873: One hundred fifty Modoc Indians surrendered to Colonel J.C. Davis near Fairchild's Ranch in California, according to army documents.

1879: General Sherman ordered General Sheridan to transport Big Snake from Fort Reno in central Indian Territory (present-day Oklahoma) back to the Ponca Reservation. Sherman decided that the court decision applied only to Standing Bear and to no one else.

1885: Fourth Cavalry soldiers and Indian scouts fought a group of Indians near Devil's Creek in the Mogollon Mountains of New Mexico. According to army documents, four soldiers were wounded.

1945: The constitution and bylaws of the Mississippi Band of Choctaw Indians were approved.

1959: An election approved Amendment 5 to the constitution and bylaws of the Lac du Flambeau Band of Lake Superior Chippewa Indians of Wisconsin.

1971: An election was held to establish a constitution and bylaws for the Shoalwater Bay Indian Organization in Washington State. It was approved by a vote of 5–0.

1974: An election for an amendment to the constitution of the Red Lake Band of Chippewa Indians of Minnesota was held. With 2,745 eligible voters, it passed by a vote of 826–273.

1976: An election for an amendment to the constitution and bylaws for the Lower Elwha Tribal Community of the Lower Elwha Reservation in Washington State was authorized. The results were 49–25 in favor.

1976: The area director, Portland area office, Bureau of Indian Affairs, had authorized an election to amend the constitution and bylaws of the Kalispel Indian Community of the Kalispel Reservation. The amendment was approved by a vote of 17–5.

1980: An election that approved an amendment to the constitution and bylaws for the Shakopee Mdewakanton Sioux Community was ratified by the acting area director, Bureau of Indian Affairs.

MAY 23

1774: Lower Creek warrior Ogulki murdered another Creek and left false clues implicating white settlers. Angry Creek attacked the settlers in retaliation. When Ogulki saw that he had accomplished his goal, he began a series of unprovoked attacks on the settlers. These attacks led to expeditions against the Creek by the local militia. Realizing that Ogulki had started the entire affair, Upper Creek chiefs demanded that the Lower Creek put Ogulki to death to end the matter. On this day, Ogulki was killed by Cussita Creek warriors.

1775: The Cherokees gave up some land.

1802: Ceremonies for a treaty conference began at Fort Wilkinson, Georgia, with the United States and the Creek. The real meetings began the next day.

1836: The New Echota Treaty (7 Stat. 478) had been ratified by the Senate by one vote. President Andrew Jackson publicly proclaimed the treaty. The treaty was signed by members of the Treaty Party, less than 500 Cherokees. Some 16,000 Cherokees opposed the treaty, but the government ignored their rejection of the document.

1837: A group of American militia captured a Creek warrior and eleven women and children in Walton County, Florida, along Alaqua Creek. All the Indians were eventually shot and killed. Their bodies were also mutilated.

1838: Under the provisions of the New Echota Treaty of December 29, 1835, this was the deadline for Cherokees to emigrate to the Indian Territory (present-day Oklahoma). Any Cherokees still east of the Mississippi River after this day were forced to leave. Only an estimated 2,000 Cherokees had emigrated to the Indian Territory by this date, according to government estimates. General Winfield Scott was charged with removing the recalcitrant Cherokees. Many were forced from their homes at bayonet point. The illegal treaty was publicly proclaimed by President Jackson two years earlier to this day.

1859: A group of Texans led by John Baylor attacked the Caddo living on the Brazos River Reservation. The pretext for the attack was a series of murders committed by nonreservation Plains Indians. After one Indian was killed, Indian Agent Robert Neighbors interceded. He arranged for the Caddo to be moved to a new reservation in Oklahoma, far from the Indian-hating Texans. Neighbors was murdered himself in September for being an "Indian-lover."

1867: According to army records, members of a stage escort fought with a band of Indians near Big Timbers, Kansas. One soldier was wounded.

1867: According to army records, members of the Second Cavalry fought with a band of Indians near Bridger's Ferry, Dakota Territory. Two soldiers were killed.

1868: Kit Carson died in Colorado.

1872: Because of his "conspicuous gallantry in a charge upon the Tonto Apache" in Sycamore Canyon, Arizona, First Sergeant Richard Barrett, Company A, First Cavalry, would be awarded the Medal of Honor.

1872: Captain E.M. Heyl and troopers from the Fourth Cavalry were attacked by Comanche on the Lost River in Texas. One soldier and one horse were killed.

1873: The Northwest Mounted Police was founded. One of the main reasons for its creation was the problems being fomented by Americans selling alcohol to Canadian Indians. This organization eventually became the Royal Canadian Mounted Police.

1880: One Bull went to Fort Buford for Sitting Bull.

1936: Secretary of the Interior Harold Ickes had authorized an election to approve a constitution and bylaws for the members of the Minnesota Mdewakanton Sioux of the Prairie Island Indian Community in Minnesota. It was approved by a vote of 35–4.

1939: The assistant secretary of the interior authorized an election to approve a constitution and bylaws for the Native Village of Gambell. The election was held on December 31, 1939.

1939: The assistant secretary of the interior authorized an election to approve a constitution and bylaws for the Eskimos of the Native Village of

Elim, Alaska. The election was held on November 24, 1939.

1944: Van Barfoot, a Choctaw, was a second lieutenant in the Forty-Fifth Infantry. For his actions against enemy troops near Anzio, Italy, he would be awarded the Medal of Honor. Among his achievements: destroying two machine-gun nests, capturing seventeen German soldiers, stopping a German tank assault, and carrying two wounded commanders to safety.

1975: The area director, Sacramento area office, Bureau of Indian Affairs, authorized an election for an amendment to the constitution and bylaws of the Manchester Band of Pomo Indians of the Manchester Rancheria.

Every: The San Juan Buffalo Dance and Feast.

MAY 24

1513: While exploring the Gulf Coast of Florida, Ponce de Leon encountered Calusa Indians near Charlotte Harbor. In a fight with the Calusa, de Leon captured four warriors.

1539: Mexican Viceroy Don Antonio de Mendoza had decided to send an expedition to search for wealthy cities north of Mexico. On March 7, 1539, Friar Marcos de Niza started the expedition from Culiacan. According to Niza's journal, he finally saw Cibola, although he never set foot in the pueblo. His report would lead to future expeditions looking for the Seven Cities of Gold.

1607: Jamestown was founded (May 14, old-style).

1721: In a letter addressed to Bienville (governor of Louisiana), de Boisbriant (governor of the Illinois District) warned of a plan by the Spanish. He had been notified that an expedition of 300 Spanish soldiers from Santa Fe was headed toward Louisiana to take over the territory from the French. According to de Boisbriant, they were attacked by "Osage and Panis" Indians. The Spanish retreated back to Santa Fe. Some of the facts were

considered to be wrong, but this report established concern among the French.

1746: Indians had surrounded Fort Number Four (at modern Charlestown, New Hampshire). The fort had twenty-one defenders. Phineas Stevens arrived and led an attack on the Indians. Five men were killed on both sides of the skirmish. Stevens, known as an excellent "Indian fighter," learned Indian ways while he was a prisoner of the Waranoke.

1802: Representatives of the Creek Nation and the U.S. government began negotiations of debts and land. A treaty was reached and signed on June 16, 1802, at Fort Wilkinson, near Milledgeville, Georgia.

1834: The Chickasaw signed a treaty (7 Stat. 450). A provision of the treaty granted protection from hostile Indians. A commission was established among the Chickasaws that had to approve the competency of any tribal member before he could sell land.

1841: Numerous Indian tribes had settled on Village Creek (near modern Arlington, Texas, between Dallas and Fort Worth). In retaliation for attacks on local settlements, seventy Texas Rangers, led by General Edward Tarrant, attacked the villages. Although outnumbered, the Texans managed to kill a dozen warriors before they were forced to retreat. Many of the Indians left the area.

1868: Sitting Bull captured riders and gave the army a warning.

According to army records, members of the Thirteenth Infantry fought with a band of Indians near the mouth of the Musselshell River in Dakota Territory. Two soldiers were killed.

1868: According to army records, members of the Thirteenth Infantry fought with a band of Indians near the Yellowstone River in Montana. No injuries were reported on either side.

1871: Lieutenant E.M. Hayes and Fifth Cavalry troops captured six hostile Indians near Birdwood Creek, Nebraska.

1872: Indians skirmished with a group of soldiers from the Fourth Cavalry near Lost Creek,

Texas, according to official army records. One soldier was wounded.

1880: Colonel Edward Hatch and a large contingent of cavalry had been searching for Victorio and his followers for some time. Chief Scout H.K. Parker and his Indian scouts fought a group of Indians near the headwaters of the Palomas River in New Mexico. The army reported that fifty-five Indians were killed in this battle.

1881: Captain O.B. Reed, the commanding officer at Camp Poplar in northeastern Montana, reported the surrender of eight lodges, equaling fifty hostiles, including twelve men.

1911: In New Mexico, Executive Order No. 1359 modified a previous order concerning lands in New Mexico.

1940: An election was held to approve amendments to the constitution and bylaws of the Tule River Indian Tribe. The results were 15–1 for both Amendments 1 and 2.

1952: An amended adoption ordinance for the Coeur d'Alene Tribe had been passed by the Tribal Council. It was approved by the acting commissioner of Indian affairs.

1969: The acting assistant commissioner of Indian affairs had authorized an election to approve a constitution and bylaws for the Hoh Indian Tribe. It was approved by a vote of 21–0.

1972: The articles of association adopted by the Twenty-Nine Palms Band of Mission Indians on March 1, 1972, were approved by Acting Deputy Commissioner of Indian Affairs Alexander Mac-Nabb.

1976: The commissioner of Indian affairs authorized an election for an amendment to the constitution and bylaws of the Manzanita Band of Mission Indians. The election was held on August 21, 1976.

1978: An election for an amendment to the constitution of the Red Lake Band of Chippewa Indians of Minnesota was held. Of the 1,490 people eligible to vote, the result was 1,028–62 in favor.

1996: Executive Order No. 13007, "Indian Sacred Sites," was issued. Its purpose was to "protect and preserve Indian religious practices."

Every: St. John Feast Day celebrated by many Pueblos.

MAY 25

1539: Hernando de Soto's Spanish expedition arrived off the shore of western Florida. Their mission was to explore Florida and the surrounding countryside.

1540: Hernando de Soto's army entered Cherokee lands. They spent the night near what is modern Highlands, North Carolina.

1637: The Battle of Mystic was fought. As a part of the Pequot War, Mohegan Chief Uncas was leading approximately 100 Indian allies, but he was doubtful of the ability of seventy-seven Europeans under Captains John Underhill and John Mason to defeat the Pequot. Regardless, they attacked a fortified Pequot village (near modern Mystic, Connecticut) before dawn. Few of the Pequot warriors were in the village, and the allies set fire to the dwellings. According to some accounts, as many as 700 old men, women, and children were burned or shot to death. Only about a dozen Pequot in the village survived. (Also recorded as happening on May 26 and June 5.)

1673: At the site of modern Niles, Michigan, the British erected Fort St. Joseph. Its garrison of sixteen men, led by Ensign Francis Schlosser, was attacked by a large Potawatomi war party. Only Schlosser and three other men survived the attack. The British were later traded for Potawatomi prisoners in Detroit.

1716: French commander Bienville had demanded the head of the Natchez chief, Oyelape, who had ordered the killing of five Frenchmen. On this day, Natchez Indians he sent with his demand to the main Natchez village returned. They said that the chief had gone into hiding and could not be found. They did return the dead Frenchmen's slaves and some of their property.

1736: As part of the French attacks on Chickasaw Indians along the Mississippi River, Major Pierre d'Artaguette, French soldiers, and Iroquois, Kaskaskia, and Miami warriors attacked the village of Hashuk-humma. The village's fortifications were formidable, and they were able to hold off the attackers. When Chickasaw reinforcements arrived, d'Artaguette's Indian allies retreated. D'Artaguette eventually surrendered after most of his remaining force was incapacitated. Most of the French prisoners, including d'Artaguette, were executed.

1776: The U.S. Congress resolved that it would be "highly expedient" if the United States could engage Indians to fight on its side of the Revolutionary War.

1782: Led by Colonel William Crawford, 480 Virginia volunteers were looking for survivors of the Gnadenhutten Massacre. As they were about to leave the abandoned village, they were attacked by a large group of Indians. The fighting continued until the next day. Crawford retreated when more Indians arrived on the scene.

1854: The U.S. Senate passed Kansas-Nebraska Act.

1868: Thirty-nine Oglala Sioux, including Sitting Bull, signed the Fort Laramie Treaty (15 Stat. 635).

1869: Indians attacked settlements in Jewell County, Kansas. According to army reports, six citizens were killed and three women assaulted.

1870: According to official army records, Indians skirmished with a group of soldiers from the First and Third Cavalry in the Tonto Valley in Arizona. Twenty-one Indians were killed and twelve were captured.

1881: Sitting Bull sat in council with Dewdney at Fort Qu'appelle through May 26.

1931: Trust Patent No. 1046692 was issued, containing 440 acres for the Pechanga Indian Reservation–Temecula Band of Luiseno Mission Indians.

1933: President Franklin Roosevelt, by executive order, abolished the Board of Indian Commissioners, created on June 3, 1869. The board had been designed to oversee Indian appropriations.

1940: Amendments to the constitution of the Tuolumne Band of Me-Wok Indians of the Tuolumne Rancheria were approved by a vote of 21–1.

1961: The U.S. government set aside lands on the Blackfeet Indian Reservation in Montana on April 9, 1954, for administrative purposes. Some of these lands were returned to Blackfeet tribal ownership.

MAY 26

1540: The "Lady of Cofitachequi" had been taken with the de Soto expedition against her will. With a large quantity of the pearls that de Soto's men took from her village, she escaped.

1540: According to Coronado's journal, he reached the "valley of the people: Called Caracones."

1637: The Battle of Mystic took place. As a part of the Pequot War, Mohegan Chief Uncas was leading approximately 100 Indian allies, but he was doubtful of the ability of seventy-seven Europeans under Captains John Underhill and John Mason to defeat the Pequot. Regardless, they attacked a fortified Pequot village (near modern Mystic, Connecticut) before dawn. Few of the Pequot warriors were in the village, and the allies set fire to the dwellings. According to some accounts, as many as 700 old men, women, and children were burned or shot to death. Only about a dozen Pequot in the village survived. (Also recorded as happening on May 25 and June 5.)

1728: According to some sources, a peace and friendship conference was held for two days between the representatives of the British in Pennsylvania and the Conestoga, Delaware, Potomac, and Shawnee Indians.

1736: A band of 500 French and another force of Choctaw warriors attacked the Chickasaw village of Ackia in northern Mississippi. The attacking force was lead by Jean Baptiste le Moyne, Sieur de Bienville, and Chevalier de Noyan. Despite repeated assaults on the Chickasaw battlements over a three-hour period, the French and, eventually, the Choctaws were repulsed. The French sustained twenty-four fatalities.

1798: During the Creek National Council meeting, Creek speaker Eau Haujo joked about cattle. He said that they "do not understand stipulations relative to boundaries." They go where the grass is.

1826: Elias Boudinot gave a speech at the First Presbyterian Church of Philadelphia about his tribe, the Cherokees. The publisher of the *Cherokee Phoenix*, Boudinot described the tribe and their recent changes.

1839: Captain John Bird and thirty-four Texas Rangers encountered a force of more than 200 Caddo, Comanche, and Kickapoo Indians (near modern Temple, Texas). Several people were killed on both sides. This was eventually called the Bird's Creek Indian Fight.

1856: Colonel Wright left troops at the Cascades while he marched to the Columbia River. On this day, Kamiakin led Yakima Indians against the Cascade garrison. The settlement was attacked, and the blockhouse where the troops were located was surrounded. This was called the Cascade Massacre by the whites.

1865: A grand council was held of the Indian Territory (present-day Oklahoma) tribes who held land in the so-called leased district. Representatives from the Kansas area and the Plains Indians were invited as well. They made a pledge not to spill any additional Indian blood.

1865: As a part of the Black Hawk War in Utah, a group of Ute Indians killed several members of a settler family named Given.

1868: The day before and on this day, fifteen Minneconjou Sioux signed the Fort Laramie Treaty

Red Cloud delegation in Washington. From left to right: Red Dog, Little Wound, John Bridgeman (interpreter), Red Cloud, American Horse, and Red Shirt (NA)

(15 Stat. 635). Twenty-four "Yanctonais Sioux" and twenty-five Arapaho also signed.

1869: Indians attacked a wagon train near Sheridan (near modern Winona), Kansas. Two drivers were wounded and 300 mules were stolen.

1869: According to army records, members of the Third Cavalry fought with a band of Indians in the Black Range of New Mexico. No casualties were reported. The fighting started on May 18.

1870: Commissioner of Indian Affairs Ely Parker (Donehogawa), concerned about war fever among the Plains Indians, let it be known that Sioux Chief Red Cloud would be a welcome guest in Washington for talks. Red Cloud decided to visit the Great Father and to see the Indian commissioner for himself. On this day, he boarded a train at Fort Laramie in southeastern Wyoming for the trip to Washington.

1874: Apache Cochinay was killed.

1877: Abbot Marty visited Sitting Bull's camp in Canada.

1881: Major D.H. Brotherton accepted the surrender of a group of hostile Indians at Fort Buford, Dakota Territory. According to army documents, thirty-two Sioux surrendered.

1885: Poundmaker, a leader in Riel's Rebellion, surrendered to Canadian forces at Fort Battleford.

MAY 27

1598: Oñate's expedition reached the Piro village of Qualacu in modern New Mexico. (Also recorded as happening on June 12.)

1607: Virginia had its first significant battle between Indians and European settlers.

1761: Cherokee Chief Attakullaculla (Little Carpenter) met with English Colonel James Grant to pursue peace between the two groups. The British refused the overture. They still wanted revenge for the attack on Fort Loudoun.

1763: Fort Miami was located at a site near what is modern Fort Wayne, Indiana. It was garrisoned by twelve British soldiers led by Ensign Robert Holmes. Pontiac's Rebellion had started, and the ensign was convinced to leave the fort by his Miami Indian girlfriend. Miami warriors killed the ensign and a sergeant who left the fort to look for the ensign. The Miami demanded the surrender of the remaining soldiers. To drive home their point, they threw the head of Ensign Holmes into the fort. The soldiers surrendered, and all but one were eventually killed.

1803: After meeting for several days, leaders of the four Southern Tribes agreed that William Bowles's scheme to unite the tribes with him as its "King of the Four Nations" was ludicrous. He was placed in chains and delivered to the Spanish governor in New Orleans. Bowles was eventually taken to Morro Castle in Havana, where in two years he would die.

1831: Explorer Jed Smith was believed to be killed by Comanche.

1842: The last soldier to die in the Seminole War succumbed to his wounds. His name was Private Jesse Van Tassel. He was shot on May 17.

1847: The Oregon Country publication *The Spectator* carried an article by its editor, George L. Curry. He blamed much of the problems with the local Indians on their use of alcohol. He asked for better enforcement of the laws prohibiting the sale of "intoxicants" to Indians.

1856: General John Wool, soldiers, and volunteers defeated the Rogue River Indians at the Battle of Big Meadows, Oregon. Tecumton (Elk Killer John) and his Rogue River Indian followers surrounded Captain Smith's camp on the Rogue River. Tecumton maintained an active assault on the troops for thirty-six hours until a relief column arrived the next day. When the relief column arrived, on May 28, Captain Augur charged the Indians. The Indians scattered. Ten whites were killed during the thirty-six-hour siege.

1862: Latta brought money to the Sioux. A party was then held.

1866: Elements of the Fourteenth Infantry fought some Indians on the Owyhee River in Idaho. One soldier was killed, seven Indians were killed, and twelve Indians were wounded, according to Fourteenth Infantry records.

1867: According to army records, members of the Seventh Cavalry under Captain M.W. Keogh fought with a band of Indians near Pond Creek Station, Kansas. Five Indians were killed and five were wounded.

1873: At the San Carlos Reservation, Chandeisi killed Lieutenant Jacob Almy and then tried unsuccessfully to kill Agent Larrabee.

1878: An attack by a group of Bannock warriors on a camp of animal herders in the Camas Valley eventually led to what was called the Bannock War.

1910: An act of Congress was passed that allowed the government to classify and dispose of surplus lands on the Pine Ridge Reservation in South Dakota.

1949: The assistant commissioner of Indian affairs authorized an election to approve a constitution and bylaws for the Confederated Tribes of the Umatilla Reservation. The election was held on November 4, 1949.

1970: The U.S. Office of the Solicitor offered an opinion for the Shoshone-Bannock Tribes of the

Fort Hall Reservation that under their constitution a convicted felon could serve upon the Fort Hall Business Council.

1978: The area director, Sacramento area office, Bureau of Indian Affairs, had authorized an election for an amendment for the constitution for the Utu Utu Gwaitu Paiute Tribe of the Benton Paiute Reservation in California. It was approved by a vote of 15–0, according to a government document.

MAY 28

1539: Hernando de Soto landed in America (also reported as May 25).

1754: Twenty-one-year-old Lieutenant Colonel George Washington led a force of Virginia militia of almost eighty men, including a band of Delaware Indians (under the Half-King Jeskakake), to aid in the building of a new fort at the forks of the Ohio (Pittsburgh, Pennsylvania). The French beat them to the area and had already started Fort Duquesne. On this day, Washington's men surprised a French detachment under Jumonville de Villiers on Chestnut Ridge in Fayette County, Pennsylvania. Washington's troops killed ten and captured the rest of the French forces. This fight in southwestern Pennsylvania was the first battle of the French and Indian War. Within a few days, Washington's forces build Fort Necessity not far from here. Among Washington's allies was Iroquois Chief Tanacharison, Half-King of the Delaware.

1763: Lieutenant Abraham Cuyler was en route to Fort Detroit with supplies and almost 100 men when he landed at Point Pelee in southern Ontario, on Lake Erie. Unaware of Pontiac's Uprising, the men were attacked by Indians after Cuyler set up camp. Only Cuyler and a few men escaped the attack.

1765: According to some reports, a meeting was held regarding questions over boundary lines between the British and the Creek.

1830: Andrew Jackson, called "Sharp Knife" by the Indians, had long fought the Indians of the

Andrew Jackson, called "Sharp Knife" by Indians

Southeast. He believed that the Indians and white settlers would not be able to peacefully live together. His solution was to renege on all of the previous treaties that granted the Indians their lands forever and to move all Indians west of the Mississippi River. Jackson made this proposal to Congress during his first congressional speech on December 8, 1829. Congress made the proposal into a law on this day.

1851: One in a series of treaties was signed with California Indians at Dent's and Ventine's Crossings. The purpose of the treaty was to reserve lands for the Indians and to protect them from angry Europeans.

1868: Fort Downer, west of Hays, Kansas, was abandoned.

1869: According to army records, members of the First Cavalry, Thirty-Second Infantry, and Indian scouts fought with a band of Indians near Mineral Springs, Arizona. Four Indians were killed and four were captured. The fighting started on May 22.

1870: In the panhandle area of Indian Territory (present-day Oklahoma), near Camp Supply, Indians attacked a wagon train. They killed one of the drivers and ran off all of the mules. Near the camp later that day, they ran off another herd and killed another man.

1871: Indians skirmished with a group of soldiers from the Eighth Cavalry Infantry in the Canadian Mountains in Texas, according to official army records. Twelve Indians were captured.

1873: Camp Shafter was established twenty-six miles southeast of Fort Duncan and Eagle Pass, Texas. It was often used as a base for operations against the Kickapoo.

1875: Indian scouts were awarded the Medal of Honor.

1885: The Frenchmens Butte Fight took place, part of Riel's Rebellion.

1888: Jim Thorpe was born.

1904: Kicking Bear, a Miniconjou Sioux, died, according to some sources.

1909: Pursuant to a Supreme Court decision on April 29, 1907, that required a new tribal roll for the Eastern Cherokee, Guion Miller reported that 45,847 separate applications had been filed, representing a total of some 90,000 individual claimants, of which 30,254 were enrolled as entitled to share in the $1 million fund set aside by the court. Some 3,203 Cherokees were residing in east and 27,051 were residing west of the Mississippi River.

1930: By Executive Order No. 5356, the trust period on allotments made to members of the Prairie Band of Potawatomi Indians in Kansas was extended.

1968: According to Federal Register No. 33FR08275, certain lands in Dakota were restored to the tribal ownership of the Cheyenne River Sioux Tribe of Indians.

1974: The area director, Bureau of Indian Affairs, had authorized an election for an amendment to the constitution and bylaws of the Lower Brule Sioux Tribe of the Lower Brule Reservation. It was approved by a vote of 56–13.

1987: The constitution of the Miami of Oklahoma was amended.

MAY 29

1643: The New England Confederation talked about Indians.

1677: Pamunkey, Roanoke, Nottaway, and Nansemond Tribes of the Powhatan Confederacy signed a treaty with the English in Virginia.

1792: William Blount held a conference with 2,000 Cherokee and Chickamauga chiefs and warriors at the village of Coyatee. He denounced the Chickamauga for murder, looting, and horse-stealing. The Chickamauga chiefs promised to stop any such incursions. But they continued.

1838: The Republic of Texas signed a treaty with the Comanche (near modern Houston).

1855: The Walla Walla conference started.

1868: According to army records, members of the First Cavalry and some Indian scouts fought with a band of Indians near the Owyhee River in Idaho. Thirty-four Indians were killed in the fighting.

1869: Indians attacked Fossil Station, Kansas, killing two and wounding four whites. That night, the Indians derailed a Kansas Pacific railroad train.

1870: According to official army records, Indians skirmished with a group of soldiers from the Ninth Cavalry near Bass Canyon, Texas. One soldier was killed.

1870: According to official army records, Indians skirmished with a group of soldiers from the Third Cavalry near Camp Apache, Arizona. One Indian was wounded and six were captured. The fighting continued through June 26.

1871: Indians skirmished with a group of soldiers from the Eighth Cavalry near Kiowa Springs, New Mexico, according to official army records. Twenty-two Indians were captured.

1876: General George Crook, this time taking personal command and Troops A, B, D, E, and I, Second Cavalry, Troops A, B, C, D, E, F, H, I, L, and M, Third Cavalry, Companies D and F, Fourth Infantry, and Companies C, G, and H, Ninth Infantry, left Fort Fetterman in southeastern Wyoming en route to Goose Creek.

1876: The Interior Department was told to cooperate with the War Department so the military could round up the hostile Indians whenever they might appear at a reservation or agency.

1877: Sixth Cavalry soldiers fought a group of Indians near Camp Bowie, Arizona. According to army documents, no casualties were reported.

1879: Captain Charles Beyer, with parts of Troops C and I, Ninth Cavalry, fought with Victorio's Warm Springs Apache in the Black Range of the Miembres Mountains at Cuchillo Negro River, near Ojo Caliente, New Mexico. One soldier and two Indians were killed. Two soldiers and two Indians were wounded in the fighting. The army captured the Indians' animals during the battle. Victorio fled into Mexico. Sergeant Thomas Boyne, Company C, would be awarded the Medal of Honor for "bravery in action."

1880: Settlers fought a group of Indians near Cook's Canyon, New Mexico. According to army documents, five citizens were killed.

1908: Congress approved an act (35 Stat. 460–463) that created the townsite of Timber Lake in the Cheyenne River Indian Reservation from lands belonging to the Cheyenne River Sioux.

1912: By Executive Order No. 1540, President Woodrow Wilson set aside lands in Arizona for the use of Walapai Indians.

1928: An act of Congress (45 Stat. 899) acquired twenty acres for the Winnemucca Shoshone Indian Colony in Nevada.

1936: The secretary of the interior authorized an election to approve a constitution and bylaws for the Hannahville Indian Community in Michigan. The election was held on June 27, 1936.

1945: The Shoshone-Arapaho tribes of Indians in Wyoming ceded to the United States a large area of their reservation in the state of Wyoming. According to Federal Register No. 10FR07542, they received part of that land back into the Wind River Reservation.

1946: The assistant secretary of the interior authorized an election for approval of a constitution and bylaws for the Nisqually Indian Community of the Nisqually Reservation in Washington. The election was held on July 27, 1946.

1954: An election for amendments to the constitution for the Omaha Tribe of Nebraska was held. It was approved by a vote of 159–2.

1958: Assistant Secretary of the Interior Roger Ernst authorized an election for the adoption of a constitution and bylaws for the White Mountain Apache Tribe. The election was held on June 27, 1958.

1958: An election for the adoption of a constitution and bylaws for the Pueblos of Laguna in New Mexico was authorized by Assistant Secretary of the Interior Roger Ernst. The election was held on October 8, 1958.

1958: Assistant Secretary of the Interior Roger Ernst authorized an election for the adoption of a constitution and bylaws for the White Mountain Apache of the Fort Apache Indian Reservation in Arizona. The election was held on June 27, 1958.

1965: Secretary of the Interior Stewart Udall ratified an election for an amendment to the constitution and bylaws of the Kaibab Band of Paiute Indians of Arizona.

1966: Ordinance No. 1 was passed by the Twenty-Nine Palms Band of Mission Indians.

1976: An amendment to the constitution of the Comanche Indian Tribe was enacted.

1980: Department of the Interior Field Solicitor Elmer Nitzschke stated that the Mille Lacs Reservation Business Committee had the right to control the Sandy Lake Indian Reservation in Minnesota. The Sandy Lake Band of Ojibwe, which lived on the reservation, felt they should have control of the reservation.

Every: San Pedro's Day celebrated by many Pueblos.

MAY 30

1540: Hernando de Soto's army arrived in the Cherokee village of Guasili (near modern Murphy in western North Carolina). This was the first recorded meeting between Cherokees and Europeans. The Cherokees gave de Soto 300 dogs to be used as food. De Soto's chroniclers described the village as having 300 homes and wide streets.

1548: Juan Diego (Cuauhtlatoatzin) was the Nahua who saw the apparition of the Virgin Mary on a hill called Tepeyacac in Mexico. The encounters took place between December 9 and 12, 1531. He died on this day at the age of seventy-four.

1650: An ordinance was passed against the making of counterfeit, or "fake," wampum by the directors of the Council of the New Netherlands. European manufacturers were producing the fakes, which were being used to pay Indians.

1778: Joseph Brant and 300–400 Indian and British loyalists attacked Cobleskill, New York, killing twenty-two American soldiers.

1779: Colonel John Bowman and 300 Kentucky militia and armed settlers attacked the Shawnee village of Little Chillicothe. The attack was in retaliation for Shawnee attacks on frontier settlements. The Americans had surrounded the village before dawn, but before they were ready to attack they gave themselves away. Chief Black Fish and approximately 100 warriors defended the village while the women and children escaped into the surrounding countryside. By the end of the fighting, the Shawnees lost five warriors, the Americans nine.

1811: In what is now modern Oregon, John Clarke and a party of men stopped to work on canoes they had left with Indians at the merging of the Lewis and Pavion Rivers. A silver cup was stolen, and Clarke threatened to hang the chief.

1842: Fort Scott, named after Winfield Scott, was established in southeastern Kansas. Its original purpose was to separate Indian lands from American settlers.

1854: The president signed the Kansas-Nebraska Act.

1854: A treaty (10 Stat. 1082) was signed by the Kaskaskia, Wea, and other Indians in Kansas. For the most part, their lands were divided up into individual plots.

1860: The Delaware signed a treaty (12 Stat. 1129) regarding land in Kansas.

1867: Indians attacked the small settlement of Downer's Station, west of Hays, Kansas. Eventually, Fort Downer would be built there.

1867: According to army records, members of the Twenty-Seventh Infantry were herding some livestock when they fought with a band of Indians near Fort Reno, Dakota Territory. One soldier was killed.

1867: According to army records, members of the Eighth Cavalry fought with a band of Indians near Beale Station, Arizona. Fifteen Indians were killed.

1868: According to army records, members of the Eighth Cavalry fought with a band of Indians in the Tonto Basin, Arizona. One civilian was reported killed and one soldier was wounded.

1869: Indians killed a settler in Salt Creek in Kansas. The Seventh Cavalry couriers were then attacked and chased for ten miles. Near Fort Hays in central Kansas, Indians attacked three government teamsters and chased them until they reached safety at the fort.

1869: According to army records, members of the Eighth Cavalry fought with a band of Indians near Camp Toll Gate in Arizona. Four Indians were killed. The fighting lasted until June 3.

1870: According to official army records, Indians skirmished with a group of soldiers from the Sixth Cavalry near Holliday Creek, Texas. One soldier and two civilians were killed.

1873: Soldiers from the First Cavalry, the Fourth Artillery, and some Indian scouts captured thirty-three Modoc Indians in Langell's Valley, California. This included Scar-face Charley, Chonchin, and Boston Charley, according to army documents.

MAY 31

Scar-faced Charley, captured Modoc scout (NA)

1877: A man named Bescento Acosta was killed by Apache approximately four miles from Fort Davis in western Texas, according to an army report.

1877: Settlers fought a group of Indians near Fort Davis in western Texas. According to army documents, one settler was killed.

1878: Several white men were driving livestock across the Big Camas Prairie in south-central Idaho. They encountered some Indians who pretended to be friendly. But the Indians shot two of the men. They escaped, and Captain Reuben F. Bernard in Boise, Idaho, was notified.

1883: After the raids near Tombstone by Chato and others, General George Crook entered Mexico to find Geronimo. When they eventually met, Crook convinced Geronimo and his people to return to the San Carlos Reservation. Crook and most of the Chiricahua left for San Carlos on this day.

1936: An election to establish a constitution for the Fort McDermitt Paiute and Shoshone Tribe in Nevada was held. It passed by a vote of 54–11.

1785: A group of inexperienced chiefs met with people from the state of "Franklin" to discuss land at Dumpling Creek on the French Broad River. Led by Chief Ancoo of Chota, who was representing Old Tassel, they signed a treaty without fully understanding its meaning. Ancoo knew they were discussing land, but he did not realize he had signed a document allowing settlers who had illegally homesteaded Cherokee lands to remain there. The treaty ceded a great deal of land east of the ridge that divided the Little Tennessee River. This treaty was repudiated by the Cherokees almost immediately, as Ancoo had no authority to sign it. The state of "Franklin" was represented by its "governor," John Sevier.

1796: The Treaty of the Seven Tribes of Canada was signed by three chiefs at New York City. The tribes gave up all claims to lands in New York except for six square miles in Saint Regis. They were paid £1,233, six shillings, and eight pence then and £21, six shillings, and eight pence annually, if five more chiefs showed up and signed the treaty.

1811: The day before in what is now in modern Oregon, John Clarke and a party of men were camped with some Indians at the Lewis and Pavion Rivers. A silver cup was stolen, and Clarke threatened to hang the chief. On this day, another Indian was caught stealing. Clarke held an impromptu trial and hanged the thief. This act led to considerable ill will among the Oregon Indians.

1834: This day marked the last edition of the *Cherokee Phoenix*. Started eight years earlier, the financially troubled publication ceased to be published.

1865: Cherokee soldiers who served as Union soldiers during the U.S. Civil War were mustered out of the army.

1867: According to army records, members of the Thirty-Seventh Infantry fought with a band of Indians near Bluff Ranch, Kansas. They were part of an escort from Fort Dodge. Two soldiers were killed.

1868: According to army records, members of the First Cavalry fought with a band of Indians at Castle Rock near the North Fork of the Malheur River in Oregon. One soldier was wounded and five Indians were captured.

1869: On Rose Creek in Kansas, Indians attacked a government wagon train. Two soldiers and five Indians were reported to be wounded in the fight.

1870: A skirmish at Carlyle Station, Kansas, netted the army two wounded and the Indians three wounded.

1870: According to official army records, Indians skirmished with a group of soldiers from the Third Infantry guarding the mail near Bear Creek, Kansas. Two soldiers and five Indians were killed. One soldier was wounded and ten Indians were captured.

1876: According to the *San Diego Union* newspaper, there were disputes over land with the Campo Indians. "One Indian took refuge in the rocks . . . and continued firing. They soon discovered his whereabouts and silenced him, shooting him through the head, killing him instantly."

1966: The U.S. government ratified the addition of Amendment 9 to the constitution and by-laws of the Swinomish Indians of the Swinomish Reservation in Washington.

JUNE 1

1716: With the exception of four Indians who were involved in the murder of five Frenchmen and two high chiefs, French commander Bienville released his Natchez prisoners. He told them that they must return all of the dead men's possessions, they must provide logs for the French to build a fort, and they must kill the Natchez chief, Oye-lape, who ordered the killings.

1763: As part of Pontiac's Rebellion, Indians asked Lieutenant Edward Jenkins, commander at Fort Ouiatenon in present-day West Lafayette in northwestern Indiana, to attend a council outside the fort. He agreed and was taken as a hostage. His garrison of almost twenty men surrendered.

1773: In Augusta, Georgia, Creek and Cherokees signed a treaty with England. The agreement gave more than 2 million acres to the Europeans. This ceding of lands eradicated debts owed by the Indians. Many Europeans were already squatting on the lands, anyway. (Also recorded as happening on June 3.)

1784: The Spanish appointed Creek Chief Alexander McGillivray, one-quarter Creek, the "Commissary" to the Creek. McGillivray sought Spanish and other tribes' help in disputing English land claims.

1812: Canadian British met with Tecumseh.

1830: Georgia laws now applied to the Cherokee.

1833: Certain Sac and Fox lands became public domain.

1836: Alabama Governor Clement Clay said there were an estimated 1,500 hostile Creek in his state.

1852: According to Major George T. Howard, superintendent of Texas Indian agents, there were approximately 22,780 Indians in Texas as of this date. The Comanche and Kiowa made up 20,000 of this number.

1867: According to army records, members of the Fourth Infantry fought with a band of Indians near Fairview, Colorado. One soldier was killed.

1868: After the Long Walk to the Bosque Redondo Reservation in New Mexico, the Navajos suffered from the poor conditions on the reservation and from homesickness for their old lands. After numerous visits from Washington representatives, General Sherman visited the Navajo. They again asked to go back to their old lands. They promised the keep the peace and the old treaties. Sherman talked with them and he listened to them. With a new treaty in hand, Sherman said he would let them go if they signed and obeyed the new treaty. The Navajos agreed, even though they lost some of their land as a part of the new agreement. On this day, Barboncito, Armijo,

Delgadito, Herrero Grande, Manuelito, and others signed the new treaty (15 Stat. 667).

1869: A party of Seventh Cavalry troopers was encamped on the Solomon River in Kansas. Indians attacked, with one person on each side being wounded. Settlements on the Solomon River were also attacked. Thirteen men were killed, 150 head of livestock were stolen, and numerous houses were burned. A cavalry search of the area proved unsuccessful.

1870: Seventh Cavalry troops pursued a band of Indians who had raided the Solomon River settlements in Kansas. Twenty Indians were killed and four wounded during the day.

1871: Indians skirmished with a group of soldiers from the Third Cavalry in the Huachuca Mountains in Arizona, according to official army records. Three Indians were killed.

1873: According to army documents, Captain David Perry of the First Cavalry supervised the capture of Modoc Chief Kintpuash (Captain Jack) at Willow Creek, California.

1873: Two weeks earlier, a group of Cree stole some horses from some American trappers. The trappers had been looking for them ever since. The trappers came upon an Assiniboin village. The Assiniboin had nothing to do with the thefts of the horses, but the trappers attacked anyway. One trapper and twenty Assiniboin were killed in the fighting.

1876: A total of 176 Indians joined the army in the fight against Sitting Bull.

1878: Two herders were killed on Colson's Ranch, twelve miles west of Camp Wood, near Del Rio, Texas, according to a report by the commanding army officer at Fort Clark, Texas.

1879: Settlers fought a group of Indians near Camp Wood, Texas. According to army documents, three citizens were killed.

1882: Sixth Cavalry soldiers and Indian scouts fought a group of Indians near Cloverdale, New Mexico. According to army documents, two Indians were killed.

1910: Congress passed an act (36 Stat. 455) that granted the government authority to dispose of "unused" lands on the Fort Berthold Reservation.

1934: A legal definition of "Indian" was made by the U.S. government.

1934: The Muckleshoot Indians listed an official tribal roll.

1979: The area director of the Bureau of Indian Affairs had authorized an election for the adoption of an amendment to the constitution and by-laws for the Ponca Tribe of Indians of Oklahoma. It was approved by a vote of 79–22.

JUNE 2

1691: According to some sources, a conference was held for the next three days between representatives of the Five Nations and the British in New York. They agreed to an alliance.

1752: Diego Ortiz Parrilla, lieutenant colonel of the Royal Armies, proprietary captain of the Dragoons of Veracruz, and governor and captain-general of the provinces of Sinaloa and Sonora in the Kingdom of New Andalucia, declared the establishment of a permanent Spanish community at what would become modern Tubac, Arizona. This would be the first significant Spanish settlement in Arizona.

1760: Cherokees had besieged Fort Loudoun in southeastern Tennessee (near modern Vonore) since March 20, 1760. The soldiers had seen little sign of the warriors for the last few days. Seeking food, the fort's surgeon, Maurice Anderson, and one of the soldiers sneaked out of the fort. The Cherokees had been lying in wait, and both men were killed within a few feet of the fort's walls.

1767: According to some reports, a conference was held by representatives of the British and the Cherokees to discuss boundary lines.

1788: Forces under General John Sevier attacked the Cherokee village of Hiwassee. The American forces were victorious, with many of the Cherokees fleeing the area. The village was burned.

1823: Aaron Stevens, a trapper, was murdered at an Arikara village. Jedediah Smith was camped nearby with forty men. There were also ninety men stationed on boats in the nearby river. They were attacked the next day.

1830: Choctaw leaders wrote Secretary of War General John Eaton. They said they would like to look at the proposed lands for their resettlement in the west before they had a conference on selling their eastern lands.

1837: Almost 500 of the 4,000 Creek Indians who were assembled in Montgomery, Alabama, in March had now reached Little Rock, Arkansas. They were under the supervision of Lieutenant Edward Deas. The remainder of the 3,500 Creek were still at Mobile Point.

1837: Many Seminole had gathered at Tampa Bay to be removed west, including Chiefs Alligator and Jumper. Chiefs Osceola and Sam Jones, who was almost seventy years old, led a force of 200 Seminole warriors into the camp. Almost 700 Seminole fled the camp into the surrounding swamps with the warriors.

1870: According to official army records, Indians skirmished with a group of soldiers from the Twenty-Fourth Infantry near Copper Canyon, Arizona. One soldier and one Indian were killed.

1875: Quanah Parker and his remaining Kwahadis Comanche surrendered to Ranald S. Mackenzie at Fort Sill, Indian Territory (present-day Oklahoma).

1877: The Pinto Horse Bluff council took place. Sitting Bull would stay in Canada.

1877: A group of Nez Perce camped along Tolo Lake in western Idaho. They were preparing to move to a reservation. Several young warriors from this group would eventually retaliate against a white settler for killing one of their relatives. This was one of the actions that led to the Nez Perce War.

1878: Captain (Brevet Colonel) R.F. Bernard and his troops from Boise, Idaho, forced the Indi-

ans at Big Camas Prairie to retreat into the nearby lava beds.

1880: One Bull stole some horses, which led to a confrontation with Canada.

1889: Eighth Cavalry soldiers captured thirty-four Indians on the north bank of the Missouri River, fifteen miles south of the Little Missouri River in North Dakota.

1911: An executive order modified the boundaries of the Hualapai Indian Reservation.

1924: A law was passed that made all American Indians born in the United States full citizens, if previous treaties had not already done so.

1945: Amendment 1 to the constitution and by-laws of the Lac du Flambeau Band of Lake Superior Chippewa Indians of Wisconsin was approved and became effective.

1986: The Lac du Flambeau Tribal Council had enacted the Reservation Water and Shoreline Protection and Enhancement Ordinance. It was approved by the secretary of the interior.

JUNE 3

1539: Having been in Florida for only a few days, Hernando de Soto formally claimed Florida for the king of Spain.

1684: According to some sources, a land-cession agreement was reached between representatives of the Delaware Indians and Pennsylvania.

1770: Gaspar de Portolá, Father Junipero Serra, and other Spanish officials performed the "possession and establishment" ceremonies that established the Spanish mission and presidio at San Carlos de Borromeo de Monterey (modern Monterey, California).

1781: The Engagement of Frankstown took place. British Lieutenant Robert was leading a group of Seneca warriors. They came across a group of Pennsylvania militiamen who were seeking the participants of a massacre of local settlers. The Seneca set up an ambush and routed the militia.

Eleven militiamen were killed, five wounded, and ten captured.

1789: Alexander Mackenzie's expedition reached the Mackenzie River delta. The river would eventually be named after him.

1798: Colonel Benjamin Hawkins was the principal agent to the southern Indian nations. His efforts to get the young Creek warriors to stop robbing settlers and, in some cases, stop committing murder had created a great deal of antagonism. He was warned by several older chiefs that a group of warriors planned to kill him during the night. Hawkins claimed his peaceful intentions and went to sleep in his quarters in the Creek village of Tuckabatchee. Several Creek chiefs guarded Hawkins during the night, and the attack was avoided.

1800: According to some sources, Choctaw Chief Greenwood was born in Mississippi.

1815: Winnebago Chief Neokautah signed a peace treaty with the Americans at Mackinac.

1816: William Clark, Auguste Chouteau, and Ninian Edwards negotiated a peace treaty (7 Stat. 144) with the Wisconsin River Winnebago in St. Louis. The treaty confirmed the end of fighting between the parties and returned prisoners.

1823: The day before, a trapper was killed in an Arikara village. The Arikara warriors attacked Jedediah Smith and forty men camped on the nearby river. There were also ninety men stationed on boats in the river. Fearing for their lives, the men in the boats refused to help Smith's men. Fifteen men were killed and almost as many were wounded in the fighting before they could swim out to the boats and flee.

1825: The Kansa Indians signed a treaty (7 Stat. 244) at Council Grove, Kansas. Representing the United States was William Clark, superintendent of Indian affairs.

1830: The governor of Georgia declared the laws passed on December 19, 1829, to officially be in effect. These laws extended Georgia sovereignty over most of Cherokee lands in the state.

Indians could no longer be witnesses in any court in the state. All Cherokee laws were now nullified. It was illegal to try to keep an Indian from emigrating to Indian Territory (present-day Oklahoma). Since gold had been discovered on Cherokee lands, the governor declared that all Cherokee lands now belonged to the state, including the gold mines.

1833: Secretary of War Lewis Cass gave orders directly to the U.S. Marshal to remove white settlers and trespassers from Creek lands in Alabama.

1846: Kearny got authority to seize California.

1850: Leaders in the Cayuse War were hanged in Oregon City. Those hanged included Tilokaikt and Tamsaky.

1868: Depending on who is telling the story, one tribe stole over 100 horses, then the other took them back. Several warriors were killed in the process. Despite the efforts of Kaw Indian Agent Major E.S. Stover, near Council Grove, Kansas, a large number of Cheyenne and Kaw warriors fought each other over the horses.

1869: President Grant, by executive order, defined the responsibilities of the newly authorized, ten-member Board of Indian Commissioners to oversee Indian appropriations. (See May 25, 1933.)

1869: According to army records, members of the Eighth Cavalry fought with a band of Indians near Camp Toll Gate in Arizona. Four Indians were killed. The fighting started on May 30.

1870: In fierce fighting at the mail station at Bear Creek, Kansas, two soldiers of the military guard were killed and one was wounded. The Indians had five killed and ten wounded. In another area, Captain George Armes, Tenth Cavalry, became separated from his escort. He was chased but escaped.

1870: According to official army records, Indians skirmished with a group of soldiers from the Third Cavalry near Fort Whipple, Arizona. Two Indians were killed.

1875: Troops of the Fourth Cavalry under Lieutenant J.A. McKinney were tracking "thieving" Indians when the advance unit came across some Osage Indians stealing a herd of cattle on Huckberry Creek in Indian Territory (present-day Oklahoma). A fight began and one Osage was killed, according to army records.

1884: The executive order of March 29, 1884, transferring certain lands for the use and occupancy of the Turtle Mountain Band of Chippewa Indians, was modified.

1995: Major Sam Steele and a group of soldiers attacked a group of Cree led by Big Bear on Loon Lake in Saskatchewan. In what was the last battle of Riel's Rebellion, three Cree were killed.

1939: The assistant secretary of the interior had authorized an election to amend the constitution and bylaws of the Oneida Tribe of Indians of Wisconsin. Amendments 1–4 were approved.

1974: Lines and laws on Colville and Spokane Reservation were modified.

1976: The constitution and bylaws of the Lower Elwha Tribal Community of the Lower Elwha Reservation in Washington State was amended.

1976: Francis Briscoe, the area director, Portland area office, Bureau of Indian Affairs, ratified an amendment to the constitution and bylaws of the Kalispel Indian Community of the Kalispel Reservation.

JUNE 4

1647: Chief Canonicus, chief of the Narragansett when the Pilgrims landed at Plymouth Rock, died. He was approximately eighty-eight years old.

1696: A second Pueblo revolt took place in New Mexico. Participating tribes were the Cochiti, Picuris, Santa Fe, Santo Domingo, Tano, Taos, and Tewa. Twenty-one settlers and soldiers and five missionaries were killed in the fighting. The revolt would not be long-lived.

1722: Germans arrived in Mobile.

1763: Indians attacked Fort Ligonier. It was the only small fort that fell during Pontiac's Uprising.

1763: Chippewa Indians come to Fort Michilimackinac on the strait between Upper and Lower Michigan. They invited the British soldiers out to watch them play a game of ball with the Sacs. The soldiers left the fort to watch the festivities. They left open the gates to the fort, and several Indian women entered the fort. When most of the soldiers were watching the ball game, the Chippewa attacked. The Chippewa killed over half of the thirty-five soldiers but did not bother any of the French traders at the fort.

1782: Colonel William Crawford and 250 Pennsylvania militia battled a similar number of Indians at Sandusky, Ohio. The next day, 140 Shawnee and Butler's Rangers arrived. Almost all of Crawford's troops were killed. Crawford was roasted on a stake in revenge for the massacre at Gnadenhutten.

1793: Pierre Falcon, a Metis singer and songwriter, was born.

1841: At a peace conference during the Second Seminole War, Miccosukee (Seminole) warrior and son of Chief Philip, Wildcat (Coacoochee) were taken prisoner by American forces under Major Thomas Childs.

1869: At Picacho Mountain in Arizona, Bugler George Gates and Private Joseph Watson, Company F, Eighth Cavalry, "killed an Indian warrior and captured his arms." For these actions, they were awarded the Medal of Honor.

1869: At Grinnell Station, Kansas, Indians started destroying the railroad tracks. A military garrison at the station ran them off.

1871: General George Crook took command of the Department of Arizona. He believed that the Indians should be treated fairly but kept under control.

1876: This day marked the start of the Rosebud sun dance.

Sioux sun dance

JUNE 5

1513: Forces under Ponce de Leon fought with Calusa Indians on the Gulf Coast of Florida. In almost two dozen canoes, the Calusa managed to kill one Spaniard before they were driven off. A force four times larger attempted another attack on the Spanish the next day, but the guns of the Spanish kept the Calusa at bay. (Also recorded as happening on June 11.)

1637: The Battle of Mystic took place. As a part of the Pequot War, Mohegan Chief Uncas was leading approximately 100 Indian allies, but he was doubtful of the ability of seventy-seven Europeans under Captains John Underhill and John Mason to defeat the Pequot. Regardless, they attacked a fortified Pequot village (near modern Mystic, Connecticut) before dawn. Few of the Pequot warriors were in the village, and the allies set fire to the dwellings. According to some accounts, as many as 700 old men, women, and children were burned or shot to death. Only about a dozen Pequot in the village survived. (Also recorded as happening on May 25 and 26.)

1728: Delaware Chief Sassoonan addressed the Pennsylvania provincial council. He complained of German immigrants settling on Indian lands in Tulpehocken Valley. The complaint was not re-

solved until 1732, when the lands were purchased from the Indians for trade goods.

1762: Cherokee Chiefs Ostenaco, Pouting Pigeon, and Stalking Turkey arrived in England. They were en route to visit King George III.

1767: According to some reports, a conference regarding trade regulations was held by the British and the Creek.

1836: Of the 407 friendly Seminole who left Tampa Bay on April 11, 1836, only 320 arrived in their new lands in the Indian Territory (present-day Oklahoma). Eighty-seven of the Seminole died during the rigorous trip.

1838: Seminole War Chief Halpatter Tustennuggee (Alligator) and 360 of his followers boarded ships in Florida. They were en route to Oklahoma as part of the American peace accords after the Second Seminole War.

1854: The Miami signed a treaty (10 Stat. 1093) in Washington, D.C. They ceded a large section of their lands.

Delaware Indian chief

1866: This day started the formal treaty conference at Fort Laramie in southeastern Wyoming. Leaders from many tribes and bands were present. The purpose of the treaty was to allow passageway for trails, roads, and railroad lines across Indian lands. The meeting was postponed for almost a week, at Red Cloud's request, to allow for the arrival of additional Indians.

1867: Indians attacked Henshaw Station on Turkey Creek in Kansas. Four soldiers were killed in the fighting. Fort Wallace was nine miles to the west, and the Indians escaped before reinforcements could arrive. The Indians also made off with many horses.

1870: According to official army records, Indians skirmished with a group of soldiers from the First and Third Cavalry in the Apache Mountains of Arizona. Thirty Indians were killed. In Black Canyon, Arizona, a different detachment from the Third Cavalry killed two Indians in a fight.

1872: The boundary of the Osage Nation was established by an act (17 Stat. 229).

1875: Fort Elliot was established in northern Texas east of Pampa. It was one of the last Texas forts built to protect settlers from Indians.

1879: General Terry sent a message to General Miles to "drive the Sioux back to Canada."

1880: Major Albert Morrow and four troops of the Ninth Cavalry attacked Victorio's Indians at Cook's Canyon in New Mexico. Ten Indians were killed, including one of Victorio's sons, three were wounded, and livestock was seized.

1943: Inquiries were made into legal "jurisdiction of the South Dakota courts to prosecute Indians for violations of the state game laws when such violations occurred on allotted lands within the boundaries of the original Lake Traverse Reservation."

1947: The acting commissioner of Indian affairs had authorized an election to approve a constitution for the Coeur d'Alene Tribe of Idaho. It would pass by a vote of 60–4.

JUNE 6

1687: According to some sources, an agreement of alliance was reached between representatives of the Five Nations and the British colonies in New York.

1838: The first group of Cherokees forced to emigrate to the Indian Territory (present-day Oklahoma) was loaded onto boats at Ross's Landing (present-day Chattanooga), Tennessee. The 800 Cherokees were guarded by soldiers led by Lieutenant Edward Deas. A total of 489 Cherokees reached Fort Coffee in eastern Indian Territory in late June. Many of the Cherokee escaped while en route.

1862: Bear's Rib was killed at Fort Pierre.

1885: Sitting Bull signed contract to work in Buffalo Bill's Wild West Show.

1868: Captain D. Monahan and troops from Troops G and I, Third Cavalry, left Fort Sumner in western New Mexico. The troops were chasing a group of Navajo Indians who had been accused of killing four settlers about twelve miles from the fort. After following their trail for 100 miles, the army surprised the Navajos, who were in a ravine. The army reported killing three Indians and wounding eleven; the rest escaped. No soldiers were killed.

1870: The District of New Mexico's chief engineering officer was attacked by Indians while surveying near Fort Selden in southern New Mexico. The post's cavalry pursued the Indians. No one on either side was hurt. In Indian Territory (present-day Oklahoma), Indians made several attacks on two wagon trains near Camp Supply in southwestern Arizona. Two Indians were injured and several mules were run off.

1870: The Missouri, Kansas, and Texas Railroad crossed the northern border of Indian Territory (present-day Oklahoma), headed south. This brought more settlers to the area.

1900: An act (31 Stat. 672) was passed that allotted land to members of the Comanche Indian Tribe.

1962: The *Fort Apache Scout* was first published.

1962: Leo Johnson of Oklahoma became the first American Indian to graduate from the U.S. Air Force Academy.

1970: Pit River Indians attempted to occupy Mount Lassen.

1971: A group of Indians set up a camp on Mount Rushmore to protest treaty violations. Several were arrested for misdemeanor charges of climbing the monument.

1973: In an election, the Articles of Association of the Pala Band of Mission Indians of California were amended.

1974: An amendment to the constitution of the Grindstone Indian Rancheria in Glenn County, California, was made.

1984: The U.S. Senate decided to have a permanent committee on Indian affairs.

1994: According to the Osage constitution, the first election for the Osage National Council was held.

JUNE 7

1494: The New World was divided between Spain and Portugal by the Catholic Church.

1539: Juan Ortiz, a Spaniard, was a member of the Narvaez expedition to Florida in 1528. He was captured by Indians. He escaped from his captors and lived with the Mococo Indians. Upon Hernando de Soto's arrival, the Mococo sent out Ortiz to mediate with de Soto. De Soto was relieved to have someone who could speak the native language. On this day, the Mococo met with de Soto and agreed to a peace.

1706: According to some sources, an agreement regarding friendship and trade regulations was made between representatives of the British in Pennsylvania and the Conestoga, Potomac, and Shawnee Indians.

1803: A treaty (7 Stat. 74) with the Delaware, Shawnee, Miami, Kaskaskia, Kickapoo, Piankashaw, Potawatomi, Wea, and two other Indian Nations was concluded at Fort Wayne on the Miami River. It included changes in boundary lines from those established in the Greenville Treaty. Lands were ceded by both sides. The United States got the salt springs of Saline Creek, and the Indians were guaranteed to get 150 bushels of salt annually. The United States got the right to have land to build inns for travelers on roads through Indian country. If any ferries were built across rivers in the area, the Indians would not have to pay to use them. The treaty was signed by William Henry Harrison and fifteen Indians.

1838: Seminole Chief King Philip was en route to the Indian Territory (present-day Oklahoma) when he died just before reaching his new lands.

1855: Head chief of the Nez Perce, Lawyer, signed the Walla Walla Treaty (12 Stat. 957). Other Indian leaders signed the treaty in the next few days.

1866: Chief Seattle died.

1869: According to army records, members of the Ninth Cavalry under Colonel R.S. Mackenzie fought with a band of Indians near the Pecos River in Texas. One soldier and one Indian were killed.

1876: General Terry and his troops established a base camp for operations against hostile Indians at the mouth of the Powder River.

1897: The boundaries of the Fort Apache Reservation in Arizona were established by an act of Congress.

1906: The James Bay Treaty Number 9 was signed. It was between the government of Canada and the Ojibwa, Cree, and other Indian inhabitants of the territory.

1945: Sacred arrows were used by the Cheyenne.

JUNE 8

1713: According to some sources, a peace agreement was reached between representatives of the Tuscarora and the British in North Carolina.

1758: General Jeffrey Amherst was leading a force of more than 10,000 soldiers on a fleet of almost fifty British ships. They landed the ships and then attacked the French fort at Louisbourg, Nova Scotia. The French forces were led by Chevier de Drucour with 3,100 soldiers, 1,000 Canadians, and 500 Indians at his disposal. The French also had a fleet in port. The fighting continued until July 26. The British were victorious. Fearing they would be executed, many of the Indians fled because the British offered terms of surrender only to the French troops.

1820: The Mi'kmaq Acadia First Nation Reserve of Wildcat was established in Nova Scotia.

1843: The Mi'kmaq Acadia First Nation Reserve of Ponhook Lake was established in Nova Scotia.

1863: According to Superintendent of Indian Affairs Clark W. Thompson, 1,945 Winnebago Indians arrived at their new reservation at Fort Randall, South Dakota. They left their old reservation in May.

1867: According to army records, members of the Seventh Cavalry fought with a band of Indians near Chalk Bluffs, Kansas. No one was injured during the fighting.

1868: According to army records, members of the Third Cavalry fought with a band of Indians near Apache Springs, New Mexico. Three Indians were killed and eleven were wounded during the extended conflict, which lasted through June 13.

1870: According to official army records, Indians skirmished with a group of soldiers from the Tenth Cavalry between Fort Dodge, Kansas, and Camp Supply, Indian Territory (present-day Oklahoma). Two soldiers were wounded and three Indians were killed.

1870: According to official army records, Indians skirmished with a group of soldiers from the Fifth Cavalry near Red Willow Creek, Nebraska. Three Indians were killed.

1871: Indians engaged in a running fight with a group of soldiers from the Third Cavalry from Verde River to the Mazatzal Mountains to Wild Rye Creek in Arizona, according to official army records. Fifty-six Indians were killed and eight were wounded. The fighting lasted through the next day.

1871: When confronted at Fort Sill in south-central Indian Territory (present-day Oklahoma) as to whether he knew anything about the attack on the wagons loaded with corn on May 15 on the Butterfield Trail, Satanta said he was the leader of the raid. Satanta told the agent that Satank, Big Tree, and others were with him. General Sherman placed the three Indians under arrest and handcuffed them. While being transported back to Fort Richardson in north-central Texas, Satank managed to work free from his handcuffs. He then attacked a guard with a hidden knife. Satank grabbed a rifle from another guard, but he was shot and killed by the remaining soldiers. His body was thrown in a ditch, and the group continued to Texas.

1874: Cochise died.

1876: General Crook's combined forces established a base camp at Goose Creek after having left Fort Fetterman in southeastern Wyoming on May 29, 1876.

1878: Near South Mountain in southern Idaho, Buffalo Horn and approximately sixty Bannock Indians fought with Captain Harper's volunteers and scouts from Captain Bernard's troops. Two soldiers were killed. Buffalo Horn was fatally wounded.

1880: President Hayes, by executive order, established the Havasupai (Suppai) Reserve. It was sixty square miles in area. The reserve was added to on November 23, 1880, and March 31, 1882.

1885: Fourth Cavalry soldiers were guarding a supply train when they were attacked by a group of Indians near Gaudalupe Canyon in Sonora, Mexico. According to army documents, three soldiers were killed.

1887: The Mi'kmaq Acadia First Nation Reserve of Yarmouth was established in Nova Scotia.

1962: Amendments to the Comanche Indian Tribe constitution were approved.

1973: Deputy Assistant Secretary of the Interior William Rogers approved an election to amend the revised constitution and bylaws for the Sisseton Wahpeton Sioux Tribe of South Dakota.

1974: An election on amendments to the constitution and bylaws of the Reno-Sparks Indian Community was held. Of the thirty-seven people voting, only a few voted against the various amendments.

JUNE 9

1647: New England Synod clergy met at Cambridge. A large number of Indians attended the meeting to hear Roxbury Minister John Eliot deliver a sermon in their own language.

1757: Indians again surrounded the troops in Fort Augusta in Shamokin on the Susquehanna River. They gave up their attempt to starve the troops, but they returned in two weeks.

1836: Government forces fought with almost 200 Seminole near the stockade at Micanopy north of present-day Ocala, Florida.

1836: A Georgia militia was tricked into an ambush in what was called the Battle of Shepherd's Plantation in Stewart County, Georgia, by the Creek. The militia had forty soldiers, the Creek six times that many.

1838: Chickasaw Chief Ishtahotapa and 129 of his followers left Pontotoc, Mississippi, with A.M.M. Upshaw for the Indian Territory (present-day Oklahoma). The Chickasaws remaining east of the Mississippi were concerned about moving west because of the epidemic of smallpox raging in the Indian Territory. During the trek west, Ishtahotapa's wife died. It was October before any significant numbers of the remaining Chickasaws set out for the Indian Territory.

1844: Captain John Coffee Hays and fourteen Texas Rangers were bivouacking on the Guadalupe River (in the area of modern Kendall County). A Ranger in a tree spotted a large group of Comanche approaching them. A series of thrusts and counterthrusts took place. After the fighting stopped, the Rangers estimated the number of Indians killed at twenty to fifty, including Chief Yellow Wolf. The Rangers lost one man. This fight goes by many names, including: the Battle of Asta's Creek, the Battle of Pinta Trail Crossing, the Battle of Sisters Creek, and the Walker's Creek Fight.

1855: The Walla Walla Treaty of 1855 (12 Stat. 957) (Governor Stevens's attempt to put Northwest tribes on reservations) was signed. Chief Peo-Peo-Mox-Mox, of the Walla Walla, signed the treaty, as did Yakama Chiefs Kamiakin, Owhi, and Skloom. The Yakama Treaty established a boarding school.

1863: The Nez Perce signed a treaty (14 Stat. 647). It dramatically reduced the size of the Nez Perce lands as established in previous treaties. The Nez Perce lose the Wallowa Valley and almost three-quarters of the rest of their land. Old Joseph (Tu-eka-kas) repudiated this treaty, which was signed by Nez Perce who had never lived in the Wallowa Valley. This treaty amended and supplanted the Treaty of June 11, 1855.

1868: According to army records, members of the Twenty-Third Infantry and some Indian scouts fought with a band of Indians near Snake Canyon, Idaho. Three Indians were killed.

1870: Ely Parker (Donehogawa), commissioner of Indian affairs, invited Red Cloud and several other Sioux to visit him and the Great Father in Washington. Red Cloud met President Ulysses Grant. Red Cloud told Grant that the Sioux did not want a reservation on the Missouri River. Red Cloud also talked about some of the promises made in the treaty that were not actually included. They had a cordial meeting, but Grant knew that the difference between the items promised and the items actually in the treaty was grounds for contention in the future. He suggested that the Indians be read the treaty in its entirety soon.

1870: In the Panhandle of Indian Territory (present-day Oklahoma) near Camp Supply, Indians attacked a government wagon train guarded by cavalry. During the fighting, three Indians were killed and ten were wounded. Three soldiers were wounded. On the same road nearby, Indians attacked a mail escort. One soldier was wounded there as well. Three Indians were killed and five were wounded. A skirmish also occurred between Fort Dodge and Camp Supply. Indians fought Lieutenant John Bodamer and Troops F and H, Tenth Cavalry. Two soldiers and three Indians were wounded. Near Fort McPherson in central Nebraska on the same day, Lieutenant Earl Thomas and Troop I, Fifth Cavalry, pursued Indians who were marauding in the area. Although the Indians escaped, the troops destroyed their village.

1871: Indians engaged in a running fight with a group of soldiers from the Third Cavalry from Verde River to the Mazatzal Mountains to Wild Rye Creek in Arizona, according to official army records. Fifty-six Indians were killed and eight were wounded. The fighting started the day before.

1876: Sioux warriors failed in their attempt to steal horses from soldiers of the Second and Third Cavalries and the Fourth and Ninth Infantries on the Tongue River in Wyoming. According to army documents, one soldier was wounded.

1977: The Federal Register (42 F.R. 33099) published the "Revocation of Termination Proclamation and Restoration of Federal Status Notice for Robinson Rancheria." It included a tribal roll.

1980: Amendment 10 to the revised constitution and bylaws of the Sisseton Wahpeton Sioux Tribe of South Dakota took effect.

JUNE 10

1761: Colonel James Grant invaded Cherokee lands with a large force. On this day, he defeated the Cherokee in a battle. He eventually destroyed many of the Cherokees' "middle towns."

1778: Settlers living in the villages of Muncy and Bald Eagle, Pennsylvania, sent a request to the Supreme Executive Council of Pennsylvania for help because of Indian attacks.

1839: Forces under John Hays and Juan Seguín chased a group of Comanche into Sabinal Canyon (near modern Utopia, Texas). They destroyed much of the village they found there.

1847: A total of 110 Choctaws of the Big Black River Band arrived in eastern Indian Territory (present-day Oklahoma) at Fort Coffee.

1851: According to sources, one in a series of treaties with California Indians was signed at Camp Persifer F. Smith. The treaty's purpose was to guarantee reserved lands and protections from the Europeans.

1859: The Comstock Lode was discovered.

1869: Indians attempted to steal livestock at an army scouting camp on the Solomon River. The troops prevented the stock from being stampeded. On Asher Creek in Kansas, Indians raided the settlements and stole fifteen head of livestock. A cavalry troop chased them for ten miles and recovered the animals.

1870: When President Grant realized that Red Cloud had never heard the real terms of the Fort Laramie Treaty (15 Stat. 635) of 1868, he ordered that Red Cloud hear the details. When Secretary of the Interior Jacob Cox read Red Cloud the treaty, Red Cloud said this was not the treaty he signed. Red Cloud blamed the differences on the interpreters, but he said he would not abide by this paper full of lies.

1870: According to official army records, Indians skirmished with a group of soldiers from the Tenth Cavalry near Snake Creek, Indian Territory. No casualties were reported.

1871: Indians skirmished with a group of soldiers from the Third Cavalry in the Huachuca Mountains in Arizona, according to official army records. No casualties were reported.

1872: Indians skirmished with a group of soldiers from the First Cavalry on Bill Williams Mountain,

Arizona, according to official army records. One Indian was killed and one was wounded.

1873: An executive order divided the Wallowa mountain area.

1896: Congress modified the San Carlos Reservation in Arizona by passing an act (29 Stat. 321,360).

1909: The U.S. Supreme Court confirmed and approved Guion Miller's new tribal rolls of the Eastern Cherokees, who were entitled to share in the distribution of a $1 million fund the Court established in 1906.

1936: According to Federal Register No. 1FR00667, a modification was made in the disposition of lands on the Pine Ridge Reservation in South Dakota.

1968: An act (82 Stat. 174) was passed by Congress to "authorize the purchase, sale and exchange of certain lands on the Spokane Indian Reservation, and for other purposes."

1972: A congressional act (17 Stat. 391) further defined the Sac and Fox Reserve in Kansas.

1974: An election approved Amendments 7–11 to the constitution and bylaws of the Lac du Flambeau Band of Lake Superior Chippewa Indians of Wisconsin.

1978: An amendment to the constitution of the Comanche Indian Tribe was enacted.

JUNE 11

1513: Forces under Ponce de Leon fought with Calusa Indians on the Gulf Coast of Florida. In almost two dozen canoes, the Calusa managed to kill one Spaniard before they were driven off. A force four times larger attempted another attack on the Spanish the next day; but the guns of the Spanish kept the Calusa at bay. (Also recorded as happening on June 5.)

1735: According to some sources, an agreement covering alliance and boundary lines was reached by representatives of the British in Georgia and the Creek Indians.

1752: Although at a conference with British authorities, Chief Shingas was named sachem (king) of the Delaware by Tanacharison of the Iroquois. The Delaware were subjugated by the Iroquois.

1755: General Edmund Braddock and two regiments arrived at Fort Cumberland in western Maryland.

1829: Major Bennett Riley and troops had just joined Charley Bent's wagon train bound for Santa Fe, near Round Grove in Kansas. A band of 100 Kiowa and Comanche stole the wagon train's herd of cattle. The Indians then started attacking the wagon train and the soldiers. Riley fired his artillery piece, and the Indians scattered.

1835: Creek leaders met in Setelechee to decide their future regarding their removal to Indian Territory (present-day Oklahoma) in the west. Creek Agent Judge Tarrant paid out the last annuity before the removal. Whites and other Indians demanded payment of debts by the Creek.

1848: Alexander Barclay established a trading post and fort at the confluence of the Sapello and Mora Rivers in northern New Mexico. The Santa Fe Trail ran past the post. It would eventually become part of the later-constructed Fort Union, one of the largest military outposts in the Southwest.

1855: This day marked the end of the Walla Walla conference. Two treaties were signed. The council had been attended by Oregon Superintendent of Indian Affairs Joel Palmer and Washington State Indian Affairs Superintendent Isaac Stevens. The Nez Perce and Cayuse tribes signed treaties, which were satisfactory to the whites.

1859: Due to a lack of protection by government troops, Texas Indian Agent Major Robert S. Neighbors had recommended the elimination of the Comanche Reservation and the reservations on the Brazos River. Orders were issued to move the affected Indians to Indian Territory (present-day Oklahoma).

1866: After the Santee Sioux Uprising in Minnesota in 1862, 1,300 Santee Sioux were moved to new lands away from Minnesota. These new lands

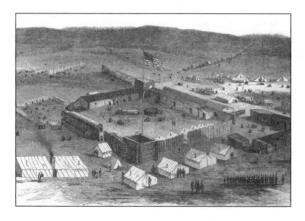

Camp Supply, built in Indian Territory, present-day Oklahoma

were on the Missouri River near Crow Creek. The results were disastrous. Within a few months, 300 people starved. After three years they were moved again. The Santee Sioux arrived at their new lands at the mouth of the Niobrara River in northeastern Nebraska Territory (near modern Niobrara).

1867: According to army records, members of the Seventh Cavalry and Third Infantry fought with a band of Indians near Big Timbers, Kansas. One soldier was killed.

1869: Indians attacked the perimeter of Captain William Graham's First Artillery command near the Solomon River in Kansas. According to the official army report, the Indians were "routed and pursued."

1870: After some confusion the day before, with Ely Parker's help Secretary of the Interior Jacob Cox reinterpreted the Treaty of 1868 (15 Stat. 635) to read that while the Powder River hunting grounds were not within the reservation they were in allowed hunting grounds. Additionally, if some Sioux wished to live in the hunting grounds, they were allowed to do so.

1870: Near Camp Supply in the Panhandle of Indian Territory (present-day Oklahoma), Indians attempted to stampede the horses at the cavalry camp. Troops A, F, H, I, and K, Tenth Cavalry, and Companies B, E, and F, Third Infantry, under Lieutenant Colonel A.D. Nelson, Third Infantry, pursued the Indians. During a fight, six Indians were killed; three

soldiers and ten Indians were wounded. Near Grinnell Station, Kansas, cavalry escorting a wagon train was attacked by Indians. A three-hour fight left no significant injuries on either side.

1880: Lieutenant Frank Mills and a group of Pueblo scouts were traveling to join Colonel Benjamin Grierson's troops near the Mescalero Agency in New Mexico. In Canyon Ojo Viejo, near Fort Davis in western Texas, they were attacked by hostile Indians. The principal Pueblo guide was killed in the fighting. Two scouts and two Indians were wounded. The fighting continued through the next day.

1883: Floods along the Canadian and Arkansas Rivers in Indian Territory (present-day Oklahoma) washed away most of the Choctaws' supplies, crops, food, livestock, and homes. The flood's highwater mark was higher than anyone's recollection of previous floods. The previous winter was the coldest in anyone's memory. All of this added to the Choctaws' difficulties in adapting to their new lands.

1936: Secretary of the Interior Harold Ickes authorized an election to adopt a constitution and bylaws by the Lac du Flambeau Band of Lake Superior Chippewa Indians of Wisconsin. The election was held on July 18, 1936.

1936: An election that approved a constitution and bylaws for the Lower Sioux Indian Community of Minnesota was ratified by the secretary of the interior. The election was held on May 16, 1936.

1948: The constitution and bylaws for the Eskimos of the Native Village of Kwinhagak were approved.

1971: Indians ended their occupation and left Alcatraz Island.

JUNE 12

1684: The La Navidad en Las Cruces Mission was established (near modern Presidio, Texas) by members of the Juan Dominguez de Mendoza expedition. It was eventually abandoned.

1690: Henry Kelsey began one of the first trading expeditions through the Canadian Plains for the Hudson Bay Company. He contacted many different tribal groups.

1755: Massachusetts posted its "scalp bounty."

1756: Delaware Indians, led by King Beaver, attacked the fortified garrison in Juniata County, Pennsylvania, called Bingham's Fort. The number of settlers killed or captured was estimated to be as many as two dozen.

1775: British General Gage wanted Indians to help in the war.

1838: The two groups of Seminole who left New Orleans on May 19 and May 23 arrived at Fort Gibson in eastern Indian Territory (present-day Oklahoma). Of the 1,160 Seminole who left New Orleans, only 1,069 survived the trip. A council was held with the Creek in the area. There was a disagreement about the lands set aside for the Seminole. Some Creek had already settled on these lands. Many of the Seminole chiefs, in particular Mikanopy, refused to leave the fort until this discrepancy in their treaty agreement was resolved.

1852: An article in *Home Journal* mentioned that there was only one saint in the Americas, Tamenend (Tammany), the Delaware sachem. According to the article, Tamenend "excited so much respect by his virtues and exploits, both among the white and red man, that, after his death, he was canonized, and the day of his birth, the first of May, regarded as a holiday."

1855: The Walla Walla conference was held. Governor Stevens bypassed the entire structure of the U.S. constitutional system, giving Congress sole power to ratify treaties.

1858: Indian and white goldseekers arrived at Bent's Fort.

1867: According to army records, members of the Seventh Cavalry fought with a band of Indians near Fort Dodge, Kansas. One soldier was wounded.

1867: According to army records, members of the Second Cavalry fought with a band of Indians near Fort Phil Kearny, Dakota Territory. One soldier was killed.

1869: Indians again raided the Solomon River, Kansas, settlements. Ten settlers were killed, and 250 head of livestock were stolen. At Edinburg, Kansas, troopers chased some Indians and recovered twenty head of stolen cattle.

1874: Apache leader Chan-Deisi was killed.

1880: Lieutenant F.H. Mills and some Pueblo scouts fought a group of Indians near Ojo Viejo, Texas. According to army documents, one scout and one Indian were killed. Two scouts and two Indians were wounded. The fighting started the day before.

1895: The Miami Tribe's "Annuity Pay-Roll" was published. It also served as a tribal roll.

1941: An order, according to Federal Register No. 6FR03300, restored "certain undisposed of surplus lands" on the Cheyenne River Reservation in South Dakota.

1941: An election that approved a constitution and bylaws for the Kialegee Tribal Town of the Creek Indian Nation of Oklahoma was ratified by the secretary of the interior.

1951: Canada's House of Commons amended the Indian Act. The change allowed some bands to decide if they wished to reinstate tribal membership to some women who had married out of their band.

1964: Associate Commissioner of Indian Affairs James Officer ratified an election to adopt a constitution and bylaws for the Paiute-Shoshone Tribe of the Fallon Reservation and Colony.

1974: The commissioner of Indian affairs authorized an election to approve a constitution and bylaws for the Upper Skagit Indian Tribe. The election was held on October 5, 1974.

1981: The Bureau of Indian Affairs received a documented petition for federal acknowledgment from the Chinook Indian Tribe, Inc.

1991: The San Carlos Apache contested the placement of a telescope on what they consider to be sacred land.

1991: Oregon allowed peyote to be used for religious purposes.

"King Philip" of the Wampanoag who met the Plymouth colonists

JUNE 13

1660: Wamsetta, a Wampanoag, and his younger brother, Metacomet (various spellings), had requested "English" names from the Plymouth court. Their names were officially changed to Alexander and Philip Pokanoket. Philip was eventually called King Philip.

1715: As a part of the Yamassee War, South Carolina militia led by George Chicken battled coastal Indians. The fight, which took place near the ponds on Goose Creek, resulted in a defeat for the Indians, with forty fatalities. Many of the coastal Indians withdrew their support for the war after this defeat.

1722: Sixty Indians attacked Brunswick, Maine, the site of Fort George. Nine settler families were captured and their farms were burned. Cannon fire from the fort and a subsequent attack from the militia forced the Indians to flee. Eighteen Indians were killed in the fighting. Europeans attacked some Indians last year at Norridgewock. This attack was believed to be a retaliatory gesture.

1783: Lyman Hall, Georgia governor (also captain-general and commander in chief), issued a proclamation forbidding the trespassing or settlement of whites in Creek or Cherokee lands.

1838: Lieutenant R.H.K. Whiteley departed from Ross's Landing (modern Chattanooga, Tennessee) with the second group of Cherokee "prisoners" to be forcibly removed to the Indian Territory (present-day Oklahoma). This group numbered 875 Cherokees. They traveled by boat to Lewisburg, northwest of Little Rock, Arkansas, where low river levels necessitated an overland march. They reached their destination on August 5.

1854: The Creek signed a treaty (11 Stat. 599). It was an amendment to the Fort Gibson Treaty signed on November 23, 1838.

1866: After postponing the Fort Laramie Treaty conference in southwestern Wyoming to allow more Indians to arrive, the conference reconvened. Later in the day, Colonel Henry Carrington arrived near Fort Laramie with almost 700 men. Standing Elk asked him why he was there. Carrington said he was there to guard the new Bozeman Trail. Standing Elk told Carrington that this trail had not been agreed upon yet, and Carrington said he would guard the trail anyway.

1868: According to army records, members of the Third Cavalry fought with a band of Indians near Apache Springs, New Mexico. Three Indians were killed and eleven were wounded during the extended conflict, which had started on June 1.

1868: According to army records, members of the Thirteenth Infantry fought with a band of Indians near Twenty-Five Yard Creek in Montana. No one was injured on either side.

1870: Indians attacked a railroad work crew near Grinnell Station, Kansas. Cavalry responded to defend the workers; three Indians were killed and ten wounded.

1870: According to official army records, Indians skirmished with a group of soldiers from the

Thirteenth Infantry near Fort Buford, Dakota Territory. Four civilians were wounded and one Indian was killed.

1872: Indians skirmished with a group of settlers near Prescott, Arizona, according to official army records. One settler was killed.

1876: General Crook left his base camp on Goose Creek to search for hostile Indians along the Rosebud.

1877: Wahlitits and two other members of White Bird's Band of Nez Perce killed a man named Richard Devine. The next day they killed three more men.

1938: Certain surplus or ceded "non-mineral, unallotted, and unreserved" lands, which had been set aside, were returned to tribal ownership on the Fort Berthold Reservation in North Dakota based on the Indian Reorganization Act.

1961: Through June 20, 1961, the American Indian Chicago Conference held a "What Indians Want" meeting. They adopted a declaration of Indian purpose.

1976: The Pit River Indian Tribe unanimously adopted a constitution in a meeting on August 16, 1964. The tribe reaffirmed that election.

1979: As part of a court case, the Sioux won money for the seizure of the Black Hills. Having other goals, they declined the money.

June 14

1671: The Sieur de St. Lusson claimed most of America for the French.

1756: According to some sources, the governor of New Jersey declared war on the Delaware.

1791: People started to arrived on the Holston River for the start of the Holston Treaty conference. Governor William Blount, forty-one chiefs, and 1,200 Cherokee warriors eventually arrived.

1846: The Bear Flag Revolt took place in California.

1866: At Fort Laramie in southeastern Wyoming, upon hearing Colonel Henry Carrington's orders to guard the trail that the Indians had never agreed to, the Indians confronted the treaty commissioners. The commissioners admitted that the army had plans to open the road. Red Cloud chastised the commissioners for pretending to bargain for something they planned on taking anyway. Red Cloud and many of the others left in disgust. A few Indians signed the treaty.

1867: According to the constitution of the Coeur d'Alene Tribe of Idaho, the Coeur d'Alene Reservation was established by executive order.

1867: According to army records, members of the Thirty-Seventh Infantry fought with a band of Indians near Grinnell Springs, Kansas. One soldier was killed.

1867: According to army records, members of the Eighth Cavalry fought with a band of Indians near Peacock Springs, Arizona. Twenty Indians were killed and nine captured.

1870: Near the Republican River in Kansas, elements of the Seventh Cavalry had a minor skirmish with hostile Indians. The Indians escaped with only the loss of one horse.

1870: According to an article published in *Frank Leslie's Illustrated Newspaper* on July 9, 1870, Indians attacked a Union Pacific train. The train coming from Cheyenne, Wyoming, hit and killed several of the Indians' horses; no humans died.

Union Pacific train under attack by Indians

1872: Indians skirmished with a group of soldiers from the Twenty-Second Infantry near Ponca Agency, Dakota Territory, according to official army records. No casualties were reported.

1877: During their forced march from their old reservation to Indian Territory (present-day Oklahoma), the Ponca arrived at the Otto Reservation. Taking pity on the Ponca, the Otto gave them some horses to help carry their people.

1879: President Hayes, by executive order, canceled the executive order of January 10, 1879. The order also added 52,000 additional acres to the Gila River Reserve in the Pima Agency for the Pima and Maricopa Tribes of Arizona south of Phoenix.

1880: Fort Harney in east-central Oregon was abandoned by the military.

1893: Natawistixina, sister of Seen From Afar, aunt of Red Crow, was buried on the Blood Reserve in Alberta, Canada, according to Lesley Wischmann at the University of Wyoming.

1954: The Sandy Lake Indian Reservation council decided to sell timber from tribal lands to cover the costs of repairing the community pump.

1960: The assistant secretary of the interior had authorized an election for an amendment to the constitution and bylaws of the Lower Brule Sioux Tribe of the Lower Brule Reservation. The vote was 105–47 in favor.

1961: The assistant secretary of the interior ratified Amendment 1 to the constitution and bylaws for the Muckleshoot Indian Tribe of the Muckleshoot Reservation.

1971: The Chicago Indian village occupied a Nike missile site.

Every: The White Earth Reservation powwow.

JUNE 15

1610: A group of Englishmen under the command of Captain Argall were on a trading expedition with the Patawomekes in Virginia. With the Indians was a prisoner named Henry Spilman, who would help the Jamestown settlement many times.

1692: According to some sources, an agreement for land cessions from the Delaware to Pennsylvania was reached.

1742: According to some reports, a conference regarding friendship and land cessions was held for the next four days between representatives of the British in New York and the Six Nations.

1763: Indians attacked Fort Pitt.

1763: A group of Seneca, Ottawa, Wyandot, and Chippewa Indians surrounded Fort Presque Isle (modern Erie, Pennsylvania). They held the fort and its twenty-seven defenders under siege until June 20.

1799: Handsome Lake had a vision.

1809: Congress passed a supplementary act to "An Act Making Appropriations for Carrying into Effect a Treaty Between the United States and the Chickasaw Tribe of Indians; and to Establish a Land-office in the Mississippi Territory."

1811: The ship *Tonquin* was sailing the waters off Vancouver Island. The Nootka captured the ship. Most of the crew were killed and the ship was destroyed.

1815: After bad weather, crop failures, and problems with the local Metis Indians, the Selkirk settlers abandoned the Red River settlements in Canada.

1831: Mushulatubbe and many other full-blood Choctaws wrote to Secretary of War Lewis Cass. They told him that they did not want any more of their annuity going to missionaries to pay for educating their children. They also did not want the missionaries going with them to Indian Territory (present-day Oklahoma). The letter stated, "We have not received a scholar out of their schools that was able to keep a grog house book."

1846: The United States accepted the Oregon Territory boundary.

1855: Mormon settlers established Fort Limhi (just south of modern Salmon) in central Idaho. This was an area inhabited by the Lemhi.

1864: Cherokee troops under Cherokee Brigadier General Stand Watie captured the steamboat *J.J. Williams*, loaded with supplies for Union soldiers. The fight took place on the Arkansas River near Fort Gibson in Indian Territory (present-day Oklahoma).

1867: According to army records, members of the Third Infantry fought with a band of Indians near Big Timbers, Kansas. Two soldiers and one civilian were killed. One soldier and two civilians were wounded.

1870: Indians attacked a ranch near Fort Bascom in western New Mexico. They assaulted, killed, and scalped a woman at the ranch. They then looted the ranch. A guard fired upon the Indians, but they escaped unharmed with five stolen horses belonging to the post's trader.

1870: According to official army records, Indians skirmished with a group of soldiers from the Third Infantry near the east branch of the Rio Verde River in Arizona. No casualties were reported.

1872: Corporal Daniel Hickey and soldiers from Company H, Eleventh Infantry, engaged in a fight with some Indians at Johnson's Station, Texas. Two Indians were reported killed.

1872: Indians skirmished with a group of settlers in the Granite Mountains of Arizona, according to official army records. Two settlers were wounded.

1873: Sioux Indians again attacked Fort Abraham Lincoln in central North Dakota. The garrison of soldiers from the Sixth and Seventeen Infantries repelled the attack, according to army documents. Four Indians were killed. One soldier and eight Indians were wounded. The fighting continued until June 17.

1876: Crook had been reinforced; he prepared to advance toward the Rosebud.

1877: The Nez Perce deadline to be on the reservation arrived. Whites were at Grangevil.

1877: Settlers fought a group of Indians near John Day's Creek, Idaho. According to army documents, four settlers were killed.

1881: Steamers arrived at Fort Yates carrying 1,700 Sioux.

1935: The Indian Reorganization Act was modified (49 Stat. 378).

1939: Amendments 1–4 to the constitution and bylaws for the Oneida Tribe of Indians of Wisconsin were approved.

1951: Assistant Secretary of the Interior Dale E. Doty approved the constitution and bylaws of the Kaibab Band of Paiute Indians of Arizona.

1952: Alberto Ruz had been excavating the Maya ruins at Palenque (Mexico). Pacal (Pakal) II's tomb was opened. A large sarcophagus was discovered. It contained Pacal's body.

JUNE 16

1598: Oñate's expedition stopped for several days at a Piro village they called Nueva Sevilla, in modern New Mexico.

1718: According to some sources, a friendship agreement was reached between representatives of the British in Pennsylvania and the Conestoga, Delaware, and Shawnee Indians.

1802: A treaty (7 Stat. 68) with the Creek was concluded near Fort Wilkinson on the Oconee River (near modern Milledgeville, Georgia). New tribal boundary lines were established, which ceded lands along the Oconee and Ocmulgee Creek and the Altamaha tract. The tribe received $3,000 annually, and some chiefs got $1,000 a year for ten years. The tribe got $10,000 now, and $10,000 was set aside to pay tribal debts to local white traders. The Creek also received $5,000 for lands that had been seized. They also got two sets of blacksmith tools and trained blacksmiths to use them for three years. The United States got the right to establish a garrison on Creek lands. The treaty was signed by thirty-nine Indians. The Americans were represented by General James Wilkinson, Benjamin Hawkins, and Andrew Pickens.

1805: Sacajawea drank mineral water to treat an illness.

1820: Lewis Cass, representing the United States, and the Chippewa Indians signed a treaty (7 Stat.

206) at St. Mary's River on the Indiana-Ohio border. The treaty provided land for the construction of a fort at Sault St. Marie, Michigan.

1832: The Battle of Pecatonica (Wisconsin) took place. As a part of the Black Hawk Wars, Kickapoo Indians killed five settlers at Fort Hamilton, Wisconsin. The Kickapoo were chased to the Pecatonica River by General Henry Dodge and thirty militiamen. During the subsequent fighting, three soldiers and eleven Kickapoo were killed. This was also known as the Battle of Bloody Pond and the Battle of Kellogg's Grove.

1863: According to a letter from Brigadier General James Carleton to Brigadier General Lorenzo Thomas, Lieutenant L.A. Bargie, First New Mexico Volunteers, was murdered and mutilated by Indians in the Jornado del Muerton in central New Mexico.

1867: According to army records, members of the Third Cavalry fought with a band of Indians near the Gallinas Mountains in New Mexico. One Indian was killed and two were wounded.

1868: According to army records, members of the First Cavalry fought with a band of Indians near Toddy Mountain in Arizona. Four soldiers and one Indian were reported killed.

1869: According to army records, members of the Eighth Cavalry fought with a band of Indians near Camp Toll Gate. One soldier and three Indians were killed. One soldier was wounded.

1870: Wood-choppers were working on Mulberry Creek in Kansas when Indians attacked. According to army reports, some of the workers were killed and their bodies were horribly mutilated.

1873: After non–Wallowa Nez Perce signed a treaty giving up the Wallowa Valley, government agents arrived to move the Wallowa Nez Perce from the land. Young Joseph (Heinmot Tooyalaket) told the agents: "It has always belonged to our people. It comes unclouded to them from our fathers, and we will defend this land as long as a drop of Indian blood warms the hearts of our men." Young Joseph asked President Grant to allow them to stay in their ancestral lands. On this day, President Grant issued an executive order prohibiting white settlers from claiming title to Wallowa Valley land.

1873: Indians fought with soldiers from the Fifth Cavalry and some Indian scouts near the forks of Tonto Creek in Arizona, according to army documents. Fourteen Indians were killed and five were captured. One soldier was wounded.

1876: General Crook and 1,000 soldiers reached the Rosebud. They found no Indians.

1878: Bannock Indians attacked and killed several settlers near Camp Harney in Oregon.

1897: The Hawaii Annexation Treaty was signed.

1938: The confines of the Port Gamble Reservation were established by an executive proclamation from Acting Secretary of the Interior E.K. Burlow for the Port Gamble Band of Clallam Indians.

1939: Assistant Secretary of the Interior Oscar Chapman approved an election that amended the constitution and bylaws of the Oneida Tribe of Indians of Wisconsin. The election was held on June 3, 1939.

1942: Aleuts were forced to leave islands in Alaska.

1947: The constitution and bylaws of the Kootenai Tribe of Idaho were approved.

1959: Assistant Secretary of the Interior Fred Aandahl ratified amendments to the constitution and bylaws of the Turtle Mountain Band of Chippewa Indians of North Dakota.

1975: Harley Zephier, area director of the Aberdeen office, Bureau of Indian Affairs, ratified an election for Amendments 1–4 to the constitution and bylaws of the Yankton Sioux. The election was held on March 20, 1975.

1980: The secretary of the interior authorized an election for an amendment to the constitution and bylaws of the Lac Courte Oreilles Band of Lake Superior Chippewa Indians of Wisconsin. The election was held on August 16, 1980.

1984: The Chinook Indian Tribe, Inc., approved a constitution that described the territory of the corporation, membership criteria, election of officers, duties of the officers, and general membership meetings.

JUNE 17

1527: Panfilo de Narvaez departed form Spain with five ships. His destination was Florida.

1579: Sir Francis Drake landed north of San Francisco, probably at Drake's Bay in California. He reported the Indians to be "people of a tractable, free and loving nature, without guile or treachery."

1654: In a meeting between the Swedes and the Delaware in Tinicum (New Sweden, Pennsylvania), Delaware Chief Naaman praised the Swedes for their righteous treatment of the native inhabitants.

1673: Father Jacques Marquette and Louis Joliet had begun an expedition to explore the Mississippi River starting from the Straits of Michilimackinac on May 17. On this day they first reached what they believed to be the headwaters of the Mississippi River near modern Prairie du Chien, Wisconsin.

1675: According to some sources, some Pokanoket returned horses to the local settlers. The horses had wandered off from their settlements, and the Indians had found them.

1824: The Office of Indian Affairs was started.

1838: The third group of Cherokee "prisoners" to be forcibly removed to the Indian Territory (present-day Oklahoma) left Ross's Landing (modern Chattanooga, Tennessee). This group numbered 1,070. Many were forced from their homes at gunpoint and had few provisions. They did not accept anything from the federal agents except food for fear of an implied acceptance of the New Echota Treaty.

1861: Brigadier General Ben McCulloch, head of Confederate forces in Indian Territory (present-day Oklahoma), asked for Chief John Ross's permission to organize Cherokee sympathizers into an army. Ross stated that he did not want to do anything that would give either side a reason to over-run and destroy Cherokee lands. Stand Watie, though, organized his own group of Cherokee fighters. They were sworn in to the Confederate Army on July 12, 1861.

1873: Fort Abraham Lincoln (formerly Fort McKeen) in central North Dakota was again attacked by Sioux Indians. Lieutenant Colonel W.P. Carlin's forces repelled the attack. One Ree scout was wounded; the Sioux sustained three killed and eight wounded. The attack started on June 15.

1876: General George Crook was in the field with less than 1,000 men to force the Cheyenne and the Sioux back to the reservation. On this day, Crook's men encountered Crazy Horse near the Rosebud River in Montana. Rather than risk a frontal attack, or the traditional riding-in-a-ring around the enemy, Crazy Horse and his mounted warriors kept attacking Crook's flanks. This change in strategy confused the soldiers. During the battle, "Chief Comes In Sight's horse was shot out from under him in front of the soldiers." He was rescued by his sister, Buffalo Calf Road Woman. Although the soldiers called this the Battle of the Rosebud, the Indians named it the Battle Where the Girl Saves Her Brother. The Indians won the day. Crook decided to return to his supply camp on Goose Creek until he could be reinforced. First Sergeants Michael A. McGann, Company F, Joseph Robinson, Company D, John Shingle, Troop I, and trumpeter Elmer Snow, Company M, Third Cavalry, would be awarded the Medal of Honor for their actions during the fighting. According to army reports, eleven Indians and nine soldiers were killed. Captain G.V. Henry and twenty other soldiers were wounded.

1877: Another battle took place between the army and the Nez Perce. The army was led by Captain David Perry. There were approximately 140 warriors in the group. This was called the Battle of White Bird Canyon. The army unit had difficulty coordinating its actions because one trumpeter had been killed and the other lost his trumpet.

According to army records, during the retreat First Lieutenant William Parnell, First Cavalry, would return and rescue a soldier whose horse had been shot out from under him. For these actions, Parnell would be awarded the Medal of Honor. Lieutenant E.R. Theller and thirty-three soldiers were killed. No Nez Perce casualties were reported. The battlefield was at White Bird, south of Grangeville, Idaho.

1892: The boundaries of the Fort Berthold Reservation were expanded by an executive order (1 Kappler 883, 884).

1909: By Executive Order No. 1090, the executive order issued on December 12, 1992, which set aside certain public domain lands for the use of the Papago Indians, was modified in the Gila Bend area.

1954: The Termination Act was passed, meaning no more federal help for Indians.

1967: Author John Stands in Timber died.

1974: W.D. Babby, the Aberdeen, South Dakota, area director of the Bureau of Indian Affairs, ratified an election for an amendment to the constitution and bylaws of the Lower Brule Sioux Tribe of the Lower Brule Reservation.

1996: A class-action suit representing 300,000 American Indians was filed in federal Court against the Bureau of Indian Affairs, the United States Treasury, and the Department of the Interior. The suit alleged that the bureau had mishandled $450 million dollars in revenues from mineral leases on lands held in trust for Indians. The suit further alleged that no accurate records were kept of the monies collected and that funds were illegally diverted to other projects.

JUNE 18

1541: Hernando de Soto's expedition had reached the Mississippi River on May 8, 1541. After exploring the near side of the river, they finally crossed to the western side.

1730: Seven Cherokee representatives met with King George II of England at Windsor Castle in London. They acknowledged him as the sovereign of the Cherokee people. Leading the Cherokees were Chief Oukah-ulah and Attakullaculla (Little Carpenter).

1744: According to some reports, a conference was held for the next three days between representatives of the British in Connecticut, Massachusetts, and New York and the Six Nations regarding friendship and alliance.

1763: As part of Pontiac's Rebellion, Seneca attacked Fort Le Boeuf (present-day Waterford in northwestern Pennsylvania). Half of the garrison of a little more than a dozen men were killed when the Indians attacked and burned the fort. The rest of the soldiers escaped.

1812: The War of 1812 was declared against the British.

1868: After signing a treaty on June 1, 1868, that gave up some of their land, the Navajo who had been held at Bosque Redondo in New Mexico were allowed to return to their traditional lands.

1870: According to official army records, Indians skirmished with a group of soldiers from the Second Cavalry near North Platte, Nebraska. One Indian was wounded.

1885: Big Brea released some prisoners.

1917: An executive order was issued to set aside 160 acres for the Winnemucca Shoshone Indian Colony in Nevada.

1934: The Indian Reorganization Act (48 Stat. 984–985) took place. Among other things, it was to "permit any Indian to transfer by will restricted lands of such Indian to his or her heirs or lineal descendants, and for other purposes. To authorize the sale of individual Indian lands acquired under the Act of June 18, 1934, and under the Act of June 26, 1936."

1956: An act (70 Stat. 290) was passed by Congress to "provide that any owner of an interest in any tract of land on the Tulalip Reservation, Washington, in which any undivided interest, is now or hereafter, held in trust by the United States for an Indian, or is now or hereafter, owned by an Indian subject to restrictions."

1968: The acting assistant commissioner of Indian affairs approved an election by the Havasupai Nation for an amendment to their constitution held on May 20, 1968.

1969: The acting assistant commissioner of Indian affairs had authorized an election to amend the constitution and bylaws of the Kalispel Indian Community of the Kalispel Reservation. It was approved by a vote of 19–3.

JUNE 19

1541: Hernando de Soto's expedition met the Casqui Indians (near modern Helena, Arkansas). There had been a drought in the area, and the padres offered to help. A large cross was erected, and the Spaniards joined in prayer. Soon it started to rain. The Casquis became allies of the Spanish.

1754: A conference was started and lasted until July 10. Representing the British from Pennsylvania were Benjamin Franklin, Isaac Norris, John Penn, and Richard Peters. The British acknowledged Iroquois claims to land in the Ohio Valley.

1767: The governor of Louisiana issued an order that recognized the Chitimacha Indians and instructed the commander at Manchac to treat them with proper deference.

1816: Robert Semple was Governor of the Red River settlement in Canada. He was trying to reestablish the settlement after many of the settlers had abandoned the area. Semple and a group of settlers encountered a group of Metis in an area known as Seven Oaks. The Metis told the settlers to give up. Shooting began, and twenty-one settlers, including Semple, were killed. Only one Metis died. This event became known as the Massacre at Seven Oaks or the Skirmish at Seven Oaks.

1833: Colonel John Abert and General Enoch Parsons met with the Creek. They suggested a new treaty to provide for rapid removal to Indian Territory (present-day Oklahoma). The Indian lands were sold to the United States, with payment in installments. The Indians' white creditors convinced the Creek not to sign the agreement.

1834: John H. Eaton, representing the U.S. government, and Andrew Ross, John and James Rogers, John West, John Drew, James Starr, Moses Smith, and T.F. Pack, representing some Cherokees, negotiated a treaty whereby the Cherokees gave up their lands in Georgia, North Carolina, Alabama, and Tennessee for a small annuity and 800,000 acres in Indian Territory (present-day Oklahoma). These Cherokees represented only a portion of the nation.

1837: Rachel Parker and four others (including her cousin, Cynthia Ann Parker) were taken captive in a Comanche raid on Parker's Fort on May 19, 1836. On this day, she was sold to Mexican traders. Unlike her cousin, she happily rejoined her family.

1838: The Cherokees were being forcibly removed to the Indian Territory (present-day Oklahoma). The South was experiencing a drought, and the weather was extremely hot this year. General Winfield Scott agreed to a petition from Cherokee leaders to delay any further shipments of Cherokees until the weather improved. Scott required that all of the Cherokees start their removal by September 1. The September deadline was extended because the drought and heat did not end until almost October.

1858: Two treaties were signed with different Indian nations.

1860: Congress divided California into two districts for Indian affairs.

1860: The original confines of the Bay Mills Reservation were purchased under an act of Congress (12 Stat. 58).

1865: The Choctaw warriors fighting for the Confederacy officially surrendered.

1867: According to army records, Indian scouts fought with a band of Indians near Steins Mountain, Oregon. Twelve Indians were killed, one wounded, and two captured.

1868: De Smet entered the Sioux camp for a peace conference.

1869: A survey crew, guarded by troops from the Seventh Cavalry, was working near Sheridan, Kansas (near modern Winona). Indians attacked the group. Two whites and twelve Indians were reported to be wounded. Four Indians were killed. An Indian attack on a government wagon train forced it to seek safety at Fort Wallace in western Kansas.

1869: According to army records, members of the Eighth Cavalry fought with a band of Indians in "Red Rock Country, Arizona." Seven Indians were killed and one was captured. The fighting continued until July 5.

1879: Lieutenant John van Orsdale and eight soldiers from the Seventh Infantry fought a small group of Sioux who had just crossed the Missouri River eleven miles above Fort Benton in north-central Montana. The Sioux had thirty stolen horses, according to army information. One of the Indians was killed. The rest of the Sioux escaped into the Badlands.

1923: Lands were taken from the Fort Hall Indian Reservation in order to build a reservoir.

1959: Amendment 5 to the constitution and by-laws of the Lac du Flambeau Band of Lake Superior Chippewa Indians of Wisconsin was approved and became effective.

1968: A modification to the constitution of the Indians of the Tulalip Tribes in Washington was approved by the U.S. government.

JUNE 20

1632: The Charter of Maryland was issued.

1675: This marks the start of King Philip's War, according to some historians.

1732: A royal land grant was issued for Georgia.

1763: As part of Pontiac's Rebellion, a force of Seneca, Ottawa, Wyandot, and Chippewa attacked Fort Presque Isle (present-day Erie in northwestern Pennsylvania). The siege had begun on June 15. The soldiers, numbering less than three dozen, surrendered when the fort went up in flames. All but Ensign John Christie and two others escaped. The rest were killed.

1775: The Wyandot gave a tract of land to James Rankin near Detroit.

1780: British Captain Henry Bird commanded a force of 1,000 men, of whom 850 were Indians. They attacked Ruddle's Station, Kentucky. Three hundred settlers had taken refuge in the station. Bird's forces had a cannon, and the settlers soon realized they were outmatched. They agreed to surrender. When they settlers opened the gate, the warriors rushed in and started killing them. Before Bird could intercede, more than 200 people were killed. This was called the Ruddle's Station Massacre. Nearby Martin's Station also surrendered. Those occupants fared better. All of the survivors were taken to Detroit as prisoners. (Also recorded as happening on June 24, 1780.)

1867: According to army records, Pawnee Scouts fought with a band of Indians near the Black Hills in Nebraska. Two hostile Indians were killed.

1868: The Jean Pierre De Smet conference began at Fort Rice, Dakota Territory.

1869: Indians raided Scandinavia, Kansas. The cavalry pursued the Indians and killed one.

1873: Colonel Stanley (with Colonel Custer) led a new expedition at Fort Rice.

1906: The James Bay Treaty Number 9 was signed. It was between the government of Canada and the Ojibwa, Cree, and other Indian inhabitants of the territory.

1936: A constitution and bylaws were submitted for ratification by the members of the Minnesota Mdewakanton Sioux of the Prairie Island Indian Community in Minnesota. It was approved by Secretary of the Interior Harold Ickes.

1939: By Proclamation No. 2339, the president transferred certain lands from the Beaverhead National Forest and made them the Big Hole Battlefield National Monument in Montana. This was the site of one of the battles on the Nez Perce flight in 1877.

1956: Elections were proposed for the Cherokees.

1977: An election to approve an amendment to the constitution and bylaws for the Lower Sioux Indian Community of Minnesota was held. It was passed by a vote of 23–12.

1987: The Chinook Indian Tribe, Inc., passed an ordinance that "replaces Section 2 of the 1984 constitution." The membership ordinance stated that membership shall consist of descendants of the Cathlamet, Wahkiakum, Willapa, and Lower Bands of Chinook Indians and the Clatsop Tribe of Indians who were living at the time of the 1851 treaties who were on the August 1, 1987, membership list and their descendants. "New members" applying after August 1, 1987, had to document their descent from persons listed on the 1919 Roblin Schedule of Unenrolled Indians, the 1906 and 1913 McChesney rolls of the Indians living at the time of the 1851 treaties or their heirs, or the 1914 annuity payment roll and had one-quarter Indian blood from the specified Chinook bands.

JUNE 21

1674: Chatot Indians had a mission established for them west of the Apalachicola River.

1752: Ojibwa, Ottawa, and Potawatomi Indians under the leadership of Frenchman Charles Langlade attacked the British and Miami at Fort Pickawillany in Ohio.

1856: Nonhostile Indians along the Lower Rogue River and at Fort Orford in southwestern Oregon were put on a boat to be moved to a new reservation between the Pacific Ocean and the Willamette River. It was called the Grande Ronde Reservation.

1867: According to army records, members of the Seventh Cavalry fought with a band of Indians near Fort Wallace, Kansas. Two soldiers were killed and two were wounded.

1867: According to army records, members of the First Cavalry and Thirty-Second Infantry fought with a band of Indians near Calabases, Arizona. Three Indians were killed, one wounded, and six captured.

1870: Indians attacked a Mexican wagon train near Carson, Colorado. Five teamsters were killed. The cavalry attempted to locate the Indians but were unsuccessful.

1874: Major C.E. Compton and a few men from the Sixth Cavalry were en route from Camp Supply, Indian Territory (present-day Oklahoma), to Fort Dodge in southwestern Kansas when they were attacked by Indians on Buffalo Creek, Indian Territory. One soldier and one civilian were wounded.

1876: After preliminary scouting in the area of the Little Bighorn by Major Marcus Reno, General Alfred Terry held a planning session with his commanders, Colonel John Gibbon and Colonel George Custer. The plan was for Gibbon's troops to reach the mouth of the Little Bighorn on June 26. Custer was to follow Reno's earlier path up the Rosebud to near the Little Bighorn. Custer was known by many names among the Indians: "Long Hair," "Yellow Hair," "Hard Bottom," and "Son of the Morning Star." Colonel Gibbon was called "The One Who Limps."

1885: Army Indian scouts fought a group of Indians near Oputo in Sonora, Mexico. According to army documents, one scout was killed.

1899: Treaty Number 8 was signed between the government of Canada and the "Cree, Beaver, Chipewyan and other Indians."

1906: The federal government, set aside land within the Flathead Indian Reservation in Montana for the purpose of establishing townsites, including Blue Bay. Many of the lots in this townsite were eventually given back over to tribal ownership due to a lack of interest in the town's development.

1906: An act (34 Stat. 325–326) was passed that allowed the federal government to extend its holding in trust of lands for Indians.

1906: The 160-acre Shingle Springs Rancheria was located in El Dorado County, California. It

Iroquois chief

was established by acts on this day and on April 30, 1908. The land was purchased by the U.S. government on March 11, 1920.

1947: An election for a proposed amendment to the constitution and bylaws of the Yavapai-Apache Tribe of the Camp Verde Reservation was held. The results were 109–2 in favor.

1978: Aleuts won compensation from the government over laws regarding furs.

Every: National Aboriginal Day celebrated as "an opportunity for all Canadians to recognize the achievements and contributions of Canada's Aboriginal peoples."

JUNE 22

1715: According to some sources, an agreement on friendship and trade was reached by representatives of the Susquehannock and the British in Pennsylvania.

1744: This was the first day of a conference between the Iroquois and the British representatives

from Maryland, Pennsylvania, and Virginia. After some haggling, much of Maryland and Virginia formerly in Iroquois hands was ceded to the British colonies.

1763: Indians killed the soldiers from Presque Isle Fort.

1768: According to some reports, a conference regarding land cessions was held between the British in Maryland and the Nanticoke.

1823: Colonel Henry Leavenworth and 200 soldiers left Fort Atkinson seeking Arikara who attacked Smith and Ashley's expedition on June 3.

1836: The Florida militia began a series of raids against the Seminole and the Creek, according to muster records. They were led by Captain William North and were in the area of Okefenokee Swamp.

1838: In a report issued on this day, General Winfield Scott estimated the disposition of the Cherokee Nation. According to his figures, 3,000 had been removed, 1,500 were in transit to the Indian Territory (present-day Oklahoma), 2,000–3,000 were in forts in the Cherokee lands awaiting movement to embarkation points, 6,750 were in concentration camps between Ross's Landing (present-day Chattanooga, Tennessee) and the eastern Cherokee Agency (present-day Calhoun, Tennessee), and there were 200 still at large in their old homelands. There were an estimated 3,000 Cherokees in North Carolina as well.

1839: Elias Boudinot, first editor of the *Cherokee Phoenix*, Chief Major Ridge (Kahnungdaclageh), and his son, John Ridge (Skahtlelohskee), were members of the Cherokee treaty party. They had generated many enemies by agreeing to the removal of the Cherokees from their lands east of the Mississippi River. They signed the peace treaty that gave away Cherokee lands east of the Mississippi River. They moved to Indian Territory (present-day Oklahoma) with the rest of the Cherokee Nation. Early this morning, John Ridge was dragged from his bed and stabbed to death. Chief Major Ridge was shot and killed at 10:00 A.M. in another part of the reservation. Later that day, Elias Boudinot was stabbed and hacked to death. These murders were committed by Cherokees for what they felt was the treasonous betrayal of their nation. A Cherokee law, which Chief Ridge helped pass, gave the death penalty to any Cherokee who sold or gave away Cherokee lands without the majority of the tribe's permission. These deaths were considered the execution of that law. Chief Stand Watie, brother to Elias and nephew to Major Ridge, managed to avoid the warriors who planned to kill him.

1867: According to army records, members of the Thirty-Seventh Infantry fought with a band of Indians near Goose Creek Station, Colorado. Two soldiers were wounded.

1867: According to army records, members of the Seventh Cavalry fought with a band of Indians near Fort Wallace, Kansas. No injuries were reported on either side.

1876: Colonel George Custer and 611 men of the Seventh Cavalry started up the Rosebud River, moving toward a reported concentration of Indians near the Little Bighorn. They traveled twelve miles. Colonel John Gibbons, with General Alfred Terry accompanying him, started out for the mouth of the Bighorn River.

1877: General Oliver "One Armed Soldier Chief" Howard left Lapwai (Apache name). He was also called "Cut Arm" for the arm he lost in the Civil War.

1885: Sitting Bull visited Washington, D.C., with Buffalo Bill.

1942: According to Federal Register No. 7FR04805, Public Land Order No. 2 was issued.

1959: Assistant Secretary of the Interior Fred Aandahl ratified two amendments to the constitution and bylaws approved by the Confederated Tribes of the Warm Springs Reservation of Oregon in an election held on April 25, 1959.

1971: Acting Associate Commissioner of Indian Affairs Eugene Suarez Sr. had authorized an election for an amendment to the constitution and bylaws of the Paiute-Shoshone Tribe of the Fallon Reservation and Colony. It was approved by a vote of 43–5.

1973: Paiute Indians got compensation over water rights.

1983: An election approved Amendment 15 to the constitution and bylaws of the Lac du Flambeau Band of Lake Superior Chippewa Indians of Wisconsin.

1988: A modification to the constitution of the Indians of the Tulalip Tribes in Washington was approved by the U.S. government.

JUNE 23

1683: William Penn and Delaware Chief Tamenend signed a peace treaty in Shackamoxon, Pennsylvania. Tamenend was also called Tammany. He was renowned for his honor. The Tammany societies were named so in his honor. William Penn purchased two plots of land from Chief Tamenend. The land was on and between the Pennypack and Neshaminy Rivers. The land was purchased for a long list of supplies.

1704: James Moore, former governor of South Carolina, was leading a force of fifty British and 1,000 Creek against Spanish settlements. They attacked the Apalachee mission of San Pedro y San Pablo at Patale in northwestern Florida. They took many Indians as slaves and killed Father Manuel de Mendoza. The mission was destroyed the next day.

1757: Indians attempted the third short siege this year at Fort Augusta on the Susquehanna River at Shamokin. They were unsuccessful.

1853: Captain John W. Gunnison left Fort Leavenworth in northeastern Kansas to start the Pacific Railroad survey along the 38th Parallel. This was a part of the government's Manifest Destiny program. (See October 26, 1853.)

1853: Major Robert S. Neighbors was appointed as a Texas Indian special agent.

1863: General James Carleton decided that the Navajos had until July 20 to report to the Bosque Redondo Reservation. This message was delivered to Delgadito and Barboncito. Any Navajos who were not on the reservation by then would be considered hostile.

1865: General Stand Watie and his Cherokee Confederate sympathizers surrendered. Stand Watie was the last Confederate general to officially surrender.

1876: President Grant, by executive order, established the Hoopa Valley Indian Reservation on the Trinity River in northern California. It contained 89,572.43 acres. The reservation was based on the congressional act of April 8, 1864.

1876: Hand-to-hand fighting took place in the Wallowa Valley.

1876: Colonel George Custer's troops advanced thirty-three miles up the Rosebud River. They saw signs that large numbers of Indians had passed through the area, but none of the signs appeared to be very recent.

1878: Captain Reuben Bernard and his Idaho troops caught up to the Bannock Indians on Silver Creek forty-five miles west of Camp Harney, which was west of present-day Burns in east-central Oregon. The soldiers reported three dead and an unknown number of Indians killed. (Also recorded as happening on June 28, 1878.)

1885: Third and Sixth Cavalry soldiers and Indian scouts fought a group of Indians in the Bapispe Mountains of Sonora, Mexico. According to army documents, one Indian was killed and fifteen were captured.

1970: An election for the adoption of a constitution and bylaws for the Chitimacha Tribe of Louisiana was authorized by the acting assistant commissioner of Indian affairs. The election was held on November 7, 1970.

1972: The Indian Education Act was passed. It funded supplementary programs to help American Indian students both on and off reservations. In so doing, it recognized that 50 percent of all Indians lived in urban areas and 75 percent lived off reservations.

1992: Executive Order No. 6450, by President George Bush, declared 1992 as the "Year of Reconciliation Between American Indians and Non-Indians."

JUNE 24

1497: Cabot claims Newfoundland.

1528: Narvaez reached the Apalachee capital.

1610: Membertou (Micmac) became the first Indian Catholic.

1675: As a part of King Philip's War, Wampanoag attacked Swansea, Massachusetts. The small community lost nine settlers before the end of the day. Skirmishes lasted until the Indians withdrew five days later.

1746: Indians attacked the settlers at Fort Bridgman in Vernon, Connecticut.

1763: As part of Pontiac's Rebellion, a group of Delaware surrounded Fort Pitt in present-day Pittsburgh, Pennsylvania. The commander, Captain Simeon Ecuyer, had 338 soldiers in the fort and would not surrender. Not having enough warriors to attack the fort, the Delaware left with a few blankets as a present. Unknown to the Indians, the blankets came from an infirmary treating smallpox. The Delaware were the first to be affected by this form of biological warfare during the rebellion. (Also recorded as happening on July 24.)

1780: British Captain Henry Bird commanded a force of 1,000 men, of which 850 were Indians. They attacked Ruddle's Station, Kentucky, where three hundred settlers had taken refuge. Bird's forces had a cannon, and the settlers soon realized they were outmatched. They agreed to surrender. When the settlers opened the gate, the warriors rushed in and started killing them. Before Bird could intercede, more than 200 people were killed. This was called the Ruddle's Station Massacre. Nearby Martin's Station also surrendered. Those occupants fared better. All of the survivors were taken to Detroit as prisoners.

1796: A treaty conference was being held between Creek and American and Georgia officials at Fort Colerain on the St. Marys River, just north of Florida. Creek speaker Oche Haujo (Alexander Cornells) said the Creek agreed to the boundary line in the New York Treaty made by Alexander McGillivray. He complained that the lands the Creek had already ceded had always been valuable, yet the goods they had received had been shoddy. No matter how far the Creek moved away from the white men, the white men always followed. Fearing they would eventually not have enough land to bury their dead, he said the Creek should give up no more land.

1821: A Cherokee war party led by Chief Walter Webber attacked a trading post on lands held by the Osage on the Grand River in Indian Territory (present-day Oklahoma). They killed one man and several children.

1832: Black Hawk and his Sac followers attacked the fort at Apple River in northwestern Illinois. The fort's defenders proved too hard to defeat, so Black Hawk looted some supplies from local farms and left. He said he did not burn the fort or the farms because the glow would attract nearby soldiers.

1832: Reverend Samuel Worcester had been arrested and convicted of living and working among the Cherokees without having a state permit or having sworn an oath of allegiance to the state of Georgia. On this day the Supreme Court ruled that the state of Georgia had unfairly tried to exercise control over the Cherokees contrary to federal law and treaties. The court struck down most of the anti-Indian laws passed by Georgia, including those seizing lands and nullifying tribal laws. Before the trial, President Andrew Jackson officially stated that he had no intention of supporting the Cherokees over the state of Georgia. Speaking to the court's decision, Jackson was quoted as saying, "John Marshall [the chief justice] has rendered his decision; now let him enforce it." Jackson ignored the Supreme Court ruling and continued in his efforts to move the Cherokees out of the South and into the Indian Territory (present-day Oklahoma).

1848: The last group of Creek to be removed to eastern Indian Territory (present-day Oklahoma) arrived at Fort Gibson.

1858: Fort Garland was established to guard against the Jicarilla Apache.

1862: By a treaty (12 Stat. 1237) signed on this day, "The Ottawa Indians of the United Bands of Blanchard's Fork and of Roche de Boeuf, having become sufficiently advanced in civilization, and being desirous of becoming citizens of the United States, it is hereby agreed and stipulated that their organization and their relations with the United States as an Indian tribe shall be dissolved and terminated at the expiration of five years from the ratification of this treaty: and from and after that time, the said Ottawas, and each and every one of them, shall be deemed and declared to be citizens of the United States."

1864: The Colorado territorial government ordered all Indians to go to their reservations.

1867: According to army records, members of the Seventh Cavalry under Lieutenant Colonel George Custer fought with a band of Indians near the North Fork of the Republican River in Kansas. One soldier was wounded.

1868: According to army records, members of the Twenty-Third Infantry fought with a band of Indians near Battle Creek, Idaho. Three Indians were reported killed and three captured.

1874: Major C.E. Compton and a few men from the Sixth Cavalry were still en route from Camp Supply, Indian Territory (present-day Oklahoma), to Fort Dodge in southwestern Kansas. They were attacked again at Bear Creek Redoubt in Indian Territory. The Indians sustained four fatalities and several wounded.

1876: Colonel George Custer and the Seventh Cavalry made twenty-eight miles on this day's march. They saw more and more signs of a large concentration of Indians. The signs were becoming fresher.

1969: An election for Amendments 1 and 2 to the constitution and bylaws of the Hopi Tribe was held; both were approved.

1972: An election to approve an amendment to the constitution and bylaws for the Wichita Indian Tribe of Oklahoma was held. It was approved.

JUNE 25

1528: Narvaez and his Spanish expedition crossed the Suwannee River. They discovered and occupied a village they called Apalachen, in Florida. There were approximately forty houses in the village and a quantity of corn. They remained there for almost a month. During that time they fought with the local inhabitants on several occasions. The local Apalachee Indians called the village Ibitachoco or Ivitachuco.

1761: The Mi'kmaq of Shediac, Pokemouche, Cape Briton, and Miramichi signed a treaty with the British of Nova Scotia.

1777: Soldiers at Fort Stanwix (modern Rome, New York) had been ordered to stay inside the fort. Captain Gregg and Corporal Madison left the walls to shoot at a large flock of birds. Not far from the fort, they were attacked by Indians. Both men were scalped and left for dead. The captain survived, though, and made it back to the fort.

1838: The third group of Cherokee prisoners to be forcibly removed to the Indian Territory (present-day Oklahoma) arrived at Bellefonte in north-central Alabama. They had heard that the government would start out no more groups of Cherokees for the Indian Territory during the summer, and they asked to be allowed to return to their concentration camps in Georgia and Tennessee until the fall. There had been a drought recently, and the weather was extremely hot. When they were told they must move on, almost 300 Cherokees grabbed their meager belongings and escaped into the nearby woods. Many of the remaining Cherokee prisoners refused to board their transport barges. General Nathaniel Smith, superintendent of the Cherokee removal, was in Bellefonte. He called for local militia to help herd the recalcitrants on the boats. Only 722 of the original group of 1,070 Cherokees reached Little Rock, Arkansas.

1868: The army reported that a detachment of troops attacked and pursued a band of hostile Indians near Fort Hayes in central Kansas. No casualties were reported.

1876: At the Battle of the Little Bighorn, Colonel George Custer was commanding Troops C, E, F, I, and L; Major Marcus Reno led troops A, G, and M; Captain Frederick Benteen led Troops H, D, and K; and Captain Thomas McDougall guarded the supply wagons with Troop B. It was a significant defeat for the U.S. Army. Army reports listed thirteen officers, 189 enlisted men, and four civilians as killed under Custer's command. Reno's troops split from Custer's. According to army documents, Lieutenant Donald McIntosh, Lieutenant B.H. Hodgson, forty-six soldiers, and one civilian were killed. Captain Benteen, Lieutenant C.A. Varnum, and forty-four soldiers were wounded in fighting that lasted through the next day. Army reports did not list how many Indians were killed or wounded in this defeat for the army. The following soldiers received congressional Medals of Honor for actions during this battle on this day and the next day: Private Neil Bancroft, Company A; Private Abram B. Brant, Company D; Private Thomas J. Callen, Company B; Sergeant Benjamin C. Criswell, Company B; Corporal Charles Cunningham, Company B; Private Frederick Deetline, Company D; Sergeant George Geiger, Company H; Private Theodore Goldin, Troop G; Private David W. Harris, Company A; Private William M. Harris, Company D; Private Henry Holden, Company D; Sergeant Rufus D. Hutchinson, Company B; Blacksmith Henry Mechlin, Company H; Sergeant Thomas Murray, Company B; Private James Pym, Company B; Sergeant Stanislaus Roy, Company A;

Private George Scott, Company D; Private Thomas Stivers, Company D; Private Peter Thompson, Company C; Private Frank Tolan, Company D; Saddler Otto Voit, Company H; Sergeant Charles Welch, Company D; and Private Charles Windolph, Company H.

1879: Army Indian scouts fought a group of Indians in the Tonto Basin in Arizona. According to army documents, six Indians were killed and one was captured.

1914: A constitution for the Standing Rock Sioux Tribe was approved by the U.S. government.

1943: Amendments 1 and 3 to the constitution and bylaws of the Lac du Flambeau Band of Lake Superior Chippewa Indians of Wisconsin was approved and became effective.

1948: The General Crimes Act (62 Stat. 757) of June 25, 1948, was passed by Congress. Its purpose was to "extend Laws of the state into Indian country except when crimes are between Indians or when tribal courts have jurisdiction."

JUNE 26

1784: The Spanish closed New Orleans to the United States.

1791: American negotiators, led by William Blount, began the Treaty of Holston negotiations with the Cherokees. The treaty was signed on July 2, 1791.

1792: A war party of Chickamauga and Creek, led by Chiefs Little Owl and Shawnee Warrior, attacked Ziegler's Station near Nashville, Tennessee. They killed five settlers and burned down the buildings.

1794: A treaty (7 Stat. 43) with the Cherokees was concluded. This treaty referred back to the Holston River Treaty of July 2, 1791, and attempted to clear up some understandings about the terms of that agreement. The Holston River Treaty was binding, and both sides agreed to the old boundary lines being marked more accurately. The treaty also referred to the Hopewell Treaty of No-

vember 28, 1785. Goods worth $5,000 were provided to the Cherokee on an annual basis, subtracting the value of any horses stolen by the Cherokee. This treaty was considered as an amendment to the Hopewell Treaty. It was signed by twelve Indians, including Doublehead of the Chickamauga.

1827: After hearing of the false rumor of the release of two Winnebago murder suspects to the Chippewa by whites, Winnebago Chief Red Bird was ordered by the tribal elders to fight. He attacked several families in Wisconsin near Prairie du Chien. After a few other attacks in the following days on settlers and riverboats on the Mississippi, the Americans ordered his surrender, or else they would destroy the entire tribe. Red Bird surrendered on September 27, 1827.

1851: Dart met with the Nez Perce in the Lapwai Valley.

1862: Colonel J.J. Clarkson was promoted to command all Confederate troops in the Cherokee Nation.

1867: According to army records, members of the Thirty-Eighth Infantry fought with a band of Indians near Wilson's Creek, Kansas. Five Indians were killed.

1867: According to army records, members of the Seventh Cavalry fought with a band of Indians near the South Fork of the Republican River in Kansas. Two soldiers were wounded and five Indians were killed.

1867: According to army records, members of the Seventh Cavalry fought with a band of Indians near Fort Wallace, Kansas. Six soldiers were killed and six were wounded.

1869: Indians rushed into Sheridan, Kansas (near modern Winona), and killed one man. The Indians escaped uninjured.

1869: According to army records, members of the Eighth Cavalry fought with a band of Indians on the Santa Maria River near Camp Toll Gate, Arizona. Four Indians were killed.

1870: According to official army records, Indians skirmished with a group of soldiers from the

Comanche chief Quanah Parker (NA)

Third Cavalry near Camp Apache, Arizona. One Indian was wounded and six were captured. The fighting started on May 29.

1871: Indians skirmished with a group of soldiers from the Second Cavalry and the Thirteenth Infantry near Camp Brown, Wyoming, according to official army records. No casualties were reported.

1874: Comanche under Quanah Parker decided to punish the white hunters for killing their buffalo herds and taking their grazing lands. Joined by Kiowa, Cheyenne, and Arapaho, they set out for the trading post known as Adobe Walls in the Texas Panhandle. Medicine man Isatai of the Comanche promised that the bullets of the white men would not harm them. A buffalo hunter named William "Billy" Dixon spotted the Indians approaching and was able to fire a warning shot before the attack. The Indians charged the trading post. There were twenty-eight men and one woman in Adobe Walls, and the buffalo hunters there had very accurate, long-range rifles with tel-

escopic sights. Dixon was reported to have knocked an Indian off his horse from 1,538 yards away with one of these rifles. The post's adobe walls provided very good cover for the defenders. Slightly more than a dozen Indians were killed in the fight, and Isatai was humiliated. The Indians gave up the fight as hopeless and left. (Also recorded as happening on June 27–July 1, 1874.)

1876: General Alfred Terry's command was marching toward the Little Bighorn from Tullock's Creek and the Yellowstone River. Just after 4:00 A.M. scouts met three Crows who claimed to have been with Custer. They told of Custer's defeat, but they were not believed.

1895: Bannock Indians were attacked near Jackson Hole. The Indians and the settlers were in a dispute over the provisions of the Fort Bridger Treaty.

1936: The Oklahoma Indian Welfare Act (49 Stat. 1967) was passed. Among other things, it was meant to provide preferential right to the secretary of the interior to purchase "any restricted Indian land or interests in land, other than sales or leases of oil, gas or other minerals therein" in Oklahoma.

1975: The shootout at Pine Ridge took place.

1976: An election to approve a new constitution and bylaws for the Cherokee Nation of Oklahoma was held. It was approved by a vote of 6,028–785.

1979: The Phoenix area office, Bureau of Indian Affairs, authorized an election for a proposed amendment to the constitution and bylaws of the Hopi Tribe. The election was held on January 30, 1980.

JUNE 27

1542: Juan Rodriguez Cabrillo left Mexico to explore up the Pacific Coast. Cabrillo was the first European to land in San Diego Bay, California. He went as far north as the Rogue River in California.

1689: At the end of King Philip's War, several Indians were killed by settlers at Cochecho, New

Hampshire. To retaliate, Pennacook Indians under Chiefs Kankamagus and Mesandowit attacked the settlement, located at the site of present-day Dover. Indian women were allowed to sleep inside the fort. At a certain time, they opened the doors and allowed the warriors to swarm into the garrison. Twenty-three settlers were killed and twenty-nine captives were sold to the French.

1760: Cherokees defeated Colonel Montgomery and his 1,500 soldiers in a battle near Franklin, North Carolina. (Also recorded as happening on June 24.)

1831: Sac Indians and the army agreed that the Indians would leave their present location.

1864: Colorado Territory Governor John Evans issued a proclamation advising all friendly Indians to stay away from the bad Indians who had been attacking white settlers. He then ordered the good Indians to report to Fort Lyon in southeastern Colorado, where the agent would provide provisions and a safe place to stay. The order neglected to mention that most of the fights with settlers were started by the settlers.

1867: According to army records, members of the Seventh Cavalry fought with a band of Indians near Fort Wallace, Kansas. No injuries were reported.

1869: According to army records, members of the Eighth Cavalry fought with a band of Indians near Great Mouth Canyon in Arizona. Three Indians were killed.

1870: Lieutenant C.T. Hall and Troop A, Second Cavalry, attacked a group of Indians, 200 strong, in the mountains at Pine Grove Meadow in Wyoming. Fifteen Indians were reported killed, and one soldier was reported wounded. The Indians retreated into the mountains.

1874: Comanche under Quanah Parker decided to punish white hunters for killing their buffalo herds and taking their grazing lands. Joined by Kiowa, Cheyenne, and Arapaho, they set out for the trading post known as Adobe Walls in the Texas Panhandle. Medicine man Isatai of the Co-

manche promised that the bullets of the white men would not harm them. A buffalo hunter named William "Billy" Dixon spotted the Indians approaching and was able to fire a warning shot before the attack. The Indians charged the trading post. There were twenty-eight men and one woman inside Adobe Walls, and the buffalo hunters had very accurate, long-range rifles with telescopic sights. Dixon was reported to have knocked an Indian off his horse from 1,538 yards away with one of these rifles. The post's adobe walls provided very good cover for the defenders. Slightly more than a dozen Indians were killed in the fight, and Isatai was humiliated. The Indians gave up the fight as hopeless and left. (Also recorded as happening on June 26–July 1, 1874.)

1875: Indians fought with soldiers from the Eighth Infantry and some Indian scouts in the Tonto Basin in Arizona. According to army documents, thirty Indians were killed and fifteen were captured. One soldier was wounded in this engagement, which lasted through July 8.

1876: General Alfred Terry joined up with Major Marcus Reno. They proceeded to the scene of Custer's defeat and found him and his entire command dead. Major Reno and Captain Frederick Benteen estimated the size of the Indian forces at 2,500.

1879: The Drifting Goose Reserve was created out of Townships 119, 120, and 121 North, Range 63 West, in the Dakota Territory. It was created for the "Mag-a-bo-das or Drifting Goose Band of the Yankatonais Sioux Indians."

1882: An executive order set aside 2,680 acres for the Pechanga Indian Reservation–Temecula Band of Luiseno Mission Indians.

1921: Treaty Number 11 was signed between the government of Canada and "Slave, Dogrib, Loucheux, Hare and other Indians, inhabitants of the territory within the limits hereinafter defined and described."

1936: The secretary of the interior had authorized an election to approve a constitution and bylaws for the Hannahville Indian Community in Michigan. It was approved by a vote of 41–0.

1951: A constitution and bylaws for the Spokane Tribe of the Spokane Reservation in Wellpinit, Washington, took effect.

1958: An election for the adoption of a constitution and bylaws for the White Mountain Apache Tribe was held. There were 1,900 eligible votes. The result was 734–67 in favor.

1971: Acting Commissioner of Indian Affairs John Crow ratified the Nez Perce vote to amendment their constitution and bylaws.

1971: The associate commissioner of Indian affairs had authorized an election to approve an amendment to the constitution of the Grindstone Indian Rancheria in Glenn County, California. It was approved by a vote of 9–2.

1981: The first regular election under the constitution and bylaws of the United Houma Nation of Louisiana was held.

JUNE 28

1719: A peace conference was held in Conestoga, Pennsylvania. Colonel John French, representing Pennsylvania, met with the kings of the local tribes: Winninchack of the Canawage, Civility and Queen Canatowa of the Conestoga, Wightomina of the Delaware, and Sevana of the Shawnee. The subject of the conference was fighting among the tribes. Although all involved promised to end their warfare, the fighting continued. Much of the fighting in the area was blamed on Iroquois war parties.

1738: According to some sources, a conference on friendship was held for the next nine days between representatives of the British in Massachusetts and the Penobscot and Norridgewock Indians.

1786: For administrative purposes, Indian Affairs was divided into north and south regions in the United States.

1827: This day marked the start of the Winnebago expedition in Wisconsin. It was also known

Bones piled together at the site where the Battle of Little Bighorn took place (NA)

as the LaFevre War, according to some sources. See June 26, 1827.

1862: The Kickapoo Reserve in the Potawatomi and Great Nemaha Agency was modified. It included twelve square miles.

1866: The Bozeman Trail was a route from Fort Laramie in southeastern Wyoming to Montana. Red Cloud vowed to never let the road go through unmolested, for this was his land. A small fort was established on the route to protect the travelers; originally named Fort Connor, it was staffed by former Confederates. On this day, the garrison was increased by men from Colonel Henry Carrington's troops. The fort was eventually renamed Fort Reno. The Sioux maintained a siege of the fort throughout the winter. The fort was located near modern Sussex, Wyoming.

1871: Indians skirmished with a group of settlers near Pawnee Fork, Kansas, according to official army records. No casualties were reported.

1876: Men from Major Marcus Reno's command buried 204 men from Colonel George Custer's command at the scene of the Battle of the Little Bighorn.

1877: First Cavalry, Twenty-First Infantry, and Fourth Artillery soldiers under General Oliver O.

Howard fought a group of Nez Perce Indians on the White Bird River in Idaho. According to army documents, no casualties were reported.

1878: Tambiago, the killer of Alex Rhoden on November 23, 1877, an event that led to the Bannock War, was hanged at the Idaho territorial prison.

1878: Lieutenant Samuel Whitall and a small group of Sixteenth Infantry soldiers assisted a U.S. Marshal in his attempt to serve a warrant on a group of Indians accused of trying to murder a man named Montgomery at Fort Sill in southern Indian Territory (present-day Oklahoma). When the warrant was served and the marshal attempted to arrest the Indians in question, the Indians pulled out knives and resisted. During the subsequent fighting, two Indians were killed and one was wounded, according to army reports.

1878: Captain Reuben Bernard and his First Cavalry Idaho troops caught up to the Bannock Indians on Silver Creek forty-five miles west of Camp Harney, which was west of present-day Burns in east-central Oregon. The soldiers reported three dead and five Indians killed. Two soldiers and two Indians were wounded. (Also recorded as happening on June 23, 1878.)

1898: The Dawes Commission was authorized by an act of Congress (30 Stat. 495) to prepare tribal membership rolls for the Cherokee, Choctaw, Chickasaw, Creek, and Seminole Tribes. These rolls were used in the allocation of land and money.

1906: An act (34 Stat. 359) according to the Osage constitution was passed regarding much of the government of the Osage Nation. The act established how the Osage tribal council would be elected and the length of their terms. It determined tribal membership qualifications. Mineral rights on the lands held by the Osage Nation were also determined.

1926: The trust period was extended for another ten years for the Papago in Arizona.

1934: The Taylor Grazing Act required compulsory school attendance by all Indian children.

1977: Amendments 10–13 to the constitution and bylaws for the Muckleshoot Indian Tribe of the Muckleshoot Reservation were ratified by the U.S. government.

1977: An election that approved a constitution and bylaws for the Lower Sioux Indian Community of Minnesota was ratified by the area director, Bureau of Indian Affairs. The election was held on June 20, 1977.

June 29

1542: Coronado reached the Arkansas River in Kansas. He was only 300 miles from Hernando de Soto's expedition, which was in Arkansas near the Oklahoma border.

1704: The same force of fifty South Carolinians and 1,000 Creek that attacked the San Pedro y San Pablo Mission in Patale on June 23 attacked the Spanish San Damian de Cupahica Mission (near modern Tallahassee, Florida). The mission was destroyed. Many of the local Indians were taken as slaves.

1778: In Pennsylvania, Cumberland County settlers sent a petition to the Supreme Executive Council asking for troops to protect them from Indian raids during their harvest. Other farmers asked for the militia to assist in gathering the crops due to the threat of Indian incursions.

1794: Approximately 2,000 Indians, including Chief Little Turtle, and British and French Rangers had surrounded Fort Recovery on the Ohio-Indiana border. Major William McMahon and 150 soldiers manned the fort. When McMahon and ninety men, not knowing of the force surrounding them, attempted to leave, they were attacked. McMahon returned to the fort. After two days of heavy fighting, the Indians gave up the fight and left.

1796: A treaty (7 Stat. 56) with the Creek Indians was concluded at Fort Colerain River on St. Marys River in southern Georgia. The previous treaty of August 7, 1790, was still binding, except as amended by this treaty. New boundary lines were established. The U.S. president was authorized to establish trade with the Creek and to build a military post on their land. When the official U.S.-Spain Treaty boundary line was drawn, two Creek chiefs accompanied the surveyors. The two chiefs received fifty cents a day for expenses. The Creek had to abide by the boundary lines drawn under the Hopewell Treaty with the Choctaws and the Chickasaw and the Holston River Treaty with the Cherokees. White prisoners held by the Creek must be given up. The Creek received $6,000 worth of goods and two sets of blacksmith tools and blacksmiths to use them. A total of 124 Indians signed the treaty. The United States was represented by George Clymer, Benjamin Hawkins, and Andrew Pickens. The 400 Creek were led by Chief Fushatchee Micco. The Creek were also represented by the adopted European John Galphin.

1812: Heading east from Fort Astoria in western Oregon territory, Robert Stuart blazed the Oregon Trail and "discovered" the South Pass of the Rockies in southwestern Wyoming.

1856: As a part of the Rogue River War, Tecumton and his band of followers surrendered.

1869: Members of the Eighth Cavalry were on patrol on the Santa Maria River in Arizona Territory. For "gallantry in killing an Indian warrior and capturing pony and effects," Private Albert Sale, Company F, would be awarded the Medal of Honor.

Indian relics (mostly arrowheads) from Enchanted Mesa (NA)

1875: Indians fought with soldiers from the Fourth Cavalry near Reynold's Ranch in Texas. According to army documents, one Indian was killed.

1878: Lieutenant James Clark's twelve Canyon City volunteers encountered fifty Bannock Indians. Being outnumbered, the volunteers fled. A running battle went for twenty miles before the Indians gave up the chase.

1879: Crow scouts skirmished with Sioux near the head of Alkali Creek twenty-five miles from Terry's Landing on the Yellowstone River. One Crow and four Sioux were killed. Four Crow scouts were wounded in the fighting. Thirty-three horses were captured.

1906: The Anasazi ruins at Mesa Verde were declared a national park.

1977: The Federal Register announced the "Revocation of Termination Proclamation and Restoration of Federal Status" notice for the California Indians of the Robinson Rancheria.

1985: An amendment to the constitution of the Comanche Indian Tribe was enacted.

JUNE 30

1520: According to some sources, Montezuma died, possibly killed by other Aztecs. Other sources said he was stabbed to death by Spaniards under Hernán Cortés.

1521: Spanish Captains Francisco Gordillo and Pedro de Quexos landed at and claimed Florida for the king of Spain.

1539: Hernando de Soto claimed Florida for Spain (according to some sources).

1598: Oñate's expedition reached the Tiwa pueblo of Santo Domingo. Other sources say it was the Keres pueblo of San Felipe.

1665: The Charter of Carolina was issued.

1798: A deed of conveyance was signed between the "Principal Chiefs, Warriors and people of the Chippewa Nation of Indians" and the Canadian government. It was regarding the island of St. Joseph in the strait between Lake Huron and Lake Superior.

Montezuma, Aztec king

1802: A treaty (7 Stat. 70) with the Seneca Indians was concluded on Buffalo Creek in Ontario County, New York. All Seneca lands in Ontario County were ceded to the Holland Land Company, and the Seneca were given new lands on Lake Erie. Nineteen Indians signed the treaty. A second treaty was also signed with the Seneca. They received $1,200 for what was called Little Beard's Reservation. John Taylor and twelve Indians signed that document.

1804: Colonel Benjamin Hawkins and Congressman David Meriwether represented the United States in a treaty conference with the Creek. The meetings were held in Tuckabatchee (near modern Tallassee, Alabama). The United States wanted more lands along the Ocmulgee River and the right to build a road through Creek lands. The conference lasted for a month.

1829: The British Band Treaty, related to the Black Hawk War, was signed.

1834: The Indian Office was made independent. An act (4 Stat. 729) was passed that intended to "prohibit the introduction of goods into the country belonging to any Indian tribe, and to revoke all licenses to trade with the Indians, and to reject all applications for trade."

1867: According to army records, members of the Eighteenth Infantry fought with a band of Indians near Fort Phil Kearny, Dakota Territory. No one was reported killed, wounded, or captured.

1869: According to army records, members of the First Cavalry fought with a band of Indians in the Burro Mountains of New Mexico. Four Indians were wounded.

1871: Indians skirmished with a group of soldiers from the Ninth Cavalry and the Twenty-Fourth Infantry in the Staked Plain (Llano Estacado) in Texas, according to official army records. One Indian was captured.

1879: Indians fought and killed a man named Anglin near the source of the North Concho River in Texas, according to army reports.

1886: The U.S. Army officially abandoned Fort Stockton in western Texas. The fort on the Comanche Trail was no longer needed to protect the frontier due to the cessation of Indian-settler conflicts. (See March 23, 1859.)

1903: The Twenty-Nine Palms Band of Mission Indians' census roll was listed.

1907: A census of the Lemhi Reservation in Idaho showed 474 Indians in residence.

1913: An act of Congress (38 Stat. 102) purchased land in Michigan for the Wisconsin Potawatomi. This eventually became the reservation of the Hannahville Indian Community.

1914: By act of Congress, the Cherokee Reservation had been split up among the Cherokees into individual plots. On this day, by another act of Congress, the Cherokee tribal government ceased to exist. The Cherokees became citizens of the soon-to-be-formed state of Oklahoma.

1976: Charles James, area director of the Bureau of Indian Affairs, authorized an election for the adoption of an amendment to the constitution and bylaws for the Ponca Tribe of Indians of Oklahoma. It was held on August 28, 1976.

July 1

1520: According to many sources, Hernán Cortés and his followers would attempt to escape from Tenochtitlán (modern Mexico City) by way of one of the causeways. They had to fight their way through large numbers of Aztec warriors. Thousands of people were killed on both sides. Many of the Spanish soldiers carried so much looted gold that when they fell in the lake they drowned. This event was often called Noche Triste (Night of Tears or Sorrows).

1675: The first scalps were taken by whites in King Philip's War. Lieutenant Oakes was en route from Reheboth to Swansea when his men encountered some hostile Indians. After the battle, Lieutenant Oakes scalped the Indians and sent his prizes to Boston for display.

1751: According to some reports, an agreement regarding peace and union was reached by representatives of the British in Connecticut, New York, and Pennsylvania and the Catawba and Six Nations tribes.

1778: As a part of the battle for the Wyoming Valley in Pennsylvania, British and Indian forces had surrounded Forts Wintermoot and Jenkins. On this day, both forts surrendered.

1793: Creek Indians killed four members of the Castleman family. They were killed outside Hay's Station Fort in the Cumberland, Tennessee, area. A relative of the killed settlers, Abraham Castleman, led five other Indian fighters in pursuit of the war party. Eventually, dressed as Indians, they found the Creek. They walked up to their camp and opened fire, killing six Creek in retribution.

1833: According to an army report, by this date the army estimated they had captured all of the hostile Creek Indians, except for the warriors from Hitchiti and Yuchi led by Jim Henry.

1835: The Caddo of Louisiana signed a treaty (7 Stat. 470) with the United States. They gave up their lands and moved out of the lands and territories held by the United States.

1836: General Scott declared the Creek War in Alabama and Georgia had ended. A few more fights took place, however.

1852: The Apache signed a treaty (10 Stat. 979) with the United States promising eternal peace, cooperation, and friendship. The peace lasted only a few years.

1855: A treaty (12 Stat. 971) was concluded in Washington Territory with the Quinault and Quileute Indians. Governor Isaac Stevens represented the United States. The treaty was signed by thirty Indians from both tribes, including Chiefs Tah-ho-lah and How-yat' l.

1863: A skirmish involving Union forces under Colonel James Williams and Confederate forces under Cherokee Colonel Stand Watie took place at Cabin Creek, Indian Territory (modern Oklahoma). The fighting would continue through the next day.

1867: According to a historical marker in Kansas, Lieutenant Lyman S. Kidder and ten soldiers of the Second Cavalry and an Indian guide were attacked by hostile Indians. All were killed in the fighting on Beaver Creek. Their mutilated remains were found by Lieutenant Colonel George Custer on July 12. (Also recorded as happening on July 2 and July 22.)

1874: President Grant, by executive order, established the Papago Reserve in the Pima Agency near Mission San Xavier del Bac in Arizona. The reservation was for the Papago Indians and covered forty-three square miles. The reservation was authorized by an act of Congress on August 5, 1882 (22 Stat. 299).

1875: First Sergeant James Mitchell and men from Troop D, Second Cavalry, skirmished with a band on Indians on the Little Popoagie River in Wyoming Territory. Two of the Indians were killed in the battle.

1876: According to a government report, there were 762 Indians at the Malheur Reservation in Oregon. However, the reservation had rations for only 454 people.

Nez Perce chief Looking Glass (NA)

1877: First Cavalry soldiers attacked Looking Glass's group of Nez Perce Indians on Cottonwood Ranch near Craig's Mountain about three miles from Kooskia, Idaho. According to army documents, Lieutenant S.M. Rains, ten soldiers, and two settlers were killed. No Nez Perce casualties were listed in the report. The fighting lasted through July 3. The army captured over 700 of Looking Glass's horses.

1878: The number of Northern Cheyenne living on the Cheyenne and Arapaho Agency at Fort Reno in central Indian Territory (present-day Oklahoma) was 942. This included Dull Knife, Wild Hog, and Little Wolf.

1902: An act of Congress (32 Stat. 726) gave the U.S. Court of Claims jurisdiction over any claim arising under treaty stipulations that the Cherokee Tribe or Band might have against the United States and vice versa.

1940: According to the constitution of the Coeur d'Alene Tribe of Idaho, an official census roll of the tribe was listed.

1955: The federal government transferred trusteeship of Alabama-Coushatta lands to the state of Texas.

1969: The assistant secretary of the interior ratified an election that approved a constitution and bylaws for the Hoh Indian Tribe. The election was held on May 24, 1969.

1971: Police removed approximately 100 Indians who had seized several buildings at an old missile site near Chicago, Illinois. They had been there since June 14, protesting the lack of available housing in the area.

1976: An election to approve an amendment to the constitution and bylaws for the Pyramid Lake Paiute Tribe of Nevada was held. Of the 240 persons entitled to vote, the results were: Amendment 5 (128–13); Amendment 6 (132–10); Amendment 7 (13–10); Amendment 7 (131–11)—all in favor of passage.

Every: Mescalero Apache Gahan ceremonial through July 4.

JULY 2

1543: The remnants of Hernando de Soto's expedition, numbering a little over 300 Spaniards led by Luis de Moscoso, boarded ships in the Indian village of Aminoya to sail down the Mississippi River to Mexico. They had spent six months in this village at the confluence of the Mississippi and the Arkansas Rivers.

1676: European and Indian forces under Major John Talcott attacked a Narragansett village as a part of King Philip's War. A total of 171 of the Narragansett were killed in the fighting.

1742: According to some reports, a conference regarding land cessions, trade, and the removal of squatters on Indian lands was held for the next eleven days between representatives of the British in Pennsylvania and Maryland Colonies and the Delaware, Nanticoke, Shawnee, and Six Nations tribes.

1744: An agreement was signed between Iroquois representatives and Maryland government officials, ceding most of the Iroquois lands in Maryland.

1754: According to some reports, a peace agreement was reached by representatives of the British in Massachusetts and the Norridgewock Indians.

1781: Near Fort Herkimer in the Mohawk Valley of New York, Lieutenant Solomon Woodworth and fifty militiamen were attacked by a large Indian war party. Only fifteen of the Europeans escaped. Of the remainder, only ten were captured.

1791: A treaty (7 Stat. 39) with the Cherokee Nation was concluded on the Holston River at White's Fort (modern Knoxville, Tennessee). The Cherokee acknowledged the sovereignty of the United States. Prisoners were returned on both sides. Boundary lines were officially established. American citizens were allowed to use a road from the Washington District to the Mero District on the Tennessee River without molestation. The United States would have the sole right to regulate trade with the Cherokee. No whites could live or hunt on Cherokee lands without Cherokee approval. Annual payments increased from $1,000 to $1,500 on February 17, 1792. The treaty was signed by thirty-nine chiefs; 1,200 other Cherokees attended the meeting. This was known as the Holston River Treaty. The Americans were represented by Governor William Blount.

1833: A total of 1,600 Creek War Indian prisoners left Fort Mitchell, Alabama, near Columbus, Georgia, en route to the west in chains and manacles. They were guarded by 300 troops.

1836: An act of Congress allowed for more government-organized Choctaw Indian removal. The Creek had been causing problems for the government in Alabama and Mississippi. This act was passed to remove the 7,000 Choctaws still in Mississippi so that they did not exacerbate the problems with the Creek. The treaty allowed any

Custer (standing in center) and his hunting party and guests at Fort Lincoln (NA)

Choctaws remaining in Mississippi after the initial removals to become citizens of that state.

1867: According to a historical marker in Kansas, Lieutenant Lyman S. Kidder and ten soldiers of the Second Cavalry and an Indian guide were attacked by hostile Indians. All were killed in the fighting on Beaver Creek. Their mutilated remains were found by Lieutenant Colonel George Custer on July 12. (Also recorded as happening on July 1 and July 22.)

1871: Indians attacked Fort Larned in southwestern Kansas. There were no reported casualties on either side, according to army records.

1874: Custer led a "science expedition" out of Fort Lincoln into the Black Hills.

1876: After a slow retreat from the scene of Custer's defeat—the wounded having to be moved slowly—General Alfred Terry's main body of troops reached the Yellowstone River and camps.

1885: Big Bear surrendered (Riel's Rebellion).

1907: Indians of the Sherwood Valley Rancheria in Mendocino County, California, started making payments to J.C. Johnson for a sixty-acre tract of land.

1936: A constitution for the Fort McDermitt Paiute and Shoshone Tribe in Nevada was approved by Secretary of the Interior Harold Ickes.

1956: According to Federal Register No. 21FR05067, mineral rights on reservation land in Wyoming were restored to tribal ownership.

1963: The Yankton Sioux Tribe in general council adopted several amendments to their constitution.

JULY 3

1676: Over 400 Europeans and Indians under Major John Talford attacked a band of Potuck's Narragansett as they attempted to surrender. After the fighting, sixty-seven Narragansett had been killed or captured.

1693: According to some sources, a two-day peace conference was held by representatives of the Five Nations and the British in New York.

1724: Frenchman Etienne Veniard de Bourgmont left Fort Orleans en route to the "land of the Padoucas." He was going there to try to establish peace and trade with them. He was traveling with "a hundred Missouris, commanded by their Grand Chief, and eight other Chiefs of war, and by sixty-four Osages, commanded by four Chiefs of war, besides a few Frenchmen."

1754: Surrounded by 500 French and 400 Indian forces under Sieur Coulon de Villiers, George Washington had only 400 soldiers at Fort Necessity (near modern Farmington in southwestern Pennsylvania). After his artillery was put out of action and with half of his men as casualties, Washington accepted de Villiers's offer of surrender. Washington led his troops back to Virginia. De Villiers was the brother of Jumonville de Villiers, Washington's counterpart in the battle not far from here on May 28. Jumonville was killed in that battle.

1761: According to some sources, the Northwest Confederacy was created at a council near Detroit. Its members included the Delaware, Miami, Ojibwa, Ottawa, Potawatomi, Shawnee, and Wyandot.

1778: A force of American militia led by Zebulon Butler embarked on an expedition into the Wyoming Valley of Pennsylvania from Forty Fort. The 400 Tory Rangers and their 700 Iroquois allies were led by Colonel John Butler. The Iroquois warriors lured the militia into an ambush in a swamp. Almost 400 of the soldiers were captured or killed during the fighting. This fight was one of many called the Wyoming Disaster.

1833: U.S. Marshal Jeremiah Austill arrived at Fort Mitchell. He was there on the Alabama-Georgia border to get troops to remove white squatters in Creek lands in Alabama. His efforts proved fruitless as Alabama militia volunteers sided with the squatters.

1836: Militia and soldiers defeated a force of Creek warriors at the Battle of Chickasawhachee Swamp in Baker County, Georgia.

1837: General Ellis Wool was charged by the New Echota Treaty with protecting the Cherokees against those who would attack them. To prevent the problems associated with whites selling alcohol to the Cherokees, General Wool prohibited the sale of liquor to Cherokees in Alabama. On this day, General Wool was charged by the state of Alabama with the crime of interfering with local laws and disturbing the peace. Wool faced a court-martial, but no one testified against him and he was acquitted of all charges.

1843: The Cherokee-Creek-Osage Covenant was signed.

1862: A Civil War battle took place near Locust Grove, Indian Territory (present-day Oklahoma). Indians fought on both sides in the battle, which was led by Union Colonel William Weer and Confederate Colonels John Drew and Stand Watie. The Union forces won the engagement, and many of Drew's Indians willingly surrendered.

1863: After the end of the Santee Sioux Uprising, Little Crow left the area. Eventually he returned to steal horses and supplies so he and his followers could survive. On this day, near

Hutchinson, Minnesota, Little Crow and his son stopped to pick some berries. Minnesota had recently enacted a law that paid a bounty of $25 for every Sioux scalp. Some settlers spotted Little Crow and opened fire. Little Crow was mortally wounded. His killer got a bonus bounty of $500. Little Crow's scalp went on public display in St. Paul. Little Crow's son, Wowinapa, escaped, but he was captured later in Dakota Territory.

1867: According to army records, members of the Third Infantry fought with a band of Indians near Goose Creek, Colorado. One soldier was wounded.

1868: The Fort Bridger Treaty (15 Stat. 673) created the Wind River Reservation for the Shoshone and Arapaho Tribes. It covered 2,828 square miles of Wyoming and was occupied by the Northern Arapaho and Eastern Shoshone.

1869: According to army records, members of the Eighth Cavalry engaged local Indians in a fight in Hell Canyon, Arizona. First Sergeant Sanford Bradbury and Corporals Paul Haupt and John Mitchell, Company L, would be awarded the Medal of Honor for "conspicuous gallantry in action."

1877: First Cavalry soldiers attacked Looking Glass's group of Nez Perce Indians on Cottonwood Ranch near Craig's Mountain about three miles from Kooskia, Idaho. According to army documents, Lieutenant S.M. Rains, ten soldiers, and two settlers were killed. No Nez Perce casualties were listed in the report. The fighting started on July 1 and continued until this date. The army captured over 700 of Looking Glass's horses.

1920: The trust period on allotments to Kickapoo Indians on the Kickapoo Reservation in Kansas was extended.

1926: An act (44 Stat. 894) was passed by Congress to "authorize the leasing of unallotted irrigable lands on any Indian reservations."

1990: Executive Order No. 6155 was issued by President George Bush, declaring Idaho Centennial Day. It acknowledged "land that had been

Santee Sioux Uprising leader Little Crow (NA)

cultivated and cherished by generations of Indian tribes, including the Kootenai, Nez Perce, Coeur d'Alene, and Shoshoni."

JULY 4

1636: Boston's Standing Committee gave orders to John Withrop Jr. to give to the Pequot. They had to turn over two murder suspects as required by the Treaty of 1634 or faced war.

1648: Father Antoine Daniel was killed by Iroquois at Teanaustaye, Canada.

1687: French General Marquis de Denonville, Jacques René de Brisay, led a force of 3,000 French and Indian soldiers against the Seneca village of Totiakton. Located in what is modern Monroe County, New York, Brisay's forces defeated a Seneca force of less than 500 warriors. The allies destroyed the town and the surrounding fields.

1710: According to some sources, a conference aimed at reaching an alliance between the British in New York and the Five Nations and the Ottawa was started. It was concluded on July 10.

1777: The Shawnees attacked Boonesborough again. Similar to their last incursion on April 15, the town's fortifications proved to be too substantial to breach.

1778: After a defeat by a vastly superior force in a nearby swamp the day before, Americans in Forty Fort in the Wyoming Valley of Pennsylvania surrendered.

1778: George Rogers Clark and almost 200 Americans defeated the British and Indian forces at Kaskaskia, Illinois.

1805: One year earlier, Presbyterian minister Gideon Blackburn opened a school for Cherokee children in the Overhill villages. He provided a demonstration by his "little Cherokees." Before an audience of Cherokee chiefs and Governor John Sevier, the children showed their ability to read and write in English and to do math. Both the Cherokees and the whites were greatly impressed by the presentation.

1805: A treaty (7 Stat. 87) with the Wyandot and six other Indian nations was concluded at Fort Industry on the Miami River in western Ohio. The treaty made references to the Greenville Treaty. A new boundary line was established. The Indians split $825 from the United States and $125 from the Connecticut Land Company, annually, for 500,000 acres of land south of Lake Erie (called Sufferers Land). The Indians were allowed to hunt and fish in their old lands if they did so peacefully. The treaty was signed by thirty-two Indians.

1827: After the death of tribal Chief Path Killer, Cherokee leaders met to pick a successor.

1837: On the Shoal River in Florida, approximately 100 Creek warriors fought with local militia led by Colonel Brown. The Creek eventually withdrew, leaving some supplies behind.

1841: As a part of the peace talks of the Second Seminole War, Wildcat (Coacoochee), a Miccosukee (Seminole) warrior, complained he had to wear chains until he convinced his people to surrender. Many years later, after being removed to Indian Territory (present-day Oklahoma), he escaped to Mexico. He was appointed as a colonel in the Mexican army.

1862: In the aftermath of the Owens Valley War in California, the cavalry established a camp on Oak Creek. In honor of Independence Day, it was named Camp Independence.

1866: The Delaware signed a treaty (14 Stat. 793) with the United States.

1874: Captain A.E. Bates, Troop B, Second Cavalry, and 160 friendly Shoshone were en route from Camp Brown in west-central Wyoming looking for a reported gathering of hostile Northern Cheyenne and Arapaho when they discovered a large group of hostiles on the Bad Water Branch of the Wind River in Wyoming. During the battle, twenty-six Indians and four soldiers were killed. Twenty Indians and six soldiers, including Lieutenant R.H. Young, were wounded. About 230 horses were captured. After this fight, many hostile Northern Cheyenne and Arapaho were convinced to return to their agencies to avoid further battles.

1876: Telegraph signals began to spread the story of the Battle at the Little Bighorn.

1877: For the next two days, the Nez Perce engaged in several skirmishes with the local settlers and the army in the Camas Prairie area of Idaho north of Tolo Lake and Grangeville. Almost two dozen whites were killed in the fighting.

1894: A group of primarily American settlers overthrew the native government of Hawaii on January 17, 1893. They established a constitution and proclaimed themselves the Republic of Hawaii.

Every: Nambe Falls ceremonial; Pawnee powwow; Salish-Kootenai powwow; the Quapaw powwow.

JULY 5

1652: According to some sources, a land-cession treaty was reached between representatives of the Susquehannock Indians and the Maryland Colony.

1697: According to some sources, a land-cession agreement was reached between representatives of the Delaware and Pennsylvania.

1754: According to some reports, a peace agreement was reached by representatives of the British in Massachusetts and the Penobscot Indians.

1796: A treaty agreement with the Creek was signed on June 29. On this day, the conference finally came to an end, with all negotiations and explanations at an end.

1831: N. William Colquhoun was appointed special agent to the Choctaws by Secretary of War Lewis Cass. Colquhoun was ordered to go to the Choctaw Nation and consult with their leaders about their removal to Indian Territory (present-day Oklahoma).

1867: According to army records, members of the First Cavalry and Indian scouts fought with a band of Indians near Dunder and Blitzen Creek in Oregon. Five Indians were killed and three were captured.

1869: Major W.B. Royall, Fifth Cavalry, commanding three Fifth Cavalry Troops and one company of Pawnee scouts, came across an Indian war party just north of the Republican River. Three Indians were killed and several were wounded. The troops then returned to General Eugene Carr's camp on the Republican.

1869: According to army records, members of the Eighth Cavalry fought with a band of Indians in "Red Rock Country, Arizona." Seven Indians were killed and one was captured. The fighting started on June 19.

1871: Arrested for murdering the wagon drivers in the raid on May 18, Kiowa Satanta and Big Tree went on trial in Jacksboro in north-central Texas, near Fort Richardson. They were found guilty after three days of testimony. Satanta told the court, "If you let me go, I will withdraw my warriors from Tehanna, but if you kill me, it will be a spark on the prairie. Make big fire—burn heap." Although they were sentenced to be hanged, the Texas governor, fearing a Kiowa uprising, decided to commute the sentences to life in a Texas prison. Eventually, Big Tree and Satanta were freed. Later, Satanta was returned to prison,

where he committed suicide by jumping off a prison balcony on October 11, 1874.

1873: A tract of land was set aside as a reserve for "Gross Ventre, Piegan, Blood, Blackfeet, River Crow and other Indians" in Montana by executive order.

1878: Forces under General Oliver Howard and Captain Reuben Bernard attacked Bannock Indians under Chief Egan near the Blue Mountains of Oregon Territory.

1973: An ordinance by the Quechan Indian Tribe, Fort Yuma, California, had created a zoning and planning commission on March 20, 1975. On this day, that action was ratified by the tribal council.

1994: Sandy Lake Band of Mississippi Ojibwe Chief Clifford Skinaway Sr. died. His tribe had been embroiled in a jurisdictional dispute with the Mille Lacs Band of Chippewa.

July 6

1534: Cartier met Micmac in Chaleur Bay, Canada.

1694: This day marked the first detailed conference between the Pennsylvania government and the Indians of the region. The meeting was attended by many tribes living in the Pennsylvania area, including the Susquehanna and the Delaware.

1724: Frenchman Etienne Veniard de Bourgmont had been charged with establishing peace among the Indians of what became Kansas. According to a journal of the expedition from Fort Orleans, he met with "the Grand Chief, six other Chiefs of war, and several Warriors of the Canzas; who present him with the Pipe of Peace, and performs the honours customary on such occasions, to the Missouri and Osages."

1754: Iroquois leaders deeded over to the British lands west of the Susquehanna from Penn's Creek to the Blue Mountains. This treaty was a part of the Albany, New York, conference.

1758: Preliminary meetings on the Easton Treaty were held in Pennsylvania. In attendance were Governor Denny and Tedyuscung.

1792: Creek Chief Alexander McGillivray had repudiated the treaty he signed in New York on August 7, 1790, with the United States. He signed a peace treaty with Spain and agreed to fight the United States to reclaim the ancestral Creek lands held by the United States.

1812: Congress passed "An Act Making Additional Appropriations for the Military Establishment and for the Indian Department for the Year One Thousand Eight Hundred and Twelve."

1820: The Ottawa and Chippewa signed a treaty (7 Stat. 207) with the United States at L'Arbre Croche and Michilimackinac in Michigan Territory.

1825: The Cheyenne signed a friendship treaty (7 Stat. 255) with the United States at the mouth of the Tongue River.

1869: According to army records, members of the First and Eight Cavalries fought with a band of Indians near "Hae qua-halla water" in Arizona. One soldier and ten Indians were wounded. Nine Indians were killed in the fight.

1869: According to army records, members of the Fifth Cavalry fought with a band of Indians near Frenchman's Fork, Nebraska. Three Indians were killed and three were wounded.

1875: Sergeant Arthur Danvers and eleven men of Company G, First Infantry, were stationed at the Ponca Agency in Dakota Territory. Approximately 200 Sioux attacked the compound. Utilizing an old piece of artillery, the soldiers drove off the Sioux after three attacks.

1883: President Grant, by executive order, established the Yuma Reserve in the Mission Tule Agency in California. The reservation covered 74.75 square miles and was home for the Yuma Apache Tribe. The reserve was modified by an order on August 15, 1894. The reservation was canceled entirely by another order on January 9, 1884.

1939: The assistant secretary of the interior authorized an election for a constitution and bylaws for the Port Gamble Band of Clallam Indians. The election was held on August 5, 1939.

1983: An amendment to the constitution and bylaws of the Suquamish Indian Tribe of the Port Madison Reservation in the state of Washington was passed in an election.

JULY 7

1540: Coronado attacked the Zuni village of Hawikuh in what became New Mexico.

1550: A conference on Indians was held in Spain.

1598: Oñate's expedition was at the village of the San Domingo pueblos. According to journals, leaders from seven different Pueblo groups met in a council with Oñate. The journals also said that the tribal leaders pledged allegiance to Spain.

1666: Robert Sanford had been exploring the coast of South Carolina for a colony site. He had found some friendly Indians at Port Royal. On this day he set sail for Barbados with the nephew of the local chief. The chief wanted his nephew to learn the white man's ways and language. Dr. Henry Woodward stayed with the Indians and learned their ways, thus making him the first European settler in South Carolina. Woodward eventually became the preeminent Indian agent in South Carolina.

Port Royal on the coast of South Carolina

1716: The Mission of Nuestra Senora de la Purisima Concepcion was established for the Hainai Indians in Texas.

1742: To retaliate for an attack on St. Augustine by English from Georgia, Spanish Florida Governor Manuel Montiano staged an attack on St. Simons Island in Georgia. Montiano's force of almost 3,000 consisted of Spaniards and Yamassee Indians. Forces under James Oglethorpe surprised the Spaniards. After killing forty Yamassee and 160 Spaniards, Oglethorpe's force, consisting of English, Chickasaws, Creek, and Yamacraw, forced the Spaniards off the island.

1836: According to government records, Jim Henry, one of the wiliest of the leaders of the Creek Indian War, surrendered to Indians fighting for the government. Henry eventually became a Methodist minister and changed his name to McHenry.

1846: Admiral Sloat claimed California for the United States.

1867: According to army records, members of the Eighth Cavalry fought with a band of Indians near Beale Springs, Arizona. One soldier was killed.

1875: Lieutenant G.H. Wright and men from Company G, Seventh Infantry, pursued a group of fifty Indians who had just stolen a small herd of horses near Camp Lewis near Lewiston, Montana. The soldiers surprised the Indians and recovered seven of the horses before withdrawing.

1876: Lieutenant F.W. Sibley, twenty-five soldiers, and a few civilians were scouting in the Bighorn Mountains near the Little Bighorn River. They encountered a great number of Indians. After a fight, Sibley and company abandoned their horses and escaped on foot to General Crook's camp. Second Cavalry soldiers fought some Indians near the headwaters of the Tongue River in Montana. According to army documents, five Indians were wounded.

1906: The James Bay Treaty Number 9 was signed. It was between the government of Canada and the Ojibewa, Cree, and other Indian inhabitants of the territory.

1977: Stanley Speaks, the area director of the Bureau of Indian Affairs, ratified the results of an election that approved an amendment to the constitution and bylaws for the Fort Sill Apache Tribe of Oklahoma.

1981: M.W. Bobby, acting deputy assistant secretary of Indian affairs, ratified an election that approved a constitution and bylaws for the Jamul Indian village in San Diego County, California.

JULY 8

1520: Hernán Cortés and his army had managed to escape from Tenochtitlán (modern Mexico City). On this day near Otumba, they encountered an Aztec army. The Spanish managed to win the battle against a much larger army.

1539: The Francisco de Ulloa expedition was designed to explore the coast of Baja, California. This expedition proved that California was not an island. Three ships, the *Santa Agueda*, the *Trinidad*, and the *Santo*, left Acapulco, Mexico.

1608: Champlain founded Quebec.

1724: French peace envoy Etienne Veniard de Bourgmont had come from Fort Orleans to visit Indians in what is modern Kansas. At the mouth of the Missouri River, he encountered the "Canza." Many of them accompany de Bourgmont on his trip to the "Padoucas."

1755: A Shawnee war party staged a series of raids in Draper's Meadows (near modern Blackburn, Virginia). They killed five settlers and captured several others. They gave a female settler a bag with the head of one of the male settlers in it. One of the captives, Mary Ingles, eventually escaped from the Shawnee. Her trek through 500 miles of the wilderness to return to her home became a legend among the Americans.

1761: The Mi'kmaq of Chignecto signed a treaty with the British of Nova Scotia, according to some sources.

1762: Cherokee Chiefs Ostenaco, Pouting Pigeon, and Stalking Turkey had an audience with King George III in London. This satisfied Ostenaco's desire to see "the Great White Father across the sea."

1776: Cherokees prepared to attack the British by having a special ceremony in which the "black drink" was prepared from the yaupon bush.

1817: Some Cherokees signed a treaty (7 Stat. 156) that ceded lands in Alabama, Georgia, and Tennessee for lands on the Arkansas and White Rivers next to the lands held by the Osage. They represented a minority group among the Cherokees; but Washington pressed the treaty. Andrew Jackson represented U.S. interests.

1852: The United States repudiated the treaties signed by California and California Indians.

1867: According to army records, members of the First Cavalry fought with a band of Indians near the Malheur River in Oregon. Two Indians were killed and fourteen were captured.

1868: According to army records, members of the First and Eighth Cavalry fought a band of Indians between the Verde and Salt Rivers in Arizona. One Indian was killed.

1869: Corporal John Kyle and three men from Troop M, Fifth Cavalry, were returning to General Carr's camp when they were attacked by Indians near the Republican River in Kansas. While wounding two Indians, Corporal Kyle was able to lead his men back to the camp. Later that night, Indians attempted to stampede the camp's horses. One of Carr's Pawnee scouts, Co-rux-the-chod-ish (Mad Bear), was wounded, but the stampede attempt failed. Mad Bear would be awarded the Medal of Honor for his action. He was acciden-

tally wounded by one of the soldiers. Corporal Kyle would also be given the Medal of Honor.

1873: Starting on this day and continuing for the next three days, members of the Eighth Cavalry from Fort Selden, New Mexico, fought local Indians. For "service against hostile Indians," First Sergeant James Morris, Sergeant Leonidas Lytle, Corporal Frank Bratling, Private Henry Wills, and blacksmith John Sheerin, Company C, would be awarded the Medal of Honor.

1875: Indians fought with soldiers from the Eighth Infantry and some Indian scouts in the Tonto Basin in Arizona. According to army documents, thirty Indians were killed and fifteen were captured. One soldier was wounded in this engagement, which started on June 27.

1878: General Oliver O. Howard had joined up with Captain Throckmorton and Captain Reuben Bernard at Pilot Rock in Oregon. Howard's scouts sighted Bannock Indians near Birch Creek in northeastern Oregon. The First Cavalry soldiers attacked. Fighting up a series of parallel ridges, the army dislodged the Indians. The soldiers likened the fight to Missionary Ridge in the Civil War. One soldier was killed; the army reported an unknown number of Indians were also killed. Captain Miles led the pursuit of the Indians.

1940: By Executive Orders No. 8471 and No. 8472, federal jurisdiction over certain lands that were acquired for the Standing Rock project under the National Industrial Recovery Act and other lands in New Mexico changed jurisdiction from the secretary of agriculture to the secretary of the interior.

1955: A "Tribal Land Enterprise" was established by the tribe pursuant to the bylaws on the Rosebud Indian Reservation. It was approved by the secretary of the interior as amended.

1965: Secretary of the Interior Stewart Udall ratified an election that approved a constitution and bylaws for the Squaxin Island Tribe of the

Squaxin Island Indian Reservation in Washington State. The election was held on May 15, 1965.

1970: President Richard Nixon asked Congress to "expressly renounce, repudiate, and repeal the termination policy as expressed in House Concurrent Resolution 108 of the 83rd Congress." He felt termination was wrong and unacceptable.

July 9

1609: Samuel de Champlain, two Frenchmen, and sixty Algonquin and Huron Indians attacked 200 Mohawks near Ticonderoga in New York. Champlain had some firearms, and they proved devastating. The Mohawks ended the battle. (Also recorded as happening on July 30.)

1716: The Mission of Nuestra Senora de Guadalupe was established for the Nacanish and Nocogdoche Indians in what eventually became Texas.

1755: General Edward Braddock's forces fought a battle. The French lost sixty men. The British had 456 killed and 421 wounded soldiers out of the 1,459 who took part in the battle. Other sources say 977 British were killed. Two-thirds of the British officers were killed or wounded. Many more British died within a few days. The French (records vary) had approximately 250 soldiers and up to 600 Indians, of which 250 were Miami. The

BRADDOCK'S EXPEDITION
June–July 1755

APPROXIMATE ROUTE OF ENGLISH TROOPS
X FRENCH AND INDIAN AMBUSH
Contour interval 1000 feet
MILES

exact number of Indian combatants was lost to history. This incident became known as Braddock's Defeat.

1867: According to army records, members of the Third Cavalry fought with a band of Indians near Fort Sumner, New Mexico. Five soldiers were killed and four were wounded.

1867: According to army records, members of the Eighth Cavalry fought with a band of Indians near Truxton's Springs, Arizona. Two soldiers were wounded, and three Indians were killed.

1877: The Ponca, forced to leave their Dakota reservation by a vindictive U.S. government, finally reached the Quapaw Reservation in Indian Territory (present-day Oklahoma). This was their new home. The tribe, used to the colder northern climate, suffered in hot Indian Territory. Almost a quarter of the tribe died during the first year in Oklahoma.

1954: Assistant Secretary of the Interior O. Lewis ratified an election for amendments to the constitution for the Omaha Tribe of Nebraska.

1969: Members of the Passamaquoddy Nation blocked a road that went through their reservation in Maine.

1970: An election on amendments to the constitution of the Zuni Tribe was held. Of the 861 eligible voters, the vote was 268–144 in favor.

1974: Secretary of the Interior John Whitaker ratified an election for an amendment to the constitution of the Standing Rock Sioux Tribe.

1981: The *Lakota Times* was first published.

July 10

1778: Settlers of the West Branch of the Susquehanna River sent a petition to the Supreme Executive Council of Pennsylvania asking for help because of attacks by Indians.

1836: About 900 Creek Indians from Eneah Emathla's Band were captured. They were shipped west in chains to catch up to the Creek that had already left for the Indian Territory (present-day

Oklahoma). The Battle of Brushy Creek also took place in Cook County, Georgia.

1843: In 1842, the Wyandot signed a treaty (11 Stat. 581) giving up their lands in Ohio for land west of the Mississippi River. On this day, 674 men, women, and children started their trip from Ohio to Kansas.

1854: According to their Indian agent, 200 Sac and Fox Indians were attacked by a force of 1,500 Comanche, Kiowa, Osage, and Apache near Smoky Hill, 100 miles west of Fort Riley in central Kansas. The Sac and Fox Indians were armed with rifles, and they prevailed over their larger adversary. The Sacs reported only six killed; the other Indians had as many as twenty-six killed and 100 wounded. Both sides were surprised that the Sac and Fox Indians won the fight.

1861: After negotiations with Albert Pike, the Confederate Indian representative, the Creek signed a treaty with the Confederate States of America. The Confederacy agreed to meet all of the old treaty provisions and allowed the Indians to send delegates to the Confederate Congress, in addition to several other significant items.

1862: The Central Pacific Railroad began construction of what became a massive railroad empire.

1868: Some 200 Kiowa set out to avenge the death of a Kiowa near the New Mexico–Texas border. The Kiowa were carrying two special talismans. Along the way, the Kiowa committed several taboos. Many of the Kiowa, sensing "bad medicine," left the war party. The remaining Kiowa met a group of forty Ute, and a battle ensued. Although the Kiowa outnumbered the Ute, seven Kiowa were killed and the Ute rode off with the Kiowa talismans. For some time, the Kiowa unsuccessfully tried to recover the talismans.

1869: According to army records, Indians attacked several stages in New Mexico. Ten civilians were killed. The fighting lasted until July 17.

1878: General Oliver Howard left Cayuse Station. Later in the day, the hostile Indians looted the station and took their booty back into the mountains. This took place in what is the state of Oregon.

1900: When the Arikara approved the severalty allotment of their lands, they became citizens of the United States.

1990: Executive Order No. 6156 was issued by President George Bush, declaring this day Wyoming Centennial Day. It included the statement: "Generations of Indian tribes—including the Crow, Cheyenne, Arapaho, and Sioux—cultivated and cherished the vast territory that is now Wyoming, establishing a rich cultural legacy that still graces the State today."

JULY 11

1598: Juan de Oñate's expedition reached the San Juan Pueblo in modern New Mexico.

1713: After the conclusion of Queen Anne's War in 1712, local settlers and the Abenaki Indians finally signed a peace treaty. This formally ended the fighting in the area. Minor incidents still occurred.

1868: According to army records, one rancher was killed and two were wounded when they were attacked by a band of Indians near the Niobrara River.

1869: General Eugene Carr's Fifth Cavalry had been following the trail of hostile Indians for several days. He found a large village on Summit Springs Creek off the South Platte, just south of present-day Sterling in northeastern Colorado. Seven troops of the Fifth Cavalry and three companies of Pawnee scouts surprised the village when they attacked. The village was captured and burned. According to the official army report, fifty-two Indians were killed, including Chief Tall Bull. Seventeen Indians were captured. No soldiers were killed in the attack. All told, 274 horses, 144 mules, a large cache of arms and ammunition, and $1,500 were seized. Two white women were prisoners in the camp. The army report said that both were shot when the soldiers attacked. One died, and the other, Mrs. Wiechell, was transported to Fort Sedgwick in the northeastern corner of Colorado, where she recovered. The army gave Mrs. Wiechell the $1,500.

1877: General Oliver Howard, called "Cut Arm" or "One Armed Soldier Chief" by the Indians, was leading 550 First Cavalry, Twenty-First Infantry, and Fourth Artillery soldiers when they spotted the Nez Perce along the Clearwater River and Cottonwood Creek. The fighting lasted until the next day, when the army got reinforcements. The Nez Perce then retreated to the north. During the fighting the army reported that it lost fifteen dead and twenty-five wounded soldiers and killed twenty-three warriors. Accounts from Nez Perce survivors put their losses at only four. First Lieutenant Charles F. Humphrey, Fourth Artillery, "voluntarily and successfully conducted in the face of withering fire, a party which recovered possession of an abandoned howitzer and two Gatling guns lying between the lines a few yards from the Indians." For his actions, Humphrey would be awarded the Medal of Honor. The fighting lasted through the next day.

1878: The hostile Indians return to Cayuse Station in Oregon Territory. This time, they burned it down.

1921: Treaty Number 11 was signed between the government of Canada and "Slave, Dogrib, Loucheux, Hare and other Indians, inhabitants of the territory within the limits hereinafter defined and described."

JULY 12

1766: The Tuscarora signed a deed for some land. They received £1,800 for 8,000 acres.

1775: A part of a legislative bill allocated $500 to Dartmouth College in New Hampshire to be dedicated to the education of Indian youth.

1784: Even though he had signed a peace treaty with the Spanish, Tonkawa Chief El Mocho was planning to join the Texas Indians together under his leadership and then attack the Spanish. The Spanish heard of El Mocho's plans. In the Presidio

of la Bahia, El Mocho was shot down in the plaza by Spanish soldiers.

1788: A small Ojibwa war party attacked a small army unit thirty miles north of Fort Harmar in Ohio. Two soldiers were killed and three were wounded. This attack hampered plans for a peace conference in Ohio.

1839: The Eastern and Western Cherokees met to discuss reuniting and establishing a new capital.

1856: Nez Perce fighters with General Cornelious disbanded.

1858: A Navajo, who was very angry with his wife, went to Fort Defiance in northeastern Arizona to sell blankets. While at the fort and for no apparent reason, he shot a black boy with an arrow. The boy died a few days later. The Navajo fled. The fort authorities demanded his return by Navajo leaders. The Navajos were given until August 11, 1858, to bring him into the fort. The murderer was never produced.

1861: After negotiations with a Confederate agent, Albert Pike, the Chickasaws and Choctaws signed a treaty with the Confederacy, almost exactly the same as that signed by the Creek two days earlier. Cherokee troops under Stand Watie were sworn in to the Confederate Army. Stand Watie was made a colonel.

Custer's soldiers discovering the remains of Lieutenant Kidder and his entire detachment who were killed by the Sioux near Beaver Creek, Colorado

Kicking Bird, Kiowa chief (NA)

1867: According to a historical marker in Kansas, Lieutenant Lyman S. Kidder and ten soldiers of the Second Cavalry and an Indian guide were attacked by hostile Indians on July 2, 1867. (Also recorded as happening on July 1 and July 22.) All were killed in the fighting on Beaver Creek. Their mutilated remains were found by Lieutenant Colonel George Custer and his men.

1870: According to army records, the Sixth Cavalry under Captain Curwen B. McClellan engaged hostile Indians along the Little Wichita River (southwest of modern Wichita Falls, Texas). They faced approximately 100 Kiowa under Chief Kicking Bird. For "gallantry in action," Corporal John Connor, Company H, Corporal John J. Given, Company K, First Sergeant John Kirk, Company L, Sergeant Thomas Kerrigan, Company H, Sergeant George H. Eldridge, Company C, Sergeant John May, Company L, Private Solon Neal, Company L, Farrier Samuel Porter, Company L, Corporal Charles Smith, Company H, first Sergeant Alonzo Stokes, Company H, Corporal James Watson, Company I, Bugler Claron Windus, Company L, and Sergeant

William Winterbottom, Company A, won the Medal of Honor.

1872: Indians skirmished with a group of soldiers from the Tenth Cavalry on the Deep River in Indian Territory, according to official army records. No casualties were reported.

1873: Captain T.J. Wint and Troop L, Fourth Cavalry, attacked a band of Indians on Live Oak Creek, Indian Territory (present-day Oklahoma). Army reports did not divulge the details of the battle.

1874: As a part of the Red River War, Kiowa Principal Chief Lone Wolf and Maman-ti managed to convince fifty warriors to join them on the warpath. Near Jacksboro, Texas, they engaged some Texas Rangers under Major John Jones. Two Rangers were killed in the fighting before they could escape. This came to be known as the Lost Valley Fight.

1877: First Cavalry, Twenty-First Infantry, and Fourth Artillery soldiers under General Oliver O. Howard fought Nez Perce near the South Fork of the Clearwater River in Idaho. According to army documents, thirteen soldiers and twenty-three Indians were killed. Captain E.A. Bancroft, Lieutenant C.A. Williams, twenty-five soldiers, and forty-six Nez Perce were wounded. Forty Indians were captured. The fighting started the day before.

1878: As a part of the Bannock War, Twelfth Infantry soldiers fought a group of Indians near Ladd's Canyon, Oregon. According to army documents, twenty-one Indians were captured. At Umatilla Agency in northeastern Oregon, early this morning, 350–400 hostile Indians were surprised to discover Captain Miles and his troops. After an eight-hour fight, an army charge forced the Indians back into the mountains. The fighting continued for the next several days.

1905: The James Bay Treaty Number 9 was signed between the government of Canada and the Ojibewa, Cree, and other Indian inhabitants of the territory.

1916: Lands allotted to the Tuscarora Indians by an act of the North Carolina general assembly in 1748 were to "revert to, and become the property of, the State, and the Indian claim thereto shall, from that time, be held and deemed forever extinguished."

1940: Assistant Secretary of the Interior Oscar Chapman ratified amendments made to the constitution of the Tuolumne Band of Me-Wok Indians of the Tuolumne Rancheria, and to the constitution and bylaws for the Kashia Band of Pomo Indians of the Stewarts Point Rancheria.

1953: Catherine Herrold Troeh, of the Chinook Tribe, Inc., submitted a list of membership applicants to the Western Washington Agency.

1967: A revised constitution and bylaws of the Kalispel Indian Community of the Kalispel Reservation was adopted in a tribal election.

1975: The commissioner of Indian affairs had authorized an election for a constitution and bylaws for the Manzanita Band of Mission Indians. It was approved by a vote of 12–0.

July 13

1573: King Philip II made new laws for Spanish conquests in the New World.

1713: Many of the northeastern Indian tribes signed a peace treaty with the British. They promised peace and became British subjects.

1866: After reinforcing and renaming Fort Reno in northeastern Wyoming, Colonel Henry Carrington set out to found a base camp from which he could protect the Bozeman Trail. He arrived at a point near Big Piney Creek with plenty of good grass for his horses. There he started building Fort Phil Kearny. The fort was in the middle of one of the best hunting grounds in the region, just south of what is present-day Sheridan, Wyoming.

1867: According to army records, members of the Twenty-Third Cavalry and some Snake Indians fought with a band of hostile Indians near the South Fork of the Malheur River in Oregon. One soldier and five Indians were killed. Two other Indians were wounded.

1869: According to army records, members of the First Cavalry and Thirty-Second Infantry fought with a band of Indians near Camp Grant in the White Mountains of Arizona. Eleven Indians were killed, two were wounded, and thirteen were captured. The fighting lasted until August 19.

1871: Indians skirmished with a group of soldiers from the Twenty-First Infantry in Cienega de Los Pinos, Arizona, according to official army records. One soldier and fifteen Indians were killed. Three enlisted men were wounded.

1872: While in the Whetstone Mountains of Arizona, Private Michael Glynn, Company F, Fifth Cavalry, encountered eight hostile Indians. He drove off the Indians single-handedly. In the process, he killed or wounded five of them. In the same engagement, First Sergeant Henry Newman, Company F, Fifth Cavalry, laid down covering fire while wounded soldiers were removed from the field of battle. Private John Nihill would "defeat four Apache." Newman and Nihill would be awarded the Medal of Honor.

1873: Captain G.W. Chilson and part of Troop C, Eighth Cavalry, from Fort McRae were near Cañada Alamosa in southern New Mexico Territory when they engaged a party of Indians. During the fight one soldier was wounded and three Indians were killed. A dozen horses, believed to have been stolen, were recovered.

1874: Captain Alfred Bates and Troop B, Second Cavalry, fought a band of hostile Indians near Sweetwater, Wyoming. One Indian was killed and several horses were seized.

1878: First Cavalry, Twenty-First Infantry, and Fourth Artillery soldiers under Captain Evan Miles fought a group of Indians at Umatilla Agency, Oregon. According to army documents, two soldiers were killed. This was a part of the Bannock War.

1973: New Mexico was told no state income taxes could be levied against reservation Indians.

1981: The Paiute Band of Indians in Utah adopted an official tribal membership roll.

JULY 14

1637: After the defeat of the Pequot force on May 26, Sassacus and most of the remaining Pequot fled. The English managed to force them into a swamp. The English demanded the Pequot surrender. The women, children, and sick were let out, but eighty warriors refused to give up. They charged the English, and twenty escaped, including Sassacus. The English then attacked the remaining Indians and killed them all.

1675: Nipmuck warriors attacked the Massachusetts town of Mendon as a part of King Philip's War. A few of the settlers were killed in the raid.

1683: According to some sources, representatives of Pennsylvania purchased several tracts of land near Schuylkill from the Delaware Indians.

1684: Naumkeag Indian and son of former Sachem Wenepoykin, James Quannapowit petitioned the English of Marblehead, Massachusetts. He complained they were giving out lands that rightfully belonged to him. On September 16, 1684, a deed was finally signed by all parties in order for the English to hold "rightful title" to the land.

1765: According to some reports, a peace agreement was signed by agents of the British and the Mingo and Shawnee Tribes.

1769: As part of a plan to explore the Northern California coast, the Gaspar de Portolá expedition, consisting of sixty-four persons (including fifteen Indians from Baja California), set out from San Diego.

1830: The Choctaws held a council meeting at the Tombigbee River "factory" store to receive their government annuity and to discuss tribal issues. Greenwood le Flore, with 1,500 of his followers, confronted Southern Chief Mushalatubbe, who had 1,000 men with him. Le Flore told Mushalatubbe that he must give up his chieftainship. Angry words were exchanged, but no fighting occurred. Mushalatubbe did not give up his chieftainship.

1836: A total of 2,498 Creek boarded two small boats at Montgomery, Alabama, bound for Indian Territory (present-day Oklahoma). This included forty warriors who were turned over to civil authorities for adjudication for their part in the Creek War. The extremely close conditions in the two boats were conducive to the spread of disease.

1837: At Fort Clark on the upper Missouri River, Francis Chardon recorded the first death of a Mandan attributed to smallpox. The outbreak of this disease spread rapidly and became extremely deadly to the people in this area.

1847: Twenty-five Choctaw Indians from Mobile Bay, Alabama, arrived in eastern Indian Territory (present-day Oklahoma) at Fort Coffee.

1862: As many as 5,000 Santee Sioux (Dakota) arrived at their upper agency in Minnesota in hopes of receiving their annuity. The money was not there. A few Indians starved during the several days they waited for it to arrive.

1865: The Chickasaw Confederate sympathizers officially surrendered.

1896: Jerry Potts was half-white and half-blood. For much of his adult life, he was an interpreter for the Northwest Mounted Police. He helped to establish friendly relations between the Canadian government and the Blackfeet. He died in Fort Macleod, Alberta, on this day.

1954: An act (68 Stat. 467) was passed by Congress to "provide that each grant of exchange on tribal lands on the Cheyenne River Sioux Reservation and the Standing Rock Sioux Reservation shall have the same force and effect as a trust patent, and for other purposes."

Every: Cochiti Pueblo festival.

JULY 15

1539: Hernando de Soto and his troops began their march inland from Tampa Bay.

1663: The Charter of Rhode Island and Providence Plantations was issued.

1673: Two Europeans, James Needham and Gabriel Arthur, arrived in the Cherokee village of Chota. They hoped to set up trade between the Cherokees and the Virginia Colony.

1675: After the start of King Philip's War, the English accosted the Narragansett. They forced them to sign an agreement to turn over any of Philip's Wampanoag who might come their way.

1682: In the name of William Penn, Deputy Governor Markham made the first recorded purchase of Indian land in Pennsylvania. Part of what is now Bucks County was purchased from fourteen Delaware chiefs for a long list of supplies.

1806: Pike began the Osage River expedition with twenty-three whites and fifty-one Osage and Pawnee.

1826: According to the journal of John Work, a horse-trading council was held with the Nez Perce. It was discovered that the Nez Perce had been promised a trading post and expected it to be built soon.

1830: William Clark and Willoughby Morgan, representing the United States, signed a treaty (7 Stat. 328) with nine different Indian Nations at Prairie du Chien. Lands in Iowa, Missouri, and Minnesota were ceded for money.

1862: In his home in the Indian Territory (present-day Oklahoma), Cherokee Principal Chief John Ross was captured by Union troops. Ross spent the rest of the war in Washington and Philadelphia.

1862: Mangas Colorado and son-in-law Cochise had been harassing settlers, wagon trains, and the army since Cochise had been wrongly accused of kidnapping by Lieutenant George Bascom in 1861. This incident led to the killing of hostages on both sides. On this day, Mangas Colorado and Cochise positioned 500 warriors on the bluffs overlooking the Apache Pass watering hole. When an army company of about 300 soldiers approached the spring-fed watering hole, the Apache attacked.

Captain Thomas Roberts and his soldiers were driven back, but they returned and captured the spring with the aid of cannon. Captain Roberts sent out five couriers to warn the next column of troops who were approaching the pass. Mangas Colorado and four dozen Apache took off after the messengers. All five of the couriers were shot, and three went down when their horses were shot. Two of the downed soldiers rode out with the other two couriers. This left Private John Teal alone against the Apache. Teal had a repeating rifle, which was new to the Apache. They remained behind cover. Teal eventually hit Mangas Colorado in the chest with a rifle shot. This effectively ended the fighting, as the Apache took their chief away. The fighting lasted until the next day.

1870: An imperial order-in-council was issued in Canada stating "any claims of Indians to compensation for lands required for purposes of settlement shall be disposed of by the Canadian Government." This extended the same rules used in the east to the western territories.

1871: Indians skirmished with a group of soldiers from the Fourth Cavalry near the Double Mountain Fork of the Brazos River in Texas, according to official army records. No casualties were reported.

1877: In the Weippe Prairie east of Weippe, Idaho, the Nez Perce held a council to decide their movements. The army was still trying to force them to move to a reservation. They wished to stay free. Looking Glass said they should go east into Montana and join the Crow. Chief Joseph (Hein-mot Too-ya-la kekt) suggested they wait for the army and fight it out in their own lands. Toohoolhoolzote joined Looking Glass in suggesting they move east into Montana. The tribe decided to move.

1878: Colonel Wheaten assumed command of the troops commanded by Captain Miles. Friendly Umatilla Indians pursued and killed Chief Egan of the Paiute and a few other Indians. This was a part of the Bannock War.

1884: Sixth Cavalry soldiers fought a group of Indians near Wormington Canyon, Colorado.

According to army documents, two citizens were killed.

1886: Geronimo eluded Captain Henry "Tall White Man" Lawton.

1948: An Arizona court said that Indians could vote.

1960: Assistant Secretary of the Interior Roger Ernst ratified the election for an amendment to the constitution and bylaws of the Lower Brule Sioux Tribe of the Lower Brule Reservation.

1966: Ordinance No. 1 was passed by the Twenty-Nine Palms Band of Mission Indians on May 29, 1966. It was approved by the area director of the Bureau of Indian Affairs.

July 16

1585: After the first encounter between the Roanoke Colony and Algonquin Indians in the village of Aquascogoc in Hyde County, North Carolina, the day before, colonists discovered one of their silver cups was missing. On this day, led by colony Governor Ralph Lane, the colonists returned to the village and demanded the return of the cup. When the cup was not returned, "we burned and spoiled all their corn," according to the governor's journal. This was one of the first significant conflicts in the area between Europeans and native inhabitants.

1709: According to some sources, an agreement of alliance was reached by representatives of the British in New York and the Five Nations.

1769: Franciscan Father Junipero Serra founded the Mission San Diego de Alcala in what became San Diego, California.

1825: Hunkpapa Sioux signed a treaty (7 Stat. 257). Henry Atkinson and Benjamin O'Fallon represented the United States. Seven Indians signed the treaty.

1836: A total of 2,498 Creek prisoners reached Mobile, Alabama, on their forced removal to Indian Territory (present-day Oklahoma). A total of 2,300 of them left tonight for New Orleans.

Flathead delegation with interpreter (standing in center) (NA)

1839: Sam Houston negotiated a treaty with the Cherokees living in Texas. They remained neutral in the Mexico-Texas conflicts in exchange for title to their lands. When Houston presented the treaty to the Texas congress, it was not ratified. A well-equipped force of almost 500 Texans under General Kelsey Douglass and Colonels Edward Burleson and Thomas Rusk defeated approximately 800 Cherokees under Chief Philip "The Bowl" Bowles at the Battle of the Neches River (near modern Tyler, Texas). Almost 100 Cherokees were killed or wounded, including Chief Bowles. The Texans lost only eight men. The Texas Cherokees left the eastern Texas area and moved north to Indian Territory (present-day Oklahoma). Burleson eventually became vice president of Texas.

1855: A treaty (12 Stat. 975) with the Flathead, Kootenai, and Upper Pend d'Oreille was concluded at Hell Gate in the Bitter Root Valley. The treaty established the Flathead Indian Reservation in Montana. This created the Jocko Reserve in the Flathead Agency of Montana. It covered 2,240 square miles and was occupied by "Bitter Root, Carlos Band, Flathead, Kutenai, Lower Kalispel,

Apache Pass in New Mexico where Chief Mangas was shot (author photo)

and Pend d'Oreille" Tribes. It also affected the Swan Creek and Black River Chippewa and Munsee in Kansas (12 Stat. 1105).

1862: The day before, as a small group of mounted soldiers attempted to leave the Apache Pass watering hole, Mangas and some warriors attacked. During the fight, Mangas was shot in the chest. The Indians abandoned the fight, with the loss of their leader. Eventually, Cochise took his father-in-law to Mexico, where he held a town hostage until a Mexican doctor healed Mangas. This battle led to the construction of Fort Bowie on July 28, 1862, according to the official National Park Service brochure. This was in modern New Mexico.

1866: Three days earlier, Colonel Henry Carrington had started construction of Fort Phil Kearny in northern Wyoming to protect travelers on the Bozeman Trail. The fort was situated in the midst of some of the best grazing and hunting in the Powder River region. Several chiefs visited the fort and talked with Colonel Carrington, called "Little White Chief" by the Sioux, and his scout, Jim "Blanket" Bridger. Carrington demonstrated his cannon. The Indians decided it would not be easy to defeat Colonel Carrington and his men in a battle.

1877: After a conference the day before, the Nez Perce decided to go to Montana to join their Crow

allies and to hopefully evade the army that was trying to force them to move to the reservation. On this day, they left their camp in the Weippe Prairie and headed toward Lolo Pass (near Missoula, Montana).

1887: A law was passed that said no Indian languages could be used in reservation schools.

1973: The deputy assistant secretary of the interior authorized an election to approve an amendment to the constitution and bylaws of the Miccosukee Tribe of Indians of Florida. The election was held on October 27, 1973.

JULY 17

1673: Father Jacques Marquette and Louis Joliet began an expedition to explore the Mississippi River on May 17. They reached the confluence of the Arkansas and Mississippi Rivers. Fearing a confrontation with the Spanish who controlled the lands farther south, Marquette and Joliet decided to end their trip and return north.

1775: Benjamin Franklin proposed a Six Nations alliance.

1781: The Mission San Pedro y San Pablo de Bicuner had been established in modern Imperial County, California, on January 7, 1781. It was where the Anza Trail crossed the Colorado River. This was land claimed by the Quechan (Yuma) Indians. After unsuccessful talks, the Quechan attacked and took over the mission and surrounding pueblo. (Also reported as 1780.)

1812: As a part of the War of 1812, British Captain Charles Roberts led a force of forty regular soldiers, 150 Canadians, and 300 Indians from Fort St. Joseph (on the waterway between Lake Huron and Lake Superior). Roberts attacked and defeated the Americans at Fort Michilimackinac, on the strait between Lake Huron and Lake Michigan. Roberts moved into the American fort and abandoned Fort St. Joseph.

1853: A dispute between a settler and some Paiute near Springville, Utah, led to the death of one of the Paiute. This would lead to what came to be known as the Walker War.

1856: Colonel Benjamin F. Shaw and his volunteer forces attacked 300 hostile Indians in the Grande Ronde Valley in northeastern Oregon. His forces suffered only five fatalities while inflicting forty upon the Cayuse, Umatilla, Walla Walla, and Yakima Indians.

1863: Union forces battled Confederates at Honey Springs, south of Muskogee. This was the biggest battle of the Civil War to take place in Indian Territory (present-day Oklahoma). The Confederate Indian forces, made up of Cherokee, Chickasaw, Choctaw, and Creek, were defeated.

1866: Early in the morning, Oglala Sioux stole almost 200 horses and mules from Fort Phil Kearny's stock in northern Wyoming. In addition to acquiring the mounts, this was a plan to draw the soldiers out of the well-defended fort. When the soldiers rode out to try to win back the animals, the Indians attacked. A running battle ensued. This was the start of a summer of constant hit-and-run attacks by the Indians.

1866: Elements of the Fourteenth Infantry fought some Indians near Steins Mountain, Oregon. One soldier was wounded. Three Indians were killed and five were wounded, according to Fourteenth Infantry records.

1866: Soldiers from the Eighteenth Infantry (Companies D, E, and F) fought with a band of Indians near Reno Creek in Dakota Territory. The army reported one soldier killed and four wounded.

1869: Between July 10 and this date, stagecoaches in New Mexico were attacked three times, according to army reports. Ten people were killed.

1876: Colonel Wesley Merritt and Troops A, B, D, G, I, K, and M, Fifth Cavalry, found approximately 800 Indians near Hat Creek (War Bonnet), Wyoming. One Indian was killed, and another was wounded. The rest were forced back to their reservation at the Red Cloud Agency. The

one Indian killed was Chief Yellow Hand. He was killed in the much heralded single combat with William "Buffalo Bill" Cody.

1877: First Cavalry soldiers, Indian scouts, and local volunteers under Major E.C. Mason fought some Nez Perce near Weippe at Oro Fino Creek in Idaho. According to army documents, one soldier and one Nez Perce were killed. One soldier was wounded.

1879: Lieutenant William Clark, a troop from Second Cavalry, a company from the Fifth and Sixth Infantries, and fifty Indian scouts were the advance unit of Colonel Nelson Miles's force seeking Sioux Indians along the Missouri River near Fort Peck in northeastern Montana. Clark encountered almost 400 Indians between Frenchmen's and Beaver Creek. A running battle took place, with Clark's soldiers eventually being surrounded by the Indians. Colonel Miles's troops rescued Clark near the Milk River. According to army reports, several hostiles and three Indian scouts were killed. A significant amount of the Indians' stores were captured. The Sioux headed off north of the Milk River.

1881: Ninth Cavalry soldiers fought a group of Indians in Alamo Canyon, New Mexico. According to army documents, one civilian was wounded.

1882: Natiotish and sixty White Mountain Apache were soundly defeated by cavalry in the Battle of Big Dry Wash (or Chevelons Fork) in Arizona. For rescuing a wounded comrade during this fight, Second Lieutenant Thomas Cruse, Sixth Cavalry, was awarded the Medal of Honor. First Lieutenant Frank West, Sixth Cavalry, also won the medal for rallying his command and leading an advance. Second Lieutenant George Morgan, Third Cavalry, and First Sergeant Charles Taylor, Company D, were awarded the medal for gallantry. According to army documents, one soldier and sixteen Indians were killed. Lieutenant G.L. Converse, Lieutenant G.H. Morgan, and seven soldiers were wounded. Some military sources cited this as the last major action between the army and Indians in Arizona.

1917: A total of 125,000 acres of land in Arizona were "reserved from entry, sale, or other disposal and set aside for the use of the Kaibab and other Indians now residing thereon."

1972: The Bureau of Indian Affairs offered the Navajos self-rule. If they accepted, they would control all functions of the Bureau of Indian Affairs on their reservation.

1973: The U.S. Census Bureau reported that the 1969 median income for Indian households was $5,832, whereas the national median was $9,590. Forty percent of all Indian households were below poverty levels; the national average was 14 percent, and blacks were 32 percent.

JULY 18

1694: Abenaki Chief Abomazine, almost 300 Penobscot warriors, and a few French attacked the settlement along the south side of the Oyster River (near modern Durham, New Hampshire). The Indians were trying to sneak into the village when their presence was discovered. Some settlers escaped, and others retreated to fortified homes. All told, 104 settlers were killed and twenty-seven were taken hostage before the Indians withdrew. Four months later, Abomazine approached the fort at Pemaquid under a white flag. He was seized by the garrison for his part in the attack.

1759: Edmund Atkins, British superintendent for Indian affairs in the Southern Department, met with Choctaws in the Upper Creek villages. They signed a treaty that established trade and a promise of mutual aid in case of war. This treaty angered the Choctaw's former allies, the French.

1764: According to some reports, an agreement regarding peace and alliance was reached by representatives of Great Britain and the Huron.

1778: Joseph Brant (Brandt) and 500 Iroquois followers attacked the small village of Springfield on Lake Otsego in New York. Fourteen men were captured, eight were killed, and most of the village was burned in the fighting.

1778: Hundreds of pro-British Indians attacked Andrustown, just south of German Flats in New York. Four settlers were killed, and the rest of the townspeople were taken prisoner. The village was then burned to the ground.

1815: At Portage du Sioux, Missouri, Potawatomi and Piankashaw Indians signed a treaty (7 Stat. 123) with the United States. William Clark, Auguste Chouteau, and Ninian Edwards represented the United States. Prisoners taken by both sides during the War of 1812 were exchanged. Twelve Indians signed the treaty.

1825: The Arikara Treaty (7 Stat. 259) was signed "at the Ricara village." Henry Atkinson and Benjamin O'Fallon represented the United States. Twenty Indians signed the treaty.

1836: A total of 2,300 Creek prisoners reached New Orleans. Heavy rains and scarce supplies made their three-day stay here miserable.

1837: The last of the 4,000 Creek who had been held at Mobile Point were moved out of the camp. Many Creek died in the unsanitary conditions at the camp.

1851: One in a series of treaties was signed at Camp Union with California Indians. The treaty was to reserve lands and to protect the Indians.

1855: A treaty was signed by the United States and the Navajo at Laguna Negra in New Mexico Territory. It was eventually rejected by the U.S. Senate.

1878: Friendly Indians at Lemhi, Idaho, killed "Bannock John," who murdered James Dempsey. They killed Bannock John so the whites would not think the Lemhi were involved in the Bannock Uprising.

1866: Soldiers from the First Cavalry fought with a band of Indians on Snake Creek in Oregon. The soldiers reported killing eleven Indians. One soldier was killed.

1936: An election to adopt a constitution and bylaws for the Lac du Flambeau Band of Lake Superior Chippewa Indians of Wisconsin was held. It was approved 182–51 according to their constitution.

1942: The Six Nations declared war on the Axis powers.

1973: An election to approve a constitution and bylaws for the Cortina Band of Indians on the Cortina Indian Rancheria in Colusa County, California, was held. It was approved by a vote of 16–8.

1979: The acting deputy commissioner of Indian affairs authorized an election to adopt a new constitution and bylaws for the residents of the Cold Spring Rancheria in Fresno County, California. The election was held on November 29, 1979.

1994: The first meeting of the Osage National Council was held according to their constitution.

Every: Northern Pueblos art show (through July 20).

JULY 19

1675: The English had trapped King Philip and some of his Wampanoag in Cedar Swamp near the Taunton River in southeastern Massachusetts. On this day, Philip lured the English into the swamp, where he attacked them. A little more than a half-dozen English were killed, and Philip escaped.

1776: The governor of Massachusetts signed a treaty with representatives of the St. Johns and Micmac Tribes.

1815: The Sioux of the Lake, the Sioux of St. Peters River, the Yankton Sioux, and the Teton Sioux signed a treaty (7 Stat. 126) with United States at Portage des Sioux.

1820: The Kickapoo signed a treaty (7 Stat. 208) in St. Louis. Auguste Chouteau and Benjamin Stephenson represented the United States. Twenty-eight Kickapoo made their marks on the document.

1837: On Alaqua Creek in Florida, the local militia, led by Colonel Brown of Jackson County, fought Creek warriors. The militia won. According to some sources, many Creek either emigrated west or went south and joined the Seminole after this defeat.

1856: By this date, all of the remaining Rogue River Indians were en route to the Grande Ronde Reservation in Oregon. They numbered 1,225.

1866: The Cherokee signed a treaty (14 Stat. 799). This was the post–Civil War treaty between the Cherokees and the U.S. government (14 Stat. 1866). Among other stipulations, they ceded lands in modern Kansas.

1867: According to army records, members of the First Cavalry fought with a band of Indians in Malheur County, Oregon. Two Indians were killed and eight were captured.

1868: According to army records, members of the Twenty-Seventh Infantry and Second Cavalry fought with a band of Indians near Fort Reno, Dakota Territory. One soldier was killed and another was wounded.

1871: Indians skirmished with a group of soldiers from the Third Cavalry at Bear Springs, near Camp Bowie, Arizona, according to official army records. Two civilians were killed and one soldier was wounded.

1879: Seventh Infantry soldiers fought a group of Indians near Camp Loder, Montana. According to army documents, one Indian was killed.

1881: After requesting the Canadian government to establish a reservation for his people, Sitting Bull (Tatanka Yotanka) was told they were not Canadians and that no reservation would be made. Many of his most trusted followers had already crossed back into the United States and were now on reservations. Sitting Bull finally decided to return to the United States. Sitting Bull rode into Fort Buford in western North Dakota. Sitting Bull was accompanied by slightly less than 190 of his beleaguered tribe. He officially surrendered to American authorities the next day.

1881: Nana, leading thirteen of the remnants of Victorio's Apache, fought with Lieutenant John Guilfoyle and his Ninth Cavalry troopers and Indian scouts near Arena Blanca River. The Indians managed to escape.

1973: An election to approve an amendment to the constitution and bylaws for the Sokaogon Chippewa Community of Wisconsin was held as authorized by the secretary of the interior. It was approved by a vote of 54–4.

1991: Congress created the Nez Perce Historical Trail Foundation. The foundation was established to mark the trail the Nez Perce took on their flight from the army in 1877. The foundation was administered by the U.S. Forest Service and the Nez Perce.

JULY 20

1528: After spending almost a month in the Apalachee village of Ivitachuco, the Narvaez expedition left. They set out in their quest for gold looking for the village of Aute (near modern St. Marks). Accompanying Narvaez was Aztec Prince Tetlahuehuetzquititzin. The prince, also known as Don Pedro, fought with the Spanish against Montezuma. He was killed by Apalachee warriors during this search for gold.

1676: Captain Benjamin Church had been joined by the Sakonett Indians in the war with King Philip. They attacked Philip's main camp and almost captured Philip. His wife and child were captured. They were sold as slaves. As many as 170 Indians were killed in the fighting.

1698: According to some sources, a peace conference was held for the next three days between representatives of the British in New York and the Five Nations.

1776: In what some call the first battle of the Cherokee War of 1776, Chickamauga Cherokee Chief Dragging Canoe led an attack on the American settlement near Eaton's Station, Tennessee, on the Great Island in the Holston River. Each side had a little over 150 fighters. The settlers had been warned of the coming attack and were prepared. Dragging Canoe sustained serious wounds, but he survived. The settlers lost four men, the Indians thirteen. As the Cherokees retreated, they attacked outlying settlements, killing eighteen

more. This fight goes by many names: the Battle of Eaton's Station, the Battle of Island Flats, and the Battle of Long Island.

1777: Continuing their efforts to stop the fighting with the English, conservative Cherokee chiefs signed a peace treaty with Virginia representatives on the Great Island on the Holston River. This treaty and the one signed on May 20, 1777, cost the Cherokees over 5 million acres of land.

1826: In the Oregon Territory, John Work's expedition camped with the "Pelushes, Colatouche" chief. Work could not afford any of the Indians' trade goods.

1843: All told, 674 men, women, and children of the Wyandot Tribe boarded a steamboat in Cincinnati, Ohio, bound for Kansas as part of a treaty they signed giving up their lands in Ohio.

1857: Lieutenant John Hood and twenty-five men from Company G, Second Cavalry, fought a group of Lipan Apache and Comanche warriors on Devils River in Texas. The army listed the Indian deaths at fifty-nine and the injuries at twice that.

1863: General James Carleton, called "Star Chief" by the Navajos, had ordered the Navajos to leave their homeland and to report to the Bosque Redondo Reservation in New Mexico. All Navajos found off the reservation after this date were to be considered hostiles and would be treated accordingly. No Navajos turned themselves in, leading to the Canyon de Chelly campaign and the Long Walk.

1867: A congressional act was passed to establish a Board of Peace Commissioners to "establish peace with certain hostile Indian tribes." Nathaniel Taylor, S.F. Tappan, J.B. Henderson, and J.B. Sanborn were appointed members by Congress. President Grant appointed Generals Sherman, Harney, Augur, and Terry to the commission.

1874: According to army records, Lieutenant Colonel George Buell and eleven soldiers and nine Tonkawa Indian scouts attacked a band of hostile Indians in Palo Pinto County, Texas. No injuries were reported, but the soldiers captured one horse.

1878: First Cavalry Lieutenant Colonel Forsyth, who had taken over Captain Bernard's Idaho Battalion, encountered part of the Bannock forces on the North Fork of John Day River near the town of Granite, Oregon. One civilian courier, and an unknown number of Indians, were reported killed.

1881: According to army records, Sitting Bull officially surrendered to Major D.H. Brotherton at Fort Buford, Dakota Territory. He was accompanied by forty-five men, sixty-seven women, and seventy-three children.

1881: According to the Oklahoma Law Enforcement Memorial, John R. Boston was a U.S. Indian police officer. Boston, a full-blood Cherokee, began tracking a gang of seven horse thieves from McAlester in July 1881. He finally caught up with them, in the Chickasaw Nation 20 miles northwest of Denison, Texas. Boston arrested two of the thieves with fourteen horses and started back with his prisoners. They were soon overtaken by the other five gang members, and Boston was killed.

1885: Louis Riel's trial began in Regina. He pleaded insanity based on his lawyer's recommendation.

1940: Assistant Secretary of the Interior Oscar Chapman ratified an election that approved two amendments to the constitution and bylaws of the Tule River Indian Tribe.

1973: Deputy Assistant Secretary of the Interior W.L. Rogers ratified several amendments to the constitution and bylaws of the Confederated Tribes of the Warm Springs Reservation of Oregon.

1989: At the Navajo tribal headquarters in Window Rock, Arizona, shooting broke out between opposing sides in a political dispute. Two people were killed.

Every: Pope Pueblo foot race.

JULY 21

1775: The United States divided the Indian Territory (present-day Oklahoma) into three divisions.

1832: General James Henry's forces defeated Black Hawk and his followers in the Battle of Wisconsin Heights. According to military records, Black Hawk lost sixty-eight warriors; however, Black Hawk said he lost only six men.

1836: The 2,000-plus Creek prisoners were loaded onto three steamboats and left New Orleans, bound for the Indian Territory (present-day Oklahoma).

1855: John W. Quinney, Stockbridge chief, died in Stockbridge, New York. Through his efforts, his tribe created a constitutional system for the election of its heretofore hereditary leaders. He was instrumental in the cessation of the sale of tribal lands to non-Indians. He led the efforts to have 460 acres of their former lands returned by the state of New York. He was elected chief of the tribe in 1852.

1866: Soldiers from the Eighteenth Infantry fought with a band of Indians on Crazy Woman's Fork in Dakota Territory. The army reported that one officer and one enlisted man were killed.

1867: According to army records, members of the Sixth Cavalry fought with a band of Indians near Buffalo Springs, Texas. One Indian was killed in the fighting.

1874: The Department of the Interior, through the War Department, authorized General John Pope and his command to "punish" the Indians raiding in Indian Territory (present-day Oklahoma). This authority allowed the army to punish these marauders even if they were found on reservations. Several expeditions were soon sent into Indian Territory to search for hostiles.

1878: First Lieutenant T.S. Wallace and fifteen men from the Third Infantry fought with a band of Nez Perce near the Middle Fork of the Clearwater River in Montana. The Nez Perce were wanted for attacking whites in Montana. They were believed to be former followers of White Bird, who left British Columbia to return to their ancestral lands in the United States. According to army documents from Fort Missoula, six Indians were killed, three were wounded, and thirty-one were captured. No soldiers were reported to have been killed. The soldiers captured thirty-one horses as well.

JULY 22

1760: In modern Presidio County, Texas, the Presidio (Fort) del Norte de la Junta de los Rios was finished. It was designed to protect local missionaries from Indians.

1790: The United States enacted a law for the formal regulation of trade with Indians, titled "An Act providing for Holding a Treaty or Treaties to Establish Peace with Certain Indian Tribes." It also enacted "An Act to Regulate Trade and Intercourse with the Indian Tribes."

1793: Alexander Mackenzie reached the Pacific on his expedition across the continent in Canada.

1814: A treaty (7 Stat. 118) with the "Wyandots, Delawares, Shawanoese, Senecas, and Miamies" was signed. The United States declared peace. It was signed by dozens of Indians.

1849: James Calhoun arrived in Santa Fe and assumed the role of Indian agent for the Navajos.

1859: The new Nez Perce agent, Mr. Cain, arrived.

1863: As a follow-up to the Owens Valley War in California, over 900 Paiute were led to the San Sebastian Reservation at Fort Tejon (north of Los Angeles).

1867: According to army records, members of the Second Cavalry fought with a band of Indians near Beaver Creek in Kansas. The unit's commander, Lieutenant Lyman S. Kidder, and ten soldiers were killed. (Also recorded as happening on July 1 and July 2.)

1869: According to army records, members of the Second Cavalry fought with a band of Indians near North Platte, Nebraska. One soldier was wounded. The fighting lasted through the next day.

1871: Indians skirmished with a group of soldiers from the Ninth Cavalry near the headwaters

American Plains Indians hunt buffalo.

of the Concho River in Texas, according to official army records. One soldier was wounded.

1872: Indians skirmished with a group of soldiers from the Tenth Cavalry near Otter Creek, Indian Territory, according to official army records. One Indian was wounded.

1876: After Custer's defeat on the Little Bighorn River (Greasy Grass), Americans sought revenge on the Plains Indians. One way to get back was to punish them all, even those who had nothing to do with the battle and were living peacefully on reservations. General Sherman received orders to impose military rule over all of the Plains reservations. All inhabitants were now considered to be prisoners of war. Congress authorized the construction of two new forts in the area of the Yellowstone River.

1878: Lemhi Chief Tendoy led a group of Indians on a buffalo hunt into Yellowstone country.

1996: In Syracuse, New York, Leon Shenandoah died at eighty-one years of age. Shenandoah was a leader of the Onondaga Indians. In 1969, he was named Tadadaho, or Spiritual Leader, of the Iroquois Confederacy. Shenandoah lived almost all of his life on the Onondaga Reservation in New York State.

JULY 23

1714: According to some sources, a peace conference was held for the next six days between representatives of the Abenaki Indians and the British in the Massachusetts Colony.

1733: José de Urrutia was appointed Captain of San Antonio de Béxar Presidio. The Spanish acknowledged him as one of their experts on Indians.

1748: According to some reports, a friendship conference was held for the next four days between representatives of the British in Massachusetts and New York and the Six Nations.

1766: According to some reports, a peace conference between representatives of Great Britain and the Huron, Ojibwa, Ottawa, Potawatomi, and Six Nations tribes was held for the next nine days.

1805: A treaty (7 Stat. 89) with the Chickasaw was completed. The Chickasaw ceded lands near the Ohio and Tennessee Rivers to pay off old debts. The tribe was paid $20,000; two individual Indians got $1,000 each. A total of $100 a year for life was paid to Chinubbee Mingo (King of Nation). No whites were to live on Chickasaw lands without Chickasaw approval. All of the old treaties still applied. Ten Indians signed the treaty.

1832: The Eastern Cherokees held a council in Red Clay, Tennessee, to discuss the proposals of President Jackson's special envoy, Elisha Chester, for their removal to Indian Territory (present-day Oklahoma). They rejected the proposal out of hand. They said they would not hold negotiations as long as the federal government was not living up to its previous treaty promises.

1836: Two men were minding the lighthouse on Key Biscayne, Florida. They were attacked by a Seminole war party. One man was killed. The other managed to signal for help from a nearby ship by exploding a keg of gunpowder.

1839: Seminole warriors under Chief Chakaika attacked elements of Colonel William Harny's Second Dragoons during the night. Hearny was camped at and around a trading post along the Caloosahatchee River. The Seminoles' attack surprised the sleeping soldiers. Harny, camped outside the post, got away only by running into the swamp in his underwear. Eighteen soldiers were killed or captured. Harny vowed revenge.

1851: At the Traverse de Sioux, Minnesota Territory, a treaty (10 Stat. 949) was concluded between the United States and the "See-see-toan" (Sisseton) and "Wah-pay-toan" (Wahpeton) Bands of Dakota or Sioux Indians. Thirty-five Indians signed the document.

1869: According to army records, members of the Second Cavalry fought with a band of Indians near North Platte, Nebraska. One soldier was wounded. The fighting started the day before.

1879: Canadians sent a message to U.S. General Miles that the Sioux who had sought refuge in Canada were behaving peacefully.

1882: A fight broke out at the Fort Stanton Agency in New Mexico. According to army documents, one citizen was wounded and three Indians were killed.

1892: The U.S. government stated no alcohol sales were allowed on Indian land.

1914: By Executive Order No. 1995, certain parts of the Navajo Reservation were set aside for the use of Company G, First Infantry, of the Arizona militia.

1936: The constitution and bylaws of the Hannahville Indian Community in Michigan were approved by Secretary of the Interior Harold Ickes.

1971: John Crow, a Cherokee, was appointed commissioner of the Bureau of Indian Affairs.

1987: The Head-Smashed-In Buffalo Jump Interpretive Center was officially opened in Alberta, Canada. It was a World Heritage Site. At this location, local Indians stampeded buffalo over a cliff, then butchered them and skinned their hides.

JULY 24

1534: Jacques Cartier erected a thirty-three-foot-high cross on a small island in Gaspe Harbor. He then claimed the area for France.

General Henry Sibley, who helped put down the Santee Sioux Uprising

1701: Fort Pontchartrain du Detroit was established.

1724: French peace envoy Etienne Veniard de Bourgmont continued his exploration of Kansas. He used the locals in his expedition, describing it as "consisting of 300 Warriors, including the Chiefs of the Canzas, about 300 woman, about 500 young people, and at least 300 dogs." His destination: the villages of the Padouca.

1766: Pontiac concluded a peace treaty and surrendered to Sir William Johnson in Oswego.

1836: Georgia militia and Creek Indians had a brief fight near Wesley Chapel in Stewart County, Georgia. The Creek appeared to have won.

1847: Brigham Young spotted the Salt Lake Valley.

1863: The Santee Sioux had engaged in an uprising in Minnesota. Some had fled the area and made their way into the Dakotas. General Henry Sibley and troops from Fort Ridgley in Minnesota had pursued them. According to reports Sibley had received, the Santee had joined up with the Teton Sioux. On this day the soldiers found an Indian village in what is now North Dakota. According to the army's report, while some scouts were talking with a couple of hundred Indians who came out to met them, someone shot and killed surgeon Josiah Weiser. The scouts shot at the Indian who shot the doctor, but he got away. More Indians arrived and started shooting. Then more soldiers arrived and opened fire. A full-scale fight took place, with some fighting lasted through early the next day. It was called the Battle of Big Mound.

1877: The Nez Perce crossed Lolo Summit on the border between Idaho and Montana.

1946: The acting commissioner of Indian affairs authorized an election to establish a constitution and bylaws for the Sisseton Wahpeton Sioux Tribe of South Dakota. The election would take place on September 24, 1946.

1953: Assistant Secretary of the Interior Orme Lewis authorized an election for Amendment 5 to the constitution and bylaws approved of the Confederated Tribes of the Warm Springs Reservation of Oregon.

1964: The assistant secretary of the interior authorized an election to approve a constitution and bylaws for the Cocopah Tribe of Somerton, Arizona. The election was held on October 8, 1964.

1967: The assistant secretary of the interior authorized an election for the adoption of an amendment to the constitution and bylaws for the Ponca Tribe of Indians of Oklahoma. The election was held on August 26, 1967.

1972: The area director for the Bureau of Indian Affairs authorized an election to amend the revised constitution and bylaws for the Sisseton Wahpeton Sioux Tribe of South Dakota. The election would take place on November 2, 1976.

1977: The Comanche and Ute ended a hunting dispute.

JULY 25

1757: A war party of five dozen Shawnees staged an attack of farms along the James River in Virginia. At one farm they killed a settler and his child. They took his wife, Hannah Dennis, prisoner. She was taken to the Shawnee village of Chillicothe. After ingratiating herself with the Shawnees, she was given run of the village. She eventually escaped. Her tale became widespread throughout the American colonies.

1759: The British attacked Fort Niagara.

1834: Crows, led by Rotten Belly, began a siege of Fort McKenzie on the Missouri River that ended in about one week.

1836: Major Jernigan was leading Georgia militiamen through an area near the swamp on the Nochaway Creek when they encountered Creek warriors. A fought ensued.

1862: Hunkpapa Sioux threatened the army at Fort Berthold.

1863: As part of the Canyon de Chelly campaign, Kit Carson decided to force the Navajos to surrender by destroying their food supply. He ordered Major Joseph Cummings to proceed along the Bonito River and to seize all livestock and crops. Anything he could not haul away was burned.

1868: The Treaty of June 1, 1868 (15 Stat. 667), between the Navajo and the United States, was ratified.

1868: According to army records, members of the Twenty-Third Infantry and some Indian scouts fought with a band of Indians near the Big Salmon River in Idaho. Forty-one Indians were captured.

1869: Troops from Fort Stanton in central New Mexico came across the trail of hostile Indians. They followed the trail to a village. The troops "totally" destroyed it, according to their report. Most of the Indians escaped into the nearby canyons.

1874: Apache Indian leader Chuntz was killed.

1877: The Nez Perce were on Lolo Creek near Rawn's Barricade.

1879: Tenth Cavalry and Twenty-Fifth Infantry soldiers fought a group of Indians near Salt Lake, Texas. According to army documents, one Indian was killed.

1881: Lieutenant John Guilfoyle and his Ninth Cavalry soldiers and Indian scouts again fought with Nana and his Apache followers (formerly with Victorio) in the San Andreas Mountains of New Mexico. Two hostile Indians and three civilians were believed to have been killed in the fighting.

1895: Bannock warriors engaged in a fight at Jackson Hole. The Indians and the settlers were in a dispute over the provisions of the Fort Bridger Treaty (15 Stat. 673) signed on July 3, 1868.

1952: Public Land Order No. 858 was modified to remove certain lands in the Fort Peck Reservation in Montana from the classification of being "opened for disposal" under public land laws.

1974: Secretary of the Interior Rogers Morton ratified an election by tribal members of the Sherwood Valley Rancheria vote to approve a constitution and bylaws. The election was held on March 9, 1974.

Every: Pueblos: Santiago's (St. James's) Day.

July 26

1763: Fort Sandusky (Ohio) was destroyed by Indians on May 16. Detroit was also being besieged. Captain James Dalyell and almost 300 soldiers arrived on the southern shore of Lake Erie. They found many bodies and the remnants of structures. His forces immediately marched against a Wyandot village (near modern Fremont).

1796: George Catlin, known for painting Indians, was born.

1824: Seminole Principal Chief Neamathla (also called Eneah Emathla) had managed to avoid removing his people from Florida to the west. Florida Governor William Duval had become convinced that Neamathla was planning another uprising. The governor officially removed Neamathla from his position as chief.

1827: The Cherokee Constitutional Convention adopted a new constitution based on the constitution of the United States.

1863: Army forces under General Henry Sibley had been pursuing the Santee Sioux after their uprising in Minnesota the year before. Two days earlier, they had a fight in Kidder County, North Dakota, called the Battle of Big Mound. They skirmished again near Dead Buffalo Lake. After a few exchanges, the Sioux retreated.

1865: Following the massacre at Sand Creek, many Indians began attacking military outposts and people crossing their territory. A group of Cheyenne led by Roman Nose wanted revenge for lost relatives. They approached a bridge across the North Platte in what is now Casper, Wyoming. The bridge was also the site of a telegraph station and a military outpost. After trying for two days to get the soldiers out of the fort, a column of troops crossed the bridge. The Indians attacked and killed many soldiers, including Lieutenant Casper Collins. Another column of troops came to the rescue, and cannon fire from the fort helped them escape. The soldiers left the fort to provide an escort for an approaching wagon train. Another band of Indians attacked the wagon train. During the fighting, Roman Nose's brother was killed. Roman Nose led a charge against the wagon train, and all of the soldiers guarding it were killed. Their anger quickly dissipated, and the Indians quit the fight and left the area.

1868: According to army records, members of the Twenty-Third Infantry fought with a band of Indians near Juniper Canyon, Idaho. Five Indians were reported killed and four captured.

1872: During the first Yellowstone expedition, Indians fought with the army on numerous occasions. The army units involved were from the Eighth, Seventeenth, and Twenty-Second Infantries and Indian scouts. They were led by Colonel D.S. Stanley, according to official army records. Over the entire expedition, two officers (Lieutenant Eben Crosby and Lieutenant L.D. Adair) and one civilian were killed or mortally wounded. The expedition lasted through October 15.

1914: Indians of the Sherwood Valley Rancheria in Mendocino County, California, finished making payments to J.C. Johnson for a sixty-acre tract of land.

1975: The constitution and bylaws of the Kalispel Indian Community of the Kalispel Reservation were amended.

1976: The area director, Aberdeen area office, Bureau of Indian Affairs, authorized an election to amend the revised constitution and bylaws for the Sisseton Wahpeton Sioux Tribe of South Dakota. The election would take place on November 2, 1976.

1997: Executive Order No. 13057, by President William Clinton, was issued "in order to ensure that Federal agency actions protect the extraordinary natural, recreational, and ecological resources in the Lake Tahoe Region." Included in the order was a provision for "recognition for traditional Washoe tribal uses."

Every: St. Anne Feast Day celebrated in many Pueblo villages.

JULY 27

1585: Sir Walter Raleigh was given a grant for Roanoke.

1755: Indians attacked the settlers at Fort Sartwell in Vernon, Connecticut.

1757: Ottawa warriors and a few French soldiers attacked a group of twenty-two barges commanded by British Lieutenant Colonel John Parker on Lake George in New York. The British forces had 160 men killed and almost 150 men captured. Only two of the barges escaped the fighting.

1777: Jane McCrea was killed. A painting was made showing her about to be scalped. It became a famous piece of American art.

1777: Three small girls left Fort Stanwix, New York, to gather berries. They were attacked by pro-British Indians. Two of the girls were killed; the third made it back to the fort.

1813: A battle took place on Burnt Corn Creek, not far from Escambia River. Creek led by Chief Peter McQueen had just recently purchased guns and ammunition in Pensacola from the British. While en route back to their villages, they were attacked by Colonel James Caller and 180 militia. After initially gaining the upper hand, someone in the militia called for a retreat, and some of the Americans took off at a run. Taking advantage of the situation, the Red Stick Creek were able to escape. This battle encouraged the Creek to engage in further battles with the Americans. Six men in McQueen's group and two soldiers died in the fighting. This first fight of the Creek War was called the Battle of Burnt Corn.

1816: The British built a fort on the Apalachicola River for the Seminole Indians to use to defend themselves. Few Seminole ever inhabited the fort, but their black allies did. About 500 Creek under Colonel Clinch and Chief William McIntosh, with an American riverboat, attacked and destroyed the fort. The fort's magazine exploded and caused an estimated 270 deaths among the 334 inhabitants. Many of the survivors fought to the death rather than face capture and enslavement. This led the Indians to believe they had to fight the Americans to keep their lands. The Americans were led by Colonel Duncan L. Clinch. The fort was well within Spanish Territory. The fort was known as Negro Fort, Fort Gadsden, and Fort Nicholls (also spelled Nicolls).

1826: John Work's trading expedition camped on the banks of the Snake and Clearwater Rivers (near modern Lewiston, Idaho). They met a group of over 200 Indians led by Chiefs Alunn and Towishpat.

1853: The Apache, Comanche, and Kiowa signed a treaty (10 Stat. 1013) at Fort Atkinson in southwestern Kansas with agent Thomas Fitzpatrick. Twenty-four Indians signed the treaty. They agreed to peace with the United States and Mexico, allowing forts and roads to be built on their lands. They got $18,000 per year for ten years.

Fort Garry, Canada, where the Stone Fort Treaty was signed

1867: According to army records, members of the First Cavalry under Lieutenant Colonel George Crook fought with a band of Indians between Forts C.F. Smith and Harney in Oregon. Forty-six Indians were reported killed or wounded.

1871: On this day through August 3, 1871, negotiations started between Cree and Ojibwa Indians and the government of Canada at Stone Fort (later Fort Garry) in present-day Winnipeg, Manitoba. This was the Stone Fort Treaty, or Treaty Number 1. They eventually sold 16,700 square miles of lower Manitoba.

1872: Indians skirmished with a group of soldiers from the Eighth Cavalry on Mount Graham, Arizona, according to official army records. One Indian was killed.

1874: Gold was found in the Black Hills.

1877: Captain Charles Rawn had built a barricade across the Lolo Canyon, east of Lolo Pass, to block the Nez Perce from passing through the mountains into Montana from Idaho. Rawn talked with the Nez Perce. The Indians promised to pass peacefully through the Bitter Root Valley if the army left them alone. Captain Rawn said he would let them pass only if they left their firearms with him, according to army records. Both parties agreed to meet again the next day. Rawn had five other officers, thirty soldiers, and 150 local volunteers. When the volunteers heard the Nez Perce were willing to travel through the area peacefully, they decided that was the safest thing for everyone. The volunteers slowly abandoned their positions and left.

1879: Captain Michael Courtney and ten troopers from Troop H, Tenth Cavalry, fought with Indians around the salt lakes near Carrizo Mountain in Texas. Two soldiers and one Indian were wounded. Two Indians died of wounds inflicted during the fighting. The soldiers also captured ten horses.

1889: Not long after the establishment of the Great Sioux Reservation the U.S. government decided to try to reduce the Indians' holdings once again. The plan was to establish several smaller reservations and to open up millions of acres for white settlement. Led by General George Crook, the treaty commission arrived at the Standing Rock Agency to convince the Sioux to sell their lands for $1.50 an acre. A previous commission's efforts to offer them fifty cents an acre failed miserably.

1939: An act (53 Stat. 1129) was passed by Congress to "provide for the distribution of the judgment fund of the Shoshone Tribe of the Wind River Reservation in Wyoming, and for other purposes."

1946: An election for approval of a constitution and bylaws for the Nisqually Indian Community of the Nisqually Reservation Washington was held. The vote for approval was 17–0.

1967: The assistant secretary of the interior ratified a revised constitution and bylaws for the Kalispel Indian Community of the Kalispel Reservation.

1973: The Nooksack Indian Tribe of Washington vote to establish a constitution and bylaws. The vote was 114–47.

JULY 28

1528: Panfilo de Narvaez and his expedition reached the Indian village of Aute, Florida.

Apache prisoners at Fort Bowie, Arkansas (NA)

1704: This day marked the end of Queen Anne's War.

1756: Delaware Chief Teedyuscung and fourteen other chiefs met with Governor Robert Morris and other Pennsylvania leaders at Easton, Pennsylvania, to discuss the Delaware Uprising. Teedyuscung agreed to visit the warring members of the tribe and to try to end the fighting.

1763: Indians attacked Fort Pitt again.

1862: Fort Bowie was established at Apache Pass in southeastern Arizona by members of Brigadier General James Charlatan's California volunteers.

1864: According to some sources, over 5,000 Santee and Teton Sioux engaged in a battle at Killdeer, North Dakota, with over 2,000 soldiers. General Alfred Sully led the army, and Chief Inkpaduta led the Sioux. Artillery eventually won the day for the soldiers.

1865: Sioux, including Sitting Bull, attacked soldiers at Fort Rice.

1868: The Fourteenth Amendment became a part of the U.S. Constitution. It granted equal rights to all men with the exception of Indians.

1868: According to army records, members of the Thirty-First Infantry fought with a band of Indians near Old Camp Sully in Dakota Territory. No injuries were reported on either side.

1872: Colonel Ranald S. Mackenzie and twelve officers and 272 enlisted men began an extended patrol of the area surrounding the Texas Panhandle. They included twenty Tonkawa scouts. They were looking for renegade Indians. One of their engagements was called the Battle of the North Fork of the Red River. It happened on September 29, 1872.

1872: Indians skirmished with a group of soldiers from the Twenty-Fifth Infantry near Central Station, Texas, according to official army records. No casualties were reported.

1877: Captain Charles Rawn was accompanied by five officers, thirty soldiers, and 150 local volunteers. When the volunteers left the night before and on this day, Rawn's force was dramatically reduced. The volunteers' withdrawal led to the barricade's derisive title: "Fort Fizzle."

1885: Army Indian scouts under Captain Wirt Davis fought with a group of Indians in Sierra Madre, Sonora, Mexico. According to army documents, two Indians were killed.

1955: An act (69 Stat. 392) was passed by Congress to "authorize the purchase, sale, and exchange of certain Indian lands on the Yakima Indian Reservation, and for other purposes."

1969: The assistant secretary of the interior ratified an amendment the constitution and bylaws of the Kalispel Indian Community of the Kalispel Reservation.

1978: An act was passed called "The Ak-chin Water Settlement Act." This act provided for equitable water for the Ak-chin Indian Community (Tohono O'odham and Pima Indians) in Pinal County, Arizona. It took six years before the law was totally enforced.

JULY 29

1706: Spaniard Juan de Uribarri was leading twenty soldiers, twelve settlers, and 200 Indian allies from Santa Fe to rescue a band of enslaved Indians held by the Cuartelejo Apache in what is now eastern Colorado. They crossed the Arkansas River at a site near modern Pueblo, Colorado.

1829: A treaty (7 Stat. 320) with the Ottawa, Chippewa, and Potawatomi Indians was signed in Prairie du Chien, at the time in Michigan Territory. The United States was represented by Caleb Atwater, Pierre Menard, and John McNeil. Lands were ceded near Lake Michigan for $16,000 a year and some goods.

1836: The 2,300-plus Creek prisoners reached Rock Roe on the White River in Arkansas. While waiting eight days for necessary supplies to arrive, the chains and manacles were removed from almost all of the Creek.

1837: Henry Dodge, representing the United States and the Chippewa Indians, signed a treaty (7 Stat. 536) at St. Peters, Wisconsin. The Chippewa traded large landholdings for $9,500 immediately, $19,000 worth of supplies, and a release from their debts.

1857: Colonel Edwin "Old Bull" Sumner, with three companies of infantry and six troops of cavalry, was proceeding down the Solomon's Fork River in western Kansas. The cavalry was a few miles ahead of the infantry when they encountered 300 Cheyenne warriors. The Indians were rested. The soldiers were tired. A running battle ensued with a few deaths on either side. Sumner's cavalry held their own against a large group of Cheyenne. The Cheyenne had been told by a medicine man they would be immune to the soldiers' bullets if the washed themselves in a sacred spring. This was one of the rare occasions when the Cheyenne faced the soldiers in an open battle. The medicine man was wrong. Disheartened by the "bad medicine," the Cheyenne took flight. The cavalry charged and followed the Indians for miles. One of the officers wounded in the battle was J.E.B. Stuart. Soldiers called this the Battle of Solomon's Fork.

1866: Soldiers from the Ninth Infantry fought with a band of Indians near Camp Cady in California. The army reported one enlisted man killed and one wounded.

1867: According to army records, members of the Eighth Cavalry fought with a band of Indians

Red Cloud, chief of the Oglala Sioux (NA)

near Willows, Arizona. No one was reported killed or wounded.

1868: After years of conflict over the Bozeman Trail along the Powder River, the War Department finally gave in to Indian demands, particularly from Red Cloud, and started abandoning its forts. Fort C.F. Smith's garrison packed up and left. The fort was located near modern Yellowtail and Bighorn Lake in southern Montana.

1876: Twenty-Second Infantry soldiers under Lieutenant Colonel E.S. Otis fought some Indians near the mouth of the Powder River in Montana. According to army documents, one soldier was wounded.

1878: Navajo Indian scouts under Lieutenant H.H. Wright fought a group of hostile Indians in the Sacramento Mountains of Arizona. According to army documents, three Indians were killed, three were wounded, and one was captured.

1879: Second Infantry soldiers fought a group of Indians near Big Creek, Idaho. According to army documents, two soldiers were wounded.

1889: On this day through July 31, the Sioux land conference was held at Standing Rock.

1905: The boundaries of the Santa Clara Pueblo Indian Reservation were modified.

1959: The Indian Claims Commission recognized eleven bands of Indians in California as the Pit River Tribe.

1967: An election to add Amendments 1 and 2 to the constitution for the Wisconsin Winnebago was held. It was approved by those who were voting.

1968: The American Indian Movement was founded.

JULY 30

1609: Samuel de Champlain, two Frenchmen, and sixty Algonquin and Huron Indians attacked 200 Mohawks near Ticonderoga in New York. Champlain had some firearms, and they proved devastating. The Mohawks quit the battle. (Sometimes listed as July 9.)

1685: According to some sources, an agreement was reached for the Delaware Indians to cede some lands to Pennsylvania.

1715: According to some sources, a peace agreement was reached by representatives of Pennsylvania and the Conestoga, Delaware, Potomac, and Shawnee Indians.

1756: Captain Jacob, a Delaware chief, his followers and a few French under Louis Coulon de Villiers attacked Fort Granville, Pennsylvania. The fort surrendered, making it one of the first well-fortified positions in the area to do so. During the fighting, Lieutenant Edward Armstrong was killed. His death led his brother, Colonel John Armstrong, on a campaign against Captain Jacob. (It was also reported that the attack started on this day and that the fort surrendered the next day.)

1819: The Kickapoo gave up their lands along the Vermilion and Illinois Rivers to the United States.

1825: The "Belantse-etoa or Minitaree" concluded a treaty (7 Stat. 261) at the Lower Mandan Village. Nine chiefs and sixteen warriors signed the document.

Nana, Apache leader (NA)

1829: In internal documents, the U.S. War Department formalized a new Indian policy. Secretary of War John Eaton believed that Indians would not be able to survive if they lived in lands surrounded by white settlers.

1863: The Treaty of Box Elder (13 Stat. 663) was signed by the Northwestern Bands of Shoshoni and Utah Territorial Governor James Duane Doty in Brigham City, Utah.

1868: The day before, the army abandoned Fort C.F. Smith in southern Montana. Red Cloud entered the fort in triumph. Red Cloud and his followers burned every building to the ground.

1868: According to army records, members of the Thirty-First Infantry fought with a band of Indians in the Tonto Valley near Camp Reno. One soldier was wounded in the fighting.

1876: Lieutenant J.L. Bullis and forty men attacked a band of hostile Kickapoo and Lipan Indians near Saragossa, Mexico. Ten Indians were killed. Four Indians and 100 horses were captured.

1880: A running fight had been going on for some time between the Tenth Cavalry soldiers of Colonel Benjamin Grierson and Victorio's Apache. They fought what some sources called the Battle of Rocky Ridge or the Battle of Tinaja de Las Palmas near Sierra Blanca in west Texas. According to army documents, one soldier and seven Indians were killed. Lieutenant S.R. Colladay and three soldiers were wounded.

1881: According to army reports, Nana and his Apache killed four Mexicans in the foothills of the San Mateo Mountains of New Mexico.

1882: According to the Oklahoma Law Enforcement Memorial, Officer Joe Barnett was one of a group of four Creek Lighthorse led by Captain Sam Scott from the National Constitutional Party faction of the Creek. The officers were guarding a "notorious character" who was a captured member of the Loyal Creek, or Sands men, at the Barnett place near Wetumka. The Sands men were a gang of about 400 led by the outlaw Dick Glass. About daybreak, a company of Sands men attacked the officers and freed the prisoner. Captain Scott was then stood up and held by the hands by a man on either side while the others filled his body with bullets. Officer Barnett was killed when he tried to go to the aid of his captain.

1957: The state of Florida recognized the Miccosukee Seminole Nation.

JULY 31

1684: According to some sources, a six-day conference started between representatives of the New York Colonies and the Mohawk, Oneida, Onondaga, and Cayuga. Some lands were ceded and allegiances were pledged.

1710: According to some sources, an agreement on peace and land boundaries was reached between representatives of Pennsylvania and the Five Nations, the Shawnees, and the Delaware.

1763: Captain James Dalyell and 280 soldiers attacked Pontiac's village at 2:30 A.M. this morning. Pontiac was informed of Dalyell's plans, so he set up an ambush at the Parent's Creek bridge with 400 Indians. When Dalyell's troops approached the bridge, the Indians attacked. Twenty soldiers, including Dalyell, and seven Indians were killed in the fighting. The creek, near Detroit, is now called Bloody Run. Major Robert Rogers helped Dalyell's survivors to escape.

1779: General John Sullivan led an expedition in retaliation against Iroquois actions in the Wyoming Valley Massacre.

1811: The city of Vincennes asked William Henry Harrison to fight the local Indians.

1837: According to government reports, of the 4,000 Creek being held at Mobile Point awaiting transport to Indian Territory (present-day Oklahoma), 177 died at the camp or in the first leg of their transport.

1851: Accompanied by Father Pierre De Smet and Alexander Culbertson, Arikara, Assiniboine, Hidatsa, and Mandan Indians left Fort Union en route to the Horse Creek Treaty conference.

1854: The Indian Appropriation Act was approved by Congress. It authorized David Meriwether, working as superintendent of Indian affairs, to conduct treaty negotiations with the "troublesome tribes under its jurisdiction."

1857: Colonel Edwin V. Sumner and the Cheyenne expedition reached the village of the Cheyenne they had already fought at Solomon's Fork. The village had recently been abandoned. Sumner destroyed the abandoned lodges and supplies.

1866: Soldiers from the Thirteenth Infantry fought with a band of Indians near Fort Rice in Dakota Territory. The army reported that one enlisted man was killed.

1867: Fort Griffin (near modern Albany, Texas) was established by Lieutenant Colonel Samuel D. Sturgis and members of the Sixth Cavalry. Its original name was Camp Wilson.

1871: Indians skirmished with a group of soldiers from the Ninth Cavalry and the Twenty-Fourth Infantry near McKavett, Texas, according to official army records. One Indian was killed.

1879: Colonel Nelson Miles, after the Battle of the Milk River on July 17, 1879, had been following the trail of a large group of Sioux Indians. On this day he reported that the Sioux had crossed over into Canada. After a brief pause, Miles returned to the Milk River.

1880: According to a report from the Fort Davis commanding officer, stage driver E.C. Baker and passenger Frank Wyant were killed by Victorio's Indians eight miles west of Eagle Springs in western Texas.

1880: Colonel Benjamin Grierson and six soldiers were attacked by Victorio's Indians between Quitman and Eagle Springs, Texas. The fighting continued as numerous cavalry soldiers came to the rescue. After many hours of fighting, seven Indians and one soldier were killed. The Indians were chased to the Rio Grande.

1881: Sitting Bull was received in Bismarck for a "big reception."

1882: An act (22 Stat. 179) was passed designed "to prevent any person other than an Indian of full blood who attempts to reside in Indian country or on any Indian reservation as a trader without license shall forfeit all merchandise and shall be liable to a penalty and may not employ a white person as clerk unless first licensed to do so, except for the Five Civilized Tribes."

1885: Louis Riel addressed the jury in his own defense. He had pleaded insanity based on his lawyer's recommendation. On this day he denied that he was insane. He said he had a mission to help all the peoples of northwestern Canada. He was found guilty by the jury.

1903: An executive order modified the boundaries of the Moapa Band of Paiute Indians Reservation.

1963: The Standing Rock Sioux tribal council recommended amending their constitution. An election was held on October 24, 1959.

1970: Congress decided that new "rolls" must be made for descendants of the Wea, Piankashaw, Peoria, and Kaskaskia Indian Tribes who were included in the May 30, 1854, treaty. The government wanted to distribute $2 million to the descendants.

AUGUST 1

1615: Champlain entered Georgian Bay.

1735: According to some sources, an agreement covering "amity and commerce" was reached by representatives of the British in New York and Western Abenaki, Housatonic, Mohegan, and Scaghticoke Indians.

1739: Several Shawnee chiefs signed a peace treaty with British Pennsylvania authorities not to become allies with any other country. The British agreed to enforce previous treaties banning the sale of rum to the Indians.

1776: General Andrew Williamson had gathered a force of 1,100 militiamen from South Carolina to fight the Cherokees. Although marching toward the Lower Cherokee villages, they were attacked by British and Cherokee forces near Esenka. The surprise attack initially gave the Indian and British forces the upper hand. The South Carolina forces regrouped, however, and they eventually beat back the attack and destroyed the town.

1813: Fort Stephenson (modern Fremont, Ohio) was attacked by British Major Henry A. Proctor and 1,200 British and Indian forces. The fort was defended by Major George Croghan and 120 men. The Americans fired only when the British and Indians were at close range. During the two-day battle, the Americans had only one man killed. The British and Indians sustained more than 1,200 casualties.

1813: British and Indians attacked Fort Malden.

1814: As an end to the Creek War, Andrew Jackson started the Fort Jackson Treaty conference (near modern Wetumpka, Alabama). The treaty (7 Stat. 120) was completed on August 9, 1814.

1829: The Winnebago signed a treaty (7 Stat. 323) in Prairie du Chien, at the time in Michigan Territory. The Winnebago gave up lands near the Rock River and the Wisconsin River for $18,000 a year.

1832: General Henry Atkinson, called "White Beaver" by the Indians, army regulars, and 3,000

civilian volunteers fought with Black Hawk's forces at the battle of Bad Axe River (a few miles south of modern La Crosse in southwestern Wisconsin). Approximately 150 Indians were killed in the fighting. (See August 3, 1832.)

1833: The Mi'kmaq Wagmatcook First Nation Reserve of Wagmatcook No. 1 was established in Nova Scotia.

1834: Reserve Margaree No. 25 was established for the Mi'kmaq Wagmatcook First Nation in Nova Scotia.

1836: A total of 2,700 Creek, including the ones who fought for the whites, were forced to leave Alabama for the Indian Territory (present-day Oklahoma). Their leader, Opothleyaholo, was with them.

1838: Although being held in the Aquohee prison camp during their forced removal from their lands east of the Mississippi River, the Cherokee tribal council held a meeting. The council and Principal Chief John Ross signed a resolution stating that the laws of the Cherokee Nation remained in effect and their right to exist as a nation could not be dissolved by the U.S. government. This official council was the only such meeting to ever be held by an Indian tribe while held prisoner by a white government.

1851: One in a series of treaties was signed with California Indians at Camp Bidwell. The treaties were to reserve lands and to protect the Indians.

1859: On February 6, 1854, Texas law allowed the federal government to establish two Indian reservations on the Brazos River in Texas. Many of the white Texans attacked the reservations without cause. To save the Indians, their federal agent, Robert S. Neighbors, led them to a new reservation on the Washita River in Indian Territory (present-day Oklahoma). With him traveled 1,430 Caddo-related Indians and 380 Penateka. Upon his return to Texas, Neighbors was murdered.

1861: Some Seminole chiefs signed a treaty with the Confederacy. It was similar to those signed by the Creek and Chickasaws on July 10, 1861, and July 12, 1861.

1866: John Ross, the principal chief of the Cherokee, died in Washington, D.C.

1867: After continued incursions into Indian lands, Indians wanted to teach the whites a lesson along the Bozeman Trail. After fasting and other ceremonies, the Indians decided to attack one of the forts along the trail. But no agreement could be reached as to which fort to attack. The Cheyenne decided to attack Fort C.F. Smith in southern Montana (near modern Bighorn Lake). Thirty soldiers and civilians were working in a field of hay a few miles from the fort when a little over 500 Cheyenne warriors come across the group. A frontal attack was repulsed at great loss to the Cheyenne because the soldiers had repeating rifles. The Indians then set fire to the hay. The soldiers were inside a log-walled enclosure when they observed a wall of flames forty feet high approaching them. Luck was on the soldiers' side, though. Just before the fire reached the soldiers, it died out. Taking this as an omen, the Cheyenne gave up the attack. According to army records, one officer (Lieutenant Sigismund Sternberg), one enlisted man, one civilian, and eight Indians were killed. Thirty Indians were wounded in the fighting.

1876: Fourth Infantry soldiers fought some Indians in Red Canyon, Montana. According to army documents, no casualties were reported.

1877: Settlers fought a group of Indians near El Muerto, Texas. According to army documents, two settlers were killed.

1881: Thirty-six civilian volunteers, led by "Mr. Mitchell," were attacked by Nana's Apache in the Red Canyon of the San Mateo Mountains in central New Mexico. They attacked while the Apache were eating dinner. One civilian was killed and seven others were wounded. The Apache seized thirty-eight of the volunteers' mounts.

1906: According to the Oklahoma Law Enforcement Memorial, at about 9:30 P.M. U.S. Indian Police Officer and Deputy U.S. Marshal Ben C. Collins was riding through the gate to his pasture on his way home. He was about 200 yards from his home, located between Emet and Nida, when he was shot from his horse by an ambusher using an eight-gauge shotgun. Collins was able to fire at his assailant four times before he was fatally shot in the face. Deacon Jim Miller was arrested for the murder but released.

1953: House Concurrent Resolution No. 108 was adopted. This law removed Indians from their "ward-of-the-state" status and brought them into equal citizenship status with all other Americans. The resolution was only advisory; it carried no legal weight and was not a law.

1966: The acting commissioner of Indian affairs had authorized an election to amend the revised constitution and bylaws of the Sisseton Wahpeton Sioux Tribe of South Dakota. The election took place this date and the next day. It passed by a vote of 123–56.

1969: Amendments 1 and 2 to the constitution and bylaws of the Hopi Tribe were approved by Assistant Secretary of the Interior Harrison Loesch.

Every: Passamaquoddy ceremonial day.

AUGUST 2

1675: Captain Thomas Wheeler, with twenty militia and three Indian guides, had arranged for a meeting with the Nipmuck on August 1. The whites hoped to make the Nipmuck allies in their fight against the Wampanoag. However, the Nipmuck had already joined up with King Philip's Wampanoag. When the Nipmuck were not at the meeting site, the English searched for them, against the advice of their Indian guides. On this day, a joint force of Nipmuck and Wampanoag attacked Wheeler's force. Half of Wheeler's force was killed in the initial attack. Wheeler retreated to Brookfield in central Massachusetts. Wheeler and the eighty local residents moved into a small wooden community fort. The Indians staged a siege and made several unsuccessful attempts to burn the building. One settler managed to escape and run for help. Within a few days Major Simon Willard and four dozen men reached Brookfield and engaged the Indians. The English claimed to have killed eighty warriors in the subsequent fighting.

1689: A small force of thirty men led by Lieutenant James Weems was occupying the fort at Pemaquid, Maine. They were attacked by almost 100 Abenaki Indians. The soldiers eventually surrendered, and those who weren't killed were taken as prisoners to Canada.

1780: At the start of Revolutionary War hostilities, Mohawks evacuated their village of Canajoharie (near modern Fort Plain, New York). White settlers then moved into the village. Joseph Brant and Mohawk warriors attacked the settlers. Fourteen settlers were killed and sixty taken prisoner. Much of the village was destroyed.

1792: Mohegan Samson Occom died in New Stockbridge, New York. A protégé of Reverend Eleazar Wheelock, Occom learned numerous foreign languages, became an ordained minister, was the first Indian to preach in England, ministered to many Indian tribes, and was instrumental in the establishment of Dartmouth College in New Hampshire.

1833: The Mi'kmaq Chapel Island First Nation Reserve of Malagawatch No. 4 was established in Nova Scotia.

1836: A total of 210 Creek "prisoners" left Montgomery, Alabama, on a boat escorted by Captain F.S. Belton. They were bound for the Indian Territory (present-day Oklahoma).

1837: The first contingent of 150 Chickasaws from Alabama arrived at Fort Coffee in eastern Indian Territory (present-day Oklahoma) on the steamship *Indian*.

1839: The Republic of Texas signed a treaty with the Shawnee in Nacogdoches. The Indians agreed to leave Texas if the government covered their expenses. The Texas senate did not ratify the treaty.

1865: According to a report, 417 Apache and 7,173 Navajo were present at the Fort Sumner Reservation (New Mexico) in July.

1867: At the same ceremonies attended by the Cheyenne earlier in the week, Red Cloud and Crazy Horse's Sioux decided to attack Fort Phil Kearny in northern Wyoming (south of modern Sheridan). Hoping to lure the soldiers out of the fort, Crazy Horse launched a diversionary attack on a woodcutter's camp near the fort. A large group of warriors went into hiding, waiting for the soldiers to come to rescue the woodcutters. For some reason, the Indians in hiding revealed themselves prematurely, and the ambush failed. Since the soldiers would not leave the fort, Red Cloud decided to direct his entire force against the woodcutters. The woodcutters had built a barricade of logs and wagon beds. Red Cloud faced the same rapid-fire rifles the Cheyenne had faced the previous day. Charges on horseback and on foot proved too costly to the Sioux. The Sioux gathered their dead and left. According to army records, one officer (Lieutenant J.C. Jenness), five soldiers, and sixty Indians were killed. Two enlisted men and 120 Indians were wounded in the fighting.

1867: According to army records, members of the Tenth Cavalry fought with a band of Indians near the Salinas River in Kansas. One soldier was killed and Captain G.A. Armes was wounded.

1868: According to army records, members of the Seventh Cavalry fought with a band of Indians near the Cimarron River in Kansas. There were no injuries reported on either side.

1869: After the Summit Springs fight with Tall Bull's followers, soldiers resupplied at Fort Sedgwick in northeastern Colorado. Colonel William Royall assumed command of the Fifth Cavalry force, previously under General Eugene Carr's command. On the first night out of the fort, as the troops were about to set up camp, a band of Indians was discovered. However, the Indians managed to escaped under cover of darkness. The cavalry followed the Indians' trail for 225 miles to the north until the army forces finally gave up near the Niobrara River in Dakota Territory.

1871: After their conviction for murder, Satanta and Big Tree were delivered to the prison in Huntsville, Texas, to serve their time.

1876: Sixth and Seventeenth Infantry soldiers fought some Indians near the mouth of the Rosebud River in Montana. According to army documents, one soldier and one Indian were killed.

1951: Raymond Harvey, a Chickasaw, received the Medal of Honor for actions during the Korean War.

1966: The revised constitution and bylaws of the Sisseton Wahpeton Sioux Tribe of South Dakota was adopted.

1983: Amendment 15 to the constitution and bylaws of the Lac du Flambeau Band of Lake Superior Chippewa Indians of Wisconsin was approved and became effective.

AUGUST 3

1492: Columbus sailed for the New World from Palos, Spain.

1716: The fort that French Commander Bienville demanded as partial reparation for the killing of five Frenchmen was finished. It was named Fort Rosalie by Bienville. It was located on a high hill near the main Natchez village on the Mississippi River. This episode was called the First War with the Natchez by the French. The Second War took place in October 1722. It was a very short encounter. The Fourth War with the Natchez saw the largest single battle at Fort Rosalie on November 28, 1729.

1761: According to some records, a conference regarding land questions and the return of prisoners was held for the next ten days between representatives of the British in Pennsylvania and the Cayuga, Conoy, Delaware, Mahican, Nanticoke, Oneida, and Onondaga Indians.

1777: British Colonel Barry St. Leger and 1,400 Indians and British soldiers started the attack and

siege of Fort Stanwix (near modern Rome, New York). The fort was defended by Colonel Peter Gansevoort and 550 men. The British and Indians continued the siege until August 22, 1777.

1788: Militia from the state of "Franklin" arrested Cherokee Principal Chief Old Tassel and Hanging Maw. They were charged with the murders of Colonel William Christian and John Donelson. Old Tassel convinced the men from Franklin that Dragging Canoe's Chickamauga followers did the deed.

1795: The Greenville Ohio Treaty (7 Stat. 49) was concluded with twelve tribes, ending Little Wolf's War. Prisoners were to be returned on both sides. New boundary lines were established. Land was given up for Fort Defiance, Fort Wayne, a British fort on the Miami River, the old fort on Sandusky Lake, the post at Detroit, Fort Michilimackinac in Michigan, the old fort on the Chicago River and Lake Michigan, Fort St. Vincennes in Indiana, Fort Massac, and Old Pioria's Fort. Certain roads were opened to unmolested travel by whites. The annuity in goods for these lands was worth $9,500. They received $20,000 now. The Indians could hunt in their old lands if they did so peacefully. No whites could live on Indian lands without the Indians' approval. The president was authorized to license all traders. All previous treaties were voided. The treaty was signed by General "Mad" Anthony Wayne and ninety Indians. The spelling of "Greenville" varies by document (sometimes Grenville and other variations).

1832: Black Hawk had been chased westward to the Mississippi River. General Winfield Scott had outfitted a steamboat, *The Warrior*, with artillery. On this day he confronted Black Hawk. Initially Black Hawk attempted to parley, but the 1,300 white forces were out for blood. In the subsequent fighting, almost 200 warriors were killed; the soldiers lost about twenty. Black Hawk escaped, but he was captured by other Indians sometime later. About 200 Sac Indians made it across the river, only to be killed by Sioux Indians on the western bank.

1869: General Alfred Sully, military superintendent of Indian affairs, wrote that lawless whites and whiskey sellers were driving the Montana Indians to warfare. In his opinion, only military force against the whites would stop a conflict.

1869: According to army records, members of the Twenty-Second Infantry fought with a band of Indians near Fort Stevenson, Dakota Territory. No casualties were reported.

1871: "Treaties 1 and 2 Between Her Majesty The Queen and The Chippewa and Cree Indians of Manitoba and County Adjacent with Adhesions" were signed. The ceremony took place at Stone Fort, later called Fort Garry (modern Winnipeg, Manitoba).

1877: To contend with the fleeing Nez Perce, Colonel John Gibbon had assembled a force of Companies A, D, F, G, I, and K, Seventh Infantry, and thirty civilian volunteers for a total of 191 men. After departing from Fort Shaw, Montana, Gibbon's force arrived in Missoula, Montana.

1880: After the fighting on July 31, 1880, Colonel Benjamin Grierson and his troops had been tracking several bands of Victorio's Indians. One band engaged in a fight on the Alamo River. Several parties were wounded on both sides. Victorio's supply camp was attacked by Captain Thomas Lebo and Troop K, Tenth Cavalry. Most of the supplies were seized, and the Indians were chased to the Escondido River. Tenth Cavalry soldiers fought a group of Indians near Sierra Diablo, Texas. According to army documents, no casualties were reported.

1881: Lieutenant John Guilfoyle and his Ninth Cavalry troops attacked Nana's Apache at Monica Springs, New Mexico. Two Indians were wounded and eleven head of livestock were seized. According to Guilfoyle's report, he estimated Nana's forces at twenty to thirty warriors.

1889: General George Crook and the other treaty commissioners were having no luck in convincing the large groups of Sioux at the Standing Rock Agency to agree to move to smaller reservations and to sell their "excess" lands for $1.50 an acre. Sitting Bull continued to "disrupt" the meetings with his angry denunciation of any attempt to sell Indian lands. Crook decided he would make more progress by talking to the tribal leaders individually. Without informing Sitting Bull, Crook held a final meeting. Local agent James McLaughlin had his tribal police surround the meeting site to prevent any of the rabble-rousers from attending. Eventually, Sitting Bull worked his way past the police and addressed the meeting. Sitting Bull was incensed because he had not been informed of the meeting. McLaughlin told those assembled that everyone knew of the meeting. At that time, Chief John Grass and many of the other chiefs came forward to sign the treaty, which broke up the large reservation. Sitting Bull vented his frustration at the other chiefs, but he was outvoted.

1948: A New Mexico court ruled that Indians could vote.

1965: A plan for the distribution of assets for the Robinson Rancheria by the undersecretary of the interior was approved. It also functioned as a tribal roll.

AUGUST 4

1528: Having just left the Indian village in Florida he called Aute, Panfilo de Narvaez and his Spanish expeditionary force reached the Gulf of Mexico again. They started to build boats for their return to Spanish civilization. It took them a month and a half to build five "barges."

1742: According to some reports, a meeting was held between representatives of the British in Massachusetts and the Maliseet, Norridgewock, Passamaquoddy, Penobscot, Pigwacket, and St. Francis Indians regarding trade problems.

1813: About 500 warriors of the White Stick faction of the Creek gathered in Coweta (across the river in Alabama from modern Columbus,

Santee Sioux Uprising in 1862

Georgia). With 200 Cherokee warriors, they made plans to attack a band of Red Stick Creek, followers of Tecumseh, over 2,500 strong. The White Sticks were led by Tustunnuggee Thlucco and Tustunnuggee Hopoie.

1824: The Sac and Fox and the Iowa Indians signed a treaty (7 Stat. 229) in Washington, D.C. They ceded to the United States all the land "lying and being between the Mississippi and Missouri Rivers." The Iowa were represented by Mah-hos-kah (White Cloud) and Mah-ne-hah-nah (Great Walker).

1845: Peter Jones (Kahkewaquonaby) was a Mississauga Ojibwa chief. While on a speaking tour of Scotland to raise money for missionary efforts in his homeland, his picture was taken. This was considered to be one of the first photographs ever made of an American Indian.

1853: Rogue River Indians were upset by the presence of gold miners in their lands. They killed Edward Edwards on Stewart's Creek, near Jacksonville. This led to widespread hostilities.

1856: Fort Randall replaced Fort Pierre.

1862: The money promised to the Santee Sioux in Minnesota was scheduled to arrived in July. When Little Crow and the other Sioux reported to their reservation's upper agency on the Yellow Medicine River, they were told the money had not arrived. The winter had been bad and the summer

crops poor. Little Crow asked Agent Thomas Galbraith to open up the local warehouse, which was full of food. Galbraith said there would be no food if there was no money. On this day, Little Crow and 500 Sioux warriors surrounded the badly outnumbered soldiers guarding the warehouse. The Santee broke in and started unloading supplies. The commanding officer of the garrison, Timothy Sheehan, understood the frustration of the hungry Indians and convinced Galbraith to officially issue the food to the Santee. Little Crow also got a promise that the lower agency would also issue supplies. The Santee then left peacefully.

1870: A "Military Reserve" and a "Hay and Wood Reserve" were established by General Order No. 19 of the War Department. It was eventually given to the Fort Mohave Tribe. The reserves contained 5,582 and 9,114 acres of land, respectively.

1873: Elements of the Seventh Cavalry engaged in two fights with Sioux Indians in the Yellowstone area. Captain Myles Moylan and Troops A and B, acting as an advance party, fought the Sioux near the Tongue River in Dakota. One soldier was reported missing and presumed dead. Lieutenant Colonel George Custer and the main body of the Seventh Cavalry encountered several hundred Sioux on the Yellowstone River in Montana. Four soldiers were killed. Lieutenant Charles Braden and three soldiers were wounded in the fighting.

1879: Captain Samuel Ovenshine and soldiers from the Fifth Infantry, a part of Colonel Nelson Miles's command, arrived at a camp of "half-breeds" on Porcupine Creek believed to be supplying the hostile Sioux with guns and ammunition. Captain Ovenshine arrested the "half-breeds" and seized forty-three carts with supplies and 193 horses.

1880: Tenth Cavalry soldiers fought a group of Indians near Camp Safford in the Guadalupe Mountains, Texas. According to army documents, one soldier was killed.

1898: An Indian Congress was formally opened in Omaha as a part of the Trans-Mississippi and

International Exposition. It had almost 500 Indians representing thirty-five different tribes.

1991: A museum returned Indian goods to the Omaha Indians.

AUGUST 5

1570: A Spanish colony expedition was sailing up the Chesapeake in Virginia when it reached the area it would call Axaca somewhere near the Rappahannock. The local Indians would force the Spanish to abandon the effort.

1763: During Pontiac's Rebellion, the Battle of Bushy Run took place in Pennsylvania. Henry Bouquet and 460 troops were marching to reinforce Fort Pitt in western Pennsylvania from Carlisle, near Harrisburg. A little over twenty miles from Fort Pitt, Bouquet's troops were attacked by a force of Wyandot, Shawnee, Mingo, and Delaware. After an inconclusive battle, both sides withdrew.

1826: The Chippewa signed a treaty (7 Stat. 290) in Fond du Lac. Dozens of Indians placed their mark on the document.

1836: Abel Pepper, representing the United States, and Potawatomi Indians signed a treaty (7 Stat. 505) in Yellow River, Indiana. The Potawatomi traded lands acquired a few years earlier for $14,080. They also agreed to move west of the Mississippi River. Twenty-seven Indians signed the document.

1838: The second group of Cherokee prisoners forcibly removed to the Indian Territory (present-day Oklahoma) arrived in their new lands. Of the 875 who originally left Ross's Landing (Chattanooga, Tennessee) on June 13, only 602 arrived. Although some of the captive Cherokees escaped, many of the 273 missing Cherokees died en route.

1840: Tucker Foley and Dr. Joel Ponton lived in Lavaca County, Texas. While traveling to Gonzales, Texas, they were attacked by twenty-seven Comanche.

1861: The Creek signed a treaty with the Confederacy on July 10, 1861. Creek from the Cana-

Field headquarters for General Crook (photograph taken after the Black Hills expedition) (NA)

dian district met and deposed their old chief. The number-two chief, Oktarharsars Harjo, called Sands, took over. He was pro-Union.

1869: According to army records, a "garrison of post and Indian scouts" fought with a band of Indians at Fort Stevenson, Dakota Territory. No casualties were reported.

1876: General George Crook, with reinforcements, moved his troops down the Tongue River toward the Black Hills looking for hostile Indians.

1877: Almost 1,000 Cheyenne left Fort Robinson in northwestern Nebraska en route to Fort Reno in central Indian Territory (present-day Oklahoma), on the Cheyenne and Arapaho Reservation, under escort by Lieutenant Henry Lawton. On the way, a few young warriors sneaked away and some of the old people died. On this day, 937 Cheyenne under Little Wolf and Dull Knife reached Fort Reno. They turned over their horses and weapons to the soldiers under Colonel Ranald Mackenzie.

1878: Ninth Cavalry soldiers and some Indian scouts fought a group of Indians near Dog Canyon, New Mexico. According to army documents, three Indians were killed, two were wounded, and one was captured.

Spotted Tail, Sioux chief (NA)

1879: Elements of Colonel Nelson Miles's command arrested four more camps of "half-breeds" believed to be supplying Sitting Bull's Sioux with food, arms, and ammunition. The army seized 308 carts of supplies.

1881: Crow Dog killed Spotted Tail on the Sioux Reservation. Eventually, the case would go to the U.S. Supreme Court and become a foundation for tribal sovereignty.

1882: Congress passed an act (22 Stat. 299) that authorized the president to establish a reservation for the Papago Indians in Arizona. The president had issued the establishing order on July 1, 1874.

1939: An election for a constitution and bylaws for the Port Gamble Band of Clallam Indians was held. The constitution was adopted by a vote of 32–7.

1947: The results of an election to amend the constitution and bylaws of the Yavapai-Apache Tribe of the Camp Verde Reservation were approved by Martin G. White, acting assistant secretary of the interior. The results were 109–2 in favor.

1965: The assistant secretary of the interior authorized an election to approve an amendment to the constitution and bylaws of the Miccosukee Tribe of Indians of Florida. The election was held on September 12, 1965.

Every: All Pueblos symbolic relay race (through August 10).

AUGUST 6

1676: Weetamoo was the sachem of the Wampanoag town of Pocasset, Rhode Island. The sister-in-law of King Philip, she led as many as 300 warriors in battle. While trying to escape from European soldiers from Taunton, Massachusetts, she drowned in the Taunton River. Her head was cut off and displayed on a pole in the town.

1687: According to some sources, an agreement of alliance was reached between representatives of the Five Nations and the British in New York.

1763: After inconclusive fighting the day before at Bushy Run in southwestern Pennsylvania, Henry Bouquet's force of almost 450 devised a plan to surprise the Wyandot, Shawnee, Mingo, and Delaware who were fighting them. Bouquet faked a retreat that led the pursuing Indians into a trap. Both sides lost a total of about 100 men in the fighting. The Indians gave up the battle, and Bouquet continued on to relieve Fort Pitt. Some of the Indians involved in Pontiac's Rebellion were less inclined to fight in the future after this battle.

1777: The Battle of Oriskany took place near Fort Stanwix, New York. For the first time, the Iroquois fought on both sides of a major engagement. General Nicholas Herkimer led a large contingent of American forces. He lost the battle, but thirty-three Seneca were killed while fighting for the British side. Many Indians left the British forces after the battle.

1836: The second group of friendly Creek Indians, led by William McGillivrey and army Lieutenant R.B. Screvens, left Wetumka, just north of Montgomery, Alabama. The group of approximately 3,000 Creek was bound for the Indian Territory (present-day Oklahoma). Many more Creek joined them en route. Also, 1,170 friendly Creek left the Talladega area led by Lieutenant Edward Deas.

1840: Hundreds of Comanche led by Buffalo Hump surrounded and attacked Victoria, Texas. In the next two days, fifteen settlers were killed in the fighting. The Comanche took several hundred head of livestock.

1846: The old settlers and the new emigrant factions of the Cherokee had been arguing over who had legal control over the Cherokee Nation since the late 1830s. It had even been proposed that the nation split into two tribes. The different sides signed a treaty (9 Stat. 871) in Washington, D.C. The treaty confirmed there would be only one Cherokee Nation.

1867: Cheyenne wrecked a train in Nebraska.

1868: According to army records, members of the Ninth Cavalry fought with a band of Indians near Fort Quitman, Texas. There were no injuries reported on either side.

1872: Indians skirmished with a group of soldiers from the Eighth Cavalry in the Chiricahua Mountains in Arizona, according to official army records. Two Indians were killed.

1880: Soldiers attacked a band of Indians in the Guadalupe Mountains in Rattlesnake Canyon, Texas. The Indians escaped in all directions. Captain John Gilmore and Company H, Twenty-Fourth Infantry, were guarding a wagon train near Rattlesnake Springs when they were attacked by Indians from the Rattlesnake Canyon fight. All total, four Indians were killed, according to army reports.

1945: The commissioner of Indian affairs modified the boundaries of certain Indian lands in New Mexico. This modified an order establishing the previous boundaries on September 1, 1939.

1975: Tribal election laws were modified by Ordinance No. 23–61 by the tribal council the Gila River Pima-Maricopa Indian Community.

1998: Executive Order No. 13096 was issued. It was titled "American Indian and Alaska Native Education." Its goal was "improving educational achievement and academic progress for American Indian and Alaska Native students is vital to the national goal of preparing every student for responsible citizenship, continued learning, and productive employment."

AUGUST 7

1670: Apache or Navajos attacked the ancient Zuni pueblo of Hawikuh. They burned the church and killed the resident missionary.

1757: According to some reports, a peace agreement was reached by representatives of the British and the Delaware, Mahican, Nanticoke, Shawnee, and Six Nations tribes.

1758: According to some reports, a peace conference was held for the next two days between representatives of the British in New Jersey and the Minisink Indians.

1760: After the start of the Cherokee War, with the killing of seventeen hostage Cherokee chiefs in Fort Prince George, the Cherokees vowed revenge. They eventually attacked Fort Loudoun on the Little Tennessee River (near modern Vonore, Tennessee). The English, under Captain Paul Demere, surrendered the fort with the proviso that they were delivered to Fort Prince George.

1786: An ordinance for the regulation of Indian affairs was passed. It established two Indian Departments for the Ohio River area. One was north of the river, the other south. A superintendent was appointed for each department. He was able to grant trade licenses.

1787: The Northwest Ordinance passed.

1790: A treaty (7 Stat. 35) with the Creek was signed in New York City. The Creek acknowledged the sovereignty of the United States. All Creek prisoners, white and black, were returned. New boundary lines were established. No whites could live in Creek lands without the Creeks' approval. The treaty was signed by Alexander McGillivray and twenty-three other Creek. The treaty was repudiated by the non-McGillivray

Creek. The treaty also required the Seminole to return all former black slaves living with them. The Seminole rejected the idea that the Creek could make treaties for them. A section of the treaty, kept secret from the Indians, made McGillivray a brigadier general in the American army. (Also recorded as happening on August 13.)

1803: A treaty (7 Stat. 77) with the Five Nations (Eel River, Wyandot, Piankashaw, and Kaskaskia Nations and the Kickapoo Tribe) was concluded at Vincennes, Indiana. The treaty referred to the Treaty of June 7, 1803, regarding the establishment of traveler's inns and entertainment houses on roads through Indian lands. The treaty was signed by William Henry Harrison and ten Indians.

1840: Calusa Seminole Chief Chakaika led a group of Indians in an attack against the settlement on Indian Key. Indian Key was midway along the Florida Keys. Thirteen whites were killed in the attack, and most of the farms were looted and burned.

1853: The *Yreka* (California) *Herald* ran the following editorial: "Now that the general hostilities against the Indians have commenced we hope that the Government will render such aid as will enable the citizens of the north to carry on a war of extermination until the last Redskin of these tribes has been killed." Extermination of the Indians was no longer a question of time, for "the time has arrived, the work has commenced, and let the first man that says treaty or peace be regarded as a traitor."

1856: The Creek and Seminole signed a treaty (11 Stat. 699) with the United States in Washington, D.C.

1869: A solar eclipse was drawn on Lone Dog's chronicle of the years.

1885: Indian scouts under Captain Wirt Davis fought with a group of Indians in Sierra Madre, Sonora, Mexico. According to army documents, five Indians were killed and fifteen were captured.

1895: On November 25, 1894, a group of nineteen Hopi hostiles were placed under arrest by the army for interfering with friendly Hopi Indian activities on their Arizona reservation. The nineteen prisoners were held in Alcatraz prison in California from January 3 to August 7, 1895.

1948: A constitution and bylaws for the Eskimos of the Native Village of Kwinhagak were approved in an election with a vote of 35–0.

1965: At the University of Oklahoma, more than 500 leaders from most of the Oklahoma tribes held a meeting. They formed the organization Oklahomans for Indian Opportunity. One of the organization's first projects worked on community improvement, job training, and leadership programs for Indian youth.

1975: An election to amend the constitution of the Yerington Paiute Tribe of Nevada was authorized by the commissioner of Indian affairs. The election was held on November 7, 1975.

1979: The area director of the Phoenix area office of the Bureau of Indian Affairs had authorized an election for an amendment to the constitution and bylaws of the Walker River Paiute Tribe of Nevada. The election results were 117–58 in favor of the amendment.

August 8

1587: A little over a week earlier, one of the English colonists in the Roanoke Colony in North Carolina was killed by an Indian. Colony leader John White led two dozen men in a raid to punish the killer. Their zeal for revenge outweighed their judgment, though. They killed a Crotan Indian, but it was the wrong one. Some historians believed this might have led to the eventual disappearance of the Roanoke Colony.

1699: The Tohome Indians lived along the Gulf Coast in Alabama and Mississippi. In Biloxi, they formally established peaceful relations with the French.

1744: France gave trader Joseph Deruisseau the sole rights to trade with Indians in the area of the Missouri and Kansas Rivers. He built Fort Cavagnial (or Fort de la Trinite, in what is now modern Kansas City).

1760: The governor of South Carolina had accused the Cherokees of murdering a white man. When he demanded that two major chiefs be turned over for execution and that twenty-four others be handed over for thinking about aggressive acts, a war developed. The Cherokees attacked a column en route to Fort Loudoun in southeastern Tennessee (near modern Vonore).

1780: American forces under George Rogers Clark attacked the Shawnee village of Piqua in Kentucky. The Americans won the fight. Clark's cousin Joseph Rogers was being held captive by the Shawnee. He was shot and killed as an Indian by the Americans.

1814: The day before the end of the Fort Jackson Treaty, which officially ended the Creek War, Tustunnuggee Thlucco, representing Jackson's Creek allies, presented him with a parcel of land three miles square, "in remembrance of the important services you have done us." The Creek, his allies, lost much of their lands under this treaty, so the purpose of the gift was not really certain. Was it sincere, or a subtle joke?

1840: A Comanche war party attacked the Texas community of Linnville on the Gulf of Mexico. They killed a few settlers and traders and destroyed much of the town. They also took some captives.

1850: Lieutenant Colonel Edwin Sumner established Fort Atkinson (west of modern Dodge City, Kansas). The fort was used as a base for the next four years to control the Indians along this stretch of the Santa Fe Trail. The fort was made entirely of sod.

1855: A treaty was signed between the United States and the Capote Band of Utah Indians in "Abiquiu," New Mexico Territory.

1856: Fort Simcoe was established at a site southwest of what is modern Yakima, Washington.

1864: Lucinda Ewbanks, another adult, and three children were taken prisoner from their home along the Little Blue River by a group of Cheyenne. She would eventually be turned over to the army.

1865: This day marked the first written use of the name "Sitting Bull" in English.

1867: According to army records, members of the Thirty-First Infantry fought with a band of Indians near Fort Stevenson, Dakota Territory. One civilian was killed.

1868: According to army records, members of the Twenty-Third Infantry and some Indian scouts fought with a band of Indians in the Juniper Mountains of Idaho. During the campaign, which lasted until September 5, sixteen Indians were captured.

1877: Traveling from Fort Robinson in northwestern Nebraska, 235 Northern Cheyenne men, 312 women, and 386 children arrived at the Cheyenne and Arapaho Agency at Fort Reno in central Indian Territory (present-day Oklahoma). The military guard turned them over to the local Indian agent. The Cheyenne had surrendered after the army campaigns of 1877.

1879: Colonel Nelson Miles's troops had been seeking out "half-breeds" believed to be supplying Sitting Bull's Sioux with food, guns, and ammunition. Miles reported that his soldiers had arrested 829 "half-breeds" and interdicted 665 carts of supplies.

1938: Legal questions were raised about the legality of the use of peyote as a sacrament in religious ceremonies by Indians on reservations in South Dakota.

1947: The constitution and bylaws of the Coeur d'Alene Tribe of Idaho were approved by Acting Commissioner of Indian Affairs William Zimmerman Jr.

1953: An election was held on a proposed Amendment 5 to the constitution and bylaws of the Confederated Tribes of the Warm Springs Reservation of Oregon. The amendment was approved by a margin of 200–47.

1961: An election that approved a resolution to adopt a constitution and bylaws for the Wichita

Indian Tribe of Oklahoma was ratified by Martin Mangan, acting commissioner of Indian affairs. The election was held on May 8, 1961.

1973: The area director of the Bureau of Indian Affairs authorized an election for amendments to the constitution for the Gila River Pima-Maricopa Indian Community.

AUGUST 9

1646: According to some sources, a treaty was reached between the Providence Plantations and the Wampanoag Indians. Peace was pledged, and the Indians gave up some lands.

1757: French and Indians under Montcalm took Fort William Henry on Lake George.

1805: Pike began his Mississippi expedition.

1814: The Treaty of Fort Jackson (7 Stat. 120) officially ended the Creek War. The Creek, including those who fought with Andrew Jackson, were forced to cede 22 million acres, almost half their lands, to the United States. Timpoochee Barnard, one of the Yuchi Indian allies of the Americans, was one of the signatories to the Treaty of Fort Jackson. Fort Jackson, formerly Fort Toulouse, was located at a site in what is modern Wetumpka, Alabama.

1823: In June, Arikara warriors attacked an American expedition. A force of 500 Sioux warriors found the Arikara, and a battle took place. Colonel Henry Leavenworth soon arrived with his force of 200 soldiers. He reported that his men killed fifty Arikara and that the Sioux killed fifteen. The Sioux lost two warriors.

1833: Representatives of the American Fur Company arrived at Fort McKenzie on the Missouri River. This was the start of the first continuous trader operations among the Blackfeet. Among those present were Iron Shirt (Blood), Bear Chief (Piegan), and Prince Maximilian of Wied-Neuwied.

1842: The United States and Britain agreed to a treaty that established a border between Maine and Canada.

1843: Penateka Comanche Chief Pahayuca signed a truce with Texas Commissioner of Indian Affairs Joseph Eldredge. A full-fledged treaty was not arranged, though.

1869: At Grinnell Station, Kansas, Indians destroyed 150 yards of telegraph lines before the station detachment could chase them off.

1877: During the Nez Perce War, the army was led by Colonel John Gibbon (they had found the remains of Custer's forces after the Battle of the Little Bighorn). Depending on the source, 183 to 191 soldiers started the fight, twenty-nine to thirty-one soldiers were killed, including Captain William Logan and First Lieutenant James Bradley, and forty soldiers were wounded, including Colonel Gibbon. The soldiers on this day mounted a surprise attack at dawn. The Nez Perce set up eighty-nine tepees in a mountain valley called the Big Hole (west of modern Wisdom, Montana). The soldiers took the upper hand in the fighting early on. When the Nez retreated, the victorious soldiers did not follow. This allowed the Nez Perce to regroup and mount a counterattack. Captain Richard Comba, in charge of the burial detail, reported finding the bodies of eighty-nine Nez Perce on the battleground. Chief Joseph reported his losses as thirty warriors and fifty women and children killed during the fight, which ended the next day. Private Lorenzo D. Brown, Company A, Seventh Infantry, Private Wilfred Clark, Company L, Second Cavalry, First Sergeant William D. Edwards, Company F, Seventh Infantry, musician John McLennon, Company A, Sergeant Patrick Rogan, Company A, and Sergeant Milden Wilson, Company I, would be awarded the Medal of Honor for their actions.

1878: As a part of the Bannock War, Captain Harry C. Egbert and his Twelfth Infantry troops found 100 hostile Indians on an island in Bennett's Creek. After several hours of sniping by both sides, the Indians escaped toward the Snake River.

1880: According to a report from the commanding officer of Fort Davis, Texas, General Byrne from Fort Worth was killed by Indians near Fort Quitman, in western Texas near the Rio Grande.

1911: Yahi Indian Ishi (portrayed in the film *The Last of His Tribe*) came into Oroville, California.

1946: An act (60 Stat. 962) was passed by Congress to "provide that any restricted Indian lands in the State of Washington may be leased for various purposes for periods not to exceed twenty-five years under regulations prescribed by the Secretary of the Interior provided that such leases are not for the exploitation of any natural resources."

1955: An act (69 Stat. 539) was passed by Congress to "provide for the leasing of restricted lands of deceased Indians for the benefit of their heirs or devisees. To restrict the payment of advance rent or other consideration for the use of land leased to be paid or collected more than one year in advance unless so provided in the lease. To provide that no lease will be approved by the Secretary that contains any provision that will prevent or delay a termination of Federal trust responsibilities with respect to the land during the term of the lease. To provide that nothing contained in this title shall be construed to repeal any authority to lease restricted Indian lands conferred by or pursuant to any other provision of law."

Every: Picuris Pueblo festival (through August 10).

AUGUST 10

1680: The Pueblo Rebellion took place in New Mexico under the leadership of a Tewa named Popé. Popé had arranged for attacks on as many of the Spanish missions as possible to take place on the same day. (Also recorded as happening on August 11.)

1703: As a part of Queen Anne's War, French officers led 500 Indians against the settlers at Wells, Maine, near the New Hampshire border. Thirty-nine settlers were killed or captured.

1707: On the fourth anniversary of the August 10 attack on Wells, Maine, Indians staged another attack. Six settlers were killed in the fighting.

1815: Skaniadariio (Handsome Lake), the half-brother of Cornplanter, had been born near Ganawagus, New York, sometime around 1735. He fought in many battles during the French and Indian Wars and during the American Revolution. Later he battled alcoholism. One day a vision led him to give up drinking and to promote traditional Indian ways among his people. He became a chief among the Seneca based on his wise council. He once spoke before President Jefferson on behalf of his people. His teachings were handed down among the Iroquois. He died on this day in Onondaga.

1823: One day earlier a force of soldiers under Colonel Henry Leavenworth allied with Sioux warriors defeated a band of Arikara. The three groups started peace talks. The Sioux left at the end of the day. The talks continued for two more days. Eventually the Arikara paid some small fines and rapidly left the area. They joined up with some nearby Mandan.

1825: The Great and Little Osage Treaty (7 Stat. 268) was signed in Council Grove, Kansas.

1843: A peace conference was held between Texans and the Comanche at Bird's Fort (between modern Dallas and Fort Worth).

1861: Stand Watie's Cherokee troops fought on the Confederate side at the Battle of Wilson's Creek in southern Missouri. The Confederates were victorious. However, the participation of the Cherokees on the side of the South led to further tensions among Cherokees who wished to remain neutral. According to some sources, the first Cherokee to die in the Civil War fell during this battle.

1868: Lieutenant Colonel Alfred Sully was in the field near the Cimarron River in Kansas with a long column of troops. A group of Indians attacked the front and rear of the column. The advance troops charged; two Indians were killed, and the soldiers lost none. In the rear, the soldiers put up a defense and lost one man. The Indians sustained ten fatalities, and twelve were reported wounded during the engagement.

1868: Approximately 225 Cheyenne, Arapaho, and Sioux descended upon settlements on the Saline River north of Fort Harker in central Kansas. After being fed by the settlers, the Indians attacked. They looted and burned six homes and brutally assaulted four females, according to official army reports.

1869: According to army records, people near Fort Buford in Dakota Territory fought with a band of Indians. Four civilians were killed.

1877: The Second Cavalry, Seventh Infantry soldiers, and local volunteers under Colonel John Gibbon fought the Nez Perce Indians in the Big Hole Basin of Montana. According to army documents, eighty-nine Indians, six volunteers, twenty-one soldiers, Captain William Logan, and First Lieutenant J.H. Bradley were killed. Colonel Gibbon, Captain Constant Williams, Lieutenant C.A. Coolidge, Lieutenant S. English, Lieutenant C.A. Woodruff, thirty-one soldiers, and four volunteers were wounded in the fighting that started the day before.

1879: Fifth Infantry soldiers under Lieutenant Colonel J.N.G. Whistler accepted the surrender of Fast Bull and fifty-six of his followers near Poplar Creek and the Missouri River in Montana.

1973: An election on July 18 had approved a constitution and bylaws for the Cortina Band of Indians on the Cortina Indian Rancheria in Colusa County, California. Marvin Franklin, assistant secretary of the interior, ratified the results.

1876: Terry and Crook joined up on the Rosebud.

1946: An act of Congress (60 Stat. 976) was passed and allowed the formation of a constitution and bylaws for the United Keetoowah Band of Cherokee Indians of Oklahoma.

AUGUST 11

1539: According to some sources, Hernando de Soto's expedition would leave the Florida village of Cale. They were en route to "Ochile."

1680: The Pueblo Rebellion took place in New Mexico under the leadership of a Tewa named Popé. Popé had arranged for attacks on as many of the Spanish missions as possible to take place on the same day. (Also recorded as happening on August 10.)

1760: In retaliation for the murder of seventeen Cherokee chiefs held hostage in Fort Prince George, Cherokee warriors killed thirty of the prisoners they took when Fort Loudoun fell a few days earlier. The Fort Loudoun Massacre led to retaliation by the English.

1762: According to some reports, a conference regarding questions over land and the return of prisoners was held for the next eighteen days between representatives of the British in Pennsylvania and the Conoy, Delaware, Kickapoo, Miami, Shawnee, and Six Nations tribes.

1802: Tecumseh predicted an earthquake, which came to be known as the New Madrid Earthquake.

1827: At Butte des Morts near Lake Winnebago, Wisconsin, Lewis Cass and Thomas McKenney signed a treaty (7 Stat. 303) with the Winnebago, Chippewa, and Menominee Indians. This established boundaries between the involved tribes and other tribes who had moved into Wisconsin.

1830: The president held a meeting about Indian removal from the southern states.'

1835: Private Kinsley Dalton became the first soldier to die in the Seminole War; he was killed by a Seminole warrior.

1873: According to army reports, Lieutenant Colonel George Custer and ten troops of the Seventh Cavalry were attacked by a large group of Sioux Indians on the Yellowstone River in Montana. Four Indians were killed. Lieutenant Charles Braden and three enlisted men were wounded.

This was considered to be a part of Stanley's Yellowstone expedition.

1874: Colonel Nelson Miles and eight companies from the Seventh Cavalry, four companies from the Fifth Infantry, some artillery, Delaware Indian trackers, and other scouts left Fort Dodge, Kansas. They were en route to Texas to take part in the Red River War.

1978: The American Indian Religious Freedom Act (92 Stat. 469) was passed by Congress. Its purpose was to "protect and preserve the American Indians' inherent right to believe, express, and exercise their traditional religion, including access to sites, use and possession of sacred objects, worship through ceremonials, traditional rites."

1988: The Aleut received restitution for losses in World War II.

AUGUST 12

3114 B.C.: According to the Maya in Chetumal, Mexico, the present creation of the world took place. It will end in 2012. Some Maya sources say this happened on August 11th or August 13th. A few sources list the year as 3113 B.C.

1676: During a skirmish with white colonists, King Philip of the Wampanoag was urged by one of his warriors to end the battle. Philip became so angry with the suggestion that he clubbed the warrior to death. The dead warrior's brother, Alderman, went to Captain Benjamin Church and offered to lead him to King Philip. On this day, good to his word, Alderman showed Church and his men King Philip's camp in a swamp at Mount Hope. The soldiers surrounded Philip. As Philip attempted to escape by a back trail, Alderman, stationed near Church, shot and killed him. Philip's head was taken to Plymouth and displayed on a pole for two decades. This ended King Philip's War. As many as 600 English and perhaps five times that many Indians were killed during the war.

1760: According to some reports, representatives of the British and the Six Nations met to discuss friendship between the two groups.

1764: According to some sources, the Wyandot signed a peace treaty at Presque Isle, Pennsylvania, with Colonel John Bradstreet as a part of Pontiac's Uprising.

1769: Kumeyaay Indians fought with Spaniards who had established the Mission San Diego de Alcala in what became San Diego, California.

1819: A council had been held in the Choctaw Nation for the last few days. Andrew Jackson, John McKee, and Daniel Burnet were trying to convince the Choctaw to move west of the Mississippi River. Chief Pushmataha bluntly told them the Choctaw would not move from their lands.

1831: George Gaines, a white man whom the Choctaws trusted, was appointed special agent to supervise the "collection and removal" of the Choctaws to the west bank of the Mississippi River. There they were turned over to the army.

1840: A band of as many as 1,000 Comanche and Kiowa Indians had been raiding the area from Austin to the Gulf Coast of Texas. While between San Antonio and Austin on Plum Creek (near modern Lockhart), they encountered General Felix Huston's troops, including Colonel Edward Burleson from the Battle of the Neches, and a few Tonkawa; a fight developed. According to reports by the Texans, eighty-six Indians and two Texans were killed in the fighting. The Tonkawa were reported to have dined on some Comanche limbs that evening in celebration of the victory.

1861: Albert Pike signed two treaties. Both gave the Indians agreements similar to those signed by the Creek on July 10, 1861. One treaty was signed by the Wichita, Caddo, and Penateka Comanche. The other treaty was signed by four bands of the Plains Comanche.

1865: The Snake Indians agreed to go to the Klamath Reservation.

1868: A large group of Indians again attacked Lieutenant Colonel Alfred Sully's troops, who were encamped near the Cimarron River in Kansas. An attempt to stampede the army horses was foiled. During several hours of heavy fighting, two soldiers were killed, three wounded. Indian losses were reported as twelve killed and fifteen wounded.

1868: According to army records, settlers fought with a band of Indians near the Solomon River in Kansas. Seventeen settlers were killed and four were wounded.

1868: The same group of Cheyenne, Arapaho, and Sioux that attacked the Saline River settlements attacked settlements along the Solomon River, Kansas. They looted and burned five homes. Fifteen people were killed and five women were assaulted. A small band of this group crossed to the Republican River and killed two people there. The main body of Indians returned to the Saline River area. There they encountered Captain F.W. Benteen and his Seventh Cavalry troopers, who had rushed to the area from Fort Zarah in central Kansas. A running skirmish took place for more than ten miles.

1868: According to the army, settlers fought with a group of Indians near the Republican River in Kansas. Two settlers were killed in the fighting.

1878: The Paiute Chief Oytes and his followers surrendered. This effectively ended Paiute participation in the Bannock War.

1881: Captain Charles Parker and nineteen Ninth Cavalry, Company K, troopers attacked Nana's Apache twenty-five miles west of Sabinal, New Mexico, in Carrizo Canyon. One soldier was killed, three wounded, and one reported missing. Captain Parker estimated the Indian losses to be similar to his own. The Indians escaped after the fighting. For his actions in defending the right side of the soldiers' position, Sergeant George Jordan would be awarded the Medal of Honor. Sergeant Thomas Shaw would

also be awarded the medal for his actions during the fighting.

1971: A trust patent was issued containing 640 acres for the Pechanga Indian Reservation–Temecula Band of Luiseno Mission Indians.

1983: Stanley Speaks, the area director of the Bureau of Indian Affairs, ratified the Nez Perce election to amend their constitution and bylaws.

Every: Santa Clara Pueblo festival.

AUGUST 13

1521: Montezuma's nephew and successor, Cuahtemoc (or Guatimozin, according to some sources), surrendered to Cortés.

1587: Manteo, a Crotan Indian, had converted to the Church of England. He was baptized by Sir Walter Raleigh. In respect for Manteo's help with Raleigh's colonists, Raleigh gave him the title "Lord of Roanoke and of Dasamonquepeuk."

1645: For several years, the Dutch and the local Indian tribes near New Amsterdam and Pavonia had been fighting. Hackensack Chief Oratamin negotiated a peace between the warring parties. It was another ten years before another major conflict erupted.

1720: A Spanish expeditionary force of forty-two Spaniards and sixty Indians led by Don Pedro de Villasur had set out to show the flag in territory claimed by Spain. They were concerned about French incursions into their territory in the Central Plains. The Spanish and their Indian allies were attacked by a force of French and Pawnee on the North Platte River. Most of the Spanish expedition was killed in the fighting. (Also recorded as happening on August 15.)

1777: Local Indians attacked three Spanish soldiers in San Juan Bautista Valley in modern San Diego County, California. Two of the soldiers escaped; the other was killed.

1786: In a letter to Colonel Benjamin Hawkins, Thomas Jefferson expressed the idea that Indians did not own their lands but were instead only "tenants at will" in lands that the United States had a mandate to own.

1803: The Kaskaskia Treaty (7 Stat. 78) was signed in Vincennes, Indiana. The Indians ceded all lands in Illinois to the United States. The treaty said they had depopulated that area and no longer needed it. The Kaskaskia got to keep 350 acres of Illinois near the township of Kaskaskia. They were granted this small spot by a congressional act on March 3, 1791. They were also allowed to keep an additional 1,280 acres of land in Illinois. The United States would protect the Kaskaskia from other Indians. Their annuity increased to $1,000. A house and a fenced field of 100 acres were provided for the chief. They got $100 a year for seven years to support a Catholic priest and $300 to build a church. They received $580 to pay for goods and debts. The Indians were able to hunt on their old lands, as long as the lands remained government property. The treaty was signed by William Henry Harrison and six Indians, including Jean Baptiste Ducoigne, principal chief of the Kaskaskia.

1866: Elements of the Fourteenth Infantry fought some Indians near Skull Valley, Arizona. One soldier was killed, another wounded. Eighteen Indians were killed and two were wounded, according to Fourteenth Infantry records.

1867: According to army records, members of the Twenty-Seventh Infantry fought with a band of Indians near O'Conner's Springs, Dakota Territory. Three soldiers were wounded.

1868: A treaty (15 Stat. 693) was signed with the Nez Perce. This was the last of 370 treaties made by the U.S. government and Indian tribes.

1868: According to army records, members of the Seventh Cavalry under Captain F.W. Benteen fought with a band of Indians near the Salinas River in Kansas. Three Indians were killed and ten were wounded.

1868: For a third time, Indians attacked Lieutenant Colonel Alfred Sully and his column of Third Infantry troops near the Cimarron River in Kansas. One soldier was killed, four wounded. Ten Indians were killed and twelve wounded, according to army reports.

1868: According to army records, members of the Eighth Cavalry fought with a band of Indians near Walnut Grove, Arizona. Three Indians were killed.

1872: A few young Indians attacked Brevet Colonel E.M. Baker's forces late at night near Pryor's Fork, Montana.

1880: Captain Nicholas Nolan, Troop A, Tenth Cavalry, Troop K, Eighth Cavalry, a few Lipan Indian scouts, and some Texas Rangers chased Victorio's Indians across the Rio Grande into Mexico twelve miles below Quitman, Texas.

1946: The Indian Claims Commission was established to settle land claims.

1949: An act of Congress (63 Stat. 604) added almost 60,000 acres to the Zuni Reservation System in Arizona and New Mexico. It also "authorize[d] the Secretary to exchange or consolidate lands or interests therein for the Pueblo or Canoncito Navajo, to include improvements & water rights. Title to lands acquired shall be in trust status."

1954: The federal Termination Act said that tribes would no longer receive federal assistance.

1970: The secretary of the interior ratified the tribal election that authorized amendments to the constitution of the Zuni Tribe on July 9, 1970.

1971: Acting Deputy Commissioner of Indian Affairs Harold D. Cox ratified an election that approved an amendment to the constitution and by-laws of the Paiute-Shoshone Tribe of the Fallon Reservation and Colony.

1973: The Office of Indian Rights was proposed by the Department of Justice.

1975: The secretary of the interior authorized an election for a constitution and bylaws for the Southern Ute Indian Tribe of the Southern Ute Reservation in Colorado. The election was held on September 26, 1975.

AUGUST 14

1559: Tristan de Luna y Arellano had been appointed to establish Spanish settlements on Pensacola Bay by the Spanish Viceroy in Mexico. His expedition of thirteen ships, several priests, 500 soldiers, and 1,000 settlers arrived in Pensacola Bay in Florida. Much of the expedition was killed or starved because of a hurricane that struck the area a few days later.

1676: Abenaki warriors attacked the village of Arrowsic, Maine. An Abenaki woman had sought refuge in the fort. Late that night, she opened the gates and let the warriors in and the fighting began.

1756: Fort George was attacked at a site in what is modern Oswego, New York.

1812: Tecumseh told Sir Isaac Brock, "We gave the forest-clad mountains and valleys full of game, and in return what did they give our warriors and our women? Rum and trinkets and a grave."

1836: Creek already established in the Indian Territory (present-day Oklahoma) held a council to decide how to deal with the forced emigrants soon to arrive. Roley McIntosh did not want the new arrivals to take over. Government forces proclaimed McIntosh the Creek leader. The new Creek arrivals acknowledged McIntosh's leadership role.

1849: Indian Agent James Calhoun and Lieutenant Colonel John Washington officially organized a military expedition in Santa Fe. They left for the lands of the Navajos on August 16.

1867: According to army records, members of the Eighteenth Infantry fought with a band of Indians near Fort Reno, Dakota Territory. No injuries or fatalities were reported.

1867: According to army records, members of the Twenty-Seventh Infantry skirmished with some Indians near Chalk Springs, Dakota Territory. One soldier was killed.

1868: On the Republican River, near Granny Creek, Indians looted and burned a home. One person was killed; one woman was captured and assaulted.

Buffalo roaming, protected by law as early as 1877 (author photo)

1868: Near Fort Zarah (near modern Great Bend) in central Kansas, Indians stole twenty mules, which were recaptured by troops later that day. During the conflict, one soldier and five Indians were wounded and one Indian was reported killed.

1872: Major E.M. Baker and Troops F, G, H, and L, Second Cavalry, and Companies C, E, G, and I, Seventh Infantry, were near Pryor's Fork, Montana, when they were attacked by several hundred Cheyenne and Sioux. According to army files, one soldier and one citizen were killed. Three soldiers were wounded. The Indian tally was two killed and ten wounded, "most of them mortally." During some of the fighting, Sitting Bull sat in an open area and smoked. He did this while soldiers shot at him. It was to prove his bravery.

1876: A steamer loaded with soldiers fired on some Indians near Fort Buford, Dakota Territory. According to army documents, no casualties were reported.

1877: The Northwest Territorial Council passed a law to protect the wholesale destruction of the buffalo (bison). The law limited the ways in which they could be killed and the purposes for which they could be killed.

1879: Lieutenant Colonel J.N.G. Whistler and soldiers under Colonel Nelson Miles's command captured fifty-seven Rosebud Agency Indians crossing the Missouri near Poplar Creek. According to army information, these Indians were headed to Canada to join Sitting Bull.

1880: En route from Redwater, Montana, to the Poplar Creek Agency, the soldiers of Company H, Fifth Infantry, encountered twenty lodges of hostile Indians who wished to surrender. Company H delivered them to Fort Keogh in eastern Montana. Also, Troop E, Second Cavalry, brought in twenty-four lodges (approximately 140 Indians) of Minneconjou captured at the Missouri River.

August 15

1514: Spanish Bishop Bartolomé de Las Casas released the Indians he held as serfs in Hispaniola.

1642: In instructions to Pennsylvania Governor John Printz of New Sweden, the queen of Sweden wished for "the wild nations" to be treated kindly and in a humane manner. She also stated that the Indians were the "rightful lords" of this land and must be treated accordingly.

1680: As a part of Tewa leader Popé's coordinated attack on the Spanish missions of New Mexico, the siege of Santa Fe began.

1749: Maliseet chiefs ratified and agreed to the Treaty of December 15, 1725.

1769: Kumeyaay Indians engaged in a second skirmished with the Spaniards who had established the Mission San Diego de Alcala in what became San Diego, California.

1782: Tonight, British Captain William Caldwell, Simon Girty, and 200 Indians surrounded Bryan's Station in Kentucky in preparation to attack the settlement the next day.

1812: British and Indian forces confronted Fort Detroit.

1812: General William Hull ordered Captain William Wells to abandon Fort Dearborn in present-day Chicago. As the occupants were leaving, almost 500 Indians attacked them. Half of the Americans were killed; the other half were taken prisoner.

1858: Lieutenant J.K. Allen and fifteen soldiers surrounded the Yakima camp of Katihotes. They captured seventy-one Indians and some livestock. A few of the captured Indians were determined to be the murderers of two local miners. They were shot. Lieutenant Allen was killed during the early-morning attack.

1861: Oktarharsars Harjo, called Sands by the whites, and Opothle Yahola, representing the pro-Union Creek, wrote to President Lincoln requesting the protection promised in their removal treaties.

1862: The Santee Sioux's annuity had not arrived on time. On August 5, the Santee surrounded the food warehouse serving the upper villages. The soldiers allowed them to take the food. The commander told Agent Thomas Galbraith to give the Indians the food on credit. The Indians got Galbraith to promise to distribute food to the Santee in the lower villages. On this day, Galbraith joined four local traders at the lower villages. The Indians soon realized that Galbraith did not plan on distributing the food until the money arrived. Galbraith asked the local traders what they wanted to do. Andrew Myrick said, "If they are hungry, let them eat grass or their own dung." This comment came back to haunt him when the Santee revolted. The Santee were furious, but they left anyway.

1869: According to army records, members of the Third Cavalry fought with a band of Indians near San Augustine Pass in New Mexico. No casualties were reported.

1872: Captain William McCleave and Troop B, Eighth Cavalry, were attacked by Indians on Palo Duro Creek in New Mexico Territory. Four Indians were killed. One soldier and eight Indians were wounded.

1876: Sixth Cavalry soldiers and some Indian scouts fought a group of Indians in "Red Rock Country," Arizona. According to army documents, seven Indians were killed and seven were captured. One soldier was wounded in the fighting.

1876: Congress passed a law requiring the Indians to relinquish their lands in the Powder River and the Black Hills regions.

1935: Cherokee humorist Will Rogers died.

1936: Secretary of the Interior Harold Ickes ratified the election to adopt a constitution and bylaws by the Lac du Flambeau Band of Lake Superior Chippewa Indians of Wisconsin.

1959: By a vote of 21–0, the Articles of Association of the Pala Band of Mission Indians, California, were adopted.

1987: The United States Post Office issued the Red Cloud stamp.

Every: Zia Pueblo festival.

AUGUST 16

1692: The Diego de Vargas campaign to reconquer New Mexico took place.

1740: According to some sources, a conference regarding a peace agreement and a "covenant with the southern Indians" was held for the next four days by representatives of Great Britain and the Six Nations.

1780: Northumberland County, Pennsylvania, settlers sent a petition to the Supreme Executive Council asking for soldiers to defend them against attacks from Indians raiding the area.

1782: About 300–400 Indians and a few whites, led by British Captain William Caldwell and Simon Girty, attacked the settlement at Bryan's Station near Lexington, Kentucky. John Craig was commanding the forty-two Americans inside the community's fort. After several skirmishes, the Indians eventually got tired of the fight and left the next day. Only a few of the settlers were killed in this fight, but many of the survivors died in the Battle of Blue Licks on August 19, 1782.

1812: Shawnee Chief Tecumseh had been commissioned as a brigadier general by the British. With his Indian forces, he was instrumental in the surrender of American forces at Fort Detroit.

1849: Indian Agent James Calhoun and Lieutenant Colonel John Washington organized a military expedition on August 14. They left Santa Fe for the Navajo lands.

1851: One in a series of treaties with California Indians was signed at Reading's Ranch. The treaty was designed to reserve lands and to protect the Indians.

1872: A fight took place at O'Fallon's Creek in Montana.

1872: Colonel D.S. Stanley and soldiers from the Twenty-Second Infantry were attacked by a large group of Indians near the Yellowstone River in Montana. Army reports did not mention the outcome of the skirmish.

1873: A tract of land was set aside as a reservation for the Crow Indians as part of an agreement.

1880: Sergeant Edward Davern with eight soldiers from Troop F, Seventh Cavalry, and three Indian scouts attacked a Sioux war party on Box Elder Creek in Montana. Two hostile Indians were killed and one was wounded.

1881: Lieutenant Gustavus Valois and Troop I, Ninth Cavalry, battled fifty Indians near Cuchillo Negro in New Mexico. Two soldiers were killed, and Lieutenant George R. Burnett was wounded twice. Lieutenant Burnett would win the Medal of Honor for his efforts in rescuing a fallen comrade. First Sergeant Moses Williams, Sergeant Brent Woods, and Private Augustus Walley would also win the nation's highest award for their bravery in the fighting, which lasted for several hours. Several Indians were reported killed by Valois. Lieutenant F.B. Taylor's Ninth Cavalry forces had a skirmish with Indians near the Black Range as well.

1954: The constitution of the Standing Rock Sioux Tribe was amended.

1964: The Pit River Indian Tribe unanimously adopted a constitution in a meeting, according to their tribal council.

1980: The secretary of the interior had authorized an election for amendments to the constitution and bylaws of the Lac Courte Oreilles Band of

Lake Superior Chippewa Indians of Wisconsin. The amendments passed.

AUGUST 17

1755: Almost 400 Indians attacked John Kilburn's stockade at Walpole, Connecticut. Some sources recorded that the Indians were led by King Philip. After a day of fighting, the Indians withdrew.

1765: Pontiac and the British signed a treaty.

1788: Losantiville (Cincinnati) was founded.

1822: The Lipan Apache signed a peace treaty with Mexico at Alcaldes de Las Villas de la Provincia Laredo.

1836: Creek Indian and West Point graduate David Moniac was promoted to captain during the Seminole War. He was killed in fighting on November 21, 1836.

1846: According to Admiral Stockton, California was now a part of the United States.

1866: Soldiers from the First Arizona Infantry fought with a band of Indians on the Salt River in Arizona. The army reported one Indian killed and one captured.

1867: According to army records, Pawnee scouts led by Captain James Murie fought with a band of hostile Indians near Plum Creek, Nebraska. Fifteen hostiles were killed and two were captured.

1868: Forty Kansans had been killed recently by Indians. The governor wrote the president asking for help.

1869: In an event that would contribute to the Baker Massacre (also known as the Marias Massacre) that took place on January 23, 1870, Malcolm Clarke was killed by several Piegan, including Owl Child, near Helena, Montana.

1872: Captain Lewis Thompson reported one of his men from Troop L, Second Cavalry, was wounded in a skirmish with Indians on the Yellowstone River in Montana.

1876: President Grant, by executive order, corrected a survey mistake and returned Uncompah-

gre Park and some prime farmland to the Ute Reservation.

1880: Seventh Cavalry soldiers fought a group of Indians near the Little Missouri River in Montana. According to army documents, two Indians were killed and one was wounded.

1936: According to Federal Register No. 1FR01226, the government ordered the purchase of land to create the Flandreau Indian Reservation in South Dakota.

1961: The boundaries of the Cocopah Tribe Reservation near Somerton, Arizona, were modified.

1983: John Fritz, deputy assistant secretary for Indian affairs, authorized an election for a proposed constitution for the Jamestown Klallam Tribe of Indians.

AUGUST 18

1804: A treaty (7 Stat. 81) was concluded with the Delaware Indians at Vincennes, Indiana. The treaty explained that the Indians wanted more money and that the government wanted a connection between the Wabash settlements and Kentucky. The Delaware ceded all of their lands between the Ohio and Wabash Rivers. They also ceded lands below the tract ceded by the Fort Wayne Treaty of June 7, 1803, and the road from Vincennes to the falls of the Ohio River. The tribe got an extra $300 for ten years. They received $300 a year for five years to teach them "agricultural and domestic arts." They got $400 worth of livestock and $800 worth of goods immediately. Stolen horses were restored to their rightful owners. The United States negotiated with the Piankashaw over lands both tribes claimed. William Henry Harrison and five Indians signed the treaty.

1854: Captain Jesse Walker attacked the Modoc on Tule Lake. Several minor engagements continued until a peace treaty was reached on September 4, 1854.

1862: Santee Sioux attacked the Lower Agency in Minnesota as one of the first moves of the Santee Sioux Uprising. As many as 400 whites died the first day.

1863: As a part of the Canyon de Chelly Campaign, Kit Carson and General James Charlatan were trying to starve the Navajos into submission. General Charlatan put a bounty on Navajo livestock. Every good horse or mule brought $20, quite a sum for those days. Each sheep earned a dollar.

1865: Colonel Nelson Cole and troops composed of Missouri infantry and artillery were marching from Nebraska to the Black Hills in southwestern South Dakota. Colonel Samuel Walker and his troops from the Kansas cavalry were marching from Fort Laramie in southeastern Wyoming to the Black Hills. Their combined forces of 2,000 troops met on the Belle Fourche River. Their orders were to meet General Patrick Connor on the Rosebud River to engage the hostile Indians in the area. The soldiers' supplies were running very short.

1868: Near Pawnee Fork in southwestern Kansas, Indians attacked a wagon train. They stopped the train, but they were not able to capture it due to resistance from the passengers. Cavalry from Fort Dodge arrived the next day and scattered the Indians. However, the Indians returned twice more. They were unsuccessful on both occasions. Five men were wounded. The Indian casualties were estimated at five killed and ten wounded.

1871: A settler was killed and his livestock was run off by Indians twelve miles from Fort Stanton in central New Mexico. Troops pursued the Indians without success.

1872: Colonel D.S. Stanley and Companies D, F, and G, Twenty-Second Infantry, skirmished with Indians at the mouth of the Powder River. After the fight, the army moved toward O'Fallon's Creek.

1877: Nez Perce Indians staged a raid at Camas Creek.

1881: Lieutenant G.W. Smith and twenty-nine cavalry troopers attacked a band of hostile Indians fifteen miles from McEver's Ranch in New Mexico. Five soldiers, including Lieutenant Smith, were killed in the fighting. A civilian volunteer, George Daly, was also killed.

1936: The secretary of the interior authorized an election for a constitution and bylaws for the Fort McDowell Band of Mohave-Apache Indians.

1976: The commissioner of Indian affairs authorized an election to approve a constitution and bylaws for the Fort Sill Apache Tribe of Oklahoma. The election was held on October 30, 1976.

1990: The Indian Law Enforcement Reform Act (104 Stat. 473) of August 18, 1990, was passed by Congress. It was intended to "clarify and strengthen the authority for certain Dept. of the Interior law enforcement services, activities, and officers in Indian country, and for other purposes."

Every: Chief Seattle Days (through August 20).

AUGUST 19

1607: English settlers officially founded "the other" English colony on North America. Unlike Jamestown, Popham was settled by just men and boys. Popham (northeast of modern Portland, Maine) was established on the bluffs overlooking the spot where the Kennebec River flows into the ocean. The colony lasted only a little more than a year. The colony's second leader returned to England, taking the settlers with him, when he inherited a sizable estate in England.

1719: Joseph le Moyne, Sieur de Serigny, had assisted his brother Jean le Moyne de Bienville with his attack on Pensacola. After the battle he returned to his fortifications on Dauphin Island, Alabama. With 160 French soldiers and 200 local Indians, he prepared for a Spanish assault. The Spanish invasion began. Two warships let loose a cannonade. When 100 Spaniards attempted to land, le Moyne and the Indians fought them off. The Spanish retreated and then gave up the fight.

1746: According to some reports, a conference was held for the next five days between representatives of the British in Massachusetts and New York and the Mississauga and Six Nations tribes regarding alliances.

1749: The Spaniards and the Apache had been trying to arrange a peace for some time. Four Apache chiefs, with their followers, buried a hatchet in a special ceremony at San Antonio, Texas.

1782: Battles had been fought in many areas around Kentucky and Virginia. On August 16, 300–400 Indians and a few whites, led by British Captain William Caldwell and Simon Girty, attacked the settlement at nearby Bryan's Station near Lexington, Kentucky. When reinforcements arrived, the Indians retreated to the area called the Blue Licks, a spring on the Middle Fork of the Linking River. Despite the advice of many frontiersmen such as Daniel Boone to wait for more soldiers, the militia took off after the Indians. The militia fell into the Indians' trap, and about seventy soldiers were killed.

1825: A treaty was signed (7 Stat. 272) by William Clark and Lewis Cass at Prairie du Chien, Wisconsin.

1830: Twenty-one Chickasaw leaders, with their agent Benjamin Reynolds, met President Jackson in Franklin. They held a formal council in a few days to discuss Jackson's removal program.

1854: A Miniconjou Sioux named High Forehead killed a sickly cow near Fort Laramie in southeastern Wyoming. The cow's owner complained to the fort's commander. Brevet Second Lieutenant John L. Grattan and thirty volunteers left the fort to find the Sioux involved. Grattan brashly went to Conquering Bear's Brule Sioux camp near Ash Hollow and demanded the Indian who shot the cow. Grattan made numerous threats to the Sioux, but they would not hand over High Forehead. During the parley, a shot rang out, and Grattan's artillery gunners opened fire on the camp. Conquering Bear tried to get both sides to stop shooting, but he was hit by an artillery round. Eventually, all but one of Grattan's men were killed in the fighting.

Santee Sioux attack on the city of New Ulme

1862: The Santee Sioux attacked New Ulm, Minnesota.

1868: On Twin Buttes Creek, Kansas, a group of woodchoppers was attacked by approximately thirty Indians. Three of the men were killed, and all two dozen of their animals were taken, according to Lieutenant G. Lewis, Fifth Infantry.

1869: According to army records, people in a wagon train from Camp Cook in Montana fought with a band of Indians near Eagle Creek, Montana. One settler and four Indians were killed. Two Indians were wounded. Settlers also fought with a group of Indians near Helena, Montana. One settler was killed and one was wounded.

1869: According to army records, members of the First Cavalry and Thirty-Second Infantry fought with a band of Indians near Camp Grant in the White Mountains of Arizona. Eleven Indians were killed, two were wounded, and thirteen were captured. The fighting started on July 13.

1873: Indians fought with soldiers from the Twenty-Fifth Infantry near Barrilla Springs, Texas, according to army documents. One Indian was killed.

1880: Indian scouts attacked a band of hostile Indians north of the mouth of O'Fallon's Creek in Montana. A dozen head of stock were recovered.

1938: A constitution and bylaws for the Alabama-Coushatta were approved. They were ratified on October 17, 1939.

1960: On March 3, 1921, the federal government set aside land on the Fort Peck Indian Reservation in Montana to establish the townsite of Lodge Pole. By Public Land Order No. 2184, several "undisposed of" lots within the townsite were returned to tribal ownership.

1974: Amendments 7–11 to the constitution and bylaws of the Lac du Flambeau Band of Lake Superior Chippewa Indians of Wisconsin were approved and became effective.

AUGUST 20

1722: According to some sources, a conference on peace and boundary lines was held between representatives of the British in New York, Pennsylvania, and Virginia and the Five Nations.

1789: Juan de Ugalde was commanding general of all Spanish forces in Coahuila, Nuevo León, Nuevo Santander, and Texas. He started a major expedition against the Apache.

1789: An "Act Providing for the Expences Which May Attend Negotiations or Treaties with the Indian Tribes, and the Appointment of Commissioners for Managing the Same" was approved by the United States.

1794: Little Turtle had seen how skillful General Wayne was at organizing his forces. Knowing this would not be like the easy encounters he had had with Harmar and St. Clair, Little Turtle suggested making peace with the whites. He was called a coward, and Turkey Foot took his place as war chief. About 800 warriors, including 100 Cherokees, were waiting for Wayne's forces near Fort Miami (near modern Toledo, Ohio). Many of the Indians had been fasting for days to be "pure for battle." Wayne took this into consideration and slowed his advance so they were weaker.

1802: According to some sources, Seminole near the town of St. Marks in northern Florida signed a treaty with the Spanish.

1819: Major Long reached a Kansa village along the Vermillion River as a part of his scientific expedition in modern Kansas.

1851: One in a series of treaties with California Indians was signed in Lipayuma. This treaty set aside lands for the Indians and protected them from Americans.

1854: Snake Indians attacked a wagon train near Fort Boise, Idaho. Nine men, two women, and eight children were killed.

1862: The Santee Sioux engaged in more fighting in Minnesota when they attacked Fort Ridgely.

1868: According to army records, members of the Thirty-First Infantry fought with a band of Indians near Fort Buford, Dakota Territory. Three soldiers were killed and three were wounded. Lieutenant C.C. Cusick was also wounded during the fighting.

1868: Comstock's Ranch on Pond Creek in Kansas was attacked this evening. Two men were killed; the others escaped by fleeing into Pond Creek.

1874: Three troops from the Eighth Cavalry led by Major William E. Price left Fort Union (New Mexico) to seek out renegade Indians in the valleys of the Canadian and Washita Rivers.

1877: Nez Perce captured 100 mules from General Oliver Howard's command at Camas Meadows, Idaho. Private Wilfred Clark, Company L, Second Cavalry, would be awarded the Medal of Honor for his actions on this day and August 9 at the Battle of Big Hole (Montana). Captain James Jackson, First Cavalry, would also be awarded the Medal of Honor for retrieving the body of his trumpeter while under heavy fire. Company L Farrier William H. Jones would also receive the Medal of Honor for his gallantry during this day's action and for his efforts in the battle of May 7, 1877, against the Sioux. Lieutenant H.M. Benson and six soldiers were wounded.

1878: Second Infantry soldiers fought a group of Indians near Big Creek, Idaho. According to army documents, one soldier was killed.

1879: First Cavalry soldiers fought a group of Indians near the Salmon River, Idaho. According to army documents, one soldier was killed.

1948: The Mi'kmaq Eskasoni First Nation Reserve of Eskasoni No. 3A was established in Nova Scotia.

AUGUST 21

1680: The Spanish left Santa Fe.

1689: Frenchmen convinced local Indians to attack British Fort Charles in Maine. Several settlers were killed in the fighting.

1739: According to some sources, an agreement covering land cession and alliance was reached by representatives of the British in Georgia and the Creek.

1805: A treaty (7 Stat. 91) was concluded with the Delaware, Miami, Eel River, Wea, and Potawatomi Nations at Grouseland near Vincennes, Indiana. The treaty referred to the Treaty of August 18, 1804. The Delaware ceded lands to the Miami. The Miami ceded lands along the Ohio River from the Kentucky River to Fort Recovery on the Ohio-Indiana line. Each tribe received the following payments per year for the next ten years: Miami, $600; Eel River, $250; Wea, $250; Potawatomi, $500. The treaty also addressed several intertribal issues. The document was signed by William Henry Harrison and nineteen Indians.

1861: John Ross had called for a meeting to be held at Tahlequah to discuss the U.S. Civil War. About 4,000 Cherokees attended the meeting in Indian Territory (present-day Oklahoma). It was decided that a united Cherokee Nation was the best policy, so they voted to side with the Confederacy. The Cherokee signed a treaty with the Confederacy in October.

1862: In Tahlequah, Indian Territory (modern Oklahoma), Stand Watie was elected principal chief during the first Confederate Cherokee Convention.

1869: Military guards repelled an attack by Indians on Coyote Station, Kansas. No casualties were sustained on either side.

1872: On this day and the next day, Colonel D.S. Stanley and Companies D, F, and G, Twenty-Second Infantry, fought with Indians along O'Fallon's Creek in Montana.

1871: Treaty No. 2 (Manitoba Post Treaty) was concluded between the Canadian government and the Chippewa, who sold 35,700 square miles of land in exchange for certain reservation lands, an annuity, schools, and other items.

1971: Southwestern Indian Polytechnical Institute was opened in Albuquerque, New Mexico.

1976: The commissioner of Indian affairs had authorized an election for an amendment to the constitution and bylaws of the Manzanita Band of Mission Indians. It was approved 14–3.

AUGUST 22

1670: Hiacoomes preached his first sermon to his Wampanoag people on Martha's Vineyard.

1694: According to some sources, a peace conference was held between representatives of the Five Nations and British colonies in Connecticut, Massachusetts, New Jersey, New York, and Pennsylvania.

1710: According to some sources, a land-cession agreement was reached between representatives of the British in New York and the Mohawk Indians.

1749: Pennsylvania authorities signed an agreement to purchase a large parcel of land between the Delaware and Susquehanna Rivers from the Iroquois, Delaware, and Shomokin Tribes. This purchase included most of what became modern Carbon, Columbia, Dauphin, Lebanon, Luzerne, Monroe, Northumberland, Pike, Schuylkill, and Wayne Counties in Pennsylvania.

1777: After maintaining a siege on Fort Stanwix (near modern Rome, New York) since August 3, British and Indian forces abandoned the siege. The Indian forces had been disheartened by rumors

Tuttassuggy, The Wind, chief of the
Little Osages (NA)

that General Benedict Arnold was leading a force of superior numbers to relieve the siege.

1806: Pike's expedition had reached a village of the Little Osage near the forks of the Osage River in modern Missouri. He held a council there with both the Grand and Little Osage. The Little Osage were led by Tuttassuggy (The Wind), and the Grand Osage were led by Cheveau Blanc (White Hair).

1830: Meeting with Secretary of War Eaton and Jim Coffee, Chickasaw leaders were told that the federal government could not protect them from state laws. The Indians were informed that their only hope was to move to the Indian Territory (present-day Oklahoma). The government offered to pay for the removal, support them for a year, and give them new land. The Chickasaw discussed the issue for a week.

1851: One in a series of treaties was signed with California Indians at the Russian Camp (Camp Fernando Felix). This treaty promised to protect the Indians from angry Europeans and to reserve them lands.

1860: Hunkpapa and Blackfeet vandalized Fort Union.

1862: A force of 800 Santee Sioux attacked Fort Ridgely in south-central Minnesota. The fort was defended by approximately 150 soldiers and two dozen volunteers. The Sioux sneaked up to the fort and tried to set it on fire. When the Sioux attacked, the army responded with an artillery barrage. Little Crow was wounded in the fighting, and Mankato took over. The artillery made the difference in the fighting, and the Sioux retreated.

1867: According to army records, members of the Fourth Cavalry fought with a band of Indians near Fort Chadbourne, Texas. Two soldiers were killed.

1867: According to army records, members of the Boise Indian scouts fought with a band of Indians near Surprise Valley, California. Two Indians were killed and seven were wounded.

1868: According to army records, members of the Eighth Cavalry fought with a band of Indians near the Santa Maria River in Arizona. Two Indians were killed and one was captured.

1872: The Sioux fought the army under Colonel David Stanley near O'Fallon's Creek.

1874: Under the new authority to pursue hostile Indians on reservations, Lieutenant Colonel J.W. Davidson and Troops E, H, and L, Tenth Cavalry, and Company I, Twenty-Fifth Infantry, from Fort Sill in southern Indian Territory (present-day Okla-

Fort Union, one of the largest forts in the West, under attack

homa), entered the Wichita Agency. They engaged Comanche and Kiowa who had taken refuge with friendly Indians on the reservation. Four soldiers were wounded in the fighting. Sixteen Indians were killed or wounded. The hostiles attempted to burn the agency, but the soldiers prevent it.

1877: The Nez Perce entered Yellowstone Park.

1883: The Dawes Commission was sent to Dakota Territory to determine if the methods used to obtain Sioux signatures on a land-cession treaty were fair. On this day, Sitting Bull addressed the commission at the Standing Rock Agency. The commissioners treated Sitting Bull as any other Sioux. Sitting Bull was offended for not being treated as a great leader. He led the Sioux out of the meeting. Eventually, he was convinced by fellow Sioux that he was not insulted, and he met with the commission a second time. This time it was the commissioners who were offended. Their efforts were to mold the Indians into white men. Sitting Bull did not accept this attitude.

AUGUST 23

1724: British forces under Captain Moulton staged a surprise attack on an Abenaki village at Norridgewock. Twenty-seven people, including a resident French priest, Father Rasles, were scalped by the English. The village was burned. This was a big blow to the spirit of the local Indians.

1732: This day marked the beginning of a peace conference held in Philadelphia with the local Indians. Attending the meeting were several Iroquois chiefs, including Onondaga Chief Shikellamy.

1862: The Santee Sioux engaged in another fight.

1867: According to army records, members of the Fourth Cavalry fought with a band of Indians near Fort Concho, Texas. One soldier was killed.

1868: The stage to Cheyenne Wells returned after being chased by thirty Indians. The Denver stagecoach was attacked between Pond Creek, Kansas, and Lake Station, Colorado, according to Captain

Bankhead, Fifth Infantry, commander of Fort Wallace in western Kansas. Eight settlers were killed.

1868: According to army reports, Indians attacked settlers in northern Texas; eight people were killed and 300 cattle were stolen. Bent's Fort in the Texas Panhandle reported that an Indian attack netted fifteen stolen horses and mules and four head of cattle.

1868: According to army records, members of the Thirty-First Infantry fought with a band of Indians near Fort Totten, Dakota Territory. Three soldiers were killed.

1876: "Treaty 6 Between Her Majesty The Queen and The Plain and Wood Cree Indians and Other Tribes of Indians at Fort Carlton, Fort Pitt and Battle River with Adhesions" was signed in Canada.

1876: Sixth Infantry soldiers on the steamers *Josephine* and *Benton* fought some Indians near the mouth of the Yellowstone River in Montana. According to army documents, one soldier was killed.

1904: An executive order modified the boundaries of the Fort McDowell Mohave-Apache Community Reservation.

1944: An election to approve a constitution and bylaws for the Metlakatla Indian Community of the Annette Islands Reserve in Alaska was authorized by the assistant secretary of the interior. The election was held on December 19, 1944.

1955: An election was authorized to adopt an amended constitution and bylaws for the Hualapai Tribe of the Hualapai Reservation in Arizona by the assistant secretary of the interior. The election was held on October 22, 1955.

AUGUST 24

1781: Joseph Brant and his Mohawk warriors ambushed Pennsylvania militia led by Archibald Lochry in Indiana on the Ohio River. Brant routed the militia. Sixty-four militiamen were killed and forty-two were captured.

1816: William Clark, Auguste Chouteau, and Ninian Edwards and representatives of the

Potawatomi, Chippewa, and Ottawa Tribes signed a treaty (7 Stat. 146) in St. Louis. The Indians received annuities for land giveaways. They were allowed to peacefully hunt on their old lands as long as the lands remained in the hands of the government.

1818: The Quapaw Indians signed a treaty (7 Stat. 176) in St. Louis covering lands along the Arkansas and Red Rivers.

1834: After Chickasaw Head Chief Levi Colbert died, the Chickasaw council voted to replace him with James Colbert.

1835: The United States signed a treaty (7 Stat. 474) with the Choctaw, Comanche, Creek (Muskogee), Cherokee, Osage, Quapaw, Seneca, and Wichita at Camp Holmes "on the eastern border of the Grand Prairie, near the Canadian River." Governor Montfort Stokes and Brigadier General M. Arbuckle represented the United States. Many Indians signed the treaty.

1853: General Lane and approximately 200 troops found some Rogue River Indians. A fight ensued near Table Rock.

1856: Eighty Cheyenne attacked a mail train near Fort Kearny in southern Nebraska.

1866: Soldiers from the First Arizona Infantry fought with a band of Indians near the San Francisco Mountains (north of modern Flagstaff) in Arizona. The army reported that one Indian was wounded and two were captured.

1868: Near Bent's Fort, three stagecoaches and one wagon train were attacked by Indians.

1869: For his actions on July 8, 1869, Mad Bear received the Medal of Honor.

1870: With the military rapidly approaching his base at Fort Garry (Winnipeg), Louis Riel decided to flee to the United States. This effectively ended the Red River Rebellion in Canada.

1877: The cabinet voted to send a commission to talk with Sitting Bull at Fort Walsh.

1982: An election approved Amendments 12, 13, and 14 to the constitution and bylaws of the Lac du Flambeau Band of Lake Superior Chippewa Indians of Wisconsin.

1636: Boston's military standing committee sent John Endecott, William Turner, John Underhill, and an expedition to Block Island. This was in retaliation for the murder of several English.

1665: Construction began on the first of four forts that were built in Chambly, Quebec, southeast of Montreal. This fort was called Fort St. Louis. Later versions were called Fort Chambly. Its primary purpose was to defend nearby settlers from attacks by the Iroquois.

1737: An agreement was signed by Thomas Penn and Munsee Chiefs Manawkyhickon and Nutimus. Teeshacomin and Lappawinzoe also signed. The agreement recognized an old deed made in 1686. The agreement called for Indian lands to be sold along the Delaware River for the distance that a man could walk in a day and a half. This was called the Walking Purchase and was performed on September 19, 1737.

1828: The United States signed treaties with five different Indian nations.

1835: The Creek wrote President Jackson telling him they were ready to move west but that they needed to sell their land to afford to go. They wanted the money promised to them by treaty.

1856: Captain G.H. Stuart and forty-one soldiers from Fort Kearny in southern Nebraska caught up to the Cheyenne who attacked a mail train the day before. The army killed ten Indians in the fight.

1856: Cheyenne attacked four wagons led by the secretary of Utah, A.W. Babbitt, on Cottonwood Creek. Two men and one child were killed and a woman was kidnapped. Babbitt was transporting money and goods for the Mormon Church.

1862: New Ulm, Minnesota, was evacuated due to the Santee Sioux Uprising.

1868: Acting Governor Hall of Colorado telegraphed the military that 200 Indians were "devastating southern Colorado." The military also received a report of Indians killing an animal herder near Fort Dodge in southwestern Kansas.

1869: According to army records, members of the Eighth Cavalry fought with a band of Indians near the Santa Maria River in Arizona. Nine Indians were killed and seven were wounded. The Eighth Cavalry also fought with a band of Indians near Camp Toll Gate at Tonto Station in Arizona. Six Indians were killed and one was captured.

1871: Indians skirmished with a group of soldiers from the Third Cavalry near Arivaypa Canyon, Arizona, according to official army records. Five Indians were killed.

1876: An act (19 Stat. 200) was passed by Congress. It was intended to "provide the Commissioner of Indian Affairs with the sole power and authority to appoint traders to the Indian tribes."

1877: At the Nez Perce camp just north of Yellowstone Lake, Captain Robert Pollock made the following observation about chasing the Nez Perce: "The whole command is weary and tired of marching. This game of hide and seek is getting mighty monotonous. . . . My men are in excellent health. They do their duty without much grousing. The lack of women and whiskey are of more concern than the Indians."

1917: A court in Calgary found Inuit Sinnisiak and Uluksuk guilty of murdering a priest who hired them as guides. The previous week they had been found not guilty of killing another priest in the same party. This was the first trial of an Inuit in Canada.

1969: Amendments 6–9 to the constitution and bylaws for the Oneida Tribe of Indians of Wisconsin were approved.

1980: Casimir LeBeau, area director, Minneapolis area office, Bureau of Indian Affairs, ratified an election for an amendment to the constitution and bylaws of the Lac Courte Oreilles Band of Lake Superior Chippewa Indians of Wisconsin.

August 26

1842: The Caddo signed a treaty in Texas. They agreed to visit other tribes and try to convince them to also sign treaties with Texas.

1858: In what was called the Battle of Four Lakes, forces under Colonel George Wright fought for about three hours with Coeur d'Alene, Columbia River, Colville, Kalispel, and Spokane Indians. The army defeated the Indians.

1866: Soldiers from the First Cavalry and First Oregon Cavalry fought with a band of Indians on Owyhee River in Idaho. The army reported that seven Indians were killed.

1869: According to army records, members of the Eighth Cavalry fought with a band of Indians near Camp Toll Gate on the Tonto Plateau in Arizona. One soldier was killed.

1872: A sergeant, six soldiers, and two Ree Indian scouts were twelve miles from Fort McKeen (later Fort Abraham Lincoln) in central North Dakota when they were attacked by more than 100 Sioux. According to army reports, the two Ree Indian scouts were killed in the fighting.

1876: General George Crook and his soldiers left General Alfred "One Star" Terry. They went east.

1876: Treaty Number 6, covering much of modern Alberta and Saskatchewan, was signed by the Cree, Chipewyan, and Saulteaux and the Canadian government.

1960: The Cold Spring Rancheria in Fresno County, California, adopt an official tribal roll.

1966: Commissioner of Indian Affairs Robert Bennett approved the results of an election to amend the revised constitution and bylaws of the Sisseton Wahpeton Sioux Tribe of South Dakota. The election took place on August 1–2, 1966.

1967: The assistant secretary of the interior had authorized an election for the adoption of an amendment to the constitution and bylaws for the Ponca Tribe of Indians of Oklahoma. It was approved in an election by the tribal members.

1985: John W. Fritz, the deputy assistant secretary of Indian affairs, authorized an election for a new constitution for the Tohono O'odham Nation.

AUGUST 27

1735: According to some sources, a peace agreement was reached between representatives of the British in Massachusetts Colony and the Iroquois of Canada.

1756: Delaware Indians staged a series of attacks along the Maryland-Pennsylvania border. Near Salisbury Plains, thirty-nine British were killed. In other fighting in the area of Franklin County, Pennsylvania, a little more than twenty soldiers and settlers were killed.

1832: Black Hawk surrendered.

1836: The Battle of Cow Creek took place between Creek warriors and the Georgia militia near the Okefenokee Swamp.

1868: According to a report filed by Captain Henry C. Bankhead, commander of Fort Wallace in western Kansas, several citizens had been killed by Indians in the last few days near Sheridan (near modern Winona) and Lake Station, Colorado. Soldiers escorting a stagecoach near Cheyenne Wells were able to fight off an Indian attack. The presence of 250 Indians caused Captain Edmond Butler, Fifth Infantry, and his wagon train to return to Big Springs. Acting Colorado Governor Hall again telegraphed the president that Arapaho were killing settlers all over southern Colorado. In a separate report, Lieutenant F.H. Beecher, Third Infantry, reported that two experienced scouts were shot in the back by Indians who had pretended to be friends. One survived by using the other's dead body as a shield.

1868: According to army records, members of the Thirty-Eighth Infantry fought with a band of Indians in the Hatchet Mountains in New Mexico. Three Indians were killed.

1869: According to an Indian taken prisoner after the Battle on Prairie Dog Creek in Kansas on September 26, 1869, Pawnee Killer and Whistler's Sioux attacked a surveying party about twenty miles south of the Platte River.

1872: Sergeant Benjamin Brown, Company C, Twenty-Fourth Infantry, and four soldiers defeated a superior force of local Indians at Davidson Canyon near Camp Crittenden, Arizona. Brown would be awarded the Medal of Honor.

1872: Indians skirmished with a group of settlers near the Santa Cruz River, Arizona, according to official army records. Four settlers were killed. Also in Arizona, soldiers from the Fifth Cavalry fought with some Indians near Davidson's Creek. Lieutenant R.T. Stewart, one soldier, and one civilian were killed.

1878: Captain James Egan and Troop K, Second Cavalry, were following a group of Bannock who had been stealing livestock along the Madison River. Near Henry's Lake, Captain Egan's forces skirmished with the Bannock and recovered fifty-six head of livestock. The escaping Bannock were starting to follow the trail taken by the Nez Perce last year.

1935: The Indian Arts and Craft Act (104 Stat. 4662) was passed by Congress. Its purpose was to "promote the economic welfare of the Indian tribes and Indian individuals through the development of Indian arts and crafts and the expansion of the market for the products of Indian art and craftsmanship."

1958: An act was passed entitled "Contracts with Indian Tribes or Indians" (72 Stat. 927). It required that all agreements made by any person with any individual or tribe of Indians for "the payment or delivery of any money or thing of value must follow certain rules and be approved by the Secretary of the Interior and the Commissioner of Indian Affairs."

1980: The constitution of the Iowa Tribe of Kansas and Nebraska was amended.

AUGUST 28

1565: Leading an expedition of 1,500 soldiers and colonists, Pedro Menendez de Aviles landed on the coast of Florida. His mission was to defeat the Protestants in the area and to claim the land for Spain. Next month he established the town of St. Augustine.

1645: The United Colonies of Massachusetts had decided to raise an army to fight the Narragansett Indians after the Narragansett started fighting with the Mohegan, who were English allies. Fearing the superior force of the English, the Narragansett agreed to a peace treaty. The treaty gave the English all of the Pequot lands the Narragansett had appropriated after the Treaty of Hartford of September 21, 1638. (Also recorded as happening on August 27, 1645.)

1676: The last Indian surrendered in King Philip's War.

1686: According to an alleged copy of a deed displaying this day's date, Delaware Chiefs Mayhkeerickkishsho, Sayhoppy, and Taughhoughsey sold lands along the Delaware River to William Penn. The deed specified that the land encompassed the distance "back into the woods as far as a man can go in a day and a half." A copy of this deed was found by Thomas Penn in 1734. The implementation of this deed was called the Walking Purchase. The walk was started on September 19, 1737. The manner in which it was done led to recriminations on both sides. (Also recorded as happening on August 30.)

1754: According to some reports, an agreement on friendship and land cessions was reached by representatives of the British in North Carolina and the Catawba Indians.

1784: Father Junipero Serra died. During his lifetime, he established many missions in what became modern California.

1811: Tecumseh spoke with Chief Big Warrior and his band of Upper Creek. He tried to get them to join his revolt.

1833: Assiniboine attacked Piegan Indians at Fort McKenzie.

1836: John Campbell, U.S. commissioner to the Creek, signed a contract with Opothleyaholo and other friendly Creek leaders. Campbell realized that the Creek needed money to move to Indian Territory (present-day Oklahoma) and to satisfy their debts in Alabama. The government gave the Creek their $31,900 annuity in advance so that they could pay their debts. The Creek agreed to provide 600–1,000 warriors to fight the Seminole. The Creek served until the Seminole surrendered totally. The Creek got to keep any plunder they could find.

1857: Fort Abercrombie was established as an outpost against the Sioux.

1868: Near Kiowa Station, Indians killed three men and stole fifty head of cattle. Kiowa station keeper Stickney was also attacked and wounded while driving a wagon. The station keeper at Reed's Spring was also attacked and driven off by Indians.

1868: Army records indicated that Pawnee scouts under Captain C.E. Morse fought with a band of hostile Indians near the Platte River in Nebraska. No injuries were reported during the fighting.

1875: Indians fought with soldiers from the Third Cavalry along the North Platte River north of Sidney, Nebraska. According to army documents, no casualties were reported in this encounter, which lasted until September 2.

1876: "Treaty 6 Between Her Majesty The Queen and The Plain and Wood Cree Indians and Other Tribes of Indians at Fort Carlton, Fort Pitt and Battle River with Adhesions" was signed in Canada.

1879: According to government sources, Indians had set numerous fires in the mountains west of Hot Sulphur Springs, Colorado. The fires rages out of control for some time.

1942: According to Federal Register No. 7FR07458, the Shoshone and Arapaho tribes of the Wind River Reservation in Wyoming got back a small part of the lands they had ceded to the United States in 1905.

1976: Charles James, the area director of the Bureau of Indian Affairs, had authorized an election for the adoption of an amendment to the constitution and bylaws for the Ponca Tribe of Indians of Oklahoma. It was approved by a vote of 40–8.

1990: The Mi'kmaq Afton First Nation Reserve of Summerside was established in Nova Scotia.

Every: Spanish and Indian fiestas in Isleta Pueblo.

AUGUST 29

1758: The First State Indian Reservation in Brotherton, New Jersey, was established. It was primarily for the Lenni Lenape.

1759: Mohegan Samson Occom was ordained as a minister by the Suffolk Presbytery of Long Island, New York. While living with Reverend Eleazar Wheelock, he had studied numerous foreign languages, including Hebrew and Greek. Eventually, he was sent to England to help raise funds for Wheelock's Indian "Charity" School. Occom was the first Indian minister to deliver a sermon in England. His fund-raising efforts were so outstanding that Wheelock's School could afford to move to New Hampshire and eventually became Dartmouth College.

1779: The Battle of Newton (near modern Elmira, New York) took place. General John Sullivan and 4,500 soldiers were part of a major expedition to defeat the Iroquois and the British in New York. British Major John Cutler and Mohawk Chief Joseph Brant commanded a British and Indian force of 600 warriors and soldiers. Being vastly outnumbered, the British and Indian forces gave up the field to the Americans. Even though the battle lasted several hours, only five Americans, five British, and twelve Indians were killed.

1796: In a speech directed to the Cherokees, President Washington announced his decision to appoint Colonel Benjamin Hawkins as the "First General or Principal Agent for all four southern Nations of Indians."

1821: Lewis Cass and Solomon Sibley signed a treaty (7 Stat. 218) with the Chippewa, Ottawa, and Potawatomi Indians in Chicago, Illinois. The Indians gave up lands in southwestern Michigan.

1858: Captains McLane and Lucero, with Indian Agent Yost and approximately sixty men, were on an expedition to Fort Defiance in north-western Arizona against the Navajos. Working on a deadline, the Navajos had failed to produce the murderer who killed a black boy at the fort on July 12, 1858. At Bear Springs, the soldiers encountered a Navajo camp and they struck. Several Indians were killed in the fighting. The soldiers then moved on to Fort Defiance.

1865: The army and Indians fought in the Powder River country. Forces under General Patrick Connor attacked an Arapaho village at a site that is near modern Sheridan, Wyoming.

1868: According to Captain William H. Penrose, Third Infantry, the commander of Fort Lyon in southeastern Colorado, Indians attacked thirteen wagons eighteen miles from the Arkansas River. The whites escaped to Fort Lyon, but the oxen were killed and the train was destroyed.

1878: As a part of the Bannock War, Fifth Infantry soldiers and some Indian scouts fought a group of Indians on Index Peak, Wyoming. According to army documents, no casualties were reported. The fighting continued through the next day.

1893: A trust patent was issued for 2,840 acres for the Pechanga Indian Reservation–Temecula Band of Luiseno Mission Indians.

1956: According to Federal Register No. 21FR6681, lands that were originally set aside to be townsites within the Flathead Indian Reservation in Montana and were "undisposed of" were returned to the tribal ownership of the Confederated Salish and Kootenai Tribes on the Flathead Reservation.

1978: The area director, Minneapolis area office, Bureau of Indian Affairs, had authorized an election for amendments to the constitution and bylaws of the Lac Courte Oreilles Band of Lake Superior Chippewa Indians of Wisconsin. The election would be held on December 15, 1978.

AUGUST 30

1645: A peace treaty between the Dutch, led by Willem Kieft, and several local tribes was signed at

Fort Orange (in modern Albany, New York). This treaty concluded a protracted conflict in the area.

1686: According to an alleged copy of a deed dated on this day, Delaware Chiefs Mayhkeerick-kishsho, Sayhoppy, and Taughhoughsey sold lands along the Delaware River to William Penn. The deed specified that the land encompassed the distance "back into the woods as far as a man can go in a day and a half." A copy of this deed was found by Thomas Penn in 1734. The implementation of this deed was called the Walking Purchase. The walk was started on September 19, 1737. The manner in which it was done led to recriminations on both sides. (Also recorded as happening on August 28.)

1690: A combined force of British, Yamassee, and Yuchi Indians attacked the Spanish mission of San Juan de Guacara in northern Florida. Many Timucua Indians in the area had been converted to Christianity or were loyal to the Franciscan monks. All of the Timucua Indians at the mission were killed in the fighting.

1813: The Red Sticks (the antiwhite faction of the Creek) attacked Fort Mims just north of Mobile, Alabama, on Lake Tensaw. About 800 Red Stick Creek warriors (some estimates range between 400 and 1,000), led by Chiefs Peter McQueen and William Weatherford (Lume Chathi–Red Eagle), rushed into the open fort at noon and killed 107 soldiers and 260 civilians, including 100 black slaves. The fort commander, Major Daniel Beasley, had done a poor job of preparing the fort for the Creek War. This laxity led to the success of the Creek attack. The defenders were brutally attacked, and only a few Americans escaped. The defense of the fort was led by militia Captain Dixon Bailey, a half-blood Creek. Bailey died in the fighting. During the five-hour battle, between thirty-six and 100 Red Stick Creek were killed, according to different sources.

1819: The Kickapoo signed a treaty (7 Stat. 202) at Fort Harrison. They ceded all of their lands along the Wabash River.

1831: The Treaty of Miami Bay, Ohio (7 Stat. 359), was signed by the Ottawa and James Gardiner. The Indians ceded lands around the Miami and Auglaize Rivers and agreed to move just west of the Mississippi River.

1838: Choctaw Chief Mushulatubbe died from smallpox near the Choctaw Agency.

1841: Kiowa skirmished with the Texas–Santa Fe expedition near the Pease River. Kiowa War Chief Adalhabakia was killed in the fighting.

1849: The expedition led by Indian Agent James Calhoun and Lieutenant Colonel John Washington camped in Tunicha Valley. Several Navajos who lived nearby visited the camp. They were informed that the Navajos were punished for not living up to previous treaties.

1855: A treaty was signed with 450 of the Penateka or Southern Comanche in Texas.

1856: Cheyenne and Arapaho attacked a wagon train eighty miles from Fort Kearny, Nebraska. One man was killed and one child was kidnapped.

1858: Oshkosh was a Menominee chief. During his lifetime he fought in many conflicts, including for the British in the War of 1812 and for the

Milky Way, a Penateka Comanche (NA)

Americans in Black Hawk's War. He was appointed as the chief of the Menominees by Lewis Cass during the negotiations of the Treaty of Butte des Morts. After surviving battles with the Europeans and other Indians, Oshkosh met his end due to a more insidious enemy: alcohol. He was killed during a drunken fight on this day.

1867: According to army records, members of the Sixth Cavalry under Lieutenant Gustavus Schreyer fought with a band of Indians near Fort Belknap, Texas. Two soldiers were killed.

1868: According to army records, members of Companies A and B of the Pawnee scouts fought with a band of hostile Indians near the Republican River in Nebraska. No injuries were reported.

1874: Colonel Nelson Miles, eight troops of the Sixth Cavalry, four companies from the Fifth Infantry, and a section of artillery encountered hostile Indians at the Washita Agency in Indian Territory (present-day Oklahoma). The opposing forces staged a running battle for several days, until the Indians were defeated eight miles from the Salt Fork of the Red River.

1878: As a part of the Bannock War, Fifth Infantry soldiers and some Indian scouts fought a group of Indians on Index Peak, Wyoming. According to army documents, no casualties were reported. The fighting started the day before.

1881: Colonel Eugene Carr had attempted to arrest a White Mountain Apache shaman named Nakaaidoklini for preaching a disruptive faith. Carr's Indian scouts revolted and then fought a battle with Carr at Cibicue Creek. Carr sustained significant losses, and Nakaaidoklini was killed in the fighting. Sergeant Alonzo Bowman and Private Richard Heartery, Company D, Sixth Cavalry, and First Lieutenant William H. Carter would be awarded the Medal of Honor for "conspicuous and extraordinary bravery in attacking mutinous scouts."

1965: The undersecretary of the interior announced the "Plan for the Distribution of Assets of Robinson Rancheria" in California.

AUGUST 31

1666: Mohawk Chief Agariata was attending a peace conference in Quebec between the Iroquois and the French. Governor Alexandre de Proville asked, during a dinner, if anyone knew who killed his son a few months earlier. Agariata bragged that he did it. The governor became so angry that he had Agariata seized and hanged. This ended the peace process. Governor de Proville led French troops against the Mohawks himself.

1700: According to some sources, an agreement was reached regarding friendship, religion, and trade between representatives of the British in New York and the Five Nations.

1715: After a history of occasional skirmishes, the Conestoga and Catawba Tribes, at the urging of Europeans living in Pennsylvania, agreed to sign a peace treaty. They agreed to stop fighting among themselves.

1735: Former Yale tutor John Sergeant was ordained as the missionary to the local Indians at Deerfield, Massachusetts.

1778: Wappinger Indian Chief Daniel Nimham was killed while fighting with American forces in the Revolutionary War battle at Kingsbridge. At the time of his death he had been chief for almost thirty-eight years. Although he sided with the British in the French and Indian War, English authorities would not help him retrieve lands appropriated by settlers in New York along the Hudson River. Nimham (sometimes spelled Ninham) and his warriors would fight on the American side during the Revolution.

1803: The Choctaw signed the Treaty of Hoe Buckintoopa (7 Stat. 80). This treaty ceded 853,760 acres, mostly in modern Alabama. Mushulatubbe was one of the signers.

1849: The U.S. expedition led by Indian Agent James Calhoun and Lieutenant Colonel John Washington arrived in Navajo territory to discuss fort-building plans and a new treaty. Among the Navajos present were Archuleta, José Largo, and Narbona. During the meeting, a fight took place and several Navajos, including Narbona, were shot.

1862: The First Cherokee Mounted Volunteers was organized. They served under Chief Stand Watie on the side of the Confederacy during the Civil War.

1865: According to some sources, Choctaw Chief Greenwood le Flore died.

1873: Captain T.A. Baldwin and Troops E and I, Tenth Cavalry, were attacked by an Indian war party near Pease River in Texas. According to army reports, one Indian was wounded.

1876: President Grant, by Executive Order No. 1221, added to the Gila River Reserve for the Pima and Maricopa Indians in the Pima Agency. This reserve was established on February 28, 1859.

1905: Ely Samuel Parker (Donehogawa) died in New York City. During his lifetime he was a Seneca chief, an engineer, a lawyer, the New York City building superintendent, a brigadier general in the Civil War (where he wrote the surrender papers signed at Appomattox), and the first Indian to be commissioner of Indian affairs. Born in 1828, he was buried in Buffalo, New York.

1925: The Mi'kmaq Membertou First Nation Reserve of Membertou No. 28B was established in Nova Scotia.

1971: An official census of the Southern Ute Indian Tribe of the Southern Ute Reservation in Colorado was listed.

SEPTEMBER 1

1640: A treaty agreement covering land cessions between the Mohegan and Connecticut was reached.

1675: According to some sources, a group of Indians staged an attack on the village of Hadley, Massachusetts. According to local legend, a man unknown to the village rushed into the church and rallied the settlers to defeat the Indians. After the fighting, the man disappeared. Other sources said there was no battle, just a call to arms. Other sources said nothing of any note happened on this day in Hadley.

1776: On July 20, 1776, Chickamauga warriors attacked Eaton Station, Tennessee. Based on this attack, a force of more than 2,000 militia and some Catawba Indians, led by General Griffith Rutherford, marched into the Tennessee Mountains. They killed a dozen Cherokee warriors and destroyed most of the Cherokee villages in Tennessee and South Carolina.

1788: Even after the Treaty of Hopewell, whites continued to settle on Cherokee lands along the Holston and French Broad Rivers. Congress issued a proclamation prohibiting whites from settling on Cherokee lands.

1813: A Creek war party attacked several farms near Fort Sinquefield, Alabama. They killed several of the settlers. One woman, Sarah Merrill, left for dead by the Creek, staggered through the woods for miles carrying her baby, also left for dead. Her ordeal sparked additional fury among the local Americans.

1826: On this day was the deadline for Creek to go west from their lands east of the Mississippi River.

1830: After discussing President Jackson's removal proposal, Chickasaw leaders signed a provisional agreement to be removed. Several of the chiefs present were offered additional lands. The treaty never went into effect because it was based on the premise that the Chickasaws would share lands with the Choctaws. The Choctaws did not agreed to give up their lands in Indian Territory (present-day Oklahoma).

1845: Tired of the continuing feud between the "old settler" and "new emigrant" factions of the Cherokee Nation, fifty-four Cherokee families left the Indian Territory (present-day Oklahoma) reservation to join relatives in Texas.

1858: Colonel George H. Wright and 600 men battled 500 Coeur d'Alene Indians and allies at the Battle of Four Lakes in western Washington. Equipped with rifled barrels and new ammunition,

Manuelito, Navajo chief (NA)

Wright's men killed five dozen Indians while suffering no mortal wounds themselves. They fought another battle on the Spokane Plains in Washington on September 5.

1866: Manuelito and twenty-three of his Navajo followers surrendered to the army at Fort Wingate.

1868: Stage agent J.H. Jones of Lake Station, Colorado, reported to the military that a woman and child were killed and scalped by Indians near the station. According to military reports, three people were killed and three people were wounded near Reed Springs.

1868: According to army records, settlers fought with a band of Indians near Lake Station, Colorado. Two settlers were killed, wounded, and captured.

1871: Indians skirmished with a group of soldiers from the Ninth Cavalry and the Twenty-Fourth Infantry near Fort McKavett, Texas, according to official army records. No casualties were reported.

1880: Ninth Cavalry and Fifteenth Infantry soldiers fought a group of Indians near Agua Chiquita in the Sacramento Mountains of New Mexico.

According to army documents, two soldiers were killed.

1881: Apache attacked Fort Apache in eastern Arizona. They were upset because Colonel Eugene Carr had tried to arrest an Apache shaman. The medicine man was killed in a fight two days earlier.

1911: Executive Order No. 1406 was issued. It set aside certain lands in New Mexico "for the benefit of the Indians of the Jemez Pueblo."

1965: An election for an amendment to the constitution and bylaws of the Moapa Band of Paiute Indians was authorized by Assistant Secretary of the Interior Harry Anderson. The election was held on November 20.

SEPTEMBER 2

1732: The first treaty between the Iroquois Confederation and the Pennsylvania Provincial Council was signed in Philadelphia. The parties agreed to peaceful relations between them. The Iroquois also promised to try to persuade the Shawnees to leave Allegheny Valley. The principal Indian chief present was Shikellamy of the Onondaga.

1777: Settlers had built a sizable stockade in Wheeling, Virginia (now West Virginia). The area was the scene of several skirmishes during the next several weeks. A force of 200 Mingo and Wyandot warriors lay in wait outside the stockade. A few Indians lured a small force of fifteen militia out of the fort into the woods, where the trap was sprung; most of the soldiers were killed. A relief force of thirteen soldiers attempted a rescue. They were attacked as well. A total of fifteen soldiers were killed; only one Indian sustained a fatal injury.

1779: General John Sullivan and his force of 4,500 men continued their attacks on Indians in New York he suspected were British allies. His forces leveled Catherine's Town.

1815: In Portage des Sioux, William Clark, Auguste Chouteau, and Ninian Edwards made a peace treaty (7 Stat. 130) with the Kickapoo for the War of 1812.

1838: The Republic of Texas signed a treaty with the Kichai, Taovaya, Tawakoni, and Waco at a site that is in modern Fannin County.

1838: Lydia Paki Kamekeha Liliuokalani, the last sovereign queen of Hawaii, was born.

1844: Tonight in Wilmington, Delaware, Cherokee Principal Chief John Ross married Mary B. Stapler.

1862: Santee Sioux engaged in another fight in the Sioux Uprising. Called the Birch Coulee Battle, it happened three miles north of Morton, Minnesota. The Minnesota forces were led by Major Joseph Brown. The Sioux were led by Big Eagle, Mankato, and Red Legs. The army had been on a burial detail. At dawn, the Sioux attacked. The soldiers lost thirteen killed and forty-seven wounded.

1868: Sergeant George J. Dittoe, Company A, Third Infantry, and four soldiers were transporting a wagon along Little Coon Creek when they were attacked by about three dozen Indians. Three of the soldiers were seriously wounded; three Indians were killed and one wounded. One soldier went to Fort Dodge in southwestern Kansas for help. Lieutenant Thomas Wallace, Third Infantry, and troops responded to relieve Sergeant Dittoe's men and chase off the Indians. One of the four soldiers, Corporal Leander Herron, was awarded the Medal of Honor for his part in the action.

1875: Indians fought with soldiers from the Third Cavalry along the North Platte River north of Sidney, Nebraska. According to army documents, no casualties were reported in this encounter, which started on August 28.

1876: The Nez Perce told settlers they had one week to leave their lands.

1877: Victorio fled the San Carlos Reservation.

1948: An adoption ordinance for the Coeur d'Alene Tribe had been passed by the tribal council. It was approved by the acting commissioner of Indian affairs.

Every: Acoma Pueblo festival.

SEPTEMBER 3

1680: Don Antonio de Otermin was the governor of the province that would eventually contain modern Santa Fe, New Mexico. The Pueblo Indians staged a revolt in August. Otermin entered Isleta Pueblo and discovered it was abandoned.

1719: Frenchman Bernard de la Harpe discovered an Indian village on the Arkansas River near Muskogee. La Harpe had traveled up the Red River, then went overland across Oklahoma. He described the land as fertile and the people (probably a Caddo tribe) as friendly and hard-working. La Harpe claimed the land for France.

1783: The Treaty of Paris was signed, ending the Revolutionary War. It left many Indian tribes without their British allies. The U.S. government considered this a victory over those tribes and soon would attempt to get reparations from the tribes.

1822: The Sac and Fox signed a treaty (7 Stat. 223) at Fort Armstrong dealing with lands in Wisconsin and Illinois.

1836: The 2,300 Creek prisoners reached Fort Gibson in eastern Indian Territory (present-day Oklahoma). Approximately eighty-one Creek died during the journey from Alabama.

1836: Colonel Henry Dodge and the Menominee Indians signed a peace treaty (7 Stat. 506) in Cedar Point, Wisconsin. In exchange for an annuity of $20,000, the Menominee ceded most of their lands along the Menominee, Wolf, and Wisconsin Rivers.

1855: Little Thunder had taken over as chief after the killing of Conquering Bear in the fight with Lieutenant Grattan's men. He had almost 250 warriors in his camp on the Blue River. General William S. Harney had 600 soldiers. After the fighting, there were 100 dead Sioux and five dead soldiers, according to Harney. Harney took seventy prisoners, almost all women and children. Based on his actions, the Sioux called Harney "the Butcher."

1863: At Whitestone, General Alfred Sully and 1,200 soldiers attacked Inkpaduta's Santee Sioux village. About 300 warriors were killed, 250 women and children captured. Sully lost twenty-two soldiers in the fighting.

1868: According to Major Joseph Tilford, Seventh Cavalry, the commander at Fort Reynolds in southeastern Colorado, four people were killed by Indians near Colorado City. Indians also attacked the station at Hugo Springs but were repelled by the occupants.

1907: In Oklahoma, the principal chief of the Creek Nation, Pleasant Porter (Talof Harjo), died.

1966: Assistant Secretary of the Interior Harry Anderson had authorized an election for amendments to the constitution and bylaws of the Lac Courte Oreilles Band of Lake Superior Chippewa Indians of Wisconsin. The amendment was approved by a vote of 152–2.

SEPTEMBER 4

1724: Indians attacked Dunstable village in Maine. They took two captives.

1801: A two-day conference began at Southwest Point, located at the confluence of the Tennessee and Clinch Rivers. Representatives of the United States and the Cherokees discussed more roads through Cherokee lands. Because of a lack of enforcement by the United States of previous treaties, the Cherokees did not agree to any U.S. proposals.

1854: A peace treaty was signed with the Modoc of Tule Lake. They were out of supplies by this time. The fighting had started on August 18, 1854.

1863: The Concow-Maidu had ancestral homes in the Butte County area of northern California. Eventually, they were forced to move to different lands. Many died or were killed along the way to these distant, hostile places. One group of 461 Concow left Chico, but only 277 would survive the two-week trip to Round Valley.

1864: At Fort Lyon, Major E.W. Wynkoop held a council with One Eye, Manimick, Cheyenne, one other Indian, and interpreter John S. Smith. Carrying a message written by George Bent, the

Apache prisoners, including Geronimo (first row, third from right), seated outside railroad car in Arizona (NA)

Cheyenne and Arapaho agreed to turn over any whites they held as prisoners. Wynkoop would leave the fort to go meet the tribal leaders on September 6.

1868: According to army records, members of the First and Eighth Cavalry and Indian scouts fought with a band of Indians near Tonto Creek, Arizona. One Indian was killed and another was captured.

1872: Indians skirmished with a group of settlers near Camp Mojave, Arizona, according to official army records. One settler was killed.

1878: Colonel Nelson Miles, 150 men of the Fifth Infantry, and thirty-five Crow scouts had been traveling up Clark's Fork of the Yellowstone, near Heart Mountain, looking for hostile Bannock Indians reported to be in the area. The soldiers came upon a camp and attacked the residents. Eleven Bannock were killed and thirty-one were captured. About 200 horses and mules were seized. An interpreter, an Indian scout, and Captain Andrew Bennett were killed in the fighting. One soldier was wounded.

1879: Members of Captain Ambrose Hooker's Troop E, Ninth Cavalry, were guarding the cavalry horses near Ojo Caliente, New Mexico, when they were attacked by Indians. Eight soldiers were killed, and the Indians captured forty-six of the soldier's mounts. The dead soldiers were African Americans, commonly referred to as buffalo soldiers by the Indians.

1882: At Whipple Barracks, General George Crook officially took over command of the Department of Arizona. The veteran Indian fighter was brought in to deal with the Apache.

1886: Geronimo and thirty-eight of his followers surrendered to General Nelson Miles at Skeleton Canyon south of Apache Pass in Arizona.

Every: St. Augustine Feast for many Pueblos.

SEPTEMBER 5

1779: General John Sullivan's forces continued their attack on suspected pro-British forces in New York. They demolished Kendaia (Appletown).

1785: Georgians continued to trespass on Creek lands. Chief Alexander McGillivray wrote Congress demanding that they protect his people from the settlers as previous treaties had promised.

1814: This day marked the start of the two-day Battle of Credit Island (near modern Davenport, Iowa). Major Zachary Taylor and 334 American soldiers were making their way up the Mississippi River, attacking British positions with considerable success. They encountered a force of 1,000 Indians and British. The allied army forced Taylor to withdraw to safety in St. Louis.

1836: A fifth group of friendly Creek, numbering 1,984, under the command of Lieutenant J.T. Sprague, left Tallassee (northwest of modern Tuskegee) for Indian Territory (present-day Oklahoma).

1858: Colonel George Wright, commanding the local army, fought with Coeur d'Alene, Columbia River, Colville, Kalispel, and Spokane Indians on the Spokane Plains. The army defeated the Indians.

1862: Little Crow heard news of Big Eagle and Mankato's battle with Colonel Henry "Long Trader" Sibley's troops at Birch Coulee. They

managed to bottle up the troops for an entire day; cannons brought up in support ended the fighting on the second day.

1865: Almost 1,000 Sioux, Cheyenne, and Arapaho fought with American forces under Colonel Cole at the Little Powder River.

1868: Indians stole five cattle at Hugo Springs Station. Later they also attacked and burned Willow Springs Station.

1868: According to army records, members of the Twenty-Third Infantry and some Indian scouts fought with a band of Indians in the Juniper Mountains of Idaho. During the campaign, which started on August 8, sixteen Indians were captured.

1869: Troops from Fort Stanton in southern New Mexico chased a group of hostile Indians. During the ensuing fight, three Indians were killed and seven were wounded. Two troopers were wounded.

1869: According to army records, members of the Eighth Cavalry and the Twelfth Infantry fought with a band of Indians near Camp Date Creek, Arizona. Three Indians were killed.

1871: The White Mountain Reservation was chosen as the site where the Apache Indians of Arizona could be "collected, fed, clothed . . . provided for, and protected." This decision was made by Vincent Colyer, commissioner, Bureau of Indian Affairs, Department of the Interior.

1871: Indians skirmished with a group of settlers in Chino Valley, Arizona, according to official army records. One settler was killed.

1877: According to many sources, Crazy Horse was fatally wounded while in captivity at Fort Robinson, Nebraska.

1878: Bannock fought with Howard's soldiers at Clark's Ford.

1968: The assistant commissioner of Indian affairs authorized an election for amendments to the constitution and bylaws of the Lac Courte Oreilles Band of Lake Superior Chippewa Indians of Wisconsin. The election was held on January 25, 1969.

1975: Commissioner of Indian Affairs Morris Thompson authorized an election to approve a new constitution and bylaws for the Cherokee Nation of Oklahoma.

SEPTEMBER 6

1689: Two hundred Indian survivors of King Philip's War had found refuge with the local Indians around Cochecho (modern Dover), New Hampshire. Boston wanted the Indians back in Massachusetts. Local settlers had signed a treaty with the local Indians. In what local legend called a mock battle, forces under Richard Walderne (Waldron) surrounded the local and refugee Indians. They removed the 200 refugees and marched them back to Boston. In Boston, most of the Indians were killed or became slaves.

1823: Seventy Seminole met with peace commissioners from the United States. This was the first such effort by the United States to reach an agreement with the Seminole after having bought Florida from Spain in 1819. A treaty was signed on September 18.

1839: A conference was held by the "old settler" and "new emigrant" Cherokees in Tahlequah, Indian Territory (present-day Oklahoma). John Ross was elected principal chief of the newly rejoined Cherokee Nation. David Vann was elected second chief. A new constitution was adopted. The convention continued until October 10, 1839. Many old settlers disavowed any actions taken by this convention. They believed that the old settlers' government was still in power.

1856: Cheyenne and Arapaho attacked a wagon train of Mormons on the Platte River. Two men, a woman, and a child were killed. One woman was kidnapped during the fighting.

1861: A Yamparika chief and another Comanche signed a treaty with Union representatives at Fort Wise, Colorado.

1864: Fort Zarah was established on Walnut Creek near the intersection of the Santa Fe Trail and the main Indian trail in Kansas. The fort served as a base of operations against hostile Indians until December 1869.

1864: Major Edward "Tall Chief" Wynkoop was the commander at Fort Lyon in southeastern Colorado. Black Kettle and as many as 2,200 Cheyenne, Arapaho, and Sioux were camped with him on Smoky Hill River. Black Kettle sent out messengers saying he would deliver white prisoners in exchange for Indian prisoners and to discuss moving to the reservation. Wynkoop received a copy of this message from One Eye and Eagle Head. Hopelessly outnumbered (he had only 127 soldiers), Wynkoop decided to go to the Smoky Hill camp to talk with Black Kettle. Wynkoop eventually took the four white children held captive and seven chiefs, including Black Kettle, to Denver to discuss ways to end the fighting in Colorado.

1867: According to army records, members of the First Cavalry fought with a band of Indians near the Silver River in Oregon. One Indian was killed and five were captured.

1868: According to army records, Indians attacked settlers in several locations in Colorado Territory. Twenty-five settlers died in the fighting during this day and the next day.

1877: Army records showed that Crazy Horse died on the night of September 6 at Fort Robinson, Nebraska.

1967: Amendments were made to the constitution of the Pawnee Indian Tribe of Oklahoma.

1967: Amendments to the Wisconsin Winnebago constitution were approved by the U.S. government.

1973: The Oklahoma Human Rights Commission requested state schools to drop rules requiring Indian students to cut their long hair. They felt the rules would "promote racial friction and community divisiveness."

1978: The Anasazi ruins at Mesa Verde were declared a World Heritage Site.

SEPTEMBER 7

1732: According to some sources, a land-cession agreement was made by representatives of the Delaware Indians and Pennsylvania.

1778: On this day through September 17, the Shawnee attacked Boonesborough. Captain Antoine Dagneaux de Quindre, with eleven soldiers and 444 Shawnees, including Chief Blackfish (Chinugalla), demanded the surrender of Boonesborough. Daniel Boone was commanding the sixty American sharpshooters in the fort. After losing thirty-five warriors to the Kentucky fighters, the Indians quit on September 20. Boone's forces reported only four men killed in the fighting. Some sources recorded the settlers' numbers as thirty men and twenty young men, with a few women and children. The losses were also reported as thirty-seven Shawnee and two settlers.

1831: Major Francis Armstrong was appointed agent to the Choctaws in Indian Territory (present-day Oklahoma). He assisted in their move to the Indian Territory.

1849: Colonel J.M. Washington, with soldiers and friendly Indians, confronted the Navajos in Canyon de Chelly. Mariano Martinez and Chapitone agreed to return stolen property and Mexican prisoners.

1850: The "Robinson Treaty with the Ojibewa Indians of Lake Superior Conveying Certain Lands to the Crown" was signed in Canada.

1862: Little Crow wrote a letter to Colonel Henry Sibley. He explained why the fighting started, that he had white prisoners, and that he wanted to negotiate. Sibley's reply was to release the prisoners and then talk. Little Crow was concerned for the Santee Indians' safety because he had heard that Governor Alexander Ramsey wanted the Santee dead or banished from Min-

nesota. Because Sibley had been a trader among the Indians, they called him "Long Trader."

1868: The "Hon. Schuyler Colfax" telegraphed the army that twenty-five people had been killed and a general uprising was going on in southern Colorado.

1880: Fourth Cavalry soldiers fought a group of Indians near Fort Cummings, New Mexico. According to army documents, one soldier was killed and three were wounded.

1917: By executive order, President Woodrow Wilson "reserve[d] from entry, sale or other disposal, and set aside for administrative purposes in connection with tribal grazing leases," 320 acres on the Crow Reservation in Montana.

1939: Assistant Secretary of the Interior Oscar Chapman ratified an election for a constitution and bylaws for the Port Gamble Band of Clallam Indians.

1957: An act of Congress gave the Chilkat Indians mineral rights to their lands near Klukwan. They were one of only a very small number of Alaskans with this provision.

1968: The Indian Council Fire awarded this year's Indian Achievement Award to Reverend Dr. Roe B. Lewis of Phoenix, Arizona. Lewis, a Pima-Papago, was cited for his efforts in educational counseling for Indians.

1972: A decision was given that said North Dakota could not tax Indians on reservations.

1979: The acting deputy commissioner of Indian affairs authorized an election for a new constitution for the Skokomish Indian Tribe. The election was held on January 15, 1980.

SEPTEMBER 8

1535: Cartier reached Stadacone, where the modern city of Quebec is located.

1565: Pedro Menendez de Aviles, accompanied by 1,500 soldiers and colonists, established the town of St. Augustine, Florida, the oldest constantly occupied European town in the United States. To secure his foothold in the area, de Aviles attacked the French settlements on nearby St. Johns River.

1598: Juan de Oñate and Vicente de Zaldivar, his nephew and second in command, completed and dedicated a church called San Gabriel (north of modern Espanola, New Mexico). Other sources said the church was called San Juan Bautist.

1755: The Battle of Lake George was fought between French and Indian forces under the command of Ludwig August Dieskau and Mohawk War Chief King Hendrick, and British and colonial troops under Sir William Johnson.

1756: Colonel John Armstrong led approximately 300 Pennsylvania soldiers against the Delaware village of Kittanning in retaliation for their attack on Fort Granville on July 30. Delaware Chief Captain Jacob was trapped in his house. He was ordered to surrender, and he refused. His house was set on fire, and he was burned to death. Armstrong estimated Delaware losses at forty killed and his own at eighteen. He recovered many English prisoners.

1779: General John Sullivan's force of 4,500 men continued their retaliatory strikes against suspected pro-British Indian villages. They destroyed Canadasaga, Kittanning, and other nearby villages in New York.

1815: William Henry Harrison, Duncan McArthur, and John Graham, representing the United States, and the Delaware, Miami, Seneca, Shawnee, and Wyandot tribes signed a treaty (7 Stat. 131) ending the warfare in the area. The treaty was signed near Detroit at Spring Wells, Michigan.

1865: A grand council of the formerly pro-Union and pro-Confederacy Indians was held at Fort Smith, Arkansas. The newly appointed commissioner of Indian affairs, Dennis N. Cooley, chaired the meeting. Most of the Indians were told that they had forfeited their lands and annuities by their traitorous support of the South. Each tribe had to plead its case for mercy.

1867: According to army records, members of the First Cavalry fought with a band of Indians near the Silver River in Oregon. Two soldiers were wounded. Twenty-three Indians were killed and fourteen were captured.

1868: Captain Henry Bankhead, commander of Fort Wallace, reported that twenty-five Indians killed and scalped two citizens near Sheridan (near modern Winona), Kansas. Indians also stole seventy-six horses and mules from Clark's wagon train on Turkey Creek.

1868: Lieutenant David Wallingford, Seventh Cavalry, arrived to help fifty men with thirty-five wagons who had fought Indians for the last four days at Cimarron Crossing. Two men had been killed, and the Indians escaped with seventy-five head of cattle. Five miles to the west, the soldiers discovered the remnants of another wagon train. Fifteen men in this train were burned to death.

1876: An advance guard under Captain Miles captured American Horse and his band of Teton Sioux at Slim Buttes, South Dakota.

1872: Elements of Company E, Fifth Cavalry, were engaging hostile Apache at Date Creek in Arizona. Sergeant Frank E. Hill managed to "secure the person of a hostile Apache Chief, although while holding the Chief he is severely wounded in the back by another Indian." For his actions, Hill would be awarded the Medal of Honor.

1877: Sixth Cavalry soldiers and some Indian scouts fought a group of Indians near the San Francisco River in New Mexico. According to army documents, twelve Indians were killed and thirteen were captured. The fighting lasted through September 10.

1880: At Fort Keogh in eastern Montana, Big Road and 200 Sioux surrendered.

1883: In Bismarck, the Northern Pacific Railroad celebrated the completion of its transcontinental railroad line. The company invited Sitting Bull, as a representative of the Indians, to make a speech to welcome the dignitaries at the celebration. Sitting Bull, speaking through an interpreter, instead said the whites were liars and thieves and that he hated all of them, smiling throughout the entire speech. The shocked interpreter, a young army officer, delivered the planned speech instead of Sitting Bull's real words. Sitting Bull was a great success and received a standing ovation. Railroad officials asked Sitting Bull to make additional speeches elsewhere based on his reception on this day.

1909: The confines of the Robinson Rancheria in California were modified.

1960: The U.S. Solicitor sent Senator Mike Mansfield a memo. The Solicitor had determined that county officials were not allowed to charge four Indians of the Flathead Reservation personal property taxes. The four men worked for the Montana Power Company at the federal Kerr Dam on the reservation. The county had tried to collect taxes from the men because, even though their job was on reservation land, it was not reservation-related.

1970: The Ramah chapter of Navajo Indians in western New Mexico established its own independent school board after the local public school was closed.

1972: The Minnesota Chippewa Tribe, consisting of the Chippewa Indians of the White Earth, Leech Lake, Fond du Lac, Bois Forte (Nett Lake), and Grand Portage Reservations, voted to approve several amendments to their constitution.

SEPTEMBER 9

426: Yax K'uk Mo established a Maya dynasty at Copán, Honduras.

1598: Juan de Oñate summoned the chiefs from the local Pueblos and made them swear oaths of allegiance to god and the king of Spain. New Mexico was divided into parishes by the Franciscans.

1836: Alexander Le Grand was appointed by Texas leader David Burnet as Indian commissioner. He was charged with negotiating a peace treaty with the Comanche and the Kiowa.

1837: Seminole Chief Philip was captured. He and a few family members were transported to St. Augustine, Florida.

1849: The United States and a few Navajo signed a treaty (9 Stat. 974). Mariano Martinez and Chapitone were among the Navajos who signed the treaty.

1850: The "Robinson Treaty with the Ojibewa Indians of Lake Huron Conveying Certain Lands to the Crown" was signed in Canada.

1868: Indians killed six people and burned a ranch between Fort Wallace and Sheridan (near modern Winona) in western Kansas. The ranch house had been burned two weeks earlier and was rebuilt.

1868: According to army records, members of the Eighth Cavalry fought with a band of Indians on the Tonto Plateau in Arizona.

1871: Cherokee leader Stand Watie died.

1872: When Lone Wolf was asked to go to Washington to discuss the government's plans for the Kiowa Reservation, he insisted that he council with Satanta and Big Tree first. They were in prison in Texas for their participation in the fighting on the Butterfield Trail on May 18, 1871. After heated negotiations with Texas officials, the United States got permission to take Satanta and Big Tree to St. Louis, a place with few Indians, to meet Lone Wolf. They left the prison in Huntsville, Texas.

1873: The confines of the Swinomish Reservation in Washington were established by executive order.

1874: Captain Wyllys Lyman and sixty men from the Fifth Infantry were escorting a supply wagon train for Colonel Nelson Miles at the Washita River, Indian Territory (present-day Oklahoma), when they were attacked by Indians. The soldiers remained barricaded for several days until relief arrived from Camp Supply in the Panhandle of Indian Territory. One soldier was killed; three other whites, including Lieutenant Granville Lewis, were wounded during the fight. First Sergeant John Mitchell, Sergeants William de Armond, Fred S. Hay, George Kitchen, John Knox, William Koelpin, and Frederick Neilon, Corporals John James, John

J.H. Kelly, and William Morris, and Private Thomas Kelly, Company I, would earn the Medal of Honor for "gallantry in action" during this engagement. (Also recorded as happening on September 10.)

1876: Nez Perce Chief Joseph talked with Major Wood. The deadline to surrender passed.

1876: Captain Anson Mills and men from the Second, Third, and Fifth Cavalries and Fourth, Ninth, and Fourteenth Infantries attacked American Horse's village of thirty-seven lodges at Slim Buttes, South Dakota, early this morning without warning. The entire village was captured. One soldier was killed and seven were wounded. Five Indians were killed, including American Horse. Numerous personal items from the soldiers of the Seventh Cavalry were discovered in the camp, including a pair of gloves belonging to Colonel Myles Keogh. After the initial morning victory, Indians from nearby villages gathered and attacked the soldiers, who had been reinforced by General George Crook's main force. Seven soldiers were wounded in the later fighting, including Lieutenant A.H. Von Luettwitz. One white scout and one soldier were killed. According to army reports, seven or eight Indians were killed in the second fight. Sergeant John Kirkwood and Private Robert Smith, Company M, would be awarded the Medal of Honor because they "bravely endeavored to dislodge some Sioux Indians secreted in a ravine."

1876: "Treaty 6 Between Her Majesty The Queen and The Plain and Wood Cree Indians and Other Tribes of Indians at Fort Carlton, Fort Pitt and Battle River with Adhesions" was signed in Canada.

1877: Fleeing from the army through the Yellowstone area, the Nez Perce Indians changed direction to Clark's Fork Canyon.

1878: According to army reports, on this night eighty-nine Northern Cheyenne men, 112 women, and 134 children abandoned their lodges and escaped from the Cheyenne and Arapaho Agency at Fort Reno in central Indian Territory (present-day Oklahoma). Dull Knife, Wild Hog, and Little Wolf were some of the leaders of the escapees. They were attempting to return to their old homelands to the north.

1881: Crazy Horse's family took his body for burial.

1891: Two Kickapoo chiefs, chosen to accompany Americans to the capital to obtain some money owed to them, were forced (in their words) to sign an "agreement" by Secretary of the Interior John W. Noble. This agreement sold the United States the Kickapoo "surplus lands" at thirty cents per acre. Many forgeries and the signatures of dead Indians and signatures of fictitious Indians were added to the agreement. Congress approved the agreement on March 30, 1893.

1946: The constitution and bylaws of the Nisqually Indian Community of the Nisqually Reservation Washington were approved by Assistant Secretary of the Interior Girard Davidson.

1989: The Cherokee tribal council made a change in the official tribal flag. A seven-pointed black star was added to the upper right corner as a reminder of the Cherokees who lost their lives on the Trail of Tears.

SEPTEMBER 10

1683: Susquehanna Chief Kekelappan sold William Penn half of his lands between the Susquehanna and Delaware Rivers.

1753: The Winchester Conference began with representatives of the Delaware and Iroquois Indians.

1782: A force of forty British Rangers and 250 Indians attacked the fort built in Wheeling, Virginia (now West Virginia). No soldiers were killed on either side, but a few Indians died in the fighting. Some historians consider this the last battle of the Revolutionary War.

1791: This day marked the start of some major fort construction projects in the Ohio Valley.

1864: Major E.W. Wynkoop met with Cheyenne and Arapaho chiefs, including Black Kettle, to discuss the release of prisoners.

1866: Soldiers from the Eighteenth Infantry fought with a band of Indians near Fort Phil Kearny in Dakota Territory through September 16. The army reported that two enlisted men were killed and two were wounded. The soldiers were led by Captain William J. Fetterman.

1867: According to army records, members of the Fourth Cavalry fought with a band of Indians near Live Oak Creek, Texas. No injuries were reported on either side.

1868: Settlements along the Purgatory River were attacked by Indians. Captain William Penrose and Third Infantry troops from Fort Lyon in southeastern Colorado arrived at the scene and pursued the marauders. The army caught up to the Indians at Rule Creek, Colorado. Four Indians and two soldiers were killed in the fight. Five army horses died from exhaustion due to the pursuit. Four miles east of Lake Station, Indians shot at a stage.

1868: According to army records, members of the Eighth Cavalry fought with a band of Indians near the Lower Agua Fria in Arizona. Four Indians were killed and three were captured.

1872: Indians skirmished with a group of soldiers from the Second Cavalry between Beaver Creek and Sweet Water, Wyoming, according to official army records. One Indian was wounded. The fighting lasted through September 13.

1874: Captain Wyllys Lyman and sixty men from the Fifth Infantry were escorting a supply wagon train for Colonel Nelson Miles at the Washita River, Indian Territory (present-day Oklahoma), when they were attacked by Indians. The soldiers remained barricaded for several days until relief arrived from Camp Supply in the Panhandle of Indian Territory. One soldier was killed; three other whites, including Lieutenant Granville Lewis, were wounded during the fight. First Sergeant John Mitchell, Sergeants William de Armond, Fred S. Hay, George Kitchen, John Knox, William Koelpin, and Frederick Neilon, Corporals John James, John J. H. Kelly, and William Morris,

Grave marker for Little Robe, Geronimo's two-year-old son (author)

and Private Thomas Kelly, Company I, would earn the Medal of Honor for "gallantry in action" during this engagement. (Also recorded as happening on September 9.)

1877: Sixth Cavalry soldiers and some Indian scouts fought a group of Indians near the San Francisco River in New Mexico. According to army documents, twelve Indians were killed and thirteen were captured. The fighting started on September 8.

1879: Settlers and soldiers fought a group of Indians near McEver's Ranch and Arroyo Seco, New Mexico. According to army documents, nine citizens were killed.

1879: White River Ute Agent N.C. Meeker wrote to the governor of Colorado requesting troops. Meeker believed the lives of settlers were in grave danger. He requested that the governor, General John Pope, and Colorado Senator Teller confer on the matter. Meeker wanted at least 100 troops to be sent immediately to his locale.

1885: According to a marker in the Fort Bowie cemetery in Arizona, Geronimo's two-year-old son Little Robe died.

1948: The assistant secretary of the interior had authorized an election to approve a constitution and bylaws for the Organized Village of Holikachuk, Alaska. It was passed by a vote of 21–0.

1967: An election to approve amendments to the constitution and bylaws for the Kashia Band of Pomo Indians of the Stewarts Point Rancheria was held. They were approved by a majority of the thirty-seven people voting.

1974: An amendment was made to the Fort Berthold Reservation constitution.

1982: Amendments 12, 13, and 14 to the constitution and bylaws of the Lac du Flambeau Band of Lake Superior Chippewa Indians of Wisconsin were approved and became effective.

SEPTEMBER 11

1609: Explorer Henry Hudson arrived at the "Hudson" River.

1856: Lasting through September 17, the second Walla Walla conference began.

1858: Colonel Miles, with five companies of soldiers and fifty Mexicans, entered the Canyon de Chelly in northeastern Arizona. The Navajos had not produced the Fort Defiance murderer of July 12, 1858. In fact, the Navajos had tried to pass off a killed Mexican prisoner as the culprit. The soldiers killed a few Navajos in the canyon. The soldiers camped in the canyon that night. The Navajos launched an ineffectual attack from the canyon walls. A captured Navajo convinced the other Navajos to stop the attack.

1868: Indians stole eighty-one head of cattle at Lake Creek from Clarke and Company hay contractors.

1868: According to army records, members of the Eighth Cavalry fought with a band of Indians near the Rio Verde in Arizona. Five Indians were killed.

1868: According to army records, members of the Seventh Cavalry and Third Infantry, under Lieutenant Colonel Alfred Sully, fought with a band of Indians near the Sand Hills in Indian Territory. The fighting lasted through September 15.

Three soldiers and twenty-two Indians were killed. Five soldiers and twelve Indians were wounded.

1874: Two scouts and four soldiers, acting as couriers between Colonel Nelson Miles and Major William Price, were attacked by Indians near the Washita River in Indian Territory (present-day Oklahoma). During a two-day fight, four of the six were wounded, one mortally. Troops rescued the survivors the next day. Sergeant Josiah Pennsyl, Company M, Sixth Cavalry, would be awarded the Medal of Honor for his actions during the fighting.

1877: General Howard found the Nez Perce trail and joined Sturgis's forces.

1881: Because of his actions in a battle near Fort Apache, Private First Class Will C. Barnes, Signal Corps, would eventually be awarded the Medal of Honor for "bravery in action."

1893: The territory of the Hoh Indian Reservation was set aside by an executive order.

SEPTEMBER 12

1609: Henry Hudson arrived at the Bay of New York.

1675: After Sunday services, English settlers were going from the Deerfield meeting house to facilities in Stockwell. A group of Pocumtuck attacked them, killing one man. The Pocumtuck quickly disappeared into the surrounding countryside.

1675: In Maine, according to settlers' records, the Abenaki attacked John Wakely's farmhouse in Falmouth. Seven people were killed; two were taken captive.

1862: Little Crow wrote to Colonel Sibley again. He said he had been treating his white prisoners kindly and wanted to know how they could end the fighting. Sibley replied that not giving up the white captives was not the way to peace.

1868: General Nichols, while traveling to Fort Reynolds in southeastern Colorado, was attacked by Indians. His escort ran them off. The Indians then stole eighty-five head of cattle near Bent's Old Fort and four more from a ranch near Point of Rocks.

1869: Troops acting as an escort to a wagon train skirmished with Indians near Laramie Peak, Wyoming. One soldier was wounded and another was killed.

1874: Major William Price and three troops of the Sixth Cavalry with a few "mountain how-itzers" battled a sizable group of Indians between the Sweetwater and the Dry Fork of the Washita River in Texas. Two Indians were reported killed and six wounded. Fourteen of the cavalry's mounts were killed or wounded. Twenty of the Indians' horses were captured. Army scouts Amos Chapman and William Dixon would be awarded the Medal of Honor for "gallantry in action." In a related action, Private John Harrington, Company H, was transporting dispatches from the battle scene when he and several other couriers were attacked by 125 Indians. "He was severely wounded in the hip and unable to move. He continued to fight, defending an exposed dying man." For his actions, Private Harrington would be awarded the Medal of Honor. Private Peter Roth, Company A, Corporal Edward Sharpless, Company H, Private George W. Smith, Company M, and Sergeant Zachariah Woodall, Company I, would also earn the country's highest award during the same fight. Private Smith would succumb to his wounds the next day. This was sometimes called the Buffalo Wallow Fight.

1878: Lieutenant H.S. Bishop, with thirty troopers and a few Shoshone scouts, attacked a band of Bannock Indians on the Big Wind or the Dry Fork of the Snake River southwest of Yellowstone Lake in Wyoming. One Indian was killed and seven were captured during the fighting. The captives said they were from the Boise Reservation and had escaped from the fight on September 4, 1878, on Clark's Fork with Colonel Miles. Although the army reported eleven Indians killed, the captives said the correct figure was twenty-eight. This was the last significant battle of the Bannock War. According to an official government report, forty whites and seventy-eight Indians were killed during the war.

1928: The secretary of the interior approved the allotment rolls of the Mission Creek Band of Indians from Mission Creek, California, according to their constitution.

1936: Secretary of the Interior Harold Ickes authorized an election to approve a constitution and bylaws for the Quileute Tribe of Washington. The election was held on October 10, 1936.

1965: The assistant secretary of the interior had authorized an election to approve an amendment to the constitution and bylaws of the Miccosukee Tribe of Indians of Florida. Twenty-seven voted in favor, two voted against.

1969: The Confederated Salish and Kootenai Tribe of the Flathead Reservation passed a resolution prohibiting the hunting or killing of mountain sheep.

SEPTEMBER 13

1700: According to some sources, a land-cession agreement was reached between representatives of the Susquehannock Indians and Pennsylvania.

1759: The Battle of Quebec took place. The French lost.

1794: A force of 550 Kentucky and Tennessee militia led by Major James Ore attacked the Chickamauga village of Nickajack on the Tennessee River. Many women and children were captured. Seventy braves were killed, including the village chief, The Breath. Ore's forces torched most of the village after the fighting.

1815: William Clark, Auguste Chouteau, and Ninian Edwards held a conference at Portage des Sioux, Missouri (St. Charles County). They got Missouri Sac and Foxes to promise not to join up with the Rock Island Sacs or to fight the United States.

1868: According to army records, members of the Eighth Cavalry fought with a band of Indians on the

Dragoon Fork of the Verde River in Arizona. Two Indians were killed, and one soldier was wounded.

1871: Indians skirmished with a group of settlers near Tucson, Arizona, according to official army records. Two settlers were killed.

1872: Indians skirmished with a group of soldiers from the Second Cavalry between Beaver Creek and Sweet Water, Wyoming, according to official army records. One Indian was wounded. The fighting started on September 10.

1873: Part of the Ute Reservation went to the United States.

1877 First and Seventh Cavalry soldiers under Colonel S.D. Sturgis fought a group of Nez Perce Indians near Canyon Creek west of Billings, Montana. According to army documents, three soldiers and twenty-one Indians were killed. Captain T.H. French and ten soldiers were wounded.

1878: Dull Knife and his Northern Cheyenne followers had left their reservation in Indian Territory (present-day Oklahoma). They were heading back to their old homelands. They crossed the Cimarron River, 150 miles north of Fort Reno, near Turkey Springs in central Indian Territory and established a camp in some canyons. A group of Arapaho talked with Dull Knife and told him the nearby soldiers wanted them to return to the reservation. Dull Knife refused, and the soldiers attacked. The Indians had the best strategic positions and pinned down the soldiers. After making their escape, the Cheyenne were pursued along their entire northward journey.

1890: First Cavalry soldiers fought a group of Indians on the Tongue River Agency in Montana. According to army documents, two Indians were killed.

1984: Activist Dennis Banks surrendered.

SEPTEMBER 14

1712: French King Louis XIV granted exclusive trade and governmental rights in Louisiana for fifteen years to wealthy merchant Antoine Crozat, Marquis de Chatel.

1726: According to some sources, a land-cession agreement was reached by representatives of Great Britain and the Cayuga, Onondaga, and Seneca Indians.

1755: Last month, Virginia Governor Robert Dinwiddie appointed George Washington commander in chief of all forces in Virginia. The governor ordered him to establish his base of operations in northern Virginia in Winchester. On this day, Washington arrived in Winchester. The villagers were either preparing for war with the local Indians, or they were in the process of moving to a safer area. Next year, Washington would begin the construction of Fort Loudoun in Winchester.

1758: British Major James Grant attacked the apparently lightly defended French Fort Duquesne with 800 soldiers. However, the French had set a trap by hiding a large force of soldiers and Indian warriors. The French and Indians defeated the British, with Major Grant and 107 of his soldiers being taken prisoner. All told, 270 British were killed and a little more than forty were wounded in the fighting. The French and Indian losses were substantially less.

1763: Seneca fought with a supply wagon train just south of Niagara as part of Pontiac's Rebellion. The train was carrying supplies from Fort Schlosser to Fort Niagara. One source cited this as the worst defeat of the war for the army.

1777: Spanish Governor Galvez issued an act in New Orleans. He ordered the military and Spanish subjects to "respect the rights of these Indians in the lands they occupy and to protect them in the possession thereof."

1779: General John Sullivan and his force of 4,500 American soldiers continued their attack on suspected pro-British Indian villages in New York. They struck Gathtsegwarohare on the Genesee River. After destroying most of the village, Sullivan's troops moved on to other villages. In all of his battles since August, he lost only forty men.

1780: Creek and British forces under British Creek Indian Superintendent Thomas Browne had captured Augusta, Georgia. A force of 500 Americans attempted to retake the town. The Creek sustained severe losses.

1814: A force of British soldiers and Red Stick Creek Indians led by Captain George Woodbine attacked Mobile, Alabama. Although the British had four warships at their disposal, the American forces held out until the British and Creek forces gave up the fight.

1816: A treaty (7 Stat. 148) ceded Cherokee lands in Muscle Shoals and Great Bend areas of northern Alabama for $11,000 annual payments for ten years. It was signed at the Chickasaw Council House.

1858: Colonel Miles had moved out of the Canyon de Chelly twelve miles to an area where the Navajos kept their herds of sheep. Miles's soldiers had captured 6,000 of the sheep. The Navajos attacked Miles's camp, but it was only a minor engagement. The troops returned to the fort the next day. There would continue to be minor skirmishes during the next several months.

1859: Robert S. Neighbors had a great deal of respect for Indians. He served as an Indian agent for the Republic of Texas and for the United States. His compassion for the Indians made him an enemy to many Texans who hated Indians. Neighbors was murdered for being an "Indian-lover" by Edward Cornett at Fort Belknap.

1866: Soldiers from the First Cavalry fought with a band of Indians near Camp Wilson in Oregon. The army reported that one Indian was killed and one was captured.

1868: According to army records, members of the Ninth Cavalry fought with a band of Indians in the Horse Head Hills of Texas. One soldier was wounded and two Indians were killed.

1869: According to army records, members of the Second Cavalry fought with a band of Indians near Popo Agie, Wyoming. Two soldiers and seven Indians were wounded. Two Indians were killed.

1869: James Camp and Private John Holt, Company K, Seventh Cavalry, were killed by Indians near the Little Wind River, Wyoming. On the

Sitting Bull, Sioux chief (LOC)

Popoagie River, Wyoming, Lieutenant Charles Stambaugh and Troop D, Second Cavalry, skirmished with Indians. Two soldiers and two Indians were killed. Ten Indians were wounded in the fight.

1876: Fifth Cavalry soldiers fought some Indians on Owl Creek (Belle Fourche River) in Dakota Territory. According to army documents, one soldier was killed.

1878: Fourth Cavalry soldiers fought a group of Indians near Red Hill, Indian Territory. According to army documents, one soldier was killed.

1961: An act (75 Stat. 505) was passed by Congress to "authorize the exchange of lands for the Pueblo Indians. Title to lands acquired will be in trust status."

1970: An election to approve a constitution and bylaws for the San Pasqual Band of Mission (Diegueno) Indians in the San Pasqual Reservation was authorized by the acting assistant commissioner of Indian affairs. The election was held on November 29, 1970.

1975: An amendment to the constitution and bylaws of the Manchester Band of Pomo Indians of the Manchester Rancheria was approved in an election by a vote of 60–4.

1989: The United States Post Office issued a Sitting Bull stamp.

Every: Jicarilla Apache fair (through September 15).

SEPTEMBER 15

1655: Esopus Indians attacked New Amsterdam in sixty-four war canoes. This retaliatory raid was for the killing of an Indian woman by a settler for stealing peaches. It was called the Peach War by many, and casualties were slight on both sides as the Dutch drove the Indians out of the settlement. Leaving New Amsterdam, the Indians attacked Staten Island and the Pavonia settlements in modern Jersey City, New Jersey. There the casualties were considerably higher. Fifty settlers were killed, and almost 100 were captured.

1797: The Seneca signed a treaty with Robert Morris and Jeremiah Wadsworth on the Genesee River in Ontario County, New York, to get a two-square-mile piece of the Tuscarora Reservation.

1830: Secretary of War John Eaton and John Coffee arrived at Dancing Rabbit Creek to talk to the Choctaws about selling their lands and moving west. They told the Choctaws that the federal government could not stop state laws that required them to move. They also told the Choctaws that if they resisted the white armies would outnumber them.

1858: The Butterfield Overland Mail route began operation from St. Louis, Missouri, and Memphis, Tennessee, through Fort Smith, Arkansas, to San Francisco, California. Contrary to many story lines in film and elsewhere, and unlike the Pony express, the Butterfield Overland Mail was attacked by the Apache only one time.

1868: Approximately 100 Indians attacked Tenth Cavalry troops led by Captain George Graham on the Big Sandy Creek, Colorado. The troops claimed eleven Indians killed and fourteen wounded while sustaining only seven injuries themselves.

1868: According to army records, members of the Seventh Cavalry and Third Infantry under Lieutenant Colonel Alfred Sully fought with a band of Indians near the Sand Hills in Indian Territory. The fighting started on September 11. Three soldiers and twenty-two Indians were killed. Five soldiers and twelve Indians were wounded.

1869: Lieutenant J.H. Spencer, leading Company B, Fourth Infantry, was attacked by 300 Indians near Whiskey Gap, Wyoming. One soldier was captured and presumed dead.

1874: "Treaty 4 Between Her Majesty The Queen and The Cree and Saulteaux Tribe of Indians at the Qu'appelle and Fort Ellice" was signed in Canada.

1876: Troop F, Ninth Cavalry, under Captain Henry Carroll fought with Indians in the Florida Mountains of New Mexico. One Indian was killed and one soldier was wounded. Eleven head of livestock were recovered.

1884: Sitting Bull appeared at Eden Musee in New York City.

1903: By executive order, the Fort McDowell Indian Reservation was established northeast of Phoenix, Arizona. It covered 24,680 acres and was home to Yavapai, Mohave-Apache, and Apache Indians.

1976: An amendment to the constitution and bylaws of the Manzanita Band of Mission Indians was ratified.

SEPTEMBER 16

1684: Naumkeag Indian and son of former Sachem Wenepoykin, James Quannapowit petitioned the English of Marblehead, Massachusetts, on July 14, 1684. He complained they were giving out lands that rightfully belonged to him. A deed was finally signed by all parties in order for the English to hold "rightful title" to the land.

1804: A Navajo war party attacked the village of Cebolleta in northwestern New Mexico. The war party of 500–1,000 Navajos found the village's three-foot-thick, ten-foot-high wall difficult to breach. After a four-day siege, with numerous casualties on both sides, the Navajos left the area. The thirty Spanish families who had settled the village in 1800 saw many more raids in the future.

1815: The Iowa signed a peace treaty (7 Stat. 136) at Portage des Sioux (modern St. Charles County, Missouri). The United States was represented by William Clark, Ninian Edwards, and Auguste Choteau.

1850: In a letter to the president of the United States, Senator John Fremont stated Spanish law gave Indians rights to their lands. He felt the United States had to enact some laws to revoke the Indians' rights. Under the Treaty of Guadalupe Hidalgo, the United States agreed to recognize Spanish land titles in the newly acquired California.

1867: According to army records, members of the Fourth Cavalry fought with a band of Indians near Fort Inge, Texas. No injuries were reported on either side.

1867: The Tenth Cavalry fought with a group of Indians near the Salinas River in Kansas. Two civilians were killed and one soldier was wounded, according to army records.

1869: According to army records, members of the Ninth Cavalry and the Forty-First Infantry fought with a band of Indians near Salt Fork of the Brazos River in Texas. Three soldiers were wounded.

1878: According to a report by Lieutenant Colonel William Lewis of Fort Dodge in southwestern Kansas, Dull Knife and his 300-plus followers had been seen raiding local ranches near Bluff Creek, Indian Territory (present-day Oklahoma).

1879: Tenth Cavalry and Twenty-Fifth Infantry soldiers fought a group of Indians in the Van Horn Mountains in western Texas. According to army documents, no casualties were reported.

1879: The secretary of war ordered the military to send troops to the White River Ute Agency to protect the local (white) inhabitants and to arrest the Indians instigating troubles in the region.

1893: About 100,000 people participated in the run for land in the recently purchased Cherokee Strip of Indian Territory (present-day Oklahoma). The Cherokees were pressured into selling the land to the federal government.

1974: A U.S. court dismissed charges against Dennis Banks and Russell Means for their activities at the Wounded Knee, South Dakota, occupation. The judge stated that the Federal Bureau of Investigation had "lied and suborned perjury" during the trial.

1974: Raymond Lightfoot, area director of the Minneapolis office of the Bureau of Indian Affairs, authorized an election for an amendment to the constitution of the Red Lake Band of Chippewa Indians of Minnesota.

SEPTEMBER 17

1718: According to some sources, a land-cession agreement was reached by representatives of the Delaware Indians and Pennsylvania.

1778: The Delaware signed a treaty (7 Stat. 13). Delaware Principal Chief Koquethagechton (White Eyes) was appointed as a colonel at the treaty signing. He worked to see the Delaware Nation become the fourteenth American state. The treaty was signed in Pittsburgh by three chiefs: White Eyes, The Pipe, and John Killbuck, as well as Andrew and Thomas Lewis.

1799: Commissioners had established a camp at the confluence of the Flint and the Chattahoochee Rivers in Creek territory. They were there to eventually draw a treaty line through Creek lands. During the summer many Creek had visited the camp to complain of the land cession. Chief Hopoheilthle Micco and some Tallassee followers attacked the camp. They stole supplies and insulted the commissioners. Later, Creek chiefs beat the Tallassee chief to death for his actions.

1812: After a series of raids into Georgia, local militia led by Colonel Daniel Newnan entered Spanish-held Florida looking for Seminole. They

Delegation of six Indians from the Mandan and Arikara Tribes with three interpreters (NA)

started a running battle with the Alachua Band of Seminole led by King Payne. This fight lasted until the militia was reinforced on October 11.

1818: Lewis Cass and Duncan McArthur, representing the United States, signed a treaty (7 Stat. 178) with the Ottawa, Seneca, Shawnee, and Wyandot Tribes on St. Mary's River on the Indiana-Ohio border. The treaty covered reservation boundaries and annuities.

1836: According to a treaty (7 Stat. 511), the Missouri Sac and Fox and Iowa tribes were given the following lands: "the small strip of land on the south side of the Missouri River, lying between the Kickapoo northern boundary line and the Grand Nemahaw River, and extending from the Missouri back and westwardly with the said Kickapoo line and the Grand Nemahaw, making 400 sections, to be divided between the said Iowas and Missouri Sacs and Foxes; the upper half to the Iowas, the lower half to the Sacs and Foxes." Years later, much of this land was ceded back to the United States.

1851: The Fort Laramie Treaty (15 Stat. 635) was signed by more tribes. The area mentioned eventually covered 1,382.5 square miles and was occupied by the Arikara, Gros Ventre, and Mandan Indians. It was called the Fort Berthold Reservation.

1858: Colonel George Wright met with some Coeur d'Alene chiefs at the Sacred Heart Mission to sign the first of a series of peace and friendship treaties.

1868: In Colorado, Brevet Colonel G.A. Forsyth (Ninth Cavalry) and fifty scouts were following the trail of Indians who had been marauding near Sheridan City. As they approached the "Arickaree" Fork of the Republican River, they were attacked by 700 Indians. The soldiers moved to an island that was 125 yards long by fifty yards wide. The army claimed that it killed thirty-five Indians while losing only six, including Lieutenant F.H. Beecher and surgeon Moore. Forsyth and his men lived on horseflesh until September 25, when a relief column of buffalo soldiers (black troops) arrived. Roman Nose died in the fighting. This was called the Battle of Beecher's Island by the soldiers.

1868: Indians attacked and burned Ellis Station in Kansas, killing one station employee in the process. The Saline settlements were attacked again. The Indians were driven off by Seventh Cavalry troops. Three miles from Fort Bascom in eastern New Mexico, Indians killed a herder and stole his thirty mules. Troops from the fort pursued the Indians for 125 miles but could not catch them.

1868: According to army records, settlers fought with a group of Indians near Fort Bascom, New Mexico. One settler was killed and one was wounded.

1869: Indians stole a some livestock, and soldiers from Fort Stanton in central New Mexico pursued them. The soldiers followed a trail to an Indian village, which they subsequently destroyed. In the process, three Indians were wounded. No one was killed. At Point of Rocks, Wyoming, a stagecoach was attacked and the driver was killed. On Twin Creek in Wyoming, soldiers escorting the mail were attacked and pursued into the mountains by Indians.

1877: Colonel Miles received orders to cut off the Nez Perce's attempt to reach Canada.

Haskell Institute football team (NA)

1878: Indian scouts for the army fought a group of Indians near Bear Creek, New Mexico. According to army documents, one soldier and two Indians were killed.

1879: According to a report by Major Albert Morrow, Ninth Cavalry, Indians fought settlers in the Black Range near Hillsboro, New Mexico. Hostile Indians killed ten citizens and seized all of their livestock.

1884: The Haskell Institute in Lawrence, Kansas, was dedicated for educating Indian youth.

1966: According to newspaper story in the *Washington Post,* "A flaming meteorite lit up the skies across the north central United States last night, frightening hundreds of persons who saw it before it broke up in bits of smoking debris over northern Indiana." The meteorite caused a few small fires as well. According to another source, "On New York State's official 'Indian Day,' Sept. 17, 1966, the Hopi delegation journeyed to the Tuscarora Reserve to join the assembled seventeen Indian Tribes and guests from all over the world. Many had asked for a sign and several expressed that hope audibly. It came that evening about 8:35 in the form of a tremendous rose-colored fireball lighting the scene as though by day, streaking across the sky above them."

1975: The area director of the Sacramento area office of the Bureau of Indian Affairs ratified an amendment to the constitution and bylaws of the Manchester Band of Pomo Indians of the Manchester Rancheria.

1975: Commissioner of Indian Affairs Morris Thompson ratified an amendment to the constitution of the Minnesota Chippewa Tribe, consisting of the Chippewa Indians of the White Earth, Leech Lake, Fond du Lac, Bois Forte (Nett Lake), and Grand Portage Reservations.

1975: Commissioner of Indian Affairs Morris Thompson ratified a constitution and bylaws for the Sauk-Suiattle Indian Tribe.

SEPTEMBER 18

524: Maya King Kan B'alam I (Great Sun Snake Jaguar) was born. Eventually, he ruled over Palenque (Mexico).

1675: Following several raids by King Philip's Indians, Deerfield, in central Massachusetts, was abandoned. Eighty residents under Captain Lathrop, from Ipswich in eastern Massachusetts, rode over to Deerfield to harvest several fields of grain. On their way home, the Europeans stopped for a rest at a brook. They were attacked by several hundred Indians, who had been following them for some time. By the time a nearby militia could come to the rescue, sixty-eight of the settlers had been killed.

1759: The French surrendered Quebec.

1813: After the massacre at Fort Mims, Alabama, by the Red Stick Creek, word of the Creek Uprising spread. In Nashville, Tennessee, Governor William Blount called on the state legislature to "teach these barbarous sons of the woods their inferiority." Cries for vengeance rang throughout the area. In a few weeks, Andrew Jackson began his campaign against the Creek.

1823: Thirty-one Seminole signed a treaty with the United States (7 Stat. 224) on Moultrie Creek in Florida. Six chiefs were given large estates to get them to agree to the treaty. Those chiefs were: John Blunt, Eneah Emathla, Emathlochee, Tuski Hadjo, Econchattemicco, and Mulatto King. The Seminole gave up lands north of Tampa Bay and returned runaway black slaves. They received an annuity of $5,000. The lands set aside for the Seminole were poor at best. The Americans were represented by James Gadsden.

1830: The Choctaw conference at Dancing Rabbit Creek officially began, with Peter P. Pitchlynn serving as chairman of the Choctaw participants. Greenwood le Flore demanded a larger delegation of Northern Choctaws. After two weeks of arguments, many of the Choctaws went home. An agreement was reached to send trusted people west to check out the new lands. A census of the Choctaw, taken this month, showed the population to be 19,554. (See September 27, 1830.)

1833: Choctaws still in the southern Mississippi District held a council and decided they would not move to the Indian Territory (present-day Oklahoma).

1851: One in a series of treaties with California Indians was signed at Camp Colus and Camp Cosumnes. The treaties were designed to reserve lands for the Indians and to protect them from Europeans.

1862: General James H. Charlatan assumed command of the Department of New Mexico. He was sent there to fight the Confederate forces and the hostile Indians.

1864: Confederate Cherokees, led by Brigadier General Stand Watie, and other Confederate forces captured a Union wagon train in modern Mayes County, Oklahoma. This supply shipment had enough food and other goods for 2,000 soldiers and was valued at $1.5 million. This was the last significant Civil War engagement in Indian Territory (present-day Oklahoma).

1873: Captain James Egan and Troops K and E, Second Cavalry, attacked a band of Sioux Indians on the North Laramie River. The troops seized eighteen horses and mules.

1876: Indian scouts fought some Indians in the caves east of Verde, Arizona. According to army documents, five Indians were killed and thirteen were captured.

1879: Captain Byron Dawson and two troops from the Ninth Cavalry found and attacked Victorio and approximately 140 Warm Springs Apache at the source of the Las Animas River in New Mexico. Two more troops of cavalry arrived under the command of Captain Charles Beyer, but the army was forced to withdraw. Five soldiers, one civilian, and two Navajo scouts were killed by the Apache. Second Lieutenant Matthias W. Day would earn the Medal of Honor for retrieving a wounded soldier while under heavy fire. Sergeant John Denny, Company C, would also win the Medal of Honor for the same actions. Second Lieutenant Robert T. Emmet would also be awarded the Medal of Honor for his actions in this day's battle.

1975: An amendment was made to the constitution and bylaws of the Manchester Band of Pomo Indians of the Manchester Rancheria.

1978: The boundaries of the Pascua Yaqui Indian Reservation were established by an act of Congress (92 Stat. 712).

1980: A base membership roll was established for the Pascua Yaqui Indians.

SEPTEMBER 19

1737: On this day was the start of the walking for the Walking Purchase from the Delaware. The walkers were Solomon Jennings, Edward Marshall, and James Yates. The walkers barely stayed below a run. By the next day at noon, Edward Marshall had covered sixty-five miles. Yates, who passed out from the exertion, died three days later. Jennings gave up the first day and was sickly for the rest of his life. Many Indians complained the "walk" did not live up to the spirit of the agreement.

1827: At Fort St. Joseph (modern Niles, Michigan), a treaty (7 Stat. 305) was signed by Lewis Cass and the Potawatomi Indians. Tribal lands were ceded, old boundaries were redrawn, and the Indians received an annuity.

1845: A peace conference was held between representatives of Texas and local Indians.

1867: In an effort to end Red Cloud's War, a new peace commission came to the end of the Union Pacific tracks near Platte City, Nebraska. The commissioners included General William Tecumseh Sherman, Indian Commissioner Nathaniel Taylor, Indian Agent William Harney, Indian Agent John Sanborn, General Alfred Terry, and a few others. The Indians were represented by Man Afraid, Pawnee Killer, Turkey Leg, Swift Bear, Standing Elk, Big Mouth, Spotted Tail, and several others. The Indians told of the problems they were having due to people invading their lands. Later, the commissioners told the Indians that the "Great Father" wanted them to move to reservations on the Missouri and Cheyenne Rivers. The Indians were not happy with this suggestion. The Indians had their own names for most of the commissioners: "Great Warrior" Sherman, "One Star Chief" Terry, "White Whiskers" Harney, and "Black Whiskers" Sanborn. The conference ended soon, and the commissioners asked the Indians to meet them at Fort Laramie in southeastern Wyoming in November.

1867: According to army records, members of the Fifth Cavalry Infantry fought with a band of Indians near Walker's Creek thirty-five miles west of Fort Harker, Kansas. One soldier was killed and three were wounded. Two Indians were killed in the fighting.

1871: Indians attacked a small detachment of troops near Foster Springs and the Red River, Indian Territory (present-day Oklahoma). One soldier was wounded, three Indians were wounded, and two Indians were killed, according to army files.

1872: Fifty Comanche Indians were attacked by an army patrol consisting of one sergeant, seven privates, and two Tonkawa Indian scouts in Jones County, Texas. According to the army report, one Mexican chief was killed and eleven stolen horses were recovered.

1879: Navajo army Indian scouts fought a group of Indians in the Miembres Mountains of New Mexico. According to army documents, two scouts were killed.

1936: An order passed on February 14, 1913, which allowed the homesteading of certain lands in the Standing Rock Indian Reservation in the Dakotas, was modified.

1974: Bonner's Ferry Kootenai Band, sixty-seven members strong, declared war on the United States. They demanded payments for seized lands, hunting, fishing, and water rights, and a 128,000-acre reservation.

1985: The Lac du Flambeau Tribal Council enacted by referendum the "Reservation Water and Shoreline Protection and Enhancement Ordinance."

Every: Laguna Pueblo festival.

SEPTEMBER 20

1654: A deed for Indian land was recorded in New England. It said, "This writing witnesseth that I Ratiocan Sagamor of Cow Harbor, have sold unto Samuel Mayo, Daniel Whitehead and Peter Wright my neck of land which makes the east side of Oyster Bay, and the west side of Cow Harbor on the north side bounded with the sound, called by the Indians Camusett."

1782: Lieutenant Richard Johnston and the York County militia were ordered to go to Pittsburgh from their patrol area in Bedford County, Pennsylvania. They joined a force led by General Hand against the Indians near Pittsburgh.

1816: A treaty (7 Stat. 150) signed by the Chickasaw paid them $16,500 a year for ten years for lands on both sides of the Tennessee River and in the Great Bend area.

1818: Lewis Cass, representing the United States, signed a treaty (7 Stat. 180) with members of the Wyandot Tribe on the St. Mary's River on the Indiana-Ohio border. The treaty involved the release of property in Michigan.

1822: Lakota Chief Red Cloud (Makhpiya-Luta) was born.

1828: Lewis Cass and Pierre Menard, representing the United States, and the Potawatomi Nation signed a treaty (7 Stat. 317) at Fort St. Joseph (modern Niles, Michigan). Land near Lake Michigan is ceded for an increase in the tribe's annuity.

1836: Lieutenant Colonel John F. Lane, 690 Creek warriors, and ninety soldiers boarded a transport from Alabama en route to Tampa Bay, Florida, to fight the Seminole. They reached Fort Drane on October 19.

1858: Camp Walbach was established near Cheyenne Pass. It was in the southeastern corner of Wyoming.

1866: Soldiers from the Eighteenth Infantry fought with a band of Indians near Fort C.F. Smith in Montana. The army reported that one officer and one enlisted man were killed.

1867: According to army records, members of the Fourth Cavalry fought with a band of Indians near Devil's River in Texas. One Indian was killed.

1869: According to army records, members of the Ninth Cavalry fought with a band of Indians near the Brazos River in Texas. One soldier was wounded. The fighting lasted through the next day.

1873: Indians fought with soldiers from the Second Cavalry near Fort Fetterman, Wyoming, according to army documents. No casualties were reported.

1874: According to his citation for the Medal of Honor, "Seminole Negro Adam Paine for Gallantry on September 20th [1874] when attacked by a hugely superior party of Indians. This man is a scout of great courage." Most sources listed this as happening on September 26.

1875: The United States wanted the Black Hills. The president sent out a commission to negotiate the issue. The U.S. representatives included Iowa Senator William Allison, General Alfred Terry, trader John Collins, and missionary Samuel Hinman. The meeting was held on the White River between the Spotted Tail and Red Cloud Agencies in Dakota. When the commissioners arrived, they were astounded by the number of Indians camping in the immediate area. It was estimated there were more than 20,000 Sioux, Arapaho, and Cheyenne. The commissioners had an escort of 120 troops from nearby Fort Robinson in northwestern Nebraska. As the conference started, thousands of Indian warriors appeared and rode around the commissioners in a dramatic show of force. After the commissioners stated their interest in the mineral rights to the Black Hills, a representative of Red Cloud (who refused to attend) asked for an adjournment for a few days so the Indians could council among themselves. The commissioners agreed to return on September 23. The United States named these representatives the Allison Commission.

1875: "Treaty 5 Between Her Majesty The Queen and The Saulteaux and Swampy Cree Tribes of Indians at Beren's River and Norway House with Adhesions" was signed in Canada.

1922: An act (42 Stat. 857) was passed by Congress. It was to "allow lands reserved for schools and Agency purposes and all other unallotted land on the Fort Peck and the Blackfeet Reservations to be leased for mining purposes."

1950: Assistant Secretary of the Interior William Warne authorized an election for the adoption of a constitution and bylaws for the Ponca Tribe of Indians of Oklahoma. The election was held on September 20, 1950.

1987: Pope John Paul II visited Fort Simpson, Northwest Territories. Called "Yahtita" (Priest of Priests) in the Dene language, his service was translated into Cree, Dene, and Slavey.

SEPTEMBER 21

1638: The Treaty of Hartford was signed. After losing their battle with the English and their Indian allies, the Pequot surrendered. The surviving members of the tribe were given as servants to the Indian allies of the English.

1721: According to some sources, the Tuscarora set out to nearby European settlements in preparation for the onset of their attacks the next day.

1753: According to some reports, an agreement to return prisoners was reached by representatives of the British in Massachusetts and the Penobscot Indians.

1866: Soldiers from the Eighteenth Infantry fought with a band of Indians on the Tongue River in Dakota Territory. The army reported that two enlisted men were wounded.

1869: According to army records, members of the Ninth Cavalry fought with a band of Indians near the Brazos River in Texas. One soldier was wounded. The fighting started the day before.

1878: Captains Joseph Rendlebrock and Charles Morse, with 150 soldiers and fifty local volunteers, finally found part of Dull Knife's Cheyenne. The two forces fought on Sand Creek, south of the Arkansas River, sometime after sunset. The Indians managed to escape.

1879: Based on the order issued by the secretary of war on September 16, 1879, Major T.T. Thornburgh, Troops D and F, Fifth Cavalry, Troop E, Third Cavalry, and Company E, Fourth Infantry, left Fort Fred Steele in southern Wyoming en route to the White River Agency in Colorado. This force was approximately 200 strong.

1904: Chief Joseph (Hinmaton-yalatkit or Hein-mot too-ya-la-kekt) died.

1936: The secretary of the interior authorized an election for a constitution and bylaws for the Covelo Indian Community of the Round Valley Reservation in California. The election was held on November 7, 1936.

SEPTEMBER 22

1528: Having completed five boats two days earlier, Panfilo de Narvaez loaded the remaining 242 men of his expedition and left to search for his sailing ships. They had been pursued by Apalachee Indians for some time. Most of Narvaez's force was lost at sea. Cabeza de Vaca landed on Galveston Island in Texas on November 6, 1528.

1711: The Tuscarora Indians, under Chief Hencock, joined the Coree, Pamlico, Machapunga, and Bear River Indians in an attack on the white settlements on the Trent and Pamlico Rivers in North Carolina. Almost 130 white adults and half that many children were killed. The war sprang from white settlement in Indian lands and Indian retaliations. A Swiss promoter, Baron Christoph von Graffenried, ordered the Indians removed when he discovered them on lands he had obtained from the Crown at New Bern in western North Carolina.

1784: This day marked the first run-in between a Russian settlement in Alaska and the local inhabitants.

1861: A series of horse races, with bets being placed by soldiers and Navajos, took place outside Fort Fauntleroy. A dispute arose during the third race. The Indians said it should be run again, but the soldiers took their winnings and went into the fort. The fort was closed and the Indians were told to stay out. As one Navajo tried to enter the fort, a shot rang out and the Indian was killed. Pandemonium ensued, and some soldiers began attacking the Navajos outside the fort. According to army records, a little over a dozen Navajos were killed during the Horse Race Fight.

1866: An executive order established the Shoalwater Bay Indian Reservation in Washington State.

1871: Indians attacked and killed two men who were herding livestock near Fort Sill in southern Indian Territory (present-day Oklahoma). The Indians escaped with fifteen head of livestock.

1877: Treaty Number 7 was signed by the Canadian government and representatives of the Blackfeet, Blood, Piegan, Sarcee, and Stoney Bands in Alberta.

1885: Army Indian scouts under Captain Wirt Davis fought with a group of Indians in the Teres Mountains of Mexico. According to army documents, one scout and one Indian were killed. One scout and two Indians were wounded.

SEPTEMBER 23

1519: Hernán Cortés and his army arrived at the gates of the Mexican city of Tlascala. A large crowd turned out to see the Spaniards.

1730: Seven Cherokee representatives in London, England, signed Articles of Agreement that established a formal alliance with England for the next fifty years. This gave the English exclusive trade rights with the Cherokees and made the Cherokees military allies. The Cherokees were led by Chiefs Oukah-ulah and Attakullaculla (Little Carpenter).

1761: According to newspaper reports, Cherokee Chief Attakullaculla (Little Carpenter) signed a peace treaty with English Governor Bull. This ended fighting that had been going on for almost two years in Charlestown, South Carolina.

Fort Snelling, Minnesota

1805: Pike bought land for Fort Snelling.

1839: The Cherokee Nation's supreme court was established.

1842: In a public meeting in Champoeg in the Oregon country, Elija White told the crowd that he had been appointed as the official U.S. Indian agent in Oregon.

1853: Major Earl Van Dorn had Camp Radziminski built as a supply base for the army's efforts against hostile local Indians. It was on the Otter Creek in Indian Territory (present-day Oklahoma). It was used off and on for the next seven years.

1858: Yakama Chief Owhi rode in unescorted to meet with Colonel George Wright. Owhi hoped to

Santee Sioux Indian camp captured by Colonel Sibley

save his son from being killed for his part in the recent fighting in the Pacific Northwest. Owhi was unsuccessful in his efforts and was placed under arrest.

1862: Approximately 700 Santee Sioux under Little Crow engaged in a fight at Wood Lake, Minnesota. They faced Colonel Henry Sibley and approximately 1,500 soldiers.

1867: According to army records, members of the Fifth Infantry fought with a band of Indians nine miles west of Cimarron Crossing, Kansas, on the Arkansas River. One soldier was killed, and Lieutenant Ephraim Williams was wounded.

1869: Elements of the Eighth Cavalry had been fighting hostile Indians at Red Creek, Arizona. For "gallantry in action" on this day, Privates George Ferrari and John Walker and Sergeant Charles D. Harris, Company D, would be awarded the Medal of Honor.

1869: After a long chase, soldiers from Fort Cummings in southwestern New Mexico caught a band of Indians with stolen horses. The troopers retrieved thirty of the mounts.

1873: Indians fought with soldiers from the Fifth Cavalry and some Indian scouts near Hardscrabble Creek in Arizona, according to army documents. Fourteen Indians were killed and five were captured.

1875: As the Black Hills conference was reconvened, Red Cloud was now present. No Indians were interested in parting with their sacred "Maha Sopa"—the Black Hills. Before Red Cloud could speak, a band of 300 of Crazy Horse's warriors rushed in on horseback. Crazy Horse's representative, Little Big Man, exclaimed he would kill any chief who agreed to give away the Black Hills. Although the Sioux police moved Little Big Man away from the commissioners, the commissioners realized that most of those present agreed that the Black Hills would not be given away. The commissioners decided to return to Fort Robinson in northwestern Nebraska.

1877: The Nez Perce reached the Missouri River and Cow Island Landing. The landing was guarded by Sergeant William Molchert and a small detachment of twelve Seventh Cavalry soldiers and four civilians. This was north of what is Winifred, Montana. According to army documents, one soldier and two volunteers were killed.

1918: Under authority of an act of Congress (34 Stat. 325–326), an executive order was issued that extended the trust period for ten years on allotments to the Iowa Indians in Kansas.

1954: Canadian Indians went to court over tariff issues.

SEPTEMBER 24

1676: Abenaki Indians attacked settlers in Wells, Maine, near the New Hampshire border. Three settlers were killed before the Indians retired.

1819: Lewis Cass negotiated a treaty (7 Stat. 203) for the United States with the Chippewa. For $1,000 a year, the services of a blacksmith, and provisions, the Chippewa gave up a large section of land. The treaty was signed in Saginaw, Michigan.

1829: George Vashon, representing the United States, and the Delaware Indians signed a treaty (7 Stat. 327) at the St. Mary's River on the Indiana-Ohio border. The Delaware gave up lands along the White River in exchange for land along the Missouri and Kansas Rivers. The Delaware also received an annuity.

1853: Command of Fort Phantom Hill north of Abilene, Texas, changed hands from Lieutenant

Colonel Carlos A. Waite to Major H.H. Sibley. The fort was often visited by the local Comanche, Lipan-Apache, Kiowa, and Kickapoo.

1858: Qualchan, son of Yakama Chief Owhi, rode into Colonel George Wright's camp. Qualchan was wanted for what the settlers considered murder for his part in recent fighting. Qualchan was taken into custody and later hanged.

1862: After realizing the futility of continuing to fight Colonel Sibley's troops, Little Wolf decided to speak to his Santee Sioux followers. Little Wolf could not understand how they lost the battle the day before. He still believed the Sioux were brave and the soldiers were weak. He felt betrayed. On this day, he and Shakopee, Medicine Bottle, and their followers left to travel west. Many other Santee surrendered to Colonel Sibley.

1867: According to army records, members of the Thirty-Seventh Infantry fought with a band of Indians near Nine Mile Ridge, Kansas. One soldier was wounded.

1868: Representing the United States, W.J. Cullen, commissioner, and James Tufts, secretary of Montana Territory, acting governor, and superintendent of Indian affairs, signed a treaty with the Shoshone, Bannock, and Sheepwater. One of the signers was Chief Tendoy of the Lemhi.

1869: After Indians raided Mexican ranches near Fort Bayard in southwestern New Mexico, troopers followed the Indians to their mountain village. In the fight there, three Indians were wounded. The soldiers destroyed the village and its contents.

1875: "Treaty 5 Between Her Majesty The Queen and The Saulteaux and Swampy Cree Tribes of Indians at Beren's River and Norway House with Adhesions" was signed in Canada.

1877: Major Ilges sighted the Nez Perce. Miles's force was at the Missouri River.

1946: The acting commissioner of Indian affairs had authorized an election to establish a constitution and bylaws for the Sisseton Wahpeton Sioux Tribe of South Dakota. It was approved by a vote of 300–146.

1970: The acting commissioner of Indian affairs authorized an election to establish a constitution and bylaws for the Winnemucca Shoshone Indian Colony of Nevada. The election was held on December 12, 1970.

1973: Deputy Assistant Secretary of the Interior W.L. Rogers ratified an election by the Nooksack Indian Tribe of Washington for a constitution and bylaws.

1973: An election that approved an amendment to the constitution and bylaws for the Sokaogon Chippewa Community of Wisconsin was ratified by Deputy Assistant Secretary of the Interior W.L. Rogers. The election was held on July 19, 1973.

1988: A "Disenrollment Procedure" was added to the constitution of the Pechanga Indian Reservation–Temecula Band of Luiseno Mission Indians.

SEPTEMBER 25

1539: Hernando de Soto's expedition built a bridge to cross the Suwannee River.

1675: The first of several attacks by Indians on the settlements on Cape Neddick, near York, Maine, began.

1714: The five Iroquois Nations sent the governor of New York a letter. They stated that the Tuscarora had joined the Iroquois Confederacy. Long ago, they had moved away. Now, they had returned.

1793: Near Knoxville, Tennessee, a group of around 300 Chickamauga, including Captain Bench, Doublehead, and John Watts, attacked Alexander Cavett's fort. Cavett and three other men were guarding ten women and children. After a few Chickamauga were killed, John Watts called for a parley. He promised not to kill the settlers if they surrendered. Finding their situation hopeless, the settlers gave up and opened the fort. Against the wishes of Bench and Watts, Doublehead killed all of the settlers except one boy saved by Watts. The boy met his own death a few days later by another angry Indian.

1868: On September 17, Brevet Colonel Forsyth and fifty scouts were attacked by 700 Indians. Two scouts escaped to Fort Wallace in western Kansas to get help. Brevet Colonel H.C. Bankhead and 100 men of the Fifth Cavalry, along with Brevet Lieutenant Colonel Louis Carpenter's company from the Tenth Cavalry, arrived to relieve Forsyth. Carpenter was awarded the Medal of Honor for his actions. General Luther Bradley, from the Department of the Platte River, also arrived to help.

1872: Indians skirmished with a group of soldiers from the Fifth Cavalry in Muchos Canyon on the Santa Maria River in Arizona, according to official army records. Forty Indians were killed.

1877: A group of local volunteers under Major Guido Ilges fought a band of Nez Perce Indians near Cow Creek Canyon, Montana. According to army documents, one volunteer was killed and two Nez Perce were wounded.

1879: The 200 men under Major T.T. Thornburgh arrived at Fortification Creek, Colorado, en route to the White River Agency. Their mission was to protect the local settlers and arrest hostile Indians. Thornburgh's thirty-man infantry company stayed at this location and established a base camp for Major Thornburgh's expedition.

1919: The Muskeg Lake Cree voted to sell 8,920 acres of land in Saskatchewan.

1935: The constitution and bylaws of the Fort Belknap Indian Community of the Fort Belknap Indian Reservation in Montana were adopted.

1975: The first Indian prayer was offered in the U.S. Senate.

1975: The commissioner of Indian affairs authorized an election for a constitution for Utu Utu Gwaitu Paiute Tribe of the Benton Paiute Reservation in California. The election was held on November 22, 1975.

SEPTEMBER 26

1675: Troops under Virginia Colonel John Washington and Maryland Major Thomas Trueman surrounded the main base of the Susquehannock Indians. They were there to determine whether these Indians were responsible for attacking colonial settlements. Trueman called out the Susquehannock for a conference under a flag of truce. Five chiefs came out of their fortified position to talk. They denied being involved in the attacks. Trueman had them led away and killed. Trueman got off with a minor fine from the Maryland assembly for this act.

1706: Miskouaki, an Ottawa from Mackinaw, met with the Marquis de Vaudreuil. He told him that the Miami and the Ottawa had been fighting each other near Detroit.

1760: Because of the recent fighting with British forces, more than 2,000 Cherokees met in Nequassee (modern Franklin, North Carolina) to hear Chiefs Oconostota and Ostenaco talk of "burying the hatchet." It was agreed that the fighting should end. The British still wanted to fight in order to avenge their losses at Fort Loudoun.

1777: Early this morning, Captain William Foreman and his company of thirty-four militia left Wheeling, Virginia, to patrol for Indians along Grave Creek. Following the creek, the militia was ambushed by forty Wyandot. Twenty-six of the militia, including Foreman, were killed in the fighting.

1833: In Chicago, George Porter and the United Potawatomi, Ottawa, and Chippewa signed a treaty (7 Stat. 431), whereby they ceded approximately 5 million acres of land in Illinois and Wisconsin for land west of the Mississippi River.

1840: On the Creek Reservation in Indian Territory (present-day Oklahoma), eventual Principal Chief Pleasant Porter (Talof Harjo) was born.

1842: The Nez Perce missionaries were reorganized.

1844: The first issue of the *Cherokee Advocate* was published in Tahlaquah, Indian Territory (present-day Oklahoma). This was the second newspaper published by the Cherokee Nation. It featured articles in both Cherokee and English.

1867: Approximately 110 members of the First Cavalry, Twenty-Third Infantry, and fifteen Warm Springs Indian scouts (Boise Indian scouts) fought with approximately seventy-five Paiute, thirty Pit River, and a few Modoc Indians in Infernal Canyon near Pitt River (south of modern Alturas, California). Lieutenant Colonel George Crook was commanding the military forces. Chief Si-e-ta led the combined Indian force. One officer, six soldiers, and one civilian were killed in this three-day fight. Eleven soldiers were wounded. Indians losses were twenty killed, twelve wounded, and two captured.

1868: According to army records, members of the Twenty-Seventh Infantry fought with a band of Indians near Fort Rice, Dakota Territory. One soldier was killed.

1869: General Thomas Duncan, leading men from Troops B, C, F, L, and M, Fifth Cavalry, Troops B, C, and M, Second Cavalry, plus two companies of Pawnee scouts, after a long march, set up camp along Prairie Dog Creek, Kansas. Duncan's advance guard of twenty troopers, led by Lieutenant William Volkmar, attacked a group of Indians trying to cut off Major North and William "Buffalo Bill" Cody, the chief scout and guide. In the ensuing fight, the cavalry chased the Indians to a village of fifty-six lodges that was being abandoned in great haste. One Indian was captured, and he identified the band as Sioux, led by Whistler and Pawnee Killer, survivors of the Summit Springs fight on July 11, 1869. In New Mexico, troopers chased a war party into the San Francisco Mountains. The troopers discovered a village, which they destroyed. They also killed two Indians.

1874: Colonel R.S. Mackenzie and Troops A, D, E, F, H, I, and K, Fourth Cavalry, had two skirmishes with Indians before they found five camps of Southern Cheyenne, Lone Wolf's Kiowa, Comanche, and other Indians in Palo Duro Canyon near Red River, Texas. The soldiers destroyed more than 100 lodges and all of the supplies. Some 1,400 horses and mules were captured; many were taken to Tule Valley and killed. One soldier was wounded and four Indians were killed, according to army reports. Lone Wolf and 252 Kiowa escaped. Many sources reported this battle as happening on September 28. Corporal Edwin Phoenix, Privates Gregory Mahoney and William McCabe, Company E, and Indian scout Adam Paine would be awarded the Medal of Honor for their gallantry during the fighting (September 26–28).

1877: Eighth and Tenth Cavalry Infantry soldiers captured five Indians near Saragossa, Mexico, according to army documents.

1877: According to army reports, Major Guido Ilges, a partial company of the Seventh Infantry, and thirty-six volunteers fought a two-hour battle with the Nez Perce. Ilges eventually retreated to Cow Island, feeling outmanned by the Nez Perce.

1879: After leaving Fortification Creek, Major T.T. Thornburgh and three cavalry troops made camp along Bear Creek in Colorado en route to the White River Ute agency. While in camp, several Ute leaders met Thornburgh and discussed his activities. The conversations were friendly, and the Indians left on a positive note.

1879: Captain Albert Morrow and 197 soldiers attacked Victorio and his Warm Springs Apache followers in the Black Range near Ojo Caliente, New Mexico. The fighting lasted until September 30. Three Apache were killed. The army reported that it recovered sixty horses and mules.

1975: An election on amendments to the constitution and bylaws of the Southern Ute Indian Tribe of the Southern Ute Reservation in Colorado was held. Of the 268 eligible voters, 92 vote in favor, 55 against.

1986: The Nez Perce amended their constitution and bylaws.

SEPTEMBER 27

1719: Charles Claude du Tisne (du Tissenet) was in northern Oklahoma near the Arkansas River. He claimed the territory for France. Eventually, a trading post was built near Newkirk.

1749: According to some reports, an agreement regarding peace and the return of prisoners was reached by representatives of the British in Massachusetts and the Norridgewock and Penobscot Indians.

1778: Forces under General John Sullivan destroyed the Indian town of Tioga (near modern Athens, Pennsylvania). The village was at the crossroads of several Indian trails and was considered the southern entrance to the Iroquois lands.

1827: According to some historians, this day marked the end of the Winnebago expedition. After the Red Bird War, which started on June 29, 1827, Winnebago Chief Red Bird surrendered in response to the army's threat to destroy the entire tribe. Red Bird was found guilty of murdering several settlers and rivermen; he died in prison before sentencing.

1830: The Dancing Rabbit Creek Treaty (7 Stat. 333) was concluded, whereby the Choctaws agreed to sell lands in Mississippi and to move to Indian Territory (present-day Oklahoma). Their new lands were bounded by Fort Smith along the Arkansas River, to the source of the Canadian Fork, to the Red River, to Arkansas Territory. This was the first treaty after the passage of the Indian Removal Act. Many chiefs got large parcels of land or money for signing, including Principal Chief Greenwood le Flore. The Choctaws had three years to complete the move. The United States was represented by Generals John Coffee and John Eaton.

1833: The Creek were in council at Wetumpka, Alabama (north of modern Montgomery). They drafted a resolution to Secretary of War Lewis Cass stating not only that whites had not been removed from their lands but also that many more had moved in. State courts had defied federal laws and ruled in favor of the local white intruders.

1850: The Donation Act was passed by Congress, allowing settlers to have lands in Washington Territory regardless of Indian claims.

Little Raven, chief of the Arapaho (LOC)

1861: About 200 Apache warriors attacked the mining town of Pinto Alto. Captain Martin and the Arizona volunteer guards helped to fight them off.

1867: Medicine Lodge Creek was sixty miles south of Fort Larned in southwestern Kansas. A peace commission had been established there to try to remove Indians from the area between the Arkansas and Platte Rivers. The government hoped to establish a reservation for the Southern Plains Indians, including the Cheyenne, Arapaho, Kiowa, Comanche, and the Apache of the region. Representing the U.S. government were Indian Commissioner Nathaniel Taylor, John Henderson, Samuel Tappen, Indian Agent John Sanborn, Indian Agent William Harney, and General Alfred Terry. Some of the Indians who attended the meeting were: Black Kettle, Ten Bears, Gray Beard, Little Raven, Little Robe, Tall Bull, Buffalo Chief, and Roman Nose. Roman Nose arrived in the Indians camp for the meeting planned on October 16. Eventually, 4,000 Indians attended the conference.

1867: According to army records, the fight that started the day before between the First Cavalry, Twenty-Third Infantry, and Boise Indian scouts and a combined force of Paiute, Pit River, and Modoc Indians in Infernal Canyon near Pitt River (south of modern Alturas, California) continued. Lieutenant J. Madigan was killed on this day.

1869: General Duncan's troops destroyed the Indian village and provisions found after the fight on Prairie Dog Creek the day before. The troopers tried unsuccessfully to follow the village residents for several days. Surveyors' tools belonging to Nelson Buck were discovered in the village. Buck and eleven others in his surveying party were killed near this area several days earlier.

1879: While proceeding toward the White River Agency, Major T.T. Thornburgh and his three cavalry troops met a White River Agency employee named Eskridge and several leading Ute Indians. Eskridge had a letter from the White River agent, N.C. Meeker. The letter stated that the Ute were agitated by Thornburgh's advance and wished him to stop. They suggested that Major Thornburgh and five soldiers come into the agency without the rest of the troops for a talk. Thornburgh agreed to come to the agency on September 29 with a five-man escort, but he asked for a representative group of Ute chiefs to visit his camp before the agency meeting. Thornburgh then continued his march.

1894: The Bureau of Indian Affairs started putting Indian kids in school with whites.

1917: By Executive Order No. 2711, President Wilson established the Cocopah Indian Reservation south of Yuma, Arizona. The reservation had 1,772 acres.

1967: The Oneida Tribe of Indians of Wisconsin listed an official membership roll, as per federal statute (81 Stat. 229).

SEPTEMBER 28

1542: Spanish explorer Juan Rodriguez Cabrillo landed at San Diego Bay, California.

1566: Father Pedro Martinez had sailed from Spain in hopes of reaching St. Augustine, Florida. He hoped to convert the Indians to Christianity. Unable to find the Spanish settlement, the priest and several others set out in a small boat to get directions from local Indians. A storm separated them from the mother ship. While still seeking directions to St. Augustine, they encountered a Timucua war party. A fight ensued, and all but four of the Spanish were killed.

1759: English Indian Superintendent Edmund Atkin met with Creek at the upper village of Tuckabatchee (near modern Tallassee, Alabama). During the meeting, one of the Creek tried to kill Atkin. Other Creek stopped the attack. Atkin's trip raised suspicion among some of the Creek, and factionalism had broken out. Atkin survived and spent a month in the village.

1778: A battle was fought between American forces and pro-British Indians near the Pennsylvania town of Wyalusing. The Americans, led by Colonel Thomas Hartley, won the fight.

1836: Two treaties were signed by the Sac and Fox (7 Stat. 520).

1839: Cherokee women could now legally marry white men.

1841: Aagaunash (Billy Caldwell) was born the son of an Indian mother and a British officer. He lived with Indians most of his life and eventually became a Potawatomi chief. He served as Tecumseh's secretary and as a liaison to the British until the end of the War of 1812. He fought for the United States against Red Bird and Black Hawk. He also signed several peace treaties for the Potawatomi. He died on this day in Council Bluffs, Iowa.

1864: Black Kettle held a parley with Colorado officials in Denver. Among the participants were: Governor John Evans, Colonel Chivington, Colonel George Shoup, Major E. Wynkoop, Indian Agent S. Whiteley; Cheyenne Chiefs White Antelope and Bull Bear; Arapahos Neva, Bosse, Heap of Buffalo, and Na-ta-nee; and interpreter John S. Smith.

1866: Soldiers from the First Cavalry fought with a band of Indians on Dunder and Blitzen Creek in Idaho. The army reported one enlisted man wounded.

1866: According to army reports, soldiers from the Second Cavalry fought some Indians along La Bonte Creek in Montana. One soldier was wounded in the skirmish.

1867: In the final day of a three-day fight, the First Cavalry, Twenty-Third Infantry, and Boise Indian scouts fought a combined force of Paiute, Pit River, and Modoc Indians in Infernal Canyon near Pitt River (south of modern Alturas, California). A total of one officer, six soldiers, and one civilian were killed. Eleven soldiers were wounded. Indians losses were twenty killed, twelve wounded, and two captured.

1869: According to army records, members of the Eighth Cavalry fought a band of Indians near Red Creek, Arizona. Approximately a dozen Indians were killed.

1874: Brevet Major General (Colonel) Ranald Mackenzie, with approximately 600 soldiers of the Fourth Cavalry, led an attack on the Indians residing in the Palo Duro Canyon in the Texas Panhandle. Four Indians and no soldiers were reported killed. However, much of the Indians' provisions were destroyed, including as many as 1,400 Indian horses killed by the soldiers. It was a major psychological blow for the few Southern Plains Indians still not living on reservations. This was called the Battle of Palo Duro Canyon. It was the major battle of the Red River War.

1968: An act (82 Stat. 884) was passed by Congress to "authorize the purchase, sale exchange, mortgage, and long-term leasing of land by the Swinomish Indian Tribal Community."

1977: The Phoenix area director of the Bureau of Indian Affairs authorized an election for Amendment 3 to the constitution for the Papago (Tohono O'odham). The election was held on January 21, 1978.

SEPTEMBER 29

1671: According to some sources, a treaty of allegiance was reached between representatives of

Sioux and William T. Sherman signing treaty at Fort Laramie, Wyoming (LOC)

the Plymouth Plantations and the Wampanoag Indians.

1753: According to some reports, an agreement to return captives was reached between representatives of the British in Massachusetts and the Norridgewock Indians.

1769: The expedition to explore the central California coast led by Gaspar de Portolá had camped at a site near what is modern Monterey. Along the Salina River, members of the expedition encountered a small Indian hunting party.

1782: General Edward Hand had been leading an expedition against the Indians in the area of Pittsburgh, Pennsylvania. General George Washington canceled the expedition.

1806: Zebulon Pike held a grand council with the Pawnee. Pike estimated that 400 Pawnee warriors attended. He hoped to win their allegiance to the United States rather than to Spain.

1817: The Treaty of the Rapids of the Miami River (7 Stat. 160) was signed. Lewis Cass and Duncan McArthur, representing the U.S. government, signed the peace treaty with the Chippewa, Potawatomi, Wyandot, Shawnee, and other tribes. The Indians got annual payments in exchange for land cessions.

1843: A treaty was signed between the Republic of Texas and the Anadarko, Biloxi, Cherokee,

Chickasaw, Delaware, Hainai, Kichai, Tawakoni, and Waco.

1866: Soldiers from the 18th Infantry fought with a band of Indians near Fort Phil Kearny in Dakota Territory. The army reported that one enlisted man was killed.

1867: According to army records, members of the Thirty-Seventh Infantry fought with a band of Indians near Fort Garland, Colorado. Two soldiers were killed.

1868: Indians attacked a house on Sharp's Creek. They killed the man living there, Mr. Bassett. The house was burned down. Mrs. Bassett and her two-day-old baby were taken captive. Mrs. Bassett was too weak to travel; the Indians assaulted her, then left her and her baby to die on the prairie.

1869: After pursuing a band of Indians for a week, troops from Fort Bayard in southwestern New Mexico found their village. The troopers destroyed the village, killing three and wounding three Indians. One soldier was wounded in the fight.

1872: Colonel R.S. Mackenzie and Troops A, D, F, I, and L, Fourth Cavalry, and some Tonkawa scouts were near the North Fork of the Red River (near modern Lefors, Texas) when they discovered a Comanche camp of 200 lodges. Mackenzie attacked and destroyed most of the encampment. According to government reports, twenty-three Indians were killed; approximately 125 warriors were captured. One soldier was killed and three were wounded. Many horses and mules were seized by the army. For "gallantry in action," Private Edward Branagan, Farrier David Larkin, Sergeant William Foster, First Sergeant William McNamara, Private William Rankin, Company F, Corporal Henry McMasters, Company A, Corporal William O'Neill, Company I, Blacksmith James Pratt, Company I, and Sergeant William Wilson would be awarded the Medal of Honor. This was Wilson's second Medal of Honor. This would become known as the Battle of the North Fork of the Red River. Some sources reported this to be the Kotsoteka Comanche village of Mow-way.

1872: After demanding their removal from prison, Lone Wolf met with Satanta and Big Tree in St. Louis. They discussed the Kiowa Indians' stand when Lone Wolf went to Washington, D.C., to discuss treaty matters. After their meeting, Satanta and Big Tree returned to prison in Texas.

1873: Indians fought with soldiers from the Fifth Cavalry, the Twenty-Third Infantry, and some Indian scouts at Sierra Ancha, Arizona, according to army documents. Two Indians were killed and four were captured.

1877: Lieutenant John Bullis and a small force from the Twenty-Fourth Infantry attacked a group of Lipan Indians in a camp four miles from Saragossa, Mexico. The army captured five women and children, twelve horses, and two mules. The camp and its contents were destroyed.

1879: After passing the Milk River in Colorado, Major Thomas T. Thornburgh split his command of three troops of cavalry. One troop continued down the road to the White River Agency with the expedition's wagons. Thornburgh and his two remaining troops followed a different route, slightly to the left of road. After crossing a high ridge, Thornburgh encountered a large group of Ute Indians. According to his report, he attempted to communicate with the Ute, but they opened fire. Being outnumbered, Thornburgh retreated back toward the troops with the wagons. Skirmishes took place while Thornburgh was retreating toward the wagons, which by now were on the Milk River. Within sight of the wagons, Thornburgh was shot and killed. The wagons were formed into a barricade, and the soldiers engaged in a battle with the Ute. The Ute set the grass on fire, and many of the wagons caught fire. Successful efforts to put out the fires led to the deaths of several soldiers. The battle lasted from 3:00 P.M. until well after dark, with many wounded and killed on both sides. Couriers slipped out of the barricade after dark to seek reinforcements. The fighting continued until October 5, 1879. According to army records, nine enlisted men, three civilians, and thirty-seven Indians were killed in the fighting. Two officers, forty-three soldiers, and three civilians were wounded. Captain Francis S. Dodge, Troop D, Ninth Cavalry, would be awarded the Medal of Honor for leading a force of forty men who came to the relief of the besieged soldiers. For retrieving ammunition for the soldiers while surrounded on three sides and under point-blank fire, Sergeant Edward P. Grimes was also awarded the Medal of Honor. Sergeant John Lawton, Company D, would also get the Medal of Honor for "coolness and steadiness under fire; volunteered to accompany a small detachment on a very dangerous mission." First Sergeant Jacob Widmer, Sergeant John Merrill, Corporals George Moquin and Edward Murphy, blacksmith Wilhelm Philipsen, and Corporal Hampton Roach would also be awarded the medal for gallantry.

1973: The House Interior Committee voted to approve a bill that reestablished federal recognition of the Menominee Indians.

1983: The area director, Bureau of Indian Affairs, ratified an amendment to the constitution and bylaws of the Suquamish Indian Tribe of the Port Madison Reservation in the state of Washington.

1984: An amendment to the constitution of the Comanche Indian Tribe was enacted.

Every: Taos Pueblo festival (through September 30).

SEPTEMBER 30

1730: In a British court in London, seven Cherokee leaders signed the Articles of Agreement with the Lords Commissioners. It was a formal alliance covering allegiance, peace, and the return of captives.

1809: William Henry Harrison, representing the United States, and the Delaware, Miami, Potawatomi, and Eel River Indians signed a treaty (7

Stat. 113) at Fort Wayne. Three million acres in Indiana and Illinois were traded for larger annuities and $5,200 in supplies.

1850: Congress authorized efforts to get treaties with the Indians of California.

1865: According to a report dated this day, 402 Apache and 7,318 Navajo Indians were present at the Fort Sumner (New Mexico) Reservation in September.

1872: Indians skirmished with a group of soldiers from the First Cavalry on Squaw Peak in Arizona, according to official army records. Seventeen Indians were killed and one was captured. Also in Arizona, Company F, Fifth Cavalry, fought some Indians near Camp Crittenden. Four soldiers were killed.

1877: On this day through October 5, according to army reports, elements of Colonel Nelson Miles's Second Cavalry captured 800 Nez Perce horses. According to army documents, Captain Owen Hale, Lieutenant J.W. Biddle, twenty-two soldiers, and seventeen Indians were killed. Captain Myles Moylan, Captain E.S. Godfrey, Lieutenant G.W. Baird, Lieutenant Henry Romeyn, thirty-eight soldiers, eight civilians, and forty Nez Perce were wounded. Almost 20 percent of the soldiers were wounded or killed during the fighting at Bear Paw Mountain (near modern Havre, Montana). The army would issue the Medal of Honor to the following soldiers during this campaign: First Lieutenant George W. Baird, Fifth Infantry, for "distinguished gallantry in action"; First Lieutenant Mason Carter, Fifth Infantry, for leading a charge "under a galling fire"; Second Lieutenant Oscar Long, Fifth Infantry, for taking over command of a troop of cavalry when their officers were killed; Second Lieutenant Edward McClernand, Second Cavalry, for using "skill and boldness when attacking a band of hostiles"; Captain Edward S. Godfrey, Seventh Cavalry, for leading his men while severely wounded; Captain Myles Moylan, for gallantry and leadership until he was severely wounded; First Sergeant Henry Hogan, Company G, Fifth Infantry, for carrying severely wounded Lieutenant Henry Romeyn out of the line of fire (this was Hogan's second award; see October 21, 1876); First Lieutenant Henry Romeyn, Fifth Infantry, for vigorously prosecuting the fight; and Major (surgeon) Henry Tilton for rescuing wounded men.

1879: Sixth and Ninth Cavalry soldiers and some Indian scouts fought a group of Indians near Ojo Caliente in the Black Range, New Mexico. According to army documents, two scouts and three Indians were killed. The fighting started on September 26.

1936: Secretary of the Interior Harold Ickes authorized an election for a proposed constitution and bylaws of the Hopi Tribe. The election was held on October 24, 1936.

1973: Inuit artist and writer Peter Pitseolak died in Cape Dorset, Northwest Territories, Canada. Using his artistic and photographic talents, he documented much of the traditional ways of life of his people.

OCTOBER 1

1539: Hernando de Soto's expedition reached the Apalachee village of Ivitachuco (also called Ibitachuco) in northeastern Florida. The Spanish set up camp near the village. Throughout the evening, the Indians shot arrows at the Spanish, with little effect. The Narvaez expedition had also visited the village in June 25, 1528, which may somewhat account for the hostile reception Hernando de Soto's expedition received.

1728: According to some sources, a conference on alliance and land cessions was held for the next four days between the British in New York and the Six Nations.

1776: About 1,800 Virginians arrived in the Overhill towns and demanded Dragging Canoe and Alexander Cameron. The two men were leaders of the Cherokees in anti-U.S. activities during the Revolutionary War. The Cherokees refused to give them up. The Virginians burned several towns.

1792: Just after midnight, almost 300 Cherokees, Chickamauga, Creek, and Shawnee attacked Buchanan's Station in the Cumberland region of Tennessee near Nashville. They were led by Chickamauga Chief John Watts, Kiachatalee, and Creek Chief Talotiskee. There were only a little over a dozen defenders in the fort. In what turned out to be a futile effort, many of the Indians were killed by the crack shots within the fort. Almost all of the Indian leaders were killed except John Watts, who was seriously wounded. When the Indians heard the sounds of a relief column coming from Nashville, they retired. None of the defenders of the fort were killed.

1800: The San Ildefonso Treaty was signed. A secret part of this treaty (signed by France and Spain) was for Spain to return to France the lands in Louisiana west of the Mississippi River.

1838: John Benge and 1,103 Cherokees left one of the concentration camps near the Tennessee Cherokee Agency. Benge's group was the first of several groups who supervised their own removal to the Indian Territory (present-day Oklahoma).

1858: Colonel Albert Sidney, four companies from the Second Cavalry, 135 Indian scouts, and Texas Rangers—all told, 350 men—fought Buffalo Hump's 500 Comanche at Rush Springs in south-central Oklahoma. Another source said the army was led by Captain Earl Van Dorn. Fifty-six Indians and five soldiers were killed in the fighting. All 120 of the Comanche lodges were burned. This campaign was part of what the army called the Wichita expedition.

1859: The Sac and Fox signed a treaty (15 Stat. 467). The United States was represented by Alfred Greenwood. The Indians ceded a large section of their reservation to the United States.

1865: According to a government report, the expense of sustaining Navajo and Apache at the Bosque Redondo Reservation from March 1, 1864, to October 1, 1865, was about $1.1 million.

1867: According to army records, members of the Ninth Cavalry on mail-escort duty fought with a band of Indians near Howard's Well, Texas. Two soldiers were killed.

1873: There were numerous fights throughout the Southwest. Captain G.W. Chilson and Troop C, Eighth Cavalry, killed three Indians and wounded one in a fight in the Guadalupe Mountains in New Mexico Territory. Sergeant Benjamin Mew and soldiers from Company K, 25th Infantry, skirmished with Indians at Central Station, Texas. Also in Texas, a sergeant and thirteen soldiers fought with a band of Comanche. One Indian was reported wounded in this fight.

1879: Captain Francis Dodge and Troop D, Ninth Cavalry, were on patrol when couriers from Major Thornburgh's troops met them. Dodge sent the message along and then pretended to camp for the evening in case his actions were being observed. After dark, he issued rations for three days and 225 rounds of ammunition. Dodge and his thirty-seven soldiers and four civilians then headed for Thornburgh's position.

1879: Army scouts captured a woman and a child from Victorio's band. The scouts then learned the location of Victorio's camp from the female captive. The army sped to the camp and captured lots of provisions, but the Apache escaped into the night.

1886: By executive order of President Grover Cleveland, certain land in Washington Territory was withdrawn from sale or other disposition and set aside for the use and occupation of the Chehalis Indians.

1962: Santa Fe's Institute of American Indian Arts opened.

1962: The *Tundra Times*, a statewide paper based in Anchorage, which served the Eskimo, Indian, and Aleut communities of the state, was first published.

1962: The Mi'kmaq Bear River First Nation Reserve of Bear River No. 6B was established in Nova Scotia.

1969: In Ridgeville, South Carolina, U.S. Marshals turned away Indian parents and children from a local school. The Indians wanted to be desegregated. A court order prohibited the Indians from attending white schools.

1969: The commissioner of Indian affairs authorized an election for amendments to the constitution of the Oglala Sioux of the Pine Ridge Indian Reservation.

1975: Commissioner of Indian Affairs Morris Thompson ratified a constitution and bylaws approved by the Southern Ute Indian Tribe of the Southern Ute Reservation in Colorado.

1990: Starting on this day, the Cherokee Nation became one of six tribes that have assumed responsibility for the disbursement of Bureau of Indian Affairs funds for their tribe. Prior to this Indian self-governance agreement, the bureau decided how the funds should be spent.

OCTOBER 2

1535: Cartier arrived in the area of what eventually became Montreal. He encountered the Wyandot there.

1685: According to some sources, an agreement was reached for the Delaware Indians to cede some lands to Pennsylvania.

1696: According to some sources, a peace and alliance agreement was reached between representatives of the British in New York and the Five Nations.

1775: George Galphin was appointed commissioner of Indian affairs for the Southern District by the Continental Congress.

1798: A treaty (7 Stat. 62) with the Cherokees was signed in Tellico. The treaty referred to the July 2, 1791, Holston River Treaty and attempted to correct some misunderstandings. It also referred to the June 26, 1794, treaty signed in Philadelphia. All treaties prior to this date were still in effect. Some Cherokee lands on the Tennessee River were ceded. Each party appointed one person to walk the new survey line. The Cherokees got $5,000 in goods up front and $1,000 annually thereafter. The Kentucky Road from the Cumberland Mountains to the Tennessee River was to remain safe and open. The Cherokee could hunt on their old lands if they did so peacefully. Thirty-nine Indians signed the treaty.

1818: Lewis Cass, Jonathan Jennings, and Benjamin Parke, representing the United States, signed a treaty (7 Stat. 185) with the Potawatomi and Wea Indians at St. Mary's River on the Indiana-Ohio border. The tribe exchanged vast holdings in Indiana for an annual payment of $2,500.

1833: Joel Bryan Mayes would become chief justice of the Cherokee supreme court. In 1887, he was elected principal chief. He was born near Cartersville, Georgia.

1853: As a part of the Walker War in southern Utah, several Ute sought refuge in the local fort. Instead of being protected, the Indians were killed by the settlers.

1858: Having been held prisoner by army forces under Colonel George Wright since September 23, Yakama Chief Owhi attempted to escaped from Fort Dalles. Chief Owhi was shot and killed.

1868: General William Hazen reported that 100 Indians had attacked Fort Zarah (near modern Great Bend) in central Kansas. The Indians then attacked a provision train and a ranch eight miles away. The Indians made off with almost 200 animals. General Alfred Sully reported that Indians had attacked a wagon train between Fort Larned and Fort Dodge in Kansas. Three citizens were killed and three wounded.

1872: Fort McKeen (later called Fort Abraham Lincoln) in central North Dakota was attacked by approximately 300 Sioux Indians. According to army reports, one soldier was wounded and three Ree Indian scouts were killed.

1879: Captain Francis Dodge reached the survivors of Major Thornburgh's troops, under siege by hostile Ute Indians on the Milk River in Colorado. Sergeant Henry Johnson, Company D, would be awarded the Medal of Honor for his actions during the next several days.

1972: The commissioner of Indian affairs authorized an election to approve a constitution for La Posta Band of Diegueno (Mission) Indians of the La Posta Indian Reservation, California. The election was held on January 26, 1973.

OCTOBER 3

1763: As a part of Pontiac's Uprising, Indians ambushed a force of five dozen Rangers in western Virginia. Fifteen of the soldiers were killed in the fighting. After tracking the Indians, a force of 150 Virginia militia and volunteers, led by Charles Lewis, found them on the South Fork of the Potomac River. The Europeans killed twenty-one of the Indians without suffering a single loss.

1764: Leaving Fort Pitt with more than 1,500 soldiers and militia, Colonel Henry Bouquet led his men into Ohio in search of hostile Indians.

1786: A group of thirty settlers, organized by the McNitt family, were moving from Virginia to Kentucky. Tonight at a site near modern London, Kentucky, they were attacked by a Chickamauga war party. Twenty-one of the Europeans were killed and five were captured. Of the four people who escaped, one, a pregnant woman, hid in a hollow log, where she gave birth.

1790: John Ross, destined to become one of the most famous Cherokee chiefs, was born in Rossville, Georgia. Although Ross was only one-eighth Cherokee, he spent his entire life working for the tribe.

1818: Lewis Cass, representing the United States, and the Delaware Indians signed a treaty (7 Stat. 188) on the St. Mary's River on the Indiana-Ohio border. The treaty traded all of the Indians' lands in Indiana for land west of the Mississippi, supplies, and an increase in annual payments from previous treaties.

1836: A total of 165 of Captain F.S. Belton's original 210 Creek "prisoners" were delivered to Indian Territory (present-day Oklahoma). Seventeen were given over to civil authorities. The rest either died in transit or were unaccounted for.

1838: Black Hawk died in Davis County, Iowa.

1854: Major Granville Owen Haller marched to avenge Indian agent A.J. Bolon's death. He encountered the Yakama on October 5.

1861: The Uintah and Ouray Reservation was established by executive order.

1866: Elements of the Fourteenth Infantry fought some Indians near Cedar Valley, Arizona. Fifteen Indians were killed and ten were captured, according to Fourteenth Infantry records.

1866: According to army records, soldiers with the Third Cavalry skirmished with a group of Indians near Trinidad, Colorado. One soldier was killed and three were wounded. Thirteen Indians were killed.

1866: In Long Valley, Nevada, the First Cavalry killed eight Indians in a fight, according to army records.

1868: According to army records, members of the Third Cavalry fought with a band of Indians in the Miembres Mountains in New Mexico. One soldier was wounded.

1872: Lieutenant Eben Crosby, Seventeenth Infantry, Lieutenant L.D. Adair, Twenty-Second Infantry, and a citizen were hunting near the Heart River in Dakota when they were attacked by Sioux Indians. In a fight that lasted until the next day, all three were killed.

1873: According to army reports, Tonkawa Indian scouts attacked a Comanche camp in Jones County, Texas. No other details were listed in the report.

1873: "Treaty 3 Between Her Majesty The Queen and The Saulteaux Tribe of the Ojibbeway Indians at the Northwest Angle On The Lake of the Woods with Adhesions" was signed in Canada.

1873: Captain Jack was hanged at Fort Klamath Oregon for his part in the Modoc War.

1936: The secretary of the interior had authorized an election to approve a constitution and by-

"Captain Jack," Modoc leader
(NA)

laws for the Fort McDowell Mohave–Apache Community in Arizona. It was approved by a vote of 61–1.

1950: Assistant Secretary of the Interior Willam Warne authorized an election to approve a constitution and bylaws for the United Keetoowah Band of Cherokee Indians of Oklahoma. It was approved by a vote of 1,414–1.

1961: An election approved Amendment 6 to the constitution and bylaws of the Lac du Flambeau Band of Lake Superior Chippewa Indians of Wisconsin.

1962: An act was passed that allowed the federal government to acquire land on the Crow Creek Sioux Reservation in South Dakota for the Big Bend Dam.

1981: The rules for the election of delegates to the Official Central Council of the Tlingit and Haida Indian Tribes of Alaska were amended.

Every: Papago festival.

OCTOBER 4

1693: In 1680, Tewa leader Popé spurred an uprising of the Pueblos against the Spanish mission in New Mexico. Diego de Vargas led an expedi-

tion to reconquer the area. His force consisted of 100 soldiers, seventy-three settler families, eighteen priests, and some Indian allies.

1779: Colonel David Rogers and some men with five boatloads of ammunition and powder were working their way up the Ohio River. As they reached the Licking River in Kentucky, Colonel Rogers spotted some Indians on the shore. He sent his four dozen men after the Indians. Lying in wait for Rogers were more than 130 Delaware, Mingo, Shawnee, and Wyandot warriors, led by Mathew Elliot and Simon Girty. All but a few of the Americans were killed in the ambush. The Indians lost only two men.

1838: Elijah Hicks and 748 Cherokees were the second group of Cherokees to leave the Tennessee Cherokee Agency area under their own supervision. They were part of the forced removal of the Cherokees to the Indian Territory (present-day Oklahoma). They arrived on January 4, 1839.

1868: Major Henry Douglass reported that Indians had wounded a Mexican near Lime-Kiln. They also attacked a wagon train, killing two men and wounding two more. An attack at Asher Creek settlement got the Indians seven horses and mules.

1868: According to army records, settlers fought with a band of Indians near Fort Dodge, Kansas. Two settlers were killed and one was wounded.

1874: Indians fought with soldiers from the Ninth Cavalry Infantry near Fort Sill, Indian Territory (present-day Oklahoma). According to army documents, one Indian was killed during this engagement, which lasted until October 31.

1876: Sixth Cavalry and some Indian scouts fought a group of Indians on the Tonto Plateau in Arizona. According to army documents, eight Indians were killed and two were captured.

1877: Between this day and the next day, 418 Nez Perce surrendered to the army.

1878: Dull Knife and his band of Northern Cheyenne crossed the Union Pacific line at Alkali Station, Nebraska. Stationed in Fort Sidney in western Nebraska, Major T.T. Thornburgh and

140 soldiers boarded a waiting train in an attempt to catch up to Dull Knife.

1922: Arizona's Fort Apache, 7,579.75 acres in size, had been established by executive order on February 1, 1877; it was expanded on this day.

1937: An election for the adoption of a constitution and bylaws for the Stockbridge Munsee Community of Wisconsin was authorized by the assistant secretary of the interior. The election was held on October 30, 1937.

1944: Van T. Barfoot got the Medal of Honor.

Every: Feast of St. Francis celebrated (Ak-chin).

OCTOBER 5

1675: As a part of King Philip's War, Springfield, Massachusetts, was attacked by Agawam and Nipmuck Indians. A scout warned the village, and most of the settlers made it to fortified dwellings. Two settlers were killed and thirty buildings were burned during the fighting.

1724: French peace envoy Etienne Veniard de Bourgmont had been charged with making peace among the Indians of what became Kansas, then part of the French Territory of Louisiana. He held a council. The council included representatives of the "Canza, Padouca, Aiaouez [Iowa?], and the Othouez [Otto?]." The various chiefs and representative all agreed to peace and smoked each other's peace pipes.

1731: Natchez warriors led by Chief Farine attacked a Natchitoches village (near modern Natchitoches, Louisiana). The Natchez took over the village. The Caddo and the French, under Louis Juchereau de St. Denis, retreated to nearby Fort St. Jean. During the fighting over the next eight days, more than six dozen Natchez were killed. The Natchez fled into the woods and were never a cohesive force again.

1813: Near the Thames River in Canada, American forces led by General William Henry Harrison, and British-Indian forces led by Henry Proctor and Tecumseh, fought a decisive battle.

Tecumseh, Shawnee chief and Indian leader allied to the British in the War of 1812

Harrison's forces were much stronger. Setting up an ambush, the British and Indian forces took up different positions. When Harrison's forces attacked the 700 British soldiers, they caved almost immediately. Tecumseh's Indians, fighting in a swamp, held out until Tecumseh was killed. At the end of the fighting, 600 British were captured and eighteen were killed. Thirty-three Indians were killed, and none were captured. The American forces lost eighteen men. (Also recorded as happening on October 15.)

1838: Reverend Jesse Bushyhead and almost 1,000 Cherokees began their emigration to the Indian Territory (present-day Oklahoma). Many of the Cherokees in the group were Baptists. They were allowed to stop on Sundays so they could conduct religious services. Their march was delayed almost a month because of thick ice on the Mississippi River. Eighty-two members of this group died before they reached Indian Territory on February 23, 1839.

1841: Recently, some Cayuse had broken some windows in Marcus Whitman's house in Waiilatpu. Whitman demanded reparations from

Cayuse Waptashtamakt. Waptashtamakt declined, but later a feast was attended by all.

1854: Troops under Major Granville Owen Haller battled the Yakama to avenge Indian agent A.J. Bolon's death. The fighting took place southwest of what is modern Yakima, Washington.

1858: The last execution by Colonel George Wright as a consequence of the Spokane War was held.

1859: A treaty (12 Stat. 1111) was concluded at the Kansas Agency between the United States and the Kansa Indians. Representing the United States was Alfred Greenwood.

1866: Elements of the First Oregon Infantry fought some Indians near Fort Klamath, Oregon. Four Indians were killed, according to army records.

1869: According to army records, members of the Twenty-First Infantry fought with a band of Indians near Dragoon Springs, Arizona. Four soldiers were killed.

1870: According to army records, members of Company M, Sixth Cavalry engage hostile Indians at Holliday Creek along the Little Wichita River in Texas. For their "gallantry in pursuit of and fight with Indians," Sergeant Michael Welch, Corporals Samuel Bowden and Daniel Keating,

Black troops and cavalry relieving federal troops during the Ute War in Colorado

Private Benjamin Wilson, and post guide James B. Doshier would be awarded the Medal of Honor.

1877: Chief Joseph, according to army reports, eighty-seven warriors, eighty-four squaws, and 147 children surrendered near Bear Paw, Montana. They were within fifty miles of their goal—the Canadian border. It was here that the chief spoke the famous words: "From where the sun now stands, I will fight no more."

1878: According to the commander of Fort Clark (near modern Del Rio, Texas), four children of the Dowdy family were killed by Indians on Johnson's Fork of the Guadalupe River.

1879: After marching 170 miles in a little over forty-eight hours, Colonel Wesley Merritt and Troops A, B, I, and M, Fifth Cavalry, numbering 350 men, reached Major T.T. Thornburgh's encircled men on the Milk River in Colorado at 5:00 A.M. During the fight, which started on September 30, 1879, the army reported that twelve men, including Major Thornburgh, were killed. Forty in Thornburgh's command were wounded. The army estimated the size of the Ute force to be 300–350. Indian sources reported the death of thirty-seven Ute during the fighting. A subsequent search at the White River Agency revealed the bodies of seven men, including the agent, Nathan C. Meeker.

Nez Perce Chief Joseph (NA)

1898: "For distinguished bravery in action against hostile Indians," Private Oscar Burkard, Hospital Corps, U.S. Army, would be awarded the Congressional Medal of Honor. This fighting was a part of the Chippewa (Ojibwa) Uprising at Lake Leech in northern Minnesota. This was the last Medal of Honor to be awarded for fighting Indians.

1966: The official approved tribal roll for the San Pasqual Band of Mission (Diegueno) Indians in the San Pasqual Reservation was issued.

1974: Commissioner of Indian Affairs Morris Thompson had authorized an election to approve a constitution and bylaws for the Upper Skagit Indian Tribe. It was approved by a vote of 65–2.

1985: The constitution and the rules for the election of delegates to the Official Central Council of the Tlingit and Haida Indian Tribes of Alaska were amended.

OCTOBER 6

1539: Hernando de Soto reached the Apalachee town of Iniahica (near modern Tallahassee). He picked this town as his winter quarters. He maintained this camp until March 3, 1540.

1598: Juan de Oñate left his base in San Juan Pueblo. He was en route to "visit" the Pueblos to the west.

1713: Indians attacked Captain Richard Hunnewel and nineteen men working in the fields outside Black Point, Maine. Only one European survived this fight, on Prout's Neck in Scarborough. A nearby pond was called Massacre Pond because of this battle.

1759: In retribution for Abenaki attacks on New England settlements, Major Robert Rogers, 180 of his Rangers, and a few Stockbridge scouts staged a predawn attack on the Abenaki village at St. Francis, Quebec. Rogers claimed to have killed 200 Abenaki at the loss of one scout. He recovered five captives and 600 "English" scalps.

1774: In Lord Dunmore's War, Virginia Governor John Murray, Earl of Dunmore, authorized an army of Virginians to go into Shawnee territory despite a royal proclamation dated October 7, 1763, that prohibited European settlements west of the Appalachian Mountains. Dunmore had granted lands to veterans in the prohibited area, and he planned on helping them get it. On this day around 800 Shawnees under Chief Cornstalk attacked Dunmore's force of 850 men at Point Pleasant on the Ohio and Kanawha Rivers (the western part of modern West Virginia). The fighting lasted all day. Both sides suffered numerous casualties. Cornstalk lost the battle and eventually signed a peace treaty with the Virginians. (Also recorded as happening on October 10.)

1786: A large force of primarily Kentucky militiamen attacked a peaceful Shawnee village on the Mad River (not far from modern Bellefontaine, Ohio). The force was led by Benjamin Logan. One of the colonels was Daniel Boone. Many Indians were killed, including Chief Molunthy, and a few prisoners were recovered.

1818: Lewis Cass, Jonathan Jennings, and Benjamin Parke, representing the United States, signed a treaty (7 Stat. 189) with the Miami Indians at the Saint Mary's River on the Indiana-Ohio border. The Miami gave up a large section of their lands for an annuity.

1851: One in a series of treaties was signed with California Indians on the Lower Klamath. The document promised lands for the Indians and to protect them from angry Americans.

1862: Articles of agreement and a convention were made and concluded at Manitowaning, or the Great Manitoulin Island in the province of Canada between the government and several tribes.

1867: According to army records, members of the Eighth Cavalry fought with a band of Indians near Trout Creek, Arizona. Seven Indians were reported killed.

1870: Troop K, Second Cavalry, was now stationed at the Carlisle Indian School in Pennsylvania.

1892: The Jerome Agreement was signed by the United States and the Apache, Comanche, and Kiowa Tribes in the Indian Territory (present-day Oklahoma). It divided much of their land into individual plots. The signatories included: David H. Jerome, Alfred M. Wilson, and Warren G. Sayre, the commissioners on the part of the United States. It was also signed by 456 others, including Quanah Parker, Lone Wolf, and Big Tree.

1972: An official tribal census for the Yankton Sioux was listed.

1986: Congress designated the path the Nez Perce took in their flight from the army in 1877 as the Nez Perce Historical Trail.

OCTOBER 7

1672: White Mountain Apache raided the Zuni pueblo of Hawikuh and killed a priest named Pedro de Abila y Ayala.

1691: The Charter of Massachusetts Bay was issued.

1701: In a farewell address to William Penn, Susquehanna Chief Oretyagh, along with other Shawnee leaders, again requested that traders be prevented from selling alcohol to the local Indians. Penn assured them that the Pennsylvania assembly was doing just that.

1719: An expedition of 800 soldiers and Indian allies and 1,000 horses were being led by Spanish Governor Antonio de Valverde. They were searching for groups of Ute and Comanche who had been raiding ranches and settlements in Colorado. Along Fountain Creek, one of their scouts, Chief Carlana, found signs of a recent campsite used by the raiders.

1759: Last year, Tawehash Indians helped to destroy the Spanish Mission of San Sabá de la Santa Cruz in eastern Texas. The Spanish had finally gathered a punitive expedition; leading 1,000 Spanish and pro-Spanish Indians, Diego Ortiz Parrilla attacked the Tawehash village. With their al-lies, the Comanche and the Tawakoni, the Tawehash fought back. The Tawehash won the day and forced the retreat of the Spanish allied forces, killing as many as 100 men in the process.

1763: As a result of Pontiac's Rebellion, the British government issued the Royal Proclamation of 1763, prohibiting Europeans from settling west of the Appalachian Mountains.

1775: In what became the Pittsburgh Treaty, congressional commissioners met with several Indian tribes. They agreed to the Ohio River as the local boundary line. The Indians agreed to release some prisoners and not to get involved in the Revolutionary War.

1844: A treaty conference was held between Texans headed by Sam Houston and the Anadarko, Lipan Apache, Caddo, Cherokee, Comanche, Delaware, Hainai, Kichai, Shawnee, Tawakoni, and Waco.

1861: With Albert Pike, the Cherokees signed a treaty with the Confederacy in Park Hill on the Cherokee Reservation in Indian Territory (present-day Oklahoma). The agreement was almost the same as that of the Creek signed on July 10, 1861. Living up to their word, three Indian delegates sat in the Confederate Congress throughout the war, something hinted at by the United States but never implemented. Pike presented the Cherokees with a special flag for their use during the war.

1863: The Tabeguache Band of Utah Indians signed a treaty (13 Stat. 673).

1868: According to army records, settlers fought with a band of Indians near the Purgatory River in Colorado. One settler was killed.

1880: A Campo Indian had been found guilty of stealing a blanket in San Diego, California. County Justice of the Peace Gaskill ordered his punishment to be 100 lashes. Gaskill was quoted as saying: "After one of these Indians has been whipped once, he will never steal again. It makes 'a good Indian' of him." The lashing almost killed the Indian.

Indian burial ground

1947: Legislation was proposed that sold the Wyandot Indian burial ground in Kansas City, Kansas.

1952: An election approved Amendment 4 to the constitution and bylaws of the Lac Du Flambeau Band of Lake Superior Chippewa Indians of Wisconsin.

1965: An amendment to the constitution and bylaws of the Miccosukee Tribe of Indians of Florida was approved by Assistant Secretary of the Interior Harry Anderson.

1969: Senator Ted Kennedy called for a White House conference on Indian problems in a speech. He criticized Bureau of Indian Affairs efforts.

1971: The commissioner of Indian affairs designated four people (Grace Cuero Banegas, Maria Sevella La Chappa, Cynthia Victoria Sevella, and Gwendolyn Ludwina Sevella) as members of the La Posta Band of Mission Indians of the La Posta Indian Reservation, California. Based on their constitution, members of the tribe were either linear descendants of these four people or adopted people.

1974: Commissioner of Indian Affairs Morris Thompson authorized an election for amendments to the Pawnee of Oklahoma constitution.

OCTOBER 8

1541: Hernando de Soto fought with Caddo Indians in Tula, Arkansas.

1758: Running through October 26, the Council of Easton began in Philadelphia, Pennsylvania. Eventually, the Iroquois and Delaware signed peace treaties. Large parts of the much-hated Treaty of Albany were abrogated.

1779: El Mocho was born an Apache, but he was captured by the Tonkawa. His bravery and natural leadership abilities eventually led the Tonkawa to make him their principal chief. He met with Spanish Governor Athanase de Mezieres in San Antonio. They signed a peace treaty, and El Mocho (Spanish for mutilated) was honored with a Medal of Honor. The peace lasted only for a few years.

1832: The Eastern Cherokees met a second time to discuss Elisha Chester's proposal for their removal to the Indian Territory (present-day Oklahoma). Although some of the lesser-bloods favored the proposal, the full-bloods voted it down. Chester warned them that if they did not agreed to move they faced the wrath of the state of Georgia.

1855: James Lupton led whites against friendly Rogue River Indians in California. They killed eight men and fifteen women and children. Survivors fled to Fort Lane in southwestern Oregon for safety.

1869: According to army records, members of the First Cavalry fought with a band of Indians in Chiricahua Pass in Arizona. Two soldiers were wounded. Twelve Indians were killed.

1873: Big Tree and Satanta were released from prison with the proviso that the Kiowa remained peaceful. After some raids by the Kiowa, Satanta was eventually returned to prison.

1873: Indians fought with soldiers from the Eighth Cavalry in the Chiricahua Mountains in Arizona, according to army documents. No casualties were reported.

1938: An election was held to approve a constitution and bylaws for the Sokaogon (Mole Lake Band) Chippewa Community of Wisconsin. It passed by a vote of 61–1.

1958: An election for the adoption of a constitution and bylaws for the Pueblos of Laguna in

New Mexico was held. It was approved by a vote of 1,331–92.

1964: The assistant secretary of the interior had authorized an election to approve a constitution and bylaws for the Cocopah Tribe of Somerton, Arizona. It was approved by a vote of 16–0.

1970: The commissioner of Indian affairs authorized and election for a new constitution for the Reno-Sparks Indian Community.

1983: The constitution and the rules for the election of delegates to the Official Central Council of the Tlingit and Haida Indian Tribes of Alaska were amended.

1984: Activist Dennis Banks was sentenced to jail for three years.

1993: A Conservation Code was amended, passed, and approved by the Bay Mills General Tribal Council in Bay Mills by a vote of 63–4, with two abstentions.

OCTOBER 9

1776: The Mission at San Francisco was started.

1844: A trade and peace treaty was signed between Texas and the Anadarko, Lipan Apache, Caddo, Cherokee, Comanche, Delaware, Hainai, Kichai, Shawnee, Tawakoni, and Waco at Tehuacana Creek.

1855: Tecumton (Elk Killer) and other Rogue River Indians retaliated for the attack the day before. They destroyed farms near Evan's Ferry. They attacked and killed eighteen people at Jewett's Ferry, Evan's Ferry, and Wagoner's Ranch. The whites called it the Wagoner Massacre.

1861: Cherokee Chief John Ross presented a treaty with the Confederate States of America to the Cherokee National Assembly for their consideration and ratification.

1868: According to army records, members of the First and Eighth Cavalries, the Fourteenth and Thirty-Second Infantries, and some Indian scouts fought with a band of Indians near the Salt River

and Cherry Creek in Arizona. Thirteen Indians were killed.

1871: Comanche under Quanah Parker stole horses from soldiers under Colonel Ranald S. Mackenzie.

1874: Lieutenant Colonel George Buell and Companies A, E, F, H, and I, Eleventh Infantry, attacked a camp of Kiowa on the Salt Fork of the Red River in Texas. One Indian was killed and the camp was destroyed. The escaping survivors were pursued for some distance. Many lodges along the way were destroyed as well.

1876: Settlers fought some Indians near Eagle Springs, Texas. According to army documents, one settler was killed.

1890: Kicking Bear visited with Sitting Bull. They talked about the ghost dance.

1940: A permit was now required for alcohol to be used as medicine in the Kiowa Indian hospital.

1940: An act (54 Stat. 1057) was passed by Congress to "allow for the leasing of any Indian lands on the Port Madison and Snohomish or Tulalip Indian Reservations in the State of Washington by the Indians with the approval of the Secretary of the Interior for a term not exceeding twenty-five years."

1955: Membership rules and regulations for the Wichita Indian Tribe of Oklahoma were adopted.

1978: The Cherokee Tribal Council adopted an official flag, designed by Stanley John.

1985: An amendment to the constitution and bylaws of the Fort Belknap Indian Community of the Fort Belknap Indian Reservation in Montana was adopted.

OCTOBER 10

1540: Hernando de Soto entered a village called Athahachi, where he met the village chief, Tascaluca. Tascaluca was taken as a hostage by de Soto to ensure the cooperation of the chief's followers.

1615: Champlain fought with the Onondaga north of what is modern Syracuse, New York.

1678: Governor Frontenac led a meeting in Quebec that debated the merits of allowing Indians to have alcohol.

1759: Shawnee Chief Cornstalk and his followers attacked settlements at Carr's Creek in Rockbridge County, Virginia. They killed a half-dozen Europeans.

1771: Spanish soldiers attacked the wife of a Kumeyaay chief. The chief attacked the soldiers and was himself killed.

1774: On a piece of land where the Great Kanawha River joined the Ohio River, called Point Pleasant, one of the biggest battles of the French and Indian War took place. Some 800 Shawnees led by Chief Cornstalk attacked a force of 850 Virginians led by Colonel Andrew Lewis at dawn. Sniping led to hand-to-hand combat. By the end of the fighting, after dark, Shawnee losses were estimated at as many as 200 warriors (some sources said forty). The Virginians had seventy-five soldiers killed, including many officers, and 140 wounded. This significant loss of warriors was a contributing force in Cornstalk's eventual decision to give up the war. (Also recorded as happening on October 6.)

1777: According to some sources, Shawnee Chief Cornstalk (Hokolesqua) was killed in Fort Randolf. He had gone to seek a peace conference and was placed in a cell. Captain John Hall and several others came into the cell and shot and killed Cornstalk.

1817: John C. Calhoun was offered the job of secretary of war by President James Monroe. In this position, Calhoun oversaw Indian affairs.

1839: The convention of Cherokees, which began on September 6, 1839, finally came to an end. During the meetings, a new constitution was adopted, new chiefs were elected, judges were appointed, and many new laws were made. However, many of the "old settlers" disavowed any actions taken at this convention. They believed the old-settler government was still in power.

1858: The Butterfield Stage arrived in San Francisco.

1865: The Miniconjou Band Sioux Treaty (14 Stat. 695) was signed. Through October 28, the Bozeman Trail Treaties would be signed.

1867: According to army records, members of the Fourteenth Infantry fought with a band of Indians near Camp Lincoln, Arizona. One Indian was killed.

1867: According to army records, members of the Thirty-First Infantry fought with a band of Indians near Fort Stevenson, Dakota Territory. One soldier was wounded.

1868: According to army records, settlers fought with a band of Indians near Fort Zarah, Kansas. No injuries were reported.

1871: According to army records, members of the Fourth Cavalry under Colonel Ranald S. Mackenzie engaged hostile Indians on the Brazos River in Texas. For his efforts in stopping the Indians from overrunning his position, Second Lieutenant Robert G. Carter was awarded the Medal of Honor. This was a part of the action that led to the Battle of Blanco Canyon.

1876: Captain C.W. Miner and Companies H, G, and K, Twenty-Second Infantry, and Company C, Seventeenth Infantry, were guarding ninety-four wagons en route from the camp at the mouth of Glendive Creek, Montana, to the force at the mouth of the Tongue River. The wagon train was attacked by several hundred Indians and retreated to the Glendive base. Soldiers replaced the drivers, and with reinforcements, including Lieutenant Colonel E.S. Otis, the force of 237 soldiers proceeded to the soldiers' camp on the Tongue River.

1878: After being forced to abandon his supply wagons four days earlier due to deep sand, Major T.T. Thornburgh's troops were out of supplies. The major gave up his pursuit of Dull Knife's Cheyenne near the Niobrara River and retreated to Camp Sheridan in northwestern Nebraska.

1883: The first Lake Mohonk-Friends conference took place.

1885: Fourth Cavalry couriers fought a group of Indians near Lang's Ranch, New Mexico. According to army documents, one soldier was killed.

1894: Indian School Superintendent Samuel Hertzog reported that thirty Hopi hostiles had seized several plots of land in Munqapi. The hostiles planted wheat in the fields.

1918: The First American (Indian) Church was incorporated in El Reno, Oklahoma. Original members included Cheyenne, Apache, Ponca, Comanche, Kiowa, and Otto.

1938: The acting secretary of the interior authorized an election to approve a new constitution and bylaws for the Ottawa Indians of Oklahoma. The election was held on November 30, 1938.

1939: An election for a constitution and bylaws of the Peoria Tribe of Indians of Oklahoma was held.

1944: Public Land Order No. 248 transferred jurisdiction of 320 acres of land in the Fort Peck Reservation in Montana from the secretary of agriculture to the secretary of the interior as a part of the Milk River Land Utilization Project.

1980: The Maine Indian Claims Act (94 Stat. 1786) took place. Its purpose was to "extend Federal recognition, provides for State jurisdiction with agreement of tribes, organization of tribal governments, and enrollment of members."

October 11

1736: According to some sources, an agreement covering friendship and land cessions was reached by representatives of the Cayuga, Oneida, Onondaga, Seneca, and Tuscarora Indians and Pennsylvania.

1794: Tennessee Governor William Blount met with Chickamauga Chief John Watts (Young Tassel) in the Tellico Blockhouse near the French Broad River in eastern Tennessee. They agreed to have a conference in November to discuss peace between the warring settlers and the Chickamauga.

1809: Meriwether Lewis died.

1812: After a series of Seminole attacks in Georgia, the local militia, led by Colonel Daniel Newnan, invaded Spanish-held Florida seeking revenge. On this day they were reinforced. They had been fighting a running battle with the Alachua Band of Seminole led by King Payne since September 17.

1838: Lieutenant Edward Deas departed with almost 700 Cherokees from the Tennessee Cherokee Agency. This group of Cherokees supported the New Echota Treaty and was given special treatment and allowances for their emigration. They reached their new lands on January 7, 1839.

1842: John Chambers, representing the United States and the Sac and Fox Indians, signed a treaty (7 Stat. 596) at their tribal headquarters in Iowa. The Indians received more than $800,000 to cede their lands in Iowa and to move to new lands along the Missouri River.

1865: Fort Fletcher was established as a military outpost in central Kansas. The fort was eventually renamed Fort Hays. It was the home of the Seventh Cavalry for a while during the Indian Wars of the late 1860s. The fort was abandoned in 1889.

1869: A confrontation had developed between Canadian surveyors and Louis Riel's Metis cousin, Andre Nault. Andre did not want the surveyors on his land. Riel and a dozen other Metis responded to help. Riel walked up, stepped on the surveyor's chain, and said, "You go no further." This was the start of a rebellion that rocked Canada.

1871: Indians skirmished with a group of soldiers from the Fourth Cavalry Infantry on the Freshwater Fork of the Brazos River in Texas, according to official army records. One soldier was killed. Colonel Ranald Mackenzie was leading the troops.

1874: Satanta had become despondent about his life-term sentence in the Huntsville, Texas, prison. He had slashed his wrists, trying to kill himself, but was unsuccessful. He was admitted to the prison hospital. Satanta jumped from a second-floor balcony. He landed head first and died.

1876: Fifteen and Twenty-Second Infantry soldiers fought some Indians near Spring Creek, Montana. According to army documents, no casualties were reported.

OCTOBER 12

1492: According to some sources, Columbus landed in the New World. According to the Taino, they were the first Native Americans to greet Columbus on the island of Guanahani (San Salvador).

1676: Mugg was an Arosaguntacook chief. At the outbreak of King Philip's War, he sought out a peace treaty with the English for his and other tribes. Rather than listen to him, the English threw him in jail. Although he was soon released, his treatment made him an enemy of the English. With 100 warriors, he attacked Black Point, Maine, in retaliation. Most of the settlers escaped, and he burned many of the structures. Mugg was killed in Black Point seven months later.

1758: British soldiers had built a fort in southwestern Pennsylvania, southwest of what is modern Johnston. The fort was named after the British commander in chief, Lord Ligonier. A force of more 1,000 French and a few hundred Indians attacked the fort. The attack was unsuccessful. The French and Indians retreated to Fort Duquesne.

1761: The Mi'kmaq of Pictou signed a treaty with the British of Nova Scotia, according to some sources.

1824: The Cherokee Legislative Council passed a law that required the loser in any court cases appealed from the district level to the Cherokee superior court to pay a fee equal to 6 percent of the judgment in the case. This fee went into the Cherokee treasury.

1833: Captain John Page left Choctaw Agency, Mississippi, with 1,000 Choctaw for the Indian Territory (present-day Oklahoma). Many of the Choctaw were old, lane, blind, or sick.

1843: The Cherokee Nation set up police force.

1863: The Shoshone-Goshute signed a treaty (13 Stat. 681) at Tuilla Valley. Goshute signers included Adaseim, Harry-nup, Tabby, and Tintsa-pa-gin.

1868: Lieutenant Edward Belger, Third Infantry, reported that Indians had attacked near Ellsworth, Kansas. One white man had been killed and several more were missing.

1868: According to army records, members of the Seventh Cavalry fought with a band of Indians on the Arkansas River in Kansas. Two Indians were killed.

1869: According to army records, members of the Eighth Cavalry fought with a band of Indians near Red Rock, Arizona. Two Indians were killed.

1888: Sioux Indians arrived in Washington, D.C., for a conference.

1936: An election was held to approve a constitution and bylaws for the Quileute Tribe of Washington. The results were 37–12 in favor.

OCTOBER 13

1528: According to some sources, Cabeza de Vaca and eighty other Spaniards came across one of the mouths of the Mississippi River. They were unable to enter the river, however, so they continued their journey west.

1864: Little Buffalo, with 700 of his fellow Comanche and Kiowa, launched a series of raids along Elm Creek, ten miles from the Brazos River in northwestern Texas. Sixteen Texans and perhaps twenty Indians were killed in the fighting with the settlers and the Rangers in the area.

1868: According to army records, members of the Second Cavalry fought with a band of Indians near the White Woman's Fork of the Republican River in Kansas. The fighting lasted until October 30. Two Indians were killed and three were wounded.

1874: A group of Navajo scouts from New Mexico, attached to Major George Price's Eighth Cavalry, attacked a group of hostile Indians near Gageby Creek, Indian Territory.

1875: Adam Paine, a private and Seminole black Indian scout, received the Medal of Honor for his actions in September 1874 in the Texas Panhandle.

1877: The Nez Perce and the army ferried across the Missouri River.

1879: Settlers fought a group of Indians near Slocum's Ranch in New Mexico. According to army documents, eleven citizens were killed.

1890: Kicking Bear was ordered to leave the reservation by Indian police officers.

1950: The acting secretary of the interior authorized an election to approve a constitution and bylaws for the Eskimos of the native village of Buckland, Alaska. The election was held on December 30, 1950.

1972: The superintendent, Northern Idaho Agency, had authorized an election to approve an amendment to the constitution and bylaws of the Coeur d'Alene Tribe. The election was held on November 18, 1972.

OCTOBER 14

1754: Anthony Henday represented the Hudson Bay Company. He was on an expedition to try to set up trade between his company and the Blackfeet. He had his first meeting with a chief of that tribe. The chief told Henday the Blackfeet had everything they needed and there was no need to trade with anyone.

1756: General Joseph de Montcalm, leading French and Indian warriors, captured Fort Oswego in New York. Montcalm fired upon his Indian allies when they attempted to kill the British forces after they surrendered.

1768: At Hard Labor, South Carolina, the British superintendent of Indian affairs met with Cherokee chiefs. They made a treaty that ceded 100 square miles of Cherokee lands. The treaty was renegotiated in two years.

1833: In Russell County, Alabama, a grand jury indicted U.S. Army soldier James Emmerson for allegedly murdering Hardiman Owen during a shootout. The army was assisting the U.S. Marshal in an attempt to remove Owen from Creek land. Owen had filled his cabin with explosives and tried to kill the marshal by setting it off. No one was killed, and Owen escaped. When Owen was later surrounded, he was shot when he tried to shoot a soldier. The army refused to give up Emmerson. Deputy Marshal Jeremiah Austill was arrested as an accessory to murder.

1837: The second group of Cherokees to emigrate from the east under the New Echota Treaty left the Cherokee Agency in eastern Tennessee on the Hiwassee River (present-day Calhoun). The 365 Cherokees were supervised by B.B. Cannon. They traveled on land rather than boat for most of their journey. They reached their new lands on December 30, 1837. During the trip, four adults and eleven children died.

1846: The Cherokee made a new law that stated that anyone who burned down a house would be sentenced to death.

1865: The Cheyenne and Arapaho signed a treaty (14 Stat. 703) with the United States. The Little Arkansas River was included in tribal lands. The treaty derided Colonel Chivington for the Sand Creek Massacre. The U.S. Senate deleted this section. The United States was represented by William W. Bent, Kit Carson, William Harney, Jesse Leavenworth, Thomas Murphy, John Sanborn, and James Steele.

1866: Elements of the First Cavalry fought some Indians near Harney Lake Valley, Oregon. One soldier was wounded, four Indians were killed, and eight were captured, according to army records.

1868: Troop L, Fifth Cavalry, was camped on Prairie Dog Creek in Kansas. A band of Indians attacked the camp. One soldier was killed, and the Indians made off with twenty-six cavalry horses.

1868: According to Captain Penrose of the Third Infantry, Satanta and his Kiowa warriors attacked a wagon train on Sand Creek, Colorado. The Indians took a Mrs. Blinn and her child cap-

Paiute Chief Truckee Winnemucca, whose granddaughter, Sarah Winnemucca, helped restore traditional tribal land to the Paiute (NA)

tive. According to Penrose, Blinn and her child were murdered by the Indians during General Custer's attack on Black Kettle's camp on November 27, 1868, on the Washita.

1869: Elements of the Eighth Cavalry were on Lyry Creek, Arizona, this morning when they encountered hostile Indians. For "bravery in action" during the encounter, Privates David Goodman, John Raerick, and John Rowalt, Company L, would be awarded the Medal of Honor.

1871: Indians skirmished with a group of settlers near Cienega Sauz, Arizona, according to official army records. One settler was killed and another was wounded.

1872: Another large gathering of Sioux Indians attacked Fort McKeen in central North Dakota. Soldiers from the Sixth and Seventeenth Infantries and eight Ree Indian scouts charged the Sioux. Three Sioux and two soldiers were killed.

1876: Men from Troop K, Second Cavalry, skirmished with a band of Indians on Richard Creek in Wyoming. One soldier was killed.

1880: Victorio's Apache were attacked by the Mexican army near Tres Castillos in Chihuahua, Mexico. Victorio was shot and killed by a Mexican sharpshooter. Many of his followers were killed as well. The Mexicans reported killing seventy-eight men and capturing sixty-eight women and children. (Also recorded as happening on October 15.)

1891: Originally named Thocmetony ("Shell Flower" in Paiute), Sarah Winnemucca was the granddaughter of Paiute Chief Truckee Winnemucca and daughter of Chief Winnemucca. She worked tirelessly to have the traditional Paiute lands returned to the tribe. She died from tuberculosis.

1907: In Collinsville, Indian Territory (present-day Oklahoma), an event called the Last Pow-Wow took place. It was intended as a ceremonial farewell of surviving American Indian chiefs. The event continued through October 19.

1924: Land was auctioned in Bismarck, North Dakota. The minimum bid was $1.25 per acre.

1936: The secretary of the interior authorized an election for amendments to the constitution and by-laws for the Oneida Tribe of Indians of Wisconsin.

1980: An amendment to the constitution and bylaws of the Suquamish Indian Tribe of the Port Madison Reservation in the state of Washington was passed in an election.

1992: An act was passed in Congress (106 Stat. 2131) that established an eighteen-member advisory committee to study policies and programs affecting California Indians.

OCTOBER 15

1606: Indians attacked Samuel de Champlain's men at Chatham, Massachusetts.

1615: Samuel de Champlain, twelve Frenchmen, and many of his Huron allies attacked the Iroquois town of Onondaga. Champlain was wounded, and several Huron were killed. Champlain gave up the attack. Because of Champlain's actions, the Iroquois fought the French for years to come.

1748: Lands were allotted to the Tuscarora Indians by an act of the North Carolina general assembly at New Bern.

1763: Earlier in the year, the father of Delaware Chief Captain Bull was burned to death by white settlers. To retaliate, his son, Captain Bull, and his followers attacked and destroyed most of the white settlements in the Wyoming Valley of Pennsylvania.

1779: After Cornstalk died, Black Fish (Chinugalla) became principal chief of the Shawnee. He led an attack on Boonesbourgh starting on September 7, 1778. He became the adopted father of Tecumseh, his four brothers, and one sister. Black Fish died from wounds he suffered during an attack on the village of Chalagawtha.

1802: Louisiana was transferred to France.

1813: Although most sources reported this as happening on October 5, some sources reported the British battling Indians on the Thames River in Canada. Tecumseh was killed in the fighting.

1836: A treaty with five different Indian nations (the "Otoes, Missouries, Omahaws, Yankton, and Santee" Bands of Sioux) was signed (7 Stat. 524).

1866: Elements of the First Oregon Infantry fought some Indians near Fort Klamath, Oregon. Two soldiers were wounded, fourteen Indians were killed, and twenty were wounded, according to army records.

1868: Indians attacked a house on Fisher and Yocucy Creek. Four people were killed and one wounded; one woman was taken captive.

1869: Troopers chased a band of Indians into the Mogollon Mountains, New Mexico Territory. After a brief struggle, the troopers recovered thirty stolen horses.

1871: Colonel Ranald S. Mackenzie's troops had been seeking the Comanche under Quanah Parker. They entered Blanco Canyon. During the next several days they had several skirmishes with Comanche. These fights become known as the Battle of Blanco Canyon.

1872: During the first Yellowstone expedition, Indians fought with the army on numerous occasions. The army units involved were from the Eighth, Seventeenth, and Twenty-Second Infantries with some Indian scouts. They were led by Colonel D.S. Stanley, according to official army records. Over the entire expedition, two officers (Lieutenant Eben Crosby and Lieutenant L.D. Adair) and one civilian were killed or mortally wounded. The expedition started on July 26.

1876: Lieutenant Colonel E.S. Otis's force of 237 soldiers and ninety-six wagons of supplies for the soldiers at the mouth of the Tongue River were attacked again on Spring Creek. This time the Indians were approximately 800 strong, according to army reports. A running battle continued. The Indians sent numerous sorties against the wagons. They also set fire to the prairie grass, forcing the wagons to drive through the flames. Several people were killed and wounded on both sides.

1880: Victorio's Apache were attacked by the Mexican army near Tres Castillos in Chihuahua, Mexico. Victorio was shot and killed by a Mexican sharpshooter. Many of his followers were killed as well. The Mexicans reported killing seventy-eight men and capturing sixty-eight women and children. (Also recorded as happening on October 14.)

1888: The Sioux Indian conference in Washington, D.C., began.

1890: Kicking Bird was removed from a reservation by Indian police.

1936: The secretary of the interior authorized an election to approve a constitution and bylaws for the L'Anse, Lac Vieux Desert, and Ontoagon Bands of Chippewa Indians residing within the original confines of the L'Anse Reservation. The election was held on November 7, 1936.

1979: The commissioner of Indian affairs authorized a vote for the approval of a new constitution and bylaws for the Ottawa Tribe of Indians of Oklahoma. The election was held on December 19, 1980.

1987: Assistant Secretary of Indian Affairs Ross Swimmer (Cherokee) authorized an election for the approval of a constitution and bylaws for the Pascua Yaqui Indians.

OCTOBER 16

1755: A band of Delaware Indians, numbering a little over a dozen, attacked the Penn's Creek Village in Snyder County, Pennsylvania. Depending on the source, nineteen to twenty-five settlers were killed and a dozen were taken captive. This was the first uprising in the area in living memory. The raids moved from settlements around New Berlin to Selinsgrove, according to account given at the time by settlers from the area.

1826: The Potawatomi Indians signed a treaty (7 Stat. 295) with the United States on the Wabash. The Americans were represented by Lewis Cass, James Ray, and John Tipton.

1833: Twenty-one Chickasaw leaders, including Levi Colbert, Henry Love, and William McGillivrey, left Tuscumbia, Alabama, to assess the lands offered to them in the Indian Territory (present-day Oklahoma) as part of their removal proposal from the U.S. government. They arrived in the Indian Territory on December 4. The government wanted them to buy land from the Choctaws.

1837: After having fought for the government in the Seminole Wars, Jim Boy "Tustennuggee Emathla" (a Creek leader) and some other Creek chiefs arrived in New Orleans en route to the Indian Territory (present-day Oklahoma).

1867: The Medicine Lodge Creek peace conference began between the United States and most of the Southern Plains Indians. The United States wanted to establish one large reservation for all of these Indians. The conference lasted until October 26.

1869: The Metis created the National Council of the Metis (Comité National des Métis). This group was charged with representing the Metis in negotiations with the Canadian government. Louis Riel was named secretary of the group.

1870: Troop B, Eighth Cavalry, under Captain William McCleave skirmished with Indians in the Guadalupe Mountains in New Mexico Territory. One Indian was killed and eight were captured.

1876: Colonel E.S. Otis and his wagon train for the soldiers at the Tongue River continued toward their destination. Indians continued to snipe at Otis's forces. An Indian was spotted leaving a message in the wagon's path. The message said: "I want to know what you are doing traveling on this road. You scare all the buffalo away. I want to hunt in this place. I want you to turn back from here. If you don't I will fight you again. I want you to leave what you have got here and turn back from here. I am your friend, Sitting Bull. I mean all the rations you have got and some powder. Wish you would write as soon as you can." Otis sent a reply stating he was going to the Tongue River and if the Indians wanted a fight he would give them one. More sniping began on both sides. Soon two Indians appeared under a flag of truce. They said Sitting Bull wanted to talk with Otis, but both sides could not agreed on the location. Three chiefs then came to Otis. They said they were hungry and wanted peace. Otis gave them 150 pounds of bread and two sides of bacon. Otis told them if they wished to surrender they could go to the Tongue River camp and talk there.

1891: President Benjamin Harrison, by executive order, extended the Hoopa Valley Indian Reservation along the Klamath River to the Pacific Ocean except for lands ceded elsewhere.

1940: A large group of Navajos enlisted in the military.

1946: The original constitution and bylaws of the Sisseton Wahpeton Sioux Tribe of South Dakota were approved by John McGue for the commissioner of Indian affairs.

OCTOBER 17

1776: In November of 1775, Kumeyaay Indians destroyed the Mission San Diego de Alcala in what became San Diego, California. The mission was now ready to be occupied again.

1782: Cherokee Indians signed the Long Swamp Treaty with General Andrew Pickens in Selacoa, Georgia. They ceded land in Georgia as reparations for the fighting during the Revolutionary War.

1788: Gillespie's Station was located near Knoxville in Tennessee. It was protected by a small group of local settlers and frontiersmen. A force of Chickamauga, led by Bloody Fellow, Categisky, Glass, and John Watts, attacked the station. The settlers were able to hold off the attack until their ammunition ran out. The Chickamauga then entered the buildings and killed all of the men and took the women as prisoners. Two warriors claimed the daughter of Colonel Gillespie as a prisoner. To settle the argument, the warriors stabbed her to death. Most of the prisoners were eventually traded for captured Indians.

1802: A treaty (7 Stat. 73) with the Choctaw was concluded at Fort Confederation on the Tombigbee River. The original British boundary line was to be redrawn and established as the new boundary. Other parcels were ceded for $1. Ten Indians signed the document.

1840: Cherokee Judge John Martin died near Fort Gibson in eastern Indian Territory (present-day Oklahoma). According to his gravestone, he was the first chief justice of the Cherokee supreme court.

1855: The United States signed a treaty (11 Stat. 657) with three major Indian nations. These were the Blackfeet Nation, consisting of the Piegan, Blood, Blackfeet, and Gros Ventre Tribes; the Flathead Nation, consisting of the Flathead, Upper Pend d'Oreille, and Kootenay Tribes; and the Nez Perce Tribe. This treaty established the Fort Belknap Reserve. It was occupied by the Gros Ventre and Assiniboin Tribes and covered 840 square miles.

Zuni Indians wearing traditional coats and leather boots (NA)

1858: Zuni warriors rescued twenty-five soldiers who were being attacked by approximately 300 Navajos near Fort Defiance on the Arizona–New Mexico border.

1863: Kit Carson had been conducting a campaign against the Navajos who had not reported to their assigned reservation. This was called the Canyon de Chelly campaign. Carson undertook a scorched-earth policy, trying to starve the Navajos into submission. Two Navajos appeared at Fort Wingate in western New Mexico under a flag of truce. One of the two was El Sordo, brother to Navajo leaders Barboncito and Delgadito. He proposed that the Navajos live next to the fort so that the soldiers could keep an eye on them at all times. They still did not wish to move away from their homelands to the Bosque Redondo Reservation. The army turned down the proposal and insisted the Navajos go to the reservation.

1865: The United States signed a treaty (14 Stat. 713) with several Indian nations: The Apache Indians, who had been confederated with the Kiowa and

Comanche, dissolved that confederation and united their fortunes with the Cheyenne and Arapaho.

1867: According to army records, members of the Sixth Cavalry fought with a band of Indians near Deep Creek, Texas. Three Indians were reported killed and one was captured.

1868: Cheyenne Indians were involved in a fight at Beaver Creek.

1874: Indians fought with soldiers from the Sixth Cavalry near the Washita River in Indian Territory. According to army documents, no casualties were reported.

1877: The Fort Walsh conference began in Saskatchewan, Canada. Participating in the conference were Sitting Bull, leader of the Lakota Sioux, American General A.H. Terry, and Major James Walsh of the Northwest Mounted Police.

1890: Indian Agent James "White Hair" McLaughlin wrote a letter to the government saying that Sitting Bull must be neutralized.

1894: Fort Bowie in southwestern Arizona was closed by the army.

1939: A constitution and bylaws for the Alabama-Coushatta, which was approved on August 19, 1938, was ratified.

1974: The acting deputy commissioner of Indian affairs authorized an election to approve the revised constitution and bylaws of the Mississippi Band of Choctaw Indians. The election was held on December 17, 1974.

1978: The Tribal Controlled Community College Assistance Act (106 Stat. 797) of October 17, 1978, was passed by Congress. Its purpose was to "provide for grants for the operation and improvement of tribally controlled community colleges to ensure continued and expanded educational opportunities for Indian students. Encourages partnership between institutes of higher learning and secondary schools serving low income and disadvantaged students to improve retention and graduation rates, improve academic skills, increase opportunities and employment prospects of secondary students."

1984: President Reagan signed the Indian Restoration Act.

1988: The Indian Gaming Regulation Act (102 Stat. 2468) of October 17, 1988, was passed by Congress. Its purpose was to "provide a statutory basis for the operation of gaming by Indian tribes as a means of promoting economic development, self-sufficiency; to regulate gaming to shield it from organized crime and other corrupting influences so that tribe is the primary beneficiary, to assure that gaming is fair and honest by operator and players; to establish an independent Federal regulatory authority for gaming, establish Federal standards for gaming, and to protect gaming as a means of generating tribal revenue."

Every: St. Margaret Mary Day (Pueblos).

OCTOBER 18

1540: Hernando de Soto arrived at the Mobile Indian village of Mabila in present-day Clark County, Alabama. As they approached the village, Tascaluca disappeared into a building. The Mobile Indians under Chief Tuscaloosa (Tascaluca) attacked de Soto's invading army. In the bloody conflict, as many as 3,000 Indians were killed by the armored Spaniards. Approximately twenty Spaniards were killed and 150 wounded, including de Soto, according to their chroniclers.

1683: According to some sources, representatives of Pennsylvania purchased several sections of land from the Delaware Indians.

1724: French peace envoy Etienne Veniard de Bourgmont had been sent from Fort Orleans to establish peace among the Indians of what became Kansas (then part of Louisiana). He met the Padouca in their home territory.

1770: The Lochabar Treaty was negotiated between Virginia and the Cherokees. This moved the Virginia boundaries to the west. Virginia was represented by John Donelson, Alexander Cameron, and John Stuart.

Fort Union, Texas, which housed troops from the Third Cavalry (author photo)

1820: A treaty (7 Stat. 210) was negotiated between Andrew Jackson and the Choctaws. The Choctaws gave up lands in Mississippi for land in western Arkansas and what became Indian Territory (present-day Oklahoma). Part of the lands Jackson promised to the Indians belonged to Spain or were already settled by Europeans. This was called the Treaty of Doak's Stand. Chief Push-mataha was one of the signators. This was the first treaty that involved the movement of tribes to Indian Territory.

1848: The Menominee signed a treaty (9 Stat. 952) at "at Lake Pow-aw-hay-kon-nay in the State of Wisconsin."

1865: The Comanche and the Kiowa signed a treaty on the Little Arkansas River in Kansas (14 Stat. 717). Twenty-four Indians signed the treaty. The United States was represented by John B. Sanborn, William S. Harney, Thomas Murphy, Kit Carson, William W. Bent, Jesse H. Leavenworth, and James Steele.

1867: Third Cavalry Soldiers from Fort Union (New Mexico) had been tracking a group of Mescalero Apache who stole a herd of cattle from near the fort. The soldiers, under Capt. Francis H. Wilson, finally caught the Mescalero in Texas. A fight ensued and the Indians fled the area.

1867: According to army records, members of the Third Cavalry fought with a band of Indians near Sierra Diablo, New Mexico. One soldier was killed and six were wounded. The army reported that twenty-five to thirty Indians were killed.

1868: Captain L.H. Carpenter and cavalry troops from Companies H, I, and M were on Beaver Creek in Kansas when they engaged a large group of Indians. According to army reports, three soldiers were wounded and ten Indians were killed.

1876: On this night, Colonel E.S. Otis's wagon train was met by Colonel Nelson Miles, who had brought out his regiment to escort them to the camp. Otis delivered his goods and returned to the Glendive Creek camp on October 26.

1886: Tenth Cavalry soldiers captured a group of eight Indians in the Black River Mountains of Arizona, according to army documents.

1969: The acting assistant commissioner of Indian affairs had authorized an election to amend the constitution and bylaws of the Oneida Tribe of Indians of Wisconsin. The results were 304–95 in favor.

1972: Amendment 1 to the revised constitution and bylaws of the Sisseton Wahpeton Sioux Tribe of South Dakota became effective when it was approved by Area Director Wyman Babby of the Bureau of Indian Affairs.

October 19

1675: Nipmuck, Norwottock, and Pocumtuck warriors under a Nipmuck sachem attacked the British settlement of Hatfield in New England. The fight was eventually terminated when neither side could get the upper hand.

1724: French peace envoy Etienne Veniard de Bourgmont finally encountered the "Padouca" in their own lands the day before. On this day he held a grand council with more than 2,000 Indians. According to a journal of the expedition, he would "exhort them to live as brethren with their neighbors, the Panimhas, Aiaouez, Othouez, Canzas, Missouris, Osages and Illinois, and to traffic and truck freely together, and with the French."

1818: Andrew Jackson and Isaac Shelby represented American interests in a treaty conference. The Chickasaws ceded their claims to lands in Tennessee (7 Stat. 192).

1836: Lieutenant Colonel John Lane, with 690 Creek warriors and ninety soldiers, reached Fort Drane northwest of present-day Ocala, Florida. They were there to fight the Seminole.

1841: Tallahassee Seminole Chief Tiger Tail (Thlocko Tustennuggee) surrendered to American forces based on the intervention of Seminole Chief Alligator (Hallpatter Tustennuggee). In only three months, though, Tiger Tail escaped from government detention in Fort Brooke.

1846: The Mormon Battalion blazed a trail through Indian country.

1868: According to army records, members of the Eighth Cavalry fought with a band of Indians near the Dragoon Fork of the Verde River in Arizona. One soldier was wounded and seven Indians were killed.

1871: Indians skirmished with a group of soldiers from the Fourth Cavalry Infantry on the Freshwater Fork of the Brazos River in Texas, according to official army records. Two Indians were killed. Colonel Ranald Mackenzie was leading the troops and was wounded in the fighting.

1888: The Sioux were engaged in a conference in Washington, D.C. They made a counteroffer to a government proposal.

1935: The constitution and bylaws of the Fort Belknap Indian Community of the Fort Belknap Indian Reservation in Montana were ratified.

1945: American Indian John N. Reese posthumously received the Medal of Honor for his actions in World War II.

1973: The Indian Tribal Funds Allotment and Distribution Act (39 Stat. 128, 87 Stat. 466, 101 Stat. 886) was passed. The act was intended "to distribute funds appropriated in satisfaction of judgments of Indian Claims Commission and the Court of Claims, and for other purposes."

OCTOBER 20

1539: Led by Juan de Ayasco, thirty cavalrymen left Hernando de Soto's winter quarters in Apalachee, Florida. They proceeded to Tampa to escort the remainder of de Soto's army to his winter quarters. En route, the Spaniards had many battles with the local natives.

1774: Georgia Governor James Wright signed a treaty with the Creek Indians in Savannah. They agreed to reestablish trade, which the Creek wanted. The Creek agreed to give up some land along the Ocmulgee and Oconee Rivers and to execute two Creek warriors accused of killing some settlers. (Also recorded as being signed on October 2.)

1832: Marks Crume, John Davis, and Jonathan Jennings, representing the United States, and Potawatomi Indians signed a treaty (7 Stat. 378) at Tippecanoe. The Indians gave up lands near Lake Michigan for $15,000 a year, debt relief, and supplies.

1832: The Chickasaws signed a treaty (7 Stat. 381) for their removal to the Indian Territory (present-day Oklahoma), at the Pontotoc Creek Council House in Mississippi. Their lands (6,422,400 acres) were sold and the government held the proceeds for them. General John Coffee represented the United States.

1865: The Sans Arcs Sioux, Hunkpapa Sioux, and Yanktonai Sioux signed a treaty (14 Stat. 731).

1869: While fighting with hostile Indians in the Chiricahua Mountains of Arizona, Corporal Charles H. Dickens, Private John L. Donahue, Private John Georgian, blacksmith Mosher A. Harding, Sergeant Frederick Jarvis, Private Charles Kelley, trumpeter Bartholomew Keenan, Private Edwin L. Elwood, Corporal Nicholas Meaher, Private Edward Murphy, First Sergeant Francis Oliver, Private Edward Pengally, Corporal Thomas Powers, Privates James Russell, Charles Schroeter, and Robert Scott, Sergeant Andrew Smith, Privates Theodore Smith, Thomas Smith,

Thomas J. Smith, William Smith, William H. Smith, Orizoba Spence, George Springer, saddler Christian Steiner, Privates Thomas Sullivan and James Sumner, Sergeant John Thompson, Privates John Tracy, Charles Ward, and Enoch Weiss, Companies B and G, Eighth Cavalry, would win the Medal of Honor for "gallantry in action." Two soldiers and eighteen Indians were killed. Lieutenant John Lafferty and two enlisted men were wounded.

1875: An executive order set aside certain lands in New Mexico to serve as a reservation for Mescalero Apache. This order canceled the executive order of February 2, 1874.

1875: By an executive order, a tract of land in Montana was "withdrawn from public sale and set apart for the use of the Crow tribe of Indians . . . to be added to their reservation." This tract covered 5,475 square miles and was occupied by Mountain and River Crow, according to government records.

1876: After being informed by Colonel E.S. Otis of Sitting Bull's request to end the warring, Colonel Nelson Miles and his regiment of 398 men set out to find Sitting Bull. Colonel Miles found him near Cedar Creek, Montana, north of the Yellowstone River. The Colonel and Sitting Bull parleyed between the lines of the Indians and the soldiers, at Sitting Bull's request. Sitting Bull wanted to trade for ammunition so he could hunt buffalo. He would not bother the soldiers if they did not bother him. Miles told Sitting Bull of the government's demands for a surrender. Although neither side was pleased, both agreed to met the next day.

1879: While leaders for the army and the Ute were negotiating the end of hostilities, the handing-over of the hostile Ute leaders, and the release of prisoners held by the Ute, soldiers and Ute clashed on the White River in Colorado. First Lieutenant William P. Hall and a scouting party of three men from the Fifth Cavalry were attacked by thirty-five Indians about twenty miles from the White River. The fighting lasted most of the day, until after sunset, when the soldiers retreated to their main camp. The army reported two people killed on each side of the battle. Lieutenant Hall would be awarded the Medal of Honor for his actions.

1959: The revised constitution and bylaws of the Sisseton Wahpeton Sioux Tribe of South Dakota was approved by a vote of 251–81.

1970: On this day through October 22 the Indian Education Conference was held in California.

OCTOBER 21

1763: Pontiac ended the siege of Detroit.

1769: The Spanish arrived in San Francisco Bay.

1770: Spanish and Opata Indian forces, led by Bernardo de Gálvez, crossed the Rio del Norte (Rio Grande) into Texas (near modern Ojinaga, Chihuahua). This was a punitive expedition directed toward the Apache. A former Apache captive was leading them to the village where he was held.

1837: Two treaties (7 Stat. 540, 7 Stat. 541) were signed by the Sac and Fox Indians. The Yankton Sioux also signed a treaty (7 Stat. 542).

1837: After helping to lead a large group of Seminole out of a relocation camp in Tampa Bay, Chief Osceola was pursued by American forces under General Thomas Jesup. Although operating under direct orders of General Jesup, soldiers invited Osceola to talk under a white flag of truce. When Osceola joined them, he was taken captive. (Also recorded as happening on October 27.)

1841: The Cherokees in Oklahoma outlawed the carrying of concealed weapons.

1867: On this day through October 28 started the biggest U.S.-Indian conference ever held, near Fort Dodge, Kansas, near what was called Medicine Lodge Creek. The name comes from a Kiowa medicine lodge that was still standing from a recent Kiowa sun dance ceremony. For the Kiowa and Comanche Treaty (15 Stat. 589), some of the ten Kiowa signers were: Satanta, Satank, Black Bird, Kicking Bird, and Lone Bear. Ten Comanche, including Ten Bears, signed, as would six Apache. The United States was represented by Commissioner N.G. Taylor, William Harney, C.C. Augur, Alfred H. Terry, John B. Sanborn, Samuel F. Tappan, and J.B. Henderson. Representing the Indians were ten Kiowa.

1868: According to army records, members of the Eighth Cavalry and Fourteenth Infantry fought with a band of Indians between Fort Verde and Fort Whipple in Arizona. One soldier was wounded.

1876: The peace conference between Sitting Bull and Colonel Nelson Miles continued. Both sides repeated their terms as stated the day before. Neither side was willing to compromise. Sitting Bull was told that by not accepting Miles's terms he was committing a hostile act. Both sides quickly separated, and fighting soon broke out. According to army reports, the 1,000 Indians were driven back for forty-two miles. They abandoned great quantities of supplies during their retreat, with five dead. Miles was referred to as "Bear Coat" by the Indians because of his fur jacket. For "gallantry in action" in the battle actions that began on this day and ran through January 8, 1877, Private Christopher Freemeyer, Company D, Fifth Infantry; musician John Baker, Company D; Private Richard Burke, Company G; Sergeant Denis Byrne, Company G; Private Joseph A. Cable, Company I; Private James S. Calvert, Company C; Sergeant Aquilla Coonrod, Company C; Private John S. Donelly, Company G; Corporal John Haddoo, Company B; First Sergeant Henry Hogan, Company G; Corporal David Holland, Company A; Private Fred O. Hunt, Company A; Corporal Edward Johnston, Company C; Private Philip Kennedy, Company C; First Sergeant Wendelin Kreher, Company C; First Sergeant Michael McCarthy, Troop H; Private Michael McCormick, Company G; Private Owen McGar,

Company C; Private John McHugh, Company A; Sergeant Michael McLoughlin, Company A; Sergeant Robert McPhelan, Company E; Corporal George Miller, Company H; Private Charles Montrose, Company I; First Sergeant David Roche, Company A; Private Henry Rodenburg, Company A; Private Edward Rooney, Company D; Private David Ryan, Company G; Private Charles Sheppard, Company A; Sergeant William Wallace, Company C; Private Patton Whitehead, Company C; and Corporal Charles Willson, Company H, would all be awarded the Medal of Honor.

1878: Red Cloud Agency Indians offered to capture Dull Knife's Cheyenne if they could keep the horses and weapons they captured.

1961: An election for a proposed amendment to the constitution of the Standing Rock Sioux Tribe was held. The vote was 775–119 in favor of passage.

1978: The area director of the Bureau of Indian Affairs, Vincent Little, authorized an election for a fourth amendment to the constitution and by-laws for the Shoalwater Bay Indian Organization in Washington State. It was held, and the amendment passed.

1980: Commissioner of Indian Affairs William Hallett approved a constitution for the "California Indians of the Robinson Rancheria."

1996: Executive Order No. 13021 was issued by President Bill Clinton. It dealt with Indian education. Among other things, it established in the Department of Education a presidential advisory committee entitled the President's Board of Advisors on Tribal Colleges and Universities.

OCTOBER 22

1784: Richard Butler, Arthur Lee, and Oliver Walcott, representing the United States, and twelve Iroquois Indians signed a treaty (7 Stat. 15) ceding much of the Indian lands in New York, Pennsylvania, and west of the Ohio River and reestablishing peace after the Revolutionary War. The treaty, signed at Fort Stanwix (near modern

Rome, New York), was repudiated by most of the Iroquois.

1785: Boats carrying seventy soldiers, under the leadership of Captain Walter Finney, landed at the confluence of the Great Miami and Ohio Rivers. They build a fort there called Fort Finney.

1790: Little Turtle and his Miami followers fought with Josiah Harmar and his 300 soldiers and 1,200 militia while they were attempting to ford the Wabash River (near modern Fort Wayne, Indiana). The Americans sustained more than 200 killed and wounded. This was a part of what was called Little Turtle's War.

1829: According to some sources, gold was found in Cherokee territory.

1859: The camp on Pawnee Fork that eventually became Fort Larned was established in Kansas. The military base was established to protect travelers on the Santa Fe Trail from hostile Indians. The fort was abandoned almost twenty years later.

1864: General James Charlatan issued General Order No. 32 to Colonel Christopher "Kit" Carson. Carson was ordered to proceed from New Mexico, along the Canadian River, into the Texas Panhandle. He was to find and "punish" the Comanche and Kiowa who had been raiding in the area. Carson's force included 335 soldiers and seventy-four Ute and Apache Indians led by Ute Chief Kaniatze.

1874: J.J. Saville was the agent at the Red Cloud Agency. He had some workers cut down a tree to make a flagpole. When the bare tree was laid down at the agency headquarters, some Indians asked its purpose. The Indians protested the idea of a flag flying at the agency. They say it was a symbol of the army and they did not like it. Saville was not moved by the Indians' complaints.

1877: Settlers fought a group of Indians near Flat Rocks, Texas. According to army documents, one settler was killed.

1878: Major George Ilges and Seventh Infantry soldiers from Fort Benton in northern Montana captured a group of thirty-five "half-breed" British Canadian Indians trespassing in Montana.

1890: In 1889, Catherine Weldon traveled to the Sioux's Standing Rock Agency in the Dakotas. She eventually became a secretary for Sitting Bull, helping him with matters in English. She ardently supported the Sioux in their efforts to keep their lands. However, due to a disagreement with Sitting Bull over the Ghost Dance religion, which she felt would denigrate the Indians in the eyes of the U.S. government, she left the reservation on this day.

1895: According to the Oklahoma Law Enforcement Memorial, a group of U.S. Indian officers went to the Quapaw Reservation to evict members of a family who had been removed once but returned. As the officers approached the house, Amos Vallier, a friend of the family, opened fire on the officers with a shotgun, shooting Officer Joe Big Knife in the head and killing him.

1955: An election had been authorized to adopt an amended constitution and bylaws for the Hualapai Tribe of the Hualapai Reservation in Arizona by the assistant secretary of the interior. It was approved by a vote of 90–17.

1985: An election approved Amendments 16 and 17 to the constitution and bylaws of the Lac Du Flambeau Band of Lake Superior Chippewa Indians of Wisconsin.

OCTOBER 23

1518: Diego de Velásquez, the governor of Cuba, appointed Hernán Cortés "captain-general" of an expedition to Mexico.

1823: According to Cherokee records, Creek Chief William McIntosh, representing U.S. Indian commissioners, attempted to bribe Cherokee leaders. For $12,000, McIntosh hoped Chiefs John Ross and Charles Hicks and Council Clerk Alexander McCoy would try to convince the Cherokees to cede lands to the United States. The Cherokee leaders refused the offer with a show of indignation.

1862: Pro-Union Delaware and Shawnee warriors attacked the Wichita Agency.

1864: Sioux Indians and Captain Pell parleyed at Fort Dill.

1866: Elements of the Second Cavalry fought some Indians on the North Fork of the Platte River near Fort Sedgwick, Colorado. Two soldiers were wounded, four Indians were killed, and seven were wounded, according to army records.

1868: In a skirmish at Fort Zarah (near modern Great Bend) in central Kansas, two Indians and two whites were killed.

1869: Following a group of hostile Indians, troopers entered the Miembres Mountains in New Mexico Territory. During a fight, three Indians were killed and three were wounded. Only one soldier was injured.

1874: This morning, a bunch of Sioux took axes to the stripped tree that Red Cloud Agency Agent J.J. Saville had planned as a flagpole. The Indians did not want a flag on their reservation. When Saville got no help from Indian leaders in stopping the choppers, he sent a worker to get help from Fort Robinson in northwestern Nebraska. As the two dozen soldiers from the fort were riding toward the agency, a large group of angry Sioux surrounded them. They tried to instigate a fight. Suddenly, the Sioux police, led by Young Man Afraid of His Horses, rode up and formed a cordon around the soldiers. The Sioux police escorted the soldiers to the agency stockade, averting a possible fight. Many Sioux were frustrated by the events and left the reservation.

1874: Indians fought with soldiers from the Fifth Cavalry and some Indian scouts near the Old Pueblo Fork of the Little Colorado River in Arizona. According to army documents, sixteen Indians were killed and one was captured.

1876: Having surrounded Red Cloud and Red Leaf's camp overnight, Colonel Ranald Mackenzie and eight troops of cavalry approached the camp after daybreak. The Indians surrendered without a fight near Camp Robinson, Nebraska. The camp had 400 warriors and numerous women and children.

1877: Miles and the Nez Perce arrived at Fort Keogh.

1878: Dull Knife and his Cheyenne followers were en route to the Red Cloud Agency to get some food from Red Cloud's people. A sudden snowstorm hit them. Out of the snow came Captain J.B. Johnson and Troops B and D, Third Cavalry. After a brief parley, the 149 Northern Cheyenne, including Dull Knife, Old Crow, and Wild Hog, surrendered near Fort Robinson in northwestern Nebraska. Little Wolf, with fifty-three men and eighty-one women and children, had split off from Dull Knife recently. They managed to avoid the soldiers and escaped into the Sand Hills. Although Dull Knife's people were marched to Fort Robinson, they hid most of their best weapons. They gave up only their old rifles and guns.

1953: Assistant Secretary of the Interior Orme Lewis ratified a constitution and bylaws approved by the Confederated Tribes of the Warm Springs Reservation of Oregon in an election held on August 8, 1953.

1978: The area director, Aberdeen area office, Bureau of Indian Affairs, authorized an election to amend the revised constitution and bylaws for the Sisseton Wahpeton Sioux Tribe of South Dakota. The election took place on November 7, 1978.

OCTOBER 24

1778: From this day until December 3, 1786, Domingo Cabello y Robles served as governor of Texas. During his term, he arranged a peace with the Comanche.

1785: U.S. representatives attempted to hold a treaty conference with the Creek. Few Indians attended the meeting.

1801: The Chickasaw Natchez Trace Treaty (7 Stat. 65) was endorsed by the Chickasaw at Chickasaw Bluffs. The United States got the right to make a road from the Mero District in Tennessee to Natchez in Mississippi for a payment of $700 in goods. Seventeen Indians signed the treaty.

1804: The Cherokee signed a treaty (7 Stat. 228) at Wafford's Settlement in the Tellico Garrison. The Cherokees ceded the area known as Wafford's Settlement. The Cherokee received $5,000 up front and $1,000 annually. The treaty was signed by Return Meigs for the United States and by ten Cherokees.

1816: The Treaty of Fort Stephens (7 Stat. 152) with the Choctaw paid them $16,000 a year for twenty years for lands between the Alabama and Tombigbee Rivers in Alabama.

1832: A treaty (7 Stat. 391) was signed at Castor Hill, the home of William Clark, with the Kickapoo. They ceded their southwestern Missouri lands for land in Kansas near Fort Leavenworth.

1834: According to government records, as part of a conference at Fort King, Florida, to relocate the Seminole, Chief Charley Emathla gave a speech. He said they had a treaty that allowed them to stay where they were for twenty years. Only thirteen years had passed at the time of the conference.

1840: Colonel John Moore, with ninety Texans and twelve friendly Lipan Indians, came upon a Comanche village on the Red Fork of the Colorado River in central Texas. The Texans sneaked up on the village and attacked. According to the Texans, 148 Comanche were killed and thirty-four were captured. Only one Texan died. The Texans also seized almost 500 horses. The village was burned.

1858: According to some sources, Lieutenant Howland and soldiers from Fort Deliverance captured Navajo Chief Terribio and twenty other Navajos.

1862: A fight took place in Indian Territory (present-day Oklahoma) near Fort Cobb. Pro-Union Comanche, Kickapoo, Kiowa, and Shawnee attacked the Indian agency. Then they struck the nearby Tonkawa village. Chief Plácido and 137 of the 300 other Tonkawa were killed in the fighting.

1871: Indians skirmished with a group of soldiers from the Third Cavalry near Horseshoe Canyon, Arizona, according to official army records. One civilian was killed and one soldier was wounded.

1874: Major G.W. Schofield and three troops from the Tenth Cavalry charged a village on Elk Creek in Indian Territory (present-day Oklahoma). The Indians surrendered under a flag of truce. Sixty-nine warriors and 250 women and children were taken into custody. Almost 2,000 horses were recovered.

1924: An order was issued that modified the Jicarilla Apache lands that had been opened for settlement. The order lasted until March 5, 1927.

1936: An election for a proposed constitution and bylaws for the Hopi Tribe was held. The results were 651–104 in favor, according to the constitution itself.

1936: An election for a proposed constitution and bylaws for the Yavapai-Apache Tribe was held. The results were 86–0 in favor.

1963: An election for an amendment to the constitution for the Standing Rock Sioux Tribe was held. The vote was 750–194 in favor.

OCTOBER 25

1755: After the attack on the Penn's Creek Village in Snyder County, Pennsylvania, on October 16, a group of men went to the area to bury the dead. The Delaware who attacked the village also attacked this group, killing several.

1764: Colonel Henry Bouquet had led a force of more than 1,500 soldiers into Ohio looking for captives of the recent wars and hostile Indians. Local Indians (near modern Coshocton, Ohio) delivered over 200 prisoners to Bouquet. Many of the smaller children did not wish to leave their "adopted" Indian parents.

1805: The Cherokee signed a treaty (7 Stat. 93) with Return Meigs on the Duck River at Tellico, covering land north of the Tennessee River in Kentucky and Middle Tennessee.

Engraving depicting the legendary origins of the Tonkawas

1841: The Cherokee council outlawed spirituous liquors.

1853: Captain John Gunnison and eight others with the Pacific Railroad surveying along the 38th Parallel were killed during a fight with Paiute Indians in the Sevier River Valley of Utah. The Paiute hunting party of twenty was led by Moshoquop. Moshoquop's father had been killed by other whites only days before. The Mormons and the Paiute had been fighting for some time. (Also recorded as happening on October 26.)

1862: The Tonkawa were living on a reservation in the Washita River in Indian Territory (present-day Oklahoma) after having been removed from a reservation on the Brazos River in Texas. The Tonkawa had earned the enmity of other tribes because they acted as scouts for the army. Delaware, Shawnee, and Caddo Indians attacked the Tonkawa village. All told, 137 of the 300 Tonkawa were killed in the raid. Some sources said the Comanche, Kiowa, and Wichita were also involved.

1867: According to army records, members of the Eighth Cavalry fought with a band of Indians near Truxell Springs, Arizona. One Indian was killed.

1868: Major E.A. Carr and Troops A, B, F, H, I, L, and M, Fifth Cavalry, encountered a large group of Indians on Beaver Creek in Kansas. During the fight, according to Carr, only one soldier was wounded; thirty Indians were killed. The Indians also lost about 130 ponies during the fight. The fight lasted two days.

1872: Indians skirmished with a group of soldiers from the Fifth Cavalry Infantry in the Santa Maria Mountains and on Sycamore Creek in Arizona, according to official army records. Nine Indians were killed in fighting that lasted until November 3.

1878: Dull Knife and his 150 Cheyenne reached Fort Robinson in northwestern Nebraska and surrendered to Major Caleb Carlton. After Carlton was replaced by Captain Henry Wessells, Dull Knife discovered his Cheyenne would be returned to Indian Territory (present-day Oklahoma). They refused to leave voluntarily, and Dull Knife said he would rather die than leave his homeland. The camp commander locked them in a barracks and slowly tried to get their cooperation by cutting off their provisions. This method did not work. (See January 9, 1879.)

1890: Sitting Bull paid his last visit to the Standing Rock Agency.

1910: The rancheria for the Tuolumne Band of Me-Wok Indians was deeded, according to their constitution.

1949: By Presidential Proclamation No. 2860, the Effigy Mounds in Iowa were designated as a national monument.

OCTOBER 26

1676: Indian fighter Nathaniel Bacon died.

1832: Marks Crume, John Davis, and Jonathan Jennings, representing the United States, and Potawatomi Indians signed a treaty (7 Stat. 394) at Tippecanoe. For $20,000 annually and $30,000 worth of supplies, the Indians gave up large sections of land.

1832: The Shawnees and Delaware signed a treaty (7 Stat. 397) at Castor Hill, William Clark's home. They ceded their land at Cape Girardeau for land in Kansas.

1853: Captain John Gunnison and eight others in the Pacific Railroad surveying along the 38th Parallel were killed during a fight with Paiute Indians in the Sevier River Valley of Utah. The Paiute hunting party of twenty were led by Moshoquop. Moshoquop's father had been killed by other whites only days before. The Mormons and the Paiute had been fighting for some time, considered a part of the Walker War. (Also recorded as happening on October 25.)

1866: Elements of the First Cavalry fought some Indians near Lake Albert, Oregon. Two soldiers were wounded, fourteen Indians were killed, and seven were captured, according to army records.

1867: According to army records, members of the Second Cavalry fought with a band of Indians near Shell Creek, Dakota Territory. No one was reported injured in the skirmish.

1867: According to army records, members of the First and Eighth Cavalry fought with a band of Indians near Camp Winfield Scott, Nevada. Three Indians were reported killed and four captured.

1868: The Beaver Creek, Kansas, fight concluded. In Central City, New Mexico, three citizens were killed by Indians.

1876: Pierre Falcon, Metis singer and songwriter, died.

1877: Chief Joseph's "I will fight no more" speech was first printed.

1880: At the Mescalero Agency in Fort Stanton Reservation in southern New Mexico, seven Apache men and seventeen women and children surrendered.

1882: The U.S. Navy shelled the Tlingit.

October 27

1795: Spain signed the San Lorenzo Treaty with the United States. The treaty allowed American boats to use the Mississippi River in Spanish Territory. It also confirmed the northern boundary of the Spanish Territories as the 31st Parallel. The Spanish were required to abandon all forts and lands north of that line. Both countries agreed to "control" the Indians within their boundaries.

1805: As a part of the Cherokee treaty (7 Stat. 95) at Kingston, the area around modern Kingston, Tennessee, called Southwest Point during that time was ceded. They also ceded the first island of the Tennessee River. It was officially given up later on January 7, 1806. This treaty was signed in Tellico.

1832: The Peoria, Lahokia, Michigamea, Tamaroa, and Kaskaskia Indians signed a treaty (7 Stat. 403) at Castor Hill, William Clark's home. They swapped their Illinois lands for lands in Kansas.

1837: After helping to lead a large group of Seminole out of a relocation camp in Tampa Bay, Chief Osceola was pursued by American forces under General Thomas Jesup. On this day, while operating under direct orders of General Jesup, soldiers invited Osceola to talk under a white flag of truce. When Osceola joined them, he was taken captive. (Also recorded as happening on October 21.)

1837: The second group of emigrating Cherokees reached Nashville, Tennessee. A few of the Cherokee leaders in this group visited President Jackson, who was visiting the area. They left the next day.

1867: After several delays, 500 Cheyenne warriors stormed down on the Medicine Lodge Creek conference. After speeches on both sides, it became apparent that the whites wanted all of the land north of the Arkansas River.

1875: Troop H, Fifth Cavalry, under Captain J.M. Hamilton from Fort Wallace in western Kansas attacked a group of Indians near Smoky Hill River, Kansas. During the fight, two Indians were reported killed and one soldier was wounded.

1876: According to army reports, 2,000 Indian men, women, and children, some 400 lodges total, surrendered to Colonel Nelson Miles on the Big Dry River in Montana.

1879: Captain Morrow followed Victorio and his Warm Springs Apache into Mexico. Twelve miles from the Corralitos River in the Guzman Mountains, Morrow attacked. The army had one scout killed and two wounded. Being low on food and water, Morrow withdrew to Fort Bayard in southwestern New Mexico.

1948: In 1905, a large part of the Wind River Reservation in Wyoming, occupied by the Shoshone and Arapaho tribes, was ceded to the United States. They got a small part of that land back, according to Federal Register No. 13FR08818.

1952: The federal government was going to build the Yellowtail Dam and Reservoir on a large part of the Crow Indian Reservation in Wyoming. The land was condemned.

1970: The Pit River Indians engaged in a skirmish with local law enforcement in Burney, California.

1973: The deputy assistant secretary of the interior had authorized an election to approve an amendment to the constitution and bylaws of the Miccosukee Tribe of Indians of Florida. Amendment 3 was approved by a vote of 44–8, Amendment 4 was approved 39–13, and Amendment 5 was approved 42–10.

1986: The Indian Alcohol and Substance Abuse Prevention and Treatment Act of 1986 (100 Stat. 3207–137) was passed. It was intended to "develop a comprehensive, coordinated attack upon the illegal narcotics traffic in Indian country and the deleterious impact of alcohol and substance abuse upon Indian tribes and their members; provide direction and guidance to program managers; modify or supplement existing programs; provide authority and opportunity for tribal participation in program management."

OCTOBER 28

1815: The Kansa Indians concluded a treaty (7 Stat. 137) in St. Louis. The United States was represented by Auguste Chouteau and Ninian Edwards.

1851: The San Saba Treaty was signed at the Council Grounds between the United States and the chiefs and head men of the Comanche, Lipan, and "Mucalaro" Tribes.

1852: Fort Chadbourne was established in western Texas (near modern Bronte). It was designed to protect the local settlers and the Butterfield Stage from the local Comanche.

1861: The Cherokee National Assembly declared war on the United States of America. They had signed a treaty with the Confederated States of America.

1863: The Cherokee capital was located in Tahlequah, Indian Territory (modern Oklahoma). The Cherokee Nation had been divided by the U.S. Civil War. Stand Watie supported the Confederacy. He and his followers burned down the capital buildings.

1865: The Upper Yanktonai Sioux and the Oglala Sioux signed treaties (14 Stat. 743, 747) with the United States.

1867: The Cheyenne and Arapaho signed a treaty with the United States (15 Stat. 593). The treaty affected approximately 2,250 Cheyenne and 2,000 Arapaho.

1869: While scouting the country surrounding the Brazos River in Texas, Forty-First Infantry Lieutenant George E. Albee and two enlisted men encountered a group of eleven hostile Indians, according to army records. During the subsequent fighting, Albee's group drove the Indians from the area. Albee won the Medal of Honor for his actions. Army records also indicated that members of the Fourth and Ninth Cavalry, Twenty-Fourth Infantry, and some Indian scouts fought with a band of Indians near the headwaters of the Brazos River in Texas. Fifty Indians were killed and seven were captured. Eight soldiers were wounded. The fighting lasted through the next day.

1869: According to army records, settlers fought with a band of Indians in the Miembres Mountains of New Mexico. One soldier and three Indians were wounded. Three Indians were killed in the fighting.

1873: Indians fought with soldiers from the Fifth Cavalry, the Twenty-Third Infantry, and some Indian scouts in the Mazatzal Mountains, Sycamore Springs, and the Sunflower Valley in Arizona, according to army documents. Twenty-five Indians were killed and six were captured. The fighting lasted through October 30.

1874: Twenty warriors and their families, with livestock, surrendered to soldiers at Fort Sill in southern Indian Territory (present-day Oklahoma) after being pursued for several days by Captain Carpenter and troops from the Tenth Cavalry. According to army documents, in total 391 Indians were captured in this expedition, led by Lieutenant Colonel J.W. Davidson, which lasted until November 8.

1880: Tenth Cavalry soldiers fought a group of Indians near Ojo Caliente, Texas. According to army documents, five soldiers were killed.

1932: The mineral rights sales ban for the Papago Reservation was canceled.

1992: According to the Osage constitution, the U.S. District Court for the Northern District of Oklahoma ruled in the case *Fletcher v. United States* (90-C–248-E). The ruling allowed members of the Osage Nation to hold an election on the adoption of a constitution. A constitution was adopted on February 4, 1994, by a vote of 1,931–1,013.

OCTOBER 29

1712: Settlers in Portsmouth, New Hampshire, held a conference to advise belligerent Indians that Queen Anne's War was over and the fighting should stop. It took almost nine months before a local treaty was signed.

1832: The Piankashaw and Wea Indians concluded a treaty (7 Stat. 410) at Castor Hill, William Clark's home. They received lands in Kansas in exchange for their lands in Illinois and Missouri.

1837: A total of 1,600 Creek under Lieutenant T.P. Sloan left New Orleans on three steamboats.

1853: Alabama Chief Antone, several subchiefs, and leading citizens of Polk County submitted a petition to the Texas legislature. The petition requested that lands in the area be set aside as a reservation for the tribe. The legislature set aside 1,110.7 acres.

1869: According to army records, members of the Fourth and Ninth Cavalries, Twenty-Fourth Infantry, and some Indian scouts fought with a band of Indians near the headwaters of the Brazos River in Texas. Fifty Indians were killed and seven were captured. Eight soldiers were wounded. The fighting started the day before.

1874: Indians fought with soldiers from the Fifth Cavalry near Cave Creek, Arizona. According to army documents, eight Indians were killed and five were captured.

1880: According to army reports, almost fifty of Victorio's Indians attacked twelve Tenth Cavalry troopers near Ojo Caliente, Texas. Four soldiers were killed. The Indians escaped into Mexico.

1926: Bannock Chief Race Horse, also known as Racehorse and John Racehorse Sr., died. He was one of the Bannock representatives in the lawsuit over the Fort Bridger Treaty that went to the U.S. Supreme Court.

1935: The secretary of the interior authorized an election for a constitution for the Indians of the Tulalip Tribes in Washington.

1949: The land needed to make the Garrison Dam was ceded from the Fort Berthold Reservation by an act of Congress (63 Stat. 1026).

OCTOBER 30

1763: Pontiac informed Major Henry Gladwin, commander at Fort Detroit, that he wanted peace and to end the fighting.

1833: Captain Page and 1,000 Choctaws arrived in Memphis. Some used ferries while others marched to Rock Roe in Arkansas, the next leg of their journey.

1866: Elements of the Twenty-third Infantry fought some Indians near Malheur County, Oregon.

Two Indians were killed, three were wounded, and eight were captured, according to army records.

1868: Indians attacked Grinnell Station, Kansas. One Indian was wounded.

1868: According to army records, members of the Second Cavalry fought with a band of Indians near the White Woman's Fork of the Republican River in Kansas. The fighting began on October 13. Two Indians were killed and three were wounded.

1870: Indians attacked a wagon train eighteen miles from Fort Stanton in southern New Mexico Territory. They stampeded fifty-nine mules. Cavalry eventually pursued them for 259 miles, destroyed their village, recovered the mules, and captured three Indians.

1873: Indians fought with soldiers from the Fifth Cavalry, the Twenty-Third Infantry, and some Indian scouts in the Mazatzal Mountains, Sycamore Springs, and the Sunflower Valley in Arizona, according to army documents. Twenty-five Indians were killed and six were captured. The fighting started on October 28.

1873: Indians fought with soldiers from the Eighth Cavalry near Pajarit Springs, New Mexico, according to army documents. Eighteen Indians were captured.

1876: President Grant, by executive order, revoked the White Mountain–San Carlos (Chiricahua) Reserve. The area bounded by Dragoon Springs to Peloncillo Mountain Summit to New Mexico to Mexico reverted to the public domain. The reserve was established on December 14, 1872.

1937: An election for the adoption of a constitution and bylaws for the Stockbridge Munsee Community of Wisconsin was held. The results were 119–13 in favor of passage.

1939: The Miami Indians of Oklahoma's constitution was ratified.

1976: Commissioner of Indian Affairs Morris Thompson had authorized an election to approve a constitution and bylaws for the Fort Sill Apache Tribe of Oklahoma. It was approved by a vote of 35–11.

1990: The law denying Indians the right to speak their own language, under certain circumstances, was repealed.

1991: Executive Order No. 6368, by President George Bush declared November as National American Indian Heritage Month.

OCTOBER 31

1755: This day marked the beginning of a raid by almost 100 Delaware and Shawnees against settlers in Fulton and Franklin Counties, Pennsylvania. Over the next several days, Indians attacked along Conolloway Creek and adjoining areas, killing or capturing half of the 100 settlers in the area. King Shingas, of the Delaware, led the raids.

1799: William Augustus Bowles, the self-proclaimed "Director General and Commander-in-Chief of the Muskogee Nation," issued a proclamation. He stated that the Treaty of San Ildefonso of 1795 was null and void because it covered ancestral Indian lands. Spain and the United States had no right to trade sovereignty over lands that belonged to others.

1818: According to the U.S. Army, this day marked the end of First Seminole War.

1833: President Jackson sent Francis Scott Key to Alabama to investigate the Owen Affair and to assist in the defense of the soldiers. (See October 14.)

1855: Soldiers from Fort Lane in southwestern Oregon fought Rogue River Indians at Hungry Hill, Oregon.

1858: General Harney pronounced that the interior was now open to settlers.

1869: The soon-to-be-named lieutenant governor of the Northwest Territory of Canada, William McDougall, received a letter from the National Council of the Metis. They told him he could not enter this area without their permission.

1869: According to army records, members of the First and Eighth Cavalries fought with a band of Indians in the Chiricahua Mountains of Arizona. Two Indians were killed.

1871: Delshay, of the Tonto Apache, met with Captain W.N. Netterville in Sunflower Valley to discuss a peace treaty. Delshay said he wanted peace, but he wanted both sides to live up to their promises, which the whites seldom did. Delshay agreed to met Peace Commissioner Vincent Colyer at Camp McDowell, near Phoenix, Arizona, on November 12, 1879. But Colyer never responded to Delshay's meeting proposal, so no peace was made.

1874: Indians fought with soldiers from the Ninth Cavalry Infantry near Fort Sill, Indian Territory. According to army documents, one Indian was killed during this engagement, which started on October 4.

1876: Hunkpapa Sioux went to Fort Peck.

1877: The Nez Perce started the boat trip to Fort Lincoln.

1879: After the *Standing Bear* trial, where it was ruled the government could not force an Indian to stay in any one reservation against their will, Big Snake decided to test the law. He asked for permission to leave his reservation to visit Standing Bear. His request was denied. He eventually left the Ponca Reservation to go to the Cheyenne Reservation, also in Indian Territory (present-day Oklahoma). Big Snake was returned to the Ponca Reservation, when General Sherman decided the Standing Bear ruling applied only to Standing Bear. Big Snake made the Ponca agent, William Whiteman, very angry. Whiteman ordered Big Snake to be arrested. On this day, Big Snake was arrested and charged with threatening Whiteman. In Whiteman's office, after denying any such actions, Big Snake refused to go with the soldiers there to arrest him. A struggle developed, and Big Snake was shot and killed.

1880: Spotted Eagle and Rain-in-the-Face surrendered at Fort Keogh.

1887: Fort Logan was established in what would become Denver, Colorado.

1923: The "Treaty Between His Majesty the King and the Chippewa Indians of Christian Is-

Rain-in-the-Face, captured Hunkpapa Sioux (NA)

land, Georgia Island, and Rama" was signed in Canada.

NOVEMBER 1

1634: Tensions in Massachusetts had risen because Niantic Indians had killed a boat captain named John Stone. Rather than wage war, the Niantic and their allies, the Pequot, concluded a peace treaty with the Massachusetts government. (Also recorded as happening on November 7, 1634.)

1770: Spanish and Opata Indian forces led by Bernardo de Gálvez were on a punitive expedition directed toward the Apache. A former Apache captive was leading them to the village where he was held near the Pecos River (modern Texas). They reached the site of the village only to discover that the Apache had gone. They continued their search during the night.

1784: The Tugaloo Treaty with the Creek was signed.

1812: Negotiations had been held between the Lower Creek and representative of the John Forbes Company, John Innerarity, at their village at Tuckabatchee. Tuckabatchee was near modern

Tallassee in east-central Alabama. Innerarity contended that the Creek owed the company $40,000 for various supplies. The Creek felt they were being overcharged and not getting a fair price for their trade goods. They reached an agreement to pay the Forbes Company a sum of $21,916.012 over a three-year period. Their current government payments for previous land cessions was $22,000 for the same period of time. This cleared their debts but left them with no outside resources for three years.

1824: Choctaws arrived in Washington, D.C., for a conference to renegotiate the Treaty of Doak's Stand of 1820.

1837: The Winnebago signed a treaty (7 Stat. 544) in Washington, D.C.

1837: The steamboat *Monmouth* had 611 Creek Indians on board heading for Indian Territory (present-day Oklahoma). During the night, while traveling upstream in a downstream lane of the Mississippi River, it struck the *Trenton*, which was being towed downstream. The *Monmouth* broke into two pieces and sunk within a few minutes. All told, 311 Creek drowned. Because of its old age, the *Monmouth* had been condemned for normal shipping. This did not stop it from being used to transport the Creek. Four of Jim Boy's children were among the dead.

1844: Cherokees passed a law saying members of the tribe could not bet on elections.

1866: Elements of the Twenty-Third Infantry fought some Indians near Trout Creek Canyon, Oregon. Four Indians were killed and three were captured, according to army records.

1873: Barbed wire was first manufactured.

1874: Elements of the Fifth Cavalry were scouting near Sunset Pass in Arizona Territory. Lieutenant Charles King was captured by local Indians. For his actions in rescuing the lieutenant, Sergeant Bernard Taylor, Company A, would be awarded the Medal of Honor.

1876: According to a story in the *Arkansas City Traveler*, Colonel William Hazen arrived at Fort

Peck. He had four companies of soldiers and supplies. The Sioux left.

1877: Lieutenant John Bullis, the Twenty-Fourth Infantry, and thirty-seven black Seminole scouts skirmished with Apache and other Indians near the Big Bend of the Rio Grande in Texas. According to army documents, no casualties were reported.

1893: Senator Henry Dawes of Massachusetts was appointed chairman of a Commission to "negotiate agreements with the Cherokee, Choctaw, Chickasaw, Creek, and Seminole Tribes providing for the dissolution of the tribal governments and the allotment of land to each tribal member." It became known as the Dawes Commission.

1978: The Education Amendments Act (92 Stat. 2143) of November 1, 1978, was passed by Congress. It was to "establish standards for the basic education of Indian children; to restructure BIA education functions; to establish criteria for dormitories. To extend and amend expiring elementary and secondary education programs."

1986: The first National War Monument for Indians was dedicated.

1999: Mamie Mullen died at 104 years of age. She was thought to be California's oldest full-blooded Maidu.

NOVEMBER 2

1770: Spanish and Opata Indian forces led by Bernardo de Gálvez were on a punitive expedition directed toward the Apache. Early on this day they discovered an Apache camp near the Pecos River in modern Texas. The Spaniards and Opata attacked. They killed twenty-eight Apache and captured thirty-six. They then returned to Chihuahua, Mexico.

1868: According to army records, a mail escort from the Fourteenth Infantry fought with a band of Indians between Prescott and Wickenberg, Arizona. One soldier was killed.

1869: While on patrol in southern Indian Territory (present-day Oklahoma), near Fort Sill, troopers recovered a white captive from a group of Indians.

1869: Metis forces took over Fort Garry, Canada. This was yet another step toward rebellion.

1875: Two troops of the Tenth Cavalry, under Twenty-Fifth Infantry Lieutenant Andrew Geddes, fought a group of Indians near the Pecos River in Texas. One Indian was killed and five were captured.

1917: Under authority of an act of Congress (24 Stat 1 388–389), an executive order was issued that extended the trust period for ten years on land allotments made to members of the "Prairie Band of Potawatomi Indians in Kansas."

1966: Assistant Secretary of the Interior Harry Anderson approved amendments to the constitution and bylaws of the Lac Courte Oreilles Band of Lake Superior Chippewa Indians of Wisconsin.

1966: An act (80 Stat. 1112) was passed by Congress to "authorize long term leases [99 years] on the San Xavier and Salt River Pima-Maricopa Indian Reservations."

1972: Some 500 Indians concluded the Trail of Broken Treaties March to Washington, D.C. They seized part of the Bureau of Indian Affairs building until November 8.

1974: The constitution of the Indians of the Tulalip Tribes in Washington was modified.

1976: An election to amend the revised constitution and bylaws for the Sisseton Wahpeton Sioux Tribe of South Dakota was held. The election results were 392–248 in favor.

1982: Peter MacDonald lost his position as chairman of the Navajo Tribe to Peterson Zah.

NOVEMBER 3

1493: Columbus landed on Dominica.

1620: The Charter of New England was issued.

1756: Delaware Indians staged a series of raids in Berks County, Pennsylvania. At least seven settlers and two Indians were killed near Fort Lebanon during the fighting.

1757: According to some reports, an agreement covering land cessions, peace, and friendship was reached by representatives of the British in Georgia and the Creek.

1757: A group of Pima and Seri attacked the Spanish settlement of San Lorenzo.

1762: As a part of the Treaty of Fountainbleau, Spain acquired all of French Louisiana west of the Mississippi River for helping France in the Seven Years War, also called the French and Indian War. (Also recorded as happening on November 8.)

1763: This day marked the beginning of a major conference between English representatives and the tribes of the Southeast. More than 700 Indians attended, representing the Catawba, Cherokees, Chickasaws, Choctaws, and Creek. Trade issues, intertribal conflicts, and tribal boundary lines were discussed.

1768: The Iroquois sold some land.

1786: The government of Georgia hoped to confirm the Creek Nation's boundaries lines. They invited Creek leaders to a conference on Shoulderbone Creek. Only a few chiefs, including Fat King and Tame King, attended. The Georgia militia threatened the attendees with execution if they did not agree to boundary lines favorable to Georgia. A treaty was signed under duress by the Creek chiefs attending the meeting. This action by the Georgians stoked the flames of the Creeks' passions against the settlers.

1791: General Arthur St. Clair had moved his force of approximately 1,400 men to some high ground on the upper Wabash River (north of present-day Greenville, Ohio). St. Clair was looking for the forces of Little Turtle, who had recently defeated General Josiah Harmar's army. More than half of St. Clair's forces were "dregs of the earth" who signed on for the $2 monthly pay. By this point 600 men had already deserted the original force of 2,000 men. The soldiers were not being paid, and they were underfed. St. Clair's regular army was having to guard what little supplies they had from the militia forces. St. Clair, feeling he had a good defensive position, deployed only minimal sentry positions.

1802: Thomas Jefferson wrote a letter to "Brother Handsome Lake." The letter discussed the selling of land to pay debts and the avoidance of alcohol.

1804: A treaty with the Creek was signed on the Flint River. The Creek gave up almost 2 million acres near the Ocmulgee River for $200,000. This amount was renegotiated several times in later treaties. The United States was represented by Benjamin Hawkins, the Creek by Hopoie Micco.

1804: A treaty (7 Stat. 84) was signed with the Sac and Fox Indians in St. Louis, Louisiana Territory. The tribes would be protected by the United States. New boundary lines were established. The Indians received $2,234.50 in goods up front and $600 (Sac) and $400 (Fox) annually. They could hunt on their old lands as long as they remained government property. Only the president could license traders. Trading-factory houses would be established. Peace would be established with the Osage tribe. A fort would be built on the Mississippi and Ouiconsing Rivers. They ceded all of their lands in Illinois (almost 15 million acres). The treaty was signed by William Henry Harrison and five Indians. Many Indians did not consider the signatories to the treaty as "official" representatives of the tribe. Dissatisfaction with the treaty led to Black Hawk's War.

1813: Colonel John Coffee and almost 1,000 men (Americans, Creek, and Cherokees) had surrounded the Red Stick Creek village of Tallasehatchee (Talishatche, Tallushatchee) on the Cousa River (near modern Anniston, Alabama). At dawn, Coffee's forces attacked. The allied forces killed more than 180 Creek while losing only five of their own men. They also captured seven dozen women and children. Davy Crockett was quoted as saying, "We shot them like dogs."

1830: Choctaw leaders Charles Hay and Ned Perry sold their lands in Mississippi. Similar lands sold after the Choctaw were mandated to leave go for only a sixth of what Hay and Perry received.

1864: After having their rations cut, the Mescalero Indians escaped from the Bosque Redondo Reservation. They stayed away for years.

1867: Elements of the Fourteenth Infantry fought some Indians near Willow Grove, Arizona. Thirty-two Indians were killed, according to Fourteenth Infantry records.

1868: According to army records, members of the Seventh Cavalry fought with a band of Indians near Big Coon Creek, Kansas. No casualties were reported.

1872: Indians skirmished with a group of soldiers from the Fifth Cavalry Infantry in the Santa Maria Mountains and on Sycamore Creek in Arizona, according to official army records. Nine Indians were killed in the fighting, which started on October 25.

1874: Colonel R.S. Mackenzie and troops from the Fourth Cavalry fought with Indians along Los Lagunas Quatro (spelled "Curato" in army papers) in Texas. Two Indians were killed and nineteen were captured. Farrier Ernest Veuve, Company A, would be awarded the Medal of Honor for the "gallant manner in which he faced a desperate Indian."

1875: In a secret government meeting in the White House, it was decided to wage war on the Indians who had not accepted and complied with U.S. authority and left the Black Hills. Attending the meeting were several senior Indian Department officials, several generals, and President Grant.

1892: Ned Christie was shot and killed by a posse outside his home. Falsely accused of killing a U.S. Marshal in 1887, Christie avoided capture for more than five years and was the most wanted fugitive in Indian Territory (present-day Oklahoma). Claiming federal marshals had no jurisdiction in Cherokee territory, the former Cherokee tribal senator refused to give himself up. Later, a witness vouched for Christie's innocence. Others said Christie did kill the marshal but did so in self-defense.

1969: The U.S. Senate declared that Indian education was in bad shape.

1976: John Artichoker Jr., the area director of the Phoenix office of the Bureau of Indian Affairs, ratified an election that approved amendments to the constitution and bylaws for the Pyramid Lake Paiute Tribe of Nevada. The election was held on July 1, 1976.

NOVEMBER 4

604: According to some interpretations of Maya engravings, Lady Kanal-Ikal (Queen Lady Yohl Ik'nal or Lady Heart of the Wind Place) of Palenque, Mexico, died. She ascended to the throne on December 21, 583.

1791: Miami Chief Little Turtle and 1,500 Miami, Delaware, Potawatomi, and Shawnee warriors had been stalking American General Arthur St. Clair and his force of 2,500 men. About 300 of the men were militia, and they had camped across a stream from the rest of the force (near the site of present-day Fort Recovery, Ohio). In a predawn move, Little Turtle's forces attacked the militia. After three hours of slaughter, St. Clair managed to retreat. All told, 900 of St. Clair's men died in what has been called the worst defeat in the history of the American army.

1833: Lieutenant Rains, disbursing agent for the Choctaws, informed General George Gibson that since the beginning of the fall approximately one-fifth of the 3,000 Choctaws near the Choctaw Agency in Indian Territory (present-day Oklahoma) had died from the climate, the flood on the Arkansas River, and lack of scientific medical care.

1851: One in a series of treaties was signed by California Indians on the Upper Klamath. The treaty was designed to set aside lands for the Indians and to protect them from angry Europeans.

1854: The Choctaws and the Chickasaws signed a treaty (10 Stat. 1116) at Doaksville.

1867: According to army records, members of the Twenty-Seventh Infantry fought with a band of Indians near Goose Creek, Dakota Territory.

1879: Will Rogers, American humorist and a Cherokee, was born. He was perhaps best known for his often repeated comment: "I've never met a man I didn't like."

1892: The Kiowa observed a total lunar eclipse. It was depicted on their annual calendar as one of the most significant events of the year.

1936: A constitution and bylaws were approved for the Southern Ute Indian Tribe of the Southern Ute Reservation in Colorado.

1949: The assistant commissioner of Indian affairs had authorized an election to approve a constitution and bylaws for the Confederated Tribes of the Umatilla Reservation. It passed by a vote of 113–104.

1968: The U.S. Post Office issued a Chief Joseph stamp.

1986: The Saginaw Chippewa of Michigan amended their constitution by a vote of 150–19.

NOVEMBER 5

1768: The Iroquois sold some land. According to many historians, the treaty signed at Fort Stanwix (near modern Rome, New York) caused such anguish among Indian tribes that it led to Lord Dunmore's War. The treaty was signed at a meeting of several thousand Indians.

1775: Kumeyaays attacked the Mission San Diego de Alcala. The mission was destroyed in the fighting.

1783: According to some sources, Chickasaw Indians, led by Chief Piomingo, signed a treaty at Nashville. The treaty ceded land along the Cumberland River to Tennessee.

1861: About 10,000 Indians left Oklahoma to avoid Confederate soldiers.

1862: The Santee Sioux were sentenced.

1864: Major Edward Wynkoop was the commander at Fort Lyon in southeastern Colorado. His

Eight Crow prisoners under guard at Crow Agency, Montana (LOC)

friendly and honorable dealings with the Cheyenne and Arapaho had angered Colorado's political leaders. Wynkoop was relieved as commander of the fort by Major Scott Anthony. One of Anthony's first acts was to cut the Indians' rations.

1867: According to army records, Lieutenant J.C. Carroll of the Thirty-Second Cavalry and a civilian fought with a band of Indians near Camp Bowie, Arizona. Lieutenant Carroll was killed and the civilian was wounded.

1868: Red Cloud signed the Bozeman Treaty.

1871: Indians attacked a mail stage near Wickenburg, Arizona, according to official army records. Six people on the stage were killed and two were wounded.

1874: According to army records, in the Staked Plain of the Texas Panhandle Corporal John W. Comfort, Company A, Fourth Cavalry, earned a Medal of Honor because he "ran down and killed an Indian."

1887: Soldiers from the First, Seventh, and Ninth Cavalries and the Third, Fifth, and Seventh Infantries fought a group of Indians on the Crow Agency in Montana. According to army documents, seven Indians and one soldier were killed. Ten Indians and two soldiers were wounded. Nine Indians were captured.

1950: Mitchell Red Cloud Jr., a Winnebago, was a corporal in the Nineteenth Infantry. While standing guard duty in Korea, his position was attacked. He withstood the attack while his unit prepared itself for the attack. For his actions against enemy forces, which cost him his life, he would be awarded the Medal of Honor.

1985: Amendments 16 and 17 to the constitution and bylaws of the Lac du Flambeau Band of Lake Superior Chippewa Indians of Wisconsin were approved and became effective.

NOVEMBER 6

1528: Cabeza de Vaca and eighty men of a Spanish expedition washed up on Galveston Island in Texas. Most of his men eventually died or became captives. Cabeza de Vaca marched across the continent to California before he reached a Spanish outpost. He was the first "white man" many Indians ever saw.

1792: Washington talked about Indians in his fourth address to Congress.

1811: William Henry Harrison arrived at Prophetstown.

1838: The Miami signed a treaty (7 Stat. 569) with the United States at the Forks of the Wabash. The Americans were represented by Abel Pepper.

1864: Colonel Kit Carson and his troops left Fort Bascom in western New Mexico en route for the Texas Panhandle to "punish" the hostile Comanche and Kiowa in the area.

1867: Engraved on a marker in the Fort Buford (North Dakota) cemetery: "Cornelius Coughing—Private, Company C, Thirty-First Infantry—Nov. 6, 1867—Killed by Indians . . . one of the wood wagons was attacked by a party of Indians in the thick brush about two miles from the post. There were four guards and a driver with the wagons. The body of Private Coughlin was found this morning in the bushes badly mutilated; he remained with the wagon discharging his piece until killed. The Indians [under Sitting Bull] captured four mules."

1868: Four Oglala Sioux, including Red Cloud, two Brule Sioux, eighteen Hunkpapa Sioux, ten Blackfeet Sioux, five Cuthead Sioux, three Two Kettle Sioux, four Sans Arc Sioux, and seven Santee Sioux signed the Fort Laramie treaty (15 Stat. 635).

1869: According to army records, members of the Eighth Cavalry fought with a band of Indians near Garde, Arizona. Two Indians were captured. Soldiers from the Second Cavalry fought with a band of Indians between Fort Fetterman and Fort Laramie in Wyoming. Two soldiers were killed.

1874: Lieutenant H.J. Farnsworth and twenty-eight men from Troop H, Eighth Cavalry, battled approximately 100 Southern Cheyenne on McClellan Creek in Texas. Their report estimated that seven Indians were killed and ten wounded. One soldier was killed and four wounded. Six cavalry horses were also killed in the fight. Near the Laguna Tahoka, also in Texas, the Fourth Cavalry fought with some Indians and killed two of them.

1920: The federal government "temporarily [withdrew] from settlement, sale or other disposition until March 5, 1922" approximately 386.85 acres of land of the Zia Pueblo in New Mexico Territory.

1960: The newly approved Articles of Association of the Pala Band of Mission Indians in California went into effect.

1972: Secretary of the Interior Harrison Loesch ratified an amendment to the constitution of the Minnesota Chippewa Tribe, consisting of the Chippewa Indians of the White Earth, Leech Lake, Fond du Lac, Bois Forte (Nett Lake), and Grand Portage Reservations.

1975: Commissioner of Indian Affairs Morris Thompson authorized an election to approve a constitution and bylaws for the Rumsey Indian Rancheria (Yocha Dehe) in Yolo County, Brooks, California.

1979: The acting deputy commissioner of Indian affairs authorized an election to approve a constitution for the Tonto Apache Tribe. The election would be held on December 22, 1979.

NOVEMBER 7

1519: According to some sources, Spaniards had their first view of Tenochtitlán (modern Mexico City).

1634: Tensions in Massachusetts had risen because Niantic Indians had killed a boat captain named John Stone. Rather than wage war, the Niantic and their allies, the Pequot, concluded a peace treaty with the Massachusetts government. (Also recorded as happening on November 1, 1634.)

1788: Representatives of the Six Nations arrived at Fort Harmar in Ohio. One chief, Captain David, presented a message to Governor St. Claire requesting a resumption of peace negotiations.

1794: After more than a year of raids by Americans and Chickamauga, the Chickamauga had been beaten down. In a meeting arranged last month, Tennessee Governor William Blount met with Cherokee and the offshoot Chickamauga chiefs at the Tellico Blockhouse near the Tennessee–North Carolina border. Forty chiefs were present, including John Watts (Young Tassel), Hanging Maw, and Bloody Fellow; they agreed to a peace. They also agreed to exchange prisoners on December 31, 1794.

1811: The Battle of Tippecanoe was fought at the confluence of the Tippecanoe and Wabash Rivers. Tecumseh's brother, Tenskwatawa (Prophet), had established a village here called Prophetstown. The village was designed as a place where Indians could return to their natural ways before the coming of the Europeans. At any given time, nearly 1,000 Delaware, Kickapoo, Ojibwa, Ottawa, Shawnee, and Wyandot Indians lived in the village. General William Henry Harrison and 1,000 soldiers approached the village when they knew Tecumseh was away. Prophet arranged for a peace conference to be held on this day. Just before dawn, predicting an easy victory because of his "strong medicine," Tenskwatawa led his followers in an attack on Harrison's camp. Alerted by sentries, the American forces fought back. When the easy victory failed to materialize and the American bullets did not dissipate in the wind, the Indians lost heart and were beaten back. Prophet lost face, and Harrison destroyed his town the next day.

1814: American forces under Andrew Jackson defeated British forces and Red Stick Creek in a fight for Pensacola, Florida. The Creek escaped to the local woods. Many of the Creek starved while trying to avoid capture.

1836: Mexican nationals in California declared independence from Mexico. This lasted for approximately one year.

1867: According to army records, members of the First and Eighth Cavalries fought with a band of Indians near Willows, Arizona. Six soldiers were reported wounded. Nineteen Indians were killed and seventeen captured.

1867: According to army records, members of the Eighth Cavalry fought with a band of Indians near Toll Gate, Arizona. Three Indians were killed.

1868: Indians attacked a stagecoach at Coon Creek in Kansas. They captured a horse.

1868: According to army records, members of the Eighth Cavalry fought with a band of Indians near Willow Grove, Arizona. Eleven Indians were killed, two were wounded, and twenty were captured. The fighting lasted until November 15.

1885: Sixth Cavalry soldiers and Indian scouts fought a group of Indians in the Florida Mountains of New Mexico. According to army documents, one soldier was killed and another was wounded.

1936: The secretary of the interior had authorized an election for a constitution and bylaws for the Covelo Indian Community of the Round Val-

ley Reservation in California. The results were 60–20 in favor.

1936: The secretary of the interior had authorized an election to approve a constitution and bylaws for the L'Anse Lac Vieux Desert and Ontoagon Bands of Chippewa Indians residing within the original confines of the L'Anse Reservation. It was approved by a vote of 239–18.

1937: The Pyramid Lake Paiute Tribe of Nevada passed an ordinance that established tribal membership rules.

1970: An election for the adoption of a constitution and bylaws for the Chitimacha Tribe of Louisiana was held. It would be approved by a vote of 85–6.

1975: An election to amend the constitution of the Yerington Paiute Tribe of Nevada was held. The results of the election would be to approve several amendments.

1978: An election to amend the revised constitution and bylaws for the Sisseton Wahpeton Sioux Tribe of South Dakota was held. Several amendments were approved.

1989: The deputy to the assistant secretary of Indian affairs, Hazel Elbert, authorized an election by the Coast Indian Community of the Resighini Rancheria for a constitutional amendment.

NOVEMBER 8

1519: According to some sources, Hernán Cortés and his soldiers first entered Tenochtitlán (modern Mexico City) by way of one of the three causeways.

1762: As a part of the Treaty of Fountainbleau, Spain acquired all of French Louisiana west of the Mississippi River for helping France in the Seven Years War, also called the French and Indian War. (Also recorded as happening on November 3.)

1873: According to the constitution of the Coeur d'Alene Tribe of Idaho, the Coeur d'Alene Reservation was modified by executive order.

1874: Lieutenant Frank Dwight Baldwin and soldiers from Troop D, Sixth Cavalry, and Company D, Fifth Infantry, attacked a Southern Cheyenne Indian camp near McClellan's Creek in Texas. Two white girls, Adelaide and Julia Germaine, five and seven years old, were rescued from the Indians during the fight. The Indians still had the girls' two older sisters (they were released in March 1875). The children's parents were killed by the Indians during an earlier raid, according to army reports. The moneys needed to support the children were deducted from the annual payments to the Cheyenne, according to a congressional act.

1874: Indians fought with soldiers from the Sixth and Tenth Cavalries, the Fifth and Eleventh Infantries, and some Indian scouts on an expedition from Fort Sill in Indian Territory. According to army documents, in total 391 Indians were captured in this expedition, which was led by Lieutenant Colonel J.W. Davidson and had started on October 28.

1882: Army Indian scouts fought a group of Indians near Tullock's Fort, Montana. According to army documents, one scout was wounded and two Indians were killed.

1956: A departmental order of September 1, 1939, that transferred certain lands to the jurisdiction of the commissioner of Indian affairs for the use of Navajo Indians was partially revoked, according to Federal Register No. 21FR08953.

1978: The Indian Child Welfare Act (104 Stat. 4544) took place. Among other things, it was to establish standards for the placement of Indian children in foster or adoptive homes to prevent the breakup of Indian families.

1978: Vincent Little, the area director of the Bureau of Indian Affairs, ratified a fourth amendment to the constitution and bylaws of the Shoalwater Bay Indian Organization in Washington State.

NOVEMBER 9

1761: The Mi'kmaq of La Heve signed a treaty with the British of Nova Scotia.

1813: General Ferdinand Claiborne was leading a large force of Mississippi recruits to fight the Creek. They entered Choctaw lands, where they were received warmly. Many Choctaws, led by Chief Pushmataha, joined Claiborne.

1837: Superintendent A.M.M. Upshaw reported he had 4,000 Chickasaws standing by at Memphis, awaiting transport to their new lands in Indian Territory (present-day Oklahoma). Upshaw arranged for their transport to Fort Coffee by ship at a price of $14.50 each. Most reached their destination by the end of the year.

1867: The peace commissioners who met on September 19, 1867, at Platte City, Nebraska, arrived at Fort Laramie in southeastern Wyoming. Commissioners Sherman, Taylor, Harney, Sanborn, Henderson, Tappan, and Terry sought out Red Cloud. But Red Cloud said he would not come to the fort until all of the soldiers had left the Powder River area. The commissioners were given a lecture by Crow Indian Bear Tooth on the ecological disaster they were spreading across Indian lands. Making no headway, the commissioners eventually left without an agreement or substantial negotiations.

1871: By executive order, President Grant established the San Carlos Apache Indian Reservation in southeastern Arizona Territory. The 2,854-square-mile reservation became the home of many Apache, Mohave, and Yuma Indians.

1875: Sitting Bull and Crazy Horse were ordered to go to the reservation.

1875: Indian Bureau Inspector E.T. Watkins reported to the commissioner of Indian affairs that the Plains Indians who lived off the reservation were well-fed, well-armed, and a threat to the reservation system. He recommended an immediate expedition against them.

1878: Part of the Ute Tribe got a new reservation.

1938: An election that approved a constitution and bylaws for the Sokaogon (Mole Lake Band) Chippewa Community of Wisconsin was ratified by Assistant Secretary of the Interior Oscar Chapman. The election was held on October 8, 1938.

1960: An amendment to the constitution and bylaws of the Fort Belknap Indian Community of the Fort Belknap Indian Reservation in Montana was adopted.

1967: Secretary of the Interior Harry Anderson ratified the results of an election that approved amendments to the constitution and bylaws for the Kashia Band of Pomo Indians of the Stewarts Point Rancheria.

1973: An amendment to the constitution and bylaws of the Miccosukee Tribe of Indians of Florida was approved by Marvin Franklin, assistant to the secretary of the interior.

NOVEMBER 10

1782: George Rogers Clark and 1,000 troops attacked the Miami Indians along the Licking River in Kentucky. This expedition had a very adverse psychological effect on the Miami.

1808: The Osage signed a treaty (7 Stat. 107) with Meriwether Lewis. This took place as Fort Osage was officially opened (east of modern Kansas City, Missouri).

1813: William Weatherford's (Lume Chathi–Red Eagle) Red Stick Creek were an antiwhite faction of the Creek Indians. About 1,000 of them had surrounded a prowhite group of Creek at Talladega in east-central Alabama. Andrew Jackson's force of 2,000 Americans and allied Indians arrived at the scene of the siege and attacked. Between the friendly Creek, called White Stick, and Jackson's men, 410 of the 700 Red Stick Creek were killed in the fighting. Jackson's force lost only fifteen men.

1837: According to Texas Ranger records, eighteen Rangers led by Lieutenant A.B. Van Benthusen were following the trail of some Indians accused of stealing horses. In Callahan County, Texas, they encountered a war party of 150 Caddo, Kichi, and Waco warriors. A battle quickly ensued. The Rangers lost ten men before they could finally escape the area.

1837: A delegation of Cherokees consisting of Reverend Jesse Bushyhead, Hair Conrad, and two others addressed the Seminole prisoners at St. Augustine, Florida. They offered to mediate between the Seminole and the United States. This action was supported by the government. The discussions led to a meeting with the warring chiefs in a few weeks.

1869: According to army records, members of the Eighth Cavalry fought with a band of Indians in the Tompkins Valley of Arizona. Four Indians were killed.

1870: Near Carson, Colorado, Indians attacked a Mexican wagon train. They made off with sixty-eight mules.

1958: Acting Secretary of the Interior Elmer Bennett ratified an election for an amendment to the constitution of the Red Lake Band of Chippewa Indians of Minnesota.

1958: An election for the adoption of a constitution and bylaws for the Pueblos of Laguna in New Mexico was ratified by Acting Secretary of the Interior Elmer Bennett. The election was held on October 8, 1958.

1970: On this day and the next day, the first college graduate was elected president of the Navajo.

1976: Harley Zephier, the area director, Aberdeen area office, Bureau of Indian Affairs, approved the results of an election to amend the revised constitution and bylaws for the Sisseton Wahpeton Sioux Tribe of South Dakota. The election took place on November 2, 1976.

1997: Annie Dodge Wauneka died at the age of 87. Wauneka became the Navajo Nation's first female legislator (tribal council) in 1951. She also traveled throughout the nation as a health educator. Among her many honors was to receive the Presidential Medal of Freedom from President Lyndon Johnson in 1963.

NOVEMBER 11

1778: Sequidongquee (Little Beard) and his Seneca followers were active participants in what was called the Cherry Valley Massacre.

1794: A treaty (7 Stat. 44) was concluded at Canandaigua (Konondaigua), New York, with the Six Nations. The United States acknowledged the treaties signed by the Six Nations and New York. Boundaries were established. The Six Nations would not submit further land claims. A wagon trail was established from Fort Schlosser to Buffalo Creek on Lake Erie. The Indians received $10,000 in goods up front. The annuity agreed to in the Treaty of April 3, 1792, was increased from $1,500 to $4,500 in goods. The treaty was signed by Thomas Pickering, for the United States, and fifty-nine Indians.

1794: A dozen Chickamauga warriors led by Chief Doublehead attacked a settlement called Sevier's Station, near Clarksville, Tennessee. Several members of the Sevier family were killed in the fighting.

1865: Medicine Bottle and Little Shakopee, two of the leaders of the Santee Sioux Uprising, were executed at Pine Knob. They both had escaped to Canada, but officials there aided Americans in their kidnapping and return to the United States.

1866: Fort Ellsworth was renamed Fort Harker in honor of Brigadier General Charles Harker. The fort (near modern Ellsworth, Kansas) was established as a supply camp and a base for actions against hostile Indians.

1867: According to army records, members of the Fourteenth Infantry fought with a band of Indians near Camp Lincoln, Arizona. Three soldiers were wounded.

1868: According to army records, members of the Eighth Cavalry fought with a band of Indians near Squaw Peak on the Tonto Plateau in Arizona. Two soldiers were wounded. Fifteen Indians were killed and forty were wounded.

1878: The governor of Kansas wrote the secretary of war that Dull Knife's Northern Cheyenne had killed forty men and "ravished" many women.

1880: Lieutenant F.F. Kislingbury, twelve Second Cavalry troopers, and ten Crow Indian scouts were attacked by hostile Sioux near the mouth of the Musselshell River in Montana. One Indian was reported killed.

1907: An executive order set aside certain lands for the Jicarilla Apache in New Mexico, modifying the original territory.

1912: The Osage Tribe had an oil-lease auction for its Oklahoma reservation. Many auctions were held under an elm tree in Pawhuska, Oklahoma. Eighteen leases sold for over $1 million. The tree was thereafter known as the Million Dollar Elm.

1917: Lydia Liliuokalani, the last sovereign queen of Hawaii, died.

1936: Secretary of the Interior Harold Ickes ratified an election that approved a constitution and bylaws for the Quileute Tribe of Washington. The election was held on October 12, 1936.

1938: The assistant secretary of the interior authorized an election for a constitution for the Havasupai Indian Tribe.

1975: Canadian federal, provincial, and native governments reached an agreement on the administration of native matters in Quebec Province. The natives were able to exert considerable control over local affairs. They controlled their schools and their lands, and they received moneys to go toward compensation and to support hunting and game conservation.

NOVEMBER 12

1602: Sebastian Vizcaino's expedition stopped in modern San Diego, California. Cautiously, the Kumeyaay briefly contacted the Spaniards.

1764: At his camp on the Muskingum River, Colonel Henry Bouquet called upon the Shawnee to deliver all of their remaining prisoners. He asked the Shawnees to treat them gently.

1825: The Cherokee legislative council voted to establish a new capital at the confluence of the

Coosawattee and Conasauga Rivers. The new town was called New Echota, Georgia. The town was located roughly in the center of the nation, making it easier for all members to come to the capital if the need or desire arose.

1834: A meteor shower took place, according to Lone Dog's buffalo-robe calendar.

1864: Cheyenne and Arapaho east of Fort Larned in central Kansas, traveling on Walnut Creek, came across a government wagon train. After pretending friendship, according to government reports, they attacked and killed all fourteen of the drivers. One boy survived after being scalped and left for dead.

1868: The Seventh Cavalry left from its bivouac at Fort Dodge, Kansas. They were searching for "rogue Indians" in Indian Territory (present-day Oklahoma).

1890: The Pine Ridge Indian agent was becoming more concerned about the way the Ghost Dance religion was affecting his charges. Among other things, the Ghost Dance religion said that the Indians would return to their old glories and that the white man's bullets would be useless against them. The agent sent out a request to Indian Affairs to get more help in dealing with the dancers.

1935: An election to establish a constitution for the Tuolumne Band of Me-Wok Indians of the Tuolumne Rancheria was authorized by the secretary of the interior.

1942: Land from the Shoshone-Arapaho Tribes was ceded to the United States. An order, according to Federal Register No. 7FR11100, returned some of that land to the Wind River Reservation in Wyoming.

1973: The assistant to the secretary of the interior authorized an election to approve amendments to the constitution and bylaws of the Tule River Indian Tribe. The election was held on January 26, 1974.

1977: The constitution and bylaws for the Menominee Indian Tribe of Wisconsin was ratified.

1991: The Oglala Sioux adopted a plan for the certification of pesticide application on their reservation.

1996: The Washita Battlefield in Oklahoma was designated as a national historic site.

Every: Tesuque Pueblo festival.

November 13

1747: According to some reports, a conference regarding alliances was held for the next four days between representatives of the British in Pennsylvania and the Miami, Shawnee, and Six Nations tribes.

1785: Federal authorities had tried to gather Creek leaders together in Galphinton, Georgia, in hopes of solving the land-grabbing efforts of the state of Georgia and head off Indian retaliatory raids. State officials told Indian leaders that the meeting was only to confirm the Long Swamp and Augusta Treaties, so only two chiefs and eighty warriors showed up. The day before, the federal representatives decided that representatives from two villages were not enough to discuss a new treaty, so they left. In their absence, Georgia signed a treaty with Fat King and Tallassee King. This treaty ceded more lands between the Oconee and Saint Marys Rivers. The Georgia officials also lied and told the Creek that they were now Georgia citizens. The two chiefs also agreed to return runaway slaves. According to federal statutes, this treaty was illegal.

1833: Just before sunrise, there was a phenomenal meteor shower, seen all over North America. This event was recorded on Kiowa picture calendars as the most significant event of the year.

1838: One group of 1,200 Cherokees was making its way to the Indian Territory (present-day Oklahoma) as a part of the Cherokees' forced removal. They were camped near Hopkinsville, Kentucky. The white settlers sympathized with the Cherokees and gave them provisions. Although many Cherokees had refused supplies from the government to avoid any inferred support of the New Echota Treaty, they accepted this generous donation.

1843: The Cherokee Nation pronounced full citizenship on the Creek who emigrated with them to the Indian Territory (present-day Oklahoma).

1867: According to army records, members of the Fourteenth Infantry fought with a band of Indians near Agua Frio Springs, Arizona. Three soldiers were wounded.

1890: The secretary of the interior and the president hold a conference on the ghost dancers.

1936: The secretary of the interior authorized an election for a constitution and bylaws for the Yerington Paiute Tribe of Nevada.

1961: Amendment 6 to the constitution and bylaws of the Lac du Flambeau Band of Lake Superior Chippewa Indians of Wisconsin was approved and became effective.

1964: The official roll of the members of the Lac du Flambeau Band of Lake Superior Chippewa Indians of Wisconsin was approved by the deputy commissioner of Indian affairs.

NOVEMBER 14

1638: According to some sources, the first Indian reservation was established in Trumbull, Connecticut.

1755: On this day and the next day, a band of Delaware Indians attacked settlers along Swatara Creek in Berks County, Pennsylvania. Approximately ten settlers were killed in the fighting.

1805: The Creek signed a treaty (7 Stat. 96) in Washington, D.C., regarding lands on the Oconee River.

1833: Francis Scott Key reported to President Jackson on the Owen Affair. Alabama officials would not let him see their murder indictments against the U.S. Marshal or the soldiers. State officials said their resistance was justified against federal intrusions into state matters.

Fort Phantom Hill near Abilene, Texas, close to many neighboring tribes (author photo)

1837: The second group of emigrating Cherokees, led by B.B. Bannon, crossed the Mississippi River near Cape Girardeau, Missouri. Many of the children were sick.

1851: Lieutenant Colonel J.J. Abercrombie and members of the Fifth Infantry began the construction of Fort Phantom Hill north of Abilene, Texas. The fort was often visited by the local Comanche, Lipan Apache, Kiowa, and Kickapoo.

1867: According to army records, Indian scouts fought with a band of Indians near Tonto Creek, Arizona. Four hostile Indians were killed and nine were captured. The fighting lasted through the next day.

1890: Indian agents were told that the army would handle the ghost dancer problem.

1936: The constitution and bylaws for the Oneida Tribe of Indians of Wisconsin were approved in an election by a vote of 790–16.

1969: Alcatraz was first occupied by Indian activists.

1983: Mary and Carrie Dann, Western Shoshone, received the Right Livelihood Award "for exemplary courage and perseverance in asserting the rights of indigenous people to their land."

1990: Executive Order No. 6230 from President George Bush declared November to be National American Indian Heritage Month.

NOVEMBER 15

1717: According to some sources, a peace agreement was reached by representatives of the British in South Carolina and the Creek Indians.

1787: George Mathews, the governor of Georgia, voiced a complaint about the Creek. He decried their killing of thirty-one citizens, the wounding of twenty, and the burning of many homes and settlements.

1824: The Quapaw signed a treaty (7 Stat. 23) and gave up their claim to land between the Arkansas Post and Little Rock, extending inland to the Saline River. They agreed to live in land promised to the Caddo Indians. The treaty was signed at Harrisons in Arkansas Territory.

1827: The Creek signed a treaty (7 Stat. 307). The United States was represented by Thomas McKenney and John Crowell.

1833: U.S. Marshals had posted warnings throughout Chickasaw lands that this day was the deadline for white squatters to get off Chickasaw lands. The deadline was not enforced, and more whites moved into the area.

1836: West Point graduate and Creek Indian David Moniac was promoted to major during the Seminole War. He led soldiers in several engagements, including the Battle of Wahoo Swamp, where he was killed two weeks from this date.

1845: A peace conference was held between representatives of Texas and the Kichai, Tawakoni, Waco, and Wichita. They agreed to the Treaty of October 9, 1844.

1861: The Potawatomi signed a treaty (12 Stat. 1191). The treaty set aside some lands for common tribal usage; other lands were set aside for individual Indians.

1867: According to army records, Indian scouts fought with a band of Indians near Tonto Creek, Arizona. Four hostile Indians were killed and nine were captured. The fighting started the day before.

1868: A unit from the Seventh Cavalry attacked a band of Indians approximately 140 miles from Fort Harker, Kansas. The cavalry pursued the Indians for more than ten miles before disengaging. The army estimated Indian casualties at five wounded.

1868: According to army records, members of the Eighth Cavalry had been fighting with a band of Indians near Willow Grove, Arizona, since November 7. Eleven Indians were killed, two were wounded, and twenty were captured.

1876: Colonel Ranald Mackenzie, ten troops of cavalry, eleven companies of infantry, and four companies of artillery left Fort Fetterman in eastern Wyoming en route to the Bighorn Mountains and the Powder River. This was called the Powder River expedition by the army.

1883: President Arthur, by executive order, added several sections of land to the Gila River Reserve in the Pima Agency to the Pima and Maricopa Indian Reservation. The reserve was established on February 28, 1859.

1890: The Wounded Knee agent asked for the army's help with the ghost dancers.

1923: The "Treaty Between His Majesty the King and the Mississauga Indians of Rice Lake, Mud Lake, Scugog Lake, and Alderville" was signed in Canada.

1937: Assistant Secretary of the Interior Oscar Chapman authorized an election for a constitution and bylaws for the Confederated Tribes of the Warm Springs Reservation of Oregon.

1938: The assistant secretary of the interior approved an election for a constitution and bylaws for the Havasupai Nation.

1944: The National Congress of American Indians held its first meeting and was established. The organization was established to "enlighten the public toward a better understanding of the Indian race, to preserve Indian cultural values, to seek an equitable adjustment of tribal affairs, to secure and to preserve Indian rights under Indian treaties with the United States, and otherwise promote the common welfare of the American Indians." Judge Napoleon Johnson (Cherokee) was elected to be the first president.

NOVEMBER 16

1805: The Choctaw signed the Treaty of Mount Dexter (7 Stat. 98). They ceded 4,142,720 acres of land in the southern parts of what are now the states of Mississippi and Alabama. In return, they received $2,500 in cash, and a trading-post bill of $48,000 was paid off. They also received an annuity of $3,000. The treaty was ratified on January 15, 1808.

1811: According to some sources, Tecumseh predicted a "light across the sky" on this night. It was supposed to have appeared, as predicted.

1838: According to a journal kept by John Burnett, one of the soldiers with a group of Cherokees with Chief John Ross marching to the Indian Territory (present-day Oklahoma), "We encountered a terrific sleet and snow storm with freezing temperatures and from that day until we reached the end of the fateful journey on March the 26th, 1839, the sufferings of the Cherokees were awful."

1869: According to army records, members of the Eighth Cavalry fought with a band of Indians near the Santa Maria River in Arizona. Two soldiers were wounded and two Indians were killed. The fighting lasted until November 28.

1874: President Grant, by executive order, expanded the Colorado River Indian Reserve. It now included part of California from Monument Peak to Riverside Mountain.

1877: An article on Sitting Bull appeared in the *New York Herald*.

1877: Settlers fought a group of Indians near Indian Creek, Texas. According to army documents, one settler was killed.

1877: The Nez Perce reached Fort Lincoln.

1885: In Regina, Saskatchewan, Louis Riel was executed by hanging.

1907: Oklahoma became a state.

1907: Actions were taken regarding the Gila Cliff-dwellings National Monument in New Mexico Territory.

1935: Secretary of the Interior Harold Ickes authorized an election to approved a constitution and bylaws of the Tule River Indian Tribe. The election was held on December 7, 1935.

1949: The superintendent of the Five Civilized Tribes Agency certified a roll of the members of the United Keetoowah Band of Cherokee Indians in Oklahoma.

1964: An election had approved a constitution and bylaws for the Cocopah Tribe of Somerton, Arizona. The assistant secretary of the interior ratified the results. The election was on October 8, 1964.

1990: The Native American Grave Protection Act was enacted.

NOVEMBER 17

1764: Part of Pontiac's army surrendered at the Muskingham River.

1785: The Galphinton Treaty was signed. The Creek were represented by Chiefs Tame King and Fat King. The Creek were plied with liquor and gave up lands belonging to the Oconee. The treaty was repudiated by the rest of the Creek leaders when they were informed of it.

1807: The United States signed a treaty (7 Stat. 103) with the Ottawa, Chippewa, Wyandot, and Potawatomi Indian Nations on the Miami and Glazier Rivers.

1856: Fort Buchanan (the first fort in the Gadsden Purchase area) was first established to operate against the Apache.

1867: According to army records, members of the Thirty-Seventh Infantry fought with a band of Indians near Fort Sumner, New Mexico. One soldier was killed.

1868: Indians attacked a wagon train seven miles from Fort Harker in central Kansas. The Indians made off with 150 mules.

1890: Pine Ridge Indian agents were becoming more concerned about the way the Ghost Dance religion was affecting the local Indians. Among other things, the Ghost Dance religion said that the Indians would return to their old glories and that the white man's bullets would be useless against them. A special Indian agent, James McLaughlin, was sent to help in dealing with the problem. On this day he saw his first ghost dance. The Ghost Dance religion and the government's reaction to it eventually led to the massacre at Wounded Knee.

1938: An election was authorized to approve a constitution and bylaws for the Thlopthlocco Tribal Town of the Creek Indian Nation of the state of Oklahoma by Oscar Chapman, assistant secretary of the interior. The election was held on December 27, 1938.

1947: The assistant secretary of the interior authorized an election to approve a constitution and bylaws for the Organized Village of Kake, Alaska. The election was held on January 27, 1948.

1961: The assistant secretary of the interior authorized an election to approve an amendment to the constitution and bylaws of the Miccosukee Tribe of Indians of Florida. The election was held on December 17, 1961.

November 18

864: The Great Ballcourt at Chichen Itza was dedicated by the Maya.

1765: According to some reports, a meeting regarding boundary lines was held by representatives of Great Britain and the Creek.

1785: Principal Cherokee Chief Old Tassel and many other Cherokees arrived at Hopewell to discuss a treaty with the United States.

1813: Members of the Hillabi Clan of the Muskogee Creek had offered to surrender to General Andrew Jackson with Scottish trader Robert Grierson acting as intermediary. Jackson agreed to the surrender. However, forces under Generals Hugh White and John Cocke were unaware of the agreement. They attacked Hillabee Village, the residents of which believed the fighting was over. Five dozen Hillabi were killed and 250 were captured. This action reversed the Hillabi decision to

surrender. They became one of the most fierce fighting units in the Creek War.

1854: A treaty (10 Stat. 1122) with the Chasta, Scoton, and Umpqua was signed by the United States.

1858: Thomas Henley, Indian superintendent in San Francisco, received a notice from J.W. Denver, of the commissioner's office of Indian affairs, dated on this day. The notice said that the secretary of the interior had decided to set aside the entire Nome Cult Valley (Round Valley, California) as an Indian Reservation.

1866: Elements of the First Cavalry fought some Indians near John Day's River, Oregon. Three Indians were killed and one was wounded, according to army records.

1868: Seven miles from Fort Hays in central Kansas, Indians attacked and killed two government scouts.

1869: After a chase of 200 miles, Lieutenant H.B. Cushing and Troop F, Third Cavalry, finally caught a band of Indians in the Guadalupe Mountains of New Mexico Territory. Two soldiers were wounded; the soldiers killed or wounded several Indians. The troopers also recovered 150 head of stolen livestock.

1877: Settlers fought a group of Indians near Sauz Ranch, Texas. According to army documents, two settlers were killed.

1890: Indian Agent McLaughlin talked to Sitting Bull.

1937: An election for the adoption of a constitution and bylaws for the Stockbridge Munsee Community of Wisconsin was ratified by the assistant secretary of the interior. The election was held on October 30, 1937.

1959: An amended constitution and bylaws were submitted for ratification by the members of the Northern Cheyenne Tribe of the Northern Cheyenne Indian Reservation in Montana. The election was held on April 12, 1960.

1972: The superintendent of the Northern Idaho Agency had authorized an election to approve an amendment to the constitution and by-laws of the Coeur d'Alene Tribe. It passed by a vote of 35–5.

1977: The Confederated Tribes of Siletz Indians of Oregon were organized by an act of Congress (91 Stat. 1415).

Every: Restoration Day celebrations (Pueblos).

NOVEMBER 19

1619: Representatives of the British colony in Virginia and the Powhatan Confederacy agreed to a treaty of alliance.

1794: According to the Jay Treaty and North-west Territory Treaty (Canada), Indians could cross borders.

1861: Opothle Yahola's pro-Union Creek fought Colonel Douglas Cooper's pro-Confeder-acy Creek and Seminole Indians, led by McIntosh and Jumper, east of Stillwell, Oklahoma. The bat-tle was inconclusive, with neither side scoring a victory. Often called the Battle of Round Moun-tain. (Also recorded as happening on December 19, 1861.)

1868: Near Little Coon Creek, Kansas, one white and five Indians were killed in a fight. Near Fort Dodge in southwestern Kansas, one white and two Indians were killed as well. Also near Fort Dodge, Sergeant John Wilson and Troop A, Tenth Cavalry, had a skirmish in which two Indi-ans were killed. A half-mile from Fort Dodge, In-dians attempted to stampede a beef contractor's herd. Lieutenant Q. Campbell and troops pursued the would-be rustlers for seven miles. Three troop-ers were wounded; four Indians were killed and six wounded.

1870: On the Wichita River in Texas, Private James Anderson, Company M, Sixth Cavalry, would be awarded the Medal of Honor for his ac-tions in the pursuit and subsequent fight with a group of hostile Indians, according to army records.

1876: John "Big Leggings" Brughier was part white and part Hunkpapa. General Miles was looking for someone to contact Sitting Bull and the other Sioux to try to arrange a peace. Big Leg-gings made a deal with Niles and worked as an in-termediary between Miles and the Sioux.

1958: Assistant Secretary of the Interior Fred Aandahl authorized an election for a proposed Amendment 6 to the constitution and bylaws of the Confederated Tribes of the Warm Springs Reservation of Oregon. The election was held on April 25, 1959.

1966: An amendment to the constitution of the Comanche Indian Tribe was voted on. It was ap-proved by a 492–483 margin.

NOVEMBER 20

1751: The second Pueblo Uprising took place at Saric, Mexico, southwest of Nogales, Arizona.

1817: Mikasuki Seminole under Chief Hornotlimed attacked a boatload of forty soldiers, seven of their wives, and four children on the Apalachicola River. Thirty-eight of the soldiers, including commander Lieutenant R.W. Scott, and all of the women and children were eventually killed. The U.S. Army considered this to be the first fight of the First Seminole War. This was also reported as November 21 and 30.

1831: While looking for rumored "lost silver mines" in Texas near the old San Sabá Mission, Jim Bowie and ten companions encountered al-most 150 Caddo and Waco Indians. A fight en-sued that became legendary in Texas history. After frontal attacks proved ineffective, the Indi-ans set fire to the brush and trees surrounding the Americans. This ploy also failed to work. After losing over fifty warriors to Bowie's one, the Indi-ans left the field.

1867: According to army records, members of the Third Cavalry fought with a band of Indians near Fort Selden, New Mexico. Two Indians were reported killed.

1868: South of Fort Dodge in southwestern Kansas, on Mulberry Creek, two government

Council of Sioux chiefs and leaders meeting at Pine Ridge, South Dakota (NA)

scouts named Marshall and Davis were killed by Indians.

1875: Indians fought with soldiers from the Third Cavalry near Antelope Station, Nebraska. According to army documents, no casualties were reported.

1890: Troops were stationed at the Pine Ridge and Rosebud Agencies. The Indian Bureau told all of its field agents to notify them of any Indians who were causing problems on the reservation relating to the Ghost Dance religion. Soon, they had a sizable list.

1935: The secretary of the interior authorized an election to approve a constitution and bylaws for the Pyramid Lake Paiute Tribe of Nevada. The election was held on December 14, 1935.

1936: The secretary of the interior authorized an election for the approval of a constitution and by-laws by the members of the Ute Indians of the Uintah, Uncompahgre, and White River Bands of the Uintah and Ouray Reservation.

1965: An election for an amendment to the constitution and bylaws of the Moapa Band of Paiute Indians was held. It was approved by a vote of 32–11.

1969: The Indians of All Tribes Proclamation was released by the activists who had seized Alcatraz Island in San Francisco Bay. The occupants stated that they now considered Alcatraz to be a reservation for all tribes.

1972: An election to approve an amendment to the constitution and bylaws for the Seneca-Cayuga Tribe of Oklahoma was authorized by the acting commissioner of Indian affairs. The election was held on January 28, 1973.

NOVEMBER 21

1724: The Rivera expedition took place.

1807: Spanish trader Manuel Lisa built Fort Raymond at the confluence of the Yellowstone and Bighorn Rivers in central Montana (near modern Custer).

1817: After American forces attacked a fort held by black allies of the Florida Indians on July 27, 1816, the Indians realized they needed to fight the Americans. The Mikasuki Seminole village of Fowltown was located on the banks of the Flint River in Georgia. Fort Scott was on the other side of the river. Chief Neamathla (also called Eneah Emathla) warned the soldiers in the fort to stay off of the Seminoles' side of the river. Angered by an "order" from an Indian, 250 troops under Major David Twiggs crossed the river to arrest the chief. A fight broke out, and five Seminole, including one woman, were killed. The Seminole evacuated the village, and the soldiers burned some of it. This action was considered by many to be the start of the First Seminole War. (Also recorded as happening on November 20 and 30.)

1836: The white man who incited the Creek to attack a mail stage near Columbus, Georgia, in May, was sentenced to hang.

1836: A battle was fought on the Withlacoochee River in the Wahoo Swamp. American forces with Indian allies were led by General Richard Call. The Seminole were led by Chiefs Osuchee and Yaholooche. After chasing the Seminole across the river, the American forces called an end to their advance when they believed the river was too deep to cross in force. Creek David Moniac was killed in the Battle of Wahoo Swamp in central Florida by Seminole. Moniac graduated from West Point. Moniac was part of a force of almost 700 Creek warriors and white soldiers.

1877: Chief Joseph was invited to a banquet in Bismarck.

1975: The Bureau of Indian Affairs received notice from the Navajo Nation announcing their plans to move sixty families from the contested Navajo-Hopi joint usage area of northeastern Arizona. This effectively ended the long-running land dispute.

1978: Amendments 5–8 to the revised constitution and bylaws of the Sisseton Wahpeton Sioux Tribe of South Dakota became effective when they were approved by Harley Zephier the area director, Aberdeen area office, Bureau of Indian Affairs.

NOVEMBER 22

1812: Potawatomi Chief Winamac was killed in fighting with Captain Logan (Spemicalawba). One of two Potawatomi chiefs with the identical name, he was a principal leader in the attacks on Forts Dearborn and Wayne in 1812. The other Winamac was pro-American.

1833: General George Gibson announced that no more Choctaws could be removed under the treaty, according to the secretary of war. The treaty allowed three years for the removal, and that time had expired. Gibson dismissed all removal agents and employees.

1836: The first part of the fifth contingent of friendly Creek, approximately 600, arrived at Fort Gibson in eastern Indian Territory (present-day Oklahoma). These were primarily the sick, elderly, and lame.

1837: The Republic of Texas signed a treaty with the Tonkawa at Bexar.

1845: Choctaw leader Nitakechi was returned to Mississippi by Superintendent Armstrong to tell the remaining Choctaws of the good conditions in the Indian Territory (present-day Oklahoma). While in Mississippi, Nitakechi got pleurisy and died.

1752: The "Mick Mack" of Nova Scotia signed a treaty with the British.

1867: According to army records, members of the Second Cavalry fought with a band of Indians near De Schmidt Lake, Dakota Territory. One Indian was killed and three were wounded.

1873: President Grant, by executive order, added to the Colorado River Agency. The land was at the old northern boundary to within six miles of Ehrenberg, Arizona. This was east of the river to the "mountains and mesas." It was eventually 376 square miles in size. It was home to Chemehuevi, Walapai, Kowia, Cocopa, Mohave, and Yuma Indians.

1875: Secretary of War W.W. Belknap said there would be dire results if the United States did not obtain the mineral-rich Black Hills from the Indians soon.

1890: Strikes-the-Kettle told government officials that Sitting Bull could not attend a council on food supplies.

1968: The acting assistant commissioner of Indian affairs authorized an election for amendments to the constitution and bylaws of the Jicarilla Apache. The election was held on December 23, 1968.

1975: The commissioner of Indian affairs had authorized an election for a constitution for Utu Utu Gwaitu Paiute Tribe of the Benton Paiute Reservation in California. The results were 29–0 in favor of the constitution.

1980: An election was held to approve a constitution and bylaws for the Spokane Tribe of the Spokane Reservation in Wellpinit, Washington. It passed by a vote of 101–33.

NOVEMBER 23

1699: According to some sources, a land-cession agreement was reached between representatives of the Bear River Indians and the British colonies in North Carolina.

1868: Custer and the Seventh Cavalry left Camp Supply looking for hostiles in the Indian Territory (present-day Oklahoma). All told, 800 soldiers started the march in a heavy snowstorm.

1868: According to army records, members of the Eighth Cavalry fought with a band of Indians southeast of the Bill Williams Mountains in Arizona. Two Indians were killed and one was wounded.

1872: Comanche Ten Bears died on the reservation. Ten Bears represented the Comanche on a visit to Washington and at many great councils.

1877: While authorities were attempting to arrest an Indian named Naught who was accused of shooting two teamsters, other Indians became agitated. One of them shot Alex Rhoden, who was walking across the street at the time, in Nalad City, Idaho. This incident led to the Bannock War.

1880: The Sioux had another council at Wood Mountain, Saskatchewan, with the Canadians.

1880: The Havasupai Reservation boundaries were modified by executive order.

1935: An election for a constitution for the Indians of the Tulalip Tribes in Washington was held. It was approved by a vote of 98–9.

1935: The secretary of the interior authorized an election to approve a constitution and bylaws for the Pueblo of Santa Clara. The election was held on December 14, 1935.

1935: A constitution and bylaws for the Rosebud Sioux were ratified and approved by Secretary of the Interior Harold L. Ickes on December 16, 1935.

1973: The secretary of the interior authorized an election for amendments to the constitution and bylaws of the White Mountain Apache Tribe. The election was held on January 24, 1974.

NOVEMBER 24

1713: Father Junipero Serra was born. During his lifetime he established many of the missions in California.

1755: According to some reports, a land-cession agreement was reached by representatives of Great Britain and the Cherokees.

Iroquois chief Joseph Brant

1755: Many Delaware, Mahican, and Munsee Indians had been converted to Christianity by Moravian missionaries. They established a group of villages on the Lehigh River (near modern Leighton, Pennsylvania). On this day a group of hostile non-Christian Munsee (Delaware) Indians, led by Jachebus, attacked one of the villages, killing fourteen of the local Indians. The Indians and the missionaries in these villages, which were known as Gnadenhuetten, were attacked on many occasions by both Europeans and Indians.

1807: Iroquois leader Joseph Brant died.

1812: As a young boy, Spemicalawba (Captain Logan or High Horn), was captured by General James Logan. General Logan raised him until he was returned to the Shawnee during a prisoner exchange. As Tecumseh's nephew, he tried to temper Tecumseh's feelings toward the Europeans. Spemicalawba scouted for the Americans during the War of 1812. He was killed on this day during a scouting expedition. He was buried with military honors; Logansport, Indiana, was named after him.

1864: Colonel John Chivington had assembled his troops fifty miles southeast of Denver. They were preparing to attack Black Kettle's camp of Cheyenne and Arapaho along Sand Creek in southeastern Colorado. Chivington's troops included members of the First and Third Colorado Volunteer Cavalries. They reached Black Kettle's camp on November 29.

1869: According to army records, members of the Ninth Cavalry fought with a band of Indians near the headwaters of the Llano River in Texas. Captain E.M. Heyl was wounded and one Indian was killed.

1874: The patent for barbed wire was granted.

1877: The Nez Perce reached Fort Leavenworth.

1890: Nelson Miles sent Buffalo Bill a message: "Bring in Sitting Bull."

1936: The assistant secretary of the interior had authorized an election to approve a constitution and bylaws for the Fort McDowell Mohave-Apache Community in Arizona. It was approved.

1939: The assistant secretary of the interior had authorized an election to approve a constitution and bylaws for the Eskimos of the native village of Elim, Alaska. It passed by a vote of 28–0.

1945: Ernest Evans got the Medal of Honor.

1976: The acting deputy commissioner of Indian affairs authorized an election to approve an amendment to the constitution and bylaws of the Miccosukee Tribe of Indians of Florida.

1980: The constitution of the Spokane Tribe approved two days earlier went into effect by a vote of the tribal business council (Resolution No. 1981–56).

November 25

1712: The commander in chief of the Carolinas' militia, Colonel Pollock, met with Chief Tom Blunt. The chief did not participate in the original attacks of the Tuscarora War. They eventually signed a treaty not to attack each other. Blunt also agreed to bring in King Hancock.

1758: The British took Fort Duquesne.

1808: A treaty (7 Stat. 112) with five different Indian nations (Chippewa, Ottawa, Pottawatami, Wyandot, and Shawanoese) was signed in Brownstown, Michigan. William Hull and several Indian tribes signed the agreement, which provided for a roadway 120 feet wide to be established from Maumee Rapids to Lower Sandusky and then south. This road helped travelers get to Fort Detroit.

1820: Many articles disparaging the Choctaws had appeared recently in the *Arkansas Gazette*. The United States had just recently arranged to move the Choctaws to land in the states of Arkansas and Oklahoma. An editorial appeared in the *Mississippi Gazette* on this day. The editorial spoke of the civilized manner in which the Choctaw conducted themselves. The editorial also suggested that when Arkansas became a state, instead of just a territory, the Arkansans could force the Choctaw farther west.

1864: During the Carson campaign, the first battle of Adobe Walls took place. On the Canadian River in the Panhandle of Texas, Colonel Kit Carson's scouts sighted Chief Dohasan's Kiowa-Apache village of 176 tepees near Adobe Walls. There were additional Comanche and Kiowa villages farther downstream. The soldiers, equipped with two howitzers, and their Ute and Jicarilla Apache allies attacked the village just after dawn. Other Indians in the villages were One-Eyed Bear, Lean Bear, Satanta (perhaps), and Stumbling Bear. The warriors held their group during the cavalry charges so their women and children could escape. Later, the Indians scattered when the howitzers were brought up and fired. Assuming that the Indians had left, the soldiers took their horses to feed and drink. The soldiers dined as well. About an hour later, approximately 1,000 warriors (according to army reports) returned. The fighting lasted most of the rest of the day. The Indians received reinforcements during the battle from other nearby villages. Lieutenant George Pettis, Company K, First California Infantry, estimated the final number of warriors to be near 3,000 (this figure could not be confirmed). Being outnumbered, Carson decided to retreat just as the Kiowa set fire to the prairie grasses. After spending a day to recover, Carson ordered a withdrawal to Fort Bascom in western New Mexico on November 27. Many sources estimated the number of combatants to be larger that those at the Battle of the Little Bighorn. Carson reported only three fatalities among his forces, with fifteen wounded. He listed Indian losses at sixty killed and 150 wounded. His report called his action a "victory."

1868: According to army reports, twenty mules were stolen and two Indians were killed in Indian Territory (present-day Oklahoma).

1868: According to army records, members of the First and Eighth Cavalry and Thirty-Second Infantry fought with a band of Indians near Camp McDowell, Arizona. One soldier was wounded and two Indians were killed. The fighting lasted until December 2.

1872: Indians skirmished with a group of soldiers from the Fifth Cavalry and some Paiute Indian scouts near Red Rocks or Hell Canyon, Arizona, according to official army records. One soldier and eleven hostile Indians were killed. Four Indians were captured.

1876: Colonel Ranald Mackenzie and ten troops from the Second, Third, Fourth, and Fifth Cavalries had camped outside a large Indian village of 173 lodges near the North Fork of the Powder River after a night march. Just after daybreak, the soldiers attacked Dull Knife's camp of Northern Cheyenne in north-central Wyoming. After an hour of fighting, the survivors fought a rear-guard action and a few skirmishes until nightfall. The soldiers destroyed the village and captured 500 horses. The soldiers confirmed twenty-five Indians were dead but suspected a much higher number. Six soldiers were killed, including Lieutenant John McKinney. First Sergeant Thomas H. Forsyth, Company M, Fourth Cavalry, would be awarded the Medal of Honor for holding his ground against "superior forces" and then rescuing fallen comrades.

1894: Members of the Gusgimukw Tribe held a "winter fest" at Fort Rupert on Vancouver Island, British Columbia.

1894: A group of nineteen Hopi hostiles were placed under arrest by the army for interfering with friendly Hopi Indian activities on their Arizona reservation. The nineteen prisoners would be held in Alcatraz prison in California from January 3, 1895, to August 7, 1895.

1992: Executive Order No. 6511, by President George Bush, declared November as National American Indian Heritage Month.

Curley, Crow scout for Custer at Little Bighorn (NA)

NOVEMBER 26

1831: David Folsom and 593 of his Choctaw followers arrived by boat at the Arkansas Post. The post now had 2,500 Choctaws with 1,000 horses. Many of the clans were at odds with each other, causing tensions.

1835: Charley Emathla was killed. Emathla signed the agreement at Fort Gibson in Indian Territory (present-day Oklahoma) committing the Seminole to their removal from Florida. He was in favor of removal. He was killed by Seminole who were against the treaty and leaving Florida. Many believed that he was killed by Chief Osceola. This was the first in a series of killings.

1864: Trader John S. Smith got permission to visit Black Kettle's people on Sand Creek to trade for buffalo hides. Major Scott Anthony let Smith go, along with army Private David Louderback and private citizen R.W. Clark in hopes that this might lull Black Kettle into a false sense of security while Chivington prepared for battle. When Chivington attacked on November 29, Smith, called "Gray Blanket" by the Arapaho, Private Louderback, and Clark were still in the village and barely avoided being killed in the fighting. Smith's half-breed son was killed in the fighting after surrendering to some soldiers.

1865: As a part of the Black Hawk War in Utah, a group of Ute Indians raided Circleville. They stole some livestock, and several settlers were killed.

1867: Fearing another Sand Creek Massacre, Black Kettle had traveled 100 miles to Fort Cobb in central Indian Territory (present-day Oklahoma) to ask General William Hazen if he could move his tribe to the fort so they would be safe. Hazen denied this request, telling Black Kettle that if his people did not break the treaties, or the law, they would have no problems from the soldiers. On this day, Black Kettle returned to his village. He warned his people to watch for angry soldiers.

1868: General George Custer's scouts came across the trail of a war party, identified as Black Kettle's Cheyenne and other Arapaho. The war party, according to army reports, had killed mail carriers between Forts Dodge and Larned in southwestern Kansas, an old hunter near Dodge, and two couriers under General Sheridan. Custer corralled his wagons, and his main force followed the fresh trail through the snow until dark.

1869: In a skirmish with hostile Indians in Arizona, Sergeant John Crist, Company L, Eighth Cavalry, earned the Medal of Honor for "gallantry in action."

1880: Gall arrived at the Poplar Agency, but he did not surrender.

1883: In *Ex Parte Crow Dog* (109 U.S. 556 [1883]), lawyers presented their cases before the U.S. Supreme Court regarding a federal court conviction of an Indian for a murder of another Indian on Indian land. The court's ruling would be made on December 17.

1884: A total of 765 square miles of land were set aside for the Northern Cheyenne Reserve by

Gall, a Hunkpapa Sioux (LOC)

executive order in the Tongue River Agency, Montana.

1890: The Seventh Cavalry arrived at Wounded Knee.

1912: An executive order modified the boundaries of the Moapa Band of Paiute Indians Reservation.

1937: A constitution was approved by Assistant Secretary of the Interior Oscar Chapman for the Pawnee Indian Tribe of Oklahoma.

1947: According to Federal Register number 13FR01589, lands were added to the Rocky Boy's Indian Reservation for the use and benefit of the Chippewa, Cree, and other Indians of Montana.

View of buildings in the Rocky Boy Agency (NA)

1960: An election to add two amendments to the constitution and bylaws of the Coeur d'Alene Tribe of Idaho was held under authority of Deputy Commissioner of Indian Affairs H. Rex Lee. They were passed on votes of 107–68 and 101–74.

1965: The acting commissioner of Indian affairs authorized an election to amend the revised constitution and bylaws of the Sisseton Wahpeton Sioux Tribe of South Dakota. The election took place on August 1 and 2, 1966.

1976: Doyce L. Waldrip, acting area director, Bureau of Indians Affairs, had authorized an election to approve an amendment to the constitution and bylaws for the Confederated Tribes of the Umatilla Reservation. The amendment passed.

NOVEMBER 27

1759: Major Robert Rogers was en route to accept custody of French forts given over to the British after the end of the French and Indian War. When he came upon the Detroit River at Lake St. Clair, he was confronted by a group of Indians. The leader of the Indians, Pontiac, an Ottawa, told Rogers he was trespassing and asked his intentions. Rogers said he was going to remove the French and gave the Indians some gifts. Pontiac allowed Rogers to pass unmolested.

1834: Cherokees in favor of the nation's removal to lands west of the Mississippi River officially formed the Treaty Party. It was led by Major Ridge, John Ridge, and Elias Boudinot.

1868: This morning before daylight, Osage Indian trackers found Black Kettle's camp on the Washita River in western Oklahoma. According to General Sheridan's official report: "Custer, who at once made the most admirable dispositions for its attack and capture. At dawn a charge is made, the village captured and burned, 800 horses or ponies shot, in accordance with positive orders, 103 warriors killed, and fifty-three squaws and children captured." Army losses in the attack on the village were Captain Louis Hamilton and three soldiers. Nearby Cheyenne, Arapaho, Kiowa, and Comanche Indians heard the "battle" and came to Custer's position. Custer drove the Indians down the Washita for several miles before withdrawing. Major Joel Elliott, Seventh Cavalry, a sergeant major, and fifteen soldiers chased a group of young boys trying to escape the fight. After capturing the boys, Elliot and his men were surrounded by superior Indian forces and were killed to a man. Three officers (Captain Albert Barnitz, Captain T.J. March, and Lieutenant T.W. Custer) and thirteen soldiers were wounded in the fighting. According to Sheridan's report, Custer found conclusive evidence, by way of property and a book with illustrations of their acts, that it was Black Kettle's band that had attacked the Saline and Solomon River settlements. The army captured 875 horses, 1,123 robes, 535 pounds of gunpowder, and 4,000 arrows. This was known as the Battle of the Washita and the Washita Massacre.

1878: According to the commander of Fort Ellis in southern Montana, Ten Doy, a friendly Lemhi Indian, had captured seven hostile Bannock Indians. They were sent under Indian guard to Colonel Nelson Miles on the Tongue River.

1885: On April 2, several Cree and Assiniboin Indians killed several people at Frog Lake as a part of Riel's Rebellion. Eight Cree and Assiniboin were convicted of murder for these killings.

1890: Teacher sent a message to Agent McLaughlin: "Sitting Bull is peaceful."

1915: Private Albert Mountain Horse was buried in Fort Macleod, Alberta. He was the only Blood Indian to go to the front lines in World War I. He died due to exposure to poison gas on the battlefield.

1978: An amendment to the constitution and bylaws of the Suquamish Indian Tribe of the Port Madison Reservation in the state of Washington was ratified by the area director of the Bureau of Indian Affairs.

NOVEMBER 28

1729: The Natchez were very upset with the new commander at Fort Rosalie. Commander Etcheparre Chepart was incapable of command. The Natchez attacked and destroyed the fort and began a revolt in the area. Approximately 200 whites were killed in the attack on the fort, which began on this day. This was called the Fourth War with the Natchez by the French. Chepart was killed while hiding in his garden. Chepart had received a warning of the impending attack from Natchez Sun (Queen) Stung Arm, but he refused to believe it.

1738: Verendrye met with the Mandan.

1745: The old frontier settlement of Saratoga, New York, was near modern Schuylerville. A combined force of 220 Indians and 400 French attacked the settlement. Most of the town and the fort was burned, 100 settlers were captured, and another thirty were killed during the fighting.

1785: A treaty (7 Stat. 18) was signed by the Cherokees at the Hopewell River. The Cherokees restored all prisoners, whether black or white. The United States reciprocated. The Cherokees acknowledged the sovereignty of the United States. New boundary lines were drawn. No whites could live on Cherokee lands without the tribe's approval. Only the United States had the right to regulate trade with the Cherokee. The treaty was signed by thirty-seven Indians. Also, 918 other Cherokees attended the meetings. They were led by Principal Chief Old Tassel. The Americans were led by Commissioners Benjamin Hawkins, Andrew Pickens, Joseph Martin, and Lachlan MacIntosh. This was called the Hopewell Treaty.

1786: Members of many of the tribes living in Ohio met in Brownstown, near Detroit. Mohawk leader Joseph Brant was one of the speakers. They discussed relations with American settlers, treaty lines, and tribal leadership.

1818: President Adams sent a message to Spain: "Control the Seminole!"

1840: The Miami Indians signed a treaty (7 Stat. 582) at the Forks of the Wabash River. The Americans were represented by Allen Hamilton and Samuel Milroy.

1842: Colonel Ethan A. Hitchcock was ordered to conduct a campaign against Seminole Chief Pascofa along the Apalachicola River.

1842: According to some reports, Florida militia forces attacked an Indian village on Wrights Creek in Holmes County. They killed twenty-two people.

1862: A skirmish involving pro-Confederacy Indians took place near Cane Hill in Arkansas.

1864: Late tonight, Colonel John Chivington, his Colorado volunteers, and Major Scott Anthony's troops—totaling 700 men—left Fort Lyon in southeastern Colorado en route to Black Kettle's camp on Sand Creek.

1869: According to army records, members of the Eighth Cavalry fought with a band of Indians near the Santa Maria River in Arizona. Two soldiers were wounded and two Indians were killed. The fighting started on November 16.

1874: Near Muster Creek, Texas, Captain Charles Hartwell and Troops C, H, K, and L, Eighth Cavalry, attacked hostile Southern Cheyenne. Two Indians were killed, and two were wounded.

1890: Buffalo Bill arrived at Fort Yates for Sitting Bull's arrest.

1969: Amendment 5 to the constitution and bylaws for the Oneida Tribe of Indians of Wisconsin was approved by Assistant Secretary of the Interior Harrison Loesch.

1969: The constitution and bylaws of the Mississippi Band of Choctaw Indians was amended.

1989: The National American Indian Museum Act was enacted.

NOVEMBER 29

1691: The Abenaki signed a peace treaty with the British. Benjamin Church had been skirmishing with them since September in the vicinity of Saco in southern Maine. The Abenaki agreed to a six-month truce to release their English prisoners and to keep the British aware of the movements of the French in the area.

1751: According to some reports, an agreement regarding trade regulations was reached by representatives of the British in South Carolina and the Cherokees.

1760: As part of the peace treaty ending the French and Indian War, the English took over Fort Detroit from the French. The British were not as good at winning friendship and cooperation from the local Indians.

1788: The North Carolina state senate adopted a resolution making it illegal for the U.S. government to grant hunting grounds within North Carolina to any Indian tribe, regardless of any treaty between the United States and Indian tribes.

1813: A battle was fought between Upper Town Red Stick Creek and the American forces in the village of Autossee in modern Macon County, Alabama. A force of almost 1,000 Georgia militia and 400 pro-American Creek (led by Efau Haujo), led by General John Floyd, attacked the Red Stick Creek stronghold. A cannonade won the day for the allies. The Red Stick Creek suffered 200 fatalities; the Americans posted only eleven dead. The village and its supplies were burned. The villages of Tallassee and Little Tallassee were also destroyed.

1836: Five years earlier, several Nez Perce traveled to St. Louis to ask for someone to come to their land to teach them about religion. In response to that request, missionary Henry Harmon Spalding traveled to Idaho. He set up a mission on this day on some land (twelve miles south of modern Lewiston) given to him by the Nez Perce.

1837: Wildcat (Coacoochee), Miccosukee (Seminole) warrior and son of Chief Philip, had been captured by American forces. He and many other Seminole were being held prisoner in the old prison in St. Augustine. By refusing to eat, they managed to lose enough weight to slip

through a barred window fifteen feet above the floor. Wildcat and nineteen other Seminole managed to escape undetected, and they were able to rejoin their people.

1847: The Cayuse engaged in a fight at the Whitman home in the Oregon country. Marcus Whitman and his wife, Narcissa, were killed. This was called the Whitman Massacre.

1854: The United States signed a treaty (10 Stat. 1125) with the Umpqua Tribe of Indians and the "Calapooias" (Kalapuya) at Calapooia Creek, Douglas County, Oregon Territory.

1864: Over 700 Colorado volunteers under Chivington attacked Black Kettle and his Cheyenne and Arapaho followers at Sand Creek in southeastern Colorado. The Indians had been told to camp in this area while they awaited a peace conference with Colorado authorities. The soldiers had four cannons with them. As a result of the fight, fourteen soldiers were killed and forty were wounded. The exact number of Indians killed was widely disputed. Chivington reported over 500 Indians dead. Other estimates ranged from 100 to 600 killed. White Antelope was killed while he was trying to surrender. This fight was most often called the Sand Creek Massacre.

1867: According to army records, members of the Second Cavalry fought with a band of Indians near Shell Creek, Dakota Territory. Four Indians were reported killed.

1872: Acting under orders from General Canby, Captain James Jackson and over a dozen members of Company B, First Cavalry, rode into Captain Jack's Modoc camp near the Lost River in Oregon. They had been ordered to arrest Captain Jack for the murder of a Klamath holy man. Gunfire broke out, and Captain Jack escaped. One soldier and eight Indians were killed. Seven enlisted men were wounded. This was considered by many to be the first battle of the Modoc Wars.

1877: Captain S.B.M. Young, 172 men from troops A and K, Eighth Cavalry, Troop C, Tenth Cavalry, and Lieutenant John Bullis's Seminole scouts attacked the same group of Lipan Indians near the "Sierra Carmel Ranch" in the Carmen Mountains, Mexico, that Lieutenant Bullis's force fought on November 1, 1877. The Indians lost most of their supplies and some livestock. Two Indians and one soldier were wounded. The fighting lasted through the next day.

1890: Buffalo Bill left Fort Yates to find Sitting Bull.

1969: The commissioner of Indian affairs authorized an election for the Pueblo of Isleta to vote on a new constitution.

1970: An election to approve a constitution and bylaws for the San Pasqual Band of Mission (Diegueno) Indians in the San Pasqual Reservation was held. It passed by a vote of 54–0.

1979: The acting deputy commissioner of Indian affairs had authorized an election to adopt a new constitution and bylaws for the residents of the Cold Spring Rancheria in Fresno County, California. It was approved by a vote of 12–3.

NOVEMBER 30

1769: Gaspar de Portolá had led an expedition to explore parts of the central California coastline. While near San Jose Creek, a group of local Indians provided them with some food.

1817: Mikasuki Seminole under Chief Hornotlimed attacked a boatload of forty soldiers, seven of their wives, and four children on the Apalachicola River. Thirty-eight of the soldiers, including commander Lieutenant R.W. Scott, and all of the women and children were eventually killed. The U.S. Army considered this to be the first fight of the First Seminole War. (Also reported as November 20 and 21.)

1830: General George Gibson ordered Lieutenant Lawrence Carter, stationed at Fort Gibson in eastern Indian Territory (present-day Oklahoma), to go to the Kiamichi River to ascertain if the area could provide food for the Choctaws arriving from Mississippi.

1836: The United States signed a treaty (7 Stat. 527) with the Wahpakoota, Sisseton, and Upper Medawakanton Tribes of Sioux Indians.

1877: Eight and Tenth Cavalry soldiers and some Indian scouts fought a group of Indians near "Sierra Carmel Ranch" in Mexico. According to army documents, two Indians were killed. Two Indians and one soldier were wounded. The fighting started the day before.

1920: The federal government extended the trust period on allotments made to Indians of the Crow Creek Reservation in South Dakota.

1927: The federal government extended the trust period on allotments on the Devil's Lake Reservation in North Dakota.

1938: The acting secretary of the interior had authorized an election to approve a new constitution and bylaws for the Ottawa Indians of Oklahoma. The voters in the tribe approved it.

1952: Charles George, a Cherokee, was a private first-class serving in Korea. During a battle, a grenade landed among George's squad. George jumped on the grenade and, by absorbing the blast, saved the other soldiers' lives. George was posthumously awarded the Medal of Honor.

DECEMBER 1

1805: To renegotiate the Flint River Treaty of November 3, 1804, the United States invited six Creek chiefs to Washington to meet with Secretary of War Henry Dearborn. The government agreed to pay the Creek $206,000 for their 2 million acres instead of $200,000. But the payments were made over more than ten years instead of in cash. The Creek also agreed to allowing a road through their lands.

1831: Peter Pitchlynn and 400 other Choctaws boarded the steamer *Brandywine* in Memphis. The steamer transported them up to the Arkansas Post on the White River.

1855: On this day marked the deadline for the Donation Land Claim Act. The law allowed certain lands to be acquired by settlers without a purchase.

1869: According to army records, members of a mail escort from the Fourth Infantry fought with a band of Indians near Horseshoe, Wyoming. Three soldiers were wounded.

1874: Indians fought with soldiers from the Fifth Cavalry and some Indian scouts near Canyon Creek in the Tonto Basin, Arizona. According to army documents, eight Indians were killed, two were wounded, and fourteen were captured.

1881: The secretary of state said Hawaii was now a part of the United States.

1886: Fort Halleck was located east of Elko, Nevada. For a while it was the headquarters for the Nevada Military District. Soldiers from the renamed Fort Halleck would participate in campaigns against the Apache, Bannock, Modoc, and Nez Perce. After almost ten years of service, it was closed.

1983: The base membership roll established for the Pascua Yaqui Indians on September 18, 1980, was approved by the Phoenix area director of the Bureau of Indian Affairs.

DECEMBER 2

1761: No land grants for Indian lands in British territories could now be made without the Crown's approval.

1794: A treaty (7 Stat. 47) was concluded with the Oneida, Tuscarora, and Stockbridge Indians at Oneida, New York. The treaty was a gesture of thanks for the tribes' help during the Revolutionary War. They received $5,000 for damages suffered during the war. Grist mills and sawmills were built, and salaries for their workers were provided for three years. They received $1,000 to build a church. No further claims were made by the tribes. The treaty was signed by Thomas Pickering for the United States and by eleven Indians.

1830: Georgia passed a law to seize Cherokee gold mines.

1833: A total of 176 of Captain Page's original contingent of 1,000 Cherokees arrived at the agency west of Fort Smith, Arkansas, on the eastern edge of the Indian Territory (present-day Oklahoma). The rest of the group had split off and gone to Fort Towson.

1838: According to a Nashville publication, 1,800 Cherokees passed through Nashville, Tennessee, on their emigration to the Indian Territory (present-day Oklahoma). The Nashville publication assumed that the Cherokees would be punished by the cold weather and the trip remaining before them.

1842: The Cherokee passed a law that called for the death penalty for any tribal member who ceded land to the United States.

1867: According to army records, members of the Eighteenth Infantry fought with a band of Indians near Crazy Woman's Creek, Dakota Territory. One soldier was killed; three soldiers and four civilians were wounded.

1868: According to army records, members of the First and Eighth Cavalries and the Thirty-Second Infantry fought with a band of Indians near Camp McDowell, Arizona. One soldier was wounded and two Indians were killed. The fighting started on November 25.

1869: While going from Fort Fetterman to Fort Laramie in southeastern Wyoming, Sergeant Conrad Bahr, Company E, Fourth Infantry, and ten men acting as a mail escort were attacked by about 150 Indians near Horseshoe Creek, Wyoming, according to the army report. One soldier was killed; several Indians were killed or wounded. On the same day, another mail escort going in the opposite direction was also attacked, with two soldiers sustaining wounds.

1872: Indians skirmished with a group of soldiers from the First Cavalry near Land's Ranch, or Tule Lake, California, according to official army records. One soldier was killed and another was wounded.

1874: Near Gageby Creek in Indian Territory (present-day Oklahoma), First Sergeant Dennis Ryan and twenty men from Troop I, Sixth Cavalry, attacked a group of Indians. A running fight developed. Many horses were killed or captured. The Indians also lost many of their provisions. For "courage while in command of a detachment," First Sergeant Dennis Ryan would be awarded the Medal of Honor.

1880: Fifteenth Infantry soldiers fought a group of Indians near South Fork in the White Mountains of New Mexico. According to army documents, two soldiers and one Indian were wounded. Four Indians were captured.

1942: The constitution and bylaws of the Kanosh Band of Paiute Indians were approved by the secretary of the interior.

1955: Assistant Secretary of the Interior Wesley D'Ewart authorized an election to approve an amendment to the constitution and bylaws for the Pyramid Lake Paiute Tribe of Nevada. The election was held on December 26, 1955.

1963: The Presidential Medal of Freedom was issued to Navajo Annie Wauneka.

1964: Land had been set aside for townsites in the Flathead Indian Reservation in Montana. Finding that certain small lots had not been disposed, the government returned that land to the tribal ownership of the Confederated Salish and Kootenai Tribes on the Flathead Reservation.

1980: Alaska National Interest Land Conservation Act (94 Stat. 2430) was enacted. It was intended to "provide for designation and conservation of certain public lands in the State of Alaska, including Implementation of Alaska Native Claims Settlement Act and Amendments."

1991: The Navajo-Hopi Settlement Act was amended by Congress. It was designed to "authorize appropriations for Navajo-Hopi Relocation Housing Program for FYs 1992, 1993, 1994, 1995. This will expire when President determines that its functions have been fully discharged."

Every: Papago festival.

DECEMBER 3

1598: Juan de Zaldivar "discovered" the Acoma.

1837: Accompanied by Cherokee mediators, Mikanopy and thirty other Seminole leaders arrived at Fort Mellon near St. Augustine, Florida, under a flag of truce to discuss peace. The Cherokee mediators were there with the approval of the secretary of war. General Thomas Jesup, much to the shame of the Cherokees, took the Seminole hostage. Jesup hoped to force the Seminole to surrender by holding their leaders as prisoners.

1866: Elements of the First Cavalry fought some Indians near Camp Watson, Oregon. Fourteen Indians were killed and five were captured, according to army records.

1875: Commissioner of Indian Affairs Edward Smith notified all of his Cheyenne and Sioux agents to order any Indians off the reservations to return by January 31, 1876, or face military action.

1901: President Theodore Roosevelt delivered his first speech on Indians.

1962: Assistant Secretary of the Interior John A. Carver Jr. authorized an election for amendments to the constitution for the Wisconsin Winnebago.

1973: A new commissioner of Indian affairs was named. Morris Thompson, an Athabascan from Alaska, got the post.

1973: Shirley Plume, an Oglala, was appointed as the first Indian woman to be an agency superintendent. She supervised the Standing Rock Agency in North Dakota.

1993: The American Indian Agricultural Resource Management Act (207 Stat. 3715) of December 3, 1993, was passed by Congress. It was meant to "carry out trust responsibilities and promote self determination by tribes of agricultural resources; provide development and management educational opportunities for Indian people and communities."

DECEMBER 4

1598: Spanish under Juan de Zaldivar had convinced the Acoma to gave them some flour. The Acoma were short of food themselves, but they decided to accommodate the Spaniards. One of the soldiers stole two turkeys, and a fight broke out. Thirteen of the nineteen Spaniards, including de Zaldivar, were killed.

1674: A mission in Chicago was established by Jesuit missionary James Marquette.

1802: North Carolina and the Tuscarora signed a treaty in Raleigh that ceded a large part of their lands. The treaty was submitted to the U.S. Senate on February 21, 1803.

1833: Twenty-one Chickasaw chiefs arrived at Fort Towson in eastern Indian Territory (present-day Oklahoma). They assessed the lands that the United States wanted them to move to when they were removed from Alabama. Meeting with local Choctaws about buying land from them proved to be unfruitful.

1858: Colonel Miles and the Navajos agreed to a truce and started negotiating a peace.

1862: The thirty-eight Santee Sioux Indians sentenced to hang by the courts for their part in the uprising were being held by Colonel Henry Sibley's troops in a prison camp on the South Bend of the Minnesota River. Tonight, an angry mob of local citizens tried to raid the camp and lynch the Indians. The soldiers were able to keep the angry crowd from getting to the prisoners.

1873: Indians fought with soldiers from the Fifth Cavalry and some Indian scouts near the East Fork of the Verde River, according to army documents. Fifteen Indians were killed.

1959: The assistant secretary of the interior authorized an election for amendments to the constitution for the Gila River Pima-Maricopa Indian Community.

1969: An election for three amendments to the constitution of the Oglala Sioux of the Pine Ridge Indian Reservation was held. All were approved by a majority of the approximately 1,200 people voting.

1974: Commissioner of Indian Affairs Morris Thompson ratified an election that approved a constitution and bylaws for the Upper Skagit Indian Tribe.

1991: The Tribal Self-Governance Demonstration Project Act (105 Stat. 1278) of December 4, 1991, was passed by Congress. It was to "amend Self-Governance legislation, including Education to extend time for demonstration project and to increase number of tribes participating, and to increase funds."

2000: Secretary of Energy Bill Richardson signed an agreement that returned to the Northern Ute approximately 85,000 acres of land in Utah. The land had been appropriated by the U.S. Congress eighty-four years earlier.

DECEMBER 5

1787: An Indian war party attacked several settlements in western Virginia along Hacker's Creek. Four settlers were killed in the fighting.

1835: Members of the Georgia Guard arrested Cherokee Principal Chief John Ross at his home. Also arrested was historian John Howard Payne. Payne, the author of the song "Home, Sweet Home," was writing a history of the Cherokee people. They were arrested so they could not attend the New Echota Treaty conference.

1836: A law passed by the Republic of Texas allowed President Sam Houston to appoint Indian agents, build forts, and several other things.

1842: Dr. Elijah White started a conference with the Nez Perce. The rules for the conference were decided.

1848: Captain Seth Eastman, commander of several companies of the First Infantry, established Camp Houston as one of the first U.S. Army posts on the western frontier of Texas. It was southeast of Fredericksburg. It was eventually renamed Fort Martin Scott.

1855: Columbia River volunteers under Nathan Olney were near Fort Walla Walla in southeastern

Washington when they encountered Pio-pio-mox-mox's (Yellow Serpent) band of Walla Walla. Pio had looted the Hudson Bay Company's Fort Walla Walla, but he had always been neutral or helped the Americans in the past. He advanced under a flag of truce and wanted to return the booty. But an agreement could not be reached. Pio refused to fight, and Olney's men took Pio and four others prisoner.

1866: Elements of the First Cavalry fought some Indians near Surprise Valley, California. No injuries or fatalities were reported on either side, according to army records.

1867: According to army records, members of the Ninth Cavalry Infantry fought with a band of Indians near Eagle Springs, Texas. One soldier was killed.

1873: Lieutenant E.P. Turner, with troopers from the Tenth Cavalry, helped local authorities recover a herd of stolen cattle. The army and a local sheriff found a group of twenty Indians with the cattle on Elm Creek in Texas. During the struggle, four Indians were killed and the others were captured. About 1,000 head of cattle were recovered.

1890: The secretary of the interior issued an order saying that Sitting Bull was not to be arrested unless he said so.

1969: The *Choctaw Community News* was first published.

1970: An election was held to adopt a new constitution for the Reno-Sparks Indian Community. It was approved by a vote of 30–10.

December 6

1748: Shikellamy (or Swataney) was an Iroquois half-king in Pennsylvania living among the Oneida. He attended many conferences in Philadelphia and was known for his oratory. He was instrumental in abolishing the sale of liquor to Indians in his area. Later becoming a Christian, he died at Sunbury (Shamokin). His name meant "Our Enlightener."

1830: President Jackson supported the Cherokee removal to lands west of the Mississippi River.

1835: Benjamin Marshall and 511 other Creek left on their westward trip to the Indian Territory (present-day Oklahoma) from Wetumka (near modern Montgomery).

1862: Lincoln refused to pardon the thirty-eight Santee Sioux sentenced to hang for their part of the uprising in Minnesota.

1866: Red Cloud, Crazy Horse, Yellow Eagle, High Back Bone, and their followers had been harassing Colonel Henry Carrington's troops from Fort Phil Kearny in northern Wyoming. They staged several raids and ambushes along the road from the fort to the nearby woods. Colonel Carrington led his troops in some of the fighting. Several soldiers were killed in the fighting. Carrington was called "Little White Chief" by the Indians. This skirmish set the stage for the Fetterman Massacre on December 21, 1866.

1866: Elements of the Second Cavalry and Eighteenth Infantry fought some Indians near Goose Creek, Dakota Territory. One officer and one soldier were wounded. Two Indians were wounded, according to army records.

1875: The government delivered a order to Indian agents that the remaining Sioux had to report to the Sioux Agency by January 31.

1886: The Dawes Severalty Act passed the Senate.

1897: President McKinley made his first speech on Indians.

1961: Assistant Secretary of the Interior John A. Carver Jr. authorized an election to approve an amendment to the constitution and bylaws for the Pyramid Lake Paiute Tribe of Nevada. The election was held on December 26, 1961.

1963: The first meeting of the Foundation of North American Indian Culture was held.

December 7

1675: In the name of Charles II, the Massachusetts Bay Colony issued a formal proclamation declaring war on the Narragansett.

1831: The Choctaw removal process had begun. Indian Commissioners John Eaton and John Coffee met with the Choctaws and the Chickasaws on Oaka Knoxabee Creek. They again discussed the possibility of the Chickasaws sharing areas in the Indian Territory (present-day Oklahoma) that had been set aside for the Choctaws. They proposed that the Chickasaws get one-fourth of the Choctaws' allotment. No agreement was reached.

1835: President Jackson delivered his seventh address on Indians.

1836: The first contingent of 2,700 friendly Creek (the tribe had split into two factions) arrived in eastern Indian Territory (present-day Oklahoma) at Fort Gibson. The rest arrived soon after.

1855: The Walla Walla attacked Nathan Olney's volunteers, who still held Pio-pio-mox-mox and four others prisoner. Pio resisted being bound, and he and three of his men were killed. His scalp and ears were paraded through white settlements. This action moved many neutral tribes toward a war status.

1862: A skirmish involving pro-Confederacy Indians took place at Prairie Grove, Arkansas.

1868: Sheridan and Custer left Camp Supply (Oklahoma) leading 1,600 soldiers and 300 supply wagons. They were en route to Fort Cobb. It was primarily meant as a show of force to the local Indians. It proved that the army could march during the winter months.

1872: Indians skirmished with a group of soldiers from the Eighth Cavalry and the Twenty-Third Infantry and some Indian scouts in Red Rock country in Arizona, according to official army records. Twelve Indians were killed. The fighting continued through the next day.

1873: Lieutenant Charles Hudson, four cavalry, and forty-one soldiers from Fort Clark in western Texas clashed with some Kiowa. During the fighting, Lone Wolf's son and nephew were killed. Lone Wolf became enraged at their deaths.

1874: The minister of the interior of the dominion of Canada purchased a section of land in the province of Nova Scotia for the use and benefit of the "Micmac" Indians in Pictou County.

1874: On Kingfisher Creek in Texas, Captain A.S.B. Keyes and Troop I, Tenth Cavalry, attacked a group of Southern Cheyenne. Thirteen warriors and thirteen women were captured.

1876: Lieutenant Frank D. Baldwin and 100 men of Companies G, H, and I, Fifth Infantry, found Sitting Bull and his village of 190 lodges. The army pursued them south of the Missouri River to the mouth of Bark Creek. The Indians escaped into the Badlands.

1886: According to a signed agreement, thirteen Crow Indian families were allowed to remain where they were now, retain their present allotment of land, and not be disturbed.

1935: A constitution for the Tuolumne Band of Me-Wok Indians of the Tuolumne Rancheria was approved by a vote of 27–0.

1935: An election was held to approve a constitution and bylaws for the Tule River Indian Tribe. They voted 43–2 in favor of the proposal.

1949: The constitution and bylaws of the Confederated Tribes of the Umatilla Reservation were ratified by Assistant Secretary of the Interior William Warne.

1974: The Pawnee of Oklahoma approved several amendments to their constitution with almost 300 people voting.

DECEMBER 8

1780: John Sevier and volunteers from North Carolina soundly defeated the Chickamauga Cherokees in a fight at Boyd's Creek, Tennessee.

1818: Secretary of War John C. Calhoun presented a report to the U.S. House of Representatives. Among the report's proposals were that tribes should no longer be treated as sovereign nations; Indians should be saved from extinction; and Indians should be taught the correctness of the concept of landownership.

1829: In his first State of the Union address, President Andrew Jackson stated his goal to remove all Indians in the southeastern part of the United States to lands west of the Mississippi. A law to that effect passed Congress on May 28, 1830.

1840: Mikasuki Seminole Chief Hallack Tustenuggee was vehemently opposed to the removal of his people from Florida. He and his followers participated in numerous battles against American forces. On this day, he attacked a party of officers' wives being escorted from Fort Micanopy by thirteen soldiers. Four soldiers, including Lieutenant Walter Sherwood, and one woman were killed in the fighting.

1847: Oregon Governor Abernathy called together the provisional government to call up troops at Oregon City. Forty-two men were dispatched within twenty-four hours.

1869: Louis Riel released his manifesto, the "Declaration of the People of Rupert's Land and the North-West." The document declared a provisional government for the area.

1872: Indians skirmished with a group of soldiers from the Eighth Cavalry and the Twenty-Third Infantry and some Indian scouts in Red Rock country in Arizona, according to official army records. Twelve Indians were killed. The fighting started the day before.

1873: Indians fought with soldiers from the Fifth Cavalry and some Indian scouts near San Carlos, Arizona, according to army documents. A total of twenty-five Indians were killed and seventeen were captured in fighting that lasted until January 20, 1874.

1874: On the Muchaque (Machague) Creek in Texas, Lieutenant Lewis Warrington and ten men from Troop I, Fourth Cavalry, attacked a group of fifteen Indians. Two Indians died, two were wounded, and one was captured. Based on this fight, the following soldiers would be awarded the Medal of Honor: Lieutenant Warrington and Privates Frederick Bergerndahl and John O'Sullivan for "gallantry in a long chase."

1882: Plains Cree Chief Big Bear signed a treaty with the Canadian government. He was one of the last major Plains Indian chiefs to do so.

1972: The constitution and bylaws of the Pyramid Lake Paiute Tribe of Nevada was amended.

DECEMBER 9

1531: According to most sources, Juan Diego (Cuauhtlatoatzin), a Nahua, first spotted the apparition of the Virgin Mary on a hill called Tepeyacac in Mexico. Many Aztec and Nahua considered Tepeyacac to be a sacred site. Juan Diego spotted her again each day until December 12.

1729: The Natchez sent two Indians to visit the Tunica. The Natchez wanted them to join in a war against the French. The Tunica refused.

1778: Virginia annexed Indian lands.

1809: The Kickapoo signed a treaty (7 Stat. 117) with the United States at Fort Wayne.

1835: By a treaty, the Cherokee got a certain area of land in Missouri near the Osage Reservation.

1854: The United States signed a treaty (10 Stat. 1130, 11 Stat. 605) with the Oto and Missouri at Nebraska City, Nebraska.

1861: Colonel Douglas Cooper again encountered pro-Union Creek and Seminole under Chief

Oto Indians wearing traditional claw necklaces and fur turbans (NA)

Opothleyaholo in a battle on Bird Creek north of Tulsa. Many of his Cherokee troops under John Drew defected and joined the pro-Union forces. Cooper withdrew to Fort Gibson. This was often called the Battle of Chusto-Talasah or the Battle of Caving Banks.

1864: Having been held as a captive for some time, Fanny Kelly was left at Fort Sully by Sioux. Fort Sully was at the confluence of the Missouri and Cheyenne Rivers. The site is now under Lake Oahe.

1873: Lieutenant C.L. Hudson and Troop B, Fourth Cavalry, had a minor skirmish with a band of Indians on the West Fork of the Nueces River in Texas.

1885: Eighth Cavalry soldiers fought a group of Indians near Lillie's Ranch on Clear Creek in New Mexico. According to army documents, two Indians were killed.

1891: President Benjamin Harrison delivered his third speech on Indian lands.

1916: A census was taken of the Winnemucca Shoshone in Nevada.

1924: By presidential proclamation, the Wupatki National Monument was established in Arizona northeast of Flagstaff.

1974: The commissioner of Indian affairs authorized an election for amendments to the constitution of the Papago (Tohono O'odham). The election was held on February 8, 1975.

arrived at Fort Gibson in eastern Indian Territory (present-day Oklahoma). The total of both groups was 2,237. The gains came from stragglers from earlier groups.

1850: Federal agents signed a treaty with the Lipan Apache, Caddo, Comanche, Quapaw, Tawakoni, and Waco Indians near the San Sabá River in Texas.

1868: According to army records, members of the Eighth Cavalry fought with a band of Indians near Walker Springs, Arizona. Three Indians were killed and six were captured.

1869: According to army records, members of the First and Eighth Cavalries fought with a band of Indians near Mount Buford, Arizona. Eleven Indians were killed and one soldier was wounded.

1873: Lieutenant C.L. Hudson, forty-two men from the Fourth Cavalry, and nine Seminole Indian scouts attacked a band of Indians near Kickapoo Springs, Texas. Nine hostiles were killed. One soldier and several Indians were wounded. Eighty-one stolen horses were recovered.

1890: Nelson Miles ordered the soldiers at Fort Yates to "secure" Sitting Bull.

1971: Assistant Secretary of the Interior Harrison Loesch approved Amendment 3 for the constitution of the Standing Rock Sioux Tribe.

1991: The name of the Custer Monument was changed to the Little Bighorn Battleground Monument.

DECEMBER 10

1831: The last of the Choctaw emigrants, approximately 200 in number, boarded a steamboat at Vicksburg and started their trip down the Mississippi River.

1834: William Marshall, representing the United States, and Potawatomi Indians signed a treaty (7 Stat. 467) at Tippecanoe. Six sections of land were traded for annual payments of $1,000 and a small amount of supplies.

1836: The second part of the fifth group of friendly Creek, approximately 1,600 in number,

DECEMBER 11

1753: French under Legardeur de Saint-Pierre were at Fort le Boeuf on French Creek (near modern Waterford) in northwestern Pennsylvania. Major George Washington arrived to deliver a message from Virginia Governor Dinwiddie. The message said the French were trespassing and to leave.

1833: Captain Page and almost 700 Choctaws reached their destination at Fort Towson in eastern Indian Territory (present-day Oklahoma). The others in the group had split off and gone to Fort Smith.

1836: The second half of the original contingent of friendly Creek arrived at Fort Gibson in eastern Indian Territory (present-day Oklahoma).

1866: Elements of the Fourteenth Infantry fought some Indians near Grief Hill, Arizona. One soldier was killed, according to army records.

1868: According to army records, members of the Eighth Cavalry fought with a band of Indians near Willow Grove, Arizona. One soldier and eight Indians were killed.

1872: Indians skirmished with a group of soldiers from the First Cavalry and the Twenty-Third Infantry and some Indian scouts on Bad Rock Mountain north of old Fort Reno in Arizona, according to official army records. Fourteen Indians were killed.

1890: Sitting Bull sent a letter to Indian Agent McLaughlin. He said he was going to the Pine Ridge Agency.

1935: The secretary of the interior authorized an election for amendments to the constitution of the Oglala Sioux of the Pine Ridge Indian Reservation.

1937: "Undisposed" lands in the Flathead Indian Reservation in Montana that had originally been designated for lots in a townsite were returned to tribal ownership.

DECEMBER 12

1531: According to most sources, Juan Diego (Cuauhtlatoatzin), a Nahua, spotted the apparition of the Virgin Mary on a hill called Tepeyacac in Mexico again. He first saw her on December 9. According to Juan Diego, the Virgin Mary instructed him to carry some roses in his *macehualli* (cloak) to the local bishop as proof of her appearance. When the *macehualli* was opened before the bishop, an image of the Virgin Mary appeared on the cloak among the rose petals. The *macehualli* is still on display in the church (Our Lady of Guadalupe) built to honor the event.

1729: The Yazoo Indians attacked French Fort St. Pierre in southern Louisiana. The Yazoo had joined the Natchez in their fight against the French. They killed all seventeen of the soldiers at the fort. They gave the women and children to the Chickasaws as slaves.

1791: Reports of St. Clair's defeat reached the army.

1806: In what eventually became Rome, Georgia, Cherokee Principal Chief Stand Watie was born. Watie figured prominently in the Cherokee removal process. His brother, Buck Watie (Elias Boudinot), was the editor of the *Cherokee Phoenix* and his uncle and cousin were Major Ridge and John Ridge. Stand Watie signed the Treaty of New Echota, ceding all of the Cherokees' lands in the east for land west of the Mississippi River. Watie managed to escape the people who murdered his three famous relatives on June 22, 1839. Watie eventually killed one of the men accused of killing his uncle. Watie enlisted as a colonel in the Confederacy in 1861 and fought in the Battle of Pea Ridge. Watie was the last Confederate general to surrender.

1842: Mount St. Helens erupted. Indians had noted many such eruptions.

1867: According to army records, Indian scouts fought with a band of Indians near Owyhee River, Oregon. Seven Indians were reported killed.

1874: Indians fought with soldiers from the Seventh Cavalry in the Standing Rock Agency. According to army documents, no casualties were reported.

1882: President Arthur, by executive order, set up the Pima Agency in the Gila Bend Reserve. It was thirty-five square miles and was occupied by the Papago. It was bounded by Township 5 South, Range 5 West, and the Gila and Salt River meridian, except for Section 18.

1890: McLaughlin received Sitting Bull's Pine Ridge letter.

1936: A constitution for the Yerington Paiute Tribe of Nevada was voted on. The results were 56–4 in favor of the proposed constitution.

1936: The Tohono O'odham Nation adopted a constitution. The secretary of the interior approved it on January 6, 1937.

1955: An election to approve an amendment to the constitution and bylaws for the Pyramid Lake Paiute Tribe of Nevada was held. They approved it 80–12.

1970: The acting commissioner of Indian affairs had authorized an election to establish a constitution and bylaws for the Winnemucca Shoshone Indian Colony of Nevada. It was approved by a vote of 15–0.

Every: Lady of Guadalupe Festival (Pueblos).

DECEMBER 13

1640: A deed for Indian land was signed in New England. It said, "It is agreed that the Indians above named shall have liberty to break up ground for their use to the westward of the creek on the west side of Shinecock plaine." From a town meeting of 1641: "It is agreed that any person that hath lotts up on Shinecocke playne in which there are any Indian Barnes or wells lying shall fill them up."

1763: Lancaster County, Pennsylvania, faced a series of Indian attacks.

1788: Northwest Territory Governor Arthur St. Claire had called for a peace conference with the tribes of the area. It convened at Fort Harmar. Among the almost 200 Delaware, Seneca, and

Northwest Territory Governor Arthur St. Clair (IMH)

Wyandot participants was Seneca Chief Cornplanter. This council led to a treaty signed on January 9, 1789.

1801: In treaty negotiations that begin at Fort Adams, Mississippi, between the Choctaw and the United States, the government agreed to provide training in the spinning of cotton and spinning wheels. The conference lasted through December 18.

1831: David Folsom's Choctaws arrived at Little Rock, Arkansas. They made camp a few miles out of town and waited for arrangements for their transport to the Red River. Many of the ill-prepared Choctaw suffered from the cold weather.

1831: Eneah Micco, principal chief of the Creeks' lower towns, wrote to Creek agent John Crowell. A total of 1,500 whites were living in Creek territory. The Creek feared they would be forced from their lands.

1863: Kit Carson was preparing to campaign against the Navajos in the Canyon de Chelly country. He had corralled a large herd of pack mules for his supplies. Barboncito and Navajo warriors stole most of the herd. Carson was without pack animals, and the Navajos had plenty of meat.

1868: According to army records, members of the Eighth Cavalry fought with a band of Indians near Walnut Springs, Arizona. Eight Indians were killed and fourteen captured.

1872: Indians skirmished with a group of soldiers from the First Cavalry and the Twenty-Third Infantry and some Indian scouts on Mazatzal Mountain north of old Camp Reno in Arizona, according to official army records. Eleven Indians were killed and six captured.

1875: Lieutenant General Philip Sheridan was sent a copy of Indian Inspector E.C. Watkins's report on the "wild and hostile bands . . . roaming about Dakota and Montana"; a report from the commissioner of Indian affairs; and the secretary of the interior's plan to require these Indians to report to their reservations by January 31, 1876, or face force.

1877: Lieutenant J.A. Rucker and Troops C, G, H, and L, Sixth Cavalry, fought a group of Indians at Ralston Flats, New Mexico Territory. One Indian was killed in the fighting.

1935: The constitution and bylaws of the Fort Belknap Indian Community of the Fort Belknap Indian Reservation in Montana were approved.

1959: The Mission Creek Band of Indians of Mission Creek, California, approved their constitution.

1973: The acting deputy commissioner of Indian affairs authorized an election for amendments to the constitution and bylaws of the Lac Courte Oreilles Band of Lake Superior Chippewa Indians of Wisconsin. The election was held on May 11, 1974.

DECEMBER 14

1703: A small militia from the Carolinas of fifty men led by Colonel James Moore and almost 1,000 Creek Indians attacked the Apalachee Indian village of Ayubale (near modern Tallahassee). After a nine-hour battle, the Carolina-Creek allies were victorious. The Apalachee were allied with the Spanish. Upon hearing of the battle, Spanish soldiers marched from a nearby fort to counterattack on January 15, 1704. Moore's force defeated the Spanish as well. According to Moore's records, more than 200 of the pro-Spanish Indians died in the fighting.

1742: Settlers had finally moved into the valley of Virginia. Indians from the north had attacked several settlements and Catawba Indians in the area. A European militia was formed to find the war party. In what was the first significant engagement in the valley, the Indians and the militia fought on the North Fork of the Potomac River. Numerous Indians and eight settlers, including Captain John McDowell, died in the fighting.

1763: A band of almost five dozen frontiersmen known as the Paxton Boys attacked a peaceful Susquehanna Indian village in Conestoga, Pennsylvania. They killed eight of the twenty-two inhabitants in this unprovoked raid. The Paxton Boys continued their rampage during the next two weeks.

1843: An agreement (9 Stat 337) was reached between the United States and the Delaware and Wyandot.

1846: According to records kept in Monterey, California, a large group of Indians raided many of the ranches in the surrounding area. According to the Mexicans, the Indians wanted the horses for food.

1852: Ned Christie was born in Indian Territory (present-day Oklahoma). During his lifetime, he was a Cherokee tribal senator and the most wanted fugitive in the territory. Falsely accused of killing a U.S. Marshal in 1887, Christie avoided capture for more than five years. He claimed that federal marshals had no jurisdiction in the Cherokees' territory, and he refused to give himself up. Later, a witness vouched for Christie's innocence. Others said Christie did kill the marshal but did so in self-defense.

1866: Elements of the Fourteenth Infantry fought some Indians near the Pinal Mountains, Arizona. Three Indians were killed, according to Fourteenth Infantry records.

1867: According to army records, some people cutting wood fought with a band of Indians near Fort Phil Kearny, Dakota Territory. Two civilians were wounded.

1872: President Grant, by executive order, established the Chiricahua Indian Reservation in the White Mountain, or San Carlos, Reserve in Arizona Territory. Camp Grant Indian Reservation in southeastern Arizona was returned to public domain. The San Carlos Reservation was created and added to the White Mountain Reservation. Various parts of the reservation were returned to the public domain on July 21, 1874, April 27, 1876, October 30, 1876, January 26, 1877, and March 31, 1877.

1872: Indians skirmished with a group of soldiers from the Fifth Cavalry near Indian Run,

Arizona, according to official army records. Nine Indians were captured.

1877: According to army records, Sergeant James Brogan, Company G, Sixth Cavalry, "engaged single-handed two renegade Indians until his horse was shot under him and then pursued them so long as he was able." For his actions, he was awarded the Medal of Honor.

1878: According to the Oklahoma Law Enforcement Memorial, Panola County was in the Chickasaw Nation of Indian Territory, an area that encompassed portions of the currant Bryan and Marshall Counties west of Durant. Deputy Culpepper "Cub" Colbert was assigned to keep the peace at a dance that went into the early-morning hours. About 4 A.M. Deputy Colbert took a gun away from a drunk man named Ben Kemp. Kemp hit the deputy on the head with a cane, and Colbert shot him in the side, inflicting a flesh wound. As Deputy Colbert was leaving, one of Kemp's sons shot the deputy in the left side with a shotgun, nearly severing his left arm and killing him almost instantly.

1886: Use of Indian language was illegal in Mississippi schools.

1891: After serving as chief justice of the Cherokee supreme court, Joel Bryan Mayes was elected as principal chief of the Cherokee Nation in 1887. Mayes served as chief until his death, on this day. Mayes's mother, Nancy Adair, was a descendant of James Adair, who wrote one of the first histories of American Indians.

1915: Red Fox James, a Blackfoot, was seeking to have a national recognition day set aside for American Indians. As a part of his campaign, he rode horseback from state capital to state capital seeking support. At the White House, James presented endorsements from twenty-four state governments.

1935: An election for amendments to the constitution of the Oglala Sioux of the Pine Ridge Indian Reservation was held. They were approved by a vote of 1,348–1,041.

1935: An election to approve a constitution and bylaws for the Pyramid Lake Paiute Tribe of Nevada was held. The 69–34 vote approved the document.

1935: The secretary of the interior had authorized an election to approve a constitution and bylaws for the Pueblo of Santa Clara. The constitution was approved by a vote of 145–8.

1971: The Alaska Native Claims Act passed Congress.

DECEMBER 15

1725: A treaty was signed in Boston between "several Tribes of the Eastern Indians viz the Penobscot, Narridgwolk, St. Johns Cape Sables & other Tribes Inhabiting within His Majesties Territorys of New England and Nova Scotia," and "His Majties Governments of the Massachusetts Bay, New Hampshire & Nova Scotia."

1855: Oregon Governor Stevens got a Nez Perce honor guard.

1869: The military guard at Bunker Hill Station, Kansas, repelled an attack by Indians with no significant injuries.

1872: In Washington, D.C., Commissioner of Indian Affairs Francis Walker told a large delegation of Kiowa, some Comanche, and other Indians that they must move to within ten miles of Fort Sill in southern Indian Territory (present-day Oklahoma) by this day's date or be killed by the army as hostiles.

1880: Major George Ilges and 180 mounted soldiers of the Fifth Infantry left Fort Keogh in eastern Montana en route to reinforce the Camp Poplar River garrison in northeastern Montana. The 200-mile trip was made in constant subzero temperatures. The reinforcement was dispatched because of a raid by Sioux from Canada.

1890: Sitting Bull was killed while being arrested at Fort Yates, South Dakota, by Eighth Cavalry soldiers and Indian police near Standing

Rock on the Grand River in Montana. Thirty-nine police officers and four volunteers were assembled to arrest Sitting Bull. Before it was all done, over 100 of Sitting Bull's supporters arrived at the scene. Several people were injured or killed in the subsequent fighting. According to army documents, four soldiers and eight Indians were killed. Of those eight were Indian Police Officers John Armstrong, Paul Akicitah, David Hawkman, James Little Eagle, Charles Shavehead, and Henry Bullhead. Three soldiers were wounded. Later this week, the editor of the *Aberdeen Saturday Pioneer* wrote a editorial about Sitting Bull. One of the passages was as follows: "The proud spirit of the original owners of these vast prairies inherited through centuries of fierce and bloody wars for their possession, lingered last in the bosom of Sitting Bull. With his fall the nobility of the Redskin is extinguished, and what few are left are a pack of whining curs who lick the hand that smites them. The Whites, by law of conquest, by justice of civilization, are masters of the American continent, and the best safety of the frontier settlements will be secured by the total annihilation of the few remaining Indians." The author of this editorial was L. Frank Baum, best known as the author of *The Wizard of Oz*.

1953: An election was authorized to approve an amended constitution and bylaws for the San Carlos Apache Tribe by the assistant secretary of the interior. The election was held on February 23–24, 1954.

1970: Blue Lake was returned to the Taos Pueblos.

1971: The Navajo Community College Act was approved. The act provided funds "to assist the Navajo Tribe of Indians in providing education to the members of the tribe and other qualified applicants through a community college."

1978: Casimir LeBeau, area director, Minneapolis area office, Bureau of Indian Affairs, had authorized an election for an amendment to the constitution and bylaws of the Lac Courte Oreilles Band of Lake Superior Chippewa Indians of Wisconsin. The amendment was passed by a vote of 158–21.

DECEMBER 16

1773: The Boston Tea Party took place. American patriots dressed up like Indians to throw British tea into Boston Harbor.

1811: The New Madrid earthquake took place on the Mississippi River around 2:30 A.M. Many tribes told tales of this event for generations. Many people said that Tecumseh predicted this earthquake.

1834: Signed in Potawattimie Mills, Indiana, a treaty (7 Stat. 468) ceded two parcels of land for $700 and cancelled some outstanding debts. It was signed by the Potawatomi Indians and William Marshall.

1841: A bill was submitted to build forts along the Oregon Trail.

1841: The Cherokee National Council established a school system for their nation. There were eleven schools in eight districts. Subjects of study included reading, writing, arithmetic, English grammar, geography, bookkeeping, and history. Within a dozen years, this system was better organized than those for whites in Missouri and Arkansas.

1868: Custer's column had continued on through severe weather after the battle of the Washita. They surprised a camp of Kiowa. Satanta and Lone Wolf were arrested, and the other Kiowa were ordered to follow Custer to Fort Cobb in southern Indian Territory (present-day Oklahoma). The Indians initially complied with the order, but they soon slipped away, except for Satanta and Lone Wolf.

1882: President Arthur, by executive order, established the Hopi (Moqui) Reservation in the Navajo Agency in Arizona. It covered 3,863 square miles.

Red Tomahawk, a Sioux policeman at Standing Rock Reservation who may have fired the shot that killed Sitting Bull (NA)

1890: According to the "official" report from Standing Rock Reservation Indian Agent James McLaughlin, "Sitting Bull was killed this morning while being arrested. Acting under orders, a force of thirty-nine policemen and four volunteers (one of whom is Sitting Bull's brother-in-law, Gray Eagle) entered the camp at daybreak on December 16, proceeding directly to Sitting Bull's house." According to the report of Captain E.G. Fechet, Eighth Cavalry, several police officers and Indians were killed or wounded. Most sources said this happened on December 15.

1935: A constitution and bylaws for the Rosebud Sioux were approved by Secretary of the Interior Harold L. Ickes.

1936: The constitution and bylaws of the Covelo Indian Community were approved by Secretary of the Interior Harold Ickes.

1971: The Coalition of Organized Indians and Natives was established. It included the American Indian Movement, the National Indian Youth Council, the National Congress of American Indians, and other organizations. They hoped to present a united front for Indian concerns in the elections of 1972.

1980: Commissioner of Indian Affairs William Hallett authorized an election to approve a constitution and bylaws for the Jamul Indian Village in San Diego County, California. The election was held on May 9, 1981.

1987: The Trail of Tears National Historical Trail was established.

DECEMBER 17

1754: According to some reports, a land-cession agreement was reached by representatives of the British and the Six Nations.

1761: According to some reports, an agreement regarding peace, the return of prisoners, and boundary lines was reached between the British and the Cherokees.

1778: British forces under Henry Hamilton and their Indian allies retook Vincennes, Indiana, from George Rogers Clark.

1801: A treaty (7 Stat. 66) with the Choctaws was signed at Fort Adams in southwestern Mississippi on the Mississippi River. A wagon road was allowed to open from the northern settlements of the Mississippi Territory to the Chickasaw lands. New boundaries were established for Choctaws lands. They received $2,000 in goods and three sets of blacksmith tools. They gave up almost 1.5 million acres (disguised as the return to an old boundary). The treaty was signed by sixteen Indians. This was called the Treaty of Fort Adams.

1803: In an address, Thomas Jefferson talked to the Choctaw. His primary topic was the trading of Choctaw lands to pay their debts.

1812: Tecumseh was unable to convince numerous tribes of Indians to join him in his fight against the Europeans. Many of these peaceful tribes had settled along the Mississinewa River. Although they had pledged to keep the peace, William Henry Harrison was dubious about leaving so many Indians along his rear flank during his expedition against Detroit. Colonel John Campbell was ordered by Harrison to take 600 men and attack Miami villages along the river. On this day, even though he was told to leave them alone, Campbell attacked Silver Heel's Delaware Indian village on the river. Eight warriors were killed. They also captured forty-two Delaware during the raid. Later, Campbell burned the peaceful village of Metocina and his Miami followers. Finally, Campbell's troops fought to a draw and then retreated from another Miami village farther downriver. Campbell returned to the area near Silver Heel's destroyed village to bivouac for the night.

1842: Pascofa surrendered to Colonel Ethan Hitchcock. He agreed to bring his Apalachicola Tribe in to the colonel.

1883: In *Ex Parte Crow Dog* (109 U.S. 556 [1883]) the Supreme Court overturned a lower federal court conviction of an Indian for the murder of another Indian on Indian land. The court reasoned that the tribe's authority to deal with such an offense was an attribute of tribal sovereignty and had not been specifically abrogated by congressional action.

1890: Sitting Bull and the police killed during his arrest were buried with honor. On this day, members of the Hunkpapa Sioux arrived at Big Foot's camp of Minneconjou Sioux, seeking refuge. However, this day would also see the issuance of an arrest warrant for Big Foot himself for his part as a "troublemaker" in the ghost dance religion.

Big Foot's band of Miniconjou Sioux in costume at a ghost dance (LOC)

1936: The constitution and bylaws of the Keweenaw Bay Indian Community were approved.

1961: The assistant secretary of the interior had authorized an election to approve an amendment to the constitution and bylaws of the Miccosukee Tribe of Indians of Florida. It was passed by a vote of 41–0.

1974: The acting deputy commissioner of Indian affairs had authorized an election to approve the revised constitution and bylaws of the Mississippi Band of Choctaw Indians. It was approved by a vote of 325–237.

DECEMBER 18

1812: After successfully attacking and burning two peaceful Miami and Delaware Indian villages and fighting to a draw in another village the day before, Colonel John Campbell and almost 600 American volunteers had camped for the night near one of the destroyed villages on the Mississinewa River. They were there to prevent the hitherto peaceful tribes from joining Tecumseh's "rebellion" and attacking William Henry Harrison's rear flank as he engaged Detroit. The Miami considered the previous day's attack on villages that had pledged not to support Tecumseh's rebellion as nothing more than an unprovoked massacre. The Miami mounted a retaliatory raid against Campbell's camp before dawn. They killed ten soldiers and wounded forty-eight more before they withdrew. Campbell gave up his expedition along the river after this attack.

1835: Near Micanopy, Florida, a military baggage caravan had separated from its main force while marching from Jacksonville to Wetumpka. A group of Seminole led by Osceola attacked the soldiers, killing most. This battle was called the Battle of Black Point. According to some historians, this was the first battle of the Second Seminole War.

1836: General Matthew Arbuckle reported that 6,000 Creek, including Chief Opothleyaholo,

Four-story dwelling at Mesa Verde (author photo)

were camped near Fort Gibson in eastern Indian Territory (present-day Oklahoma). They were ill-prepared for the winter conditions. Many of the people contracted to transport the Creeks' belongings had not done so. This left the Creek without winter clothing.

1860: A sergeant and twenty troopers from the Second Cavalry, Captain Sul Ross and a contingent of Texas Rangers, and several Tonkawa scouts and volunteers under Captain Jack Cureton were on an expedition against the Comanche. On the Pease River near Crowell, Texas, they discovered a Comanche village. The soldiers attacked and easily defeated the Indians. During the fighting, Cynthia Ann Parker, captured on May 19, 1836, was "rescued" by the soldiers. Despite her pleas to be allowed to stay with the Comanche, Parker was forced to return to "civilization" with the troops. Peta Nocona, husband of Cynthia Ann Parker and father of Chief Quanah Parker, was killed in the fighting, according to some sources.

1876: In Montana at Redwater Creek, Lieutenant Frank Baldwin captured an entire village (122 lodges), goods, and sixty horses, mules, and ponies. This was a group of Sitting Bull's followers.

1877: Lieutenant J.A. Rucker and Troops C, G, H, and L, Seventh Cavalry, fought the same group of Indians they had fought on December 13, 1877. This time, fifteen Indians were reported killed in the fight in the Las Animas Mountains, New Mexico Territory.

1888: According to the Mesa Verde National Park Service in Colorado, "Richard Wetherill and his brother-in-law, Charles Mason, rode out on what is now Sun Point in search of lost cattle and first saw Cliff Palace. That afternoon, Richard found Spruce Tree House, and the next day, the two men discovered Square Tower House. Al Wetherill, Richard's brother, saw Cliff Palace sometime the year before, but he did not enter the dwelling, so the credit for 'discovering' the dwelling has been given to Richard Wetherill and Charles Mason." Thus the most famous of the Anasazi ruins was discovered.

1892: Congress approved a monthly pension of $30 for Lemhi Chief Tendoy.

1937: The questions of tribal power and membership were addressed regarding the Potawatomi of Kansas and Wisconsin.

1937: An election was held to adopt a constitution and bylaws by the Confederated Tribes of the Warm Springs Reservation of Oregon. The vote was 181–77 in favor.

1963: An election to approve a constitution and bylaws for the Paiute-Shoshone Tribe of the Fallon Reservation and Colony was held. It was approved by a vote of 40–22.

1971: Congress established the Alaska Native Claims Settlement Act (85 Stat. 688), according to the Kootznoowoo Incorporation papers.

1974: Congress passed Senate Bill 1296, which President Ford signed into law on January 3, 1975 (Public Law 93–620). This act enlarged the Havasupai Indian Reservation by 185,000 acres and designated 95,300 contiguous acres of the Grand Canyon National Park as a permanent traditional use area of the Havasupai people.

1976: The Pit River Indian Tribe was named as the "beneficial owner" of the XL Ranch in California by William Finale, area director, Sacramento office, Bureau of Indian Affairs. The tribal constitution was modified accordingly.

DECEMBER 19

1597: The Oñate expedition into what became New Mexico began.

1675: Narragansett under Chief Canonchet battled with Plymouth Governor Josiah Winslow with 970 men from Massachusetts, Connecticut, and Plymouth. The colonists lost 70–80 men, with 150 wounded; the Indians lost 600 dead, half of them warriors.

1813: A combined force of Indian warriors and British soldiers attacked and captured Fort Niagara in New York. The American defenders sustained sixty fatalities, and 350 were captured. Later, the victorious Indians also captured nearby Lewiston.

1829: The state of Georgia enacted a law that extended state boundaries over a sizable section of the Cherokee Nation. The law stated that anyone within this area after June 1, 1830, was subject to Georgia laws. All Cherokee laws became null after that date as well. The act also stated that an Indian could not be a witness in any court in the state. It was also a crime for anyone to promote the cause of not emigrating to Indian Territory (present-day Oklahoma).

1837: Jumper (Ote Emathla) and 250 of his Seminole and free black followers surrendered to Colonel Zachary Taylor. They were sent to the Indian Territory (present-day Oklahoma).

1842: Hawaiians visited Congress.

1861: Opothle Yahola's pro-Union Creek fought Colonel Douglas Cooper's pro-Confederacy Creek and Seminole Indians, led by McIntosh and Jumper, east of Stillwell, Oklahoma. The battle was inconclusive, with neither side scoring a victory. (Also recorded as happening on November 19, 1861.)

1867: According to army records, members of the First Cavalry fought with a band of Indians near Camp Wallen, Arizona. One Indian was reported killed.

1885: Eighth Cavalry soldiers fought a group of Indians near Little Dry Creek, or White House, New Mexico. According to army documents, assistant surgeon T.J.C. Maddox and four soldiers were killed. Lieutenant R.C. Cabell and one soldier were wounded.

1936: The Ute Indians of the Uintah, Uncompahgre, and White River Bands of the Uintah and Ouray Reservation approved a constitution and bylaws by a vote of 347–12.

1936: Secretary of the Interior Harold Ickes ratified an election that approved a constitution and bylaws for the Hopi Tribe. The election was held on October 24, 1936.

1944: An election to approve a constitution and bylaws for the Metlakatla Indian Community of the Annette Islands Reserve in Alaska was held as per an authorization by the assistant secretary of the interior. It was approved by a vote of 105–17.

1980: The commissioner of Indian affairs had authorized a vote for the approval of a new constitution and bylaws for the Ottawa Tribe of Indians of Oklahoma. It was approved by the tribe with a vote of 547–17.

1980: Chaco Canyon (New Mexico), the site of many Anasazi ruins, was officially designated as the Chaco Culture National Historic Park.

DECEMBER 20

1803: New Orleans became part of the United States.

1812: Sacajawea died at Fort Manuel, South Dakota, according to some sources.

1833: Creek met again at Wetumpka, Alabama, and sent another message to Secretary of War Lewis Cass about the state authorities overruling the federal authorities. The troops were leaving the area to jubilant white squatters.

1841: Seminole warriors under Chief Hallack Tustenuggee attacked Mandarin, Florida, located thirty-five miles north of St. Augustine. The Seminole overpowered the local forces. They captured and looted the town. Four Europeans were killed in the fighting.

1935: The constitution and bylaws of the Pueblo of Santa Clara were approved by Secretary of the Interior Harold Ickes.

1939: Assistant Secretary of the Interior Oscar Chapman authorized an election for a constitution for the Ketchikan Indian Corporation.

DECEMBER 21

1759: According to some reports, a conference covering peace and the resumption of trade was held for the next eight days between representatives of the British in North Carolina and the Cherokees.

1804: The two treaties the Cherokees signed with Return Meigs were sent to the U.S. Senate for consideration. The Cherokees gave up more than 4 million acres for almost $20,000.

1836: The fifth contingent of Creek wrote a letter to Lieutenant Sprague: "Tell General Jackson if the white men will let us, we will live in peace, and friendship. But tell him these agents [people paid to supply and help transport the Creek] came not to treat us well, but make money, and tell our people behind not to be drove off like dogs. We are men, we have women and children, and why should we come like wild horses." They thanked Lieutenant Sprague for his kindness.

1836: A constitution and bylaws were approved for the Oneida Tribe of Indians of Wisconsin.

1837: Four Chickasaws and Captain G.P. Kingsbury set out from Fort Coffee in eastern Indian Territory (present-day Oklahoma) to blaze a trail to the Chickasaws' new lands to the west.

1841: According to some sources, one of the last battles in the Second Seminole War was fought. Billy Bowlegs (Holtamico) led the Seminole; the American army was led by Major William Belknap. Fighting in a swamp, the Seminole escaped after both sides lost several men.

The Battle of the Hundred Killed, also known as the Fetterman Massacre, where more than eighty soldiers were killed by a band of Sioux warriors

1866: Red Cloud, Crazy Horse, Yellow Eagle, High Back Bone, and their followers had been harassing Colonel Henry Carrington's Second Cavalry and Twenty-Seventh Infantry troops from Fort Phil Kearny in northern Wyoming. They staged several raids and ambushes along the road from the fort to the nearby woods. Captain William J. Fetterman had once said, "A company of regulars could whip a thousand, and a regiment could whip the whole array of hostile tribes." A convoy of wagons carrying wood left the fort. It was attacked by a decoy group of Indians. Following up on his claim that he "could ride through the Sioux Nation" with just eighty men, Fetterman pursued the decoying Indians away from the fort. The Indians' trap was sprung. Fetterman's entire force of three officers, forty-seven infantry, twenty-seven cavalry, and two civilians were killed in the fighting. The soldiers called this the Fetterman Massacre. The Indians called it the Battle of the Hundred Killed.

1873: Indians fought with soldiers from the Fifth Cavalry near Ehrenberg, Arizona, according to army documents. Six Indians were killed and one was captured.

1875: An order was issued that modified the boundaries of the Hot Spring Reservation in New Mexico Territory.

1882: By executive order, a tract of land was set aside for the use and occupancy of the Turtle Mountain Band of Chippewa Indians in Dakota Territory.

1936: Secretary of the Interior Harold Ickes approved the election for the constitution and bylaws for the Oneida Tribe of Indians of Wisconsin.

1959: Acting Commissioner of Indian Affairs Leon Langan approved an election to amend the revised constitution and bylaws of the Sisseton Wahpeton Sioux Tribe of South Dakota.

1978: Casimir LeBeau, area director, Minneapolis area office, Bureau of Indian Affairs, ratified an election for an amendment to the constitution and bylaws of the Lac Courte Oreilles Band of Lake Superior Chippewa Indians of Wisconsin.

1988: The U.S. Environmental Protection Agency's proposed National Contingency Plan generally defined Indian tribes as states (53FR51479).

2012: According to some Maya sources, the present creation will end on this day. (December 23 or 24, 2012, according to some other sources.)

December 22

1769: The Shawnee captured Daniel Boone.

1830: The state of Georgia prohibited whites from being on Cherokee land without a permit.

1836: Between November 22, 1836, and this day, the Alabama Emigrating Company had delivered 9,833 Creek to Fort Gibson and the Verdigris River. During 1836, 14,609 Creek, including 2,495 hostiles, were removed to eastern Indian Territory (present-day Oklahoma), according to government reports.

1890: Captain J.H. Hurst of the Twelfth Infantry accepted the surrender of 294 Indians near Cherry Creek in South Dakota. According to army documents, these were members of Sitting Bull's band.

1898: President McKinley, by executive order, established the Hualapai Indian School Reserve for the purpose of educating the Hualapai Indians in Arizona Territory. The reserve was in Section 10, Township 23 North, Range 13 West.

1973: The Menominee Restoration Act was passed.

1974: The Hopi-Navajo Joint Use Act was passed.

1979: The acting deputy commissioner of Indian affairs had authorized an election to approve a constitution for the Tonto Apache Tribe. It was approved by a vote of 30–1.

December 23

1813: Almost 850 militia from Natchez, led by Brigadier General Ferdinand Claiborne, and 150 Choctaws, led by Chief Pushmataha, attacked the Red Stick Creek at a secret holy site called the Hickory Ground in present-day Lowndes County, Alabama. Although Red Stick Creek Chief William Weatherford (Lume Chathi–Red Eagle) survived by jumping off a cliff on his horse into the Alabama River, the Creek lost the battle. This was called the Battle of Econochaca or the Battle of the Holy Ground. Along with losing approximately thirty-three Red Stick warriors, the Creek lost many prophets as well. This was a serious blow to their morale. The Americans reported only one soldier killed.

1814: In northwestern Florida, Major Uriah Blue led a force of American militia against a Creek village near the Yellow River. Thirty Creek, including Alabama King, were killed and six dozen were captured.

1847: The Ogden conference was held at Fort Walla Walla with the Cayuse.

1855: White volunteers surrounded a friendly Rogue River Indian village they had visited the day before. The village was mostly unarmed. The whites attacked, and nineteen Indian men were killed. The women and children were driven into the cold. The survivors arrived at Fort Lane in southwestern Oregon with severe frostbite and frozen limbs.

1866: Sitting Bull attacked the Fort Buford sawmill.

1872: George Catlin died in New Jersey.

1873: An executive order set forth the confines of the Tulalip Reservation in Washington.

1873: Indians fought with soldiers from the Fifth Cavalry and some Indian scouts near Cave Creek, Arizona, according to army documents. Nine Indians were killed and three were wounded.

1877: Settlers fought a group of Indians near Van Horn's Wells in Bass Canyon, Texas. According to army documents, two settlers were killed.

1890: Big Foot left his village to go to Pine Ridge.

1923: Cherokee activist and educator Ruth Muskrat long promoted the concept of Indian self-determination. At a meeting of a reform group called the Committee of One Hundred, she presented President Calvin Coolidge a copy of the book *The Red Man in the United States*.

1963: Assistant Secretary of the Interior John Carver Jr. ratified an election that adopted an amendment for the constitution of the Standing Rock Sioux Tribe. The election was held on October 24, 1963.

1968: An election for amendments to the constitution and bylaws of the Jicarilla Apache was held. The results were 107–27 in favor.

1974: The constitution and bylaws of the Lac Courte Oreilles Band of Lake Superior Chippewa Indians of Wisconsin were amended.

1975: William Finale, area director, Sacramento area office, Bureau of Indian Affairs, authorized an election for amendments for the constitution of the Tuolumne Band of Me-Wok Indians of the Tuolumne Rancheria.

2012: One interpretation of the Maya calendar predicted that this day would be the end of world or the present creation.

DECEMBER 24

1721: French explorer Benard de la Harpe started an expedition up the Arkansas River. Leading sixteen men, he traveled all the way to the mountains. He returned and recommended establishing trading posts along this route to New Mexico.

1776: Washington asked the Passamaquoddy for help in the Revolutionary War.

1791: A Shawnee war party from Chillicothe attacked John Merrill's farm in Nelson County, Kentucky. Merrill was seriously wounded when the Shawnees first attacked. In what became a frontier legend, Merrill's wife killed six Shawnees as they tried to break into the cabin. After they broke off the attack, the Shawnees called Mrs. Merrill "Long Knife Squaw" out of respect.

1809: Kit Carson was born.

1814: The Treaty of Ghent ended the War of 1812.

1824: Choctaw Chief Pushmataha was in Washington, D.C., hoping to negotiate a better treaty for his people. He suddenly got sick and died in Tennison's Hotel. Pushmataha led Choctaw warriors many times in battle for the Americans. He told President Jackson that he wished to be buried with military honors. Jackson led the thousands of mourners when Pushmataha was buried in the congressional cemetery.

1824: The Mexican government awarded one square mile of land to each Shawnee warrior.

1866: Soldiers from the Thirteenth Infantry at Fort Buford led by Captain W.G. Rankin attacked Sitting Bull and his followers. According to army records, three Indians were killed in the fighting.

1872: The Missouri, Kansas, and Texas Railroad crossed the Texas border, completing the north-south crossing of Indian Territory (present-day Oklahoma).

1880: Crow King went to Fort Buford for Sitting Bull.

1886: According to the Oklahoma Law Enforcement Memorial, Samuel Sixkiller was son of Redbird Sixkiller, who came to Goingsnake District, Indian Territory. Redbird held many public offices for the tribal council and as judge. Sam kept many of his father's traits. Sam was appointed sheriff in Tahlaquah, Oklahoma. Later, he was appointed sheriff in Muskogee, Oklahoma. He was killed by Dick Vann on Christmas Eve for a grudge that Vann held for an earlier arrest. Sam was unarmed and could not defend himself.

1890: Big Foot and 333 of his followers made it to the Badlands.

1969: Acting Commissioner of Indian Affairs A.O. Allen approved an amendment to the constitution of the Oglala Sioux Tribe of Indians of the Pine Ridge Indian Reservation endorsed by the tribe.

2012: One interpretation of the Maya calendar predicted that this day would be the end of world or the present creation.

Every (through December 25): Matachina dances (Pueblos).

DECEMBER 25

1611: In September, Sir Thomas Dale was leading a band of Jamestown colonists up the James River with the intention of establishing a new settlement. When they reached an Appomattoc village, twenty men were killed in the night by Appomattoc women who had invited them to spend the night with them. On this day, Dale burned the main Appomattoc village as retribution for the earlier attack. Dale eventually built a settlement called Bermuda Hundred at that spot.

1780: John Sevier and additional troops from Virginia burned the Cherokee town of Chota, Tennessee, and several nearby villages.

1837: Colonel Zachary Taylor and 1,000 troops fought with the Seminole on the northern edge of Lake Okeechobee, Florida. The Seminole lost fourteen dead. Taylor's forces lost a little over two dozen dead and 112 wounded during the battle. This was one of the largest battles of the war. Seminole war Chief Halpatter Tuatennuggee (Alligator) led a group of 150 Seminole, and seventy-year-old Chief Sam Jones led 200 warriors during the fighting. The Seminole escaped into the swamps after the battle. Chief Jones was one of the Seminole who never left Florida.

1839: After the defeat at the Battle of the Neches on July 16, 1839, Cherokees under Chief "The Egg" attempted to escape to Mexico. They made it as far as the Colorado River before they met resistance. Colonel Edward Burleson, leading Texan and Tonkawa forces, engaged them in a fight. Seven Cherokee warriors were killed and twenty-four women and children were captured. Among the dead was The Egg.

1854: A force of 100 Ute and Jicarilla Apache, led by Tierra Blanco, ravaged a settlement on the Arkansas and Huerfano Rivers, killing fifteen men. They also captured some women and children.

1858: Colonel Miles and the Navajos signed a peace treaty. The Navajos agreed to boundary lines to the south and east. Reparations had to be made to the victims of the fighting. The army could establish a fort on Navajo lands. The peace lasted a little less than six months.

1868: Brevet Lieutenant Colonel A.W. Evans and troops from the Third Cavalry and the Thirty-Seventh Infantry had moved from Fort Bascom in western New Mexico, along the Canadian River, to the headwaters of the Red River. There he discovered a band of hostile Comanche. He attacked and, according to his report, killed twenty-five Indians, captured and burned the village, and destroyed a large amount of the Indians' supplies. The Indians were followers of Horse Back.

1869: According to army records, members of the Ninth Cavalry fought with a band of Indians near Johnson's Mail Station, Texas. No casualties were reported.

1968: As a part of an amended constitution, the Havasupai Nation held an election for tribal council.

DECEMBER 26

1620: The Plymouth Plantation was established.

1734: Reverend Richard Treat of Glastonbury, Connecticut, started teaching English and religion to the Wangunk close to Middletown.

The mass hanging of thirty-eight Indian leaders of the Great Sioux Uprising, Mankato, Minnesota

1759: South Carolina Governor William H. Lyttleton held a conference with six Cherokee chiefs at Fort St. George. The six chiefs agreed to a peace treaty that was repudiated by most of the Cherokee chiefs who did not attend the meeting.

1814: In northwestern Florida, Major Uriah Blue led a force of American militia against the Indian settlement called Holmes' Village on the Choctawhatchee River. The Creek who had been living there escaped before the attack.

1854: A treaty (10 Stat. 1132) was signed at Medicine Creek with the "Nisqually, Puyallup, Steilacoom, Squawskin, S'Homamish, Stehchass, T' Peek-sin, Squi-aitl, and Sa-heh-wamish tribes and bands of Indians, occupying the lands lying round the head of Puget's Sound."

1861: The Battle of Chustenahlah took place. Pro-Union Indians under Creek leader Opothle Yahola had established a fortified encampment on Hominy Creek northwest of Tulsa, Oklahoma. Confederate forces from Arkansas attacked them. The Indians deployed on a forested hill. It took fierce, hand-to-hand fighting to win the day. The Indians abandoned their supplies and 1,134 head of livestock. The Indians escaped during a blizzard, and many people froze to death in Kansas. They finally stopped in central Kansas with 3,168 Creek, 777 Seminole, a few other Indians, and ninety-

one blacks. The Union would provide them with some supplies. Eventually, over 7,500 survivors made it to the camp. The men were organized into the First Regiment of Indian Home Guards. This was also called the Battle of Shoal Creek.

1862: The thirty-eight Santee Sioux condemned for their actions in the Santee Sioux Uprising were hanged in Mankato, Minnesota. This was the largest mass hanging in American history.

1866: Elements of the First Cavalry fought some Indians near Owyhee Creek, Idaho. Two soldiers were wounded, fourteen Indians were killed, and seven were captured, according to army records.

1867: According to army records, members of the Ninth Cavalry fought with a band of Indians near Fort Lancaster, Texas. Three soldiers were killed. Twenty Indians were reported killed and eleven were wounded.

1869: In Sanguinara Canyon in the Guadalupe Mountains of New Mexico Territory, Lieutenant Howard Cushing and Troop F, Third Cavalry, engaged a band of Indians. During the fight, Lieutenant Franklin Yeaton was mortally wounded.

1869: According to army records, members of the Second Artillery fought with a band of Indians near Fort Wrangle, Alaska. One civilian was wounded. One Indian was killed and another was wounded.

1961: An election to approve an amendment to the constitution and bylaws for the Pyramid Lake Paiute Tribe of Nevada was held. It was approved by a vote of 80–20.

DECEMBER 27

1761: Europeans had established several settlements in the Long Canes area of southern Carolina. Creek, under Chief "The Mortar," attacked the area, killing fourteen settlers.

1763: Angry white vigilantes known as "the Paxton Boys" broke into a building housing the fourteen Conestoga, Pennsylvania, Indians not killed in the attack on December 14. The whites killed all of the Indians, including women and children, while they prayed. Benjamin Franklin wrote a broadside ("Narrative of the Late Massacres in Lancaster County") condemning the white attackers for brutalizing the innocent Conestoga.

1837: The second group of Cherokees to emigrate after the New Echota Treaty arrived in Indian Territory (present-day Oklahoma) just southwest of the Missouri-Arkansas border. During the march, four adults and eleven children died.

1845: According to a *New York Morning News* editorial: "Our manifest destiny to overspread and to possess the whole of the continent which providence has given us for the development of the great experiment of liberty and federated self-government entrusted to us."

1846: Shuk-ha-nat-cha and 360 other Choctaws arrived at Fort Coffee in eastern Indian Territory (present-day Oklahoma).

1858: Twenty Texans, led by Indian fighter Peter Garland, attacked a peaceful group of Anadarko and Caddo camped on Keechi Creek near the Brazos River Reservation. The Texans killed seven Indians while they were sleeping. According to some reports, the Texas Rangers refused to arrest Garland for the unprovoked murders. A grand jury set up to investigate the murders charged Anadarko Chief Jose Maria (Iesh) with horse-stealing instead.

1873: Corporal John Wright and soldiers from the Twenty-Fifth Infantry fought with Indians on Deep Red Creek in Indian Territory (present-day Oklahoma). One Indian was wounded.

1875: President Grant, by executive order, established reservations for the Portrero, Cahuila, Capitan Grande, Santa Ysabel, Pala, Agua Caliente, Sycuan, Inasa, and Cosmit Mission Indians primarily in San Diego County, California. This order was modified on: May 3, 1877; August 25, 1877; September 29, 1877; January 17, 1880; March 2, 1881; March 9, 1881; June 27, 1882; July 24, 1882; February 5, 1883; June 19, 1883; January 25, 1886; March 22, 1886; January 29, 1887; March 14, 1887; and May 6, 1889.

1938: An election to approve an amendment to the constitution and bylaws for the Thlopthlocco Tribal Town of the Creek Indian Nation of the state of Oklahoma was held. It was passed by a vote of 95–4.

1946: Indians were relocated in North Dakota due to dam construction.

1980: The U.S. Post Office issued the Sequoyah stamp.

DECEMBER 28

1520: According to some sources, Hernán Cortés and his army started their second excursion to Tenochtitlán (modern Mexico City) from Tlascala, Mexico. This time they had made and brought a group of small boats to use on the lake surrounding the city.

1791: Cherokee Chief Bloody Fellow and others arrived in Philadelphia to meet with President Washington. The meeting was delayed by Secretary of War Knox until the Cherokees had been outfitted in "more proper" clothing. The eventual meeting led to an addenda to the Holston Treaty that was signed on February 17, 1792.

Secretary of War Henry Knox (IMH)

1835: Seminole Agent Wiley Thompson, Lieutenant Constantine Smyth, and Erastus Rogers were killed by antiremoval Seminole at Fort King (near modern Ocala) in the north-central part of Florida. Major Francis L. Dade's company of troops was marching from Fort Brooke on Tampa Bay to Fort King. Near the Little Withlacoochee River (near modern Bushnell), they were attacked by 180 Seminole. Of a total of 112 soldiers, only three survived. Chief Mikanopy was credited by many as firing the first shot that killed Major Dade. Chief Jumper killed Dade's adjutant. Only three Seminole were killed. Osceola led the Seminole on several skirmishes during the day. This was considered the start of the Second Seminole War by the U.S. Army.

1840: Five soldiers and a civilian were killed by Seminole warriors just outside of Micanopy, Florida.

1847: Oregon troops led by Colonel Gilliam attacked some Indians in the first battle of the Cayuse War. Captain Lee fought des Chutes's warriors. Half of the Indians were killed; no soldiers were killed, according to government reports.

1870: From a marker in the Fort Buford (North Dakota) cemetery: "Daughter of Bloody Knife— December 28, 1870—Disease."

1872: Events in the Tonto Basin campaign took place. Apache and Yavapai warriors were defeated by the army near Skull Canyon, Arizona. Indians skirmished with a group of soldiers from the Fifth Cavalry and some Indian scouts in the Salt River Canyon in Arizona, according to official army records. One soldier and fifty-seven Indians were killed. One soldier was wounded and twenty Indians were captured.

1874: Captain A.S.B. Keyes and Troop I, Tenth Cavalry, had been following a group of Southern Cheyenne for eighty miles. On the Canadian River in Texas, the entire group of fifty-two Indians and seventy horses surrendered, according to army records.

1890: Seventh Cavalry and First Artillery soldiers accepted the surrender of 106 Indians near Porcupine Creek, South Dakota.

1985: The Quarter Blood Amendment Act (99 Stat. 1747) of December 28, 1985, was passed by Congress. Its purpose was to "define eligible Indian students for Indian education programs and tuition-free attendance at [Bureau of Indian Affairs] or contract schools."

Every: Children's dances (Pueblos) and Holy Innocence Day.

DECEMBER 29

1776: John McClelland's station was located near what is modern Lexington, Kentucky. Mingo under Chief Pluggy attacked the stockade. Men were killed on both sides, including both force's leaders. The Indians eventually gave up the attack.

1830: Nine local missionaries issued a proclamation defending the Cherokees against the actions of Georgia. Georgia was trying to remove the Cherokees from their lands in New Echota. Eventually, Georgia passed a law sentencing anyone living in Cherokee territory to four years of hard labor if they had not sworn allegiance to Georgia.

1831: David Folsom's Choctaws began their march to the Red River. Bridges must be built, roads improved, bogs crossed, and rivers forded. The muddy roads and river crossings slowed the trip.

1831: Cherokee leaders sent a memorandum to the secretary of war stating their grievances against the actions of the state of Georgia. Georgia had taken their lands at gunpoint, carried off their people in chains, taken their gold mines, and planned to sell off their lands to white settlers. A delegation of John Ross, Judge John Martin, William Shorey Coodey, and John Ridge went to Washington to follow up on their complaints.

1835: The United States informed the Cherokees that they were to appear in their capital city, New Echota, Georgia, to negotiate a treaty with the United States. They were informed that anyone not attending the council was assumed to support any agreement reached there. Several Cherokee leaders opposed to the movement of the tribe to Indian Territory (present-day Oklahoma) were physically restrained so they could not attend the meeting. Chief John Ross was held prisoner, without charges, for twelve days by Georgia militia. Of the estimated 18,000 Cherokees, less than 500 attended the treaty council. On this day, a treaty (7 Stat. 478) was signed by less than 100 Cherokees that ceded all of the Cherokee lands in the east. The treaty-signers, led by Elias Boudinot, Major Ridge, and John Ridge, agreed to the treaty with the provision that it receive approval from the majority of the Cherokee Nation. Although representatives of almost 16,000 Cherokees informed the government they did not endorse or support the treaty, the U.S. Senate ratified it by a one-vote margin.

1876: Colonel Nelson Miles, companies A, C, D, E, and K, Fifth Infantry, Companies E and F, Twenty-Second Infantry, and two pieces of artillery—436 men total—left Fort Keogh (at the mouth of the Tongue River) in eastern Montana in search of Crazy Horse and hostile Northern Cheyenne and Sioux.

1890: The Battle of Wounded Knee, or Wounded Knee Massacre, took place. According to army records, one officer (Captain G.D. Wallace), twenty-four soldiers, and 128 Indians were killed. Thirty-five soldiers and thirty-three Indians were wounded in the fighting. The army would give Congressional Medals of Honor to the following soldiers: Sergeant William G. Austin, for "using every effort to dislodge the enemy"; Company E musician John E. Clancy, who "twice voluntarily rescued wounded comrades under fire of the enemy"; Private Mosheim Feaster, Company E, for "extraordinary gallantry"; First Lieutenant Ernest A. Garlington, for "distinguished gallantry"; First Lieutenant John C. Gresham, for leading an attack into a ravine; Sergeant Richard P. Hanley, Company C, for recovering a pack mule loaded with ammunition while under heavy fire; Private Joshija B. Hartzog, Company E, First Artillery, for rescuing his wounded commander while under heavy fire; Second Lieutenant Harry L. Hawthorne, Second Artillery, for distinguished conduct; Private Marvin C. Hillock, Company B, for distinguished bravery; Private George Hobday, Company A, for conspicuous and gallant conduct; Sergeant George Loyd, Company I, for bravery, especially after being severely wounded through the lung; Sergeant Albert McMillian, Company E, for leading by example; Private Thomas Sullivan, Company E, for conspicuous bravery; First Sergeant Frederick Toy, Company C, for bravery; First Sergeant Jacob Trautman, Company I, for "killing a hostile Indian at close quarters" and remaining with the troops even though he was entitled to retire; Sergeant James Ward, Company B, for fighting after being severely wounded; Corporal Paul Weinert, Company E, for assuming command of his artillery piece when his officer was wounded; and Private Hermann Ziegner, Company E, for conspicuous bravery.

1915: Lands were ordered to be set aside for agency and school purposes in connection with the administration of the Cheyenne and Arapaho Indians.

1955: An election held to adopt an amended constitution and bylaws for the Hualapai Tribe of the Hualapai Reservation in Arizona was ratified by Assistant Secretary of the Interior Wesley D'Ewart.

1964: The secretary of the interior had authorized an election to approve a constitution and bylaws for the Squaxin Island Tribe of the Squaxin Island Indian Reservation in Washington State. The election was held on May 15, 1965.

1990: An anniversary gathering was held at Wounded Knee.

DECEMBER 30

1806: Thomas Jefferson wrote a letter to "Wolf and People of the Mandan Nation." It extolled the virtues of peace.

1847: During the Cayuse War, Colonel Gilliam and 160 men were attacked by some Indians near Waiilatpu. The Indians lost twenty warriors and lots of supplies.

1853: The Gadsden Purchase was made, adding land to the United States in the southern parts of Arizona and New Mexico. Most of these lands were claimed by Indians.

1869: According to army records, members of the Third Cavalry fought with a band of Indians near Delaware Creek in the Guadalupe Mountains of Texas. No casualties were reported.

1872: Indians skirmished with a group of soldiers from the Fifth Cavalry near the mouth of Baby Canyon in Arizona, according to official army records. Six Indians were killed, one was wounded, and two were captured.

1890: In the aftermath of the battle at Wounded Knee, the Drexel Mission Fight happened just north of the Pine Ridge Agency in South Dakota.

1890: While pursuing Sioux Indians at White Clay Creek, South Dakota, elements of the Seventh Cavalry engaged in a skirmish. Captain Charles Varnum, Company B, First Sergeant Theodore Ragnar, Company K, and farrier Richard Nolan, Company I, would win the Medal of Honor for bravery.

1950: A constitution and bylaws for the Eskimos of the Native Village of Buckland, Alaska, were ratified by a vote of 17–13.

1982: The Indian Claims Limitation Act (96 Stat. 1976) of December 30, 1982, was passed by Congress. It was intended to "provide guidelines for revision to file claims based on dates of publication in Federal Register, submission of legisla-

Mandan chief

tion or legislative report, or decision of suit by Secretary of the Interior."

DECEMBER 31

1590: Spaniard Gaspar Castaño de Sosa was exploring the area of what is now New Mexico. A few days earlier, several men in his group had a fought with some of the residents of the Pecos Pueblo. Sosa's main body reached the pueblo. There was a brief fight, and Sosa took some of the Indians captive. Sosa would later return to the pueblo and get a better reception.

1794: After agreeing to a peace with the United States on November 7, the Cherokee and Chickamauga Indians and the United States exchanged prisoners, effectively ending the Chickamauga War.

1813: Indian and British forces under General Phineas attacked Buffalo, New York, burning the small village to the ground. Settlers soon returned and rebuilt.

1835: A census of the Cherokees in Georgia, Alabama, North Carolina, and Tennessee was concluded. It showed 16,542 Cherokees living in those four states. They owned 1,592 black slaves, and 201 whites had married into the tribe.

1835: During the Second Seminole War, Chiefs Osceola and Alligator led a force of 250 Seminole against an army detachment of 750 men, led by Generals Duncan Clinch and Richard Call, on the Withlacoochee River near Tampa Bay, Florida. This was one of the few pitched battles the Seminole engaged in. The Seminole opened fire when the Americans tried to cross the river. Only a few soldiers and warriors were killed in the fighting. A bayonet charge led by Colonel Alexander Fanning helped to end the fighting, but Clinch was forced to retreat from the area.

1873: Near Eagle Springs, Texas, fifteen Indians attacked a sergeant and soldiers from Company B, Twenty-Fifth Infantry. Only one Indian was wounded in the fight.

1873: Indians fought with soldiers from the Fifth Cavalry in the Sunflower Valley near Fort Reno, Arizona. According to army documents, seven Indians were killed and eleven were captured.

1880: Major Ilges held a council with Crow King at Poplar Agency.

1881: The Osage Nation adopted a constitution at Pawhuska, Oklahoma.

1939: The assistant secretary of the interior had authorized an election to approve a constitution and bylaws for the native village of Gambell. It was passed by a vote of 76–3.

1954: According to Federal Register No. 20FR00181, certain tracts of Indian Reservation land were "withdrawn from all forms of disposal under the public lands laws, including the mining and mineral leasing laws."

1958: The assistant secretary of the interior authorized an election for a constitution for the Standing Rock Sioux Tribe. The election was held on February 11, 1959

1960: The federal government terminated the Menominee Tribe.

1964: An amendment to the constitution and bylaws of the Fort Belknap Indian Community of the Fort Belknap Indian Reservation in Montana was adopted.

APPENDICES

Tribal Names

Many tribal names mean "people," "us," "human beings," or similar words. The names below are for those groups whose name has another meaning. Some tribes' names were acquired from Europeans using a second tribe's name for the first tribe. The "New Name" was used so much, it gained an "official" status or became the common name. In many cases, tribal name origins are lost in the mists of history. Some definitions below are based on conjecture by historians. In some cases, some tribal members would agree with the names below, while other members will not. In essence, this is a list of commonly used definitions.

Abenaki . . . . those living at the sunrise
           (easterners)
Achomawi . . . . . river
Acolapissa . . . . . those who listen and see
Ahtena . . . . ice people
Akwesasne . . . . . land where the partridge drums
Alabama . . . . I clear the thicket
Apache . . . . enemy (Zuni word)
Apalachicola . . . people of the other side
Apalachee . . . . . people of the other side
Arikara . . . . horns or elk people, or corn eaters
Assiniboin . . . . . ones who cook using stones
           (Ojibwa word)
Atakapa . . . . man eater
Atsina . . . . white clay people
Atsugewi . . . . . . hat creek Indians
Avoyel . . . . people of the rocks
Ahwahneechee
           people of the deep grassy valley
Bayogoula . . . . . . people of the bayou
Bidai . . . . brushwood (Caddo word)
Brule . . . . burned thighs
Caddo . . . . true chiefs
Cayuga . . . . place locusts were taken out, people at the mucky land

Cayuse . . . . stones or rocks (French-Canadian word)
Chakchiuma . . . red crawfish people
Chehalis . . . . sand
Cherokee . . . . cave people (Choctaw word), people of different speech (Creek word)
Chetco . . . . close to the mouth of the stream
Cheyenne . . . . . . red talkers (Dakota word)
Chickahominy . . hominy people
Chippewa . . . . . . to roast till puckered up
Chipewyan . . . . . pointed skins (Cree word)
Chitimacha . . . . they have cooking vessels
Chontal . . . . stranger (Nahuatl word)
Choula . . . . fox
Chowanoc . . . . . people at the south
Chumash . . . . . . people who make the shell bead money
Clallam . . . . strong people
Clatsop . . . . dried salmon
Cocopah . . . . river people
Comanche . . . . anyone who wants to fight me all the time (Ute word)
Coeur d'Alene . . those who are found here
Crow . . . . crow, sparrowhawk, bird people
Dakota . . . . ally

Dihai-kutchin .. those living farthest downstream
Ehdiitat
   Gwich'in .... people who live among timber or
            spruce
Erie .... log tail or cat people (Iroquois
            word)
Fox .... red earth people
Gwich'in ...... people who live at a certain place
Gros Ventre .... big bellies, one who cooks with a
            stone, he cooks by roasting (see
            Atsina)
Hach winik .... true people
Han .... those who live along the river
Havasupai ..... people of the blue-green water
Hidatsa .... willow (speculation)
Hiute .... bowmen
Honniasont .... wearing something around the
            neck
Hopi .... peaceful ones
Houma .... red, red crawfish
Huchnom ...... mountain people
Hunkpapa ..... campers at the opening of the
            circle
Hupa .... trinity river
Huron .... ruffian (French word)
Hwal'bay
   (Hualapai) ... people of the tall pines
Ihanktonwan ... dwellers at the end
Ihanktonwana .. little dwellers at the end
Iowa .... sleepy ones (Dakota word)
Iroquois .... real adders (Snake) or we of the
            extended lodge
Jatibonicu ...... people of the great sacred high
            waters
Jatibonuco ..... great people of the sacred high
            waters
Jicaque .... ancient person (Nahuatl word)
Jicarilla .... little basket weaver (Spanish word)
Kainai .... many chiefs
Kalispel .... camas
Kan-hatki ...... white earth
Kanienkahaka .. people of the place of flint
Kansa .... people of the south wind
Karok .... upstream

Kato .... lake
Kawchottine ... people of the great hares
Ketsei .... going in wet sand
Kickapoo ...... he stands about
Kiowa .... principal people
Klallam .... strong people
Klamath ...... people of the lake
Kotsoteka ..... buffalo eaters
Kutcha-kutchin .. those who live on the flats
Kwuda .... people coming out
Lakota .... friend or ally (same with Dakota
            and Nakota)
Latgawa .... those living in the uplands
Lenni Lenape ... genuine men
Lillooet .... wild onion
Loucheux .... people with slanted or crossed eyes
Machapunga ... bad dust
Mahican .... wolf
Makah .... cape people
Maliseet .... broken talkers
Manso .... mild (Spanish)
Massachuset .... at the hills
Mdewan
   -kantonwan .. dwellers of the spirit lake
Menominee .... wild rice men
Miami .... people on the peninsula, cry of
            the crane, pigeon
Michigamea .... great water
Miniconjou .... planters by water
Minnetaree .... they crossed the water
Minqua .... stealthy
Missouri .... great muddy, people with wooden
            canoes
Moapa .... mosquito creek people
Moatokni ...... southerners
Modoc .... southerners
Mohave .... three mountains
Mohawk .... the possessors of the flint, coward
            or man eater (Abenaki words)
Mohegan ...... wolf
Moneton ...... big water people
Muklasa .... friend, people of one nation
Munsee .... at the place where the stones are
            gathered together

Nahane .... people of the west
Narragansett ... people of the small point
Nanticoke ..... people of the tidewaters
Natsit-kutchin .. those who live off the flats
Navajo .... cultivated field in an arroyo
        (Tewa word)
Nez Perce ...... Pierced Nose
Nihtat
   Gwich'in ..... people living together as a mixture
Nipmuck ...... freshwater fishing place
Nokoni .... those who turn back
Nooksack ...... mountain men
Nootka .... along the coast
Oglala .... scatters their own
Ojibwa .... to roast till puckered up
Okelousa ...... blackwater
Okmulgee ...... where water boils up
Omaha .... upstream people or people going
        against the current
Oneida .... a boulder standing up, people of
        the standing stone
Onondaga ..... people on top of the hills
Opata .... hostile people (Pima word)
Ottawa .... to trade
Otto .... lechers
Pahodja .... dusty nones
Pakiutlema ..... people of the gap
Pamunkey ..... rising upland
Pantch-
   pinunkansh .. men altogether red
Papagos .... desert people, bean people
Pascagoula ..... bread people
Passamaquoddy . plenty of pollock
Paugusset ...... where the narrows open out
Pawnee .... horn people, men of men, look
        like wolves
Penateka ...... honey eaters
Pennacook ..... down hill
Penobscot ...... it forks on the white rocks, the
        descending ledge place, at the
        stone place
Pensacola ...... hair people
People of the
   lakes .... tribes near the great lakes

Peoria .... carrying a pack on his back
Pequot .... fox people or destroyers
Piegan .... scabby robes
Pilthlako ...... big swamp
Pima .... "no" in Nevome language when
        responding to question from
        Spanish if they knew their name,
        river people
Pojoaque ...... drinking place
Potawatomi .... people of the place of the fire,
        keepers of the fire, fire nation,
        fire people
Powhatan ...... falls in a current of water
Pshwanwapam .. stony ground
Puyallup .... shadow
Quahadi .... antelope
Quapaw .... downstream people
Sac .... people of the yellow earth or
        people of the outlet
Salish .... flatheads
Sans Arc .... without bows
Schaghticoke ... at the river forks
Sekani .... dwellers on the rocks
Seminole ...... separatist or breakaway, peninsula
        people, those who camp away
Seneca .... place of stone, people of the
        standing rock, great hill people
Shawnee .... south or southerners
Sihasapa Sioux .. blackfeet
Siksika .... blackfeet
Sioux .... snake (French version of other
        tribe's name)
Sisitonwan ..... dwellers of the fish ground
Skokomish ..... river people
Snake .... river dwellers
Taino .... we the good people
Takelma .... those living along the river
Tanima .... liver eaters
Tangipahoa .... corn gatherers
Tantawats ..... southern men
Tarahumara .... running plant, those with light
        feet
Tatsanottine ... people of the copper water
Tawakoni ...... river bend among red hills

Teetl'it

   Gwich'in . . . . people who live at the head of the waters

Tejas . . . . friendly

Tenawa . . . . downstream

Tennuth-

   ketchin . . . . . . middle people

Teton . . . . dwellers of the prairie

Tewa . . . . moccasins

Thlingchadinne

   . . . . dog-flank people

Titonwan . . . . . . dwellers of the plains

Tonawanda . . . . confluent stream

Tonkawa . . . . . . they all stay together or most human of people

Tsattine . . . . lives among the beavers

Tsetsaut . . . . people of the interior (Niska word)

Tubatulabal . . . . pinenut eaters (Shoshone word)

Tukudeka . . . . . . sheep eater

Tuscarora . . . . . . hemp gatherers, the shirt-wearing people

Two Kettle . . . . . two boilings

Unalachtigo . . . . tidewater people

Viniintaii

   Gwich'in . . . . people who live on or by the caribou trail

Vuntut

   Gwitch'in . . . . dwellers among the lakes

Vvunta-

   ketchin . . . . . . those who live among the lakes

Wahpekute . . . . shooters among the leaves

Wahpetonwan . . dwellers among the leaves

Wailaki . . . . north language (Wintun word)

Wakokai . . . . blue heron breeding place

Walapai . . . . pine tree people

Walla Walla . . . . little river

Wampanoag . . . . eastern people

Wappo . . . . brave

Waptailmin . . . . people of the narrow river

Wasco . . . . cup, those who have the cup

Wichita . . . . big arbor (Choctaw word)

Winnebago . . . . filthy water people

Wiwohka . . . . . . roaring water

Wyandot . . . . people of the peninsula, islanders

Yakima . . . . runaway

Yamparika . . . . . root eaters or yap eaters

Yavapai . . . . people of the sun, crooked mouth people

Yoncalla . . . . those living at ayankeld

Yuchi . . . . situated yonder

Yuki . . . . stranger (Wintun word)

Yurok . . . . downstream (Karok word)

Zuni . . . . the flesh

Alternative Tribal Names

Many tribes have more than one name. Some tribes have a name they give to the world, with another name meant to be used only among themselves. Some tribes became known by the names that other tribes called them. For example, *Cherokee* was a name given to that tribe by others. Eventually so many Europeans, Americans, and other tribes called them by that name that the tribe adopted it. Below is an example of the many names given to the Cherokee. It comes from *The Indian Tribes of North America* by John R. Swanton:

Alligewi or **Alleghanys,** a people appearing in Delaware tradition who were perhaps identical with this tribe.

Ani'-Kitu'hwagi, own name, from one of their most important ancient settlements and extended by Algonquian tribes to the whole.

Ani'-Yun'-wiya', own name, meaning "real people."

Baniatho, Arapaho name (Gatschet, MS., B.A.E.).

Entari ronnon, Wyandot name, meaning "mountain people."

Manteran, Catawba name, meaning "coming out of the ground."

Ochie'tari-ronnon, a Wyandot name.

Oyata' ge'ronon, Iroquois name, meaning "inhabitants of the cave country."

Shanaki, Gaddo name.

Shannakiak, Fox name (Gatschet, Fox MS., B.A.E.).

Talligewi, Delaware name (in Walam Olum); see Alligewi.

Tcaike, Tonkawa name.

Tcerokieco, Wichita name.

Uwatayo-rono, Wyandot name, meaning "cave people."

There are many variations on how Europeans spelled tribal names. Lewis and Clark referred to the Iowa (pronounced EYE-oh-way) Indians with spellings that varied from page to page in their journal. I have not included every possible phonetic spelling, just some of the major ones. One additional point: Some tribes have been referred to by a name that is not their real name, and neither do they officially acknowledge that name. However, because it has been misused so often, I have listed the incorrect name so readers can understand the references in the dates section of this book.

Abenaki
  (western) .... Alnonba, Abnaki
Adai .... Nateo
Adamstown .... Upper Mattaponi
Alabama .... Alibamu
Aleut .... Alutiiq, Unangan
Anadarko ...... Nadaco
Apache .... N'de, Inde, Tinneh, Dine, Tinde,
              Unde, Shis Inde, Jicarilla, Lipan,
              San Carlos, Chiricahua,
              Mescalero, Pinal, Arivaipa
Apache Mohave
  .... Yavapai
Appomattoc .... Apamatuks
Arapaho .... Inunaina, Atsina
Arikara .... Northern Pawnee, Ricara, Ree
Assiniboin ..... Hohe
Atasi .... Muskogee
Athabascan .... Dene
Atsina .... Haaninin
Aztec .... Nahua, Nahuatl
Bannock .... Panaiti, Digger
Bear River Indians
  .... Niekeni
Bellabella ...... Heiltsuqu, Heiltsuk
Bellacoola ..... Nuxalk
Blackfeet ...... Nitsi-tapi, Piegan, Pikuni (north-
              ern); Siksika, Sisaka (southern),
              Sihasapa
Blood .... Kainai
Brule Sioux .... Si can gu
Caddo .... Adai, Eyeish, Hasinai, Hainai,
              Kadohodacho, Kadohadacho
              Confederacy, Natchitoches,
              Anadarko Cahuilla Kawia
Calusa .... Calos, Carlos, Muspa
Campo .... Kumeyaay
Carrier .... Wet'suwet'en
Catawba .... Esaw, Ushery
Cayuga .... Kweniogwen, Iroquois
Cayuse .... Wailetpu, Te-taw-ken
Chakchiuma ... Shaktci Homma
Chastacosta .... Shista-kwusta
Chemehuevi ... Tantawats

Chetco .... Tolowa
Cherokee ...... Tsa-la-gi, Ani-yun-wiya, Aniki-
              tuhwagi, Keetowah
Cheyenne ...... Dzi tsi stas, Sowonia (southern),
              O mi sis (northern)
Chippewa ...... Ojibwa
Chitimacha .... Pantch-pinunkansh
Choctaw ...... Chakchiuma, Chatot
Chumash ...... Santa Barbara Indians
Clackamas ..... Guithlakimas
Clallam .... S'klallam, Nusklaim, Tlalem
Clowwewalla ... Willamette
Cocopah .... Xawitt Kunyavaei
Coeur d'Alene .. Skitswish, Schee chu'umsch
Comanche ..... Detsanayuka, Kotsoteka, Nermer-
              nuh, Noconi, Nokoni, Numunuu,
              Padouca (Sioux word), Penateka,
              Pennande, Quahadi, Yamparika
Comox .... Catloltx
Conoy .... Canawese, Ganawese, Kanawha,
              Piscataway
Copane .... Kopano, Quevenes
Cora .... Nayarit
Coushatta ..... Koasati, Acoste
Cree .... Kenistenoag, Iyiniwok
Creek .... Muskogee, Abihika, Abeika,
              Hitchiti
Crow .... Absaroke
Cupeno .... Kupa
Cuthead .... Pabaksa
Delaware ...... Lenni Lenape, Lenape, Abnaki,
              Alnanbai, Wampanoag, Munsee,
              Unami, Unalachtigo, Powhatan-
              Renápe
Dieguenos ..... Comeya, Tipai, Ipai, Kumeyaay
Eskimo .... Inuit, Inupiat, Inuvialuit, Yupik
Fox .... Mesquaki
Gabrieleno ..... Tongva
Ganawese ...... Conoys, Piscataways
Goshute .... Kusiutta
Gros Ventre .... Atsina (prairie), Hidatsa (Mis-
              souri), Ah-ah-nee-nin, Minnetaree
Gwich'in ...... Loucheux
Hainai .... Ioni

Hasinai . . . . Caddo
Havasupai . . . . . Suppai, Supai
Hidatsa . . . . Gros Ventre
Hopi . . . . Hopitu, Shinumu, Moqui, Hapeka
Hualapai . . . . Hwal'bay, Walapai
Huchnom . . . . . . Redwood
Hupa . . . . Natinnohhoi
Huron . . . . Wendat, Wyandot
Ingalik Athabascan
. . . . Deg Het'an
Iowa . . . . Pahodja
Iroquois . . . . Haudenosaunee, Hodenosaunee,
Ongwanosionni, Hotinonshonni,
Cayuga, Mohawk, Onondaga,
Seneca, Tuscarora, Oneida
Jemez . . . . Tuwa, Ha'mish
Jicarilla Apache . Tinde
Kalispel . . . . Pend d'Oreilles
Kamia . . . . Tipai
Kansa . . . . Hutanga, Kansas, Kanza, Kaw
Kato . . . . Tlokeang
Keres . . . . Pueblo, Acoma, Cochiti, Isleta,
Laguna, San Felipe, Santa Ana,
Santo Domingo, Zia
Ketsei . . . . Kitsei, Kichai
Kickapoo . . . . . . Kiwigapawa
Kiowa . . . . Kwuda, Tepda, Tepkinago,
Gaigwu
Kiowa Apache . . Nadiisha Dena
Klamath . . . . Eukshikni Maklaks, Auksni
Klickitat . . . . Qwulhhwaipum
Kootenai . . . . . Kuronoqa, Kutenai, Asanka
Koso . . . . Panamint
Kutchin . . . . Gwich'in
Lancondon . . . . . Maya
Loucheux . . . . . . Gwich'in
Lillooet . . . . Lil'wat, St'át'imc
Lipan . . . . Naizhan
Lower Sioux . . . . Mdewakanton, Wahpekute
Lumbee . . . . Cheraw
Machapunga . . . dusty
Makah . . . . Kwenetchechat
Mandan . . . . Metutahanke or Mawatani (after
1837), Numakaki (before 1837)

Manhattan . . . . . Rechgawawank
Manso . . . . Maise, Mansa, Manse, Manxo,
Gorreta, Gorrite, Tanpachoa
Maricopa . . . . . . Xalchidom Pii-pash, Pipatsje,
Pipatsji, Pee-posh
Miami . . . . Twightwis, Twa-h-twa-h,
Oumameg, Wea
Micmac . . . . . . Mi'kmaq
Missouri . . . . Niutachi
Moapa . . . . Moapariats
Mobile . . . . Mabila
Modoc . . . . Moatokni, Okkowish
Mohave . . . . . . Mojave, Tzinamaa,
Ahamakav
Mohawk . . . . . . Kanienkahaka, Kaniengehage,
Abenaki, Iroquois
Molala . . . . Latiwe
Mono . . . . Monache
Moratoc . . . . . . Nottoway
Mosopelea . . . . . Ofo
Munsee . . . . Minasinink
Muskogee . . . . . Alabama, Atasi, Eufaula, Hilibi
Nanticoke . . . . . Unalachtigo
Navajo . . . . Diné, Dineh, Tenuai, Navaho,
Tewa Navahu
Nez Perce . . . . . Nee-me-poo, Nimipu, Kamuinu,
Tsutpeli, Sahaptin, Chopunnish
Nootka . . . . Nuu-chah-nulth
Nottaway . . . . . . Cheroenhaka
Ofo . . . . Mosopelea
Oglala . . . . Okandanda
Ojibwa . . . . Chippewa, Anishinabe, Mis-
sisauga, Saginaw
Northern Ojibwa
. . . . Saulteaux
Okanagon . . . . . Isonkuaili
Oneida . . . . Iroquois
Onondaga . . . . . Iroquois
Osage . . . . Wakon, Wazhazhe
Ottawa . . . . Adawe
Otto . . . . Chewaerae
Oulaouaes . . . . . Necariages
Parianuc . . . . . . White River Utes
Paiute . . . . Numa, Nuwvi, Snake

Papagos . . . . Tohono O'odham, Ak-chin, Yohono Au'autam

Passamaquoddy . Peskedemakddi

Patchogue . . . . . Unkechaug

Pawnee . . . . Pariki, Chahiksichahiks, Ckirihki Kuruuriki, Awahi

Pawokti . . . . Alabama

Pecos . . . . Pueblos from Jemez

Pend d'Oreilles . . Kalispel

Penobscot . . . . . . Pannawanbskek, Penaubsket

Petun . . . . Khionontateronon, Tionontati

Piegan . . . . Blood, Kainai, Pikuni, Pigunni

Pima . . . . Onk Akimel Au-authm, Tohono O'odham, A-atam, Akimul Au'autam, Akimel O'oodham

Piro . . . . Tortuga

Pit River . . . . . . Achomawi, Atsugewi

Poosepatuck . . . . Unkechaug

Pshwanwapam . . Upper Yakima

Pueblo . . . . Acoma, Cochiti, Hano, Hopi, Isleta, Isleta del Sur, Jemez, Keresan, Laguna, Nambe, Pecos, Picuris, Piro, Pojoaque, San Felipe, San Ildefonso, San Juan, Sandia, Santa Ana, Santa Clara, Sia, Santo Domingo, Senecu, Taos, Tano, Tesuque, Tewa, Tiwa, Zia, Zuni

Quapaw . . . . Quapah, Akansea, Ouaguapas

Quechan . . . . . . Yuma

Quileute . . . . Quil-leh-ute

Quinault . . . . Qui-nai-elts

Sac and Fox . . . . Sauk, Meshkwakihug, Fox

Sahwnee . . . . Shawadasay

Salish . . . . Okinagan, Flathead

Sans Arc . . . . Itazipco

Santee . . . . Sisseton

Saponi . . . . Monasukapanough

Scioto . . . . (Five Nations of the Scioto Plains) Shawnee, Wyandot, Delaware, Munsee, Seneca

Seminole . . . . . . Ikaniuksalgi, Alachua, Mikasuki

Seneca . . . . Iroquois

Serrano . . . . Cowangachem, Mohineyam

Shawnee . . . . . . Savannah, Chillicothe, Hathawekela, Mequachake, Piqua

Shoshone . . . . Shoshoni, Snake, Nimi, Tukudeka

Sioux . . . . Brule, Dakota, Hunkpapa, Isanyati, Itazipco, Lakota, Mnikowoju, Nakota, Ocheti Shakowin, Oglala, Oohenunpa, Sicangu, Sihasapa, Teton, Titunwan

Sissipahaw . . . . . Haw

Skagit . . . . Humaluh

Skoskomish . . . . Twana

Snake . . . . Northern Paiute, Takelma

Squinamish . . . . Swinomish

Slotas . . . . Red River Metis

Songish . . . . Lkungen

Southern Paiute . Numa

St. Francis . . . . . Abenaki

St. Regis Mohawk Akwesasne, Kaniengehage

Stockbridge . . . . Mahican

Susquehanna . . . Susquehannock, Conestoga, Minqua, Andaste

Taidnapam . . . . . Upper Cowlitz

Tarahumara . . . . Rarámuri

Taviwac . . . . Uncompahgre Ute

Tawasa . . . . Alabama

Tejas . . . . Hasinai, Cenis

Tenino . . . . Melilema

Teton . . . . Brule, Hunkpapa, Itazipco, Mnikowoju, Oglala, Oohenunpa, Sicangu, Sihasapa, Titunwan

Tewa . . . . Pueblo, Nambe, Pojoaque, San Ildefonso, San Juan, Santa Clara, Tesuque

Thompson . . . . . Nlaka'pamux

Tigua . . . . Pueblo, Tiwa, Tortuga

Tillamook . . . . . Killamuck

Timucua . . . . . . Utina, Acuera

Tiwa . . . . Pueblo, Tortuga

Tlingit . . . . Lingi't, Kolushan

Tobacco . . . . Khionontateronon, Tionontati

Toltec . . . . Chiaimeca Mochanecatoca

Tonkawa . . . . . . Titskan Watitch, Titskanwatitch, Tonkaweya

Tubatulabal . . . . Bahkanapul, Kern River

Tunica . . . . Yoron

Tuscarora . . . . . . Skaruren, Iroquois, Coree

Tututni . . . . Tolowa

Twana . . . . Tuadhu

Two Kettle . . . . . Oohenunpa

Umpqua . . . . Etnemitane

Uncompahgre Ute . . . . . . Taviwac

Upper Chehalis . Kwaiailk

Upper Sioux . . . . Sisseton, Wahpeton

Ute . . . . Noochi, Notch, Nuciu, Yamparka,
Parianuc, Taviwac, Wiminuc,
Kapota, Muwac, Cumumba,
Tumpanuwac, Uinta-ats, Pahvant,
San Pitch, and Sheberetch

Wampanoag . . . . Pokanoket

Warm Springs . . Tilkuni

Wasco . . . . Galasquo

Watlala . . . . Katlagakya

Whilkut . . . . Redwood Indians

Winnebago . . . . Winipig

Wichita . . . . Kitikiti'sh, Wia Chitch
(Choctaw word)

Winik . . . . Maya

Wishram . . . . . . Ilaxluit, Tlakluit

Wyandot . . . . . . Huron, Talamatans

Yakima . . . . Waptailmin, Pakiutlema

Yazoo . . . . Chakchiuma

Yoncalla . . . . Tchayankeld

Yuchi . . . . Chisa

Yuma . . . . Quechan, Euqchan

Zuni . . . . Ashiwi, Taa Ashiwani,
Sunyitsi

North American Indian Calendars

As you will note below, some listings include one entry per month. In these cases, usually, the name in that language may be more properly a name for the month, instead of the "moon," since there are more than 12 moons per year. Over a long enough period of time, the moons will shift through the seasons.

There are occasional multiple names for one moon or month. This could be caused by the overlapping of some moons in a month, different groups in the tribe using different names, or from different translations of the same common name. Also, some groups within a tribe might have a name for a moon or month, while other groups within the same tribe may have no name for the same moon or month.

	Month Names	Moon Names
Abenaki		
January	Alamikos	Greetings Maker Moon
February	Piaodagos	Makes Branches Fall in Pieces Moon
March	Mozokas	Moose Hunter Moon
Mid-March	Sigwankas	Spring Season Maker Moon
April	Sogalikas	Sugar Maker Moon
May	Kikas	Field Maker Moon
June	Nokahigas	Hoer Moon
July	Temaskikos	Grass Cutter Moon
August	Temezôwas	Cutter Moon
September	Skamonkas	Corn Maker Moon
October	Penibagos	Leaf Falling Moon
November	Mzatanos	Freezing River Maker Moon
December	Pebonka	Winter Maker Moon
Algonquin		
January	Squochee Kesos	Sun Has Not Strength to Thaw
February	Wapicuummilcum	Ice in River Is Gone
March	Namossack Kesos	Catching Fish
April	Suquanni Kesos	When They Set Indian Corn
May	Moonesquanimock Kesos	When Women Weed Corn
June	Twowa Kesos	When They Hill Indian Corn

	Month Names	Moon Names

Algonquin (continued)

July	Matterllawaw Kesos	Squash Are Ripe and Indian Beans Begin to Be Edible
August	Micheenee Kesos	When Indian Corn Is Edible
September	Pohquitaqunk Kesos	Middle Between Harvest and Eating Indian Corn
October	Pepewarr	White Frost on Grass and Ground
November	Quinne Kesos	Same as Pepewarr
December	Papsapquoho	

Anishnaabe (Chippewa, Ojibwa)

January	Gichi-manidoo-giizis	Great Spirit Moon
February	Namebini-giizis	Sucker Moon
March	Bebookwaadaagame-giizis(oog)	Snow Crust Moon
April	Iskigamizige-giizis(oog)	Broken Snowshow Moon
May	Waabigwani-giizis	Blossom Moon
June	Ode'imini-giizis	Strawberry Moon
July	Aabita-niibino-giizis	Raspberry Moon
August	Miini-giizis	Berry Moon
September	Manoominike-giizis	Rice Moon
October	Binaakwe-giizis	Falling Leaves Moon
November	Gashkadino-giizis(oog)	Freezing Moon
December	Manidoo-gizisoons	Small Spirits Moon

Apache

January	Time of Flying Ants	
April		Moon of the Big Leaves
May	Season When the Leaves Are Green	
July		Moon of the Horse/Time of Ripeness
October	Time When the Corn Is Taken In	

Northern Arapaho

January	When the Snow Blows Like Spirits in the Wind	
February	Frost Sparkling in the Sun	
March	Buffalo Dropping Their Calves	
April	Ice Breaking in the River	
May	When the Ponies Shed Their Shaggy Hair	
June	When the Hot Weather Begins	
July	When the Buffalo Bellows	
Late July	When the Chokeberries Begin to Ripen	
August	Geese Shedding Their Feathers	
September	Drying Grass	
October	Falling Leaves	
November	When the Rivers Start to Freeze	
December	Popping Trees	

Month Names		Moon Names

Assiniboin

January	Wicogandu	Center Moon
February	Amhanska	Long Dry Moon
March	Wicinstayazan	Sore Eye Moon
April	Tabehatawi	Frog Moon
May	Indiwiga	Idle Moon
June	Wahequosmewi	Full Leaf Moon
July	Wasasa	Red Berries Moon
August	Capasapsaba	Black Cherries Moon
September	Wahpegiwi	Yellow Leaf Moon
October	Anukope	Joins Both Sides Moon
	Tasnaheja-hagikta	Striped Gopher Looks Back Moon
November	Cuhotgawi	Frost Moon
December	Wicogandu-sungagu	Center Moon's Younger Brother

Aztec (Different Calendar System)

Izcalli	Resurrection
Atlcahualco	Departure of the Waters
Tlacaxipehualiztli	Slaughtering of Dogs
Tozoztontli	Little Vigil
Hueytozoztli	Grand Vigil
Toxcatl	Dry Thing
Etzalcualiztli	Meal of Corn and Bean
Tecuilhuitontli	Little Feast of Lords
Hueytecuilhuitl	Grand Feast of Lords
Miccailhuitontli	Little Feast of the Dead
Hueymiccailhuitl	Grand Feast of the Dead
Ochpaniztli	Sweeping
Pachtontli	Small Hay
Hueypachtli	Large Hay
Quecholli	Flamingo
Panquetzaliztli	Raising of the Banners
Atemoztli	Lowering of Water
Titl	Shrinking
Nemontemi	Empty Days

Cherokee (Months with Help from Tu'ti)

January	Unolvtana	Cold Moon
February	Kagali	Bony Moon
March	Anvhyi	Strawberry or Windy Moon
April	Kawohni	Flower Moon
May	Ansgvti	Planting Moon
June	Dehaluyi	Green Corn Moon
July	Kuyegwona	Ripe Corn Moon
August	Galohni	End of the Fruit or Drying Up Moon

Month Names	Moon Names

Cherokee *(continued)*

September	Dulisdi	Nut or Black Butterfly Moon
October	Duninhdi	Harvest Moon
November	Nvdadegwa	Trading Moon
December	Vskihyi	Snow Moon

Eastern Cherokee (Moons thanks to Robert Graybear)

Nvda Kanawoga	Cold Moon
Nvda Kola	Bone Moon
(So Little Food, People Gnaw on Bones and Eat Bone Marrow Soup)	
Nvda Unole	Wind Moon
(When Strong Winds Strip Away the Dead Wood and Foliage and Prepare the Land for Renewal)	
Nvda Atsilusgi	Flower Moon
(When Plants Come to Life and Bloom Again and the Earth Is Renewed)	
Nvda Gahlvsga	Planting Moon
(Strict Translation "The Putting It in a Hole Moon")	
Nvda Seluitseiyusdi	Green Corn Moon
(When the Corn Is Up and Showing Itself as an Identifiable Crop)	
Nvda Utsi'dsata'	Corn in Tassel Moon
(When the Corn Is Displaying a Tassel)	
Nvda Seluuwa'nûûññ'sa	Ripe Corn Moon
Nvda Udatanvagisdi Ulisdv	End of Fruit Moon
Nvda Udatanûûññ	Nut Moon
Nvda Tsiyahloha	Harvest Moon
Nvda Ganohalidoha	Hunting Moon
Nvda Gutiha	Snow Moon
(When the First Snows Fall in the Mountains)	

Cheyenne

January	Moon of the Strong Cold
April	Moon When the Geese Lay Eggs
May	Moon When the Horses Get Fat
September	Drying Grass Moon
October	Moon When the Water Begins to Freeze on the Edge of the Streams
November	Deer Rutting Moon
December	Moon When the Wolves Run Together

Cree

January	When the Old Fellow Spreads the Brush	Gishepapiwatekimumpizun
February	Old Month	Cepizun
March	Eagle Month	Migisupizum
April	Gray Goose Month	Kiskipizun
May	Frog Month	Aligipizun
June	The Month Leaves Come Out	Sagipukawipizun
July	The Moon When Ducks Begin to Molt	Opaskwuwipizun

	Month Names	Moon Names

Cree (continued)

August	The Moon Young Ducks Begin to Fly	Opunhopizun
September	Wavy or Snow Goose Month	Weweopizun
October	The Moon the Birds Fly South	Opinahamowipizun
November	The Moon the Rivers Begin to Freeze	Kaskatinopizun
December	When the Young Fellow Spreads the Brush	Papiwatiginashispizun

Creek

May		Mulberry Moon
July		Little Ripening Moon
August		Big Ripening Moon
September		Little Chestnut Moon
November		Moon When the Water Is Black with Leaves
December		Big Winter Moon

Creek (Alternative; starts in August)

Much Heat or Big Ripening
Little Chestnut
Big Chestnut
Iholi-frost
Big Winter
Little Winter
Wind
Little Spring
Big Spring
Mulberry
Blackberry
Little Heat or Little Ripening

Diegueno (Starts in November; six names, repeat with slight variation)

Ilya-kwetl	Cold
Heha-nimsup	Snow
Hatai	Cold
Heha-psu	Rain
Hatya-matinya	Rain
Ihy-anidja	Growth
Kwurh	
Namasap	
Tai	
Pswi	
Matanai	
Anaha	

Hopi

January	Paamuya	Joyful Moon
February	Powamuya	Purification Moon

Month Names		Moon Names

Hopi (continued)

March	Osomuyaw	Whispering Wind Moon
April	Kwiyamuyaw	Windbreaks Moon
May	Hakitonmuyaw	Waiting Moon
June	Wukouyis	Major Planting Moon
July	Kelmuya	Fledgling Raptor Moon
August	Paamuya	Joyful Moon
September	Nasanmuyaw	Full Harvest Moon
October	Angaqmuyaw	Long Hair Moon
November	Kelmuya	Fledgling Raptor Moon
December	Kyaamuya	Respect Moon

Huchnom (Starts in Winter; two names per moon)

Mipa'ohot	Old Man Finger, thumb-march
Mipa-koye	Long Finger
Mipa'-olsel	
Yoht-umol	May
Olpalmol	Tree Leaves
Im-pomol	
Yoht-wanmol	
Im-tomol	
Im-pusmol	
Yoht-pomol	Dry
Yoht-usmol	
Olom-tomol	Mountains Burned over
On-tutwin	
On-woi-mol	Earth Smoky (August–September)
Lehpwanmol or	
Lehpwene	Beginning of Autumn
Huwol-huntusmol	Acorns Ready to Drop
Huwol-chukmol	Acorns Fall
Munl-nantmol	Ice on Streams
Yem-tamol	Fire _____?
Hunw-tankmol	Fish Frozen

Inuit (Eskimo)

January	Avunniviayuk
February	Avunnivik
March	Amaolikkervik
April	Kriblalikvik
May	Tigmiyikvik
June	Nuertorvik
July	Padlersersivik
August	Krugyuat Tingiviat
September	Aklikarniarvik
October	Tugluvik

Month Names		Moon Names

Inuit (continued)

November	Itartoryuk
December	Kaitvitjuitk

Juaneno (Starts at Winter Solstice; only ten names)

A'apkomil (Winter Solstice)
Peret
Yarmar
Alasowil
Tokoboaich
Sintekar (Summer Solstice)
Kukwat
Lalavaich
Awitskomel
A'awit

Keresan

January	Nadzi-kisraiti
February	Y'amuuni Daawaatra
March	Shch'ami Daawaatra
April	Bashch'atsishe Daawaatra
May	Shawiitsishe Daawaatra
June	Sauhua Daawaatra
July	Sina Kisraiti
August	Y'aamuni Daawaatra
September	Kinati Daawaatra
October	
November	
December	Nachuweenu Daawaatra

Kiowa

Early February	Little Bud Moon	Kaguat P'a San
Early March	Bud Moon	Kaguat P'a
Early April	Leaf Moon	Aiden P'a
Late April	Summer	Aganti (I'll Make It Hot Soon, Pai Aganti)
Late May	Summer	Tepgan (Geese Go North, Pai Tepgan P'a)
June	Summer Moon	Pai Ganhina P'a
Late July	Little Moon of Deer Horns Dropping Off	Tagunotal P'a San
August	Yellow Leaves Moon	Aidenguak'o P'a
September	Moon When the Leaves Fall Off	
Early October	Ten-Colds Moon	Gakinat'o P'a
Late October	Wait Until I Come	Aganti
Late November	Geese-going Moon	Tepgan P'a
Late December	Real Goose Moon	Ganhina P'a

Month Names	Moon Names

Klamath (Starts in August; counted on fingers)

T-hopo	Thumb, Berries Dried
Speluish	Index-finger, Dancing
Tat-helam	Middle-finger, Leaves Full
Kapchelam	Ring-finger, Snow
Kapcha	Little Finger, Heavy Snow
T-hopo	Thumb, Lakes Frozen
Speluish	Index-finger, Rain and Dancing
Tat-helam	Middle-finger, Sucker Fishing
Kapchelam	Ring-finger, "Ipos" Gathering
Kapcha	Little-finger, Suckers Dried
T-hopo	Thumb, "Wokas" Harvest
Speluish	Index-finger, Return from Harvest

Kumeyaay

September	Halakwol
October	Halanyimcep
November	Halatai
December	Halapisu
January	Halamrtinya
February	Halanitca
March	Halakwol
April	Halanyimcep
May	Halatai
June	Halapisu
July	Halamrtinya
August	Halanitca
September	Halakwol (Kumeyaay New Year)

Foothill Maidu (Starts in March)

Kono	
Win-uti	Black Oaks Tassel
Tem-diyoko	Fawns
Nem-diyoko	Big Mouth
Kaui-tson	Ground Burn
Eslakum	Middle
Mat-meni	Acorn Bread
Bapaboka	
Bo-lye	Trail _____?
Sap	
Into	
Omi-hintsuli	Squint Rock

Mountain Maidu (Starts in March)

Bom-tetno	Trail Sit Along
Kono	

Month Names	Moon Names

Mountain Maidu *(continued)*

Kulokbepine	Old Woman ____?
No Name June	
No Name July	
No Name August	
Se-meni Seed	
Tem-tsampauto	Small Tree Freeze
Tetem-tsampauta	Large Tree Freeze
Kanaipino	Under Burn
Bom-hintsuli	Trail Squint
Bo-ekmen	Trail Breaks Open

Valley Maidu (Starts in March)

Shawi or Sha-kono	Flowers
Laila	Grass
Kon-moko	Seeds, fish, geese
Neng-kaukat	Big Summer
Tumi	Smoky
Tem-simi	Acorns Ripen
Kum-menim She-meni	Acorns Gathered
Shahwodo	Acorns Cached
Yapakto	Winter Divided
Omhincholi	Ice Lasts All Day
Yeponi or Bom-pene	Ceremonial Initiate or Two Trails
Kaka-kano	Pattering Showers

Mandan-Hidatsa

April	Moon of the Breaking Up of the Ice
November	Moon When the River Freezes

Maya (Different calendar system)

Pop	Mat
Uo	Frog
Zip	Stag
Zotz	Bat
Tzec	Skull
Xul	End
Yaxkin	Tender Sun (Green)
Mol	Reunion
Chen	Well
Yax	Green
Zac	White
Ceh	Deer
Mac	Cover
Kankin	Mature Sun (Yellow)

	Month Names	Moon Names
Maya *(continued)*		
Muan	Owl	
Pax Music		
Kayab	Turtle	
Cumhu	Dark God	
Uayeb	Specters	
Mohawk		
January	Tsothohrhko:wa	The Big Cold
February	Enniska	Lateness
March	Ennisko:wa	Much Lateness
April	Onerahtokha	Budding Time
May	Onerahtohko:wa	Time of Big Leaf
June	Ohiari:ha	Ripening Time
July	Ohiarihko:wa	Time of Much Ripening
August	Seskehko:wa	Time of Freshness
September	Seskhoko:wa	Time of Much Freshness
October	Kentenha	Time of Poverty
November	Kentenhko:wa	Time of Much Poverty
December	Tsothohrha	Time of Cold
Muscogee (Creek)		
January	Rv'fo Cusee	Winter's Younger Brother
February	Hotvlee-hv'see	Wind Month
March	Tasahcucee	Little Spring Month
April	Tasahcee-rakko	Big Spring Month
May	Kee-hvsee	Mulberry Month
June	Kvco-hvsee	Blackberry Month
July	Hiyucee	Little Harvest
August	Hiyo-rakko	Big Harvest
September	Otowoskucee	Little Chestnut Month
October	Otowoskv-rakko	Big Chestnut Month
November	Echolee	Frost Month
December	Rvfo-rakko	Big Winter
Natchez (Starts in March)		
		Deer Moon
		Strawberry Moon
		Little Corn Moon
		Watermelon Moon
		Peaches Moon
		Mulberries Moon
		Maize Moon
		Turkey Moon

Month Names	Moon Names

Natchez (continued)

	Bison Moon
	Bear Moon
	Cold Meal Moon
	Chestnuts Moon
	Nuts Moon

Nisenan

January	Ashy Season
February	Big Moon
March	Brush-Leafing
April	Flower Season
May	Fine Seeds Ripe Season
June	Hot Season
July	Small Hot Season
August	Big One Season

Omaha

January	Moon When Snow Drifts into Tepees
February	Moon When Geese Come Home
March	Little Frog Moon
June	Moon When the Buffalo Bulls Hunt the Cows
July	Moon When the Buffalo Bellow
September	Moon When the Deer Paw the Earth

Osage

May	Moon When the Little Flowers Die
August	Yellow Flower Moon

Passamaquoddy

January	Opolahsomuwehs	Whirling Wind Month
February	Piyatokonis	When the Spruce Tips Fall
March	Siqon	Spring Moon
April	Ponatom	Spring Moon
May	Siqonomeq	Alewife Moon
June	Nipon	Summer Moon
July	Accihte	Ripening Moon
August	Apsqe	Feather Shedding Moon
September	Toqakiw	Autumn Moon
October	Amilkahtin	Harvest Moon
November	Kelotonuhket	Freezing Moon
December	Punam	Frost Fish Moon

	Month Names	Moon Names

Pima

January	Gi'ihothag Mashath	The Weight Loss Month (When Animals Lose Their Fat)
February	Kohmagi Mashath	The Gray Month (When Trees Are Bare and Vegetation Is Scarce)
March	Chehthagi Mashath	The Green Month
April	Oam Mashath	The Yellow Month
	S-gevk Mashath	The Strong Month (When the Trees Begin to Bloom)
May	Ko'ok Mashath	
June		
July		
August		
September		
October		
November		
December		

Pomo (Starts approximately in January)

Bashelamatau-la	Buckeyes Ripe
Sachau-da	Cold Winds
Kadamchido-da	Growth Begins
Chidodapuk	Flowers
Umchachich-da	Seeds Ripen
Butich-da	Bulbs Mature (The "Brodiaca")
Bakaichich-da	Manzanita Ripens
Luchich-da	Acorns Appear
Shachluyiau-da	Soaproot Dug for Fish Poison
Kalemkayo	Trees Felled by Fire at Butt
Kasi-sa	Cold Begins
Stalpkel-da	Leaves Yellow and Fall

Ponca

January	Snow Thaws Moon
March	Water Stands in the Ponds Month
June	Hot Weather Begins Moon
July	Middle of Summer Moon
August	Corn Is in the Silk Moon
October	Moon When They Store Food in Caches

Potawatomi

January	Mkokisis	Month of the Bear
February	Mnokesis	Month of Rabbit Conception
March	Cicakkises	Month of the Crane
April		
May	Te'minkeses	Month of the Strawberry

	Month Names	Moon Names
Potawatomi (continued)		
June	Msheke'kesis	Month of the Turtle
July	We'shkitdaminkese	Month of the Young Corn
August	E'mnomukkises	Month of the Middle
September		
October	E'sksegtukkisis	Month of the First Frost
November	Pne'kesis	Month of the Turkey and Feast
December		
Sioux		
January		Moon of Strong Cold/Frost in the Tepee/ Wolves Run Together
February		Raccoon Moon/Dark Red Calves
March		Moon When Buffalo Cows Drop Their Calves/of the Snowblind/Sore Eye Moon
April		Moon of Greening Grass/Red Grass Appearing
May		Moon When the Ponies Shed
June		Moon of Making Fat/Moon When Green Grass Is Up/Strawberry Moon
July		Moon When the Wild Cherries Are Ripe/ Red Cherries/Red Blooming Lilies
August		Moon When the Geese Shed Their Feathers/Cherries Turn Black
September		Moon of Drying Grass/When Calves Grow Hair or Black Calf/ When the Plums Are Scarlet
October		Moon of Falling Leaves/Changing Season
November		Moon of the Falling Leaves
December		Moon of Popping Trees/When Deer Shed Their Horns/Buffalo Cow's Fetus Is Getting Large
Tewa Pueblo		
February		Moon of the Cedar Dust Wind
March		Moon When the Leaves Break Forth
June		Moon When the Leaves Are Dark Green
September		Moon When the Corn Is Taken In
November		Moon When All Is Gathered In
Winnebago		
February		Fish-running Moon
April		Planting Corn Moon
May		Hoeing-corn Moon
July		Corn-popping Moon
November		Little Bear's Moon
December		Big Bear's Moon

	Month Names	Moon Names

Wishram

January		Her Cold Moon
February		Shoulder to Shoulder Around the Fire Moon
March		Long Days Moon
April		The Eighth Moon
May		The Ninth Moon
June		Fish Spoils Easily Moon
July		Salmon Go up the Rivers in a Group Moon
August		Blackberry Patches Moon
September		Her Acorns Moon
October		Travel in Canoes Moon
November		Snowy Mountains in the Morning Moon
December		Her Winter Houses Moon

Yuchi

January	Frozen Ground	Salatcpi
February	Wind	Hodadzo
March	Little Summer	Wadasine
April	Big Summer	Wadaa
May	Mulberry Ripening	Deconendzo
June	Blackberry Ripening	Cpaconendzo
July	Middle of Summer	Wagakya
August	Dog Days	Tseneaga
September	Hay Cutting	Tsogalinetsee
October	Corn Ripening	Tsotohostane
December	Middle of Winter	Hoctadakya

Yurok (Starts in late December)

Kohtsewets	
Na'aiwets	
Nahksewets	
Tsona'aiwets	
Meroyo	
Kohtsawets	
Tserwerserk	
Knewoleteu	
Kerermerk or Pia'ago Red Berries Gathered	
Wetlowa or Le'lo'o	
Nohso	Time of Acorn Gathering
Hohkemo	
Ka'amo	Cold Time

Zuni

January	Dayamcho Yachunne	Moon When Limbs of Trees Are Broken by Snow
February	Onon U'la'ukwamme	No Snow in Trails Moon
March	Li'dekwakkya Ts'ana	Little Sand Storm Moon

Month Names		Moon Names

Zuni (continued)

April	Li'dekwakkya Lana	Great Sand Storm Moon
May	Yachun Kwa'shi'amme	
June	Ik'ohbu Yachunne	Turning Moon
July	Dayamcho Yachunne	Moon When Limbs of Are Trees Broken by Fruit
August	Onan U'la'ukwamme	
September	Li'dekwakkwya Ts'ana	Miyashshe:nak'ya
		When Everything Ripens and Corn Is Harvested
October	Li'dekwakkwya Lana	Big Wind Moon
November	Yachun Kwa'shi'amme	
December	Ik'ohbu Yachunne	Turning Moon or the Sun Has Traveled South to His Home to Rest Before He Starts Back on His Journey North

Season Names

Abenaki

Spring	Sigwan
Summer	Niben
Fall	Tagwogo
Winter	Pebon

Cree

Early Spring	Sigun
Late Spring	Miluskamin
Early Summer	Nipin
Late Summer	Megwanipiu
Early Fall	Tukwagun
Late Fall	Migiskau
Early Winter	Pichipipun
Late Winter	Megwapipun

Powhatan
(They Had a Fifth Season, Nepinough, for the "Earing of the Corn")

Winter	Popanow
Spring	Cattapeuk
Summer	Cohattayough
Fall	Taquitock

Yuchi

Winter	Wicta
Spring	Hina Wadele
Summer	Wade
Fall	Yacadile

Day Names

Abenaki

Sunday	Sanda
Monday	Kizsanda
Tuesday	Nisda Alokan
Wednesday	Nsida Alokan
Thursday	Iawda Alokan
Friday	Skawatukwikisgad
Saturday	Kadawsanda

Cherokee

Sunday	Unadodagwasgvi
Monday	Unadodagwohnvi
Tuesday	Taline Iga
Wednesday	Joine Iga
Thursday	Nvhgine Iga
Friday	Junhgilosdi
Saturday	Unadodagwidena

Chickasaw

Sunday	Nitak Hullo
Monday	Munti
Tuesday	Chosti
Wednesday	Winsti
Thursday	Soisti
Friday	Nam Ulhchifa Nitak
Saturday	Nitak Hullo Nukfish

Chippewa (Ojibwe)

Sunday	Ana'mi'e-gijigad
Monday	Nitam-gijigad
Tuesday	Nijo-gijigad
Wednesday	Abitoose-gijigad
Thursday	Niwing-gijigad
Friday	Naning-gijigad
Saturday	Ningoot'wasso-gijigad

Bibliography

Adair, James. *Adair's History of the American Indians*. 1775.

Avant, David A. Jr. *J. Randall Stanley's History of Gadsden County*. Tallahassee, Florida: L'Avant Studios, 1985.

Axtell, James. *The Invasion Within*. New York: Oxford University Press, 1985.

Baum, L. Frank. "Sitting Bull, most renowned Sioux of modern history, is dead." *Aberdeen Saturday Pioneer*. 1890.

Beach, William Wallace. *The Indian miscellany; containing papers on the history, antiquities, arts, languages, religions, traditions and superstitions of the American aborigines; with descriptions of their domestic life, manners, customs, traits, amusements and exploits; travels and adventures in the Indian country; incidents of border warfare; missionary relations, etc*. Albany, New York: J. Munsell, 1877.

Boorstin, Daniel J. *The Discoverers*. New York: Random House, 1983.

Bourne, Russell. *The Red King's Rebellion*. New York: Oxford University Press, 1990.

Bowman, John S. *The World Almanac of the American West*. New York: Pharos Books, 1986.

Brimlow, George F. *The Bannock Indian War of 1878*. Caldwell, Idaho: Caxton Printers, 1938.

Brown, Dee. *Bury My Heart at Wounded Knee*. New York: Bantam Books, 1970 .

Brown, William Compton. *The Indian Side of the Story*. Spokane, Washington: C.W. Hill, 1961.

Brownell, Charles De Wolf. *The Indian Races of North and South America*. Hartford, Connecticut: Hurlbut, Scranton, 1864.

Burnett, John G. *Story of the Removal of the Cherokees*. Self-Published. 1839.

Burns, Ken. *The Way West*. PBS Television Series, 1995.

Burt, Henry M. *Burt's Illustrated Guide of the Connecticut Valley*. Northampton: New England Publishing Company, 1867.

Cantor, George. *North American Indian Landmarks*. Detroit: Visible Ink, 1993.

Carswell, E.W. *Florida's Twelfth County*. Tallahassee, Florida: Rose, 1991.

Carswell, E.W. *Holmsteading: The History of Holmes County, Florida*. Tallahassee, Florida: Rose, 1986.

Clark, Agnew Hilsman. *History of Stewart County, Georgia*. Vol. 2. Waycross, Georgia.

Coues, Elliot, Ed. *The History of the Lewis and Clark Expedition*. New York: Dover, 1893.

Crowder, David Lester. *Tendoy: Chief of the Lemhis*. Caldwell, Idaho: Caxton, 1969.

Cutler, William G. *History of the State of Kansas*. Chicago: A.T. Andreas, 1883.

Debo, Angie. *A History of the Indians of the United States*. Norman: University of Oklahoma Press, 1970.

Dennis, Henry C. *The American Indian, 1492–1976: A Chronology and Fact Book*. Dobbs Ferry, New York: Oceana, 1977.

DeRosier, Arthur Jr. *The Removal of the Choctaw Indians*. Knoxville: University of Tennessee Press, 1970.

Dillon, Richard H. *North American Indian Wars*. Greenwich, Connecticut: Brompton, 1983.

Dunn, J.P. Jr. *Massacres of the Mountains: A History of the Indian Wars of the Far West.* New York: Capricorn, 1969.

Eagle/Walking Turtle. *Indian America: A Traveler's Companion.* Santa Fe, New Mexico: John Muir, 1989.

Elliott, T.C., ed. "Journal of John Work, July 5–September 15, 1826." *Washington Historical Quarterly* 6 (1915).

Ferguson, T.J., and E.R. Hart. *A Zuni Atlas.* Norman: University of Oklahoma Press, 1985.

500 Nations. Television Program, 1995.

Flanigan, James C. *History of Gwinnett County, Georgia.* Vol. 1. Hapeville, Georgia: Tyler, 1943.

Foreman, Grant. *Indian Removal: The Emigration of the Five Civilized Tribes of Indians.* Norman: University of Oklahoma Press, 1932.

Gahan, Laurence K. "The Nipmucks and Their Territory." *Massachusetts Archaeological Society Bulletin* 2, no. 4 (July 1941).

Gardener, Lion. *Leift Lion Gardener, his relation of the Pequot Warres.* Boston, 1833.

Glassley, Ray H. *Indian Wars of the Pacific Northwest.* Portland, Oregon: Binfords and Mort, 1972.

Heard, J. Norman. *Handbook of the American Frontier: Four Centuries of Indian-White Relationship.* Vols. 1–2. Lanham, Maryland: Scarecrow Press, 1990.

Henri, Florette. *The Southern Indians and Bejamin Hawkins.* Norman: University of Oklahoma Press, 1986.

Hirschfelder, Arlene, and Martha Kreipe de Montaño. *The Native American Almanac.* New York: Prentice Hall, 1993.

How the West Was Lost. Television Program, 1993.

Hutchinson, Ira A. *Some Who Passed This Way.* Panama, Florida: Self-Published.

Huxford, Folks. *The History of Brooks County, Georgia.* Quitman, Georgia: Hannah Clarke Chapter, D.A.R., 1948.

Kappler, Charles. *Indian Affairs: Laws and Treaties.* Washington, D.C.: Government Printing Office, 1904.

Kroeber, A.L. *Handbook of Indians of California.* Berkeley, California: California Book Company, 1925.

Lavender, David. *Let Me Be Free.* New York: HarperCollins, 1992.

Malone, H.T. *Cherokees of the Old South: A People in Transition.* Athens: University of Georgia Press, 1956.

Marcy, Randolph B. *Thirty Years of Army Life on the Border.* New York: Harper, 1866.

Martin, Simon, and Nikoli Grube. *Chronicle of the Maya Kings and Queens.* London: Thames and Hudson, 2000.

Mason, John. *A Brief History of the Pequot War.* Boston: 1736.

Mayhall, Mildred P. *Indian Wars of Texas.* Waco, Texas: Texian, 1965.

McDonald, Archie P. *In Celebration of Texas: An Illustrated History.* Northridge, California: Windsor, 1986.

Mooney, James. *Calendar History of the Kiowa Indians.* Washington, D.C.: Government Printing Office, 1898; rpt., Washington: Smithsonian Institution Press, 1979.

Morgan, Ted. *Wilderness at Dawn.* New York: Simon and Schuster, 1993.

Neihardt, John G. *Black Elk Speaks.* Lincoln: University of Nebraska Press, 1932.

Orr, Charles, Ed. *History of the Pequot War.* Cleveland, Ohio: Helman-Taylor, 1897.

Prescott, William Hickling. *The History of the Conquest of Mexico.* 1843.

Reader's Digest. *Story of the Great American West.* Pleasantville, New York: Reader's Digest Association, 1977.

San Diego Union-Tribune. Newspaper.

Schele, Linda, and Peter Mathews. *The Code of the Kings.* New York: Scribner, 1998.

Sheridan, Lt. Gen. P.H. *Record of the Engagements with Hostile Indians, Department of Missouri, 1868–1892.* Chicago, 1882.

Sipe, C. Hale. *Indian Wars of Pennsylvania.* Pennsylvania: 1929.

Smithsonian Institution. *The Native Americans: The Indigenous People of North America.* New York: Smithmark, 1991.

Special Archives Publication Number 149, Florida Department of Military Affairs, St. Augustine, Florida.

Spencer, Robert F., et al. *The Native Americans*. New York: Harper and Row, 1965.

Stands in Timber, John, and Margot Liberty. *Cheyenne Memories*. Lincoln: University of Nebraska Press, 1967.

Starr, Emmet. *History of the Cherokee Indians*. Tulsa: Oklahoma Yesterday, 1993.

Swanton, John R. *Final Report of the United States De Soto Expedition Commission*. 76th Cong., 1st sess., House Document no. 71. Washington, D.C.: Government Printing Office, 1939.

Swanton, John R. *Indian Tribes of North America*. Washington, D.C.: Government Printing Office, 1952.

Tebbel, John, and Keith Jennison. *The American Indian Wars*. New York: Bonanza, 1960.

Thomas, David, et al. *The Native Americans*. Atlanta: Turner, 1993.

Unknown. *Chronological List of Actions, &c. With Indians, January 1, 1866, to January 1891*. Washington, D.C.: Adjutant General's Office.

Unknown. *History of Lowndes County, Georgia, 1825–1941*. Valdosta, Georgia: General James Jackson Chapter, D.A.R., 1942.

United States. *Condition of the Indian tribes. Report of the joint special committee, appointed under joint resolution of March 3, 1865*. Washington, D.C.: Government Printing Office. 1867.

Utley, Robert M. *The Lance and the Shield*. New York: Henry Holt, 1993.

Utley, Robert M., and Wilcomb E. Washburn. *The American Heritage History of the Indian Wars*. Boston: Houghton Mifflin Company, 1977.

Van Doren, Charles, and Robert McHenry. *Webster's Guide to American History*. Springfield, Massachusetts: G. and C. M Company, 1971.

Various. New Handbook of Texas (online). Texas State Historical Association. Available at http://www.tsha.utexas.edu/handbook/online/index.html.

Various. EnviroText (online). Available at http://envirotext.eh.doe.gov/.

Various. Costanoan Ohlone Indian Canyon Resource (online). Available at http://www.rahunzi.com/costano/.

Various Editors. *Handbook of North American Indians*. Washington, D.C.: Smithsonian Institution, 1978.

Viola, Herman J. *Exploring the West*. New York: Harry Abrams, 1987.

Vogel, Virgil J. *This Country Was Ours*. New York: Harper and Row, 1972.

Waldman, Carl. *Atlas of North American Indians*. New York: Facts on File, 1985.

Waldman, Carl. *Timelines of Native American History*. New York: Prentice Hall, 1994.

Ward, Geoffrey C. *The West: An Illustrated History*. New York: Little, Brown, 1996.

Woodward, Grace Steele. *The Cherokees*. Norman: University of Oklahoma Press, 1963.

▼▼▼

Index